# Praise for *Libertari...*
## *Politics in Black and...*

M000210286

"*Libertarian Socialism: Politics in Black and Red* is an invaluable contribution to historical scholarship and libertarian politics. The collection of essays contained in the book has the great virtue of offering both analytical perspectives on ideas, and historical perspectives on movements. The contributions examine classical themes in anarchist politics such as individual liberty, whilst also exploring more neglected thinkers and themes from a libertarian standpoint, such as C.L.R. James and race. There can be little doubt that the volume will be of major interest to historians, theorists, students and activists."
> —Darrow Schecter, reader in Italian, School of History, Art History and Philosophy, University of Sussex

"This is a welcome and essential collection that is sure to spark debates and support ongoing efforts to build a liberatory movement in which Marxists and anarchists can find common ground and practice mutual respect and humility. In this period of late-capitalism, survival itself is at stake. Theory and practice, whether Marxism or Anarchism in their many manifestations, lead to dead ends without careful assessment of the world as it is now."
> —Roxanne Dunbar-Ortiz, author of *An Indigenous Peoples' History of the United States*

"An important, redemptive collection of essays that questions narratives of sectarian difference without resorting to easy answers. In exploring the productive frictions, convergences, agonisms and affinities that have created and re-created the 'black and red,' the contributors recover the neglected histories of a capacious Left, one that repudiated ideological rigidity and sterile orthodoxies without abandoning its socialist commons. Itself a model of such capaciousness, this is a stimulating and necessary work."
> —Raymond B. Craib, associate professor, Department of History, Cornell University

"Just what we need as we move into a new phase of revolt against the obscenity of capitalism: a recovery of the richness of our different traditions of struggle, with their weavings and bumpings. Time to move on, time to redeem the struggles of the past. A valuable and welcome collection."
> —John Holloway, author of *Change the World Without Taking Power* and professor of sociology, Autonomous University of Puebla

# Libertarian Socialism

# LIBERTARIAN SOCIALISM
# Politics in Black and Red

Edited by Alex Prichard, Ruth Kinna, Saku
Pinta, and David Berry

2017

*Libertarian Socialism: Politics in Black and Red*
Alex Prichard, Ruth Kinna, Saku Pinta, and David Berry © 2017
This edition © 2017 PM Press

ISBN: 978-1-62963-390-9
Library of Congress Control Number: 2016959590

Cover by John Yates/Stealworks.com

10 9 8 7 6 5 4 3 2 1

PM Press
PO Box 23912
Oakland, CA 94623
www.pmpress.org

Printed in the USA by the Employee Owners of Thomson-Shore in Dexter, Michigan.
www.thomsonshore.com

# Contents

# Acknowledgements

We would like to thank our contributors to the volume for their patience and for responding so positively to editorial requests. We gratefully acknowledge the support of everyone at PM Press, who have enabled us to bring out this expanded, accessible edition of the book. We would also like to thank all the participants at the 'Is Black and Red Dead?' conference held at the Centre for the Study of Social and Global Justice, University of Nottingham, UK, in September 2009, which provided the original inspiration for this collection. Sue Simpson and Tony Burns deserve a special mention for their help and support throughout. We would also like to acknowledge the generosity of the UK Political Studies Association's Marxist Specialist Group and the PSA Anarchist Studies Network, who, in supporting this conference, made it possible for some of the contributors, and many others whose excellent papers could not be included, to meet and exchange ideas face-to-face in a convivial environment.

# Contributors

**Jean-Christophe Angaut** has been Assistant Professor of Philosophy at the École Normale Supérieure de Lyon since 2006. His fields of research and teaching are nineteenth-century philosophy, political philosophy and connections between socialist, communist and anarchist thought. He has published two books on the young Bakunin's thought: *Bakounine jeune hégélien – La philosophie et son dehors* (2007) and *La liberté des peuples – Bakounine et les révolutions de 1848* (2009). He has also published articles on Marx, Bakunin, Kropotkin, the Young Hegelian movement and the situationists. He is a member of the editorial committee of the French anarchist journal *Réfractions*.

**David Bates** is a principal lecturer and Director of Politics and International Relations in the Department of Applied Social Sciences at Canterbury Christ Church University, UK. His interests are focused primarily in the area of radical politics, including anti-capitalist forms of thinking. He has a particular concern with Marxist and post-Marxist approaches to socialist emancipation. More recently he has been interested in the critical relationship between Marxist and libertarian radical politics.

**David Berry** is Senior Lecturer in History at Loughborough University, UK. He was awarded his DPhil in French labour history from the University of Sussex, UK. His research area is the history of the Left and of labour movements in twentieth-century France. He has worked mostly on the French anarchist movement and 'alternative Left', and is currently working on the life and ideas of Daniel Guérin (1904–1988) and the libertarian communist tradition from 1917 to the present. His publications include *A History of the French Anarchist Movement, 1917–1945* (2009) and (edited jointly with Constance Bantman) *New Perspectives on Anarchism, Labour and Syndicalism: The Individual, the National and the Transnational* (2010). Having been involved for some years with the *Journal of Contemporary European Studies* (formerly the *Journal of Area Studies*), he is currently an associate editor and reviews editor of the journal *Anarchist Studies*. He is a member of the Centre International de Recherches sur l'Anarchisme, Lausanne and Marseille, of the Association for the Study of Modern and Contemporary France and of the Anarchist Studies Network.

**Paul Blackledge** is Professor of Political Theory and UCU Branch Secretary at Leeds Beckett University, UK. He is author of *Marxism and Ethics* (2012), *Reflections on the Marxist Theory of History* (2006) and *Perry Anderson, Marxism and the New Left* (2004). He is co-editor of *Virtue and Politics* (2011), *Alasdair MacIntyre's Engagement with Marxism* (2008), *Revolutionary Aristotelianism* (2008) and *Histor-*

*ical Materialism and Social Evolution* (2002). He has written on Marxism and anarchism in *The Edinburgh Critical History of Nineteenth-Century Philosophy* (2011) and in *International Socialism*. He is a member of the Socialist Workers Party.

**Toby Boraman** is a lecturer in politics at Massey University Te Kunenga Ki Pūrehuroa, New Zealand. His research interests are labour history from below, (anti-state) communism and extra-parliamentary protest of the 1960s and 1970s. He received his PhD in 2006 from the University of Otago in Dunedin, New Zealand, on the subjects of the New Left and anarchism in New Zealand. Afterwards, he published a history of anarchism and anti-Bolshevik communism in New Zealand from the 1950s to the 1980s called *Rabble Rousers and Merry Pranksters* (2007). He has also published a book chapter and articles on the subjects of the New Left and working-class resistance to neoliberalism, and historical pieces on strikes and near riots in New Zealand.

**Benoît Challand** is an associate professor of sociology at the New School for Social Research and a lecturer at the University of Bologna, Italy. He works in the field of political and historical sociology, with a particular interest in Arab politics and political theory. His publications include *La Ligue Marxiste Révolutionaire, 1969–1980* (2000) and *Palestinian Civil Society and Foreign Donors* (2009). He is co-author, with Chiara Bottici, of *The Myth of the Clash of Civilizations* (2010) and *The Politics of Imagination* (edited 2011).

**Andrew Cornell** is a visiting assistant professor of American studies at Williams College, MA. He holds a PhD in American studies from New York University, New York, USA, and is completing a study of anarchism in mid-twentieth-century USA. He is the author of *Oppose and Propose! Lessons from Movement for a New Society*. His writing appears in periodicals such as the *Journal for the Study of Radicalism, Perspectives on Anarchist Theory* and *Left Turn* magazine. He has also contributed to the collections *The University against Itself* (2008) and *The Hidden 1970s: Histories of Radicalism* (2010).

**Christian Høgsbjerg** is a UK-based historian and recently was teaching fellow in Caribbean history at the UCL Institute of the Americas. He completed his doctoral thesis, *C.L.R. James in Imperial Britain, 1932–38*, in the Department of History at the University of York, UK, and is the editor of a special edition of C.L.R. James's 1934 play about the Haitian Revolution, *Toussaint Louverture: The Story of the Only Successful Slave Revolt in History* (2012). He is a member of the editorial board of the journal *International Socialism*.

**Ruth Kinna** is Professor of Political Theory at Loughborough University, UK. She is the author of *William Morris: The Art of Socialism* (2000) and the *Anarchism: A Beginner's Guide* (2005, 2009). She has published numerous articles on late nineteenth- and early twentieth-century socialism, including 'Guy Aldred: Bridging the Gap between Marxism and Anarchism' (*Journal of Political Ideologies*, 16 (1) 2011), which explores themes examined in this collection.

**Carl Levy** is a professor in the Department of Politics, Goldsmiths, University of London, UK. He is the author of six books. His interests include comparative European politics, history, policy-making and the history of ideas since 1860, with particular interest in anarchism and specialising in Italy and Italian anarchism. He is currently writing a biography of Errico Malatesta.

**Renzo Llorente** teaches philosophy at Saint Louis University's Madrid Campus, Spain. His research centres on issues in social philosophy, ethics and Latin American philosophy, and he is the author of numerous papers in these and other areas. His recent publications include *Beyond the Pale: Exercises in Provocation* (2010), a chapter on Marxism in *A Companion to Latin American Philosophy* (2010), 'The Moral Framework of Peter Singer's *Animal Liberation*' in *Ethical Perspectives* (2009) and 'Sobre el humanismo especista de Víctor Gómez Pin', in *Razonary actuar en defense de los animales* (2008). He is currently working on a study of the moral foundations of Marxism.

**Lewis H. Mates** is a tutor in history and politics at Durham University, UK. He has published several journal articles and book chapters on aspects of interwar British political history, and a monograph titled *The Spanish Civil War and the British Left* (2007). He is currently working on two projects: membership and activism in the Labour and Conservative parties (1945–1974), and rank-and-file movements and political change in the Durham coalfield before 1914.

**Saku Pinta** is a documentary filmmaker, sheet-metal worker and independent scholar. He completed his doctoral thesis, titled 'Towards a Libertarian Communism: A Conceptual History of the Intersections between Anarchisms and Marxisms', at Loughborough University, UK in 2011. His current research focuses on the history of the Finnish membership of the Industrial Workers of the World (c.1905–1975) in Canada and the USA. An essay on this topic – 'Educate, Organize, Emancipate: The Work People's College and the IWW' – is set to appear in *Anarchist Pedagogies: Collective Actions, Theories, and Critical Reflections on Education* (2012).

**Alex Prichard** is senior lecturer in International Relations at the University of Exeter, UK. He gained his PhD from Loughborough University, UK, in 2008, and has since held research and teaching posts at the University of Bath, UK, and the London School of Economics, UK, and an ESRC postdoctoral fellowship at the University of Bristol, UK. He has published articles on anarchism and world politics in the *Review of International Studies*, *Millennium: Journal of International Studies* and *Anarchist Studies*. He is the founder of the PSA Anarchist Studies Network and co-editor of the new monograph series *Contemporary Anarchist Studies*, published by Continuum Books. His first monograph, *Justice, Order and Anarchy: The International Political Theory of Pierre-Joseph Proudhon*, was published in 2012.

# Preface

Saku Pinta, Ruth Kinna, Alex Prichard, and David Berry

A century has now passed since the 1917 October Revolution in Russia ushered in the world's first 'workers' state'. Aside from its significance as one of the defining historical moments of the twentieth century, the ten days that shook the world reshaped the contours of the revolutionary Left, casting a long shadow over later global movements. The clampdown on radical left formations that followed the Bolshevik seizure of power generated considerable hostility and mutual recrimination, bringing to an end the reasonably good relations that groups of anarchists and Marxists had forged in opposition to the European capitalist war and against reformist social democracy.[1] This was especially so after the suppression of the Makhnovists in Ukraine and the Kronstadt uprising in 1921, though the antagonism was symbolised most dramatically in Europe in 1936 when Franco's failed coup gave a green light to the Soviet communist suppression of anarchist social revolution. For anarchists, Marxism emerged as the undisputed victor of the Russian Revolution and indisputably the revolution's undoing. In 1970, Stuart Christie and Albert Meltzer wrote that the 'old battles between Marxism or Marxist-Leninism on the one hand and Anarchism on the other left Marxism stronger than ever, sustained not only in State communist countries with all the violence of criminal Statism, but by schools of philosophy churning these out in all countries of the world'.[2]

The effects of the Soviet Union's assumption of the leadership of the world revolution were felt in local movements across the globe. The disastrous effects of alignment with the Comintern, resulting in the imposition of Soviet-led policy, are well known. 'At the end of the twenties', Jorge Semprun wrote, 'the Spanish Communist party was a tiny sect, torn apart by internal conflicts . . . and neutralized as a possible vanguard force by the capricious, authoritarian, and manipulative leadership of the all-powerful delegates of the Comintern, who forced the party into constant contradictory shifts of policy and changes of the party line'.[3] Anarchists of course had no place in this new International, but the Bolshevik coup not only aggravated historic tensions between anarchists and Marxists, it created strains within anarchist and Marxist movements, too.

Just as the dispute between Makhno's platformists and Voline's synthesists fractured anarchist communist and syndicalist movements, in the Marxist camp antiparliamentary and left communists, dubbed infantile by Lenin, turned their fire against the Bolsheviks and two significant elements of their international revolutionary strategy: parliamentary participation and 'boring from within', designed to transform established trade union federations.

Changes with the Soviet leadership, resulting in the identification of successive fifth columns, inevitably created new divisions. To borrow Marie-Louise Berneri's formulation: 'In order to prevent the past from condemning the present, in order to prevent Lenin from judging Stalin, the militiamen from condemning the Stalinist commissars, the communist militants from denouncing the Communist Party, the victims of the G.P.U. from accusing their persecutors, it is necessary to shut their mouths'.[4]

Once the Soviet Communist Party had established itself as the authoritative voice of world socialism, virtually everyone who identified with the Left was obliged to position themselves in relation to it: anarchists and Marxists, reformists and revolutionaries alike.[5] As the British libertarian communist journal *Aufheben* noted:

Ever since the Russian Revolution in 1917, all points along the political spectrum have had to define themselves in terms of the USSR, and in doing so they have necessarily had to define what the USSR was. This has been particularly true for those on the 'left' who have sought in some way to challenge capitalism. In so far as the USSR was able to present itself as 'an actually existing socialist system', as a viable alternative to the 'market capitalism of the West', it came to define what socialism was.[6]

Undoubtedly, the fracturing of the socialist movement was organisationally significant and it mapped, albeit imperfectly, on to some important disagreements about strategy. To be sure, the story of its development – typically traced back to the break-up of the First International in 1872 and the subsequent ejection of anarchists from the congresses of the Second International in 1896 – has also played an important part in forging movement identities, and has certainly been retold in ways that reinforce oppositional political loyalties. The intellectual domination of Marxism over anarchism in political and academic debate has created barriers to dialogue and exchange, and these continue to resonate, as the recent discussion between Simon Springer and David Harvey demonstrates.[7]

Although there is considerable disagreement about the proper labelling of the axes separating Marxism from anarchism, there is also a discernible pattern in the prevailing shorthand: Marxism's head to anarchism's heart, Marxism's theory to anarchism's practice, Marxism's science to anarchism's utopianism, Marxism's modernism to anarchism's primitivism are some of the most potent and deeply rooted oppositions. A more recent variation, rehearsed in the recent Critchley-Žižek debate, which mostly rumbled on after *Libertarian Socialism* was first published, compares Marxism's strategy to anarchism's ethics, perhaps picking up on the post-anarchist strategy-tactics distinction.

While not underestimating the significance of these traditions and representations, our principal aim in this book was to show that the anarchist-Marxist schism that the Bolshevik seizure of power ostensibly cemented was in fact neither final nor complete. The consolidation of Bolshevik power left an indelible mark on revolutionary socialism, yet the divisions it buttressed were always partial. Relationships between anti-Bolshevik and anti-Soviet Marxists and anarchists remained in flux and shifts in anti-Fascist and later cold war politics stimulated a huge body of critical theory and often biting analysis of the appalling results of Soviet-led policy, opening up consensual spaces for activists who placed themselves on different sides of the socialist divide.

Viewed as a tension and not a breach, the relationship between the black and the red – the red of communism, the black of anarchism – reveals a creative dynamic and a space for the articulation of libertarian socialism. Contributors to this volume illustrate the obstacles to its development – the misunderstandings, deliberate distortions, and misrepresentations of ideas – as well as the potential for its expression, by looking at late-nineteenth and twentieth-century, primarily European, socialist thought. A subsequent collection of essays, developing from this volume, examines the space and need for ideological convergence and has a more contemporary focus, with a third in preparation examining the ideological composition of the contemporary non-European Left.[8]

There is considerable scope to open up other fields for analysis, probing the politics of workers' self-management, reformulated by a new postwar generation in the aftermath of the Hungarian Revolution in 1956, and the critique of bureaucratic control in the West and the East; revisiting the development of socialist feminisms in the spirit of Selma James and bell hooks by looking at the resonances between militants such as Alexandra Kollontai and Emma Goldman; examining the cross-pollination of ideas in postcolonial critique and the ways that activists breathed new life into old revolutionary principles, transcending traditional Marxisms and anarchisms.[9] Peace activism and ecology are equally rich grounds for thinking about libertarian socialist experimentation.[10]

As the contributors to this volume show, there has always been a rich, fertile ground for the configuration of 'anarchism,' and of 'Marxism', and for the construction of their interrelation. By shedding light on the character of the disagreements that divided anarchists from Marxists, exploring how these played out in theory and practice and revealing the intersections between groups and individuals who located themselves in (and outside of) rival traditions, our aim has not been to deny the tensions that existed – and exist – within the socialist movement, but to show how processes of convergence in black and red politics have always run alongside the polarisation of ideological and theoretical positions.

A quarter of a century has now passed since the collapse of the Soviet Union, with Fukuyama's triumphalist 'end of history' thesis following closely in its wake. What have been the political implications of the post-Soviet era on the relationships between anarchisms and Marxisms?

Without a doubt several variants of Marxist-Leninism remain influential and maintain a viable presence, especially through the Maoist insurgencies on the Indian subcontinent, to say nothing of the remaining one-party 'workers' republics'. Nevertheless, in the period since the fall of the Berlin Wall, two events stand out as examples of libertarian socialist experimentation: the Zapatista uprising in Chiapas, Mexico in 1994 and the Rojava revolution, in progress since 2011. These are very different models of revolutionary practice, but each may be seen as an example of nonsectarian, inclusive, libertarian self-organising. Subcomandate Marcos's well-known declaration 'I shit on all the revolutionary vanguards of this planet' was not only a rejection of Leninism but a rebuke to all socialists (especially Europeans) who sought to recommend models of best revolutionary practice to non-European peoples.[11] The uprising emerged as the first sustained rebellion in the post-Soviet period. It rejected the well-worn model of capturing state power and broke with doctrinaire state socialism, serving as a key reference point for anti-state Marxists like John Holloway and Harry Cleaver and some anarchists (though it was not recognised as anarchist by others). The movement continues to exercise a bottom-up form of self-governance over a large territory in Chiapas.

The Rojava revolution is the most important recent example of a convergence of Marxist and anarchist-inspired ideas since *Libertarian Socialism* was first published.[12] Abandoning Marxist-Leninist ideology and seemingly the emphasis on national liberation, the social experiment in the Rojava region of northern Syria rose to prominence after the uprisings connected to the Arab Spring shook the foundations of established political power in North Africa. The dramatic Stalingrad-esque defence of the city of Kobane by the Kurdish People's Protection Units captured international headlines. Kurdish forces, eventually supported by American-led bombing missions, finally gained control of the city after a six-month battle against the Islamic State. Aside from the highly visible role of women fighters in the militias, this conflict has drawn attention to the ideological transformation of the Kurdish radical Left which has been developing since the mid-2000s, resulting in the shedding of a Leninist heritage and the adoption of practices that look similar to those of the Zapatistas; some have even drawn parallels between the Kurdish-led struggle in northern Syria against the Islamic State and the Spanish anarchist revolutionary uprising against Franco in 1936.[13]

The Movement for a Democratic Society (Tev-Dem) in Rojava supports a political programme that is informed by the work of Murray Bookchin: a non-statist vision of networked, self-governing communities as an alternative to the nation-state, or what has been termed democratic confederalism by its imprisoned figurehead Abdullah Ocalan.[14] It remains unclear to what degree the democratic forms celebrated by the Tev-Dem have been extended into the economy as a direct challenge to capitalist property relations. Left critics and feminists have also questioned the cult of personality that surrounds Abdullah Ocalan, and there are claims of ethnic cleansing in Rojava. However, international supporters of the movement highlight the relative religious, ethnic, and gender equality that exists in Rojava, and regard the self-governing cantons of northern Syria as a viable libertarian socialist alternative to the colonially established state boundaries in the Middle East, as well as providing an antidote to the social tensions generated by the comprador bourgeoisie.

As the inter-imperialist conflict continues to play out through highly complex, often contradictory and shifting alliances, it seems that the real choice before us is the one Rosa Luxemburg outlined: socialism or barbarism. Perhaps there's some consolation in thinking that as the memory of the Bolshevik coup dims and new traditions of libertarian socialist resistance become established, Marxists and anarchists will stop fighting each other and look to commonalities and mutual strategies for realignment and renewal. The chapters in this volume should give historical context and pause for reflection in the context of calls for a new left party,[15] or for a fully automated luxury communism.[16] The future demands debate and engagement, and on the basis of sound historical understanding.

## Notes

1.  Lucien van der Walt, 'Counterpower, Participatory Democracy, Revolutionary Defence: Debating Black Flame, Revolutionary Anarchism and Historical Marxism', *International Socialism* 130 (2011), accessed 19 February 2017, http://isj.org.uk/revolutionary-anarchism-and-historical-marxism/.

2.  Stuart Christie and Albert Meltzer, *The Floodgates of Anarchy* (London: Kahn & Averill, 1970), 6.

3.  Jorge Semprun, *Communism in Spain in the Franco Era: The Autobiography of Federico Sanchez*, trans. Helen R. Lane (Sussex: Harvester, 1980), 7.

4.  Marie-Louise Berneri, *Neither East Nor West: Selected Writings 1939–1948* (London: Freedom Press, 1988), 66.

5.  Benjamin Franks, 'Between Anarchism and Marxism: The Beginnings and Ends of the Schism . . .,', *Journal of Political Ideologies* 17:2 (2012), 207–27, accessed 15 February 2017, http://www.tandfonline.com/doi/full/10.1080/13569317.2012.676867.

6.  'What Was the USSR? Part I: Trotsky and State Capitalism', *Aufheben* #06 (Autumn 1997), accessed 19 February 2017, http://libcom.org/library/what-was-the-ussr-aufheben-1.

7.  'Simon Springer and David Harvey Debate Marxism, Anarchism and Geography', *Progressive Geographies*, accessed 27 January 2017, https://progressivegeographies.com/2015/06/10/simon-springer-and-david-harvey-debate-marxism-anarchism-and-geography/.

8.  Alex Prichard and Owen Worth, 'Left-Wing Convergence: An introduction', *Capital & Class* 40/1 (2016), 3–17, accessed 15 February 2017, http://journals.sagepub.com/doi/pdf/10.1177/0309816815624370.

9.   Benedict Anderson, *Under Three Flags: Anarchism and the Anti-Colonial Imagination* (London: Verso, 2005); Maia Ramnath, *Decolonizing Anarchism: An Antiauthoritarian History of India's Liberation Struggle* (Oakland: AK Press, 2011).

10.  Murray Bookchin, *Post-scarcity Anarchism*, 2nd edition (Montreal: Black Rose, 1986).

11.  Subcomandante Marcos, 'I Shit on All the Revolutionary Vanguards of This Planet' (January 2003), accessed 27 January 2017, http://flag.blackened.net/revolt/mexico/ezln/2003/marcos/etaJAN.html.

12.  Michael Knapp, Anja Flach, and Ercan Ayboga, *Revolution in Rojava: Democratic Autonomy and Women's Liberation in Syrian Kurdistan* (London: Pluto, 2016).

13.  David Graeber, 'Why is the world ignoring the revolutionary Kurds in Syria?', *The Guardian*, October 8, 2014, accessed 30 January 2017, https://www.theguardian.com/commentisfree/2014/oct/08/why-world-ignoring-revolutionary-kurds-syria-isis.

14.  Knapp *et al.*, *Revolution in Rojava*.

15.  Jodi Dean, *Crowds and Party: How Do Mass Protests Become an Organised Activist Collective?* (London: Verso, 2016).

16.  Nick Srnicek and Alex Williams, *Inventing the Future: Postcapitalism and a World without Work* (London: Verso, 2015).

# 1
# Introduction

*Ruth Kinna and Alex Prichard*

> *Crowned heads, wealth and privilege may well tremble should ever again the Black and Red unite!*
>
> Otto Von Bismarck[1]

This book is about two currents of ideas, anarchism and Marxism. It examines their complex interrelationship and mutual borrowings in history, theory and practice and it probes the limits and possibilities of co-operation by looking at the institutional and social contexts in which both heretical and orthodox expressions of these movements have operated. In presenting this collection, we have not attempted to fix the ideological content of either of these two currents but to show instead how this content has itself been shaped by a process of engagement, theoretical debate and political activity. To begin with definitions is to restart the long and wearisome tradition of demarcating difference and establishing doctrinal purity. This tradition has dominated in the past and its historical significance can hardly be underestimated, and we discuss it by way of introduction in order to contextualise the aims of the collection. But its practical effect has been to establish exclusive boundaries and to encourage a view that a politics of black *and* red is impossible, impractical or dangerous. The essays in this book suggest that such a politics might well be problematic, but that it nevertheless provides a welcome counter to sectarianism.

To turn, then, to the context: the history of European revolutionary socialism is usually told as a story of factionalism and dispute, and the politics of black and red – black being the colour of anarchism, and red of communism – is usually understood as dysfunctional and oppositional. The antagonism at the core of the relationship is often traced back to 1871 when the collapse of the First International appeared to mark the neat division of socialism into Bakuninist and Marxist currents. Suggestions that the significant marker was earlier, in the 1840s, when Proudhon refused collaboration with Marx, tend to reinforce the importance of this later split: 1871 cemented the formation of an ideological divide that Marx and Proudhon's mutual suspicion presaged.[2] Criticisms of Max Stirner, voiced since the 1890s – sometime after Marx and Engels sketched their critique of 'Saint Max' in *The German Ideology* – similarly bolstered the view that the political disputes that divided Marxists and anarchists were grounded in very different, perhaps irreconcilable, philosophical traditions, always latent in the socialist movement.

A second influential story of the relationship is the account promoted by Lenin and it consists of the view that the differences between Marxists and anarchists have been overstated: both groups of socialists are committed to the realisation of a common end, they disagree only about the means of transformation. In the 1970s this case was advanced by the historian Eric Hobsbawm. The rejection of anarchism, he argued, had a number of dimensions, but its leading idea was that '[t]here is no difference between the ultimate objects of Marxists and anarchists, i.e. a libertarian communism in which exploitation, classes and the state will have ceased to exist'.[3] Hobsbawm attempted to explain the apparent tension between this theoretical accord and the actual history of the revolutionary socialist movement by showing how revolutionary Marxists – Marx, Engels and Lenin – combined a rejection of anarchist thought with benevolence towards anarchist and anarcho-syndicalist movements. The agreement on ends reflected the shared practical experience of revolution, but it was also consistent with a firm denial of anarchist means to that end, and the theory that supported those means. His explanation implied a clear separation of ideas from practice in the development of ideology. Although Hobsbawm acknowledged the imprecision of 'doctrinal, ideological and programmatic distinctions' in rank-and-file movements, contrary to contemporary treatments of ideological formation, he failed to see how the ideas of 'ideologists and political leaders', of both Marxist and anarchist varieties, were *also* shaped by political engagements and events – not just theory.[4] The result was to reinforce the principle of theoretical division whilst providing a positive account of Leninism that, for anarchists, was unpersuasive.

Hobsbawm's elaboration of the apparent dovetailing of Marxist and anarchist positions points to a line of division that many anarchists have wanted to highlight – a third account of difference. This turns on the relationship between the means and ends of revolutionary struggle and the anarchist rejection of the idea that the transition from capitalism to socialism requires a period of transition in which state power is captured and used as an instrument of change, before 'withering away'.[5] For anarchists, the adoption of such means necessarily compromises the ends of the revolution and it points to a model of socialist organisation that most have rejected. Although he passed over the theoretical grounds of the anarchist complaints, Hobsbawm pinpointed precisely the nature of the concern: Marxists not only accepted the 'withering away' thesis[6] they also adopted a 'firm belief in the superiority of centralization to decentralization or federalism and (especially in the

Leninist version), to a belief in the indispensability of leadership, organization and discipline and the inadequacy of any movement based on mere "spontaneity" '.[7] From an apparent agreement about the ends of the revolution, Hobsbawm identified a combined package of ideas that was antithetical to anarchist thought and which, in parts and in whole, many self-identifying Marxists also rejected.[8]

A fourth story of the relationship between Marxism and anarchism relates to the relative significance of these two currents of thought. One version of this story focuses on practical activity, the other on emergence and re-emergence, dominance and subservience. As to the first, the place of Marxism as the dominant current within socialism is sometimes assumed without qualification. Indeed, such has been the dominance of Marxism that recent histories of the Left simply conflate socialism with Marxism and ignore the anarchists completely.[9] Others assign anarchism little more than a footnote in a wider narrative of Marxist infighting and factionalism.[10] A second version of the poor relation thesis centres on the assessment of the relative intellectual merits of Marxist and anarchist ideas. Anarchism fares badly here, too. The blunt claim of Murray Bookchin's essay 'The Communalist Project' is that anarchism 'is simply not a social theory'.

> Its foremost theorists celebrate its seeming openness to eclecticism and the liberatory effects of 'paradox' or even 'contradiction,' to use Proudhonian hyperbole. Accordingly, and without prejudice to the earnestness of many anarchistic practices, a case can made that many of the ideas of social and economic reconstruction that in the past have been advanced in the name of 'anarchy' were often drawn from Marxism.[11]

Bookchin's evaluation is not untypical. As Graeber and Grubacic note, anarchism's most distinctive contribution to socialism is often identified with revolutionary commitment. It is the passionate, idealistic heart to Marxism's sober and realistic head. In a discussion of 'small-a anarchists' they note: 'Marxism . . . has tended to be a theoretical or analytical discourse about revolutionary strategy. Anarchism has tended to be an ethical discourse about revolutionary practice . . . where Marxism has produced brilliant theories of praxis, it's mostly been anarchists who have been working on the praxis itself.'[12] Although there is now talk of an 'anarchist turn' in radical political theory, it is not yet clear that anarchism's relationship to Marxism has fundamentally altered.[13] Nor is it clear which Marxism the new Left today are turning from or which anarchism is it moving towards. The danger of 'turns' is that they reinforce existing, often caricatured, assumptions of difference and ossify identity. The reality is that the terms of debate have evolved and resist easy pigeon-holing, as the chapters in this volume testify.

The imbalance between Marxism and anarchism is also sometimes expressed through the language of emergence and re-emergence. In this discourse, anarchism is treated as a somewhat juvenile expression of inter-mittent protest. The year 1968 is often referred to as a moment of rebirth for anarchism and the new Left.[14] Likewise, 1999 is a marker for the appearance of a new anarchistic 'movement of movements' and the reappearance of anarchism, now galvanised by the struggle for global justice.[15] At the height of the Paris *évènements*, Daniel Cohn-Bendit identified both the continuities and the important critical interchanges that these movements actually represented. His unusual formulation of 'Leftism' was based on an under-standing of socialism as a continuous theoretical dispute which gave equal weight to opposing views: 'Marx against Proudhon, Bakunin against Marx, Makhno against Bolshevism', and what Cohn-Bendit called the studentwork-ers' movement against the 'transformation and development of the Russian Revolution into a bureaucratic counter-revolution, sustained and defended by Communist Parties throughout the world'.[16] Moreover, Cohn- Bendit's approach pointed to a process of political development based on continu-ous constructive critique: if Leftism was new, it borrowed from anarchism – anarchism had not re-emerged, it was merely that new groups were only just discovering it. Yet Cohn-Bendit's dialogic approach did not predominate and the sense that anarchism follows a phoenix-like existence, albeit with a shorter life-cycle, is still powerful.

The dominance of Marxism over anarchism might be explained in a number of ways. The tendency to read a utopian prehistory back into sci-entific socialism and to tie revolutionary socialism tightly to the rise of an urban, industrialised working-class movement has undoubtedly played a role in sealing Marxism's good reputation. The sense that anarchism was attractive to predominantly rural populations – though itself contestable – has encouraged a view that it was irrelevant to the modern world and attractive only to an uneducated and therefore theoretically unsophisti-cated audience. The inspiration that Marxism has provided for a range of socialist regimes and political parties also helps explain why anarchism has often been seen as Marxism's poor relation. The working assumption of Donald Sassoon's seminal study of European socialism was that the only socialist organisations to alter the trajectory of European society were the 'traditional socialist parties' (Communist and Social Democratic) which emerged from 1889. This blotted all sorts of revolutionary organisations out of socialist history, especially the anarchists, even though, as Tony Judt noted, the fringe groups that fell under Sassoon's radar nevertheless exerted a significant (albeit unwelcome in his view) influence on socialist thought. Moreover, as recent research has confirmed, other mass move-ments – notably the syndicalist – occupied a pivotal place in many parts of the world.[17]

The approach to socialism that measures success in terms of a competitive struggle for power in the state naturally disadvantages anarchism, particu-larly since no anarchist ideology is likely to find the statist patrons that have sustained and nurtured nationalist, Marxist, religious and other ideological movements. The subordination of anarchism to Marxism in accounts of socialism also owes something to the way in which political 'success' and 'defeat' are estimated and understood. The defeat of the anarchist revolution in Spain in 1939 is sometimes interpreted as a symbol of the collapse of anarchism, both in theory and practice. For Hobsbawm it provided further proof of the ideological bankruptcy of anarchism and the 'failure' of the revolution itself, evidence of the inadequacy of anarchism as a practical goal.[18] George Woodcock's view was not much different. In *Anarchism*, Woodcock argued that the 'actual anarchist movement . . . stemmed from the organization and inspiration activities of Michael Bakunin in the 1860s' and that it 'ceased to have any real relevance in the modern world' after the Spanish defeat.[19] The inability of the anarchists to stand up to Hitler, Stalin, Franco and Mussolini – practically alone – is judged as a weakness of ideology rather than of material capability. Admittedly, in the aftermath of 1968 Woodcock suggested that this had been an overly pessimistic judgement. However, its implication, which he accepted, was that anarchism was a mere tendency, a current of thought that was likely to receive only sporadic expression for it lacked institutional longevity.

Accounts of the relationship between anarchism and Marxism have helped to define and delimit the focus of critical study: anarchism is linked only to its nineteenth-century 'fathers' and Marxism tied tightly to Bolshevism, opening the way to charting Marxism's rise through the Soviet regime and its satellites and the emergence of the composite doctrine, Marxism–Leninism, at the cost of say, Trotskyism, autonomism or other currents of ultra-Left dissent. Interest in party-political success and the analysis of practical activity in the state only extends this bias. Following the logic of this approach it is easy to see why the collapse of the Berlin Wall was widely treated as the beginning of the end for European Marxism and the dawn of 'a new anarchism'.[20] Impressions such as these are today widely contested. Notions of 'the old Left' resonate in our imagination, while those who discover the antecedents of 'the new Left' find that these antecedents are often the same groups and people that populated 'the old Left' but who were marginalised or forgotten: the dissenters and heretics, but also often the acolytes or (self-appointed) vanguard. This book ought to help give more shape to this ideological morphology, but so much more remains to be done.

This reading of history leads to a similar delimitation in anarchist historical analysis. The twin claims that anarcho-syndicalism was the most important current in the anarchist movement and that it had its origins in Bakunin and his heirs, and can only be traced back to him, is one example.[21] An important consequence of the argument is that Proudhon's influence, which was particularly strong in France, Spain, Switzerland and Russia, long before Marx sought his collaboration and for a good period after, is bypassed. As a result, the republicanism of Pí-y-Margall, the pluralism of G.D.H. Cole and Harold Laski, Tolstoy's anarchism or the French tradition of 'personal-isme' and pluralist syndicalism to give a few examples, appear anomalous in socialist traditions, and the currents of thought they developed and of which they were a part are stripped of integral aspects of their substance in efforts to force them into one or other 'tradition' of socialist thinking.[22]

Reviewing these traditional accounts of anarchism and Marxism here helps illuminate the subterranean trends in socialist thinking that have always given the lie to that easy dichotomy and helps us understand the complexity of the lines of division. Continual reference to the 'anarchist core' of contemporary activist movements, illuminated and developed at length by David Graeber elsewhere,[23] belies the explosion of alternative socialist groups in the post-cold war period that are neither red nor black but draw on the politics of both. Autonomists, Council Communists, open Marxists, the Zapatistas, primitivists, nowtopians and post-anarchists all share space with longer-established groups of anarchists and Marxists, Trotskyists and Leninists, sometimes within the fuzzy intellectual plurality of the Climate Camps and the horizontalism of the wider protest move-ments, often in specific labour struggles or revolutionary moments. The relationships between the groups that make up this contemporary kalei-doscope are by no means clear or uncontested.[24] Few of their members are perhaps aware of, and probably more are indifferent to, the equally messy history of the movements which preceded their own. Yet the leading con-tention of this book is that they have something to gain from re-engaging with and reflecting on the past, on the complexity of socialist history and on the problems which previous generations of activists encountered. The drive to action and the mythological but 'tainted history' shared by anar-chists and Marxists have ignited a desire for novelty and ingenuity, and a flourishing of revolutionary vitality. An understanding of the processes of ideological formation or ossification, of the ways in which ideas translate into and are transformed by practice, helps reveal the contestability of claims made about both traditions – about both the permanence of the past or the shape of the future. There is much to be gained from opening up this rich seam.

In mining it, this collection has three main aims that have been hinted at above but are worth stating clearly. The first is to challenge conventional accounts of socialist interrelations and reopen analysis of the relationship of Marxism to anarchism. This is to suggest that the ideological boundaries are far more complex, fluid and porous than these potted histories indicate; that the diversity of views within broadly anarchist and Marxist groups is wider than the alignment with key figures allows; and that the conceptual differences between socialists who identify with different currents of thought are more interesting and nuanced than the means–end dichotomy suggests. A second aim is to reconsider the overlaps and tensions between and within different Marxisms and anarchisms and highlight the plural forms that both main currents have taken since the end of the nineteenth century. The aim here is to begin to map a more contemporary history of the Left.[25] The third aim is to delve into areas of the relatively neglected history of the socialist movement to show both how socialist ideas have played out at specific times and in particular locations and how the borrowings and mutual critiques of well-known activists – Morris, Sorel, C.L.R James, Castoriadis – who refused to adopt orthodox positions, were importantly shaped through engagement in particular struggles.

The methodological bias of the collection is towards the history of ideas.[26] While the essays are written from a range of different theoretical standpoints and advance very different normative claims, they do so by contextualising arguments rather than through appeal to abstract theoretical debate alone. This volume proceeds from the view that politics without history is directionless and that attempts to renegotiate an alignment between red and black would benefit from a sense of historical precedent rather than more theory.[27]

This book is not designed as a bridge-building project or as a search for similarity, nor is it one that presumes uniformity or homogeneity to be a suitable platform for future Left-wing strategy.[28] Moreover, the essays in this collection do not pass over the sectarianism of revolutionary socialism, but variously attempt to pinpoint what the conceptual fault lines are, show why they are significant, how they might be bridged and/or reflect on the trade-offs and creative tensions within socialism and the limits to co-operation in context. In some cases, the argument points to the irreconcilability of socialist ideologies and to insurmountable philosophical problems in bridging gaps between different factions. In other cases, spaces for negotiation are identified and encouraged. Some have found some correspondence between black and red, others have not, but even where some correspondence has been identified, the terms are divergent because the contexts are often distinct, or even – less prosaically – people simply have not understood one another. Studies that focus on key individuals show how the interplay between anarchist and Marxist currents has been captured in their writings and can be seen to have been lived through the lives of these individuals in particular intellectual and social contexts. Other chapters illustrate how attempts at engagement failed. Historical analyses of particular social or labour movements also arrive at starkly different conclusions, and while some case studies show how groups and individuals successfully exploited overlaps, others highlight sectarian collapse.

There are no general lessons here, but a number of important insights can be gleaned about the ways in which ideas translate into and through different practices, how revolutionary ambitions have changed over time and how the experience of struggle has exercised a common influence on activists in very different geographical and historical locations. In their own ways, each of these essays presents a realistic and representative platform for debate and

each contributes to our understandings of ideological division and formation on the Left, and within ideologies more broadly.[29] In the conclusion to this volume, David Berry and Saku Pinta set out what they
understand to be the most productive terms on which red and black have
engaged, and show how ways and means of thinking the past into the
present might be given a particular content. But we leave it to readers to
decide which (indeed, if any) of the versions of socialism presented here
is feasible or attractive and reflect on the future prospects of synthesis or
reconciliation.

No history is ever complete, and no collection of papers that seeks to provide a snapshot of an epochal series of such disparate debates as this can be
anything more than a beginning. The present collection includes chapters
that collectively span nearly 150 years of socialist wrangling, with all its
practical achievements and huge disappointments. In spite of our best efforts we were unable to source a chapter on historical feminist engagements
with the black and red divide or a feminist perspective on the history of this
split. This was particularly disappointing, given the practical and theoretical
contribution feminist activists on the Left have made to the understanding
of ideological division and its effective negotiation, and to the practical
achievements of women's groups in the socialist movement. But perhaps it
is telling that the voices of Lucy Parsons, Emma Goldman or groups such
as the *Mujeres Libres*, and innumerable other women's movements, do not
feature prominently in the historiography of anarchism or Marxism. As will
become clear, socialism has been recorded predominantly as a man's game
over the past century and it is a shame that this collection has failed to re-
dress this notable imbalance.[30]

Alongside this gender imbalance, there is also a geographical one. Discussion is mainly, though not exclusively, centred on European and North
American subjects and their influence elsewhere. This is another regrettable
limit on the collection.[31] So, too, is the narrowly 'political' focus. Unfortunately, the collection lacks a wider discussion of the cultural and artistic
movements that emerged across and between black and red divides.[32] But
despite these glaring lacunae, we are confident that the present volume
provides rich enough material to introduce the broad contours of the red
and black divide, give cause to pause for reflection and kick-start wider discussions. The essays have been organised to trace a history of engagement
and to give some sense of the chronology of anarchist and Marxist relations.
The volume begins with a robust defence of Marxism and presents an analysis of anarchism which identifies its theoretical and political weakness in
a model of human nature that is deemed liberal and, therefore, essentially
individualist. Paul Blackledge argues that one of Marx's great achievements
was to present a historicised conception of nature which, in showing how
human essence is transformed in and through the process of revolutionary
action, also highlighted Marxism's democratic character. Blackledge sees a

potential for dialogue with some forms of anarchism, but argues that the commitment to liberal individualism (here identified with Stirner) leaves anarchists without the practical means of revolutionary organisation and results in failure to develop a plausible theory of democracy. Until anarchists accept Marx's Hegelian conception of history, division will remain. Indeed, the anarchists' rejection of this conception not only puts them at odds with Marxism, it explains why they have characteristically misunderstood and misrepresented Leninism.

Ruth Kinna's chapter, which follows, picks up some of these themes. It examines William Morris's rejection of anarchism as individualist, and shows how this critique fed into Morris's conception of collective decision-making. The discussion looks at the ways in which anarchism and individualism were understood at the end of the nineteenth century in order to show that Morris's treatment conjured up a ghoul, an anarchism that was individualist and hence antithetical to socialism. Morris contributed to the stigmatisation of a tradition of thinking that was far richer than he was prepared to give it credit for, and his critique forced him to substantially revise some of his own democratic principles. It also demonstrated how a lack of care and clarity in the terms of debate helped narrow the scope for co-operation. Morris, like Blackledge, saw little room for negotiating black and red traditions. In unpicking the relationship between anarchism and individualism, Kinna argues that there is at least some scope for the reappraisal of the terms of this split.

Lewis Mates' chapter provides a powerful and complex counterpoint and development to the preceding chapters. Through an analysis of the lives of George Harvey (an industrial unionist) and Will Lawther (an anarchist syndicalist) in pre-war Durham, Mates shows how the urge to collective action and communist ends were led by idealistic and highly motivated individuals in and around the pit villages during these momentous years. Influenced by the writings of De Leon, Morris, Kropotkin and Aldred, and the practical iniquities and challenges they experienced daily, the socialism that emerged largely eschewed parliamentary action and sought collective direct action for socialist ends. But there were significant ideological tensions between the purist Lawther and pragmatic Harvey, which were played out in the course of the miners' struggle. The struggle for autonomy and self-management in Durham is a microcosm of wider struggles elsewhere at that time and bears careful reading precisely for the light it sheds on the lived attempts to realise communal ends through individual initiative and revolutionary commitment.

In Chapter 4, Renzo Llorente reopens the question of ideological division through a reappraisal of George Sorel. Llorente's main concern, however, is to classify Sorel as an anarcho-Marxist: someone in whom certain key features of both traditions were united and around whom both black and red might be able to unite. Llorente shows how Sorel's direct engagement with the writings of Marx, Proudhon and Bakunin did not lead to theoretical paradox but to hybridisation. In some respects, Llorente shows us that anarchist means can lead to communist ends. Sorel distinguished between the violence perpetrated by the state, individual acts of violence and the revolutionary violence of the working classes – the latter essentially a synonym for strikes. He claimed that it was through the marshalling of forces for the general strike that the working class was educated both in its own agency and revolutionary potential. Democratic participation in the organisation of the general strike was the direct means to empowerment. The links to Lenin, Kropotkin and Bakunin are clear – the question raised is whether they are convincing enough to help us move beyond black and red, towards some sort of viable synthesis.

The cross-currents of socialist thought are further probed in Carl Levy's analysis of Gramsci, a figure who, perhaps more than any other either before or after him, is identified with the fusion of anarchism and Marxism. Levy's chapter brings this out to good effect, but contests this view. In Gramsci we see the eschewal of orthodoxy and the turn to small(er)-scale voluntarism as the motor of progressive counter-hegemonic blocs – the role of the intellectual and moral vanguard notwithstanding. But his thought was shaped by his early engagement with Croce and by involvement in the complex politics of the Italian Left. His relationship with the anarchists reflected the depth of his disagreements with other activists and was not an indication of deep empathy with anarchist ideas. Indeed, his criticisms of Malatesta and other anarchist intellectuals ran alongside an appreciation of Leninism, only to be replaced by councillism once the orthodoxies of Second and Third International Marxism came to prominence.

Saku Pinta's chapter takes the historical narrative of the volume to the onset of the Second World War. While the First World War proved disastrous for the anarchist movement as a whole, the Second World War and the defeat of the Spanish anarchists killed off what was left of a mass anarchist revolutionary movement, at least in Europe.[33] What came later, as the following chapters show, is a far stronger Leninist form of libertarianism than the anarchist-flavoured synthesis that preceded it. In this respect, the perspectives of the Council Communists on the Spanish revolution provide an important historical marker in the twentieth-century history of anarchism and Marxism, while at the same time showing that even in the so-called death throes of anarchism alternative hybrids of libertarian socialism were already well established.

Christian Høgsbjerg's chapter covers the unique life experiences of the Trinidadian socialist C.L.R. James. As the complementary chapters of Berry and Cornell show, James' connections with anarchist, syndicalist and black civil rights activists make him a hugely significant figure in the history of the Left. James' criticism of Trotsky also presents us with a glimpse into the personal and political that shaped this 'bohemian freelancer'. Høgsbjerg argues that despite an early flirtation with Kropotkin's work on the French Revolution, James was no anarchist and his criticism of the direction of the Soviet state and later his break with official Trotskyism are no more indication of this than his appreciation of Kropotkin's work. James was an anti-anarchist who, despite drawing on and developing the ideas of many around him, remained a committed Marxist. His intellectual legacy lies in autonomism.

David Berry examines the work of Daniel Guérin, a friend of James. His essay considers Guérin's attempt to synthesise anarchism and Marxism, an attempt which sprang from a desire for 'total revolution', a dissatisfaction with the economic reductionism and authoritarianism of Trotskyism, and from the inspirational works of Bakunin and Proudhon. The way in which Guérin appropriated anarchism after his break with Trotskyism is remarkable precisely because it mirrored the path taken by James, Gramsci and others. And yet Guérin was far more open in his admiration for Proudhon, Stirner and Bakunin and seemed remarkably more open to engagement with their ideas in finding an audience for his own synthesis of anarchism and Marxism. Berry argues that Guérin's importance lies in his practical engagement with French movements and in his eschewal of abstract theory. He identifies his legacy in the emergence of the new Left in France and elsewhere, highlighted during the events of May '68 and beyond.

Benoit Challand provides an analysis of one of the key intellectual markers in the pre-'68 French revolutionary Left: the group of writers that coalesced around the publication *Socialisme ou Barbarie*, in particular Cornelius Castoriadis. The life and times of these characters provides an excellent case study of the role of authoritarian personalities in the formation and trajectory of intellectual movements and the failure of revolutionary socialist movements to bridge the divide between anarchism and Marxism – anarchism here identified with Council Communism. The Council Communist tradition and the particular brand of Trotskyism outlined by Lefort and Castoriadis were both productive and suggestive, but ultimately the factionalism and the contrast between the libertarian politics of '*S ou B*' and the authoritarianism of the group's leader proved too much for the smooth running of the group. This factionalism is probably the lived experience of day-to-day socialism for innumerable activists. What every expulsion and every act of intellectual dissidence shows, of course, is that 'red' and 'black' have been, and still are, deeply and passionately contested concepts.

Jean-Christophe Angaut's essay examines the politics of the Situationist International (SI). While he acknowledges the important influence that the SI exercised on the events in 1968, his analysis is designed to reveal the significance of the critiques that Guy Debord and others levelled against anarchist anti-authoritarians and Marxist anti-capitalists. His intellectually and socially contextualised analysis draws out the Hegelianism of the SI. The SI's view, he argues, was that the *unity* of revolutionary theory was to be found in an original critical relation of both black and red with

Hegelian thought – a current from which Bakunin, Marx, Engels and Stirner all emerged. Their attempt to go beyond the subsequent separation (outlined in different ways by Blackledge and Kinna), brings us back to a point of unity. Angaut's point is not to endorse the unity and totality that the SI found, but to return to this starting point. Historical versions of Marxism and anarchism are both redundant, he argues. Today, 'black and red' means 'the multiplicity of real social alternatives, avoiding hierarchy and the rule of the commodity' (p. 441).

Andrew Cornell takes us back over the Atlantic to a contemporaneous revolutionary movement and shows us how today's anarchist tactics influenced, morphed into and then once again developed out of the tactics of the black civil rights activists between the late 1930s and the mid-1970s. Anarchists went into the US penitentiary system as conscientious objectors, campaigned against racial separation while inside and also helped radicalise the future leaders of the civil rights movement – their fellow inmates. Once outside, the anarchist-inspired black civil rights movement in the USA evolved further through encounters with the doctrines of Marxist national liberation ideology – particularly the writings of C.L.R. James and the Johnson Forest Tendency – and erupted through both violent and nonviolent civil disobedience, direct action and 'black bloc' tactics. The latter were to feed back into the radical undercurrents of anarchist politics in the run up to mass protests surrounding Seattle in 1999.

As Toby Boraman makes clear, Australasian revolutionary socialists were at the fringes of the global movement but in many respects the experiences of the main characters in his micro-drama are familiar to us all. Boraman's case study sheds light on a neglected area of anarchist research. It shows us the typical rather than the extraordinary, the everyday rather than the high politics of revolution, and is enlightening for precisely that reason. Boraman examines how ideas translated in the Australasian context; how situationists, Council Communists and class struggle anarchists intermingled; and how their acolytes fell out with one another and struggled together for social change and self-expression. He draws on this analysis to reflect on the splits between carnival anarchists and class warriors as an example of a division between the ideologically pure and the pragmatists of life. Many will recognise some aspect of Boraman's detailed picture and doubtless agree that with the collapse brought about by factional disputes it is likely that the moniker 'libertarian socialism' – understood here as 'a many-sided struggle to change not only work, but also everyday life' – will supersede those that went before (p. 470).

Bates brings our collection up to date with the most recent and perhaps the most famous rearticulation of contemporary socialist politics: Michael Hardt and Antonio Negri's work. Their writings are controversial and, as he shows, open to a wide variety of interpretations. Bates explains these disagreements by discussing their self-identification as communists, their reinterpretation of Leninism and vocal rejection of anarchism. His analysis also shows the complex historical processes and intellectual lineages that shaped their ideas, both opening up our understanding of them as well as asking a range of difficult questions about the political efficacy of a politics founded on multitude, a rejection of class conflict and a celebration of 'foundationlessness'. Hardt and Negri are without doubt original; the questions Bates raises are in relation to what, and at what cost?

Pinta and Berry's conclusion draws on some of the cross-currents of socialist thinking expressed in these chapters and identifies the most powerful areas of convergence in the gap between social democracy and Bolshevism on the one hand, and anarchist individualism on the other. Their analysis treats libertarian socialism as a form of anti-parliamentary, democratic, antibureaucratic grass roots socialist organisation, strongly linked to workingclass activism. Locating libertarian socialism in a grey area between anarchist and Marxist extremes, they argue that the multiple experiences of historical convergence remain inspirational and that, through these examples, the hope of socialist transformation survives. The potential for revolutionary change continues to rest on the possibility of convergence rooted in social struggles, because it is here that affinities are forged and mutual dialogue takes place.

To bring this introduction to a close, it is important to emphasise that this book is simply a collection of reflections on the antecedents and emergent hybrids of contemporary socialist thought. Many will recognise the pictures painted here and many others will disagree with particular inflections, interpretations and biases. This would be to engage with precisely the historical recovery and rearticulation this book seeks to defend and would be a necessary first step towards developing alternatives. Ideas do not spring ready-formed from our minds, but emerge out of the confluence of quiet reflection and the tumult of social struggle. That is what these chapters show and they undoubtedly suggest that political agency and ideological morphology are born of and live through specific times and places. The past might not hold lessons, but a better appreciation of history provides a counterweight to presentism, expands the terms of political praxis and checks political myopia. In this respect, this book is for those who seek to realise new possibilities from within the shell of the old.

## Acknowledgements

We would like to thank David Berry, Lucien van der Walt and Gabriel Kuhn for comments on an earlier draft of this Introduction.

## Notes

1.  These are the words that Bismarck was reported to have said on hearing of the split between the anarchists and Marxists in the First International. They appear in Burnette G. Haskell's statement of the principles for the reunification of red and

black, written in 1883. Haskell was the secretary of the West Coast International Workingmen's Association, and his project failed. See Chester McA. Destler, 'Shall Red and Black Unite? An American Revolutionary Document of 1883', *Pacific Historical Review*, 14, no. 4 (December, 1945), p. 447.

2.  For a critical revisionist account of the debate between Marx and Proudhon, see Iain McKay, *Property Is Theft! A Pierre-Joseph Proudhon Anthology* (Edinburgh: AK Press, 2011), pp. 64–79.

3.  Eric Hobsbawm, 'Bolshevism and the Anarchists', *Revolutionaries* (London: Quartet Books, 1977), p. 57.

4.  Hobsbawm, ibid., p. 59. For a discussion of ideology and politics see Michael Freeden, 'Thinking Politically and Thinking Ideologically', *Journal of Political Ideologies*, 13, no. 1 (2008), pp. 1–10; Michael Freeden, *Ideologies and Political Theory: A Conceptual Approach* (Oxford: Clarendon, 1996).

5.  This is not to imply that all anarchists accepted the idea of violent revolution: Proudhon is a notable exception and others, including Stirner and Tolstoy, also rejected revolution on this model. However, both the idea of prefiguration – that the means of struggle are inextricably linked to its ends – and the rejection of state-led transformation are also common themes in non-revolutionary anarchist writing. For a recent exchange on the question of means and ends, revolutionary violence and the idea of the state, see Paul Blackledge, 'Marxism and Anarchism', *International Socialism: A Quarterly Journal of Socialist Theory*, 125 (2010), at http://www.isj.org.uk/index.php4?id=616&issue=125 (accessed 14 May 2012), and Lucien van der Walt, 'Detailed reply to *International Socialism*: debating power and revolution in anarchism, *Black Flame* and historical Marxism', at http://lucienvanderwalt.blogspot.com/2011/02/anarchism-black-flame-Marxism-and-ist.html (accessed 27 July 2011).

6.  A critique of the thesis is presented by Solomon F. Bloom, 'The Withering Away of the State', *Journal of the History of Ideas*, 7, no. 1 (1946), pp. 113–121, and Richard Adamiak, 'The Withering Away of the State: A Reconsideration', *Journal of Politics*, 32 (1970), pp. 3–18.

7.  Hobsbawm, 'Bolshevism and the Anarchists', p. 58. The division on the question of centralisation is noted in E. Yaorslavsky's *History of Anarchism in Russia* (London: Lawrence & Wishart, 1937) and by Ivan Scott, 'Nineteenth Century Anarchism and Marxism', *Social Science*, 47 (1972), pp. 212–218.

8.  The extent to which the Marxism(s) against which anarchism is assessed has any relationship to Marx is a moot point. Daniel Guérin tackled the question of interpretation in 'Marxism and Anarchism', in D. Goodway (ed.) *For Anarchism: History, Theory and Practice* (London: Routledge, 1989), pp. 109–125. For a discussion of Marxist distortions of Marxian thought see Paul Thomas, *Marxism and Scientific Socialism: From Engels to Althusser* (London: Routledge, 2008). Thomas's Marxian analysis of anarchism does not result in a substantially more sympathetic account of anarchism than other Marxist readings. See Paul Thomas's *Karl Marx and the Anarchists* (London: Routledge, 1985).

9.  See, for example, Subrata Mukherjee and Sushila Ramaswamy, *A History of Socialist Thought: From the Precursors to the Present* (Delhi: Sage, 2000).

10. Darrow Schecter, *The History of the Left from Marx to the Present: Theoretical Perspectives* (London: Continuum, 2007), pp. 127–134.

11. Murray Bookchin, 'The Communalist Project', *The Harbinger*, 3 (1) (2002), at http://www.social-ecology.org/2002/09/harbinger-vol-3-no-1-the-communalistproject/ (accessed 14 June 2011).

12. David Graeber and Andrej Grubacic, 'Anarchism, or the Revolutionary Movement for the 21st Century', at http://www.zmag.org/content/showarticle. cfm?ItemID=4796 (accessed 14 June 2011).

13. The claim that there has been a fundamental shift is made by Duane Rousselle and Süreyyya Evren in *Anarchist Developments in Cultural Studies*, vol. 1, 2010, at http:// anarchist-developments.org (accessed 17 June 2011). A link to papers presented at 'The Anarchist Turn' conference held at the New School for Social Research, New York, 5–6 May 2011, at http://anarchist-developments.org/index.php/adcs/issue/ view/4 (accessed 14 June 2011).

14. See the collection 'Anarchism Today' edited by David Apter in *Government and Opposition*, 5, no. 4 (1970).

15. Barbara Epstein, 'Anarchism and the Alter-Globalization Movement', *Monthly Review*, 53, no. 4 (2001), at http://www.monthlyreview.org/0901epstein.htm (accessed 01 November 2010).

16. Daniel Cohn-Bendit, *Obsolete Communism the Left-Wing Alternative*, trans. A. Pomerans (London: André Deutsch, 1968), p. 18.

17. Donald Sassoon, *One Hundred Years of Socialism: The West European Left in the Twentieth Century* (London: Fontana, 1996), p. xxi; Tony Judt, *Times Literary Supplement*, 8 November 1996, p. 21. Judt was dismissive of the 'multifarious socialist "sects" ' but argued their impact gave historians sufficient reason to study them. For a recent study of anarcho-syndicalism see Michael Schmidt and Lucien van der Walt, *Black Flame: The Revolutionary Class Politics of Anarchism and Syndicalism* (Edinburgh: AK Press, 2009).

18. Eric Hobsbawm, 'The Spanish Background', *Revolutionaries* (London: Quartet Books, 1977), p. 75; Eric Hobsbawm, *The Age of Extremes: The Short Twentieth Century 1914–1991* (London: Abacus, 1999), p. 74.

19. George Woodcock, *Anarchism* (Harmondsworth: Penguin, 1975), p. 452.

20. David Graeber, 'The New Anarchists', *New Left Review*, 13 January/February 2002, pp. 61–73.

21. Schmidt and van der Walt make this claim, though their analysis of the broad anarchist tradition and anarcho-syndicalist strategy also discusses a variety of other anarchisms. Schmidt and van der Walt, *Black Flame*.

22. See, for example, Benedict Anderson, *Under Three Flags: Anarchism and the Anti-Colonial Imagination* (London, Verso 2005); Cécile Laborde, *Pluralist Thought and the State in Britain and France, 1900–1925* (Basingstoke: Palgrave Macmillan, 2000).

23. David Graeber, *Direct Action: An Ethnography* (Edinburgh: AK Press, 2010).

24. The extent to which the horizontal politics of the alter-globalisation movement is rooted in anarchism, for example, is contested. See, for example, Uri Gordon, *Anarchy Alive! Antiauthoritarian Politics from Practice to Theory* (London: Pluto, 2008).

25. Cf. G. D. H. Cole, *A History of Socialist Thought 1789–1939* (VII vols) (London: Macmillan, 1953–1961).

26. Quentin Skinner, *Visions of Politics Volume 1: Regarding Method* (Cambridge: Cambridge University Press, 2002).

27. See also Ruth Kinna and Alex Prichard, 'Anarchism: Past Present and Utopia', in Randall Amster et al. (eds.), *Contemporary Anarchist Studies: An Introductory Anthology of Anarchy in the Academy* (London: Routledge, 2009), pp. 270–279.

28. For an example of this see William T. Armaline and Deric Shannon, 'Introduction: Toward a More Unified Libertarian Left', *Theory in Action*, special edition, 'Building Bridges Between Anarchism and Marxism', 3,

no. 4 (2010), at http://www.transformativestudies.org/publications/theory-in-action-the-journal-of-tsi/past-issues/volume-3-number-4-october-2010/ (accessed 17 June 2011). See also Howard Zinn on Anarchism and Marxism in an interview with Sasha Lilley, at http://www.youtube.com/watch?v=DbaizDSg1YU (accessed 17 June 2011).

29. For a discussion of the morphological character of ideologies see Freeden, *Ideologies and Political Theory*.

30. On the historiography of anti-feminism in anarchist studies see Sharif Gemie, 'Anarchism and Feminism: A Historical Survey', Women's History Review 5, no.3 (1996), pp. 417–444, or a recent account of women's involvement in a range of early twentieth-century movements and campaigns and a useful bibliography, see Sheila Rowbotham, *Dreamers of a New Day: Women Who Invented the Twentieth Century* (London: Verso, 2010).

31. For an important and interesting collection of papers that traces a global history of anarcho-syndicalism see Steven Hirsch and Lucien van der Walt (eds) *Anarchism and Syndicalism in the Colonial and Postcolonial World, 1870–1940: The Praxis of National Liberation, Internationalism, and Social Revolution* (Leiden: Brill, 2010).

32. See the work of Allan Antliff, for example, *Anarchist Modernism: Art, Politics and the First American Avant-Garde* (London: University of Chicago Press, 2001).

33. Elsewhere, anarchism maintained a healthy if subterranean existence. See Hirsch and van der Walt, *Anarchism and Syndicalism* for far more on this.

# 2
# Freedom and Democracy: Marxism, Anarchism and the Problem of Human Nature

*Paul Blackledge*

## Introduction

In this paper I argue that anarchist[1] criticisms of Marx's 'statism' inherit themes from liberalism that serve as a brake on the democratic aspirations of anarchist practice. While superficially attractive, especially when deployed to explain the character of both Stalinism and social democracy, this liberal element of anarchist theory prevents anarchist practice developing from a mode of resistance to capitalism to become an adequate strategic alternative to it. Further, I argue that classical Marxism offers tools by which to overcome this problem and suggest that Marx is best understood not as the statist other to libertarian socialism, but as the most coherent exponent of human emancipation. I conclude that anarchists would do well to re-engage with his critique of liberalism to help move beyond the politics of perpetual opposition.

The overlap between anarchism and liberalism is evident, for instance, in the parallels between Bakunin's suggestion that 'power corrupts the best'[2] and Lord Acton's famous aphorism that 'all power tends to corrupt and absolute power corrupts absolutely'.[3] Underlying Acton's claim is a highly contentious concept of human nature which undermines not only the assertion of papal infallibility – Acton's specific target – but also the democratic aspirations of the socialist movement. Acton was a liberal Roman Catholic whose comments on power are perhaps best understood as a particularly pithy expression of the political implications of the Christian conception of original sin as secularised through the liberal idea of egoistic individualism. To accept that power corrupts implies something like this model of human essence. One implication of this idea is liberalism's contradictory view of social organisation and thus the state as simultaneously alien and essential: 'a necessary evil' in Tom Paine's felicitous phrase.[4] For the socialist movement the implications of this idea were drawn out most forcefully by Robert Michels. He insisted that an 'iron law of oligarchy' followed from humanity's 'natural love of power',[5] and argued that the utopian nature of the socialist project was tacitly registered by Marx through his concept of the dictatorship of the proletariat – 'the direct antithesis of the concept of democracy'[6] – and practically negated by the German Social Democratic Party's reproduction of the kind of guiding aristocratic 'political class' that ran traditional elitist parties.

Michels wrote that '[a]narchists were the first to insist upon the hierarchical and oligarchical consequences of party organisation. Their view of the defects of organisation is much clearer than that of the socialists.'[7] Interestingly, not only did Michels register anarchism's insights about the tendency to oligarchy, but anarchists have often returned the compliment. Most recently, for instance, Michael Schmidt and Lucien van der Walt have borrowed the concept of 'iron law of oligarchy' in their analysis of trade union organisation – though they mediate it through reference to a counter 'tendency towards democracy'.[8] Schmidt and van der Walt's positive reference to Michels is not unusual in anarchist literature. Indeed, it has been suggested that Bakunin 'foreshadowed' Michels' analysis.[9] And it is clear that there is at least a family resemblance between Michels' iron law of oligarchy and Bakunin's claim that 'all political organisation is destined to end in the negation of freedom.'[10]

In this essay I explore some broader implications of these theoretical parallels with a view to challenging what Chomsky called Bakunin's 'all too perceptive' warnings about the inevitable logic of Marxist authoritarianism towards the creation of a 'red bureaucracy'.[11] I argue that the parallels between social anarchism and Michels' elite theory actually illuminate aspects of a shared model of human essence that weakens anarchism's revolutionary intent. Moreover, I argue that the theoretical roots of this weakness are to be found in what is often portrayed as one of anarchism's strengths: the liberal moment of its dual inheritance from socialism and liberalism. So, whereas Rudolf Rocker, in his oft-repeated claim that anarchism represents the 'confluence of...socialism and liberalism',[12] implied that anarchism had forged a synthesis from the best of modern political and economic theory, I argue that far from working a synthesis of these two traditions, anarchism's inheritance from liberalism acts as a barrier to the full realisation of the revolutionary implications of its socialist side. I therefore suggest that if anarchism is to move beyond the politics of resistance to point to an adequate revolutionary alternative to capitalism it needs to reassess the liberal side of its heritage.

Marx pointed to the kind of root and branch critique of liberalism necessary for such a manoeuvre. In arguments first articulated in response to Max Stirner's anarchism, he responded to the naturalisation of egoism not by positing an opposite socialistic essence, but rather by extending Hegelian insights to suggest a fully historicised conception of our nature.[13] Marx's critique of Stirner is of general significance because it acts as the theoretical core of his critique of the liberalism underpinning Acton's aphorism about the corrupting influence of power. Against liberalism's embrace of a transhistorical conception of human nature,[14] Marx grasped the socio-historic co-ordinates of modern egoism in the rise of capitalism, and conversely pointed to the seeds of its potential transcendence in the solidaristic movements of the 'newfangled' working class. His was a historical model of human essence that underpinned a historical model of human freedom.[15] It was through these arguments that he was able to conceptualise socialism as, in the words of Ernst Bloch, a 'concrete utopia': a tendency towards political power rooted in the workers' movement against capitalism.[16]

This argument illuminates an important difference between Marxism and anarchism. Both of these tendencies on the revolutionary Left emerged in the nineteenth century as aspects of a democratic revolt against capitalism. However, whereas Marx was able to conceive of new forms of democracy that overcame the capitalist separation of economic and politics, as we shall see anarchism's tendency to embed a transhistorical conception of human egoism acts as a barrier to its conceptualisation of any such project. I suggest that if the potential of the democratic impulse behind class-struggle anarchism is to be realised, anarchism needs to address underlying ontological assumptions about human nature.

## Marx's critique of anarchism: Human nature and democracy

The first significant engagement between Marxism and anarchism was Marx's critique of Stirner in the 1840s. It is important to note that Marx did not reject Stirner from a pre-established position, but rather developed his vision of socialism in no small part in answer to Stirner's critique of 'true socialist' moralism in the context of the emergence of the collective workers' struggles against capital in the 1840s.[17]

Stirner argued that all political systems lead in practice to the authoritarian suppression of the individual ego. Even revolutions, by claiming to be in the common interest, lead to the suppression of individual egoism. Consequently, he conceived 'self-liberation' to be possible through an act of rebellion rather than through revolution.[18] In a comment on the French Revolution which he believed to have general salience, he suggested that this upheaval was not directed against '*the establishment*, but against the *establishment in question*, against a particular establishment. It did away with *this* ruler, not with *the* ruler'. That the French Revolution ended in reaction should therefore come as no surprise: for it is in the nature of revolutions that one authority is merely exchanged for another.[19] 'Political liberalism's' embrace of the post-revolutionary state revealed its authoritarian implications, implications that were also inherent in socialism and communism (ideologies he subsumed under the revealing heading 'social liberalism'), for these too would merely repeat the transference of power from one authority to another.[20]

Stirner embraced an absolute model of freedom, according to which '*freedom* can only be the whole of freedom, a piece of freedom is not *freedom*'.[21] From this perspective, he concluded that all moral approaches, because they preached self-sacrifice in the name of some metaphysical notion – god, man, the state, class, nation and so on – were the enemies of freedom. If 'the road to ruin is paved with good intentions', the correct egoistic response was not revolution in the name of some 'good' but a more simple rebellion of the ego against authority.[22] For Stirner, therefore, there exists a fundamental opposition between individual ego and society, which could not be overcome by any form of social organisation.[23] Indeed, he believed that communism ('social liberalism') was not so much a radical alternative to the *status quo* as it was its latest moralistic variant.[24]

In his reply to Stirner, Marx argued that, far from being an abstract moral doctrine, solidarity was becoming a real need within the working-class movement whose emergent goal was, as he was later to write in *The Communist Manifesto*, an 'association, in which the free development of each is the condition for the free development of all'.[25] From this perspective there would be no need to impose the idea of community on the working class from without because solidarity/community would emerge from below. This historical model of freedom was rooted in a historical model of human nature. Marx argued that communism is, for Stirner:

> quite incomprehensible ... because the communists do not oppose egoism to selflessness or selflessness to egoism ... communists do not preach morality at all ... on the contrary they are very well aware that egoism, just as much as selflessness, is in definite circumstances a necessary form of self-assertion of individuals.[26]

As we shall see, Marx was interested in the definite historical context through which human essence evolved and the definite circumstances of the contemporary movement for freedom against capitalism. Concretely, he argued that it was through the movement from below that workers begin to challenge the narrow confines of egoism in a way that allows them to conceive society (and thus authority) positively as real democracy. This was no mere political movement, for, as he wrote in *On the Jewish Question*, 'political emancipation' does not overcome the 'egoistic, independent individual' of civil society. In fact, it is only when humanity 're-absorbs in [itself] the abstract citizen' that it recognises its own forces 'as social forces, and consequently no longer separates social power from [itself] in the shape of political power, only then will human emancipation have been accomplished'.[27]

This idea of dialectical development and the model of emancipation it supported is foreign not only to Stirner but also to the most important voices within social anarchism – Proudhon, Bakunin and Kropotkin. By contrast with Marx's fundamental critique of the liberal conception of individual egoism, social anarchists tend rather to mediate this concept by mixing it with more social conceptions of human nature. According to David Morland, Proudhon, Bakunin and Kropotkin all embraced models of human nature that included transhistorical conceptions of both egoism and sociality, and which consequently tended to conceptualise history as an 'everlasting battle in human nature between good and evil'.[28] Proudhon, he argues, wrote that 'man is essentially and previous to all education an egoistic creature, ferocious beast, and venomous reptile...only transformed by education', while Bakunin insisted that man is 'not only the most individual being on earth – he is also the most social being'.[29] Even Kropotkin, who is by far social anarchism's most sophisticated spokesperson, was only able to make sense of the evils of modern society by embedding a transhistorical conception of egoism as the necessary counterweight to the idea of mutual aid within his model of human nature. Kropotkin suggested that throughout human history two opposed traditions have vied with each other. As he wrote, this timeless struggle is concretely realised in history as struggles between 'the Roman and the Popular; the imperial and the federalist; the authoritarian and the libertarian'.[30] Moreland concludes that social anarchism 'rests on the twin pillars of egoism and sociability'.[31] Consequently, and despite social anarchism's attempts to articulate a social vision in which society is 'perceived as an organic whole within which individual freedom is mediated through some notion of communal individuality',[32] in practice the attempt to forge a creative synthesis of socialism and liberalism results in an 'irresolvable stalemate over the question of human nature'.[33] From this we might conclude that although social anarchists reject Stirner's extreme individualism they tend not to make a root and branch critique of egoism but rather reify it as an important facet of human essence.

The political implications of this general perspective were forcefully expressed by Bakunin in his *Revolutionary Catechism* where he insisted that anarchism involves the 'absolute rejection of every authority'. While the negative implications of this statement is clear – it informs anarchism's resistance to all forms of domination – it is less clear how Bakunin, despite his claim that forms of authority are acceptable if they are 'imposed on me by my own reason',[34] is able to move from this standpoint to a more positive project of building a democratic alternative to capitalism. Indeed, the worry that Marxists have about Bakunin's position is that his own criticisms of democracy show no evidence that he even considered the possibility that it could have a deeper social content than bourgeois democracy.[35] This ambiguous relationship to the idea of a real democratic alternative to capitalism seems evident elsewhere in anarchism and is perhaps best expressed by Malatesta, who, despite writing that the worst democracy is preferable to the best dictatorship, remained of the opinion that 'democracy is a lie, it is oppression and is in reality, oligarchy'.[36] Arguments such as this open the door to George Woodcock's claim that 'no conception of anarchism is farther from the truth than that which regards it as an extreme form of democracy'.[37] Similarly, Uri Gordon has recently asserted that anarchism's defence of the absolute rights of the individual against the state means that, despite its congruence with certain aspects of democratic social movements, it is best understood as 'not "democratic" at all'.[38]

These arguments have been challenged from within the anarchist movement by, among others, Schmidt and van der Walt, Todd May and Wayne Price. According to Schmidt and van der Walt, 'anarchism would be nothing less than the most complete realisation of democracy',[39] while May and Price insist, respectively, that anarchism represents the democratic unfolding of social practices or the 'most extreme, consistent and thoroughgoing democracy'.[40] Given the forthright nature of these claims it is interesting that these authors do not address the kind of anarchist criticisms of democracy noted above – though Price admits that 'the historical relation between anarchism and democracy is highly ambiguous'.[41] Ruth Kinna's discussion of the relationship between anarchism and democracy goes further in registering this problem. She points out that while anarchists are drawn towards democratic politics, they have had little of substance to say about democracy beyond a desire for consensus decision-making. And as she acknowledges, this approach is open to the famous criticism levelled by Jo Freeman at the North American anarcha-feminist movement in the 1960s. What she called *The Tyranny of Structurelessness*,[42] or the ability of the most articulate (usually middle class) members of structureless groups to hold *de facto* power within them.

In his attempt to develop the anarchist position, Price argues that anarchism and democracy can be married once it is recognised that it is possible to distinguish between the kind of power that 'it will be necessary for the oppressed to take' in the struggle for socialism, and 'state power'.[43] Against the broad current of anarchist and autonomist thinking which associates Marxism with the idea of state 'seizure', Price argues that this position was, in essence, shared by Marx and Lenin. Interestingly, van der Walt suggests something similar when he argues that the revolution should be defended through workers' own democratic organisations. In a reply to my own and Leo Zeilig's rehearsals of the Marxist understanding of the dictatorship of the proletariat as a form of extreme democracy, he writes that:

> If (and I stress, only if) we concede such definitions, then we *must* argue that Bakunin, Kropotkin ... [and] the majority of the broad anarchist tradition were *for the state* – at least, that is, *for* the 'workers' state' and *for* the 'dictatorship' of the proletariat.[44]

Clearly, it is safe to say that this statement would be very contentious in anarchist circles – even Price insists that Lenin's 'libertarian interpretation of Marxism is contradictory to the totalitarian state' he developed.[45] Nevertheless, Price and van der Walts's position seems to open a potential space for dialogue, and assuming anarchists, like Marxists, are able to embrace the Paris Commune as a model of socialism any such dialogue must at some point engage with the problem of adequately conceptualising it.

In a critique of reformism, Engels famously wrote 'of late, the Social Democratic philistine has once more been filled with wholesome terror at the words: Dictatorship of the Proletariat. Well and good, gentlemen, do you want to know what this dictatorship looks like? Look at the Paris Commune. That was the Dictatorship of the Proletariat'.[46] The concept of the dictatorship of the proletariat sits at the very core of the divide between Marxists and anarchists, and forms the basis for anarchist criticisms of Marx's 'state socialism'. The tension between the idea of the dictatorship of the proletariat and Marx's vision of socialism from below was labelled by Alexander Berkman as 'the great contradiction of Marxian socialism'.[47] Obviously 'authoritarian', Daniel Guérin argues that the idea of the dictatorship of the proletariat represents the medium through which the Jacobin tradition found its way into modern socialism. In Marx, he suggests, elements of this tradition sit alongside more libertarian tendencies. Anarchism developed the libertarian side of socialist theory, Guérin argues, and Marxists generally and Lenin in particular embraced the more authoritarian aspect of socialism.[48] More recently John Holloway has argued that although classical Marxists such as Lenin, Trotsky, Gramsci and Luxemburg believed that modern states could be used for progressive ends, in practice Lenin and Trotsky were conquered by the states they believed they were mastering.[49]

According to this interpretation, Lenin's claim that 'we do not at all differ with the anarchists on the question of the abolition of the state as aim' is undermined by his insistence that socialism can only be won through revolution in which workers would need temporarily to organise 'the instruments, resources and methods of state power against the exploiters'.[50] Arguments of this type are, of course, a long-standing anarchist criticism of Marx and Marxism going back at least as far as the debates in the First International.

By contrast, a minority of anarchist critics of Lenin accept that it was through the concept of the dictatorship of the proletariat that Marx sought 'a method of achieving the liberty that neither falls into chaos nor into state authority'.[51] I think that this argument is, in essence, correct. However, to fully grasp Marx's arguments we need to engage with his historical conception of human essence. This is because his perspective is so alien to the liberal tradition from which anarchism borrows that without making these ontological assumptions explicit anarchists and Marxists are inclined to talk past each other.

## Marx's concept of human essence

In sharp contrast to even social anarchism's naturalisation of one or other aspect of modern egoism, we have noted that one of Marx's great contributions to social theory was to outline the first historical account of human essence, on which he built his political theory. In the *Grundrisse* he developed arguments he had first suggested in the 1840s in his critique of Stirner. He pointed out that the further one looks back into history 'the more does the individual...appear as dependent, as belonging to a greater whole.' Through prehistory and on through pre-capitalist modes of production, the individual's sense of self was mediated through familial and clan units. Conversely, it is only with the rise of capitalism that social relations between people 'confront the individual as mere means towards his private purposes, as external necessity'.[52] The 'private interests' assumed to be natural by liberals are in fact a product of history. They are 'already a socially determined interest, which can be achieved only within the conditions laid down by society and with the means provided by society'.[53] Alasdair MacIntyre comments that whereas in pre-capitalist societies individuals conceive themselves through mutual relations involving obligations, liberalism reflects the way that in modern capitalist society individuals appear 'unconstrained by any social bonds'.[54]

If Marx therefore historicises what liberalism takes as its universal ontological starting point – the egoistic individual – his political opposition to liberalism is similarly rooted in a historical conception of emergent forms of solidarity and association. He claimed that though the division of labour separated and fragmented the 'new fangled' working class,[55] this class's struggle for freedom takes a new form as a growing need and desire for association. Against any romantic notion of a natural human solidarity, he claimed that 'individuals cannot gain mastery over their own social interconnections before they have created them'. If 'in earlier stages of development the single individual seems to have developed more fully', this was only because these individuals had not yet fully worked out their mutual 'relationships'.[56] Because modern capitalism greatly deepens our mutual interconnections, it creates the potential for us to flourish as much richer social individuals. The problem Marx addresses is not whether workers have the capacity to recreate some pristine humanity out of their alienated existence. Rather, he criticises the existing social order from the point of view of real struggles against it, judging that workers' struggles point towards a fuller realisation of human freedom. This is why, as Hal Draper points out, rather than use the abstract word socialism to describe their goal, Marx and Engels more usually wrote of workers' power.[57]

Marx and Engels first drew these conclusions in the 1840s on the basis of their engagement with the Silesian weavers' revolt, Chartism in Manchester, and socialist circles in Paris.[58] As I have argued elsewhere, Marx generalised from these experiences to argue that in struggling against the power of capital, workers begin to create modes of existence which underpin a virtuous alternative to egoism.[59] This is the reason why he places the working class at the centre of his political project. Of course Marx argued that a degree of social surplus is a necessary prerequisite for socialism, but this is a necessary not sufficient prerequisite. Beyond the development of the forces of production, Marx's political project is predicated upon the emergence of new social relations which underpin novel forms of solidarity and community. It is for this reason that, he argues, the existence of the modern proletariat is a necessary prerequisite for socialism, and that its emergent unity through struggle is the process through which this potential is realised in history.

The novelty of Marx's model of revolution was based upon his recognition that workers' unity could only be won through the process of class struggle. In *The German Ideology* he suggested two reasons for revolution. First, in common with revolutionaries such as Robespierre and Blanqui, he argued that the ruling class (and the state) could not be overthrown by any other means. Second, and much more profoundly, he differentiated his conception of revolution from those associated with these earlier revolutionaries by insisting that 'the class overthrowing it can only in a revolution succeed in ridding itself of all the muck of ages and become fitted to found society anew'.[60] From this perspective, revolutionary activity is not merely system changing, it is also individually transformative: it is the necessary means through which workers may come to realise in consciousness their emergent needs, first, for solidarity and then for a new socialised mode of production.

Moreover, because the revolutionary activity through which workers transform themselves is from the bottom up it will not be uniform. There will, therefore, be more and less advanced sections of the working class – that is (so to speak) vanguards and rearguards. Once this simple fact is grasped it is easy to see, first, that the idea of socialist leadership is actually presupposed by the concept of socialism from below, and, second, that this idea has little in common with the caricatured critiques of vanguardism that are all too common in anarchist circles.[61] Interestingly, despite widespread rumours to the contrary, Lenin said nothing about the role of a Central Committee, omnipotent or otherwise, in *What Is to Be Done?* His actual argument was much more prosaic: Russia's disparate socialist movement could progress from its existing fragmented state to challenge for political power if the various groups were unified through a newspaper into a single organisation.[62]

Far from being a rehash of Blanquism, this general model of revolutionary practice is based upon Marx and Engels' critique of Blanqui's Jacobinism. Though Marx agreed with Blanqui that capitalism had made workers unfit to rule, he departed from Blanqui's revolutionary elitism by insisting that workers could *become* fit to rule through the revolutionary process itself: 'the coincidence of the changing of circumstances and of human activity or self-changing can be conceived and rationally understood only as *revolutionary practice*'.[63] Indeed it was the collective struggles in the revolutionary process that did away with the need for Blanqui's elitist model of 'revolutionary dictatorship'. Discussing arguments put forward by the Blanquists in the wake of the Paris Commune (1871), Engels suggested that they were 'socialists only in sentiment', because their model of socialism was not underpinned by anything like an adequate account of either the class struggle or of the historical basis for socialism itself. He thus dismissed Blanqui's proposal that the revolution be a '*coup de main* by a small revolutionary minority', and claimed that the Blanquist conception of politics involved an 'obsolete' model of revolution as 'dictatorship'.[64]

It is because Marx's perspective is rooted in a historical materialist analysis of the emergence of a new social class with novel needs and capacities (that is, a new nature), that it is woefully inadequate to characterise his political project in terms of Jacobinism or Blanquism. Anarchist suggestions that Marx reproduced one or other (insurrectionary or reformist) form of statist politics betray a failure to recognise how his novel conception of human nature underpinned a model of the social that escaped liberalism's naturalisation of the egoism of civil society. The consequences of this misunderstanding are most clearly apparent from the perspective of debates over what Marx and Engels took to be the concrete realisation of the dictatorship of the proletariat: The Paris Commune.

## The Paris Commune

For the purposes of this essay the significance of the Paris Commune lies in the light it casts on Marx's and Bakunin's conceptions of socialism. For though both wholeheartedly embraced the Commune, they interpreted it in very different ways: while Bakunin argued that it amounted to the abolition of politics, Marx conceived it as the transcendence of politics.[65] This difference reflected their very different conceptions of human nature.

Within the First International the social content of the division between Proudhonists and Marxists can, in part, be illuminated by their divergent conceptions of human nature. Whereas Marx's critique of capitalism was made from the standpoint of the struggles of the 'new fangled' working class, Proudhon criticised nineteenth-century French society for its deviation from the 'natural order': France had become a 'fractitious order' with 'parasite interests, abnormal morals, monstrous ambitions, [and] prejudices at variance with common sense'.[66] The dominant voice of socialism in France at the time was Louis Blanc's reformism. According to Proudhon, Blanc was heir both to Robespierre's statism, and through him to the dictatorial methods of 'the scoundrel' Rousseau.[67] What these figures shared was a common focus on reform through the state. This approach, or so Proudhon believed, confused legitimate with illegitimate forms of authority: the state transferred patriarchal authority from its proper abode in the family to an unnatural situation.[68] This was just as true of revolutionary socialists such as Blanqui as it was of reformists such as Blanc; Proudhon claimed that both were counter-revolutionary because they failed to see that political power and liberty were absolutely 'incompatible'.[69] It was against these socialists that Proudhon insisted that the key issue of the day was not which kind of government but rather 'Government or No-Government', or absolutism versus anarchy, and the aim of the revolution was 'to do away with...the state.'[70] In place of the state, Proudhon envisioned a social contract which was the opposite of Rousseau's statism because it was to be freely entered into by independent producers.[71]

From 1867 to 1868 onwards the torch of anarchism was taken up within the International by Bakunin. He described his version of anarchism as 'Proudhonism greatly developed and pushed to its furthest conclusion'.[72] Concretely, this meant that while Bakunin agreed with Proudhon's general argument that natural social harmony was possible only through the erad- ication of government and the state, he went further than Proudhon in a collectivist direction.[73] Within the International, the gap between Marx and Bakunin was, initially at least, less than it had been between Marx and Proudhon.[74] However, areas of convergence were soon overshadowed by renewed debates on the question of political power and the state, where Bakunin's position 'was of a piece with Proudhon's'.[75] Indeed, Bakunin was keen to stress that Marx was a statist who reproduced a top-down politics that he inherited from the Jacobins through Blanqui.

Despite this criticism, both Marx and Bakunin embraced the Paris Com- mune of 1871 as an example of real living socialism. According to Bakunin, whereas 'the communists believe it is necessary to organize the workers' forces in order to seize the political power of the State', 'the revolutionary socialists organise for the purpose of destroying or – to put it more politely – liquidating the State'. Concretely, Bakunin proclaimed his support for the Commune not only because it was made by 'the spontaneous and contin- ued action of the masses' but also because it was the 'negation of the state'.[76] By contrast, he insisted that Marx was 'a direct disciple of Louis Blanc' and as 'an Hegelian, a Jew, and German' he was both a 'hopeless statist' and 'state communist'.[77]

Passing over this casual racism, Bakunin's criticism of Marx illuminates the social content of the claim that Marx was a state socialist. At one level this is manifestly false: at the time Bakunin wrote, Marx had already written in a document published under the auspices of the International that though 'the working class cannot simply lay hold of the ready-made state machin- ery, and wield it for its own purposes', it must be 'smashed'. Nevertheless, the rational core of Bakunin's argument is evidenced by Marx's claim that though the Commune was the 'direct antithesis to the Empire' it nevertheless was 'a working-class government'.[78] The problem for Bakunin was that Marx was palpably correct: the Commune was a novel form of government and indeed a novel form of state.

Given this fact, the most consistent way to maintain the anarchist variant of an anti-statist position implied developing a much more critical perspective on the Commune. This was Kropotkin's perspective. He produced what was in effect an immanent critique of Bakunin's analysis of the Commune. According to Peter Marshall the Commune exemplified not Marx's concept of the dictatorship of the proletariat but rather Bakunin's 'bold and outspoken negation of the state'.[79] Nonetheless, it is difficult to reconcile Bakunin's self-image as the enemy 'of every government and every state power' with the reality that the Commune organised itself as a military force or state.[80] For Kropotkin the Commune's key failing was its embrace of a representative structure, which meant that it reproduced the typical vices of parliamentary governments. The weaknesses of the Commune, he insisted, were due not to the men who led it but to the 'system' it embraced.[81]

If Kropotkin's comments point to anarchist difficulties with the Commune, Marx shows that to embrace the Commune involved embracing a novel form of state. He was able to square this perspective with his own anti-statist insistence that socialism could only come through the smashing of the old state on the basis of a deeper conception of the social. Thus in a draft of *The Civil War in France* he described the Commune in language reminiscent of that he deployed in the 1840s:

> The Commune – the reabsorption of the State power by society, as its own living forces instead of as forces controlling and subduing it, by the popular masses themselves, forming their own force instead of the organized force of their suppression – the political form of their social emancipation, instead of the artificial force (appropriated by their oppressors) (their own force opposed to and organised against them) of society wielded for their oppression by their enemies. The form was simple like all great things.[82]

This argument suggests Bakunin's charge that Marx was a Jacobin or Blanquist was not simply wrong (though it clearly was) but rather involved a complete misunderstanding of Marx's project. It is not merely that for Marx the dictatorship of the proletariat meant the rule of the working class rather than a dictatorship of an elite,[83] more importantly Bakunin's criticism does not begin to rise to the level demanded of the theoretical breakthrough underpinning Marx's position. If, from the standpoint of the egoistic individual, the demand to smash the state can only be understood negatively as the removal of public power, Marx's historicised conception of human nature – his 'new materialism'[84] – allowed him a much more positive interpretation of this concept: it would involve not merely the removal of an alien form of public power that stands over society but also its replacement by a public authority that is 're-absorbed' into society.

Unfortunately, Bakunin's failure to understand Marx is a recurring characteristic of anarchist criticisms of his work. For instance, Peter Marshall is so caught up in is rhetoric about Marx's statism that he is quite unable to comprehend how Marx, Engels, Lenin, Trotsky and Luxemburg could embrace the Commune as a model of the dictatorship of the proletariat except as an 'irony of history'.[85]

Interestingly, this inability to grasp the novel social content of Marx's anti-statism informs the tendency within anarchism to conflate Marxism and social democracy and thus to misunderstand both the break between the two towards the end of the nineteenth century, and conversely the profundity of Lenin's renewal of Marxism at the beginning of the twentieth century.[86] Whereas Marx and Engels insisted that socialism could only be won through a revolutionary 'smashing' of the old state, German social democracy evolved on the basis of fudging this question. Thus at both the Gotha conference (1875) and the Erfurt Conference (1892) the party elided over what Engels claimed was the main issue, that 'our party and the working class can only come to power under the form of a democratic republic. This is even the specific form of the dictatorship of the proletariat.'[87]

It was one of Lenin's great contributions to Marxism to recognise that German Social Democracy's reformism (statism) had roots in this elision over the issue of state power.[88] Consequently, his critique of Kautskyism opens a space for a powerful challenge to Michels' attempt to deploy German social democracy as a proxy for Marxism. For, despite its rhetoric, the German Social Democratic Party was a reformist organisation, and rather than Michels proving the iron law of oligarchy to be of universal significance, he merely showed, as Colin Barker has argued, that it applies to those modern parties which aim to win state power. It is because Marx's project cannot be reduced to these terms that Michels' critique misses its target.[89] And to the extent that anarchists share Michels' conflation of Marxism and social democracy, they too miss their mark. Indeed, it is not so much that anarchists disagree with Marx on the state as they misunderstand his project, and this helps explain the tendency for anarchists and Marxists to talk past each other.

## Conclusion

In a brilliant early essay, Gramsci made the interesting suggestion that anarchism was a universal and elemental form of opposition to oppression. He argued that, because 'class oppression has been embodied in the state, anarchism is the basic subversive conception that lays all the suffering of the oppressed class at the feet of the state'. However, he noted that because different states have structured different forms of oppression the concrete form of 'anarchism's' victory is distinct in each determinate epoch: each new class substantiates 'its own freedom'. From this perspective, the bourgeoisie had been the 'anarchist' opponent of the feudal state, and their victory was the victory of liberalism: the freedom of free trade. By contrast, the 'anarchist' opponent of the modern bourgeois state is the working class whose victory takes the form of 'Marxist communism'.[90]

Whereas Gramsci's argument assumes something like Marx's historicisation of the concept of human essence/freedom, anarchism's reduction of Marx's politics to a new form of statism illuminates its own understanding of human essence. As we have seen, social anarchism embeds one or other variations on the liberal conception of individual egoism/freedom, and this informs the parallels between its critique of Marxism and Acton's and Michels' comments on power and oligarchy. The problem for anarchism with this perspective is that liberalism falsely universalises a definite, historical conception of human essence, and this idea of essence acts as a fundamental barrier to conceptualising a real democratic alternative to capitalism. Indeed, Bakunin's *a priori* comments on Marxism as a prospective 'red bureaucracy' reflect not a perceptive grasp on reality but rather the fundamental problems associated with conceiving democracy from an anarchist perspective and thus the limitations of anarchism as an anti-capitalist ideology. As David Morland suggests, 'the rationale behind the anarchist objection to Marxism is, to put it very simply, that Marxist-Leninists have misunderstood human nature. There is, anarchists caution, a lust for power in humankind that will jeopardise the very outcome of the revolutionary process itself.'[91] This suggests, notwithstanding Marx's nominal convergence with anarchism over the desire to 'smash' the state, that it would be wrong to claim that the differences between them were of a merely tactical kind.[92] On the contrary, because the anarchists do not have, as did Marx, a historical conception of human nature, they do not understand, as he did, the overthrow of the state to mean that 'socialised man...man freely associated with his fellows, could control the totality of his social existence, and become master of his own environment and activity.'[93]

From this perspective, anarchism is best understood as sitting at a political fork in the road: to the extent that it remains a mix of a socialist critique of capitalism and a liberal critique of communism it is limited to a form of perpetual opposition. Of course it is possible to take the right-hand road from this fork towards a type of radical liberalism – this is effectively the substance of Bookchin's charge against lifestyle anarchism.[94] On the other hand, the democratic impulse behind class-struggle anarchism tends towards Marxism. To realise the potential of this movement demands both that we unpick Marx's anti-statism from its caricatured distortion at the hands of the Stalinists and that we reconstruct his positive democratic alternative to alienated capitalist politics.

According to István Mészáros, 'the central theme of Marx's moral theory is how to realise human freedom' against the capitalist system of alienation.[95] The social content of this conception of freedom is, according to George Brenkert, a model of social self-determination through democracy.[96] The realisation of this project assumes a historical model of human essence which denaturalises both the exchange relations characteristic of civil society and the liberal conception of the social as an alien power. So, whereas liberalism can conceive the state only as an alien power, Marx's model informs his claim that freedom consists 'in converting the state from an organ superimposed upon society into one completely subordinate to it'.[97] Far from being a 'statist' project, this goal assumes the existing state must be 'smashed' and replaced by organs of workers' power. Surely authoritarian in the sense that such an organisation must aim at suppressing the counter-revolution, Marx's goal was, as Herbert Marcuse insisted, the democratisation of authority based upon the emergence of a new class rooted in new relations of production and with a new need and desire for solidarity.[98] Class-struggle anarchism is part of this movement, but it is hindered in realising its potential by its inheritance from liberalism. Marx pointed beyond this inheritance, and class-struggle anarchism would do well to re-engage with his political theory to develop its own.

## Notes

1. In this essay I will use anarchism as a synonym for class struggle anarchism.
2. Michael Bakunin, *Power Corrupts the Best* (1867), online at http://dwardmac.pitzer. edu/anarchist_archives/bakunin/bakuninpower.html
3. Antony Jay, *Oxford Dictionary of Political Quotations* (Oxford: Oxford University Press, 1996), p. 1.
4. Paul Blackledge, 'Marxism and Anarchism', *International Socialism* II/125 (2010), 144.
5. Robert Michels, *Political Parties* (New York: Collier Press, 1962), p. 326.
6. Ibid., pp. 342, 349.
7. Ibid., p. 325.
8. Michael Schmidt and Lucien van der Walt, *Black Flame: The Revolutionary Class Politics of Anarchism and Syndicalism, vol. 1, Counter-Power* (Edinburgh: AK Press, 2009), p. 189.
9. Paul Thomas, *Karl Marx and the Anarchists* (London: Routledge & Kegan Paul, 1980), p. 252.
10. Peter Marshall, *Demanding the Impossible: A History of Anarchism* (London: HarperCollins, 2008), p. 23.
11. Noam Chomsky, *Government in the Future* (New York: Seven Stories Press, 2005), p. 33.
12. Rudolf Rocker, *Anarcho-Syndicalism* (London: Pluto Press, 1989), p. 21; cf. David Goodway, *For Anarchism: History, Theory and Practice* (London: Routledge, 1989), p. 1; Noam Chomsky, *Introduction to Daniel Guérin, Anarchism* (New York: Monthly Review Press, 1970), p. xii; Marshall, p. 639.
13. Sean Sayers, *Marxism and Human Nature* (London: Routledge, 1998).

14. Maureen Ramsay, *What's Wrong with Liberalism?* (London: Leicester University Press, 1997), p. 7.
15. Scott Meikle, *Essentialism in the Thought of Karl Marx* (La Saale: Open Court, 1985).
16. Ernst Bloch, *The Principle of Hope* (Oxford: Blackwell, 1986), pp. 173, 199. Paul Blackledge, *Marxism and Ethics* (New York: SUNY Press, 2012).
17. David McLellan, *The Young Hegelians and Karl Marx* (London: Macmillan, 1969), p. 134.
18. John Martin, *Introduction to Stirner's The Ego and His Own* (New York: Dover, 2005), p. xiii; Thomas, *Marx and the Anarchists*, p. 130.
19. Max Stirner, *The Ego and His Own*, p. 110.
20. Ibid., pp. 122, 130.
21. Ibid., p. 160.
22. Ibid., pp. 75, 54.
23. Hal Draper, *Karl Marx's Theory of Revolution*, vol. IV (New York: Monthly Review Press, 1990), p. 156.
24. Stirner, pp. 18, 164, 258.
25. Karl Marx and Friedrich Engels, *Manifesto of the Communist Party*, in *The Revolutions of 1848* (London: Penguin, 1973), p. 87; cf. Thomas, *Marx and the Anarchists*, p. 154.
26. Karl Marx and Friedrich Engels, *The German Ideology* in *Collected Works* (New York: International Publishers, 1976), p. 247.
27. Karl Marx, *On the Jewish Question* in *Collected Works*, vol. 3 (New York: International Publishers, 1975), p. 168.
28. David Morland, *Demanding the Impossible? Human Nature and Politics in Nineteenth-Century Social Anarchism* (London: Cassell, 1997), pp. 38, 78.
29. Ibid., pp. 62, 78.
30. Ibid., p. 141.
31. Ibid., p. 23.
32. Ibid., p. 3.
33. Ibid., pp. 188–189.
34. Michael Bakunin, *God and the State* (1871), online at http://www. Marxists.org/reference/archive/bakunin/works/godstate/index.htm
35. Marshall, *Demanding the Impossible*, p. 296.
36. Errico Malatesta, *Democracy and Anarchy* (1924), online at http://theanarchist library.org/HTML/Errico_Malatesta__Democracy_and_Anarchy.html; cf. *Neither Democrats nor Dictators* (1926), online at http://www.Marxists.org/archive/malatesta/1926/05/neither.htm
37. George Woodcock, *Anarchism* (London: Penguin, 1962), pp. 7, 30.
38. Uri Gordon, *Anarchy Alive! Anti-authoritarian Politics from Practice to Theory* (London: Pluto, 2008), p. 70.
39. Schmidt and van der Walt, *Black Flame*, p. 70.
40. Todd May, 'Anarchism from Foucault to Ranciere', in Randall Amster and Others, *Contemporary Anarchist Studies: An Introductory Anthology of Anarchy in the Academy* (London: Routledge, 2009), p. 16; Wayne Price, *The Abolition of the State* (Bloomington: AuthorHouse, 2007), p. 164.
41. Ibid., p. 165.
42. Ruth Kinna, *Beginner's Guide to Anarchism* (Oxford: Oneworld, 2005), pp. 114–115; Jo Freeman (1970), *The Tyranny of Structurelessness*, online at http://struggle.ws/pdfs/tyranny.pdf
43. Price, *Abolition of the State*, p. 10.

44. Lucien van der Walt, *Anarchism, Black Flame, Marxism and the IST: Debating Power, Revolution and Bolshevism* (2011), online at http://lucienvanderwalt. blogspot.com/2011/02/anarchism-black-flame-Marxism-and-ist.html; 'Debating Black Flame, Revolutionary Anarchism and Historical Marxism', *International Socialism* II/130 (2011), pp. 195–196.
45. Price, *Abolition of the State*, p. 50.
46. Friedrich Engels, 'Introduction to *K. Marx's The Civil War in France'*, in *Collected Works*, vol. 27 (New York: International Publishers, 1990), p. 191.
47. Alexander Berkman, *What Is Communist Anarchism?* (London: Phoenix Press, 1989), pp. 76–77.
48. Daniel Guérin, 'Marxism and Anarchism', in Goodway, p. 120.
49. John Holloway, *Change the World without Taking Power* (London: Pluto, 2002), p. 18.
50. V.I. Lenin, *The State and Revolution* in *Selected Works* (Moscow: Progress Publishers, 1968), p. 304.
51. Kojin Karatani, *Transcritique* (London: MIT Press, 2003), p. 178.
52. Karl Marx, *Grundrisse* (Harmondsworth: Penguin, 1973), p. 84.
53. Ibid., p. 156.
54. Alasdair MacIntyre, *A Short History of Ethics* (London: Routledge, 1967), pp. 121–128.
55. Karl Marx, 'Speech at the Anniversary of The People's Paper', in *Collected Works*, vol. 14 (New York: International Publishers, 1980), p. 656.
56. Marx, *Grundrisse*, pp. 161–162.
57. Hal Draper, *Karl Marx's Theory of Revolution*, vol. II (New York: Monthly Review Press, 1978), p. 24.
58. Stephen Perkins, *Marxism and the Proletariat* (London: Pluto, 1993), p. 33.
59. Blackledge, *Marxism and Ethics*, pp. 140–145.
60. Marx and Engels, *German Ideology*, p. 53.
61. Lars Lih, *Lenin Rediscovered, What Is to Be Done? In Context* (Amsterdam: Brill, 2006), p. 556.
62. Ibid.
63. Karl Marx, *Theses on Feuerbach* in *Karl Marx Early Writings* (London: Penguin, 1975), p. 422.
64. Friedrich Engels, 'Programme of the Blanquist Commune Refugees', in *Collected Works*, vol. 24 (New York: International Publishers, 1989), p. 13; Hal Draper, *Karl Marx's Theory of Revolution*, vol. III (New York: Monthly Review Press, 1978), p. 35.
65. Donny Gluckstein, *The Paris Commune* (Chicago: Haymarket Press, 2011), pp. 181–207.
66. Pierre-Joseph Proudhon, *What Is Property?* (Cambridge: Cambridge University Press, 1989), p. 75.
67. Ibid., pp. 118, 152–153.
68. Ibid., p. 171.
69. Thomas, *Karl Marx and the Anarchists*, pp. 180, 212.
70. Proudhon, *What Is Property?*, pp. 105, 128, 153, 286.
71. Ibid., 113ff; pp. 130, 206
72. Guérin, *Anarchism*, p. 4.
73. Ibid., p. 12.
74. Henry Collins and Chimon Abramsky, *Karl Marx and the British Labour Movement* (London: Macmillan, 1964), p. 228; cf. Thomas, *Karl Marx and the Anarchists*, p. 268.

75. Thomas, *Karl Marx and the Anarchists*, p. 294.
76. Michael Bakunin, *The Paris Commune and the Idea of the State in Bakunin on Anarchy* (London: Allen and Unwin, 1973), pp. 263, 264, 268.
77. Michael Bakunin, *Statism and Anarchy* (Cambridge: Cambridge University Press, 1990), pp. 142–143.
78. Karl Marx, *The Civil War in France* in *The First International and After* (London: Penguin, 1974), pp. 206, 208, 212.
79. Marshall, *Demanding the Impossible*, p. 288.
80. Bakunin, *Statism and Anarchy*, p. 136.
81. Peter Kropotkin, 'Revolutionary Government', in *Peter Kropotkin: Anarchism* (New York: Dover, 2002), pp. 237–242.
82. Karl Marx, 'Drafts of the Civil War in France', in *Collected Works* vol. 22 (New York: International Publishers,1986), p. 487.
83. Hal Draper, *The Dictatorship of the Proletariat* (New York: Monthly Review Press, 1987), p. 29.
84. Marx, *Theses on Feuerbach*, p. 421.
85. Marshall, *Demanding the Impossible*, p. 301.
86. George Lukács, *History and Class Consciousness* (London: Merlin Press, 1971), pp. 34–35.
87. Friedrich Engels, 'A Critique of the Draft Programme of 1891' in *Collected Works*, vol. 27 (New York: International Publishers, 1990), p. 227.
88. Lenin, *The State and Revolution*.
89. Colin Barker, 'Robert Michels and the "Cruel Game"', in Colin Barker and others (eds.) *Leadership and Social Movements* (Manchester: Manchester University Press, 2001), pp. 24–43.
90. Antonio Gramsci, 'Address to the Anarchists' in *Selections from the Political Writings, 1910–1920* (London: Lawrence and Wishart, 1977), p. 186.
91. Morland, *Demanding the Impossible?*, p. 13; cf. David Miller, *Anarchism* (London: Dent, 1984), p. 93.
92. Thomas, *Karl Marx and the Anarchists*, p. 13.
93. Ibid., p. 106.
94. Murray Bookchin, *Social Anarchism or Lifestyle Anarchism* (Edinburgh: AK Press, 1995).
95. István Mészáros, *Marx's Theory of Alienation* (London: Merlin, 1975), p. 162.
96. George Brenkert, *Marx's Ethics of Freedom* (London: Routledge, 1983), pp. 87–88; Paul Blackledge, 'Marxism, Nihilism and the Problem of Ethical Politics Today', *Socialism and Democracy* 24/2 (2010), 126–127.
97. Karl Marx, *Critique of the Gotha Programme* in *The First International and After*, p. 354.
98. H. Marcuse, *A Study on Authority* (London: Verso, 2008), p. 87.

# 3

# Anarchism, Individualism and Communism: William Morris's Critique of Anarcho-communism

*Ruth Kinna*

## Introduction

William Morris's commitment to revolutionary socialism is now well established, but the nature of his politics, specifically his relationship to Marxism and anarchist thought, is still contested. Perhaps, as Mark Bevir has argued, the ideological label pinned to Morris's socialism is of 'little importance' for as long as his political thought is described adequately. Nevertheless, the starting point for this essay is that thinking about the application of ideological descriptors is a useful exercise and one which sheds important light on Morris's socialism and the process of ideological formation in the late nineteenth-century socialist movement. Bevir is surely right when he says that 'ideologies are not mutually exclusive, reified entities' but 'overlapping traditions with ill-defined boundaries'.[1] Yet the struggle to reify these boundaries in a messy political world is a dominant feature in the history of the Left and one in which Morris was not afraid to engage. Indeed, towards the end of his life he made a concerted attempt to draw an ideological boundary between his preferred form of revolutionary socialism and anarchism. This not only makes him an interesting subject for the analysis of Marxist–anarchist relations, it also raises questions about the adequacy of the familiar charge that anarchism is both inherently individualistic and, as a consequence, ill-equipped to develop a coherent approach to democratic decision-making.

Morris defined his ideological position between 1883 and 1885 and called himself a communist. In 1890, when he withdrew from the Socialist League and established the Hammersmith Socialist Society he described this position negatively: neither state socialist nor anarchist.[2] In adopting this formulation Morris did not mean to suggest that he straddled these two ideological poles. Rather he wanted to indicate his independence from both. However, in 1893–1894 he repositioned himself once more, representing communism as a rejection of anarchism. His claim, that anarchists were individualists, was a recurrent charge in the non-anarchist socialist press, but Morris was an unusual critic of anarchism because he was sensitive to the different currents that ran through anarchist and individualist thought. Moreover, his late application of the individualist tag was extended to include anarchists with whom he had worked most closely: anarchist communists. Coming from him, the charge appears as an obvious reduction that grouped together a set of ideas that were based on very different, not always compatible, political, economic and ethical principles.

The undiscriminating and angry tone of his critique can be explained by his rejection of the political violence of the late nineteenth century, a tactic that seemed all the more futile once Morris had acknowledged the failure of the anti-parliamentary revolutionary strategy he had adopted in the 1880s. He developed the theoretical justification for the critique in a discussion of the limits of freedom and individual–community relations.[3] This discussion drew on concepts of slavery, tyranny and mastership that he had elaborated in the 1880s. Morris's claim was that anarchism wrongly denied limits to freedom and that it was therefore socially disintegrative: individualist. The fatal flaw of anarchism was illustrated, he further suggested, by the inability of anarchists to show how individuals might enter into a process of decision-making and, therefore, to develop any practical socialist alternative. Unfortunately for Morris, this argument revealed that the ideological divide he sought to establish – between communism and anarchism – could be sustained only by his adoption of a model of decision-making that ran counter to his own radical principles of mastership and tyranny because it demanded the identification of democracy with the subordination of individual to class interests.

The argument is developed in three sections. The first discusses Morris's late critique of anarchist communism and his treatment of this strain of anarchism as a generic form. It examines his motivations and sets out the key concepts on which he later relied to develop his analysis of decision-making. The relationship between anarchism and individualism is discussed in the middle section, both in order to contextualise Morris's understanding of these terms and to demonstrate how his awareness of anarchist and individualist politics gave way to the narrower system of ideological classification. His attempt to demonstrate how the inherent individualism of anarcho-communism ruled against collective agreement is the subject of the concluding part. It should become clear that the conjunction of anarchism and individualism that Morris sought to cement is dubious and that the boundaries between socialist traditions are more porous than he wanted to admit.

## Morris's critique of anarchism

On 1 May 1893 leading members of the Social Democratic Federation, the Fabian Society and Morris's Hammersmith Socialist Society issued the *Manifesto of English Socialists*. This document, to which Morris was a signatory, was intended to outline 'the main principles and broad strategy on which ... all Socialists may combine to act with vigour' and it called on socialists to 'sink their individual crochets in a business-like endeavour to realise in our own day that complete communization of industry for which the economic forms are ready and the minds of the people are almost prepared'.[4] Notwithstanding its apparent inclusiveness, the *Manifesto* specified the limits of socialist co-operation:

> ... we must repudiate both the doctrines and tactics of Anarchism. As Socialists we believe that those doctrines and tactics necessarily resulting from them, though advocated as revolutionary by men who are honest and single-minded, are really reactionary both in theory and practice, and tend to check the advance of our cause. Indeed, so far from hampering the freedom of the individual, as Anarchists hold it will, Socialism will foster that full freedom which Anarchism would inevitably destroy.[5]

Morris's willingness to put his name to the *Manifesto* was not entirely surprising: the deterioration of his relationship with the anarchists in the Socialist League, which eventually forced his withdrawal from the party and the editorship of *Commonweal*, the League's paper, helped explain the gradual but increasing hardening of his attitude. He had already voiced misgivings about anarchism in *News From Nowhere* and in the year following the publication of the *Manifesto* this light ridiculing turned into uncompromising rejection. In 1894 two important articles appeared. The first was an interview, 'A Socialist Poet on Bombs and Anarchism', published at the start of the year in *Justice*, the journal of the Social Democratic Federation. The second, an essay titled 'Why I Am a Communist', appeared in James Tochatti's anarchist paper *Liberty* the following month. Morris made two claims: that anarchism was an individualist doctrine and that its individualism was reflected in the recent and unacceptable turn to political violence.

His critique of anarchist individualism focused on two points, what Stefan Collini identifies as its methodological and moral principles. These were often used to support a politics of individualism, but were not necessarily presupposed by it.[6] Morris's objection to methodological individualism was that it was impossible to make sense of individual behaviours by abstracting individuals from their social context. The moral principle, which he tied to it, was that that the communal bonds that he believed essential to individual flourishing, were wrongly represented by individualists as only so many potential constraints. Anarchism, he argued, embraced both ideas and the two articles that he published in 1894 advanced this case.

In *Justice* Morris argued: 'man is unthinkable outside society. Man cannot live or move outside it. This negation of society is the position taken up by the logical Anarchists...'.[7] In 'Why I Am a Communist' he reiterated the point. One of the distinctive features of the communist position, he argued, is the conviction that 'mankind is not thinkable outside of Society'.[8] In contrast, 'Anarchism, as a theory, negatives society, and puts man outside it.' Although Morris accepted that anarchists like Kropotkin, who he knew quite well, were not in fact 'against society altogether',[9] having once granted this exception he refused to acknowledge that anarcho-communism described a coherent politics. This term, he argued, was a 'flat contradiction': 'In so far as they are Communists they must give up their Anarchism' because anarchism 'is purely destructive, purely negatory'. Comrades like Kropotkin who called themselves anarchists were deluded, Morris argued. They 'cannot be Anarchists in the true sense of the word'.[10]

Morris's understanding of moral individualism was underpinned by the interrelated concepts of 'tyranny', 'slavery', 'mastership' and 'fellowship'. Perhaps ill-advisedly using tyranny to describe the nature of social existence, he reasoned that because individuals could not be understood in the abstract and must always be considered as members of particular communities, they were always necessarily constrained by social arrangements. Tyranny was thus an unavoidable feature of all social life. Naturally, Morris recognised that social tyranny could take different forms and that it was not necessarily empowering or benign. In other words, some social systems were also tyrannical. The distinction Morris made was between 'true' and 'false' or 'arbitrary' society. Commercial society plainly fell in the latter category, since here social relations were based on class coercion, or what Morris called 'force' and 'fraud'. In socialism, tyranny would assume 'true' form. This was the position Morris outlined in the *Statement of Principles of the Hammersmith Socialist Society*:

> For here we must say that it is not the dissolution of society for which we strive, but its reintegration. The idea put forward by some who attack present society, of the complete independence of every individual, that is, for freedom without society, is not merely impossible of realization, but, when looked into, turns out to be inconceivable.[11]

The goal of revolutionaries, Morris argued, was to rid society of slavery rather than tyranny, since when slavery was abolished tyranny's tyrannical features would also disappear. As Susan Buck-Morss notes 'slavery had become the root metaphor of Western political philosophy' by the eighteenth century, 'connoting everything that was evil about power relations'.[12] Morris appeared to follow this convention and defined slavery as a relation based on compulsion, rooted in nature and institutionalised in economic power. In nature, he argued, all life was enslaved by the necessity of labour. The stark choice was to work or perish. In human societies, nature's compulsion was overlaid by secondary systems of enslavement. These could take different forms but Morris believed that each historical type reflected the attempt of a minority to escape the force of nature and the dictates of labour, and he argued that the differences between them were irrelevant to their classification. Bond-slavery, feudalism and wage-labour were not moral equivalents but they all enabled the elite to live from the labour of others and stripped those charged with the burden of labour of effective choice in production. This group were thus doubly enslaved.

Morris applied the same reasoning to women, yet he argued that there was a difference between labour and the way that slavery operated in this context. Women were dependent on men as well as slaves to capitalism, and they were therefore triply enslaved. Even accepting that there was 'the closest of relations between the prostitution of the body in the streets and of the body in the workshops',[13] he concluded that the liberation of women required a social as well as an economic change: dependence on men in addition to the abolition of capitalism and, above all, the abolition of bourgeois marriage laws which enshrined the power relations that compelled women to prostitute themselves for the sake of economic security, controlling their reproduction in addition to their labour.

Tyrannical societies (that is, those based on slavery) operated through mastership. In *The Dream of John Ball,* a story of the 1381 Peasants' Revolt, Morris tells the eponymous hero of the story that

> men shall yet have masters over them who have at hand many a law and custom for the behoof of masters, and being master can make yet more laws in the same behoof; and they shall suffer poor people to thrive just so long as their thriving shall profit the mastership and no longer.[14]

Mastership blinded individuals to their exploitation by masking naked greed with false ideas of duty, natural hierarchy and political obligation. John Ball tells his listeners: 'sooth it is that the poor deemeth the rich to be other than he, and meet to be his master, as though, forsooth, the poor were come of Adam, and the rich of him that made Adam, that is God'.[15] Yet in principle, Morris associated mastership with wilfulness and was more concerned with its location than its existence. As one of the fictional characters of his prose romances says: ' "So it is then the world over, that happy men are wilful and masterful." '[16] The same idea is expressed by the fourteenth-century peasants. Morris observes how the artisans sing a song 'concerning the struggle against tyranny for the freedom of life ... of the life of a man doing his own will and not the will of another man commanding him for the commandment's sake.'[17] The promise of mastership was that it could be recovered by and devolved to individuals, so that instead of satisfying another's will each was able to realise their own. Structurally, this demanded economic equality (which Morris defined as a principle of distribution according to need), an end to both the artificial hierarchies that facilitated slavery and the compulsion that forced labour. Yet none of these conditions released individuals from the duties and obligations that unjust, tyrannical societies perverted. In just social conditions, these obligations and duties would persist.

In a future communist society, Morris anticipated duty and obligation transformed. As masters, individuals exercised their own will but they did so co-operatively or, as Morris put it, in fellowship. Although he did not pinpoint precisely what he meant by this concept, he captured the essence of the social relations he desired in his discussions of art. His principle assumption was that the democratisation of art in communism would free individuals by transforming work.[18] As artists, individuals would meet their essential needs by engaging in productive leisure. Working voluntarily, they would no longer perceive labour as compulsion but instead as pleasure. However, the freedom they experienced as artists would meet a communal as well as an individual need. As Morris explained to James Tochatti in 1894, in communism artists 'will work for the benefit of ... the whole people: whereas now they work for the masters, the rich class, that lives on the labour of others.'[19] Free to do what they willed, individuals would produce things that were thought to be 'beautiful and pleasant' and which they hoped would give pleasure to others. They would have full scope for creative expression – mastership – but would find meaning for their art in fellowship. In the true sense, Morris argued, art was impossible,

> except by means of the co-operation of labour that produces the ordinary wares of life; and that co-operation again they cannot have as long as the workmen are dependent on the will of a master. They must co-operate consciously and willingly for the expression of individual character and gifts which we call art.[20]

While the theoretical weakness that Morris eventually identified in anarchism rested on the claim that individualism ruled against the possibility of co-operation and collective agreement, his late critique also fastened on what he considered to be the practical implications of the anarchists' individualist stance. His charge was that because anarchists failed to understand that individuality must issue from, or in tandem with co-operation, their individualism played itself out in violence. Evidence to support the charge was readily available. In the early 1890s a series of trials provided a platform for anarchists accused of committing a range of high-profile assassinations and bombings to justify the use of violence as a revolutionary tactic. In his interview for *Justice*, Morris referred to some of the more notorious characters involved, notably Ravachol and Vaillant. His complaint against them was two-fold: insofar as their acts involved the targeting of 'non-combatants' they were immoral and as a revolutionary strategy violence was futile. Quite a lot of anarchists – including Kropotkin – agreed. Yet Morris appeared to draw the arguments together to suggest that the anarchists' lack of feasible alternative highlighted a lack of constraint that was implicit in their individualism.

His view was mediated by a longer reflection about the prospects for revolution. During the whole period of his active involvement in socialism (1883–1896) Morris's expectations about revolution altered considerably and his relationship with anarchism varied in turn. His warmest relations with the anarchists coincided with a period of optimism in the mid- to late 1880s when he combined a commitment to 'making socialists' with a policy of anti-parliamentarism, in preparation for the anticipated collapse of capitalism. His sympathies began to wane after 1887 when the disaster of Bloody Sunday (a mass demonstration in London's Trafalgar Square which met with extraordinary police violence, leaving three dead and hundreds injured) gave him a glimpse of the sheer might of the state's reactionary force. No longer sanguine about the willingness or capability of the workers to immediately confront or resist it, Morris became convinced that his efforts to make socialists through anti-parliamentary activity were hopeless and that the strategy would likely end in disaster. By the early 1890s his criticisms of anarchism became more strident as he reluctantly reconciled himself to the idea that parliament offered the only available route to change.[21] Having taken stock of the reality of class struggle, he tired of talk of revolution and felt that those who indulged in such arguments were deluded.

Morris's reassessment of revolution not only coincided with the wave of political violence explicitly associated with anarchism but, equally importantly, with its enthusiastic embrace by self-identifying anarchists in the League. At precisely the point that Morris accepted parliamentarism as the only available route to socialist change, some League anarchists found their inspiration in assassination and random killing and adopted a rhetoric of revolutionary violence that filled him with frustration and despair. Although he continued to offer financial support to former comrades who fell foul of the incitement laws and *agent provocateurs*, the co-operation he had once enjoyed with anarchists both in an out of the League as an anti-parliamentarian gave way to a deep hostility. When James Tochatti first requested a statement of his politics in *Liberty*, Morris told him that he could not 'in conscience' allow his name to be 'attached' to an 'anarchist paper' because of the 'promiscuous slaughter' which anarchists had adopted as 'a means of converting people'.[22] The significance of this reappraisal was not missed by observers. One anonymous anarchist correspondent to *Liberty* wrote that Morris now counter-posed violence to political action as if there were no other possibility, a view that wrongly dismissed the revolutionary potential of 'trade combinations' and of waging precisely the kind of extra-parliamentary struggle that he outlined in the chapter 'how the change came' in *News From Nowhere*.[23] Having put his name to the *Manifesto*, Morris appeared to be persuaded that there were only two routes to socialism: parliament or terror. Even if the former was likely to lead to a type of socialism that he did not like, the refusal of all anarchists to accept it and the willingness of some to choose terror indicated the extent of their individualism. Only those who prioritised this concept above all others would fail to see the necessity of supporting the collective struggle or perform blatantly immoral acts that ran counter to ordinary political calculations.

As individualists, Morris concluded, anarchists were not prone to violence as such, but to assertive and transgressive behaviours which might be expressed violently and which were at root, anti-social. Taking August Vaillant (the anarchist executed in 1894 for throwing a bomb into the French Chamber of Deputies) as his model, Morris linked individualism to vain-gloriousness.

> Prepared to sacrifice his life in order to gratify his vanity; he is a type of men [sic] you meet in all grades all professions. You and I have met some of them; even among artists and poets they are not unknown; men who would do, in their art, what they knew to be quite wrong and outrageous in order to gain notoriety rather than work honesty and well and remain in obscurity.[24]

In Morris's mind, anarchists like Vaillant were artists of a particular stripe. Failing to understand their social obligations and duties, they denied fellowship and so wrongly interpreted mastership as a principle of individual domination. Morris found another model of this brand of individualism in capitalism and in the experimentation of elite art where, what passed as creativity was increasingly driven by the desire to secure a niche in the market through notoriety: false claims to 'originality' fuelled by 'competition for the guineas of the Manchester patron'.[25] In this competitive environment 'everybody must at least pretend to be a master: for, look you, it no longer *pays* an artist to work hard to correct the faults which he himself cannot fail to recognize'.[26] This analysis tapped into discussions of decadence, which as Regenia Gagnier shows, cut across late Victorian literary, political and scientific fields.[27] Although it was clear that individualism in the arts represented a different level of attention-seeking to assassination and terror, Morris was not alone in thinking that it came from the same root and that it expressed a similar anarchistic distain for social engagement, co-operation and mutual support as well as integrity and self-reflection.

To summarise: Morris's attempt to classify all anarchists as individualist appeared to establish a clear ideological boundary between anarchism and communism. Violence was symptomatic of this division, but it was rooted in an understanding of individual–community relations that Morris derived from his concepts of fellowship, mastership and tyranny: a social condition of co-operative interdependence, supported by economic equality. Morris's position was certainly clear, yet as an accurate description of ideological difference it was deeply flawed. The sweep of his late designation of anarchist thought was muddied by the complexity of political debate and the contestation of both of his central terms: 'anarchism' and 'individualism'. As will be seen below, these terms were used to describe free market anti-statism at one end of the spectrum and the anti-capitalist, anti-authoritarianism of Bakunin and Kropotkin at the other. Morris directed his critique at both, but his blanket rejection of anarchism assumed a questionable conflation that was belied by divisions within Victorian individualism and the anarchist movement itself.

## Anarchisms and individualisms: From politics to ideology

Individualism was a central term in late Victorian political debate and disagreements about the role of the state, in particular, were conceptualised in terms of its opposition to collectivism.[28] In late nineteenth- and early twentieth-century revolutionary socialist circles this debate took a distinctive turn. Revolutionaries also probed the rights and wrongs of state intervention – the delivery of welfare services, questions of individual rights and responsibilities – but looked as well at the state's class composition, its transformative potential, its ethical status and long-term existence. These interests affected the ways in which key terms of debate were couched. For example, socialists did not so much use collectivism as a synonym for socialism, as was the habit of anti-collectivists, but to describe a commitment to a principle of common ownership which could be interpreted either to mean centralised state ownership, decentralised communal and/or direct workers' control. The goal of revolution was usually described in other ways: socialism, communism, mutualism, anarchy, the co-operative commonwealth, and sometimes democratic socialism and, pejoratively, state socialism. Anarchists sometimes defined 'collectivism' even more narrowly, to describe the principle of distribution according to work – or deeds – as opposed to the communist system of needs. Kropotkin's adoption of this usage enabled him to gloss over his differences with Bakunin while also disputing the claim that Marx was a communist.[29]

Naturally, discussions conducted in the anti-collectivist circles had an impact on socialist debates and on perceptions of anarchism in particular. The pre-eminent position that Herbert Spencer occupied in the individualist camp meant that individualism was habitually associated with anti-statism, opening the way for anarchism to be linked to the defence of the free market, the economic doctrine that socialists typically mapped to individualist political theory. In the Liberty and Property Defence League (LPDL), a Spencerite organisation whose co-authored manifesto *A Plea for Liberty* was published in 1891, all these relationships were examined. Auberon Herbert, one of the group's leading lights called himself a 'voluntaryist', a stance which combined resistance to the state, 'the great machine' as Herbert called it, and the 'many systems of State force' with recognition of the 'free and open market'. His political ideal was one which released the 'living energies of the free individuals' and left them

> free to combine in their own way, in their own groups, finding their own experience, setting before themselves their own hopes and desires, aiming only at such ends as they truly share in common, and ever as the foundation of it all, respecting deeply and religiously alike their own freedom, and the freedom of all others.[30]

Herbert rejected the label anarchist because he supported a system of regulation to 'repress aggression or crime'[31] but other members of the LPDL – notably J.H. Levy – did not and in embracing it further blurred the boundaries between different anarchisms. Dividing anarchists into three camps – 'conservative', 'communist' and 'individualist' – he acknowledged that communism occupied the main ground of the movement, but argued that none of the factions could claim exclusive rights over its application. Moreover, the generic use of the term 'anarchist' did not worry him since he believed that there was an important family resemblance between these varieties. United in their opposition to 'coercive co-operation' or government – what he called socialism – anarchists differed only on the structural mechanisms required to achieve their aims: whether to maintain full rights of ownership, abolish property rights or allow property in use.[32] The secretary of the LPDL, Wordsworth Donnisthorpe, took yet another approach. At first resisting the label, he later identified himself as an anarchist because he believed that anti-statists were more interested in defending privilege by entrenching market advantage in monopoly than in genuinely expanding the sphere of liberty. According to Wendy McElroy, he was steered in this direction by Benjamin Tucker, having been for many years a correspondent to *Liberty* and the paper's most frequent British contributor.[33]

Outside the LPDL, anarchist opinion about the proper designation of anti-collectivist individualism was similarly divided. For Max Nettlau, an associate of Kropotkin, Herbert's voluntaryism was 'humane and vigorously anti-statist' but ultimately dilettante and not 'anarchist'.[34] In contrast, Tucker described Herbert as a true anarchist.[35] Victor Yarros, an associate of Tucker, made the same claims for Levy.[36] These responses broadly mapped to sub-divisions between so-called individualist, egoist, mutualist and communist principles. As a rule of thumb, anarchists who put themselves in one of the first two groups tended to be more receptive to anti-collectivist individualism than mutualists or communists. Yet, as discussions within and between these groups show, anarchist conceptions of individualism were far more complex and messy. For example, notwithstanding the common ground that anarchist individualists sometimes found with anti-collectivists, anarcho-communists did not reject individualism out of hand. Indeed, while Kropotkin felt that Tucker's Spencerite leanings ultimately pointed to the defence of a minimal state, he endorsed key tenets of his anti-statist critique. On Spencer's death, *Freedom*, the anarchist paper Kropotkin helped establish, feted Spencer as 'the greatest philosopher of the nineteenth century'. His two virtues were that he had 'vigorously shaken the foundation stone of the idea of God, or authority and of superstition on which the power and privileges of the rich oppressors are based' and that he had 'denounced the State as a pernicious establishment bequeathed to us by the barbarians and strengthened by those idle and oppressing social classes living on the labour of the people'.[37] Kropotkin offered another appreciation, highlighting his common commitment to Spencer's rationalism, love of naturalistic science and celebration of the idea that 'the welfare of the individual' was the single most important postulate of the social and physical sciences.[38] Spencer had shown that individuals had a capacity to reason, co-operate and develop social behaviours without compulsion and without recourse to religion or other metaphysical speculation. In this he had followed the tradition established by Proudhon. Anarchists, Kropotkin argued, endorsed both his analytical approach and his anti-statism.

Anarchist communists were intolerant of anti-collectivist economics, however, and parted company equally with anti-collectivists and anarchist individualists on questions of property and exchange. Nettlau, together with another of Kropotkin's comrades, Varlaam Tcherkesov, argued that these issues were the real determinants of individualist and non-individualist doctrines. Insofar as Nettlau and Tcherkesov's arguments treated varieties of anarchism as mere 'economic forms' their understanding bore some relation to Levy's.[39] The difference was that Levy's Spencerite leanings led him to identify all anarchists (including communist) as individualists and anti-socialist, whereas Tcherkesov changed the ideological poles of debate to argue that individualism represented a deviation from a socialist-anarchist norm. By his reckoning, the division between anarchists and individualists was marked by the anarchist's rejection of private ownership and the market. Thus placing '[Max] Sterner' [sic] in the same category as Spencer, he dismissed both as 'bourgeois'.[40] In 1893 *Freedom* published a full statement of this view:

> Communist anarchists claim as the basis of the new social order *common property,* whereas Individualists defend private property as the necessary foundation of society...Nor is that the only difference between Communist and Individualist Anarchists. Communist Anarchists maintain that

the necessary accompaniment of private property is government; a government of some kind, whether a parliamentary one, or a sort of East India Company, or a Pinkerton Police Force salaried by the capitalists. And as to the 'voluntary' taxation and other 'voluntary' things advocated by Individualists, we fail to see how, in a society based on private property and individual competition, the people who 'voluntarily' submit to a tax could be prevented from shifting the burden on to their neighbours; or how those who join in a Defence Association would be prevented from using this organized force against others than themselves.[41]

Tying anarchism to a particular politics rather than an economic form, mutualists challenged Tcherkesov's anarchist–individualist dichotomy. Mutualism, they argued, was not a mere economic system, even if liberty of production, or the right of producers to determine how goods were to be distributed and disposed of, was central to it.[42] Importantly, mutualism differed from the anti-collectivist individualism associated with Herbert and Spencer, because it did not justify unlimited accumulation or authority through private property.[43] Some communists accepted the ethical distinction that the mutualists sought to make between their own position and unqualified anti-statism. As a correspondent to *Freedom* noted, plain individualism was Lockean: it described 'the right of the individual to appropriate the result of other people's labor over and above what he pays them in wages, though he generally has to share this surplus according to agreement with the usurer, landlord and government'.[44] Mutualism, by contrast, was egalitarian and it did not allow such appropriations. Treating mutualist claims seriously, these anarchists nevertheless criticised mutualists for calling themselves individualists because it wrongly implied 'a tautology between Individualism and Anarchism' and misleadingly conflated an agreement (between communists and mutualists) about ethics with a disagreement about the operation of markets.[45] Rejecting this implication, the anarcho-communists argued that they were as committed to individual freedom as the mutualists were and that communism was the only economic system capable of securing the liberties that both groups of anarchists cherished. Kropotkin made a similar point in a discussion of Proudhon and Stirner, but introduced a modification to the terms of debate. Proudhon, Kropotkin argued, understood correctly that moral conscience, by which he meant a conception of justice and equality, had a basis in social life. Stirner argued that morality existed only by convention and wrongly concluded that it was necessarily rooted in authority.[46] On this reading, mutualism described a system of anarchist ethics based on the principle of individuality; egoism, by contrast, was an individualist doctrine which sanctioned selfishness in the name of self-expression.[47]

These were a complex set of debates and because they involved a range of individuals who assumed a number of different theoretical perspectives, there was little consensus about where or how to draw the lines of ideological division. Perhaps not surprisingly, therefore, outside observers sometimes simply passed over the complexity of anarchist politics and failed to acknowledge the different ways in which the relationship between anarchism and individualism was understood. For example, in a sweeping critique of *a priori* political philosophy, T.H. Huxley identified two important trends in the history of European thought: regimentation and anarchy. The first was defined by the view that 'the blessings of peace' required the surrender of rights to authority. In the modern period Hobbes stood at its head. The second, anarchy, typically treated individuals as 'highly intelligent and respectable persons, "living together according to reason, without a common superior on earth, with authority to judge between them" '.[48] This was the tradition of Locke. On this system of classification Auberon Herbert – who rejected the label – was as much an anarchist as Levy who was willing to accept it or, as Huxley in fact suggested, as Stirner and Bakunin.[49] Nonanarchist socialist critics tended to treat the divisions within the anarchist movement in an equally cavalier manner and even more mischievously. In 1893 *Freedom* noted that social democrats usually 'disposed' of anarchism in one of three ways. One was to claim that it was 'too perfect an ideal' and utopian. Another was to suggest that anarchy was identical to the social democratic vision and that 'anarchism and anarchy' were just 'bad neologisms'. The third was to argue that anarchism was 'a return to barbarism . . . a new form of the old and discredited laissez-faire doctrine', 'reactionary' to boot.[50] This last claim touched directly on the nature of anarchist individualism and it became one of the dominant themes in social democratic writing, not least because it was taken up at the turn of the century by Lenin.[51] Writing in 1896, William Liebknecht advanced precisely this case. On account of the influence that Stirner had exercised on the anti-socialist Eugene Richter (whose 1891 satire *Pictures of a Socialistic Future* mocked German social democracy as a hopelessly inefficient and frighteningly utopian tyranny), Liebknecht traced the origins of anarchism to Stirner and thus denounced it as an individualist doctrine.[52] While Stirner's egoism was indeed open to individual property ownership, the elision of egoism with limited state doctrines and the extension of this combination to anarchism in general was – as Tcherkesov protested – highly misleading. Still, Liebknecht argued:

> There is, in fact, nothing in common between Anarchism and Socialism. Anarchism . . . has individualism for its basis; that is, the same principle on which capitalist society rests, and therefore it is essentially reactionary, however hysterical may be its shrieks of revolution.[53]

How did Morris approach these debates? The answer is that the view he expressed in 1893–1894 was based on a classification equally reductive as Huxley's and Liebknecht's. Yet it was unusual because it was also based on both a familiarity with the anarchist movement (that Huxley lacked) and a much closer and sympathetic involvement with anarchist politics than Liebknecht had ever enjoyed.

Morris's diary for 1887 distinguished three groups. The first were what he called the 'orthodox' anarchists who met at Cleveland Hall and he identified Victor Dave – with whom he and Belfort Bax co-wrote their history of the Paris Commune – as their 'leading spirit'. The second were the anarchists of the Autonomy group and the third the Freedom group organised around Kropotkin and Charlotte Wilson. Morris was aware of these groups' different constituencies. He noted, for example, that Dave's 'orthodox' anarchists were fervent internationalists, largely French- and German-speaking refugees. A newspaper cutting from the *Daily News* pasted into his diary described Charlotte Wilson as a 'South Kensington or British Museum art student' type, an 'aesthete with views', capturing an image of the Freedom group that was usually painted in less polite terms by the anarchists of the Socialist League.[54]

Apart from noting their different meeting places and memberships, Morris seemed unsure of the issues that divided these groups. For example, he admitted ignorance of the grounds of the 'quarrel' – a spying scandal – which divided Dave's anarchists from the Autonomy group, though later becoming involved in the affair, he designated the latter as 'unrespectable'.[55] Yet, as Florence Boos notes, Morris appreciated that there were significant divisions between 'orthodox Anarchists', 'collectivists' and Kropotkin's anarcho-communists.[56] Moreover, he identified the distinctively communist position with the rejection of government, of parliamentarism and the characterisation of bourgeois politics as a condition of war – a most tyrannous tyranny. What Morris called the 'anarchical' tendencies of Charlotte Wilson's 'Utopian Anarchist Superstition' referred, additionally, to the communists' unwavering faith in the latent power of spontaneous grass roots resistance, a faith which he did not share.[57]

Morris's observations of the anarchist movement hardly touched on the theoretical issues discussed in the anarchist press, but he was certainly familiar with the anti-collectivism of the LPDL. The text of a speech by Wordsworth Donnisthorpe, published in Henry Seymour's paper *The Anarchist,* earned a scornful review in *Commonweal* in 1887.[58] Donnisthorpe's critical dissection of the *Socialist Catechism* by Morris's friend J.L. Joynes might well have influenced his judgement, but either way Morris described the speech as an example of the 'pessimistic paradoxical exercises which are a disease of the period, and whose aim would seem to be the destruction of the language'.[59] Morris's judgements of Auberon Herbert were hardly warmer. He had worked with Herbert in the Eastern Question Association in the 1870s, and thereafter followed debates about 'voluntaryism' in the liberal reviews, but this personal association failed to encourage an appreciation of his ideas. The critique Grant Allen presented in the essay 'Individualism and Socialism' was too tame for Morris, but he agreed with Allen that the LPDL's defence of property in use would result in the very monopoly that undercut the equal enjoyment of individual liberty the group championed.[60] As Morris put it: by supporting a principle of distribution according to deed, these anarchists 'wished to abolish *organised* monopoly but supported unorganised monopoly, or the rule of the strongest individual . . . upholding . . . private property with no association.'[61]

However confusing Morris found the internal politics of the anarchist movement, he was certainly familiar with some of the issues that divided anarchist communists from limited-state anti-collectivists. Nevertheless, in his late critique of anarchism he subordinated these differences to capture both groups under the common principle of anti-authoritarianism. This approach to anarchism was well rehearsed in the non-anarchist socialist press, though *Freedom's* commentary on social democratic objections to anarchism overlooked it. For example, finding agreement neither in 'object, policy, nor methods' with the anarchists, *Justice* argued that the anarchist, 'will have no authority on any account' and that 'the Social-Democrat believes that a certain amount of authority will always be necessary'.[62] Anarchist anti-authoritarianism was also central to Engels' critique and, just as Liebknecht used Stirner to link laissez-faire economics to anarchism, he drew on the same source to reveal the chaotic destructiveness of anarchist doctrines. Identifying Bakunin as the transmitter of 'Stirnerian "rebellion" ' he jibed: 'the anarchists have all become "unique ones", so unique that no two of them can agree with each other'.[63] Morris arrived at his position by a different route, fastening on collective agreement rather than abstract authority, but his claims were similar. He attempted to show that anarchist moral individualism rendered agreement in socialism impossible. His discussion drew back to the concepts he had elaborated in the 1880s: social tyranny, slavery and fellowship. Rejecting 'social tyranny', he contended, anarchists also denied fellowship, leaving individuals exposed to new forms of slavery, rooted in the unconfined principle of individual mastership. The difficulty of the charge was that it ran counter to a process of decision-making that Morris also supported, suggesting that the ideological reduction that he had distilled from his engagement with anarchist politics was perhaps faulty.

## Communism, anarchism and democracy

Accusing the anarchists of being 'somewhat authoritative' on the issue, Morris argued that the individualism of the anarcho-communists was expressed through their rejection of collective agreement.64 His starting point was that anarchists opposed agreement on the grounds that it gave power to majorities and was therefore coercive. For Morris, this argument was self-defeating. To illustrate why, he imagined a dispute about the building of a bridge. Should opinion be divided, he asked: 'What Is to Be Done?

Which party is to give way?' The anarchist answer, Morris thought, was to 'say it must not be carried by a majority'; Morris responded, 'in that case, then, it must be carried by a minority'.[65] The illogicality of the anarchist position pointed to an important theoretical principle: anarchists prioritised the rights of individuals over all forms of collective power.

Failing to recognise that equal freedom necessarily involved a coercive limit on the liberty of all, anarchists not only tied themselves in knots on the question of majoritarianism, they also committed themselves to the negative moral individualism that genuine communism – Morris's doctrine – rejected. To the anarcho-communist readers of the *Commonweal* Morris argued that 'if freedom from authority means the assertion of the advisability or possibility of an individual man doing what he pleases always and under all circumstances, this is an absolute negation of society'.[66] No matter how much these anarchists openly disagreed with the 'voluntaryists' on questions of economics, they shared the same moral outlook.[67]

The strength of Morris's conclusion lay in his claim that the anarcho-communists in fact understood authority as he suggested. Yet as the debates about individualism make clear, this argument was difficult to sustain. Admittedly, the clearest statements of anarchist-communist ethics appeared only after Morris had died. However it was clear from discussions in *Freedom* that anarcho-communists were extremely wary of non-communist anarchist doctrines and their impact on individual–community relations. Two particular examples were that mutualism failed to provide adequate safeguards to protect the egalitarian relations it espoused and that egoism gave free reign to individual competition. Morris expressed precisely the same worry about 'voluntaryism' and the individualism of the LPDL. More tellingly, Morris's further explorations of democracy suggested that the fault line that he identified between communism and anarcho-communism was not based on the presumed incompatibility of anti-authoritarianism with unrestrained individual freedom, at all. Indeed, he located the problem of individualism in the tension between anti-authoritarianism and class interest. This argument secured the ideological division he wanted to cement, but it did not sit easily with the model of decision-making that he presented in his utopian romance, *News from Nowhere*.

Morris opened up the gap in the debate in his letter to the readers of *Commonweal* where he attempted to show how anarchist defences of liberty conflicted with the idea of a common good. He imagined two scenarios: one where the long-term stability of society was threatened by the rise of a tyrannous interest, for example, the attempt to reintroduce some form of slavery (like monopoly), and a second, short term dispute where opinions about a particular policy diverged. Both scenarios, he argued, legitimised coercion, but the tyranny assumed different forms. The first case, the threat of new enslavement, convinced Morris that there was a need for an organisation or a 'central body', at least for a temporary period, to enforce commitments to socialist principles.[68] The second dispute – the policy disagreement – did not demand this kind of regulatory body, but resolution depended on observance of socialist principles, or an idea of collective good. To illustrate, Morris imagined how a proposal to cut down 'all the timber in England' and turn the 'country into... a market-garden under glass' might be challenged. Opponents, he suggested, might prefer the landscape to remain wild and to preserve its natural beauty.[69] However, if the majority backed the proposal, it was only right that the imagined objectors (Morris put himself among them) subordinate their own interests to the general interest of the community. No matter how significant their differences might be – and the example Morris chose was designed to highlight how divisive he felt the issue was – the minority would 'give up the lesser for the greater'.[70]

On this account, Morris perceived communism to be anti-anarchist in two ways. On the one hand, the imagined central body institutionalised the social tyranny on which socialism depended, and on the other it gave priority to majority over minority or individual interests. Yet in 1894 he drew still further from anarchist thinking by adopting a position which relied on the recognition of a universal interest, not just the priority of the numeric majority. The pluralism which explained the policy disagreements that socialists were likely to face was now denied. Majority rule, he argued, 'is only harmful where there is conflict of interest'.[71] In socialism, 'there would be no opposition of interests, but only divergences of opinion' because the 'struggles between *opposing interests* for... mastery', that were part and parcel of the existing parliamentary system, would be a thing of the past.[72] Morris's argument was consistent with his earlier rejection of representative democracy as a system of class rule,[73] but it suggested that majorities could never injure minorities once class divisions based on private ownership had been abolished. As Morris put it, 'community cannot compel the community'.[74] This very Rousseauean view meant that individuals would be expected to identify with a higher authority, even while their opinions were being trampled on or ignored.[75]

Morris's unqualified defence of simple majoritarianism, let alone his assumption of universal class interest certainly put him at odds with a good proportion of anarchists, communists and individualists alike.[76] He was probably right to think that his proposal for a central defensive body would alarm all sorts of anarchists, ever mindful of the potential for the state's reconstitution. However, his claim that the anarchist rejection of 'the tyranny of society' meant 'that every man should be quite independent of every other'[77] – as he phrased the critique in *News From Nowhere* – wrongly assumed that the rejection of these two models of decision-making exhausted the possibilities of radical democracy. This assumption was faulty because it overlooked the possibility of stepping *between* the tyranny of class interest and moral individualism, even though his own work contained an outline model of a non-tyrannous democratic system. Indeed, he fleshed out the point in *News from Nowhere,* where he again discussed the building of a bridge.[78]

In his second hypothetical context, disagreements about the proposal are resolved through dialogue and a continuous process of direct, open balloting, neither by the submission of the minority to majority interests, nor by the recognition of the common good. In this picture of communism, agreement is reached through a deliberative process, supported by ordinary tyranny, capable of determining policy outcomes through the resolution rather than the subordination of differences. Morris fleshed out a similar process of consensual and deliberative debate in *Commonweal*. Assuming that 'a dozen thoughtful men' would have 'twelve different opinions' on 'any subject which is not a dry matter of fact', he argued that the group would negotiate a compromise to 'get their business done'. Morris described the 'common rule of conduct' that underpinned this process as a 'common bond' of 'authority'. In this context, however, 'authority' referred only to the background concept of tyranny, which he believed essential to any society, not the positive commitment to the common good – or class interest – that he subsequently adopted to distinguish his brand of communism from the individualism of the anarchists.[79]

Having developed a model of decision-making which assumed that individuals might reach voluntary agreement through open discussion and consensus, Morris shifted his position when it came to distinguishing communism from anarchism. When it came to pinpointing anarchism's ideological distinctiveness, agreement appeared to require more than the observance of moral norms and respect for individual autonomy (tyranny and mastership), which were the only conditions for consensus. In addition, it demanded the enforcement of majority rule (the relocation of mastership from individuals to the group) or, even more stringently, the recognition of a universal interest (the institutionalisation of mastership as an abstract idea). The elision of ordinary tyranny with majoritarianism substantiated Morris's claim that anarchists were individualists, but the integrity of his consensual alternative was the price he paid.

One way of thinking about the alternatives Morris explored is to return to his understanding of mastery and art. His conception of anarchist antiauthoritarianism pointed to egotism, or a form of competitive, vain-glorious mastership which was consciously transgressive. Against this, he posited a defence of majoritarianism and universal interest. This mapped onto an idea of mastership which subordinated the interests of individual artists to the well-being of the community. A third possibility, one that he sidelined in his late critique of anarchism, was outlined in *News from Nowhere*. It suggested that creativity was primary but that the pleasure artists derived from their production was linked to its reception in the wider community. This assumed the existence of social tyranny, but one that was shaped by the expression of individual wills.

## Conclusion

Morris's rejection of anarchism was fuelled by his frustrations with the Socialist League and the political violence of the early 1890s. It can be explained by the refusal to accept compromise on parliamentary action – and perhaps the discomfort Morris felt in adopting a strategy that he knew to be flawed. His concerns about anarchist individualism were informed by principles of fellowship, mastership and tyranny which derived from deeply held convictions about social relations in communism, but his critique depended on reductive ideological labelling which smothered the politics of the anarchist movement. Morris's critique of anarchist individualism succeeded when couched in terms of 'anti-authoritarianism', but the costs of success were high: his discussion of decision-making and collective agreement was not easily reconciled with the idea of mastership he sought to defend. Anarchists might have found aspects of Morris's communism troubling. But his attempts to dismiss anarchism as individualistic by showing that it was wholly incompatible with it, failed.

## Acknowledgement

Thanks to Alex Prichard for repeated attempts to bring clarity to the argument.

## Notes

1. Mark Bevir, 'WilliamMorris: TheModern Self, Art and Politics', *History of European Ideas* 24 (1998), 176.
2. William Morris, *Statement of Principles of the Hammersmith Socialist Society,* (London: Kelmscott Press, 1890), p. 6.
3. On Morris's divergence from Kropotkin on this issue see 'Morris, Anti-statism and Anarchy', in Peter Faulkner and Peter Preston (eds), *William Morris: Centenary Essays* (Exeter: University of Exeter Press, 1999), pp. 215–228.
4. *Manifesto of English Socialists,* (London: Twentieth Century Press, 1893), p. 8.
5. *Manifesto,* p. 5.
6. Stefan Collini, *Liberalism and Sociology: L.T. Hobhouse and Political Argument in England 1880–1914,* (Cambridge: Cambridge University Press, 1983), p. 16.
7. William Morris, 'A Socialist Poet on Bombs and Anarchism: An Interview with William Morris', *Justice* (27 January 1894), p. 6.
8. William Morris, 'Why I Am a communist', *Liberty* (February 1894), pp. 13–15.
9. Morris, 'Socialist Poet'.
10. Ibid.
11. Morris, *Statement of Principles,* p. 5.

12. Susan Buck-Morss, 'Hegel and Haiti', *Critical Inquiry* 26 (2000), 821.
13. William Morris, *Journalism: Contributions to Commonweal 1885–1890*, Nicholas Salmon (ed.) (Bristol: Thoemmes Press, 1996), p. 27.
14. William Morris, 'The Dream of John Ball', in A.L. Morton (ed.), *Three Works by William Morris* (London: Lawrence & Wishart, 1986), pp. 94–95.
15. Morris, *John Ball*, p. 56.
16. William Morris, *The Story of the Glittering Plain* (Bristol: Thoemmes Press, 1996), p. 322.
17. Morris, *John Ball*, p. 45.
18. For a recent discussion see Laurence Davis, 'Everyone an Artist: Art, Labour, Anarchy and Utopia', in Laurence Davis and Ruth Kinna (eds), *Anarchism and Utopianism* (Manchester: Manchester University Press, 2009), pp. 73–98.
19. Norman Kelvin (ed.), *The Collected Letters of William Morris, vol. IV: 1893–1896* (New Jersey: Princeton University Press, 1996), p. 209.
20. William Morris, *Political Writings: Contributions to Justice and Commonweal*, Nicholas Salmon (ed.) (Bristol: Thoemmes Press, 1994), p. 397.
21. This shift is sometimes interpreted as a principled reversal of his earlier position, but can be explained as a pragmatic response to his disappointment with the failure of the League and his perception that workers were more interested in electoral power and welfare reform than revolution and the realisation of communism in the society of art. In 1895 Morris wrote that while he saw the 'necessity' of the 'political side' of the struggle, this was still an element with which he could not work. Norman Kelvin (ed.), *The Collected Letters of William Morris, vol. IV: 1893–1896* (New Jersey: Princeton University Press, 1996), p. 285.
22. *Letters* IV, p. 113.
23. Morris, *Liberty*, p. 18.
24. Morris, 'Socialist Poet'.
25. Morris, *Political Writings*, p. 37.
26. Ibid., pp. 37–38.
27. Regina Gagnier, *Individualism, Decadence and Globalization* (London: Palgrave/Macmillan, 2010), p. 2.
28. Collini, *Liberalism and Sociology*, pp. 14–15.
29. Peter Kropotkin, in R. Baldwin (ed.), *Kropotkin's Revolutionary Pamphlets* (New York: Dover, 1970), pp. 166, 295.
30. Auberon Herbert, *The Voluntaryist Creed: Being the Herbert Spencer Lecture Delivered at Oxford, June 7, 1906* (London: Henry Frowde, 1908), pp. 6–7, http://files.libertyfund.org/files/1026/0545_Bk.pdf (accessed 17 September 2010).
31. See C. Tame, 'The Libertarian Tradition no. 1: Auberon Herbert', *Free Life, The Journal of the Libertarian Alliance*, 1/2 (1980), 2; E. Mack, 'Voluntaryism: The Political Thought of Auberon Herbert', *Journal of Libertarian Studies*, 2/4 (1978), 306; Wendy McElroy, *The Debates of Liberty: An Overview of Individualist Anarchism, 1881–1908* (Lanham, Boulder, New York, Oxford: Lexington Books, 2003), p. 33.
32. J. Levy, Appendix to Auberon Herbert, *Taxation and Anarchism: A Discussion between the Hon. Auberon Herbert and J.H. Levy* (London: Personal Rights Association, 1912), http://app.libraryofliberty.org/?option=com_staticxt&staticfile= show.php%3Ftitle=2257&chapter=212934&layout=html&Itemid=27 (accessed 17 October 2010).
33. McElroy, *Debates of Liberty*, pp. 7, 164.
34. Max Nettlau, *A Short History of Anarchism*, ed. H.M. Becker, trans. I.P. Isca (London: Freedom Press, 1996), p. 40.

35. Mack, 'Voluntaryism', p. 306.
36. McElroy, *Debates of Liberty*, p. 164.
37. *Freedom*, January 1904.
38. Peter Kropotkin, *Freedom*, April 1893.
39. *Freedom*, July 1895.
40. Varlaam Tcherkesov, 'Socialism or Democracy', *Supplement to Freedom*, June 1895.
41. *Freedom*, July 1893.
42. *Freedom*, June 1895.
43. Mutualists distinguished between property and possession and argued that anything more than one's tools, personal possessions and dwelling, must always be co-operatively organised and co-ordinated.
44. *Freedom*, July 1895.
45. Ibid.
46. Kropotkin, *Revolutionary Pamphlets*, p. 297; Peter Kropotkin, *Ethics: Origin and Development*, trans. Louis S. Friedland and J. R. Piroshnikoff (Montreal/New York: Black Rose, 1992), pp. 269–270, 338.
47. Kropotkin, *Revolutionary Pamphlets*, p. 172.
48. T.H. Huxley, 'Government: Anarchy or Regimentation' (1890), in *Collected Essays*, http://aleph0.clarku.edu/huxley/CE1/G-AR.html (accessed 17 October 2010).
49. Ibid.
50. *Freedom*, July 1893.
51. V.I. Lenin, 'Anarchism and Socialism', in *Marx, Engels, Lenin: Anarchism and Anarcho-Syndicalism* (Moscow: Progress Publishers, 1972), pp. 185–186.
52. Eugene Richter, *Pictures of the Socialistic Future* (London: Swan Sonnenschein & co. 1907), http://www.econlib.org.
53. William Liebknecht, 'Our Recent Congress', *Justice*, 15 August 1895.
54. 'Celebrating the Commune', *Daily News*, 18 March 1887.
55. Florence Boos, 'William Morris's Socialist Diary', *History Workshop* 13 (1982), 38.
56. Ibid., 28 n. 56–58.
57. Ibid., 38 n. 106.
58. Morris, *Political Writings*, pp. 180–183.
59. Ibid., p. 180. For Donnisthorp's comments on Joynes see *Socialism Analyzed. Being a Critical Examination of Mr. Joynes's 'Socialist Catechism'* (London: Liberty and Property Defence League, 1888).
60. W. Morris, *Collected Letters of William Morris, vol. III: 1889–1892*, Norman Kelvin (ed.) (New Jersey: Princeton University Press, 1996), p. 59; Grant Allen, 'Individualism and Socialism', *Contemporary Review* LV (1889), 730–734.
61. Morris, *Letters* III, p. 88.
62. *Justice*, 5 September 1896.
63. Friedrich Engels, Letter to M. Hildebrand, in *Marx, Engels, Lenin*, p. 179.
64. Morris, *Letters* III, p. 63.
65. Ibid., p. 87.
66. Ibid., p. 63.
67. Ibid., p. 64.
68. Morris, *Letters* II, p. 769.
69. Morris, *Letters* III, p. 63.
70. Ibid., p. 64.
71. Morris, 'Socialist Poet', p. 6.
72. Morris, *Liberty*, p. 14.
73. Morris, *Letters* II, p. 768.

74.  Ibid., p. 766.
75.  Morris, *Liberty*, p. 14.
76.  For a qualified anarchist defence of majoritarianism see A. Bertolo, 'Democracy and Beyond', *Democracy and Nature: An International Journal of Inclusive Democracy*, 5(2) (1999), http://www.democracynature.org/vol5/vol5.htm (accessed 28 November 2010).
77.  William Morris, *News from Nowhere*, David Leopold (ed.) (Oxford: Oxford University Press, 2003), p. 77.
78.  Ibid.
79.  Morris, *Letters* III, p. 64.

# 4

# The Syndicalist Challenge in the Durham Coalfield before 1914

*Lewis H. Mates*

## Introduction

The British 'labour revolt' immediately before the outbreak of the First World War saw millions of working days lost in strike action and the mushrooming of trade unions. This unrest, which included the first British national miners' strike in 1912, coincided with a growth in revolutionary agitation. The emergence of syndicalist ideas, essentially revolutionary trade unionism, seemed fortuitously timed to give coherence and revolutionary temper to an urge to revolt evident in important sections of the organised (and previously unorganised) British working class.

'Syndicalism' is deployed here in its 'broadest sense' to refer to 'all revolutionary, direct-actionist' organisations.[1] As Lucien van der Walt and Michael Schmidt have recently argued, syndicalism's ideological origins lay in the works of the anarchist Mikhail Bakunin. That said, self-defining Marxists also developed ideas and approaches that fed into syndicalism.

Consequently, revolutionaries who self-identified as Marxists, anarchists and others all contributed to the syndicalist canon and operated on its ideological terrain; syndicalism thus fed from, and into, both anarchist and Marxist traditions.[2] Nevertheless, the traditional divisions between Marxist and anarchist approaches persisted within syndicalism; there were both points of convergence as well as of divergence even over fundamentals. Syndicalism, therefore, offers a unique forum to study at close quarters the relations between revolutionary activists of the red and the black.

This chapter explores the impact of ideology on the conduct of revolutionary struggle among activists in the Durham coalfield, in north-east England. Coal miners, especially those of south Wales, were fundamental to the syndicalist project in Britain. The single most significant British syndicalist propaganda document was *The Miners' Next Step*, written by Welsh miners in 1911 and published in January 1912. It expressed lessons militants had taken from the defeat of the Cambrian Combine dispute. At its peak, the dispute involved 30,000 south Wales miners striking over conditions and wages, and it saw serious rioting at Tonypandy in November 1910.[3]

The unusual socio-economic conditions and radical cultural milieu in south Wales – its miners were 70 per cent more likely to strike than their counterparts in any other British coalfield before 1910 – proved particularly conducive to generating and sustaining syndicalism.[4] Yet contemporaneous upheaval in the Durham coalfield – of a similar size and, like south Wales, dependent on the vicissitudes of the unpredictable export market – offered promising ground for fruitful syndicalist intervention.

The Durham coalfield witnessed some of the first skirmishes in the wave of late Edwardian industrial unrest when, in January 1910, a considerable proportion of lodges affiliated to the 130,000 strong Durham Miners' Association (DMA) struck against an agreement signed by their executive to institute a 'three shift system' in the coalfield. For the vast majority of Durham miners this was an incredibly unpopular change because it demanded they work night as well as morning and afternoon shifts and consequently brought significant disruption to family and social life. The unpopularity of the DMA leaders – and especially the most influential, general secretary and Liberal MP John Wilson – grew with their high-handedness during the national miners' strike of 1912.

Anger from disenchanted sections of the Durham rank and file after the 1912 national strike was manifest in two main ways: first, in the growth of an aggressive and unofficial (that is, not officially endorsed by the DMA's official leadership) lodge strike policy and, second, with the institutionalisation of efforts to reform the DMA (as well as fight for increased wages), in the form of the Durham Forward Movement.[5] This was a well-supported rank-and-file initiative headed by a group of miner activists of the Independent Labour Party (ILP). Established nationally in 1893, the ILP had become one of the founders of the Labour Party, and had since made some (contested) progress in establishing itself in the coalfield.

This chapter begins by discussing the ideological strands that informed the development of syndicalism in Britain. It then considers the ideological development of Durham coalfield's two most significant pre-1914 revolutionary activists, Will Lawther and George Harvey, before examining their activities and evidence of their immediate impact. After brief consideration of the wider syndicalist influence in the coalfield, the chapter ends by examining some of the ways in which both Harvey and Lawther's politics arguably inhibited their potential impact on the wider radical milieu.

## Ideological origins of syndicalism

Three currents, involving both Marxists and anarchists, were crucial in shaping the tendencies that arose within British syndicalism. The first major influence came from America in the form of the writings of Daniel De Leon (a self-identifying Marxist) and the subsequent emergence of the Industrial Workers of the World (IWW or 'Wobblies'). De Leon developed a theory of revolutionary working-class advancement that demanded both 'political action' – defined in this context as standing for elections at local and national levels on a revolutionary platform – and industrial action. The latter took the form of 'industrial unionism' (rather than 'syndicalism' as such): revolutionary trade unions of skilled and unskilled workers in the major industries. These industrial unions were to work alongside the pre-existing unions until they supplanted them; this was dual unionism. De Leon was influential in establishing the Chicago IWW in 1905, successfully proposing an amendment to the IWW's preamble that committed it to political action. Though ratified, the issue of political action soon split the IWW between De Leon and Wobblies under Big Bill Haywood of the Western Federation of Miners, as well anarchists like Thomas Hagerty (who penned the first draft of the original preamble) and veteran anarchist organiser Lucy Parsons, wife of the Haymarket martyr Albert Parsons. This grouping prevailed at the fourth IWW convention (1908) and the amended preamble precluded affiliation to any political party. Using sadly characteristic language, De Leon denounced the victorious 'bummery', 'slum proletarians' and 'anarchist scum' and left to form a rival IWW based in Detroit, which soon faded away.[6]

In 1903 and under the influence of De Leon, most of the Scottish branches of the Marxist Social Democratic Federation (SDF) broke away, eventually forming the Socialist Labour Party (SLP).[7] In its early years, the party was an exclusive sect, but it gained importance in the trade union-sponsored working-class educational institution Ruskin College, Oxford. This was evident during the strike of 1908, when the majority of Ruskin students and the college's principal resigned in protest at its failure to place Marx at the centre of the teaching curriculum. The protest led to the founding of the Central Labour College, in London. De Leon's influence was clear in the choice of 'Plebs' League' (inspired by a De Leon pamphlet) as the name of the organisation formed to support the Central Labour College.[8] The SLP began to place an increasing emphasis on the industrial sphere and it grew with the labour revolt after 1910. However, its increasing relaxation of certain sectarian positions also lost it members and the still less sectarian and more flexible syndicalists began to outmanoeuvre it in the industrial sphere.

The second major influence was French. In 1910, Tom Mann, a veteran of the New Union struggles of the late 1880s who had been agitating in Australia, visited French syndicalists with fellow socialist Guy Bowman. Mann had also seen the North American IWW at close quarters. However, indigenous ideas, and particularly those of self-styled 'communist' William Morris, also influenced Mann as well as nurturing the development of British syndicalism more generally.[9] Morris had left the rather dogmatic SDF to form the Socialist League. While Morris developed a distinct brand of anti-statist and revolutionary anti-parliamentarianism based on Marxism, many other Socialist League activists gravitated towards anarchism.

On his return to Britain, Mann established the Industrial Syndicalist Education League (ISEL) and began producing the *Industrial Syndicalist* from July 1910. Mann played a leading role in the industrial unrest in Liverpool in 1911 and his paper, *The Transport Worker*, achieved an astonishing circulation of 20,000. Mann became even more prominent after reprinting the famous 'Don't shoot' appeal to soldiers policing the picket lines in *The Syndicalist* of January 1912. His and Bowman's subsequent imprisonment became a *cause celebre* for the Left. Nevertheless, the SLP criticised the ISEL's overemphasis on the use of the 'general strike' and its consequent denigration of working-class political action. The SLP also disparaged the ISEL's apparently weak and informal organisation and its industrial sabotage tactic, which they regarded as a counter-productive sign of weakness.[10]

Still, *The Miners' Next Step* emerged from this second syndicalist strand. Its authors were the self-styled 'Unofficial Reform Committee of the South Wales Miners' Federation' which included Marxist miners who, like Noah Ablett, had been to Ruskin, were important at Central Labour College, and who had been influenced by De Leon.[11] Aiming for the 'elimination of the employer', *The Miners' Next Step* was quite clearly revolutionary.[12] This would occur when the union in each industry was 'thoroughly organised, in the first place, to fight, to gain control of, and then to administer that industry'.[13] Yet it was also a pragmatic document, laying out in some detail a strategy for making the mines unprofitable so that the workers could assume control. But this would be full workers' control, not that exercised by the state in some form of nationalisation. While the document contained a powerful critique of trade union bureaucracy and leadership in general terms, it still – crucially – advocated internal union restructuring rather than dual unionism. The only area of contradiction in *The Miners' Next Step* was around political action, where different sections endorsed and rejected it outright.[14] The emphasis on industrial action (as well as the rejection of dual unionism) meant the SLP denounced the authors of *The Miners' Next Step* as 'anarchist freaks'.[15] But their pejorative use of 'anarchist' was merely rhetorical – the word 'anarchist' only appeared in *The Miners' Next Step* to describe how the mine owners feared the miners' radicalisation.[16] Nevertheless, the inconsistency in *The Miners' Next Step* over political action, as well as its strong critique of leadership and power within organisations, meant that it was open to anarchist interpretations.

The third strand of syndicalism was more libertarian and grouped around Guy Aldred's *Herald of Revolt* (and its successor from May 1914, *The Spur*). Bakunin was the major influence, certainly on Aldred, who published translations of Bakunin's writings in the *Herald of Revolt* and in his later papers (*The Spur*, 1914–1921; *The Commune*, 1923–1929; and *The Council*, 1923–1933), and, in 1920, an abridged edition of Bakunin's works and a biography. This strand claimed Mann was too unclear and non-committal on the issue of political action and that Mann's criticisms of parliament did not go far enough. Aldred's efforts to establish an 'Industrial Union of Direct Actionists' after 1908, however, made little headway.[17] Aldred self-identified as 'communist' or 'anti-parliamentarian'. Others in this strand explicitly adopted the word 'anarchist' to describe their position. While it was possible that a British activist, Sam Mainwaring, first coined the term 'anarcho-syndicalist' before 1914, it did not come into widespread use until the interwar period.[18] In essence, then, this group's ideology was a precursor of anarcho-syndicalism.

In the Durham coalfield itself, early anarchist influences were rather different. Russian anarchist Peter Kropotkin spoke at the 1882 Durham miners' gala, as well as elsewhere in the region. Kropotkin's influence was also evident in the founding of the anarchist commune at Clousden Hill in Forest Hall, just outside Newcastle. In the 1890s, there were anarchist meetings in a handful of scattered Durham pit villages and in several of the larger conurbations bordering the coalfield where anarchist propaganda circulated.[19] While there was a renewed phase of anarchist activity from around 1907 in Newcastle and Sunderland, the growth after 1910 was unprecedented. The form of anarchism also altered in the region, away from Kropotkin's anarcho-communism towards a syndicalist emphasis on workplace and trade union struggle.

This regional development reflected a countrywide trend (Aldred was critical of Kropotkin); as anarchism became more syndicalist orientated so the anarchist current in syndicalism became stronger. Indeed, by 1914, anarchist syndicalism, partly because of 'the refusal of many of its supporters to uphold dual unionism', was in the ascendancy.[20] The new weekly journal *The Voice of Labour* (launched in early 1914) helped to draw together disparate anarchist groups around the country, though there remained the divide with the predominately Scottish dual unionist anarchists around *The Herald of Revolt*. What was the interplay of these influences on George Harvey and Will Lawther, the two main Durham coalfield revolutionary activists before 1914?

## Harvey and Lawther's political development

Both Harvey and Lawther were politically active before they moved to revolutionary syndicalism. Harvey, born in 1885 (and four years Lawther's senior), spent his early political life as a fairly moderate member of the ILP. Harvey's radicalisation took place at Ruskin College (which he attended from 1908–1909) probably, according to Ray Challinor, under the influence of tutors W. W. Craik and Noah Ablett.[21] While at Ruskin, Harvey joined the Plebs' League, and the SLP. His rise through the Party's ranks was evident when he became editor of its journal, *The Socialist*, between 1911 and 1912. Harvey remained committed to the SLP and industrial unionism throughout the pre-war period. Nevertheless, there was nothing inevitable about either his radicalisation or his move into the SLP. Jack Parks, a Northumberland miner and boyhood friend, was Harvey's roommate at Ruskin. He too became radicalised, though over a longer period, leaving the ILP in 1910 and becoming linked with Mann's *Industrial Syndicalist* by March 1911.[22]

Will Lawther's more complex political trajectory deserves further scrutiny. Born into a Northumberland mining family in 1889, Lawther was initially influenced by Robert Blatchford's *Merrie England* and was aware that his grandfather had been imprisoned for involvement in the Chartist agitation (though his own parents were not politically active). Like Harvey, Lawther began his political life (at the age of 15) by helping to establish an ILP branch in his pit village. A year later, the Lawthers moved to Chopwell, a new pit in the north-west Durham coalfield. Lawther soon became secretary of Chopwell ILP branch.[23] He later wrote that his 'groping for a philosophy hardened into a positive conviction that militant socialism was the answer to most of the problems that beset the working class...'.[24] Perhaps more significantly, Lawther rapidly rose in the union; in 1906 he was elected vice-chair of Chopwell lodge and soon after he became its delegate to the DMA.

Lawther's conversion to syndicalism came at the newly established Central Labour College, which he attended for a year from October 1911, aided by funding from his family and lodge. As an 'exhibitioner', he had already received free education in his spare time at Rutherford College in Newcastle, having been unable, as the eldest of a big family, to take up a scholarship he won to a local grammar school. At Labour College Lawther studied sociology, economics, politics and history. Sociology lectures, delivered by Dennis Hird, considered the work of Herbert Spencer. In economics, the emphasis was, unsurprisingly, almost exclusively on Marx. Lawther read *Capital* twice and studied other works of his including *Critique of Political Economy* in addition to well-known studies of Marx by Louis Boudin and Daniel De Leon and Ricardo's *Political Economy*. Lawther also read Morris, Bernard Shaw and John Ruskin.[25] Of these, Marx was obviously a significant influence. Lawther's favourite work was the *Eighteenth Brumaire*, especially the line: 'Him whom we must convince we recognise as the master of the situation', which he quoted frequently throughout his life.[26]

What of the individuals Lawther met at college? As with Harvey, Craik, who delivered Lawther's economics lectures, must have been influential, as was Ablett, who Lawther later regarded as 'the greatest of all pre-war Marxists'.[27] Indeed, Ablett's influential role was probably crucial; his influence on the two Durham miners was quite different, as Ablett's own politics had changed significantly between the times Harvey and Lawther came into contact. Ablett had moved from activism in the SLP to rejecting its dual unionism and gravitating instead towards Mann's less doctrinaire, but more 'anti-political' syndicalism.

Lawther also joined the Plebs' League and, already fired by a militant brand of ILP socialism, he had less political distance to travel than the initially relatively moderate Harvey. While he was still at Labour College, Lawther had clearly imbibed much of the syndicalist case, condemning, in a letter to the *Daily Chronicle*, DMA secretary John Wilson's 'old fashioned notion of conciliation', and arguing instead that the union's attitude should embody the class war.[28] Writing in retirement in 1955, Lawther remained clear about the appeal that the revolutionary doctrine held at that time: 'to us it was new and exciting. It was the ultimate in extremism, the demand for direct action, and the professed disgust, not only with the class ridden structure, but also with all gradual means of getting rid of that form of society'.[29]

In his last months at Central Labour College, Lawther seemed to endorse a basic syndicalist case in the vein of *The Miners' Next Step*. This was evident in the first syndicalist propagandising Lawther conducted in his own coalfield in May 1912 when he supported south Wales syndicalist miner W. F. Hay's speaking tour of county Durham.[30] As the chair of these meetings, Lawther's rhetoric was indistinguishable from Hay's. After returning to Chopwell in August 1912, much of Lawther's rhetoric remained in tune with *The Miners' Next Step*. For example, there was Lawther's revolutionary critique of nationalisation and advocacy of workers' control. Speaking in October 1912, Lawther 'found that nationalisation of the mines, state ownership, was nothing more or less than state capitalism ...'.[31]

Indeed, the inspiration of *The Miners' Next Step*, and particularly its emphasis on aggressive class conflict, the need for workers' direct action and self-empowerment and the rejection of leaders and bureaucracies, remained evident in Lawther's rhetoric throughout the pre-war period. For example, in October 1913, Lawther wrote in a letter to the local press, that activists of the 'New [revolutionary] Movement [...] will not wait for the "lead" to come from a chosen few, for they will be conscious of their own desires and destination and their mandate will therefore be supreme'.[32] Yet these were all features of *The Miners' Next Step* that readily lent themselves to an anarchist interpretation.

One indication that Lawther's politics were shifting came in his flirtation with dual-unionism. Thus, in October 1912 Lawther based part of his speech at a conference he had helped organise in Chopwell on the IWW's preamble, saying that 'they were out for the whole of the workers to be in one organisation'.[33] Yet Lawther's position on dual-unionism is difficult to discern, not least because he was not particularly vocal on this essential issue. Indeed, Lawther later appeared to have a foot in both anarchist camps, contributing to the dual-unionist *Herald of Revolt* and becoming a leading supporter of the *Voice of Labour*, which rejected dual-unionism.[34]

There was no mystery where Lawther stood on another fundamental issue though, as he became increasingly vocal on his rejection of political action. At a public debate in Chopwell Miners' Hall in September 1913, for example,

Lawther argued in support of the motion 'That the emancipation of the working class can be brought about more readily by direct action than by legislation.'[35] He followed this up with a lengthy letter in the local press titled 'Direct Action or Legislation. Which?'[36] This increasingly overt anti-political attitude suggested Lawther's syndicalism was moving in an anarchist direction, and, when he began to contribute to the *Herald of Revolt*, he was in good company. Lawther then began using the term 'anarchist' explicitly to describe his politics (as he did when writing about this period of his life as a retired miners' leader in 1955), though it was clear that he continued to see revolutionary trade unionism as the vehicle for 'direct action'.[37]

What caused Lawther's more Marxist-influenced syndicalism to develop into a self-proclaimed anarchism? In terms of his studies at Central Labour College, Morris' interpretation of Marx must have been pivotal, and seemed particularly evident in Lawther's anti-parliamentary rhetoric.[38] Lawther later said that Morris 'made an appeal for life against the machine horrors'.[39] While in London Lawther also met the anarchist engineer Jack Tanner and they later collaborated on several anarchist projects, including the *Voice of Labour*.[40] Probably the most influential individual was George Davison, who Lawther first met at the 1911 TUC conference in Newcastle (before he went to Central Labour College). A follower of Kropotkin, Davison was an 'eccentric and courageous millionaire ... who held very advanced views on politics and theology.'[41] From a humble background, Davison rose to become a civil servant. He was also a pioneer of photography and a Kodak shareholder. By 1900, Davison was Kodak's managing director, though his political activities (and alleged lack of business acumen) forced his resignation from the company's board in 1912.[42] By this time, Davison's desire to support progressive causes was manifest in his funding of the nascent Central Labour College in 1910. As financial backer of W. F. Hay's speaking tour of the Durham coalfield in 1912, his path crossed with Lawther's once more.[43] Davison's wealth was to impact in at least one corner of the Durham coalfield before 1914.

While Harvey and Lawther shared very similar backgrounds both socio-economically and politically, the precise timing of the periods they spent in full-time working-class educational institutions helps to explain their adoption of significantly different forms of revolutionary syndicalism, Harvey's more Marxist and Lawther's increasingly anarchist. Scrutiny of their activities shows that they also developed their political activism in different ways.

## Activities

Harvey and Lawther's conversions to syndicalism demanded that they propagandise. That they did so to some extent in different ways was more a reflection of their relative strengths as political activists and their access to different resources rather than a result of differing Marxist and anarchist approaches within syndicalism. Harvey, a diminutive and unimpressive presence on the public platform whose head would wobble from side-to-side as he spoke, nurtured a talent for writing reports in *The Socialist* and information-rich propaganda pamphlets.[44] His first, titled 'Industrial Unionism and the Mining Industry', appeared in August 1911.

In June 1912, Harvey produced a second pamphlet, 'Does Dr. John Wilson MP, secretary of the Durham Miners' Association, Serve the Working Class?' This was an enraged response to a 'joke' Wilson cracked at the retirement ceremony of Charles Fenwick (Liberal MP for Wansbeck and a miners' leader). Lord Joicey, a mine owner, gifted Fenwick £260 and, at the presentation ceremony, Wilson remarked that he would like a similar 'bribe' on his retirement. Harvey wrote that Wilson's 'aim has always been to bolster up capitalism, and he, more than any other leader perhaps, has swayed the miners to take that particular action which is either harmless or beneficial to the capitalist class...If £260 is the price, then miners' leaders are cheap and worth getting at.'[45] Wilson demanded that Harvey withdraw the accusation. Harvey refused. The libel case went to court in November 1912 where Harvey maintained that Wilson was an enemy of the working-class and servant of capitalism, citing Wilson's agreement to a 5 per cent reduction in miners' wages (which even an arbitrator had deemed unwarranted) in evidence. The judge, however, found in favour of Wilson, and awarded £200 damages and £100 costs.

By contrast, Lawther was less of a theorist than Harvey. He did not write detailed propaganda pamphlets.[46] Yet he was active from the point of his return from Central Labour College. Lawther soon established a 'Workers' Freedom Group' based on similar groups in the south Wales coalfield, which engaged in energetic and varied propagandising.[47] Lawther reported in July 1913, for example, that: 'by selling FREEDOMS [the London-based anarchist newspaper] and pamphlets and by discussion circles, the kind of propaganda that matters is being kept up...'.[48] Lawther also performed a pivotal role in organising a conference to discuss syndicalism in October 1912, which attracted representatives from seven Durham lodges to Chopwell.

Furthermore, Lawther contributed to public debates, corresponded with the local press and involved himself in community struggles. In spring 1913, there was intense agitation throughout the coalfield against a 50 per cent increase in the doctors' fee for miners, a result of recent National Insurance legislation. Lawther was central to the campaign in Chopwell for a return to pre-Act fees.[49] Retaining his commitment to working-class education, Lawther also ran Plebs' League classes three times a week in Consett and South Shields as well as Chopwell.[50] He clearly regarded this form of education as essential propaganda work; Lawther later commented 'that the Labour College was of the utmost influence...'.[51]

Political ambition was evident in this frenetic work. Lawther and the Chopwell anarchists' aims extended well beyond creating a stronghold in their own pit village. In July 1913, the Chopwell group wanted 'the message of direct action to be carried right throughout the coalfield and no help is refused'.[52] Thus, the previous month, Lawther had spoken at the 'new ground' of Crawcrook (another Durham pit village), while in July he spoke at the miners' annual gala on the 'need for direct action and revolution'.[53] The DMA annual gala, or 'Big Meeting', was a day out for all Durham miners and their families, and tens of thousands thronged to Durham racecourse to hear speeches from local and national leaders. It was an obvious place to take propaganda efforts. Lawther was also concerned that anarchists should organise effectively together in the region and nationally. In April 1914, for example, he took a delegation and spoke at an anarchist conference in Newcastle. The conference concerned itself with national organisational issues such as supporting a new anarchist newspaper and international topics such as the (recently state-executed) Spanish freethinker Francisco Ferrer's 'modern schools', as well as organising an international anarchist conference in London in September 1914.[54] Lawther spoke at a modern school in east London in summer 1913.[55] To maintain the lines of communication, Lawther supplied regular reports to the national anarchist paper *Freedom* as well as contributing to other anarchist and syndicalist publications. In summary: both Harvey and Lawther were committed activists. Harvey's strength was theoretical and embodied in his written propaganda, while Lawther excelled as a speaker. These strengths, which reflected their personal abilities and inclinations, fuelled the syndicalist movement of the Durham coalfield. But what was the impact of their efforts?

## Specific and immediate impacts

Clearly, Harvey and Lawther's specific activity had some degree of immediate impact. That Harvey, Lawther and their groupings were also (in Lawther's words) 'fellow slave[s] of the lamp and pick' must have encouraged a sympathetic reception at a time of intense industrial and socio-political flux in the Durham coalfield.[56] Harvey's pamphlets were particularly important. 'Industrial Unionism and the Mining Industry' sold 2,000 copies, and Harvey received invitations to speak all over the Durham coalfield about it in summer 1911. An audience of 3,000 saw Harvey speak at a Chester-le-Street meeting on 'Industrial unionism and fakirdom in the DMA.'[57] Similarly, the libel case surrounding Harvey's June 1912 pamphlet attacking John Wilson received extensive press coverage. The verbatim reports read like a trial of the old methods by the new revolutionary ideas; this trial encapsulated the revolutionary challenge to the old DMA leadership. Certainly, the press coverage enhanced Harvey's reputation and raised the profile of his politics. Indeed, Harvey's very public championing of the Durham miner in 1912 must have played an important part in his securing a checkweighman post only a year later, at Wardley pit near Gateshead (see below).

The 1912 trial also gave Harvey's political project a welcome boost. A matter of days after the court-case, Harvey launched the 'Durham Mining Industrial Union Group', what the *Durham Chronicle* deemed somewhat wearily 'still another organisation anxious to reform the Durham Miners' Association'.[58] The group formed after a meeting of 'about twenty representatives' at Chester-le-Street, and decided to issue lodges with a copy of its industrial unionist manifesto.[59] This built on Harvey's own local grouping, 'Chester-le-Street and District Industrial Union'. Harvey certainly maintained a strong local support base wherever he worked in the Durham coalfield throughout his life. One example of the longer-term influence he exercised came in the form of Tom Aisbitt, one of his Chester-le-Street industrial unionist converts. The same age as Harvey, Aisbitt had also been a member of Chester-le-Street ILP (he was its secretary) as well as helping to found Chester-le-Street trades council.[60] Aisbitt later secured an influential post in the Newcastle trades council with which he influenced regional labour politics in the interwar period.[61]

While Lawther did not introduce anarchism to the region, he certainly brought its syndicalist version into the Durham coalfield in a concerted and energetic way. Naturally, it was in Lawther's home pit village of Chopwell that his direct influence was most obvious, and in the form of bricks and mortar. Lawther's wealthy anarchist contact George Davison agreed to sponsor a 'Communist Club' in Chopwell. One of only three in the country, it opened in December 1913. The police were certainly impressed with the club's members, who were apparently 'mostly young men and are above the average miner in intelligence'.[62] Only four months after its opening, there was an anarchist conference in Newcastle. *Freedom* reported that 'the Chopwell boys came in their dozens, each an embryo fighter, from whom more will be heard anon, we hope'.[63] Many of these must have been Lawther's converts, directly or indirectly.

However, not all Chopwell radicals were convinced by this new gospel. Certainly, the response to the war effort from Chopwell – 500 went to fight, including two of Lawther's own brothers – suggested that the village's revolutionary nucleus had had a distinctly limited impact. Only a small hardcore, that included Lawther and two other brothers, took a militant stand against the war and became conscientious objectors.[64] This response to Harvey and Lawther's propagandising efforts suggests a rather circumscribed degree of influence of syndicalist ideas in the Durham coalfield. A possible explanation is that the activists concerned lacked conviction, their propaganda deficient in substance. Since this charge has been levelled at Lawther, in particular, it bares considering, before turning to an alternative understanding.

## The syndicalists' wider influence?

In assessing syndicalist influence in Durham, commentators have tended to focus on Harvey and Lawther (and to a lesser extent their groupings), though their conclusions have been quite different. Roy Church and Quentin Outram, for example, claimed that syndicalist influence was negligible in County Durham, basing this on an interpretation of Lawther's role and politics.[65] Specifically, they endorsed John Saville's view that in his early years Lawther 'described himself as a Marxist, syndicalist, anarchist and member of the ILP' (which echoed Robin Smith, a prospective biographer of Lawther, in the North-east Labour History Society journal).[66]

In one respect Saville was right, for, as we have seen, syndicalism was attractive for some self-defined Marxists as well as anarchists. But syndicalism's emphasis on direct action and eschewal of parliamentary or 'political' action easily lent itself to anarchist interpretations within what was a fairly broad church. Neither the theories nor (most of) the organisations formed to advocate them were exclusive, ideologically pure and self-contained in this time of flux.[67] Indeed, Robin Smith employed his (the original) claim about Lawther's politics to illustrate this very point, though Smith was referring to the whole period before 1926 (when Lawther was aged between 15 and 36). This *was* unhelpful, as the period before 1926 saw considerable change in Lawther's politics, which reflected developing events on the international scene. The 1917 Bolshevik Revolution had had a tremendous impact on the revolutionary Left in Britain, resulting in the formation of a British Communist Party from sections of the SLP, shop stewards' movement activists, left-wing ILP members and others in 1920. Lawther was thus a communist-supporting Labour Party activist by the early 1920s. Furthermore, the birth of the British Communist Party heralded a slow drift towards more exclusivity and sectarianism among the Left.

Nevertheless, the implication of Smith's claim and the accounts of those who endorsed it was that Lawther was something of a dilettante, a political butterfly, flitting between parties and political programmes at whim, or that he was confused about his true political home. That Lawther ended his career as a right-wing national miners' leader after 1945 has also thrown doubt over his early revolutionism. In reality, there were distinct and logical phases in the development of Lawther's politics between 1905 and the early 1920s. There is no reason to question the sincerity of his conversion to syndicalism from activism in the ILP in 1912 and his subsequent move to anarchist syndicalism before August 1914. The very intensity of his activity is sufficient evidence of the extent to which his political conversion was felt. The shorter pieces Lawther published in the local press in the war period reveal an individual capable of grasping and expressing applied theory including that of Marx. Certainly, it is rather facile to claim that, because Lawther ended up on the political Right, that this was where he was always destined to go. If the authenticity of Lawther's politics is the yardstick for measuring syndicalism in the Durham coalfield then it *was* a significant force.

Unlike Smith, Bob Holton took Lawther and Harvey's politics very seriously. Indeed, his study of the two informed his judgement that the Durham coalfield provided the second most important ground for syndicalism after south Wales.[68] Unfortunately, Holton's wider discussion of the Durham coalfield was insubstantial, and suggested a relationship between syndicalism and militancy that was difficult to sustain. He noted the particularly strong unrest in the coalfield over the return to work after the 1912 national strike, but later acknowledged that the major coalfield to vote *for* a return to work in 1912 was south Wales (where syndicalism was strongest). While Holton explained this vote by the peculiar conditions in south Wales including a lack of resources after the Cambrian Combine dispute that engendered strike weariness, there was clearly no simple correlation between industrial militancy and syndicalist influence.[69] While there remains considerable research to do in this area, Holton's work makes clear that, thanks to Harvey, Lawther and their groupings, syndicalism *did* have an impact in the Durham coalfield, but that it was not as far reaching as that in south Wales. In Durham, the ILP had been remarkably effective in channelling miners' grievances through the Durham Forward Movement. But by the same token, the Forward Movement's success testified to the continued existence of considerable grievances among Durham miners. Syndicalists, too, could have spoken to this rank-and-file discontent. How, then, did Harvey and Lawther apply their politics and how might this have blunted their potential impact in the Durham coalfield?

## Dogma, pragmatism and sectarianism

Two intertwining aspects of the Durham syndicalists' own politics – their puritanism (or, more negatively put, their dogmatism) and their sectarianism – militated against their influence. First, some aspects of their politics inhibited their ability to propagate their message, thereby helping to isolate them from the wider movement. Second, the revolutionary alternative Harvey and Lawther offered in the Durham coalfield was, and remained, to some extent divided both theoretically and organisationally (as elsewhere in Britain).

In terms of dogmatism, Lawther's politics suffered the most. His anarchism demanded a rejection of any form of constitutional office and he did not stand for any lodge, DMA or party position (until 1915). This was significant as Lawther had been a Chopwell lodge official in one of the largest and most militant pits in county Durham before going to Labour College. Being a lodge official earlier in his life had brought Lawther into contact with influential Durham miners throughout the coalfield, as well as with significant national and international figures within the movement.[70] Lawther's principled decision not to stand for any constitutional office was undoubtedly laudable. It further testified to Lawther's complete commitment to his politics at this time. But it denied Lawther access to important means of exercising local and regional influence. By contrast, two significant south Wales syndicalists, Noahs Ablett and Rees, were elected to the SWMF Executive Committee in 1911, thereby demonstrating their prominence in the coalfield and enhancing their authority.

George Harvey did not have these particular qualms. Indeed, the (in some respects) more pragmatic Harvey had been instrumental in altering the SLP's proscription on members standing for trade union office. Harvey pointed out that in Durham any prospective party member would have to relinquish trade union office to join the party. Naturally, they refused to do this, and yet the lodges in which these individuals were officials were also those that bought the most SLP propaganda.[71] The newly unshackled Harvey then won a checkweighman post in 1913. This development was of considerable significance, as this prestigious position demanded a high degree of trust from the pit's miners. In his application letter, Harvey clearly stated he was 'a Revolutionary Socialist and a strong believer in Industrial Unionism'.[72] Harvey's election both reflected his already established reputation as well as entrenching and widening his influence.

The growing interest in syndicalism between 1910 and 1914 seemed to allow for a blurring of the barriers between Marxism and anarchism, at least at the level of theory. The relative ease with which individuals could move between the two traditions, exemplified by the (rapid) development of Lawther's politics, reflected the wider socio-economic flux of the times. This blurring of the boundaries between Marxism and anarchism was also evident, for example, in the explanation Lawther gave (during the time of the cold war) for the naming of the Edwardian 'communist clubs' such as that in Chopwell. They were 'supposed to be the rallying grounds for those interested in communism and anarchism, a communism, by the way, which bore little resemblance to the Russian brand today [1955]'.[73] Marx and Marxists had clearly influenced Lawther, though he soon branded himself an anarchist, and in a similar way the Chopwell 'Communist Club' (which was also known in this period as the 'Anarchist Club'), was a forum for the discussion of various revolutionary ideas that were in many respects difficult to disentangle.

Ray Challinor wrote of the SLP's diminishing sectarianism in this period too.[74] However, sectarian divisions remained between the syndicalists in the Durham coalfield. Harvey was the main offender. This was evident at the Chopwell syndicalist conference in October 1912, where Harvey and Lawther vied to convince the audience of their case. Lawther glossed over the differences in politics between himself and Harvey, concluding his speech, 'they were out for the whole of the workers to be in one organisation. They could call that Industrialism, Unionism [sic. presumably a press mistake for 'industrial unionism'] or syndicalism, or what they liked…'[75] Harvey, speaking after Lawther, suggested his audience should propagandise for a Durham mining industrial union. There was certainly overlap: Harvey's call for education and organisation, his claim that 'Leaders and politicians could do nothing' and that the 'hope of the working-class lay in the working-class themselves' all echoed Lawther. Harvey's description of industrial unionism – working on the principle 'that an injury to one is an injury to all' (an IWW slogan) – also resonated with Lawther's speech.[76]

However, Harvey then underlined where he and Lawther differed in explicit terms:

> they ought not to go in for syndicalism, because if it were a halfway house they had to recognise sooner or later that they must go to the higher pinnacle of organisation. He contended that the scientific weapon was industrial unionism. They were out for industrial and political action. The two must go hand in hand.[77]

This political action included fighting all elections, not for votes as such but on a 'revolutionary issue' to 'create a fever heat of industrial revolution and they could only do that by industrial and political propaganda'.[78] Indeed, the extent to which Harvey argued in favour of political action caused problems in his own party. His claim in *The Socialist* (March 1912) that SLP candidates would be the best parliamentarians as only revolutionaries could win reforms, sparked extensive internal criticism. It provoked the secession of most of the party's members in Lancashire, claiming that the SLP had become reformist.[79]

More unfortunately, Harvey, like many SLP activists, replicated aspects of De Leon's language, denouncing other revolutionary groupings as 'fakirs'. Harvey was similarly a 'virulent critic' of Tom Mann's syndicalism.[80] In response to Mann's imprisonment for publishing the famous 'Don't shoot' article appealing for soldiers not to fire on strikers, Harvey wrote in *The Socialist* (of April 1912) that his Party were not syndicalists and 'have no sympathy with syndicalism'. That said there were limits to Harvey's sectarianism. On this occasion, the SLP reprinted Mann's banned article because they were 'fighters for freedom and the free press'.[81] It was perhaps then rather unfortunate that sectarianism was apparently the most noteworthy aspect of Harvey's politics for authors such as Robin Page Arnot.[82]

In County Durham, Lawther seemed prepared to accept Harvey's attempts to mark a clear ideological divide between them; and Harvey's support for 'political action' remained anathema to Lawther's anarchism. Nevertheless, Lawther continued to promote solidarity with Harvey. In February 1913, Lawther made an impassioned appeal for Harvey in the aftermath of the Wilson case:

> It is up to us, as miners, to show to George Harvey, by word or deed, that we believe that what he said [about Wilson] was true... And I believe that, during the forthcoming summer, the gospel of revolt, of direct action, of anti-leadership will spread, not because Harvey or any other person

believes in it, but because of the oppression and tyranny that is taking place in the mines . . . [83]

In July 1913, the two men, among others, shared a platform at the Durham miners' annual gala.[84] Notwithstanding a willingness to share public platforms, Lawther and Harvey offered two distinct brands of syndicalism in the Durham coalfield. Their differing visions of revolutionary politics and the theoretical terms they used to express them to an interested, but not necessarily informed miner audience (for example, at the Chopwell conference of October 1912), must have confused more than just the local press.

Lawther revealed another kind of sectarianism, however, and, while it underscored his revolutionary credentials, it hampered his ability to operate effectively, denying him access to the platforms of potentially influential and sympathetic organisations and individuals in the DMA. One of the first to address the syndicalist conference in Chopwell in October 1912, Lawther opened his speech by explaining why they 'were out for the new movement. They were out against the "forward movement"'.[85] Lawther was clearly keen to distinguish himself and his followers from the Forward Movement's project – indeed, defining them as opponents – from the outset. He did so by first attacking nationalisation, the aim of key Forward Movement activists, and thus effectively marked the gap between the apparent reformists of the Forward Movement and the revolutionaries. That the Forward Movement leaders were intent on making reputations and careers for themselves on the back of the miners' discontent was a fairly common theme in Lawther's rhetoric[86] (and, ironically, a charge that was later made, unjustly, against Lawther himself).

Again, Harvey displayed a little less principled idealism and a little more pragmatism in relations with the wider rank-and-file movement. At his libel trial in November 1912, Harvey asked Wilson if he was aware that he had been heavily criticised by the Forward Movement. Harvey quoted part of a speech by John Jeffries, a Forward Movement leader, claiming that Wilson's evident talents were 'from time to time not used for the purpose they ought to be' and, explicitly, that Jeffries was referring to the conciliation doctrine that Wilson 'continually dinned into their ears'. Harvey's defence here was significant, as he was taking the logic of Forward Movement rhetoric a step further, clearly aligning himself with it as he did so. Indeed, Harvey claimed (slightly disingenuously) that he 'had said no more than what had been said by other bodies during the last decade – by the socialists or the "Forward Movement" – and the action had only been taken against him because he was a working miner'.[87] The extent to which Harvey's more conciliatory approach to the larger rank-and-file movement in Durham benefited him in terms of his ability to propagate his politics is difficult to measure. But it certainly seems to have secured him a prominent position on the platform of at least one Durham Forward Movement mass meeting. In April 1912, Harvey seconded a motion of censure of the DMA agents, with a speech complaining that the men had been 'sold-out' by their leaders. Harvey argued that the leaders should receive the same wage as the miners; then perhaps the leaders would fight for their demands, as 'every time the men got a rise they would also be better off'.[88] Lawther, unsurprisingly, never appeared on a Durham Forward Movement platform as such – although he did speak at a meeting on the miners' minimum wage in Newcastle in December 1913, this was not apparently under their auspices.[89] That said, Lawther's attitude did not prevent co-operation in Chopwell with Forward Movement activists. For example, Lawther sat on the local negotiating committee in the doctor's fee agitation in early 1913 with Vipond Hardy, who Lawther had failed to convince of syndicalism and who was, instead, active in the maligned Durham Forward Movement.[90]

## Conclusion: an opportunity missed?

Revolutionary activists are often confronted with a dilemma when faced with favourable circumstances in which to propagate their politics. To what extent should they soft-pedal or compromise on fundamentals in order to be able to access platforms and provide a message that has the potential to chime with large numbers of individuals in some form of struggle? If they compromise too much they are open to the jibe of being opportunistic, while too little compromise means they could be denounced as zealots: inflexible, too dogmatic.

In the period of industrial strife 1910–1914, Lawther, certainly, adopted a purity of praxis that denied him access to certain platforms and alienated him from some potential allies. Harvey, on the other hand, seemed too sectarian, fixated on the finer points of the policy of his infinitesimal party. This is not to argue that Lawther, in particular, should have abandoned the principled political positions he held. However, it is to recognise that maintaining such ideological positions had clear consequences and that in certain circumstances what was sacrificed for the sake of principle was potentially considerable.

Arguably, Lawther's anarchist syndicalism was more theoretically coherent and defensible than the looser syndicalism of the south Wales 'Unofficial Reform Committee'. Yet, even when better co-ordinated in 1914, anarchism remained a minority strand within the minority revolutionary syndicalist section of the mass labour movement. Harvey's SLP, though more tightly organised for a longer period, also remained a minority tendency within syndicalism. Furthermore, in its efforts to break out of this ghetto (often prompted by Harvey himself), the SLP often lost as much as it gained. By the outbreak of war, like the other Left parties, both revolutionary and reformist alike, the SLP was losing members.[91] Clearly, conditions were not as favourable for syndicalism in the Durham coalfield as they were in south

Wales. Still, in their interpretation and application in syndicalism, both Marxism and anarchism fell short in the pre-1914 upheaval in the Durham coalfield.

## Acknowledgements

Thanks are due to Trevor Bark, Emmet O'Connor, Kevin Davies, Nick Heath, Ken John, Don Watson, Chris Williams, John Patten, and to Dave Douglass, Peter Mates and the anonymous reviewers for their comments on earlier drafts. I would like to dedicate this chapter to the late, great Dr Ray Challinor.

## Notes

1. Marcel van der Linden, 'Second Thoughts on Revolutionary Syndicalism', *Labour History Review*, 63/2 (1998), 182.
2. Lucien van der Walt and Michael Schmidt consequently include De Leonism as part of the broad anarchist tradition, notwithstanding De Leon's self-identification as a Marxist. This is problematic not least because De Leon consistently defined his position against the 'anarchists' and with good reason. The issue of political action was crucial. Regardless of the weight that De Leon attached to political action, attitudes to its utility were significant in his and his followers' rejection of the rest of the syndicalist milieu and especially of the anarchists. See *Black Flame: The Revolutionary Class Politics of Anarchism and Syndicalism (Counter-Power)* (Edinburgh: AK Press, 2009), pp. 16–17, 161–162.
3. See D. Smith, 'Tonypandy 1910: Definitions of Community', *Past and Present*, 87 (1980), 158–184.
4. David Egan, 'The Miners' Next Step', *Labour History Review*, 38 (1979), 10; D.K. Davies, *The Influence of Syndicalism, and Industrial Unionism in the South Wales Coalfield 1898–1921: A Study in Ideology, and Practice* (Ph.D. thesis, University of Wales, 1991).
5. C. Marshall, *Levels of Industrial Militancy and the Political Radicalisation of the Durham Miners, 1885–1914* (M.A. thesis, Durham University, 1976), pp. 92–95, 99–100, 310–311.
6. See Melvyn Dubofsky and Joseph McCartin, *We Shall Be All: A History of the Industrial Workers of the World* (Chicago: Quadrangle, 1969).
7. Ray Challinor, *The Origins of British Bolshevism* (London: Croom Helm, 1977).
8. See John Atkins, *Neither Crumbs nor Condescension: The Central Labour College, 1909–1915* (Aberdeen: Aberdeen People's Press, 1981).
9. Bob Holton, *British Syndicalism 1900–1914. Myths and Realities* (London: Pluto, 1976), p. 38.
10. Holton, *British Syndicalism*, pp. 114–116; Challinor, *British Bolshevism*, pp. 95–96.
11. Egan, 'The Miners' Next Step', p. 11.
12. *The Miners' Next Step* (1912) Reprinted with introduction by Dave Douglass (Doncaster: Germinal and Phoenix Press, 1991), p. 30.
13. Ibid., p. 31.
14. Ibid., pp. 16–17, 21; Holton, *British Syndicalism*, p. 87.
15. G. Walker, *George Harvey: The Conflict Between the Ideology of Industrial Unionism and the Practice of Its Principles in the Durham Coalfield* (M.A. thesis, Ruskin College, 1982), pp. 36–39.

16. *The Miners' Next Step*, p. 13.
17. John Caldwell, *Guy A. Aldred (1886–1963)* (Glasgow: The Strickland Press, 1966).
18. This chapter employs the term 'anarchist syndicalist' where specificity is necessary. Albert Meltzer, *The Anarchists in London 1935–1955* (Sanday: Cienfuegos Press, 1976), p. 9; David Berry, *A History of the French Anarchist Movement, 1917–1945* (London: Greenwood Press, 2002), pp. 134–135.
19. G. Pattison 'Anarchist Influence in the Durham Coalfield Before 1914', *The Raven*, 11 (1990), 239; John Quail, *The Slow Burning Fuse: The Lost History of British Anarchists* (London: Paladin, 1978), pp. 250–254.
20. Holton, *British Syndicalism*, p. 142.
21. Challinor, *British Bolshevism*, p. 116.
22. *The Industrial Syndicalist*, 1(9), March 1911 in Geoff Brown, *The Industrial Syndicalist* (Nottingham: Spokesman Books, 1974), pp. 314–315; Ray Challinor, 'Jack Parks, Memories of a Militant', *Bulletin of the North-east Group for the Study of Labour History*, 9 (1975), 34–38; Dave Douglass 'The Durham Pitman', in Raphael Samuel (ed.), *Miners, Quarrymen and Salt Workers* (London: Routledge & Kegan Paul, 1977), pp. 286–287.
23. *Newcastle Journal*, 8, 10, 11, 15 March 1955; R. Smith 'Obituary Article: Sir William Lawther', *Bulletin of the North-east Group for the Study of Labour History*, 10 (1976), 27–28; J.F. Clarke, 'An Interview with Sir Will Lawther', *Bulletin of the Society for the Study of Labour History*, 18 (1969), 20.
24. *Newcastle Journal*, 15 March 1955.
25. Ibid., 11 March 1955; 15 March 1955; Lawther's Notebooks of Economics and Sociology Lectures, October 1911–July 1912 (both in possession of the late Jack Lawther); Smith, 'Obituary Article', 28–29, 33; Clarke, 'Lawther Interview', 14, 19.
26. Smith, 'Obituary Article', 33.
27. Holton, *British Syndicalism*, p. 169.
28. Smith, 'Obituary Article', p. 29.
29. *Newcastle Journal*, 17 March 1955.
30. *Durham Chronicle*, 31 May 1912; *Blaydon Courier*, 1 June 1912.
31. *Blaydon Courier*, 19 October 1912.
32. Ibid., 18 October 1913.
33. Ibid., 19 October 1912.
34. Holton, *British Syndicalism*, pp. 142–143.
35. *Freedom*, September 1913; *Blaydon Courier*, 20 September 1913.
36. *Blaydon Courier*, 18 October 1913.
37. See for example the *Newcastle Chronicle*, 13 April 1914.
38. Ibid.
39. Smith, 'Obituary Article', 28.
40. Holton, *British Syndicalism*, pp. 142–143.
41. *Newcastle Journal*, 16 March 1955.
42. Colin Harding, 'George Davison', in John Hannavy (ed.) *Encyclopedia of Nineteenth-century Photography* (London: Routledge, 2008), pp. 387–288.
43. Quail, *Slow Burning Fuse*, p. 254; Atkins, *Crumbs nor Condescension*, p. 63.
44. Challinor, *British Bolshevism*, p. 117.
45. *Evening Chronicle*, 7 November 1912.
46. Lawther did, however, contribute fairly short theoretical pieces to the local press from 1916. See Lewis H. Mates, *From Revolutionary to Reactionary: the Life of Will Lawther* (M.A. Thesis, Newcastle University, 1996), pp. 11–16.
47. Quail, *Slow Burning Fuse*, pp. 278–279.

48. *Freedom,* July 1913.
49. *Blaydon Courier,* 25 January 1913.
50. Smith, 'Obituary Article', 33.
51. Holton, *British Syndicalism,* p. 169.
52. *Freedom,* July 1913.
53. Ibid., September 1913.
54. Ibid. May 1914; *Evening Chronicle,* 13 April 1914.
55. Paul Avrich, *The Modern School Movement: Anarchism and Education in the United States* (Edinburgh: AK Press, 2006), p. 263.
56. *The Herald of Revolt,* February 1913.
57. G. Walker 'George Harvey and Industrial Unionism', *Bulletin of the North-east Group for the Study of Labour History,* 17 (1983), 21.
58. *Durham Chronicle,* 15 November 1912.
59. *Evening Chronicle,* 7 November 1912.
60. Labour History Archive and Study Centre, Manchester, CP/CENT/PERS/1/01, Tom Aisbitt biography by Horace Green.
61. Lewis H. Mates, *The Spanish Civil War and the British Left: Political Activism and the Popular Front* (London: I.B. Tauris, 2007).
62. Tyne and Wear Archive Service T148/1 Copy letter, 27 December 1913, p. 71. My thanks to Kevin Davies for drawing my attention to these files.
63. *Freedom,* May 1914.
64. L. Turnbull, *Chopwell's Story* (Gateshead: Gateshead Borough Council, 1978), (no page numbers).
65. Roy A. Church and Quentin Outram, *Strikes and Solidarity: Coalfield Conflict in Britain, 1889–1966* (Cambridge: Cambridge University Press, 2002), pp. 62, 68.
66. John Saville, 'Will Lawther', in J. Bellamy and J. Saville, *Dictionary of Labour Biography. Vol. VII* (London: Macmillan, 1984), 141; Smith 'Obituary Article', 29.
67. White 'Syndicalism', 110.
68. Holton, *British Syndicalism,* p. 169.
69. Ibid., pp. 117–119.
70. *Newcastle Journal,* 11 March 1955.
71. Challinor, *British Bolshevism,* pp. 116–118.
72. Walker, 'Harvey thesis', p. 40.
73. *Newcastle Journal,* 16 March 1955.
74. Challinor, *British Bolshevism,* p. 117.
75. *Blaydon Courier,* 19 October 1912.
76. Ibid.; Dubofsky and McCartin, *We Shall Be All,* p. 118.
77. *Blaydon Courier,* 19 October 1912.
78. Ibid.
79. Challinor, *British Bolshevism,* pp. 120–121.
80. Brown, Introduction, *Industrial Syndicalist,* p. 19.
81. Challinor, *British Bolshevism,* p. 85.
82. R. Page Arnot, *South Wales Miners to 1914* (London: George Allen and Unwin, 1967), p. 376.
83. *The Herald of Revolt,* February 1913.
84. *Freedom,* September 1913.
85. *Blaydon Courier,* 19 October 1912.
86. See, for example, *The Herald of Revolt,* February 1913.

87. *Evening Chronicle,* 7 November 1912.
88. *Durham Chronicle,* 12 April 1912.
89. Ibid., 5 December 1913.
90. *Blaydon Courier*, 19 October 1912; 25 January 1913.
91. Challinor, *British Bolshevism*, pp. 118–121.

# 5

# Georges Sorel's Anarcho-Marxism

*Renzo Llorente*

> *When one considers the tragic history of the international working-class movement since 1914, one is inclined to regard the doctrine of revolutionary syndicalism advocated... by the 'new school' of Georges Sorel, Edouard Berth, and Arturo Labriola as one of the most interesting and promising forms in which Marxian thought has experienced a renaissance.*
>
> Maximilien Rubel[1]

## Introduction: Sorel's uncertain legacy

Georges Sorel (1847–1922) was an important figure in the development of radical left-wing theory during the early decades of the twentieth century, and his ideas strongly influenced the work of some major Marxist thinkers, including Antonio Gramsci,[2] Georg Lukács,[3] José Carlos Mariátegui[4] and Antonio Labriola.[5] Today, however, the Left shows very little interest in Sorel's writings. This lack of interest is regrettable, for Sorel's works address many of the central themes in emancipatory social theory: the permissible use of violence in political struggles; the possibilities and limits of parliamentarism; the role of intellectuals in revolutionary movements; the advantages and disadvantages of various revolutionary strategies and organisational structures; the contrast between reform and revolution; the relationship between left-wing political parties and those whose interests they claim to represent; the transformation of the bourgeois state; and the moral aims of socialism.

At the same time, the contemporary tendency to ignore Sorel is perhaps not so surprising after all, considering the great divergence of opinion regarding the value of Sorel's contribution to political thought. On the one hand, there are the views of scholars and thinkers such as Eugene Kamenka, John Gray and José Carlos Mariátegui. Kamenka, a philosopher and Marx scholar, ranks Sorel among the 'most perceptive exponents' of socialism,[6] while Gray endorses Croce's description of Sorel as 'the most original and important Marxist theorist after Marx himself'.[7] For his part, Mariátegui, Latin America's greatest Marxist writer, considers Sorel 'Marx's most vigorous follower [*continuador*] in... [a] period of social-democratic parliamentarism.'[8] On the other hand, George Lichtheim, a historian of Marxism, calls Sorel an 'irresponsible chatterbox' and a 'romantic littérateur',[9] and Lenin himself dismisses Sorel as a 'notorious muddler'.[10]

These highly divergent judgements regarding Sorel have arisen not only in connection with the calibre and value of his writings; there is also considerable disagreement when it comes to the basic political orientation of his texts: Does Sorel belong to the Left or to the Right? If his place is with the theorists of the left, should we include him among the Marxists or among the anarchists? With respect to the first question, I think it is clear, in light of Sorel's most significant political writings, that we ought to situate him on the Left, and for our present purposes I will simply assume that those who depict Sorel as a right-wing thinker are fundamentally mistaken.[11] How, then, to respond to the second question? Which label best describes Sorel – 'Marxist' or 'anarchist'?

To be sure, in *Reflections on Violence*, his most important work as a political theorist (first published in 1908), Sorel unequivocally identifies his enterprise with Marxism, and most works in political philosophy tend to classify Sorel as a Marxist of sorts.[12] Yet it is also true that Sorel has, as Jeremy Jennings puts it, 'traditionally been regarded as one of the most controversial figures in the history of Marxism'.[13] While there are many factors that account for Sorel's controversial status in the history of Marxism, one reason is undoubtedly his debt to Pierre-Joseph Proudhon, whose works had a profound and lasting influence on Sorel's thought. In fact, as Sorel scholar John Stanley points out, 'it is Proudhon who is cited most frequently in his [Sorel's] early writings', and Stanley goes on to claim that 'the thinker who is closest to Sorel is... Pierre-Joseph Proudhon'.[14] It is partly owing to this affinity that some commentators, such as Lichtheim, tend to consider Sorel a 'Proudhonist',[15] while others view him as an outright anarchist. Indeed, Irving Louis Horowitz not only includes a selection from *Reflections on Violence* in his 1964 anthology of anarchist texts, but actually refers to Sorel, along with Bakunin, Malatesta and Kropotkin, as one of 'the classical anarchists',[16] and James Joll's well-known study of anarchism also devotes several pages to Sorel's thought.[17]

What is one to make of so much disagreement in interpreting Sorel? In my view, the disagreement and uncertainty stem from the fact that the theoretical basis for the position developed in *Reflections on Violence* is in essence neither Marxism nor anarchism, but rather a fairly coherent, if idiosyncratic, variety of *anarcho-Marxism*. Accordingly, I would propose the term 'anarcho-Marxism' to describe Sorel's perspective, as this term is more accurate than either 'Marxism' or 'anarchism' and, on the other hand, much more illuminating, theoretically speaking, than 'anarcho-syndicalism', the customary label for his views.

Before discussing the anarcho-Marxist features of Sorel's thought in the *Reflections* (and elsewhere), I should perhaps explain that I shall be using this term to designate (non-evaluatively) any theoretical perspective that combines fundamental elements of anarchist doctrine with fundamental elements of Marxism. In the case of Sorel's anarcho-Marxism, this blend involves, in essence, a commitment to Marxist social and historical analysis (including Marx's philosophy of history, with the theoretical justification for socialism that it entails) coupled with an espousal of what is, in effect, an anarchist political practice. In short, the political profile I have in mind in labelling Sorel an 'anarcho-Marxist' is not unlike that which Donald Clark Hodges evokes in claiming that Bakunin was 'the first anarcho-Marxist', Bakunin being an anarchist 'who accepted his [Marx's] theories but rejected his politics as authoritarian'.[18] Whether or not Hodges is correct in characterising Bakunin as an anarcho-Marxist, a careful examination of *Reflections on Violence* and other texts reveals the aptness of this description as applied to Sorel, as we shall see.

My aim in the remainder of this chapter is to sketch the justification for construing Sorel's theoretical outlook, as articulated in *Reflections on Violence*, as first and foremost a form of anarcho-Marxism. To this end, my essay focuses on four themes, or rather positions, that figure prominently in the *Reflections*: anti-statism; the condemnation of parliamentary socialism; the advocacy of revolutionary syndicalism; and defence of the revolutionary general strike. Starting from the premise that these four positions are characteristically anarchist views, I argue that Sorel's adherence to them entails an acceptance of some important components of anarchism. I also argue, however, that many Marxists could endorse these same views, provided that they attach as much importance as Sorel does to *workers' self-emancipation* as a fundamental Marxist commitment. Since it turns out, therefore, that Marxists could endorse the *Reflections'* anarchist views and, as I also contend, anarchists could adopt the *Reflections'* Marxist views, we may safely say that *Reflections on Violence* both combines Marxist and anarchist theses and does so in a way that makes each group's theses acceptable to the other group. To the extent that this is the case, *Reflections on Violence* proves successful as a statement of *anarcho-Marxist* doctrine. The final part of the chapter briefly discusses some ways in which Marxists might benefit by revisiting Sorel's anarcho-Marxism.

## Reflections on Violence

Before turning to each of the themes mentioned above, it will be useful to review briefly the main argument in *Reflections on Violence*. As the book's title indicates, Sorel's central topic is violence, but the violence that interests Sorel is a specific manifestation of political violence, namely the violence that workers use or administer in doing battle with the bourgeoisie in strikes and militant labour actions. Sorel's central claim holds that this kind of 'proletarian violence'– an absolutely indispensable element of class struggle in his view – is the most effective method for establishing socialism.

His reasoning is as follows. Following Marx, Sorel assumes that capitalism must produce the maximal development of the forces of production before socialism becomes possible; in other words, capitalism will give way to socialism only when capitalist relations of production become a fetter on the forces of production and an impediment to their further development. Capitalism, in short, must exhaust the possibilities for development and expansion of the productive forces within the framework of capitalist relations of production before we can undertake the transition to socialism. According to Sorel, capitalists, or the bourgeoisie, will be effective in developing the forces of production, and hence in achieving the complete development of capitalism, to the extent that they focus single-mindedly on maximising profit. An exclusive focus on profit maximisation entails, in turn, a refusal to grant any concessions to the workers (for example, higher wages, a reduced working day, measures to improve conditions in the workplace, expansion of employee benefits, or establishment of worker rights requiring new expenditures or investments) which might hamper or retard the utmost development of the forces of production.

What does this have to do with violence? In Sorel's view, proletarian violence facilitates the bourgeoisie's pursuit of profit – and thus contributes to and hastens the creation of socialism – by dissuading capitalists (and others) from making concessions to the workers. For if workers unfailingly 'repay with *black ingratitude* the *benevolence* of those who wish to protect the workers',[19] that is to say, if they respond to welfare-enhancing concessions from the bourgeoisie with heightened militancy (with new strikes and more violent resistance), the capitalists will conclude that nothing is to be gained by making such concessions and they will cease to offer them. Consequently, instead of squandering their time, energy and resources on measures designed to enhance the workers' well-being, capitalists will devote themselves single-mindedly to the pursuit of profit and the development of the forces of production. In short, proletarian violence, and consistently militant opposition from labour more generally, helps to sustain the bourgeoisie's spirit or ethic of capitalist ruthlessness and antagonism; thanks to this attitude on the part of the workers, *capitalists remain capitalists*, and are prevented from succumbing to any of the impulses that might distract them from the business of producing surplus value. To put the same point a bit differently: acts of proletarian violence and the workers' disposition to meet concessions with ingratitude serve to 'reawaken' the bourgeoisie 'to a sense of their own class interests', thereby reinvigorating the bourgeoisie and 're-establish[ing] the division into classes'.[20] As Sorel explains:

> ... proletarian violence comes upon the scene at the very moment when the conception of social peace claims to moderate disputes; proletarian violence confines employers to their role as producers and tends to restore the class structure just when they seemed on the point of intermingling in the democratic morass.... This violence compels capitalism to restrict its attentions solely to its material role and tends to restore to it the warlike qualities it formerly possessed. A growing and solidly organized working class can force the capitalist class to remain ardent in the industrial struggle; if a united and revolutionary proletariat confronts a rich bourgeoisie eager for conquest, capitalist society will reach its historical perfection.[21]

In short, violence promotes the optimal development of capitalism, thereby helping to establish the material preconditions for, and accelerating society's advance towards, socialism. It is precisely for this reason that proletarian violence 'may save the world from barbarism'.[22]

In summarising Sorel's argument it is important to emphasise that his concept of 'proletarian violence' refers to acts of violence flowing from the resistance that forms a part of militant strikes and other labour struggles involving intransigent opposition on the workers' part. For Sorel, moreover, such acts of violence, and strikes in particular, are 'acts of war',[23] the war in question being the class war (if revolutionary strikes are inherently violent, it is precisely because they constitute acts of war). Sorel is careful to distinguish this type of violence from acts of violence committed by the *state*: whereas the purpose of the latter is to preserve and strengthen the state, proletarian or 'syndicalist' violence consists in acts of violence 'perpetrated in the course of strikes by proletarians *who desire the overthrow of the State*'.[24] In other words, the workers' violence does not aim at replacing one (authoritarian) state structure with another, but rather at doing away with the state altogether, along with the domination and exploitation which the state makes possible.

It is also worth emphasising that Sorel defends proletarian violence not only on account of its role in the consummation of capitalism, but also because of its beneficial effect on the workers themselves. In preparing and executing acts of violence in strikes, proletarians develop self-confidence, acquire political independence, develop skills and abilities necessary for self-management, and of course gain greater class consciousness.[25] And to the extent that acts of proletarian violence achieve one of their primary purposes, namely to 'mark the separation of classes',[26] these acts are likely to heighten workers' militancy and combativeness (which will of course encourage capitalists to devote their energies exclusively to developing the forces of production...which should provoke, in turn, even more proletarian violence).

Yet the greatest benefit of all from acts of violence has to do with their role in preparing workers for a *revolutionary* (or 'syndicalist') *general strike*, an idea which, in Sorel's opinion, 'contains within itself the whole of proletarian socialism'.[27] Unlike mere political strikes (or even a *political* general strike), a proletarian general strike does not produce a mere change of government, but the destruction of the state as such: as Sorel succinctly puts it in one of the appendices ('Apology for Violence') to *Reflections on Violence*, the revolutionary or proletarian general strike involves 'an overthrow in the course of which both employers and the State will be removed by the organized producers'.[28] Besides being the event that puts an end to capitalism, the general strike is important insofar as it functions as a *myth* for revolutionary workers. For Sorel, myths are 'expressions of a will to act',[29] compelling images and conceptions of a (future) collective enterprise that serve to inspire, motivate and mobilise the actors who will be engaged in this enterprise.[30] Sorel maintains that only those who embrace some such myth will prove capable of great endeavours,[31] and it is the 'myth' of the general strike, the very idea of which 'produces an entirely epic state of mind',[32] which serves as an indispensable inspiration and motivation for the revolutionary worker.

## Marxist and anarchist themes in Sorel

*Reflections on Violence* is a somewhat eccentric and highly uneven work. While it contains incisive analyses of trends and developments in fin-de-siècle socialism and many provocative arguments concerning the struggle for a socialist society, Sorel's text often appears rather disjointed, and his reasoning can be exasperatingly quirky. Moreover, some of his principal theses are undeniably unsettling. For example, Sorel's approach to the emancipation of the working class is, as we have seen, an incomparably robust version of *the worse, the better*, albeit cast in the form of *the better, the worse*: the more welfare-enhancing concessions the workers exact from capital, the poorer the prospects for their emancipation. (Sorel's defence of this viewpoint is, I would suggest, one of the chief reasons that the *Reflections* 'remains a profoundly disturbing book', as Jennings says in his introduction to the text.[33])

In any event, while Sorel's *Reflections* raises numerous questions, I would like to focus on the book's fundamental political orientation, which, as I shall try to demonstrate, is best interpreted as a variety of anarcho-Marxism. My remarks will deal mainly with the anarchist dimension of *Reflections on Violence*, for two reasons. First, as I indicate below, I believe it is more difficult for Marxists to assume Sorel's properly 'anarchist' commitments than it is for anarchists to assume his essentially 'Marxist' views. Second, as noted earlier, the fact is that Sorel is most often classified as, if anything, a Marxist of sorts, however idiosyncratic his interpretation of Marxism may turn out to be. In other words, the identification of Sorel with Marxism is somewhat less controversial than his assimilation to anarchism. Since my discussion centres mainly on the 'anarchist Sorel', let me first summarise very briefly the grounds for regarding Sorel as a Marxist.

To begin with, one can hardly ignore the various passages in *Reflections on Violence* and other texts in which Sorel expressly affirms the Marxist affiliation of the 'new school' of theorists to which he belongs.[34] The 'new school' ('nouvelle école') was a name used by the group that included, along with Sorel himself, Edouard Berth and Hubert Lagardelle, and was associated with *Le Mouvement socialiste*, a journal founded by Lagardelle in 1899. According to Sorel, the new school 'rejected all the formulas which came from either utopianism or Blanquism; it thus purged Marxism of all that was not specifically Marxist and it intended to preserve only what, according to it, was the core of the doctrine'.[35] Furthermore, it does 'not in the least feel itself bound to admire the illusions, the faults and the errors of the man [Marx] who did so much to work out revolutionary ideas',[36] but rather seeks 'to remain faithful to Marx's spirit' and to 'what is really true in Marxism'.[37] For Sorel, what is 'really true' in Marxism is above all the notion that class struggle comprises 'the alpha and omega of socialism'.[38] Sorel and the 'new school' identify class struggle with a principled opposition to 'social peace' – Sorel himself tends to conflate 'class struggle' and 'class war'[39] – and advance an uncompromisingly anti-reformist, anti-parliamentarist theoretical orientation and, in positive terms, a commitment to revolutionary syndicalism and a political strategy aimed at producing the conditions necessary for a successful revolutionary general strike (the culmination of revolutionary praxis in the present era, according to Sorel).[40] Sorel's allegiance to these core ideas sets him apart from 'the official [i.e. parliamentary] socialists', who, he remarks, 'wish to admire in Marx that which is not Marxist'.[41] If Sorel's Marxism appears heretical, it is, he suggests, because the prevailing schools of socialism have distorted the essential elements of Marxist doctrine, which he and the other members of the 'new school' seek to recover and renew in a Marxist fashion.[42]

In addition to providing this self-identification, and perhaps even more important, Sorel explicitly endorses many Marxist theses and assumptions (a few of which have already been noted) over the course of his *Reflections*. For example, Sorel accepts many of Marx's central assumptions regarding the material preconditions for socialism and the philosophy of history; he agrees, as just noted, with Marx's emphasis on the centrality of class struggle in social life and social development, and its role in the fight for socialism; like Marx, Sorel views the state as an instrument of class domination and advocates its abolition; he rejects utopias and utopian socialism; Sorel acknowledges, like Marx, the primacy of production, as this notion is understood in historical materialism; he, too, affirms the desirability of a cataclysmic socialist revolution that abolishes capitalism once and for all, and the importance of helping workers to bring it about; as with Marx, Sorel envisions socialist society as a classless social order in which the forces of production are collectively owned, and managed by the workers themselves; and, finally, Sorel, like Marx, steadfastly adheres to the principle of proletarian self-emancipation.[43] As a matter of fact, it is precisely because of Sorel's commitment to Marx's essential views and doctrines – or rather what Sorel takes them to be – that he denounces 'the anti-Marxist transformation which contemporary socialism is undergoing',[44] and it is also for this reason that the *Reflections* is in part a polemic against distortions or (neutralising) corruptions of Marx's thought attributable to figures who claim to champion socialism.

But what about anarchism? As it turns out, in addition to his enthusiastic endorsement of numerous Marxist views, Sorel also defends some essentially and indisputably anarchist positions in the pages of *Reflections on Violence*. I will mention four of them.

The first plainly anarchist position to note is Sorel's uncompromising *anti-statism*. He advocates the abolition of the state, and he regards the abolition of the state as a *condition* of the revolution, or rather as a measure that coincides with the overthrow of capitalism, and not as a more or less distant occurrence resulting from a process of 'withering away'. Indeed, the goal of the general strike, and hence the ultimate end of proletarian violence, is nothing other than the suppression or destruction of the state, or as Sorel writes in one passage, the elimination of 'both employers and the State'.[45]

Significantly, this uncompromising stance vis-à-vis the state leads Sorel to reject 'the dictatorship of the proletariat' – a principle which, according to Lenin, constitutes 'the very *essence* of Marx's doctrine'.[46] The dictatorship of the proletariat would, Sorel maintains, perpetuate a division between 'masters' and 'servants',[47] and is therefore unacceptable.

A second essentially anarchist position advanced in the *Reflections* is the *condemnation of parliamentary socialism*. Sorel stresses time and again in this work the inherently anti-revolutionary, conservative nature of parliamentary institutions, and their baneful effect on socialists willing to serve these institutions. He acknowledges that the anarchists were correct in warning that participation in bourgeois institutions, with its exposure to bourgeois influences, would lead to a political *embourgeoisement* of revolutionaries.[48] The 'official socialists' (Sorel's term for parliamentary socialists) 'boast to the government and to the rich bourgeoisie of their ability to moderate revolution', for parliamentary socialism basically '*sells peace of mind to the conservatives*'.[49] A revolution that brought official socialists to power would change little,[50] since parliamentary socialists desire above all to preserve, and if possible expand, their own power and that of the parties they represent, and this objective presupposes the preservation and fortification of the state. Proletarian violence, carried out in the proper fashion, will put an end to parliamentary socialism, which is plainly one of the reasons that the parliamentary socialists themselves condemn it.[51]

A third anarchist position can be found in Sorel's *espousal of revolutionary syndicalism*. According to the doctrine of revolutionary syndicalism, autonomous trade unions, acting independently of political parties and institutions, must be both the agent of revolution and the fundamental organisational components of the future socialist society, understood as an arrangement in which these units will control production. Unlike parliamentary socialism, revolutionary syndicalism is resolutely opposed to the state, which it aims to destroy.[52]

The final important anarchist position that Sorel champions in *Reflections on Violence* is a commitment to the *revolutionary* or *syndicalist* (or *proletarian*) *general strike*. This form of strike is, Sorel insists, very different from a merely 'political strike' (whether or not it is a 'political *general* strike'). The latter does not presuppose, as does the proletarian general strike, an absolute class confrontation between the bourgeoisie and the proletariat.[53] Nor do merely 'political' strikes pose any fundamental threat to politicians,[54] since such actions aim at reforms and improvements within the existing socio-political order, whose fundamental legitimacy remains unquestioned by those who organise and carry out 'political' strikes. The revolutionary or proletarian general strike, on the other hand, 'entails the conception of an irrevocable overthrow', followed by the creation of a new civilisation.[55] Since the concept of the revolutionary general strike also includes the definitive defeat of the bourgeoisie and the destruction of the state, it is an 'idea ... [which] contains within itself the whole of proletarian socialism'.[56]

Each of the four positions that I have mentioned constitutes either an essential anarchist commitment (anti-statism, the rejection of parliamentarism), or a position that has been defended and embraced mainly by anarchists (revolutionary syndicalism, the general strike),[57] or both (anti-statism and the rejection of parliamentarism). Indeed, some major anarchists, such as Rudolph Rocker and Emma Goldman, hold all four positions.[58] At any rate, even those anarchists who reject revolutionary syndicalism and the general strike would surely acknowledge that these positions are not fundamentally at odds with essential anarchist values.[59] Accordingly, just as few Marxists would dismiss as essentially un- or anti-Marxist any of the 'Marxist' positions (listed above) that Sorel defends, few anarchists would dismiss as un- or anti-anarchist any of the 'anarchist' positions that he defends.

## An anarcho-Marxist synthesis?

So, in *Reflections on Violence* we find a number of standard Marxist positions alongside a number of standard anarchist positions. One might be inclined to conclude, on the basis of my remarks and given the differences between Marxism and anarchism, that the result is a rather incoherent amalgam, or at best a very unstable synthesis of two political doctrines widely believed to be grossly incompatible with each other. As it turns out, however, *Reflections on Violence* is actually fairly successful as a model of anarcho-Marxism, owing to the fact that *anarchists could embrace Sorel's Marxist commitments, while Marxists could embrace his anarchist commitments.*

Let me begin with first of these last two claims. It is, I believe, the case that most anarchists could subscribe to all of the theses and views that make *Reflections on Violence* a 'Marxist' text, or at least to those mentioned earlier. Recall that these were: i) Marx's view of the material preconditions for socialism; ii) his perspective on the role of class struggle in social evolution and the struggle for socialism; iii) Marx's concept of the state as an instrument of class domination, and his belief that it must, therefore, be abolished; iv) Marx's rejection of utopian socialism; v) Marx's emphasis on the 'primacy of production'; vi) Marx's support for a cataclysmic socialist revolution, which one should help the workers to bring about; vii) Marx's conception of socialist society as a classless social order in which the forces of production are collectively owned, and managed by the workers themselves; and viii) Marx's commitment to proletarian self-emancipation. If I am correct in claiming that anarchists could endorse all of these views, and hence both the anarchist *and* Marxist commitments present in *Reflections on Violence*, it is difficult to understand how they could reject, in general terms, Sorel's anarcho-Marxism.

What about Marxists? Could they subscribe to Sorel's anarchist theses and views, or at least to those discussed above? This is, in my view, the main issue in assessing the 'success' of Sorel's anarcho-Marxism. One might naturally approach this issue by examining the works of more mainstream Marxist theorists and thinkers, thereby determining whether or not many other Marxists have endorsed the anarchist views defended by Sorel. I will, however, follow a different approach, which consists in considering Sorel's stated rationale for defending positions that are almost invariably associated with anarchists. This approach seems especially appropriate, considering that Sorel himself conceives of the *Reflections* as a non-dogmatic development and updating of Marx's theories, but one that recovers, and draws its inspiration from, the most essential and authentic elements in Marx's thought.[60]

Let us begin with Sorel's commitment to revolutionary syndicalism, which he claims is 'on the true Marxist track'.[61] Can one make a plausible Marxist case for revolutionary syndicalism, a doctrine that is usually synonymous with *anarcho*-syndicalism?

For many Marxists, revolutionary syndicalism appears suspect, and impossible to embrace, owing to its decidedly *anti-political* character: revolutionary syndicalism rejects political parties, condemns participation in parliament or collaboration with governmental authorities, denies political institutions any role in the post-revolutionary period and so on. This stance, which gives economic struggle absolute priority over political activity, is anathema to most Marxists, who typically accord primacy to political activity.[62]

Sorel, like the anarchists, insists on the primacy of economic struggle (for example, militant initiatives in the workplace, strikes, industrial mobilisations, direct challenges to employers' domination), but he suggests, in effect, that this is in reality the more authentically Marxist view. For Sorel attaches extreme importance to *proletarian self-emancipation*, and this principle, so central to the Marxist outlook,[63] can plausibly be construed as providing warrant for privileging economic struggle over political struggle. After all, if one adheres to the principle that the emancipation of the working class must take the form of *self*-emancipation, and the sphere in which workers enjoy the best prospects for exercising their collective agency is in the economic realm (that is, in the world of production), then it is hardly unreasonable to embrace something like revolutionary syndicalism, with its emphasis on industrial agitation, direct action, and mobilisation of the rank and file. Furthermore, self-emancipation requires a certain degree or level of worker militancy, a point that Marx insists on, according to Sorel: 'Marx wishes us to understand', writes Sorel, 'that the whole preparation of the proletariat depends solely upon the organization of a stubborn, increasing and passionate resistance to the present order of things'.[64] If this spirit of resistance is as decisive as Sorel says, and revolutionary syndicalism promotes and sustains this spirit (or morale) better than rival doctrines, then perhaps it really is the case that revolutionary syndicalism affords workers a 'truly proletarian ideology'.[65]

Let us turn now to Sorel's impassioned defence of the revolutionary general strike. While it is true that Rosa Luxemburg once wrote that the strike is 'the external form of struggle for socialism',[66] Marxists have generally attached considerably less importance to strikes, and the notion of the revolutionary general strike, first popularised by Bakuninites, has almost invariably been associated with anarchist doctrines and movements.[67] Indeed, the German trade union leaders of Sorel's day, whose views were shaped to one degree or another by the 'Marxism' upheld by German social democracy, were given to saying that 'General Strike is General Nonsense'.[68] Yet Sorel holds that 'the fundamental principles of Marxism are perfectly intelligible only with the aid of the picture of the general strike and, on the other hand, the full significance of this picture . . . is only apparent to those deeply versed in Marxist doctrine'.[69] Moreover, in several passages in the *Reflections* he underscores alleged similarities and affinities between Marxism's general theoretical framework and that which justifies the revolutionary general strike.[70] What are these alleged similarities and affinities?

First of all, the revolutionary general strike, like Marx's revolution, is a 'catastrophic' occurrence – Sorel uses 'catastrophe' or 'catastrophic' many times in connection with the general strike[71] – which evokes and symbolises, but also precipitates the passage from capitalism to socialism, and thus from oppression to liberation. Owing to the awesome, epic images that it conjures up, the 'catastrophic' notion of the revolutionary general strike serves, much like Marx's concept of socialist revolution, to inspire and motivate workers (which is why Sorel regards both the general strike *and* 'Marx's catastrophic revolution' as 'myths', in the sense noted above).[72] What is more, 'It is through strikes [including the general strike] that the proletariat asserts its existence'[73]: the strike is the method or strategy of struggle most readily available to the workers, and so they naturally use strikes in order to emerge from invisibility, establish their social presence, and express their needs and demands. (Furthermore, to the extent that these actions are accompanied by, or rather give rise to, a new class consciousness among the workers, it may also be said that strikes help the proletariat to become a 'class for itself'.) In this sense, an insistence of the supreme political value of the revolutionary general strike, and strikes more generally, seems to follow quite straightforwardly from an unqualified commitment to proletarian self-emancipation. If Marx himself does not appreciate this, it is, Sorel suggests, partly because Marx gave little thought to the actual organisation of workers for revolutionary struggle,[74] and partly because he could not possibly have foreseen developments that occurred after his death, developments which make it clear that adoption of the revolutionary general strike as a political strategy represents a correct adaptation of Marxist thought to contemporary realities.[75]

As for anti-parliamentarism, it would also seem clear that Sorel can derive his position from a bedrock commitment to proletarian self-emancipation, in that parliamentarism substitutes mediation and representation for the workers' own activity and initiatives, and also fosters passivity among them. For these reasons, the acceptance of parliamentarism seems be at odds with the principle of *self*-emancipation. What is more, parliamentarism is, on Sorel's view, inherently de-radicalising and corrupting; in a word, an obstacle to class struggle and revolution. As noted above, Sorel contends that revolutionaries and radicals who participate in parliament inevitably end up devoting themselves to 'preserv[ing] the old cult of the state', from which they benefit, and limit themselves to 'attack[ing] the men in power rather than power itself'.[76] If 'official socialists' are unable to understand proletarian violence, it is precisely because the perpetrators of this violence wish not to take over the state, but rather to eliminate it.[77]

This brings us, lastly, to Sorel's radical anti-statism, which represents an essentially anarchist perspective on the abolition of the state: the suppression of the state is to coincide with the advent of the revolution, and constitutes a necessary condition of its success. '[T]here is an absolute opposition between revolutionary syndicalism and the State',[78] writes Sorel, making it clear that he departs from Marxist orthodoxy when it comes to the fate of the state following the revolution. Sorel seems to assume, however, that to insist on the abolition of the state as a condition of the revolution is in fact more consistent with Marx's basic outlook, inasmuch as Marx held that 'the socialist revolution ought not to culminate in the replacement of one governing minority by another'.[79] (Recall that Sorel rejects the dictatorship of the proletariat because it would perpetuate a division between 'masters' and 'servants').[80] Yet whether or not it is true that one can find in 'authentic' Marxism this type of justification for a position that is in essence the anarchist view on the state, one could presumably also appeal to the principle of workers' self-emancipation in order to justify the same position. After all, the main impediment to *self*-emancipation (as well as self *emancipation*) is the state, insofar as it upholds the employers' interests and serves as their instrument of domination (that is, it is the 'central nucleus' of the bourgeoisie).[81]

These are, it seems to me, the arguments available to Sorel if pressed to explain how he can endorse his four *anarchisant*, or outright anarchist, positions without departing from Marxism.[82] As I have tried to show, it turns out that the key commitment in making a Marxist case for each of the positions is the thesis of proletarian self-emancipation. To the extent that Marxists' commitment to proletarian self-emancipation would in fact enable them to endorse the four positions examined here (with some important qualifications, perhaps, in the case of Sorel's 'radical anti-statism') and assuming, on the other hand, that most anarchists could embrace Sorel's indisputably Marxist convictions, it is fair to say that Sorel's theory furnishes a fairly coherent model of anarcho-Marxism.[83]

## Learning from Sorel

Sorel's anarcho-Marxism has, I believe, much to recommend it to Marxists; but even if they do not find his theory wholly satisfactory, Marxists can still profit from a careful consideration of Sorel's reasons for advocating such a theory. Consider, for example, a problem that bedevilled Marxists throughout the twentieth century and that continues to provoke debate among Marxists and others to this day: the failure of workers in industrialised nations to become the agent of socialist revolution. Whatever other factors may have contributed to this failure, it was certainly due in part to a lack of 'class consciousness' among the workers, who were, for whatever reason(s), largely unaware of their collective capacities and true class interests, and were consequently disinclined to engage in militant forms of class struggle to defend these interests. Although Sorel himself could hardly have foreseen the extent to which the working class would fail to assume the role of 'revolutionary subject', he was acutely aware of the challenges to the development of a 'revolutionary' orientation among workers. Indeed, one of the reasons that Sorel advocates revolutionary syndicalism arises from his belief that this is the only approach to political action that can succeed in fostering the necessary kind and degree of 'consciousness' among the workers themselves. Sorel thus represents and articulates a view that is in some sense the very antithesis of Lenin's influential position. Whereas Lenin famously claims that 'class political consciousness can be brought to the workers *only from without*, that is, only from outside the economic struggle, from outside the sphere of relations between workers and employers', 84 Sorel maintains that 'class political consciousness' can only arise *from within*, as it were, and that acceptance of this thesis implies a commitment to something like revolutionary syndicalism. Indeed, if revolutionary syndicalism is, for Sorel, a 'great educative force',85 it is precisely because it teaches workers to combat capitalism by asserting themselves and developing class solidarity, while at the same time preparing them for their role in the socialist future, with its worker-managed system of production. In any event, whether or not Sorel's overall estimation of revolutionary syndicalism ultimately proves justified, it should be clear that he has good *Marxist* reasons for granting the 'economic struggle' priority vis-à-vis the 'political struggle',86 and that Marxists would therefore be well-advised to reflect on these reasons.

Of course, as should be clear from my earlier remarks, Marxists are not the only ones who would benefit from (re-)acquainting themselves with Sorel's *Reflections on Violence*: anarchists can also learn a great deal from re-reading Sorel, if only because his work reveals that the 'spirit of Marx'87 may in many ways be much closer to 'the spirit of anarchism' than most anarchists (and Marxists) tend to realise. If Marxists and anarchists alike do re-examine Sorel's contribution to socialist theory, we shall surely find ourselves one step closer to a much-needed reconciliation of these two formidable political movements.

## Notes

1. Maximilien Rubel, *Rubel on Karl Marx*, J. O'Malley and K. Algozin (eds. and trans.) (Cambridge: Cambridge University Press, 1981), p. 78, n. 119.

2. M. Charzat, 'A la source du "marxisme" de Gramsci' in M. Charzat (ed.), *Georges Sorel* (Paris: Éditions de l'Herne, 1986), pp. 213–222; David McLellan, *Marxism After Marx*, 3rd edn. (London: Macmillan, 1998), p. 193.

3. I. Mészáros, *Lukács' Concept of Dialectic* (London: The Merlin Press, 1972), p. 21.

4. H. García Salvatecci, *Georges Sorel y Mariátegui. Ubicación ideológica del Amauta* (Lima: Delgado Valenzuela, 1979); R. Paris 'Mariátegui: un sorelismo ambiguo' in J. Aricó (ed.), *Mariátegui y los orígenes del marxismo latinoamericano* (Mexico City: Pasado y Presente, 1978), pp. 155–161.

5. Antonio Labriola, *Socialism and Philosophy*, P. Piccone (trans.) (St. Louis: Telos Press, 1980).

6. Eugene Kamenka, 'Marxism and Ethics – A Reconsideration' in Shlomo Avineri (ed.), *Varieties of Marxism* (The Hague: Martinus Nijhoff, 1977), p. 119.

7. John Gray, *Post-Liberalism: Studies in Political Thought* (New York and London: Routledge, 1993), pp. 100–101. Leszek Kolakowski also ranks Sorel highly in comparison with other Marxists; see *Main Currents of Marxism*, vol. 2, *The Golden Age*, P.S. Falla (trans.) (Oxford: Oxford University Press, 1981), p. 153.

8. J.C. Mariátegui, *Mariátegui Total*, vol. 1 (Lima: Empresa Editora Amauta S.A., 1994), p. 1292 (my translation).

9.  George Lichtheim, *The Concept of Ideology and Other Essays* (New York: Random House, 1967), p. 261; *Marxism: An Historical and Critical Study*, 2nd edn. (New York and Washington: Praeger, 1965), p. 229, n. 2.
10.  V.I. Lenin, *Materialism and Empirio-Criticism* in *Collected Works*, vol. 14 (Moscow: Progress Publishers, 1972), p. 292.
11.  Significantly, many of the commentators who link Sorel's thought with reactionary or fascistic ideas and claim that Sorel was a right-wing thinker furnish very little evidence to support their claim. See George Woodcock, *Anarchism: A History of Libertarian Ideas and Movements* (New York: Meridian, 1962), p. 323; Irving L. Horowitz, 'A Postscript to the Anarchists' in Horowitz (ed.), *The Anarchists* (New York: Dell Publishing, 1964), p. 592; George Lichtheim, *From Marx to Hegel* (New York: The Seabury Press, 1971), p. 116; James Joll, *The Anarchists*, 2nd edn. (Cambridge, MA: Harvard University Press, 1980), p. 194; Peter Marshall, *Demanding the Impossible: A History of Anarchism* (London: Fontana Press, 1993), p. 442. Woodcock's judgement is especially puzzling, considering that he both shares Sorel's enthusiasm for syndicalism and writes from an anarchist perspective; cf. note 57 below.
12.  See Jeremy Jennings, 'Sorel, Georges' in T. Bottomore et al. (eds), *A Dictionary of Marxist Thought* (Cambridge, MA: Harvard University Press, 1983), pp. 453–454; R.A. Gorman, 'Sorel, Georges' in R.A. Gorman (ed.), *Biographical Dictionary of Neo-Marxism* (Westport, CT: Greenwood Press, 1985), pp. 390–392; Kolakowski, *Main Currents of Marxism*, p. 14.
13.  Jennings, 'Sorel', p. 453.
14.  J.L. Stanley, 'Editor's Introduction' in *From Georges Sorel* (New York: Oxford University Press, 1976), pp. 7, 17. In his 'In Defence of Lenin' Sorel characterises the *Reflections* as 'Proudhonian in inspiration', *Reflections on Violence*, J. Jennings (ed.) (Cambridge: Cambridge University Press, 1999), p. 292.
15.  'But one must always bear in mind that Sorel was really no Marxist, but a Proudhonist', Lichtheim, *Marxism*, p. 113.
16.  Horowitz, p. 17; cf. Horowitz's *Radicalism and the Revolt Against Reason* (New York: The Humanities Press, 1961), p. 160.
17.  Joll, *Anarchists*, pp. 188–195. Just as some Marxists dispute Sorel's Marxist credentials, some anarchists and writers sympathetic to anarchism tend to minimise Sorel's affinities with the anarchist tradition. George Woodcock scarcely discusses Sorel's ideas in *Anarchism*, while Peter Marshall devotes but two (ill-informed) paragraphs to Sorel in *Demanding the Impossible*, p. 442.
18.  D.C. Hodges, *The Literate Communist: 150 Years of the Communist Manifesto* (New York: Peter Lang, 1999), p. 113.
19.  Sorel, *Reflections*, p. 77; italics in the original.
20.  Ibid., pp. 77, 85; cf. p. 78.
21.  Ibid., pp. 78–79.
22.  Ibid., p. 85; cf. p. 251.
23.  Ibid., p. 279.
24.  Ibid., p. 108; emphasis added.
25.  Ibid., pp. 74–75.
26.  Ibid., pp. 105–106.
27.  Ibid., p. 150.
28.  Ibid., pp. 279–280.
29.  Ibid., p. 28.

30. '[M]en who are participating in great social movements always picture their coming action in the form of images of battle in which their cause is certain to triumph. I propose to give the name of "myths" to these constructions . . . ' (Ibid., p. 20).

31. Ibid., p. 140.

32. Ibid., p. 250.

33. J. Jennings, 'Introduction' in G. Sorel, *Reflections on Violence*, J. Jennings (ed.) (Cambridge: Cambridge University Press, 1999), p. xxi.

34. See, for example, Sorel, *Reflections*, p. 40.

35. G. Sorel, *La Décomposition du Marxisme* (Paris: Riviere, 1908), pp. 63–64, cited in Jennings, Introduction, p. 34, note 'p'.

36. Sorel, Introduction, p. 172; italics in the original.

37. G. Sorel, 'The Socialist Future of the Syndicates' in *From Georges Sorel*, ed. J.L. Stanley (New York: Oxford University Press, 1976), p. 72; 'Préface de 1905', in *Matériaux d'une théorie du proletariat* (Paris and Geneva: Slatkine Genève-Paris, 1981), p. 67 (my translation).

38. Sorel, 'Préface', p. 67 (my translation).

39. See for example, Ibid., pp. 68, 75, and Sorel, *Reflections*, pp. 105, 279.

40. Sorel, *Reflections*, p. 213; cf. 'Préface', p. 63. This 'Preface' articulates many of the 'new school's' characteristic views.

41. Sorel, *Reflections*, p. 172.

42. See, for example, G. Sorel, 'Mes raisons du syndicalisme' in *Matériaux d'une théorie du proletariat*, p. 253.

43. On the material preconditions for socialism and the philosophy of history see Sorel, *Reflections*, pp. 73, 80, 128, 129; on class struggle, pp. 34, 85, 126, 182; on the state, pp. 18, 30, 161; on utopias and utopianism, pp. 28–29, 118–119, 129, 132, 224; on 'the primacy of production', p. 138; on socialist revolution, pp. 126, 140, 155; on the conception of socialist society, pp. 155, 171, 238; and on the principle of proletarian self-emancipation, p. 32. All the views listed here are conventionally ascribed to Marx and Engels. On Marx and Engels' commitment to 'the principle of proletarian self-emancipation', which is relevant to my central thesis, I furnish some textual references in note 63.

44. Sorel, *Reflections*, p. 73.

45. Ibid., p. 279; cf. pp. 18, 107, 161, particularly as regards the suppression of the state. Sorel's conception of the state as an instrument of *class* domination would probably not be endorsed by many anarchists, but what I wish to focus on here are practical political commitments, rather than their theoretical justifications.

46. V.I. Lenin, *The Proletarian Revolution and the Renegade Kautsky* in *Collected Works*, vol. 28 (Moscow: Progress Publishers, 1974), p. 233.

47. Sorel, *Reflections*, p. 163.

48. Ibid., p. 34.

49. Ibid., p. 67 (italics in the original). On the failings of parliamentary socialism, see Ibid., pp. 67–68, 111, 154.

50. Ibid., p. 83.

51. Ibid., pp. 79, 118–119.

52. Ibid., pp. 107, 108.

53. Ibid., p. 151.

54. Ibid., p. 147.

55. Ibid., pp. 281, 280.

56. Ibid., p. 150; cf. pp. 110, 113, 118, and Sorel, 'Préface', p. 59.
57. On Bakunin's espousal of the general strike, see Michael Bakunin, 'Geneva's Double Strike' in *From Out of the Dustbin: Bakunin's Basic Writings, 1869–1871*, R. M. Cutler (ed. and trans.) (Ann Arbor, Michigan: Ardis, 1985), pp. 149–150. His views on the value of strikes more generally sound like an anticipation of Sorel's (see, for example, 'The International and Karl Marx', in *Bakunin on Anarchy*, S. Dolgoff (ed. and trans.) (New York: Alfred A. Knopf, 1972) pp. 304–307. According to Emma Goldman syndicalism constitutes 'the economic expression of Anarchism'; see 'Syndicalism: Its Theory and Practice' in A.K. Shulman (ed.), *Red Emma Speaks: Selected Writings and Speeches by Emma Goldman* (New York: Vintage Books, 1972), p. 68. Woodcock similarly claims that 'syndicalism is the industrial manifestation of anarchism'; see 'Syndicalism Defined' in G. Woodcock (ed.), *The Anarchist Reader* (Fontana Paperbacks, Glasgow, 1977), p. 208.
58. See Rudolf Rocker, *Anarcho-Syndicalism* (London: Pluto Press, 1989); Goldman, 'Anarchism: What It Really Stands for' and 'Syndicalism' in *Red Emma Speaks*, pp. 47–77.
59. Malatesta both criticised syndicalism – largely, it seems, because he equated it with conventional trade unionism – and expressed reservations about the general strike. On syndicalism, see 'Syndicalism and Anarchism' in Vernon Richards (ed.), *The Anarchist Revolution: Polemical Articles 1924–1931* (London: Freedom Press, 1995), pp. 23–27; on the strategy of the general strike, see 'Syndicalism: An Anarchist Critique' in Woodcock *Anarchist Reader*, pp. 223–225.
60. See, for example, Sorel, *Reflections*, p. 120.
61. Ibid., p. 132.
62. The separation of 'the political' and 'the economic' is in many ways quite artificial, an analytical construct – and one that often serves 'bourgeois' interests, as Marxists, among others, point out. Even so, the distinction seems useful with respect to the contrast that I wish to establish here.
63. According to the First International's 'Provisional Rules', drafted by Marx in 1864, 'the emancipation of the working classes must be conquered by the working classes themselves'. See 'Provisional Rules of the Association' in Karl Marx and Friedrich Engels, *Collected Works*, vol. 20 (New York: International Publishers, 1985), p. 14. Marx subsequently cited the formulation in the 'Critique of the Gotha Program' (*Collected Works*, 1989, vol. 24, p. 88) in 1875. In their 1879 'Circular Letter' to Bebel, Liebknecht and others, Marx and Engels reaffirm the paramount importance of this principle (*Collected Works*, vol. 24, p. 269), as does Engels in his 'Preface' to the 1888 English edition of the *Communist Manifesto* (*Collected Works*, 1990, vol. 26, p. 517). One of Marx and Engels' pre-*Manifesto* expressions of this principle is in *The Holy Family* in *Collected Works*, vol. 4 (New York: International Publishers, 1975), p. 37. For discussion, see Hal Draper, 'The Principle of Proletarian Self-Emancipation in Marx and Engels' in Ralph Miliband and John Saville (eds), *The Socialist Register 1971* (London: The Merlin Press, 1971); *Theory*, vol. I, pp. 213–234; and *Theory*, vol. II, pp. 147–165. For Lenin's commitment, see Lenin, 'Draft Programme' in *Collected Works*, vol. 2 (Moscow: Progress Publishers, 1972), p. 97.
64. Sorel, *Reflections*, p. 126.
65. Ibid., p. 226. Elsewhere Sorel unreservedly equates syndicalism with 'proletarian socialism', which he contrasts with 'political socialism'. See, for example, 'Mes raisons du syndicalisme', in *Matériaux d'une théorie du proletariat*, pp. 268–269.

66. Rosa Luxemburg, 'Our Program and the Political Situation' in P. Hudis and K.B. Anderson (eds), *The Rosa Luxemburg Reader* (New York: Monthly Review Press, 2004), p. 368.

67. For Marxist views on strikes, see R. Hyman, 'Strikes' in Tom Bottomore et al. (eds), *Dictionary of Marxist Thought*, pp. 469–471; N. Harding, *Leninism*, pp. 68–69. On the Bakuninite origins of the revolutionary general strike, see Hyman 'Strikes', p. 470; Joll, *Anarchists*, p. 179.

68. Joll, *Anarchists*, p. 193.

69. Sorel, *Reflections*, p. 122.

70. Ibid., pp. 120, 130–131.

71. Ibid., pp. 126, 140, 182.

72. Ibid., p. 20.

73. Ibid., p. 279.

74. Ibid., p. 169.

75. Ibid., p. 213.

76. Ibid., pp. 103, 107.

77. Ibid., pp. 18–19.

78. Ibid., p. 108.

79. Ibid., p. 107.

80. Ibid., p. 163.

81. Ibid., p. 18.

82. For a detailed attempt to demonstrate that Marx upholds an essentially anarchist outlook on the question of the state, see Maximilien Rubel, 'Marx, Theoretician of Anarchism', available at http://www.Marxists.org/archive/rubel/1973/Marx-anarchism.htm (accessed 12 April 2011).

83. By 'model of anarcho-Marxism' I mean only the four political positions discussed here, together with an adherence to the various Marxist theses enumerated earlier. I do not include, for example, Sorel's advocacy of 'the ethics of the producers' (the theme of the *Reflections'* last chapter), his theses regarding 'myths', or his conception and defence of violence.

84. V.I. Lenin, *What Is to Be Done?* in *Collected Works*, vol. 5 (Moscow: Progress Publishers, 1961), p. 422 (italics in the original).

85. Sorel, *Reflections*, pp. 243, 126.

86. E.H. Carr underscores this point. See *Studies in Revolution* (London: Frank Cass, 1962), p. 157.

87. Sorel, *Reflections*, p. 120.

# 6
# Antonio Gramsci, Anarchism, Syndicalism and *Sovversivismo*

*Carl Levy*

## Introduction

The relationship between Antonio Gramsci's Marxism and the anarchist and syndicalist traditions is complex and intriguing but it is overlooked by most of his scholarly interlocutors. I have argued that there are a number of elective affinities between the young Gramsci's unorthodox Marxism and the libertarian socialist tradition, and that Gramsci's concept of industrial democracy, elaborated during the era of the factory councils in Turin (1919–1920), was shaped through his encounters with anarchists, self-educated workers and formally educated technicians employed by Fiat and others. His relationship to the anarchists runs far deeper than an Italian variation of the tactical political ploy, which Lenin indulged in his anarchist-sounding pronouncements in revolutionary Russia during the spring and early summer of 1917.

Here I focus on the pre- *'Biennio Rosso* Gramsci', in order to show that Gramsci's amalgam of libertarian and authoritarian thought was already formulated before he encountered the Leninist model. Three aspects of the pre-Leninist Gramsci's Marxism serve as benchmarks to evaluate the interaction of libertarian thought and action with Gramsci's social thought: voluntarism, prefiguration and his nascent conception of hegemony as is evident in his attitudes towards language, education and free thought.

Gramsci's introduction to Marxism was filtered through a philosophical culture of voluntarism that permeated the Italian universities of antebellum Italy, whose myriad variations on the theme were found in European and North American philosophy (actualism, pragmatism, Bergsonism and so on) and were rigorously denounced by Lenin and later by Bukharin (who was roasted for naïve materialism by Gramsci in *Prison Notebooks*).[1] The theme of voluntarism is directly connected to Gramsci's concept of prefiguration.[2] Simply put, prefiguration implies that the institutions of the future socialist society should be foreshadowed in the democratic institutions of the working class in civil society under capitalism. Not only does this solve the dilemma of how one gets from the capitalist to socialist stage of history, it also implies the libertarian potential of working-class self-organisation. For Gramsci, *theoretical* Marxist voluntarism is embodied in self-organisation in civil society.

Gramsci was no anarchist or syndicalist, but anarchism and syndicalism served as foils to forge Gramscian social thought and political action. In his arguments with the libertarians before his encounters with Lenin and what became known as Leninism, Gramsci had already opened his thought to a ready acceptance of the authoritarian solutions proposed in Russia. The authoritarian aspects of the young Gramsci, however, paradoxically are derived from the libertarian-like voluntarism of his political thought, not from the determinism of Second Internationalist Marxism, even Lenin's radical variant.[3] In the remainder of this chapter, among other things, I will examine how the early Gramsci's concept of prefiguration and his master term, hegemony, are fleshed out in this dialogue with anarchist, syndicalist, and libertarian culture more broadly conceived. But it is his form of pedagogical socialism, drenched in Gentilean assumptions, which demonstrates the theoretical gulf separating his apparent libertarian socialism from the positivist culture of the anarchists and syndicalists.

A second theme of the discussion, relevant to Gramsci's relationship with the anarchists, is his concept of the subaltern. The term 'subaltern' relates to Gramscian keywords: common sense, good sense, and *sovversivismo* ('subversivism'),[4] and it reopens the controversy between Marxists and anarchists concerning the class basis of revolutionary politics. Is the Gramscian concept of the subaltern merely a more sympathetic but ultimately patronising and paternalist version of that old Marxist canard, the lumpenproletariat?[5] And is Gramsci's seemingly sympathetic account of 'primitive rebels' just an open-minded version of the anthropological gaze?[6] Indeed, the gaze Eric Hobsbawm adopted, since he claimed Gramsci inspired his 1959 study of 'primitive rebels'?[7] Were the anarchists and syndicalists merely politically pernicious modern versions of less threatening (to Marxist political hegemony) earlier religious-based millenarians? Thus a discussion of Gramsci's encounter with anarchists and syndicalists is inherently interesting for his intellectual biography and his type of Marxism, and echoes an earlier pattern of encounters by Marx with Stirner, Proudhon and Bakunin.[8] The question of Gramsci's take on the subaltern and the primitive rebels is also a fruitful way of interrogating Gramsci's relationship to the historiography of Italian anarchism, which I have discussed elsewhere.[9]

## Prefiguration and the 'libertarian Gramsci'

Gramsci, Antonio Labriola and the anarchists Gramsci employed the daily concerns of Turin's labour and co-operative movements as laboratories to develop and illustrate his more complex theoretical conceptions very early in his career – one or two years before Gramsci began to promote the 'Sovietist', Western European or incipient Turinese versions of Council Communism.[10]

It was precisely during his discussion of the co-operative that Gramsci carried out a sustained analysis of Marxist philosopher Antonio Labriola (1843–1904).[11] It was Labriola's reading of the philosophy of praxis that allowed Gramsci to use a distinguished if politically marginal Marxist scholar to challenge the orthodoxies of Second Internationalist Marxism during the war years (1915–1918).

Although they were from different generations, their relationships with the anarchists were strikingly similar. Both men worked with proletarian anarchists, but just like Gramsci, Labriola differentiated between Jacobinical '*capi*', the *spostati della borghesia* (bourgeois dropouts), the intellectual proletariat, in contrast to the anarchist workers whom Labriola had helped during the Roman builders' strike in the early 1890s. Although Labriola was capable of differentiating between the 'reasonable' anarchism of Errico Malatesta and terrorist bombers and assassins, he never took the intellectual premises of anarchism very seriously.

Gramsci and Labriola based the superiority of Marxism over other forms of socialism on its ability to forge a world view that required little borrowing from other systems of philosophical thought, and this caused them to fight against the marriage of positivism and Marxism. They denied the intellectual validity of other systems of socialism, particularly anarchism, but in their search for autonomous working-class institutions immersed in civil society and with a shared hostility to state help or interventionism, they found an appreciation in the work of Georges Sorel, a close correspondent of Labriola in the 1890s and, in his last years, an admirer of Gramsci and his young comrades in Turin in 1919–1920.

## The young Gramsci, Sorel and the anarchists

Most accounts of Gramsci emphasise his sharp differentiation between the trade union, a reformist institution immersed in the logic of the capitalist marketplace and the factory council, representative of the rank and file, subversive of labour as a commodity, reflecting the productivist and functionalist prerequisites of future socialised industry.

An article on consumer co-operatives by Gramsci, 'Socialism and Co-operation' (30 October 1916, published in the local journal of the Turinese socialist co-operative movement, *L'Alleanza Co-operativa*), is bathed in Sorelian allusions and thought patterns.[12] First, he made it abundantly clear that socialism had to be productivist, echoing Sorel. Consumer co-operatives were not, nor could they be, central to these politics. Socialism, he wrote 'is not simply to solve the distribution of finished products', but one must accelerate production, so that, 'collectivism will serve to accelerate the rhythm of production itself, by eliminating all those artificial factors of productivity'.[13]

Socialist co-operatives had to steer clear of the meddlesome and corrupting influences of bourgeois legislation and the state. If co-operatives did not serve the entire working class they were protectionist, parasitical organisations that gave rise to a group of privileged workers, who were successful at freeing themselves partially from capitalist exploitation, but whose actions were harmful to their class specifically and costly to production more generally. Thus Gramsci's early radicalism can be placed within the cultural context of the pre-war syndicalist wave, which enveloped the globe and embraced a critique of crony and state capitalism. Similarly, in London the exiled Italian anarchist, Errico Malatesta, adapted Hillaire Belloc's critique of a 'Servile State' and imported it into the Italian Left's opposition to statist reformism, mirroring the early Gramsci.[14]

Gramsci's general tenor of discussion is linked to his earlier connections with free-trade socialists and syndicalists in Sardinia and Turin.[15] Previously, Gaetano Salvemini, the free-trade socialist who criticised 'the dictatorship' of the north of Italy over the downtrodden south, had been a major influence, and during the war Gramsci edited a special issue of the local Turinese socialist newspaper, *Il Grido del Popolo*, devoted to the necessary connections between free trade and socialism. Free trade, Gramsci believed, would help to lessen the north/south divide but it was also central to the definition of his form of socialism.

Gramsci was also attracted to the English radical liberals who founded the Union for Democratic Control, and particularly Norman Angell, whose wartime writings, Gramsci claimed, showed that protectionist state socialism or state capitalism were universal evils arising from the inherent demands of the world conflict. This pervasive 'Prussianism' (his revealing synonym for the Servile State), Gramsci felt, threatened democratic liberties won before the war.[16] But free trade was not only the guarantor of civil rights; free trade also served as a metaphor for Gramsci's *maximalist programme*. Concurrently, Lenin, who appreciated the mechanics of power and production, was *praising* the wartime German Empire as being a step closer to socialism: cartels, trusts and indeed state-assisted cartels and trusts preparing the way for socialism; these did not corrupt the workers, but trained them for a future socialist industrial society. For the early free trade and 'libertarian' Gramsci, trusts, cartels and state capitalism undermined the unity of the working and peasant classes in Italy and also stunted the productivity of the capitalist economy and thus delayed the socialist stage of history.[17]

He also believed that 'reform from above' or 'state socialism' had too long been uncritically accepted within pre-war socialism and even within Marxist theory itself. This became evident in an article written on 8 April 1917 when Gramsci argued:

> Many of our comrades are still imbued with doctrines concerning the state that were fashionable in the writings of socialists twenty years ago. These doctrines were constructed in Germany, and perhaps in Germany might still have their justification. It is certain that in Italy, a country even less parliamentary than Germany, due to the prevailing political corruption and the lack of parliamentary consciousness, the state is the greatest enemy of citizens (of the majority of citizens) and every growth of its powers, of its activity, of its functions, always equals a growth of corruption, of misery for citizens, of a general lowering of the level of public, economic and moral life.[18]

Gramsci's complex, and at times confused, form of anti-statism is further shaped by his appropriation of Sorel's concept of cleavage, namely the sharp separation of the working-class from bourgeois culture and lifestyles.[19] But while there were similarities with Sorel, differences were also evident in the early 'libertarian' Gramsci.

Gramsci and Sorel shared a belief in a non-Jacobinical transition to socialism based upon the daily experiences of workers in their own trade unions and co-operatives, with Gramsci alluding to Sorel's highly influential book *l'Avenir socialiste des syndicats*, circulated by Italian left-wing socialist and syndicalist activists before the war.[20] This work predates Sorel's departure into myth-making and the celebration of violence, and is firmly grounded in his encounters with Eduard Bernstein, Antonio Labriola and the former Italian anarchist Francesco Saverio Merlino, which arose during the so-called revisionist debate (concerning the revision of Marxism) at the turn of the century.[21] From diverse starting points these three thinkers sought institutions within civil society, which might temper or suppress state socialism.

Italian anarchists became sharply critical of Sorel, especially after he showed little regret for the execution in 1909 of Francisco Ferrer, the anarchist Spanish educationalist (who he considered a muddle-headed Freemason), but in any case Gramsci's 'Sorel' was different from the majority of pre-war Italian syndicalists, who remained attracted to the Frenchman's works, albeit, it has been argued, that a certain reading of Sorel helped shaped Gramsci's concept of hegemony during his prison years – the young 'libertarian' Gramsci's transition to socialism relied upon the conscious, reasoned intervention of social actors, rather than myths. He did not share the fascination expressed by syndicalist intellectuals with the exotic, indeed the 'Orientalist', imagery of raw, anti-intellectual and uneducated workers such as the syndicalist professor Enrico Leone.[22]

Gramsci's early libertarianism is not merely found in his 'free-trade socialism', as discussed previously, it can also be seen as Gramsci's interpretation of

Marxist praxis, which he deployed to undermine the Second Internationalist concept of scientific socialism – a concept embraced by social democrats and Bolsheviks – or equally the alternative positivist determinism of Kropotkinite anarcho-communism, which some Italian anarchists, most notably Malatesta, believed the Russian advanced.

This led Gramsci to passionate denunciations of the division of socialism between a leadership caste imbued with the correct formulae and followers who were easily manipulated by their 'scientific' magic tricks. So he imbibed cautiously the ideas of the sociologist Robert Michels, especially the 'iron law of oligarchy' from the exiled German professor of politics at the University of Turin[23]; and indeed Gramsci sometimes advanced anarchist-like critiques of the Italian socialist party machine:

> The proletariat is not an army; it does not have officers, subalterns, corporals and soldiers. Socialists are not officers of the proletarian army, they are part of the proletariat itself, perhaps they are its consciousness, but as the consciousness cannot be divided from an individual, and so socialists are not placed in duality with the proletariat. They are one, always one and they do not command but live with the proletariat, just as blood circulates and moves in the veins of a body and it is not possible for it to live and move inside rubber tubes wrapped around a corpse. They live within the proletariat, their force is in the proletariats' and their power lay in this perfect adhesion.[24]

We have seen how libertarian themes permeated Gramsci's thought even before the Council Communist phase of 1919–1920. His socialism was anti-statist. He was suspicious and on guard against the creation of a socialist hierarchy: he was against Jacobinical socialism. He promoted socialism grounded in civil society and prefiguration. But he was also ill at ease with syndicalist workerist arguments concerning socialist and working-class movements. But neither should the socialist leadership patronise or order about the rank and file, flaunting their well-developed consciousness over the less well-educated grass roots. However, that did not mean that conscious socialists did not have a duty to educate the movement. And it was over the question of education and the anarchist concept of 'free thought' and the 'free thinker' that Gramsci engaged in his most extended theoretical debate with the anarchists before his clashes during the Factory Council Movement of 1919–1920.

## Free thought and educated thought

Turin, Gramsci argued, lacked a cultural organisation controlled by and acting on behalf of workers. The *Università Popolare* was, he felt, a purely bourgeois humanitarian venture. In contrast, his proposed Association of

Culture would supply trained intellectuals suitably socialised for adequate tasks within the socialist movement, to help workers in their struggles. Although he did not quote Robert Michels directly, he was certainly thinking of his pre-war study of German socialism, particularly Michels' description of the ways in which rootless intellectuals became the object of an unhealthy hero worship within the movement.[25] Gramsci equated the authoritarianism of the movement with the generally low level of education enjoyed by the rank and file of the Italian socialist movement.

Against Michels, he argued that an Italian socialist party, filled with educated comrades, would be sustainably democratic and libertarian because it would function through the spontaneous rationality he detected in the micro-institutions (such as the Clubs of Moral Life, the suburban circles and newspaper editorial groups) in which he was involved in these first years of socialist activism.

Gramsci's conception of socialist education and culture was democratic, participatory and libertarian, but it had little in common with the rationalist free thought that dominated socialist and anarchist political culture in Liberal Italy.[26] Gramsci believed that fuzzy-minded rationalist free thought played into the hands of the fickle and bombastic leadership of the pre-war Italian Socialist Party, because it denied the rank-and-file critical faculties to control this leadership. An educated party would be more democratic and libertarian because it would function through a spontaneous 'socratic' rationality acquired in such micro-institutions as the 'Clubs of Moral Life'.

For Gramsci, the educators could not be found among the pre-war leaders of the socialist movement – Enrico Ferri, Filippo Turati or Claudio Treves – since they had been corrupted by positivist social thought and shared with working-class popular culture, including anarchist culture, the misleading assumptions of free thought. During the war Gramsci drew these concerns together in a vitriolic attack on the favourite shibboleth of pre-war anarchism and socialism: Esperanto. Esperanto was prominent at the *Università Popolare* and among the anarchists, for example, Tolstoy.

Gramsci's attacks on Esperanto highlighted an aspect of Gramsci's training as a very promising student of linguistics at the University of Turin.[27] Umberto Cosmo, his professor of linguistics at the University of Turin, had taught him that languages were unique representations of national or regional culture; thus he dismissed Esperanto as nonsense, and argued that the attachment to Esperanto by Italian anarchists and socialists merely represented an artificial form of cosmopolitanism that was likely to prevent Italian socialism from developing a realistic form of internationalism.[28] Yet Gramsci's savaging of Esperanto was just part and parcel of the broader syndrome known as 'free thought', his chief target, which he associated with the intellectual weakness of anarchist and socialist culture in Italy.

As a follower of both Croce and Sorel, who were well known for their attacks on masonic free thought, it is not surprising that Gramsci would be extremely hostile to one of the Italian Left's most long-cherished beliefs.[29] In March 1918 Gramsci's ideal typical Free-Thinker happened to be the anarchist editor of Milan's *L'Università Popolare*, Luigi Molinari, who had published in pamphlet form, a lecture he gave in 1917 on the Paris Commune (*Il dramma della Comune*), which Gramsci thought was a perfect example of the culture of free thought.[30] Gramsci received a drubbing in the anarchist press, but in response to Molinari's final rejoinder (he died soon after) Gramsci revealed a deeper argument which lifted the debate from personalities and particulars to high theory.

In 'Libero Pensiero and Pensiero Libero' ('Free Thought and Liberated Thought'),[31] Molinari's world-view is characterised as 'libero pensiero' ('free thought'): a philistine, bourgeois expression associated with Jacobin individualism – an association 'that', Gramsci writes, explains 'why we find grouped around it Freemasons, Radicals and...libertarians'. Free thought was equated with pre-war *bloccardismo* (the front that included the socialists and the free thought radicals, liberals and libertarians). In contrast, his Marxist 'pensiero libero' ('liberated thought') was a form of libertarian historicism that broke with this tradition and looked to Benedetto Croce and Antonio Labriola for its inspiration.

Gramsci advanced the opinion that the anarchists, or at least their leaders and theoreticians, were less libertarian than the Marxist socialists of the anti-positivist historicist stamp because they were incapable of thinking critically: 'historistically', and dialectically, digesting contradictory arguments and enriching their own thought by overcoming them. He argued: 'in as much as the libertarians are intolerant dogmatists, slaves to their own particular opinions', they 'sterilize' debate with their petty arguments'.[32]

The debate with Molinari also reveals that the mental apparatus behind that key couplet found in the *Notebooks* (1929–1935) – *senso comune* (common sense as naïve sense) and *buon senso* ('good sense' meaning educated and critical sense) – was already present by 1918 in the contrast between *pensiero libero* and *libero pensiero*.[33] Anti-positivist historicist socialism is imbued with *buon senso* and *libero pensiero* whereas, 'subversive', immature socialists and anarchists (even if they might argue between themselves about the need for the state) shared assumptions which reflected their banal culture of *senso comune* and *pensiero libero*. Such mindsets could never create counter-hegemony, which would lay the foundations for a new workers' state and in turn this culture shared much with the superstitious folkways of the powerless subaltern classes.

Thus Gramsci's encounters with the free thinkers helped more clearly to define his unique position within Italian socialist political culture. At his best, on the one hand he refused to accept a patronising spoon-feeding of culture to the working classes, and on the other he refused to be hoodwinked by a simple-minded celebration of populism, the provincial and the parochial. His conclusion was that the workers needed to master the humanist and scientific codes of educated Italy in order to develop the mental equipment and self-confidence to challenge the ruling classes and the threat of the 'dictatorship' of the socialist professors within the Italian Socialist party.[34] Having said this, there is more than a dose of authoritarian condescension in Gramsci's remedies. Gramsci dismissed Molinari's efforts at vulgarisation, but Molinari's efforts in the fields of science and history for over 20 years had been enormously influential among the less educated socialists and trade unionists.[35]

Gramsci's type of socialism was more libertarian than Lenin's scientific socialism, but it too assumed that an elite of educated socialists was needed to set the tone and parameters for effective politics. Furthermore, although Gramsci was prepared to work with and argue against the anarchists and syndicalists in a more tolerant and engaging manner than Lenin had done, nevertheless his attitude did have some similarities with Lenin's vigilant guardianship of orthodoxy. Lenin's orthodoxy was his version of Second Internationalist gospel – Gramsci's odd mixture of Gentile, Croce, Sorel and Antonio Labriola may have made him appear wildly unorthodox to other Italian socialists, but this did not prevent Gramsci from invoking ortho-doxy when he discussed the potential for the formation of political alliances with the libertarians. In fact, in order to expose the muddleheaded nature of Italian positivist socialism, he argued that his approach was more Marxist and therefore more rigid in its conditions for accepting alliances with the libertarians than the mainstream socialists. As we have seen, Gramsci argued that the culture of free thought had defined the pre-war socialists and the libertarians and that his form of socialism transcended this murk and thus there was always a limit to the alliances with anarchists and syndicalists of which Gramsci was willing to countenance.

## Gramsci and the anarchists: the barriers to alliances

During the war a new international Left arose from a fortuitous combina-tion of formerly mutually hostile groups: some were pacifist, some social democrat, some anarchists or syndicalist.[36] Intellectuals and journalists such as Henri Barbusse, Romain Rolland, Jacques Mesnil and Max Eastman trans-mitted ideas from one part of the network to another, sustained by reportage in *Avanti!*, *L'Humanité*, the *Liberator* or the *Workers' Dreadnought*, by pri-vate correspondence, but above all by the imagery and myths surrounding international conferences at Zimmerwald and Kienthal, as well as over the controversies stirred by the never convened Stockholm Congress, called by the Petrograd Soviet in 1917.

While politicians and intellectuals attempted to mould mass movements from the initial radicalisation of 1916–1918, differences quickly reappeared. Gramsci's debate with the anarchists and syndicalists is symptomatic of a broader story played out against the backdrop of events unfolding in Russia.

But his peculiar theoretical background presents an interesting variation on a continental, indeed global, theme.

For the young Gramsci, the bustling working-class suburbs of Turin were proletarian unity-in-action and one of its earliest manifestations was the march of the suburbanites on the bourgeois centre during the Red Week of 1914, when anarchists, syndicalists, left-wing socialists and republicans united in a quasi-insurrectionary movement against militarism and the Italian monarchy. Recalling the events of 1914 in an article of 1916, Gramsci remembered how 'our city made through military order and tradition', a city centre of looming piles of aristocratic townhouses, arrayed 'like a regiment of the army of their old Savoyard Dukes', witnessed the march past of well-ordered proletarian ranks.[37] 'Coarse men descended on the city boulevards and marched in front of the closed shop shutters, past the pale little men of the city police who were consumed by anger and fear.'[38]

These Sorelian images of the gruff, productive working class marching from its suburban strongholds to challenge the clerical or parasitical café society were present in much of Gramsci's writings.[39]

However, Gramsci opposed politically inspired united fronts of socialists and anarchists in Turin or nationally. Between 1916 and early 1918, Gramsci took part in a debate in the Italian socialist press on this subject, sparked off by the private and public exchanges of the anarchist Luigi Fabbri and the leading maximalist socialist Giacinto Menotti Serrati, as well as other discussion between anti-war anarchists, syndicalists and socialists.[40] Fabbri was inspired by a letter from Errico Malatesta to Armando Borghi (the anarchist leader of the *Unione Sindacale Italiana* (USI)) written from his exile in London, which proposed a new international (*La Mondiale*) that would include anti-war socialists, anarchists and syndicalists. It would heal the schism caused by the expulsion of the libertarians from the Second International in 1896 but would have had little in common with the militarised disciplined organisation that Lenin would found in 1919.

Gramsci contested the commonly held opinion in the Italian socialist Left that anarchists or syndicalists were more revolutionary and 'purer' socialists than the socialist themselves. Gramsci also wanted to distance his socialism from the anarchists' heterodoxy. Here he argued that the antiparliamentarianism of Malatesta and the anarchists posed an obstacle to formal unity and, recalling his arguments against Free Thought, that their mentality was ahistorical and doctrinaire. International organisations such as Malatesta's *La Mondiale* undermined Gramsci's prefigurative conception of socialist politics. The concept of prefiguration may have evolved in Gramsci's theory by 1917, before he encountered the Soviet model, but his type of prefiguration, while not Leninist, was still linked to a well-organised and distinctive socialist party, though this was a party not founded on the culture of free thought or positivist socialism. Rather, the consensual discipline of a party based on the educational principles of Gramsci's 'clubs of moral life', linked to the creativity of prefigurative institutions such as the co-operatives, would produce a distinctive socialist politics.

## The early Gramsci and the Gramsci of the *Biennio Rosso*

I have argued that just as Gramsci's key conceptions were already operating in his mind before 1918, his attitudes towards the anarchists and syndicalists were already operationalised before he worked closely with them in *L'Ordine nuovo*. Thus Gramsci's thought before his encounter with Lenin did not signal a break between a libertarian and an authoritarian viewpoint; rather, his youthful 'libertarianism' was based on first premises, which tended towards a critique of the ideologies of anarchism and syndicalism, even if superficially he seemed close to these camps. Thus, as I have shown elsewhere, anarchist 'organic intellectuals' were cultivated but anarchist 'traditional intellectuals', the friends and colleagues of Molinari, were denounced as muddled demagogues; anarchist workers as organically tied to the point of production, could be saved from their misguided ideas, anarchist ideologues were beyond redemption. Just as the Sorelian and productivist legacies were so important to catalyse Gramsci's prefigurative and civil-society-based socialism of pre-1917–1918, his Council Communism of 1919–1920 was merely a variation on this theme reinforced by international examples. The libertarian productivist Taylorism of the anarchist engineer Pietro Mosso was the lynchpin, which held together the Council Communism of 1919–1920; meanwhile anarchist metalworkers in FIOM (the socialist engineers and metalworkers union) were essential to propagate the ideas of *L'Ordine Nuovo* throughout the movement in its Turinese industrial heartland. When Gramsci fell out with his colleagues, Angelo Tasca and then Palmiro Togliatti in 1920, over the boundaries between the trade union and factory council, his only remaining allies were the anarchists.[41] The arguments Gramsci advanced in the early war years were merely repeated and placed in a more super-charged and propitious atmosphere, the vehicle of prefiguration – the factory council came into its own, even if the theory was fleshed out in his discussion of co-operatives in 1916.

One benchmark did change, however, and is a clue to his uncritical acceptance of Lenin's way, even after his earlier misinterpretation of Lenin (temporary, necessary charismatic *capo* of a system of soviets and workers' councils) seemed to be discredited by the reality: Lenin as the dictator of a monopoly party-state. The change in his attitude towards Jacobinism is linked to his criticism of masonic free thought, which reformist socialists, most maximalist socialists and the anarchists all suffered from. Gramsci's evaluation of Jacobinism changed drastically from the war years to 1920.[42]

At first Jacobinism was not used in the context of Russian politics, but that of pre-war Italian political culture. He used it in the same breath as his invocation of Sorel's and Croce's attacks on the culture of Masonic Free

Thought. Jacobinism 'is a messianic vision of history: it always responds in abstractions, evil, good, oppression, liberty, light, shade, which exist absolutely, generically and not in historical forms'.[43] In other words, like Free Thought, Jacobinism lacked grounding in historicism.

But by 1920 he associated Jacobinism with Paris heroically seeing off the internal and external enemies of the Revolution, and finding a parallel in the Bolsheviks' civil and foreign wars with the myriad enemies of their new state.[44] Jacobinism took on another positive, different valence when Gramsci approached the question of the city and the countryside in Italy (in various and indeed contradictory forms appearing in his essay on the Southern Question, his approach to the New Economic Policy (NEP) and even War Communism and later forced collectivisation). Jacobins were then cast as pitiless against the enemies of the revolution but also strengthened by forming alliances with those elements in the countryside willing to accept the political hegemony of the Bolsheviks as the representatives of the urban working-class. Similarly, in the mid-1920s Gramsci argued for the hegemony of the Italian Communist Party over peasant, syndicalist or autonomist movements in the south, not for an open-ended co-operative support for competitors in the rural Left: he was not a pluralist. His early mistaken praise of Chernov was replaced by venomous attacks on the Socialist Revolutionaries and Makhno's 'anarchist experiment' in Civil-War Ukraine.[45] The anti-Jacobinical socialism of pre-1918 and the negative interpretation of the Jacobins he learned from Croce, Salvemini or Sorel was replaced by a praise of the Jacobins' rigour and their successful linkage to the 'healthy' forces in the countryside. No longer socially divorced pedants, arid ideological fanatics or the imbibers of shallow anti-clerical positivist nostrums, Jacobins were the models for the creative but implacable Bolshevik elite. Gramsci did not abandon this revision before his death in 1937, even if he probably agreed that Stalin had become a cruel tyrant, a Genghis Khan with a telephone, as Bukharin, his former ally in the 1920s, described him.

As Gramsci endorsed all things Bolshevik, particularly the Twenty-One Points, he became increasingly militantly anti-anarchist. However, throughout the early 1920s, he was placed in a tactical dilemma. Before the Kronstadt rebellion, the suppression of all factions in the Russian Communist Party, and the failure of negotiations between various syndicalist trade unions and the Comintern, Gramsci had to tread carefully. While he mercilessly criticised the leadership of the USI, he could not burn all his bridges, since the Russians saw merit in cultivating the Italian anarchists and syndicalists, especially when a pro-Comintern faction was formed in the USI itself. In Turin his anarchist allies were marginalised in FIOM after the occupation of the factories and some were murdered by the Fascists in late 1922, but before the March on Rome, and indeed until 1925–1926, Gramsci saw the advantage in keeping feelers open to the social interventionist Left, Gabriele D'Annunzio and even briefly with the suspiciously libertarian *Arditi del Popolo*, the only anti-Fascist militia in these years which caused Mussolini and the Fascists some concern. But while Gramsci and his comrades maintained a non-stop tirade against the 'child-like' antics of Malatesta and Borghi, Zinoviev and even Lenin, recognised in Malatesta a revolutionary and in Borghi a man to be wooed in Moscow. Gramsci reverted to the same twin-track approach he used in 1916 – organic intellectual anarchists good, 'traditional' intellectual anarchists bad – and chose to finesse the tactical cunning of the Russians as much as possible.[46]

## Anarchism as the highest form of *sovversivismo*[47]

In the *Notebooks*, Gramsci engaged in historical and comparative sociological examination of the modern world and particularly the collapse of liberal Italy and the destruction of the Left within it. Thus the nature of Italian Fascism and its enduring success was the red thread, which ran throughout his notes. The failure of the Left *and* the triumph of Fascism and its transformation of the Italian state were understood through the term *sovversivismo*. This term may be taken as a tool of historical and sociological analysis, but it is drenched with highly partisan political first premises that assume that Gramsci's historicist Marxism offered a master-key for unlocking the secrets of the past as well as the solutions for the future. He may have been writing his notes for eternity, and it is unlikely he would have sanctioned their publication in the form they were produced, but he certainly had not left his politics at the cell door. Even if there was good deal of frustration and perhaps justifiable paranoia about party comrades and the murderous ways of the Georgian tyrant, he was still a militant Marxist who wrote in such a spirit.[48] The troubling aspect of Gramsci's historicising Marxism is that mere empiricism and 'information' is looked upon as the greatest of mortal sins. In short, unlike the rather inelegant, plodding notes of Angelo Tasca on utopian socialism and anarchism that are deposited in Milan's *Biblioteca Feltrinelli*, for example, Gramsci did not let facts get in the way of theory.[49]

Gramsci was less concerned with an in-depth account of the anarchists and syndicalists, more in using them in his construction of the all-purpose analytical term *sovversivismo*. But this had been honed from his debates with the anarchists and syndicalists before 1922, and bore all the traces of a political term of art or an artifice of historicist metaphysics. Just as detailed knowledge of the factory councils and soviets and the Bolsheviks did not prevent Gramsci from creating a fantastically libertarian Lenin in the early years of the Russian regime, lack of detailed analysis of the anarchists and syndicalists before 1926 in Italy did not prevent him from shoe-horning them into his neat and politically charged term, *sovversivismo*. This is frustrating, because the term certainly has its uses as a tool to interrogate that anarchist past, but as a provisional probe, an ideal-type, not as a form of political abuse.

For Gramsci, the Italian concept of the subversive and *sovversivismo* were based on a populist positioning of the people pitched against the ill-defined *signori*. This *sovversivismo* was a product of Italy's bastard modernity. Subversives could come from the Left and Right, and there was even a *sovversivismo* from above. Subversives could be reversible, as was the case of the social interventionists, who interested Gramsci when he was a newspaper editor in Turin in 1921 and 1922. Thus, Gramsci argued, a lack of modern political institutions, a weak ethical political culture and an incorrect reading of Marxism or social theory, especially among the anarchist and syndicalist subversives, characterised these currents. The touchstone of Gramsci's early radicalism, the Red Week of 1914, and Malatesta, one of its leaders, became symbolic of this 'subversive' type of Italian radicalism. But the ghost at this banquet was his gaoler, and Gramsci felt this personally, for he had been drawn into politics partially by the socialist and 'Stirnerite' Mussolini, and he almost spoiled his copy book by his torturous flirtations with Mussolini's war interventionism in 1914.[50]

*Sovversivismo*, Gramsci argued, had fed off the role of volunteers from the *Risorgimento* and the example of Garibaldi and 'the Thousand' toppling the Bourbon Kingdom and setting in train the Piedmont conquest of the peninsula. The anarchists were merely one variation on this theme, which included the republicans but also of course the Fascist militia of the early 1920s. The Italian state was also nourished by reformed *sovversivi* from Crispi to Mussolini. So, Gramsci concluded that the dependence on charismatic politics, reflected in the political culture of anarchist and socialist leaders of pre-Fascist Italy, demonstrated the low level of education of the Italian people and weakly constructed institutions of the socialist and labour movement.

But contrary to Gramsci's generalisations, Italian anarchists such as Errico Malatesta were well aware of the dangers of hero worship.[51] Malatesta preached organisation, organisation and more organisation. Anarchism, Malatesta argued, was not about the lack of organisation, which was essential if anarchists were serious about dealing with the exigencies of the modern industrial city. He may have been naïve, but Malatesta pleaded with the factory occupiers in 1920 to recommence trade with other factories without the aid of the capitalist system. For Gramsci, the lesson one learned from the factory occupations was that 'the spontaneity in the factory council movement was not neglected, even less despised. It was *educated*, directed, purged of extraneous contamination; the aim was to bring it into line with modern theory.'[52] But nowhere in Gramsci do we find an open acknowledgement of the authoritarianism of 'modern theory' (communism) and possibility that socialism had failed to take another more libertarian path in the way the tarnished Tasca (he was accused of collaboration with Vichy France during the Second World War) did in the preface to his postwar edition of his wonderful history of the rise of Fascism, where he invoked the libertarian potential of the pre-Fascist Chambers of Labour.[53] When Gramsci recalled another exemplar of Italian grass roots socialism, the factory councils, their most important contribution was not their inherent democracy, but their contribution to 'modern theory'.

One can flesh-out a Gramscian critique of the Stalinist Soviet Union but he never questioned the Marxist monopoly of legitimate thought and action and he never even granted the anarchists the title of gadflies of the revolution, their warnings about the untrammelled powers of the new Soviet state were never accepted by Gramsci even in his deepest pessimistic moments, because their way of thinking was alien to his very being.

## Conclusion: Gramsci in the twenty-first century

Much of this chapter has been an exercise in historical reconstruction. However, it is not without its contemporary applications. For the anarchist Richard Day Gramsci is dead because the politics of hegemony can have no place in the alter-globalisation movement.[54] Day argues that the concept of hegemony in both its international relations realist and Gramscian interpretations share a similar attachment to the state as prime actor. Day's book is inspired by aspects of post-anarchism, which disowns the concept of the revolutionary moment and draws on the maverick classical anarchist Gustav Landauer's earlier formulation of anarchism.[55] Day's proposals involve changes in personal relations, in casting out the spooks in our heads and starting to build anarchism at the interpersonal level, or as the recently deceased British anarchist Colin Ward argued,[56] creating reformist projects, which undermine the solidity of state power, or, to paraphrase another alter-globaliser, 'change the world without taking power'.[57] But this is different to creating counter-hegemony: the building of an alternative form of hegemony involves state formation or reformation. Gramsci would not have disagreed with Day's criticism, he would have embraced it: libertarian tools in the Gramscian intellectual toolkit were used to create a new state and not to abolish state power, at least until some distant point in the future when the state would be replaced by the rather disturbing sounding formulation in the *Quaderni*, 'regulated society'.

Another aspect of Gramsci's thought is relevant to an encounter between varieties of post-anarchism, post-colonialism, post-modernism, Gramsci and the 'classical anarchists'. If the concept of hegemony has launched a thousand academic Gramscian boats since the 1960s, the term subaltern, used by the self-same school of studies from the Indian subcontinent and present of course in the work of the Palestinian American Edward Said, revived the study of Gramsci, so that after 1989 and the fall of State Communism, Gramscian studies outside of Italy did not miss a heartbeat, while the increasingly moribund conditions of Gramscian studies inside Italy experienced a renaissance through the importation of cultural and post-colonial studies, which in turn had been supercharged by this rearranged 'diasporic Gramsci'.[58] As I mentioned in the introduction, even if the recent popularity of the concept of the subaltern in Gramsci is not without its problems, because it is unclear whether Gramsci uses this term as a synonym for the Italian male working-class, for those at the margins of society (women, minorities and poor peasants) or merely as the *lumpenproletariat*, a certain reading might allow one to interrogate Italian anarchist culture and history more sympathetically – although this may merely be Gramsci's elaborate reworking of a mode of reasoning already evident in his early polemics with Luigi Molinari and the 'subversive' advocates of Esperanto.

Gramsci is also attractive to modern thought because of his post-positivist position. The theoretical foundations of Gramsci's voluntarism are in sharp contrast to the determinism of Lenin's social thought. Lenin's political activism was informed by the problem of power, how to seize and conserve it.[59] Lenin was a political voluntarist of the first order, but his social thought never left the straitjacket of the most rule-bound 'scientific socialism', except perhaps in the late *Philosophical Notebooks*. Indeed Lenin spent an inordinate amount of time throughout his life stamping out a bewildering variety of 'heresies', which threatened his love affair with 'scientific socialism': monists, 'God-builders' and infantile communists were all chosen targets.[60] Unorthodox and ruthless in seizing and holding power, his political thought was perhaps more rule-bound and orthodox than his fallen idols', Kautsky and Plekhanov. It should be remembered that in 1916 and 1917 Lenin (and Bukharin) argued that historical time could be sped up precisely because of the emergence of a new stage of history: world war that flowed from the imperialist capitalist stage of historical development sanctioned his anarchist-like heretical political behaviour in the spring of 1917. But it did not sanction a rethinking of the orthodox Marxism he had mentally ingested before 1914 – the Marxism of historical stages was never disavowed, imperialism was merely the highest stage of capitalism, which sanctioned anarchist-like direct action on the part of the scientific Bolsheviks. Karl Kautsky was a 'social traitor' because he had betrayed his political principles, not because their mutually shared theory of scientific socialism was incorrect.

Gramsci's approach was different. He read Lenin through his own synthesis of Italian neo-idealist voluntarism, which owed more to Giovanni Gentile and Georges Sorel than early twentieth-century orthodox Marxism. Indeed Gramsci's first lengthy analysis of the Bolshevik Revolution was titled the 'The Revolution Against Capital', that is, Marx's *Das Kapital*.[61] Thus this anti-capitalist revolution was also a theoretical revolution against the positivist encrustations, which had enveloped Marxism and implicitly might have tarnished the master himself. In Italy reformist and maximalist socialists were outraged by this article and Gramsci earned an unsavoury reputation as a Bergsonian, which just reinforced a general suspicion about his soundness due to his earlier flirtation with the pro-war interventionism of the former *Duce* of Italian maximalist socialism, Benito Mussolini. In this case, Gramsci's behaviour might have been understandable to Lenin,[62] who liked to shape events, not to be the passive recipient of beneficial outcomes; Gramsci, it can be argued, thought that socialists could not be above the fray in a world historical event such as world war, without becoming utterly marginalised. Indeed, the Italian Socialist Party ended by taking a confusing temporising position, which ill-prepared it for the tumultuous *Biennio Rosso* (1919–1920).

However, if we turn the telescope around and imagine a counterfactual history in which Gramsci had encountered Lenin's Marxist orthodoxy *before* he had successfully piloted the Bolsheviks to state power, Gramsci would have certainly had a dim if not sarcastic reaction to it. Therefore in 1917 and 1918 Lenin was a fantastical projection of Gramsci's radicalism, not the flesh and blood Lenin in command of the new Soviet state. In the *Quaderni* Lenin is praised as the prime innovator of the concept of hegemony. While this had led many commentators (most famously Perry Anderson)[63] to discount the myriad sources of the concept and essence of hegemony,[64] which preceded Gramsci's deepening knowledge of Russian Marxism during his sojourn in the Soviet Union in the early 1920s, the 'young' and 'mature' Gramsci both thought Lenin's most important contribution to the theory of Marxism was Lenin's actions in the autumn of 1917, action not thought, which is equated to the Marxian conception of praxis. Whether this is an accurate description of what Marx meant by praxis is questionable: at the end of the day it seems a case of the old adage of 'nothing succeeds like success'. Gramsci's Gentilean actualism, his politics of pragmatism, were finessed by verbal acrobatics, which were never adequately reconciled with his grander version of what he called the philosophy of praxis. The disjunction between his political thought and the model, which proved successful in actually gaining power in the Soviet Union, would threaten the coherence of his project for the rest of his life.[65]

## Notes

1. Michelle Maggi, *La filosofia della rivoluzione. Gramsci, la cultura e la guerra Europea* (Rome: Edizione di storia letteratura, 2008).
2. Carl Boggs, *Gramsci's Marxism* (London: Pluto Press, 1976).
3. Richard Bellamy and Darrow Schecter, *Gramsci and the Italian State* (Manchester: Manchester University Press, 1993).
4. Carl Levy, ' "*Sovversivismo*": The Radical Political Culture of Otherness in Liberal Italy', *Journal of Political Ideologies*, 20.2 (2007), pp. 147–161.
5. Peter Stallybrass, 'Marx and Heterogeneity: Theorizing the Lumpenproletariat', *Representations*, 32 (1990), pp. 69–95.
6. Marcus Green, 'Gramsci Cannot Speak: Deconstruction and Interpretation of Gramsci's Concept of the Subaltern', *Rethinking Marxism*, 13.1 (2001): pp. 1–24; K. Crehan, *Gramsci, Culture and Anthropology* (London: Pluto Press, 2002); K. Smith

'Gramsci at the Margins: Subjectivity and Subalternity as a Theory of Hegemony', *International Gramsci Journal*, 2 (April 2010), pp. 39–50.

7. Eric Hobsbawm, *Primitive Rebels: Studies in Archaic Forms of Social Movement in the 19th and 20th Centuries* (Manchester: Manchester University Press, 1959).

8. Paul Thomas, *Karl Marx and the Anarchists* (London: Routledge & Kegan Paul, 1980).

9. Carl Levy, 'Gramsci's Cultural and Political Sources: Anarchism in the Prison Writings', *Journal of Romance Studies*, 22.3 (2012).

10. Carl Levy, 'A New Look at the Young Gramsci', *Boundary 2*, 24.3 (1986), pp. 31–48; Carl Levy, *Gramsci and the Anarchists* (Oxford and New York: Berg/NYU Press, 1999).

11. Paul Piccone, 'From Spaventa to Gramsci', *Telos*, 31 (1977), pp. 35–66.

12. Darrow Schecter, 'Two Views of Revolution: Gramsci and Sorel, 1916–1920', *History of European Ideas*, 22 (1990), pp. 636–653; Darrow Schecter, *Gramsci and the Theory of Industrial Democracy* (Aldershot: Ashgate, 1991), Levy, *Gramsci*.

13. Antonio Gramsci, *Pre-Prison Writings*, edited by Richard Bellamy (Cambridge: Cambridge University Press, 1994), p. 15.

14. Carl Levy, '"The Rooted Cosmopolitan": Errico Malatesta, Syndicalism, Transnationalism and the International Labour Movement' in David Berry & Constance Bantman (eds.) *New Perspectives on Anarchism, Labour & Syndicalism: The Individual, the National and the Transnational* (Newcastle: Cambridge Scholars Press, 2010), pp. 61–79.

15. L. Michelini, 'Antonio Gramsci e il liberismo italiano (1913–1919)' in F. Giasi (ed.) *Gramsci e il suo tempo*, Vol. 1 (Rome: Carocci, 2008), pp. 175–196.

16. Antonio Gramsci, *Il nostro Marx: 1918–1919*, edited by Sergio Caprioglio (Turin: Einaudi, 1980), pp. 236–237.

17. C. Natoli, 'Grande Guerra e rinnovamento del socialismo negli scritti del giovane Gramsci (1914–1918)' in F. Giasi (ed.) *Gramsci e il suo tempo*, Vol. 1 (Rome: Carocci, 2008), pp. 51–76.

18. Antonio Gramsci, *La città futura: 1917–1918*, edited by Sergio Caprioglio (Turin: Einaudi, 1980).

19. Nicola Badaloni, *Il Marxismo di Gramsci: dal mito alla ricomposizione politica* (Turin: Einaudi, 1975).

20. J. J. Roth, *The Cult of Violence. Sorel and the Sorelians* (Berkeley: University of California Press, 1980).

21. G. Morabito, 'Antonio Gramsci e l'idealismo giuridico italiano. Due tesi a confronto', *Storia e politica*, 6.4 (1979), pp. 744–755.

22. Antonio Gramsci, *Cronache torinesi*, edited by S. Caprioglio (Turin: Einaudi, 1980), pp. 99–103.

23. F. Lucarini, 'Socialismo, riformismo e scienze sociali nella Torino del giovane Gramsci (1914–21)' in F. Giasi (ed.) *Gramsci e il suo tempo* (Rome: Carocci, 2008), pp. 219–240.

24. Gramsci, *La città futura*, p. 332.

25. Ibid., p. 498; Carl Levy, 'The People and the Professors: Socialism and the Educated Middle Classes in Italy, 1870–1914', *Journal of Modern Italian Studies*, 4.2 (2001), pp. 205–208.

26. P. Audenino, 'Non più eterni iloti: valori e modelli della pedogogia socialista' in L. Rossi (ed.) *Cultura, istruzione e socialismo nell'età giolittiana* (Milan: Franco Angeli, 1991), pp. 37–54.

27. F. Lo Piparo, *Lingua intellettuali egemonia in Gramsci* (Bari: Laterza, 1979); Peter Ives, *Gramsci's Politics of Language. Engaging the Bakhtin Circle & the Frankfurt School* (Toronto: University of Toronto Press, 2004); Peter Ives, *Language and Hegemony in Gramsci* (London: Pluto, 2004); F. Lussana & G. Pissarello (eds.) *La lingua/le lingue di Gramsci e delle sue opera. Scrittura, riscritture, letture in Italia e nel mondo* (Soveria Mannelli: Rubbettino, 2008); P. Ives & R. Lacorte (eds), *Gramsci, Language and Translation* (Lanham, MD: Lexington Books, 2010).

28. G. Fiori, *Antonio Gramsci: Life of a Revolutionary* (London: NLB, 1970), pp. 74–75, 93, 104, 113: G. Bergami, *Il giovane Gramsci e il marxismo: 1911–1918* (Milan: Feltrinelli, 1977), pp. 70, 92.

29. G.B. Furiozzi, *Sorel e l'Italia* (Florence: D'Anna, 1975).

30. Gramsci, *La città futura*, pp. 751–752.

31. Gramsci, *Il nostro Marx*, pp. 113–117.

32. Ibid., pp. 113–114.

33. A. M. Cirese, 'Gramsci's Observations on Folklore' in A. Showstack Sassoon (ed.) *Approaches to Gramsci* (London: Writers and Readers Publishing Co-operative, 1982), pp. 212–247; J. Nun, 'Elements for a Theory of Democracy: Gramsci and Common Sense', *Boundary 2*, 14.3 (1986), pp. 197–230; M. Green and P. Ives, 'Subalternity and Language: Overcoming the Fragmentation of Common Sense', *Historical Materialism*, 17.3 (2009), pp. 3–30; G. Liguori, 'Common Sense in Gramsci' in J. Francese (ed.) *Perspectives on Gramsci. Politics, Culture and Social Theory* (London: Routledge, 2009), pp. 122–133.

34. Levy, 'The People and the Professors'; Deb Hill, *Hegemony and Education. Gramsci, Post-Marxism and Radical Democracy Revisited* (Lanham, MD: Lexington Books, 2007).

35. L. Zanardi, *Luigi Molinari. La Parola, l'azione, il pensiero* (Mantua: Sometti, 2003).

36. For overviews see, A. S. Lindemann, '*The Red Years': European Socialism and Bolshevism, 1919–1921* (Berkeley: University of California Press, 1974); D. Kirby, *War, Peace and Revolution. International Socialism at the Crossroads 1914–1918* (London/Aldershot: Gower, 1986); C. Levy, 'Anarchism, Internationalism and Nationalism in Europe, 1860–1939', *Australian Journal of Politics and History*, 50.3 (2004), pp. 330–342; R. Darlington, *Syndicalism and the Transition to Communism. An International Comparative Analysis* (Aldershot: Ashgate, 2008).

37. Levy, *Gramsci*, pp. 94–99.

38. Gramsci, *Cronache torinesi*, pp. 76–77.

39. Levy, *Gramsci*, pp. 63–118.

40. Ibid., pp. 102–103.

41. M. Clark, *Antonio Gramsci and the Revolution that Failed* (New Haven: Yale University Press, 1977).

42. Levy, *Gramsci*, pp. 197–206; R. Medici, 'Giacobinismo' in F. Frosini & G. Liguori (eds.) *Le parole di Gramsci. Per un lessico di Quardern del Carcere*, Vol. 1 (Rome: Carocci, 2004), pp. 112–130; R. Shilliam, 'Jacobinism: The Ghost in the Gramscian Machine of Counter-Hegemony' in A.J. Ayers (ed.) *Gramsci, Political Economy and International Relations Theory. Modern Princes and Naked Emperors* (Basingstoke: Palgrave Macmillan, 2008), pp. 189–208.

43. Gramsci, *Il nostro Marx*, p. 149.

44. I. Tognarini, 'Giacobinismo e bolschevismo: Albert Malthiez e l'Ordine Nuovo', *Ricerche storiche*, 6 (1976), pp. 523–549.

45. L. Paggi, *Le strategie del potere in Gramsci* (Rome: Riuniti, 1984).

46. Levy, *Gramsci*, pp. 221–228.
47. Levy, ' "*Sovversivismo*" '.
48. F. Benvenuti & S. Pons (eds), 'L'Unione Sovietica nei *Quarderni del Carcere*' in G. Vacca (ed.) *Gramsci e il novecento* (Rome: Carcocci, 1999), pp. 93–124; A. Kolpakidi & J. Leontiev, 'Il peccato originale: Antonio Gramsci e la fondazione del PCd'I' in S. Bertelli & F. Bigazzi (eds.) *P.C.I. La storia dimentica* (Milan: Arnaldo Mondadori, 2001), pp. 25–60; A. Rossi & G. Vacca, *Gramsci tra Mussolini e Stalin* (Rome: Fazi, 2007); E. Saccarelli, *Gramsci and Trotsky in the Shadow of Stalin. The Political Theory and Practice of Opposition* (London: Routledge, 2008).
49. G. Berti (ed.), ' "Problemi del movimento operaio". Scritti critiche e storiche inediti di Angelo Tasca', *Annali della Biblioteca G.G. Feltrinelli*, X (1968), pp. viii–721; S. Soave, 'Gramsci e Tasca' in F. Giasi (ed.) *Gramsci nel suo tempo*, Vol. 1 (Rome: Carocci, 2008), pp. 99–125.
50. Levy, 'Gramsci, Anarchism'.
51. Carl Levy, 'Charisma and Social Movements: Errico Malatesta and Italian Anarchism', *Modern Italy*, 3.2 (1998), pp. 205–217.
52. Antonio Gramsci, *Quaderni del carcere*, Vol. 1 (Turin: Einaudi, 1975), p. 330.
53. A. Tasca, *Nascita e avvento del fascismo* (Florence: Le Monnier, 1950), Preface.
54. Richard J. F. Day, *Gramsci Is Dead. Anarchist Currents in the Newest Social Movements* (London: Pluto Press, 2005).
55. Gustav Landauer, *Revolution and Other Writings. A Political Reader*, edited and translated by G. Kuhn (Oakland: PM Press, 2010).
56. Colin Ward, *Anarchy in Action* (London: Allen & Unwin, 1973); S. White, 'Making Anarchism Respectable: The Social Philosophy of Colin Ward', *Journal of Political Ideologies*, 12.1 (2007), pp. 11–28; C. Levy (ed.), 'Colin Ward (1924–2010)', *Anarchist Studies*, 19.2 (2011), pp. 7–15.
57. John Holloway, *Change the World Without Taking Power* (London: Pluto Press, 2002).
58. S. Chattopadhyay and B. Sarkar, 'The Subaltern and the Popular', *Postcolonial Studies*, VIII.4 (2005), pp. 357–363; T. Brennan, *Wars of Position. The Cultural Politics of Left & Right* (New York: Columbia University Press, 2006); G. Baratta, *Antonio Gramsci in contrappunto. Dialoghi al presente* (Rome: Carocci, 2007); A. Davidson, 'The Uses and Abuses of Gramsci', *Thesis Eleven*, 95.1 (2008), pp. 68–94; G. Schirru (ed.), *Gramsci, le culture e il mondo* (Rome: Viella, 2009).
59. Robert Service, *Lenin A Biography* (Basingstoke: Macmillan, 2000).
60. C. Read, *Revolution, Religion and the Russian Intelligentsia* (Basingstoke: Macmillan, 1979); R. C. Williams, *The Other Bolsheviks. Lenin and His Critics, 1904–1919* (Bloomington: University of Indiana Press, 1986).
61. Gramsci, *Pre-Prison Writings*, pp. 34–42.
62. D. Settembrini, 'Mussolini and the Legacy of Revolutionary Socialism', *Journal of Contemporary History*, 11.4 (1976), pp. 239–268.
63. Perry Anderson, 'The Antinomies of Antonio Gramsci', *New Left Review*, 100, (1976–1977), pp. 5–78.
64. P. Ghosh, 'Gramscian Hegemony: An Absolutely Historicist Approach', *History of European Ideas*, 27 (2001), pp. 1–43; D. Boothman, 'The Sources of Gramsci's Concept of Hegemony', *Rethinking Marxism*, 20.2 (2008), pp. 201–215; A. D'Orsi (ed.), *Egemonie* (Naples: Libreria Dante & Descartes, 2008).
65. 65. Carl Levy, *Antonio Gramsci. Machiavelli. Marxism and Modernism* (Cambridge: Polity, 2013).

# 7

# Council Communist Perspectives on the Spanish Civil War and Revolution, 1936–1939

*Saku Pinta*

## Introduction

Council Communism is often regarded as a current within the revolutionary Marxist tradition that bears a close resemblance to what some now refer to as 'class struggle' anarchism[1] and is routinely considered to belong to a broader 'libertarian communist' tendency.[2] In so far as those anarchist currents which embrace a revolutionary class politics are delineated from individualist or other variants, the common emphasis on direct action and forms of self-organisation as the prefigurative organs of revolutionary change, distrust of bureaucracy and officialdom, and critique of both reformism and Bolshevism all lend credence to suggestions of convergent perspectives between councilism and class struggle *anarchisms*. Moreover, much like the broadly defined anarchist tradition, Council Communism became submerged during the Second World War – and overshadowed during the political climate of the postwar bipolar system[3] – only to resurface with the upsurge of antisystemic movements of the new Left and the post-68 era.

However, while theoretical similarities have been acknowledged, historically-situated examinations of the evolving relationship between anarchist and Marxist praxis have been sorely lacking in Left and labour historiography.[4] An approach sensitive to historical conditions and concrete political manifestations may provide some insight into the relationships between the 'red' and 'black' largely missing from what strictly analytical or normative approaches can tell us. Moreover, they may also serve as correctives to simplistic treatments counter posing a singular, 'capital-M' Marxist *bête noire* to a more varied and robust anarchism, or vice versa. Indeed, the view of ideologies as dynamic, conceptual products of their social, political, and economic environments, morphing in relation to changed circumstances, is an approach gaining ground in contemporary political theory.[5]

This chapter will examine Council Communist perspectives on anarcho-syndicalist participation in the Spanish Civil War and Revolution 1936–1939 through the writings of the American Group of Council Communists and its most outstanding theorists Paul Mattick and Karl Korsch. This conflict represents a pivotal episode in the international working-class movement, bookending the interwar period (1918–1939). The anti-Fascist struggle in Spain provided the backdrop against which ideological tensions were dramatically played out, and one in which the political aims and objectives of nearly all political actors involved were subject to revision: some anarchists participated in government, Stalinists actively defended liberal democracy and private property, and sections of the liberal bourgeoisie made common cause with self-styled socialists. The two main councilist journals of this period – *Rätecorrespondenz* in the Netherlands and *International Council Correspondence* in the USA – followed the events in Spain closely. In his 1969 introduction to a reprinted collection of the North American Council Communist journal, Paul Mattick reflected on this period, stating that:

> The anti-Fascist civil war in Spain, which was immediately a proving ground for World War II, found the council communists quite naturally – despite their Marxist orientation – on the side of the anarcho-syndicalists, even though circumstances compelled the latter to sacrifice their own principles to the protracted struggle against the common Fascist enemy.[6]

The chapter will begin with a brief outline of the origins and development of the Dutch–German Council Communist current, before providing a sketch of the American Group of Council Communists. It will then consider the critical, but sympathetic, support of the Spanish anarcho-syndicalists by the American councilists, highlighting the critique of the Popular Front, the positive appraisal of anarchist collectivisation, and the main councilist critiques of anarcho-syndicalism in Spain. In conclusion, councilist attitudes to the performance of anarchism in Spain will be discussed in relation to similar self-critiques made by rank and file formations such as *La Agrupación de Los Amigos de Durruti* (the Friends of Durruti Group). The Friends of Durruti were an anarcho-syndicalist affinity group, formally launched on 17 March 1937, named after the legendary anarcho-syndicalist militant Buenaventura Durruti who was killed in the defence of Madrid in 1936.[7] The group functioned as a Left opposition formation within the two main institutional expressions of anarchism and anarcho-syndicalism in Spain, the CNT (*Confederación Nacional del Trabajo*; National Confederation of Labour) and FAI (*Federación Anarquista Ibérica;* Iberian Anarchist Federation), and rose to prominence during the 'May Days' of 1937 in Barcelona.[8]

Beyond strictly historical interest, the councilists' critical appraisal of the revolutionary movement in Spain, and its counterpart within the radical Left of the CNT-FAI, reveals a series of common considerations between

revolutionary *anarchisms* and *Marxisms* with regards to the dynamics of revolutionary struggle: the limitations of anti-Fascism within the framework
of liberal democracy; internationalist perspectives on the risks and benefits
of extending isolated 'national' or regional revolutionary struggles beyond
their frontiers; the relationship between mass-based working-class organisations and avant-garde political groupings in pre- and post-revolutionary
periods; and finally, the very thorny question of what, exactly, is meant by
'taking power'?

## Workers' councils and Council Communist praxis

The Dutch–German Council Communist tendency, represents one of the
most significant and original revolutionary Marxist tendencies of the interwar period. The best-known Council Communist theorists include Anton
Pannekoek, Paul Mattick, Herman Gorter and Otto Rühle, while arguably
the most famous and controversial councilist activist, Marinus van der
Lubbe, was responsible for setting the fire that destroyed the Reichstag
building in February 1933 as an act of protest against the Nazis. In the
early 1920s, Council Communism had a mass audience and considerable
influence within the Dutch and German working-class movement.

The centrepiece of Council Communist theory is the notion that workers' councils constitute the main unit of revolutionary working-class struggle
and the basis on which post-capitalist arrangements should be constructed.
In his *Workers' Councils,* one of the most widely read expositions of Council
Communist ideas, Anton Pannekoek described councils as forms of working-
class self-organisation rooted in the myriad organs of production. These
councils, typically created in situations in which workers attempt to wrest
control of their workplaces and communities, would replace parliamentary
political institutions and the state with collaborating bodies of recallable
delegates responsible for democratically administering production as well
as activity in other spheres. This form of organisation would amount to a
'total revolution' in human affairs and result in the dissolution of the separation between politics and economics under capitalism.[9] Like class struggle
anarchists, Council Communists believe that democracy is a sham unless
extended to the economy and other areas of social life.

From these premises, the Council Communists developed a critique of
bureaucracy and mediated forms of political action as running directly
counter to the emancipatory aims of the workers' movement. As Rachleff
wrote in his 1976 study of councilist history and political theory:

> The councilists ... rejected the party structure because it recapitulated the
> capitalist division between mental and manual labor, between order-
> givers and order-takers. With their emphasis on the importance of the
> connection between the means and ends of the class struggle, they

recognized that socialism – workers' self-management of production and society – cannot be achieved through a form of organization that hindered self-emancipation. Rather than stimulating the capabilities of workers, parties function to stifle them.[10]

Council Communists also rejected the trade union form, for similar reasons, arguing that conventional unions had failed as instruments of revolution, being integrated into the functioning of advanced capitalism as agents of social control and collaborationist capital–labour mediation. By acting *above* or *on behalf* of the workers, the councilists reasoned that both trade union and party officials restrained and usurped the creative potential and agency of the working class. In doing so, a bureaucratic stratum formed, developing and defending its own privileges and class interests as the managers, rather than gravediggers, of capitalism. These hierarchical organisations were argued to be obstacles to human emancipation, a goal that could only be realised through collective social action and institutions powered 'from below'.

## From Left radicalism to Council Communism, 1900–1924

The ideas outlined above were not considered as abstract theoretical positions. Rather, councilist ideas were informed through the study of mass workers' struggles – particularly in the emergence of workers' councils (soviets) in Russia in 1905 and again in 1917, as well as the appearance of councils in Germany, Hungary and Italy in the uprisings, factory occupations, military mutinies, and insurrections that swept central and southern Europe in the years immediately following the First World War.[11]

In Germany and the Netherlands, Council Communist praxis originated in the early twentieth century from a radical Left minority in the German Social Democratic Party[12] and the Dutch 'Tribunist' group, both of whom collaborated extensively.[13] Perhaps the most important proponent of this radical Left faction was the German–Polish revolutionary Rosa Luxemburg. Her writings, especially *Reform or Revolution*,[14] first published in 1900, and her 1906 *The Mass Strike, the Political Party and the Trade Unions*,[15] helped lay the intellectual foundations of the Left radical and, later, councilist currents. Luxemburg's famous libertarian dictum – directed as a criticism of Lenin in the early stages of the Russian Revolution – presaged later conflicts between the heirs of this radical current and the Bolsheviks. 'Freedom,' she maintained, 'is always and exclusively freedom for the one who thinks differently... its effectiveness vanishes when "freedom" becomes a special privilege.'[16]

Frequently denounced as an 'anarchist deviation', Broué, in his study of the German revolution (1917–1923), noted that 'The German left radicals had been in conflict for years with the authoritarian organisation of their own party.'[17] Intraparty divisions within the social democratic camp came to a head during the crisis on the political Left provoked by the First World War, and, at a later stage, the overall reconfiguration of the international working-class movement in the years following the Russian Revolution in 1917. Those who had maintained anti-war positions and had welcomed the revolutionary events in Russia formed the Communist Party of Germany (KPD, *Kommunistische Partei Deutschlands*). Similar to many Western European Communists, the majority of this party held anti-parliamentary and anti-trade union positions. Perhaps initially taking Lenin's early 1917 revolutionary writings at face value, like his *April Theses* or *State and Revolution*[18] – much as many Russian and international anarchists had done during the October revolution[19] – workers and intellectuals in the Dutch–German Communist movement argued that the Russian Communists had revealed the emancipatory potential of the workers' councils.

A series of bureaucratic manoeuvres within the KPD by a small section of the party was successful in capturing important positions in the central committee, and through this influence expelled left-wing branches. The strategic aim of these expulsions centred around efforts to attract members of other, more moderate, parties to the KPD in the hope of building a mass party.[20] The insistence of the Communist International for all affiliated parties to participate in electoral campaigns in their national parliaments as well to work *within* the trade unions in order to radicalise them were also divisive issues for many Western Communists.[21] For the Dutch–German Communist Left, the function of the trade unions and political parties had already been called into question from their performance before, during and after the war. In response, Lenin's 1920 polemic, *Left-Wing Communism: An Infantile Disorder*[22] explicitly aimed at destroying the influence of the anti-parliamentary and radical sections of the Communist movement in Western Europe.[23]

The expelled sections of the KPD regrouped to form the Germany Communist Workers Party (KAPD, *Kommunistische Arbeiter-Partei Deutschlands*) in 1920, and participated as an observer group within the Communist International until the Third Congress of that body in 1921. Although increasingly critical, following the KAPD exit from the Comintern councilists engaged in a much more detailed critique of Bolshevism and the Soviet Union.[24] Perhaps the two definitive councilist statements against Bolshevism include Herman Gorter's 1920 *Open Letter to Comrade Lenin*[25] and Helmut Wagner's *Theses on Bolshevism*.[26] Both writings express the view that conditions in Western Europe precluded the adoption of parliamentary and unionist methods for revolutionary ends. Wagner's analysis of Bolshevism, which became the standard councilist view, further argued that the Bolshevik Party had carried out a bourgeois revolution in a predominantly agrarian society (rather than a proletarian revolution) against the remnants of Russian feudal absolutism and a weak liberal capitalist class, and installed the revolutionary intelligentsia as masters of a dictatorial party-state.

The programme of the KAPD explicitly stated that they were 'not a party in the traditional sense'. Rather than participating in the electoral process or seeking to capture state power, the political organisation was given a more modest role, namely, uniting and co-ordinating the efforts of the most politically advanced segments of the working-class under a Communist programme. The factory organisations or 'workers' unions' (*Unionen*) were considered as constituting 'the foundation of the communist society to come'[27] Parallel to the KAPD (peaking in 1920 with some 40,000 members) was the 200,000 strong General Workers' Union of Germany (AAUD *Allgemeine Arbeiter Union Deutschlands*), a network of factory organisations modelled on the Industrial Workers of the World (IWW). Of all early twentieth-century labour organisations, the 'revolutionary industrial unionism' of the IWW had the most significant and lasting impact on councilist industrial strategy.[28]

Differences emerged within the councilist Left in the early 1920s.[29] A split from the AAUD, led by Otto Rühle, led to the creation of the AAUE (*Allgemeine Arbeiter-Union – Einheitsorganisation*), as a political-economic 'unitary organisation'. Militants of the AAUE denied the necessity of a revolutionary political organisation separate from workers' economic organisations.[30] This underpinned the main debates within the councilist movement regarding the utility of a revolutionary party. Three different positions emerged. Rühle argued that efforts should be directly at forming workplace groups as a synthesis of economic and political organisation, and that attempts to form separate political organisations should be abandoned. This position was laid out most clearly in Rühle's pamphlet *The Revolution is Not a Party Affair*[31] , and in several respects, resembled that of revolutionary syndicalism.[32] Herman Gorter argued for a revolutionary party and defended the role of the KAPD as a political organisation for militants, carrying out propaganda work and linking members in a common organisation under a common platform. Pannekoek and Mattick in some ways oscillated between the two positions: with the former settling on a somewhat 'spontaneist' perspective which asserted that any outside intervention in working-class struggles would ultimately be harmful,[33] and the later considering these differences (in retrospect) to be of little practical significance.[34]

Despite differences, the conceptions of a Leninist-type party or activity in parliamentary politics were strategies rejected by Council Communists. The councilist notion of a 'party', as 'a group which share[s] a general common perspective and [seeks] to clarify and publicise the issues of class struggle',[35] in this sense, did not fundamentally differ from some anarchist conceptions of a revolutionary, anti-parliamentary political organisation.[36] In the radical political atmosphere of the Weimar Republic, historian Hans Manfred Bock considered the German Council Communists to be, along with the *Föderation der Kommunistischen Anarchisten* (FKAD, Federation of Communist Anarchists of Germany) and the *Freie Arbeiter Union Deutschlands* (FAUD, Free Workers' Union of Germany), a part of a common, 'relatively widespread antiauthoritarian movement' with 'open borders and fluid crossings and interactions between' these 'components of the antiauthoritarian camp'.[37]

## Post-1924 Council Communism in the USA

By 1924 the combined membership of councilist organisations in Germany had dwindled to some 2,700 active militants.[38] Those who remained committed to advancing social revolutionary perspectives focused primarily on developing theory and carrying out propaganda and educational work. One such group was the American UnitedWorkers Party, later renamed the Group of Council Communists, formed in 1934 through the initiative of Paul Mattick. Mattick, a former KAPD and AAUD worker-intellectual, emigrated to the USA in 1924, first moving to Benton Harbor, Michigan, later settling in Chicago, Illinois in 1927. Bonacchi writes that German radical émigrés like Mattick:

> ... saw the U.S. as the strongest capitalist country with the most radical labor tradition (the IWW)... providing the ideal conditions for the rapid development of that class autonomy which in Europe had been handicapped by capitalism's structural backwardness and by the labor movement's tradition of reformism.[39]

Indeed, Mattick attributed the formation of autonomous councils of the unemployed in the USA during the Great Depression as creating the conditions for the emergence of a Council Communist movement in that country.[40] Prior to the formation of an explicitly councilist organisation, organising and propaganda related to unemployment issues was conducted through the IWW. Mattick was an active member, and drafted a Germanlanguage revolutionary programme for the union in 1933 based on the theories of Henryk Grossman – *Die Todeskrise des kapitalistischen Systems und die Aufgaben des Proletariats* (The death crisis of the capitalist system and the tasks of the proletariat)[41] – which did not make the impact Mattick anticipated. In 1931 Mattick attempted to revive the *Arbeiter-Zeitung* newspaper in Chicago, a German-language radical publication famously associated with the Haymarket Martyrs.

As the movement of the unemployed declined, Mattick left the IWW[42] and regrouped with other Council Communists, Wobblies, members of the left-wing faction of the American Proletarian Party, and unemployed workers in 1934 to create the United Workers Party (UWP).[43] This group, with members based in Chicago, Buffalo, Washington D.C., and New York,[44] functioned primarily as a 'propaganda organization advocating the self-rule of the working class'.[45] The party's manifesto – *World-wide Fascism or World Revolution?* – outlined the role of the party, similar to that of the KAPD:

> The communist revolutionary party is an instrument of revolution and as such it must serve that purpose. It has no interests separate from the working class, but is only an expression of the fact that minorities become consciously revolutionary earlier than the broad masses . . . It does not look for power for itself or for any bureaucracy, but works to strengthen the power of the workers councils, Soviets. It is not interested to hold positions, but to place the power in the hands of workers committees, exercised by the workers themselves. It does not seek to lead the workers, but tells the workers to use their own initiative. It is a propaganda organization for Communism, and shows by example how to fight in action.[46]

In October 1934, the UWP began publishing *International Council Correspondence*. Mattick, who edited the journal, characterised it as a 'forum for discussion, unhampered by any specific dogmatic point of view, and open to new ideas that had some relevance to the council movement'.[47] Soon after, in 1936, the UWP changed its name to the Group of Council Communists. They explained that since the UWP 'was not a "party" in the traditional sense, the retention of the word has led to a lot of needless misunderstandings'.[48] In 1938 the journal changed its title to *Living Marxism*, and in 1942 the title was changed to *New Essays*. The name changes did not reflect revisions to the journal's political orientation. A membership decline prompted the first title change to *Living Marxism* as the journal 'did not promote the growth of the organization but was practically no more than a vehicle for the elucidation of the ideas of Council Communism'.[49] Mattick wrote that the overall decline of radicalism with the outbreak of the Second World War 'made the name *Living Marxism* seem rather pretentious, as well as a hindrance in the search for a wider circulation',[50] and the journal appeared as *New Essays* until it ceased publication in 1943. Aside from Mattick, Karl Korsch, a Marxist intellectual who emigrated to the USA in 1936, was perhaps the most prominent regular contributor to the journal. The writings of key figures in the European council movement, like Anton Pannekoek and Otto Rühle, appeared regularly as did translations from their Dutch sister publication *Rätekorrespondenz*.[51] In keeping with their open attitude to other working-class groups, the journal also published contributions by other figures on the radical Left, notably an article by Max Nomad (formerly a follower of Jan Wacław Machajski) and Daniel Guérin's 'Fascist Corporatism' (a translation from the revolutionary syndicalist journal *La Révolution prolétarienne*).[52]

## The Spanish Civil War and revolution

The events surrounding the Spanish Civil War are well-known and documented, and there is no need to go into any great detail into the causes
and outcomes of the conflict. Of note, however, is the way in which the
conflict has generally been portrayed, namely, as one between Fascism and
democracy.[53] The fact that a mass-based revolutionary movement exerted
considerable influence, particularly in anarchist-dominated areas such as
Catalonia, has not figured prominently in the literature on the Spanish
conflict until recent times. Conversely, the existence of this revolutionary
element, at the time, was actively concealed in the interests of advancing
the aims of Soviet foreign policy. For the American councilists, the revolutionary element and the tensions *within* the Popular Front were central to
any understanding of events in Spain.

Between October 1936 and April 1939, *International Council Correspondence*, and its later incarnations, ran no fewer than eight articles and three
book reviews directly related to the conflict in Spain, in addition to a
reprinted appeal from the CNT-FAI for international class solidarity.[54] Of the
articles, a total of five were written by Paul Mattick, one by Helmut Wagner
(a translation from *Rätezcorrespondenz*), and two by Karl Korsch. The extensive coverage of the Spanish conflict within the pages of *International Council
Correspondence* is all the more notable given the lack of information – from
a revolutionary perspective – outside of Spain and in particular, North
America. The 'conciliatory approach towards the CNT'[55] positioned the
journal as a mediator between the sometimes uncritical support for the Popular Front by some anarchist groups and the routinely inflexible approach
displayed by some Left Communists. Unlike some councilist-oriented organisations, there is no evidence to suggest that the American Group of Council
Communists had any physical presence in Spain during the war in the
militias or as journalists.[56]

## Anti-Fascism, revolution, and the reaction

The first full-length article on Spain appeared in October 1936, less than four
months after General Franco launched his military rebellion against the Second Spanish Republic. Written by Paul Mattick, entitled 'The Civil War in
Spain', this essay constituted the full issue of *International Council Correspondence*. It began by outlining the 'semi-feudal' social and political conditions
in Spain in the years prior to the outbreak of the civil war, with an emphasis on the powerful grip of the church, landowners, and military on the
state apparatus and economy, and an assessment of the various forces within
the anti-Fascist front.[57] Semi-feudal conditions, argued Mattick, retarded the
development of capitalism in Spanish industry and agriculture as well as the
emergence of an effective liberal-democratic reform movement which could

impose modern capitalist relations on the feudal interests, the working class, and peasantry. Despite the electoral victory of the Popular Front coalition of the liberal and parliamentary labour parties in 1936, the weakness of the Spanish liberal bourgeoisie was further exposed. Moderate government policy in land, labour, and education reforms alienated the traditional Spanish ruling elite and did little to ease tensions or placate the increasingly revolutionary class movement. 'The reaction,' wrote Mattick, 'simply realized that any concession which the bourgeois government made to the workers had to be made at the expense of the reactionary elements'.[58] In rebelling, the Spanish generals, and the class interests they represented, sought to impose its own order by means of a dictatorship which, to the right-wing plotters, was directed 'against a government which by its previous policy seemed liable to become the prisoner of the labor movement'.[59]

The conflict that ensued, pitting the reaction against anti-Fascist forces, was characterised by political fragmentation, but nonetheless polarised competing elements into two camps. Mattick asserted that:

No doubt the struggle for the power in Spain is between three different tendencies; practically, however, the struggle has as yet been confined to the one between Fascism and Anti-Fascism ... The reactionary forces taking up for Fascism are confronted by those of a bourgeois-democratic and social-reformist caste, tho at the same time by a movement aiming at socialism, so that each individual group is fighting against two tendencies: Fascism against Democracy and Revolution, this Democracy against Fascism and Revolution, the Revolution against Fascism and bourgeois democracy.[60]

Mattick noted that while divergent trends coexisted within the anti-Fascist camp, the immediate threat that the reaction posed compelled these forces to unite as a matter of survival, just as the Fascists concerned themselves with the class aspirations of workers rather than on differences in their organisations and policies.

Neither the groups of fascists nor those of the workers are allowed the time or opportunity to go their own special ways, and it is idle to ask whether the Spanish workers under the present conditions should fight against fascism and for bourgeois democracy or not.[61]

Mattick perceptively speculated that '[i]n case the reaction should be struck down, then ... the struggle of the bourgeois-democratic forces against those which are aiming to set aside the exploitation society must again come into the foreground'.[62] In other words, the frictions within the anti-Fascist front would, due to irreconcilable interests and objectives, come into conflict sooner or later; frictions 'which must become the greater the longer the civil war is drawn out, since in such conditions the real socialisation is bound to spread and the social-reformist forces challenged to greater resistance'.[63]

With these considerations, Mattick turned to an analysis of the different factions within the anti-Fascist front. Spanish social democracy was characterised as the 'left wing of the bourgeoisie', politically concerned with maintaining parliamentary and capitalist institutions. The small but disproportionately influential Spanish Communist Party maintained a similar outlook having 'given up every policy of its own, other than that of further attenuating the workers' struggle. Like the Social Democracy it wants nothing more than to defend capitalist democracy against fascism.'[64] If the Spanish Socialist Party represented a centre-left position in the Popular Front, the Communist sections were to the right of it on the political spectrum. Only the dissident Marxist POUM (*Partido Obrero Unificación Marxista*, Workers' Party of Marxist Unification), of the Popular Front forces, could be considered to be the carriers of a genuine Leninist or Bolshevik position, advancing a programme of state ownership of the economy similar to that of the Soviet Union.[65] Of the Spanish anarchists, Mattick wrote:

> Over against these 'marxist' organizations, which have nothing more in common with Marxism than the name, stands the anarcho-syndicalist movement, which, even though it has not the organizational strength of the popular-front parties, can nevertheless be rated as their worthy adversary, capable of bringing into question the aspirations of the pseudo-marxist state capitalists.[66]

The development of anarcho-syndicalist federalism in Spain was considered by Mattick to be a product of the disorganisation of the ruling class – divided between liberal-democratic and reactionary elements – and uneven and regional industrial concentrations in Spain, meaning less emphasis on centralised control and direction of the movement:

> The localizing of the workers manifestations was...an inevitable product of the circumstance that only industrial oases existed in the feudal desert...In the course of the further industrializing of Spain, this syndicalist movement...will be obliged, regardless of its previous attitude, to take up with more coordinated and centralized forms of organization, if it is not to go under. Or, possibly, the centralistic control and coordination of all political and economic activity will be imposed overnight by a successful revolution; and in these circumstances the federalistic traditions would be of enormous value, since they would form the necessary counter-weight against the dangers of centralism.[67]

Combining centralism and federalism was not understood by Mattick or other councilists as being contradictory. For example, in an earlier article in *International Council Correspondence* entitled 'Anarchism and Marxism' the author 'WRB' argued that a communist economy needed co-ordination to satisfy human needs and desires, requiring elements of centralism and federalism. Autarkic, totally self-sufficient units were deemed at best to be unfeasible, and at worst, could develop 'competitive tendencies' if autonomous communes engaged in exchanging surplus products with other communes. Decision-making power in a communist society would have to be as decentralised and federative as possible as a corrective to the formation of bureaucracy: thus, a combination of centralised industrial co-ordination and federal decision-making and control.[68] While the CNT *syndicatos unicos*, or industrial unions, sought to remedy the decentralised craft or trade union structure, Daniel Guérin and others, have also criticised some of the 'rather naive and idealistic'[69] conceptions of a localist libertarian communism, expressed by Isaac Puente[70] and dominant in the 1936 Saragossa CNT conference, along the same lines.[71] Guérin, in fact, explicitly rejected Puente's notion of libertarian communism as an 'infantile idyll of a jumble of "free communes", at the heart of the Spanish CNT before 1936 [...] This soft dream left Spanish anarcho-syndicalism extremely ill-prepared for the harsh realities of revolution and civil war on the eve of Franco's putsch.'[72]

Overall, Mattick praised the self-organised nature of the CNT, its rejection of both parliamentarism and soviet-style state capitalism. 'In the course of the present civil war', he wrote, 'anarcho-syndicalism has been the most forward-driving revolutionary element.'[73]

Mattick maintained that a workers' revolution in Spain would encounter multiple difficulties. Aside of the immediate threat posed by Fascism stood the likelihood that the Spanish revolutionary movement would be confronted with Popular Front counterrevolution or foreign intervention. To be successful, Mattick held that the revolutionary workers had to encompass an internationalist outlook and extend the revolutionary class struggle beyond its national boundaries, instigating insurgent movements in neighbouring France and North Africa in particular.[74] This, he reasoned, would naturally provoke imperialist powers to protect their colonial possessions while controlling domestic dissent, in effect transforming the Spanish conflict into an international class war. Mattick's view on this was nearly identical to that of Italian anarchist militant Camillo Berneri (1897–1937).[75] Chomsky summarised Berneri's position:

He argued that Morocco should be granted independence and that an attempt should be made to stir up rebellion throughout North Africa. Thus a revolutionary struggle should be undertaken against Western capitalism in North Africa and, simultaneously, against the bourgeois regime in Spain, which was gradually dismantling the accomplishments of the July revolution.[76]

In proposing such a strategy, Berneri hoped that Franco's base of military support in North Africa would be severely weakened and that the response by Western capitalist nations would help ignite revolution outside of Spain.

Aside from extending the struggle outside of Spain, according to Mattick, a political anti-Fascist struggle would only bring limited returns, at best ushering in soviet-style state capitalism, so a broader anticapitalist struggle was necessary: 'The workers' struggle must be directed not exclusively against Fascism, but against Capital in all its forms and manifestations.'[77]

In the next issue of *International Council Correspondence*, Mattick wrote a shorter follow-up article entitled 'What Next in Spain?' Here Mattick underscored his previous assertion that the revolutionary movement in Spain faced major obstacles and hostilities from the imperialist powers:

> The extent of the civil war, the anarchist element in it, allowed for the possibility that in Spain capitalism itself may be wiped out. This would have meant the open intervention of many capitalist powers in Spain and a sudden clash of imperialist interests which probably would have marked the beginning of the world war.[78]

The Russian intervention, claimed Mattick, had put the anarchists at a disadvantage, and severely limited the scope of their activity. 'Recognizing that Franco would win, in case help from the outside was denied to the loyalists, the anarchists had to accept the Russian bribe and domination of the anti-Fascist front which automatically worked against the anarchists.'[79] In this early stage of the war, Mattick reiterated his position that a joint struggle against Fascism was unavoidable: 'All political organizations had to fight Franco and postpone the settlement of all other questions [. . .] It would be foolish to blame the revolutionary groups for the one or the other wrong step, as even a correct policy would have meant nothing,' and continued that 'The circumstances force the policies of the anarchists, not their own decisions.'[80]

## Karl Korsch and anarchist collectivisation

Karl Korsch's major contribution to the councilist perspectives on the war and revolution in Spain was his positive assessment of the anarchist attempts at collectivising the economy, which he outlined in two articles, 'Economics and Politics in Revolutionary Spain' and 'Collectivization in Spain', both published in 1938 as the prospects of an anti-Fascist victory appeared slim. Both of these articles were originally intended for publication in the Frankfurt School's Institute for Social Research journal in New York but disagreements between Korsch and the Institute, arising from editorial revisions, compelled him to publish them in *Living Marxism*.[81]

In 'Economics and Politics in Revolutionary Spain' Korsch argued that the Spanish revolution and its achievements in collectivisation represented a new period of class struggle worthy of serious attention and could not be mechanically evaluated 'with some abstract ideal or with results attained under entirely different historical conditions'.[82] Korsch maintained that the Spanish revolution 'should not be compared with anything which happened in Russia after October, 1917'.[83] In this assertion, Korsch sought to defend the revolutionary movement in Spain against unnamed Leninist critics who 'extol the revolutionary consistency of the Bolshevik leadership of 1917, to the detriment of the "chaotic irresolution" displayed by the dissentions and waverings of the Spanish Syndicalists and Anarchists of 1936–1938'.[84] Against these critics, Korsch argued that the 'Bolshevik leadership of 1917 was in no way exempt from those human wavering and want of foresight which are inherent in any revolutionary action'.[85] Specifically, Korsch cited Lenin's support of the Kerensky government in Russia against General Kornilov's counter-revolutionary rebellion showing 'how little the minor followers of Lenin are entitled to criticise the deficiencies of the syndicalist achievements in revolutionary Catalonia'.[86] Politically, Korsch's defence of the Spanish anarchists and syndicalists was aimed at removing the 'deep shadow thrown on the constructive work' of Catalonia's revolutionary workers by Stalinists, and exposing the socialist content of collectivisation as opposed to state capitalist nationalisation.[87]

Korsch's follow-up article, 'Collectivization in Spain', maintained that the Spanish workers had achieved a greater degree of success in constructing a self-managed economy than their early twentieth-century predecessors. Basing his account on a CNT-FAI pamphlet – *Collectivisation: The constructive work of the Spanish Revolution* – Korsch asserted that '[t]he syndicalist and anarchist labor movement of Spain' were 'better informed and possessed a much more realistic conception of the necessary steps to achieve their economic aims than had been shown, in similar situations, by the so-called "Marxist" labour movements in other parts of Europe'.[88] While anarchist and syndicalist attempts at realising workers' self-management were restricted by reactionary forces as well as the moderate, Soviet-backed Popular Front government, for Korsch, despite these limitations, the historical importance and lessons of the Spanish revolution were to be placed alongside the 1871 Paris Commune, the 1918 Hungarian and Bavarian revolutions, and the early revolutionary achievements of the Russian Revolution in 1917.[89]

Korsch emphasised that the Catalan workers were able to expropriate vast sections of industry, transportation, and other sectors of the economy after their owners and managers, many of whom had supported the military rebellion, fled after its defeat in Barcelona and other areas. This revolt which 'resembled a war against an invisible enemy,' showed the 'relative ease with which under equally fortunate circumstances . . . deep and far reaching changes in production management and wage payment can be accomplished without great formal and organizational transformations'.[90]

Korsch concluded with an analysis of his main interest, namely, the Spanish syndicalist form of organisation. 'These syndicalist formations,' he stated, 'anti-party and anti-centralistic, were entirely based on the free action of the working masses.' This feature of Spanish syndicalism was considered by Korsch to be an asset, as its activity was based on non-bureaucratic methods, 'managed from the outset not by professional officialdom, but by the elite of the workers in the respective industries'. Further, '[t]he energy of the anti-state attitude of the revolutionary Spanish proletariat, unhampered by self-created organizational or ideological obstacles explains all their surprising successes in the face of overwhelming difficulties'.[91]

## Problems of political organisation: syndicates or soviets?

While acknowledging the difficult circumstances in Spain during the years of the civil war – and importantly, circumstances which compelled the CNT-FAI to participate in the Popular Front government – both Mattick and Korsch also criticised anarchist attitudes towards political organisation, or perhaps more accurately, the separation of the political from the economic in the revolutionary period. For Korsch, this was the single most important lesson, not only of the Spanish revolution, but of the entire post-First World War revolutionary period:

> The very fact that the CNT and FAI themselves were finally compelled to reverse their traditional policy of non-interference in politics under the pressure of increasingly bitter experiences, demonstrated [. . .] *the vital connection between the economic and political action in every phase and, most of all, in the immediately revolutionary phase of the proletarian class struggle.* This, then is the first and foremost lesson of that concluding phase of the whole revolutionary history of post war Europe which is the Spanish revolution.[92]

In keeping with councilist perspectives on emergent social forms that develop through the revolutionary process, Korsch's critique underscored the position that revolutionary organisations cannot be formed prior to a revolutionary period and must develop in accordance with the tasks at hand by placing all power in the workers' councils, rather than maintaining traditional leadership roles and sectional interests. In a review of anarchist Diego Santillan's *After the Revolution*, Mattick also gave a clear picture of the function of syndicates, formed in a pre-revolutionary period, and the problems associated with maintaining this organisational form in a revolutionary period:

It must be borne in mind that syndicates, including the anarchist CNT, are pre-revolutionary organizations which were organized principally to wrest concessions from the capitalist class. In order to do this most efficiently, a staff of organizers, an apparatus, was necessary. This staff became the new bureaucracy, its members the leaders and guides.[93]

The failure of the anarchists to assert a new form of working-class political power meant that state and capitalist power, which had largely, but not entirely, dissolved in vast areas of Spain (particularly Catalonia) in the aftermath of Franco's coup d'etat, was able to reassert itself and regain its former position of dominance. This also meant that, in the absence of an alternative political-economic framework, the CNT-FAI were ultimately forced to compromise their anti-statist principles by entering the government.

## The Barcelona May Days, 1937

Ultimately, in May 1937 in Barcelona, the logical end of this compromise between the CNT-FAI and the Popular Front government culminated in the defeat of the workers' movement.[94] This historical moment revealed the tensions within the broad 'Republican' camp in the struggle against Fascism, and the divergent strategies in conducting the war and the economy. 'No historical episode,' claimed historian Burnett Bolloten, 'has been so diversely reported or defined.'[95] For the anarchists and POUM, the May Days were simply a response from the working class to communist provocations. Bolloten observed that few accounts of May 1937 'were reconcilable, which partially explains why the May events, despite numerous attempts to clarify them, are still . . . shrouded in obscurity'.[96]

Tensions began in early April when the PSUC (*Partit Socialista Unificat de Catalunya*, Unified Socialist Party of Catalonia, the only Comintern-affiliated organisation in Catalonia) and UGT (*Unión General de Trabajadores*, General Union of Workers, a union aligned politically with the PSUC) announced a 'Victory Plan' for Catalonia, seeking to create a regular army in the region, nationalise war industries and transport, create an internal government security force, and concentrate all arms and munitions into the hands of the government: in effect, reassert state power and authority in Catalonia.[97] The political assassinations of Communist officials Rodriquez Salas and Roldan Cortada and AntonioMartin, the anarchist president of a revolutionary committee in Puigcerda, were quickly followed by the seizure of 'frontier posts along the Franco–Spanish border hitherto controlled by revolutionary committees', dispatched by finance minister Juan Negrin from Valencia, the seat of the Popular Front government.[98] In this politically sensitive atmosphere, May Day celebrations in Barcelona were cancelled for fear that openly displaying political allegiances in the city could trigger violence. Finally, on May 3, government forces seized the *telefónica*, or central telephone exchange. The telephone exchange had been operated by a joint UGT-CNT committee where 'the Anarcho-syndicalists were the dominant force, and their red and black flag, which had flown from the tower of the building ever since July, attested to their supremacy'.[99] The people of the working-class districts of Barcelona, where anarcho-syndicalists were firmly entrenched, were enraged by the seizure of the telephone exchange. Strategically located buildings were quickly occupied and barricades erected. Intense street-fighting between armed workers and government forces continued for four days. Only after the CNT-FAI leadership appealed for a cease-fire were the barricades dismantled and the workers disarmed. Graham concluded that:

> The meaning of the May Days was not, in the end, about 'breaking the CNT' *per se* – its leadership was already a willing part of the liberal Republican alliance. Rather it was about breaking the CNT's organizational solidarities in Barcelona to deprive its constituencies . . . of the mechanisms and political means of resisting the state. 'May' was about a process of forcible 'nationalization': in the immediate term about war production, but ultimately about state building through social disciplining and capitalist control of national economic production.[100]

Mattick commented on these developments in two articles. In 'Civil War in Catalonia' he stated that 'The clash between the Generalidad and the Anarchists is a natural outgrowth of the politics of the "Peoples Front" . . . The logic of the Peoples Front politics dominated by Russian diplomacy makes the shooting and suppression of revolutionary workers inevitable.'[101] Mattick's second article on the Barcelona May Days, 'Moscow-Fascism: The Barricades Must be Torn Down!', forcefully condemned the Popular Front policy:

> The workers' revolution must be radical from the very outset, or it will be lost. There was required the complete expropriation of the possessing classes, the elimination of all power other than that of the armed workers, and the struggle against all elements opposing such a course. Not doing this, the May Days of Barcelona, and the elimination of the revolutionary elements in Spain were inevitable. The CNT never approached the question of revolution from the viewpoint of the working class, but has always been concerned first of all with the organization. It was acting for the workers and with the aid of the workers, but was not interested in the self-initiative and action of the workers independent of organizational interests.[102]

Mattick noted in passing that 'The "Friends of Durruti" split away from the corrupted leaders of the CNT and FAI in order to restore original anarchism, to safeguard the ideal, to maintain the revolutionary tradition,' but did so too late.[103] He concluded that the revolutionary movement would have to reassert itself, declaring that 'The barricades, if again erected, should not be torn down.'[104]

## Conclusions

The American councilists, while sympathetic to the cause of the Spanish anarcho-syndicalists, directed two major criticisms at their performance in a revolutionary situation. First, the anarchist workers failed to create unified economic-political organs of workers' power in areas in which they clearly held a dominant position and suppress counter-revolutionary elements. In neglecting to do so, they allowed a weakened state power to re-emerge, culminating in the Barcelona May Days. Second, and related to the first, was a theoretical weakness, which recognised the dangers of statist bureaucracy but did not extend this understanding to the syndicates, where the CNT-FAI leadership became gradually separated from the self-organised activity of the working class. These attitudes were tempered by an intimate understanding of the very difficult circumstances, and isolation, in which the Spanish anarchist movement found itself.

Within this historical juncture, these critiques rather than creating a further gulf between Marxist-councilist and anarchist revolutionary theory, indicate a more considerable sphere of theoretical convergence. This is particularly evident when considering the positions adopted by the Friends of Durruti (FoD), one of the few organised elements in Barcelona in 1937 which actively discouraged the armed workers from abandoning the barricades.

The FoD was formed primarily to combat what they regarded as the reformist positions of the leadership of the CNT-FAI and the gradual surrender of the revolutionary gains of July 1936. The two of the most important political decisions which they were opposed were the CNT-FAI entry into the Republican central and regional Catalan governments and the acceptance of the militarisation of the workers' militias under the political direction of the government. On the first point, the rejection of CNT-FAI 'ministerialism', the FoD criticised the 'treason' of the CNT leadership in collaborating with elements in the state apparatus who were hostile to the main social revolutionary achievements of the working-class movement: particularly the collectivisation of large segments of industry and agriculture and the workers' patrols in place of government security or police agencies. That this collaboration was conducted as the only viable option, for anti-Fascist unity in the war effort, was totally rejected by the FoD. The war and the revolution were inseparable, and to postpone the revolution was to destroy the morale of the working-class base of support which sustained the war effort. On the second point, the reorganisation of the workers' militias into a regular army, the FoD were not opposed to a co-ordinated, well-organised military. In fact, the group outlined the basis for such a formation, which they referred to as a 'confederal army' which they envisaged as being co-ordinated by a 'single collective command,' under the guidance of working-class organisations.105 What they objected to was the hierarchy, military formalism, and above all, the state direction of the military under the guise of being a non-political formation.

The FoD, while a small grouping inside the CNT-FAI, might be said to have some influence beyond their small numbers,[106] and certainly, reflected the opinions of the rank and file of those organisations, at least if the spontaneous fighting of the May Days is taken as a barometer. These events were under-stood as a turning point, signalling the defeat of the revolutionary movement. During the street fighting in Barcelona between government forces and the armed working-class, the FoD openly defied the appeals of the CNT-FAI lead-ership for a cease fire, and went one step further, agitating for the creation of a 'revolutionary junta'. This 'junta' or council was envisaged as an organ of working-class political power, suppressing the forces that were in open conflict with the revolutionary movement. In the aftermath of the May Days Jaime Balius, the most prominent intellectual voice of the group, presented a cri-tique of the CNT-FAI and outlined a proposed alternative political-economic structure in the pamphlet *Towards a Fresh Revolution*. In this pamphlet, Balius sought to resolve the contradictions of official CNTFAI policy while advancing a more consistent interpretation of 'libertarian communism'. Balius argued that the CNT lacked a coherent vision and was not prepared to face the tasks of building and defending the revolution.

> What happened was what had to happen. The CNT was utterly devoid of revolutionary theory. We did not have a concrete programme. We had no idea where we were going . . . By not knowing what to do, we handed the revolution on a platter to the bourgeoisie and the marxists who sup-port the farce of yesteryear. What is worse, we allowed the bourgeoisie a breathing space; to return, to re-form and to behave as would a conquer-or.[107]

The CNT-FAI, argued Balius, 'collaborated with the bourgeoisie in the affairs of state, precisely when the State was crumbling away on all sides [. . .] It breathed a lungful of oxygen into an anaemic, terror-stricken bourgeoisie.' CNT-FAI collaboration with the state, then, not only violated anti-statist principles but allowed the Popular Front forces time to revive state power and limit collectivisation in Barcelona and other areas. Balius argued that 'One of the most direct reasons why the revolution has been asphyxiated and the CNT displaced, is that it behaved like a minority group, even though it had a majority in the streets.'[108] The proposed 'revolutionary junta' of the FoD was not envisaged as a 'substitutionist body', separate from the work-ing-class, but rather an elected body drawn exclusively from working-class organisations with the tasks of managing the war effort, maintaining public order, international affairs, and conducting revolutionary propaganda. The council would include a recall process and a regular rotation of members to prevent a bureaucratic class from developing, and would be subordinate to the unions in economic affairs. Syndicates would thus be the main organ from which the council would draw its political power and legitimacy, and would have the responsibility of directing the economy on the principles of workers' self-management. As Balius noted at a later stage, the FoD advocated 'all power to the syndicates,' or unions, rather than soviets, as the revolutionary committees of the CNT were regarded as possessing the organisational attributes necessary for carrying out libertarian communist reconstruction.

> We did not support the formation of Soviets; there were no grounds in Spain for calling for such. We stood for 'all power to the trade unions'. In no way were we politically oriented. The junta was simply a way out, a revolutionary formula to save the revolutionary conquests of July 1936. We were unable to exercise great influence because the Stalinists, helped by the CNT and FAI reformists, undertook their counter-revolutionary aggression so rapidly.[109]

The FoD differed slightly with the councilists on this point, however, in other ways their self-criticism were nearly indistinguishable from the views of Mattick and Korsch. 'Taking power' would mean nothing less than the direction of the economy, war effort, and all other areas by workers' organisations and the suppression of counter-revolutionary groups by workers' militias directly tied and accountable to these organisations. Halfway measures and compromises with social forces hostile to social revolution would only result in defeat.

In terms of the significance of these historical revolutionary movements towards anarchist-Marxist convergences, these may be considered to have underscored a common emphasis on working-class self-organisation as both method and non-dogmatic source of inspiration. Mattick, in reflecting on Korsch's contributions to revolutionary Marxism, perhaps best sums up this attitude:

> Korsch turned to the anarchists without giving up his Marxist conceptions; not to the petty-bourgeois anarchists of *laissez faire* ideology, but to the anarchist workers and poor peasants of Spain who had not yet succumbed to the international counter-revolution which now counted among its symbols the name of Marx as well . . . The anarchist emphasis on freedom and spontaneity, on self-determination, and, therefore, decentralisation, on action rather than ideology, on solidarity more than on economic interest were precisely the qualities that had been lost to

the socialist movement in its rise to political influence and power in the expanding capitalist nations. It did not matter to Korsch whether his anarchistically-biased interpretation of revolutionary Marxism was true to Marx or not. What mattered, under the conditions of twentieth-century capitalism, was to recapture these anarchist attitudes in order to have a labour movement at all.[110]

It is on this level that we begin to see some of the broad outlines of a libertarian communist politics in the interwar period, expressed less as a doctrinal system or tradition, but rather as a series of common considerations and political commitments forged during heightened revolutionary periods, and further developed upon reflection in defeat. The workers' councils of the Dutch–German councilists, the 'revolutionary junta' of the Friends of Durruti, as well as the 'free soviets' and calls for more coherent forms of political organisation by the Makhnovschina in an earlier period, amongst others, reflect a common organisational focus on forms of workers' autonomy and a view to generalising these emergent social forms as the basis for a free society.

## Notes

1.   For example B. Franks, *Rebel Alliances: The Means and Ends of Contemporary British Anarchisms* (Edinburgh/Oakland: AK Press and Dark Star, 2006), pp. 12–16; W. Price, *The Abolition of the State: Anarchist and Marxist Perspectives* (Bloomington/Milton Keynes: Authorhouse, 2007), pp. 3–5.

2.   For example R. Hahnel, *Economic Justice and Democracy: From Competition to Cooperation* (New York: Routledge, 2005), pp. 392–393, n. 1 and n. 2; D. Guérin, *Towards a Libertarian Communism* (1988): http://libcom.org/library/towards-libertarian-communism-daniel-guerin (accessed 8 February 2010); and N. Chomsky, *Government in the Future* (New York: Seven Stories Press, 2005), pp. 23–30.

3.   Steve Wright notes that 'if anything, the climate of the Cold War would be even more inhospitable for those who saw the rival blocs as simply different forms of capitalist imperialism'. 'Radical traditions: Council Communism', *Reconstruction* 4 (1995): www.libcom.org/library/radical-traditions-council-communism-stevewright (accessed 04 August 2009).

4.   A notable exception to this is the definitive though largely unknown outside of a German readership: H. Bock, *Syndicalismus und Linkskommunismus von 1918 bis 1923. Zur Geschichte und Soziologie der Kommunistischen Arbeiterpartei Deutschlands (K.A.P.D.), der Allgemeinen Arbeiterunion (A.A.U.D.) und der Freien Arbeiterunion (F.A.U.D.)* (Meisenheim: Verlag Anton Hain, 1969). On the relationship of German syndicalism to Council Communism in the Weimar Republic, see H. Bock, 'Anarchosyndicalism in the German Labour Movement' in W. Thorpe and M. van der Linden (eds.), *Revolutionary Syndicalism: An International Perspective* (Aldershot: Scolar Press, 1990), pp. 59–79.

5.   M. Freeden, *Ideologies and Political Theory: A Conceptual Approach* (Oxford: Oxford University Press, 1996).

6.   P. Mattick, 'Introduction', *New essays: a quarterly dedicated to the study of modern society* (Westport, Conn.: Greenwood Reprint Corporation, 1969), viii–ix. As will

be discussed below, this journal changed its title twice between 1934 and 1943: *International Council Correspondence*, then *Living Marxism* and finally *New Essays*. These will be referred to collectively hereafter as *New Essays*.

7. For a discussion of the 'deaths' of Durruti, see A. Paz, *Durruti in the Spanish Revolution* (Edinburgh, Oakland: AK Press, 2007), pp. 637–681.

8. The two most important studies are A. Guillamón, *The Friends of Durruti Group: 1937–1939* and the definitive Spanish-language treatment M. Amorós, *La revolución traicionada: La verdadera historia de Balius y los Amigos de Durruti* (Barcelona: VIRUS editorial, 2003). See also G. Fontenis, *The Revolutionary Message of the 'Friends of Durruti'* (1983), available online: www.flag.blackened.net/revolt/spain/FODtrans/intro.html (accessed 09 July 2010); P. Sharkey, *The Friends of Durruti – A Chronology* (1984), available online: www.flag.blackened.net/revolt/spain/fod_chron.html (accessed 09 July 2010); and B. Bolloten, *The Spanish Civil War: Revolution and Counterrevolution* (Chapel Hill: The University of North Carolina Press, 1991), pp. 420;428;866–867, n.49.

9. A. Pannekoek, *Workers' Councils* (Oakland/Edinburgh: AK Press, 2003), pp. 44–50.

10. P. Rachleff, *Marxism and Council Communism: The Foundation for Revolutionary Theory for Modern Society* (Brooklyn: Revisionist Press, 1976), p. 207.

11. See P. Rachleff, *Marxism and Council Communism*, p. 106; Mattick, 'Introduction' in *New essays*, v.; A. Pannekoek, *Workers' Councils*, pp. 76–77.

12. For a summary of the left, right, and centrist currents in German pre-war social democracy, represented by Luxemburg, Eduard Bernstein, and Karl Kautsky respectively see R. Gombin, *The Radical Tradition: a study in modern revolutionary thought* (London: Methuen & Co Ltd., 1978), pp. 93–94.

13. Bourrinet writes that 'There is not on the one hand a German Left and on the other a Dutch Left, but truly a German-Dutch Communist Left, with Gorter as its leading political figure.' P. Bourrinet, *The Dutch and German Communist Left: a contribution to the history of the revolutionary movement* (London: Porcupine Press, 2001), p. 9.

14. R. Luxemburg, *Reform or Revolution* (New York: Gordon Press, 1974). Karl Korsch and Paul Mattick regarded this as a central text, and in general, Luxemburg as a key figure in the development of the councilist current. See K. Korsch, 'The Passing of Marxian Orthodoxy', *New Essays* 3:11/12 (December 1937), pp. 7–11; P. Mattick, 'Luxemburg vs. Lenin', *New Essays* 2:8 (July 1936), pp. 17–35.

15. R. Luxemburg, *The mass strike, the political party, and the trade unions and The Junius pamphlet* (London: Harper and Row, 1971).

16. R. Luxemburg, *The Russian Revolution* (1918): http://www.marxists.org/archive/luxemburg/1918/russian-revolution/ch06.htm (accessed 28 September 2010).

17. P. Broué, *The German Revolution 1917–1923* (Chicago: Haymarket Books, 2006), p. 39.

18. V. Lenin, *April Theses* (1917): www.marxists.org/archive/lenin/works/1917/apr/04.htm (accessed 15 October 2010) and V. Lenin, *State and Revolution* (1918): www.marxists.org/archive/lenin/works/1917/staterev (accessed 15 October 2010).

19. G.P. Maximoff, wrote that 'The slogans formulated by the Bolsheviks (Communists) voiced, in a precise and intelligible manner, the demands of the masses in revolt, coinciding with the slogans of the Anarchists: "Down with the war," "Immediate peace without annexations or indemnities, over the heads of the governments and capitalists," "Abolition of the army," "Arming of the

workers," "Immediate seizure of land by the peasants," "Seizure of factories by the workers," "A Federation of Soviets," etc. [. . .]Wasn't it natural for the Anarchists to be taken in by these slogans, considering that they lacked a strong organisation to carry them out independently? Consequently, they continued taking part in the joint struggle.' G.P. Maximoff, *Syndicalists in the Russian Revolution* (n.d., c.1940): www.libcom.org/library/syndicalists-in-russian-revolutionmaximov (accessed 24 August 2009). See also P. Avrich, *The Russian Anarchists* (Princeton: Princeton University Press, 1967), pp. 128–129;171–203; M. Bookchin, *The Third Revolution: Popular Movements in the Revolutionary Era*, Volume 3 (London: Continuum, 2004), p. 199; K. Zimmer, 'Premature Anti-Communists?: American Anarchism, the Russian Revolution, and Left-Wing Libertarian Anti-Communism, 1917–1939', *Labor: Studies in Working-Class History of the Americas*, 6:2 (Summer 2009), pp. 45–71; I. de Llorens, *The CNT and the Russian Revolution*, trans. Paul Sharkey (London/ Berkeley: Kate Sharpley Library, 2007); D. Berry, 'Sovietism as Council Anarchism' in *A History of the French Anarchist Movement, 1917 to 1945* (Edinburgh/Oakland: AK Press, 2009), pp. 55–83; R. Gombin, *The Radical Tradition*, p. 34.

20. P. Broué, *The German Revolution 1917–1923*, pp. 393–491.
21. See the 'Conditions of Admission into the Communist International' in *Minutes of the Second Congress of the Communist International* (1920): www.marxists.org/ history/international/comintern/2nd-congress/ch07.htm (accessed 24 October 2009).
22. V. Lenin, *Left-Wing Communism: An Infantile Disorder* (1920): www.marxists.org/ archive/lenin/works/1920/lwc/ (accessed 12 October 2010).
23. P. Mattick, 'Introduction', *New Essays*, vi.
24. See for example 'What was the USSR? Towards a Theory of the Deformation of Value under State Capitalism Part III: Left Communism and the Russian Revolution', in *Aufheben* 8 (Autumn 1999): http://libcom.org/library/what-wasussr-aufheben-left-communism-part-3 (accessed 05 August 2009).
25. See H. Gorter, *Open Letter to Comrade Lenin, A Reply to 'Left-wing' Communism, an Infantile Disorder* (1920): www.marxists.org/archive/gorter/1920/open-letter/ index.htm (accessed 23 June 2009).
26. H. Wagner, 'Theses on Bolshevism', *New Essays* 1:3 (December 1934), pp. 1–18.
27. *Programme of the Communist Workers Party of Germany* (KAPD) (1920): www.libcom. org/library/programme-communist-workers-party-germany-kapd-1920 (accessed 06 July 2009).
28. See P. Rachleff, *Marxism and Council* Communism, p. 172. As early as 1912, Pannekoek had regarded the principles of the IWW as 'perfectly correct': P. Bourrinet, *The Dutch and German Communist* Left, p. 78. See also A. Pannekoek, *Workers' Councils'*, pp. 65–66. John Gerber writes that 'Familiarity with the IWW came from the Hamburg left radical Fritz Wolffheim, who had edited an IWW publication in the USA, and from the activities of American IWW sailors in the ports of Bremen and Hamburg.' John Gerber, 'From Left Radicalism to Council Communism: Anton Pannekoek and German Revolutionary Marxism', *Journal of Contemporary History* 23 (1988), 169–189: www.libcom.org/library/left-radicalism-council-communismanton-pannekoek-german-revolutionary-marxism-john-gerb (accessed 21 September 2009); Broué also notes the influence of the IWW on Wolffheim and the KAPD/AAUD, P. Broué, *The German Revolution*, p. 66. The ideas of the Dutch–German Left Radicals found a major platform for an American

audience in the *International Socialist Review*. This journal was published by the Chicago-based Charles H. Kerr Publishing Company between 1900 and 1918 and was politically close to both the left-wing of the Socialist Party of America and the IWW. The *International Socialist Review* regularly published articles by Luxemburg, Liebknecht, Pannekoek and other major voices within the radical and Zimmerwald lefts.

29. For a more detailed discussion of these divisions see M. van der Linden, *On Council Communism* (2004) www.kurasje.org/arkiv/15800f.htm (accessed 5 July 2009); M. Shipway, 'Council Communism' in M. Rubel and J. Crump (eds.), *Non-Market Socialism in the Nineteenth and Twentieth Centuries* (London: MacMillan Press, 1987), pp. 104–126; R. Gombin, *The Radical Tradition*, pp. 104–114.

30. See O. Rühle, *From the Bourgeois to the Proletarian Revolution* (1924) www.marxists.org/archive/ruhle/1924/revolution.htm (accessed 05 August 2009).

31. O. Rühle, *The Revolution is Not a Party Affair* (1920): www.marxists.org/archive/ruhle/1920/ruhle02.htm (accessed 01 August 2009).

32. Bock writes that 'The contacts between the AAUE and the FAUD [a German syndicalist union] were never wholly severed; AAUE representatives, for example, participated regularly as guests at the congresses of the FAUD.' Bock, 'Anarchosyndicalism in the German Labour Movement', p. 66. Thorpe speculates that the 'policy of admitting only one affiliate from each country also prevented the councilist AAUE from joining [the syndicalist international IWMA], as the FAUD was the German IWMA section.' W. Thorpe, *Revolutionary Syndicalism: An International Perspective*, p. 250.

33. M. van der Linden, *On Council Communism*.

34. Mattick wrote that 'History bypassed both groups; they argued in a vacuum. Neither the Communist Workers Party nor the anti-party section of the General Labor Union overcame their status of being "ultra-left" sects. Their internal problems became quite artificial for, as regards activities, there was actually no difference between them.' Paul Mattick, 'Anti-Bolshevist Communism in Germany', *Telos 26* (Winter 1975–1976): www.libcom.org/library/antibolshevist-communism-germany-paul-mattick (accessed 8 August 2009). See also Mattick's correspondence with members and supporters of the British Anti-Parliamentary Communist Federation on the question of revolutionary parties, 'Party and Class' in *Class War on the Home Front* (1998): www.libcom.org/library/apcf-class-war-home-front-4 (accessed 26 August 2009).

35. P. Rachleff, *Marxism and Council Communism*, p. 208.

36. This is particularly true of the conclusions of the 'platformist' current of anarchist-communism which developed out of the experiences of several former Makhnovist militants in the Russian Revolution and Civil War (1917–1921). Wolodomyr Holota, in the most comprehensive account of the Makhnovist movement, argued that the Council Communist conception of the 'party' closely resembled platformist conceptions of revolutionary organisation, and were also similarly devised as anti-statist alternatives to Bolshevism with a basis in workers' councils. *Le Mouvement machnoviste ukrainien 1918–1921 et l'évolution de l'anarchisme européen à travers le débat sur la plate-forme 1926–1934* (Unpublished PhD, Strasboug Université des sciences humaines, 1975), pp. 513–514.

It bears mention that the questions surrounding the role of a specific revolutionary political organisation has remained a recurring, often divisive, and arguably unresolved issue for many groups on the anti-statist revolutionary Left – cutting across 'anarchist' and 'Marxist' lines – as have issues of 'boring from within' traditional unions rather than forming independent 'dual unions' or autonomous workers' groups.

37. H. Bock, 'Anarchosyndicalism in the German Labour Movement', pp. 63–64.

38. M. van der Linden, *On Council Communism*.

39. G. Bonacchi, 'The Council Communists Between the New Deal and Fascism' (1976): www.libcom.org/library/council-communism-new-deal-fascism (accessed 15 August 2010).

40. Paul Mattick, 'Introduction', *New Essays*, vi.

41. P. Mattick, *Die Todeskrise des kapitalistischen Systems und die Aufgaben des Proletariats* (1933): www.workerseducation.org/crutch/pamphlets/todeskriese. html (accessed 20 July 2009).

42. Mattick still maintained correspondence and good relations with IWW members. See for example the letter from *Industrial Worker* editor Fred Thompson to Paul Mattick, Dec. 6, 1946, Paul Mattick Papers, International Institute for Social History.

43. P. Mattick, 'Introduction' *New Essays*, xi.

44. *New Essays*, 1:1 (October 1934), p. 9.

45. P. Mattick, 'Introduction' *New Essays*, i.

46. United Workers Party of America, *World-wide Fascism or World Revolution? Manifesto and Program of the United Workers Party of America* (1934): www.marxists. org/archive/mattick-paul/1934/fascism-revolution.htm (accessed 20 July 2009).

47. P. Mattick, 'Introduction' *New Essays*, vii.

48. *New Essays*, 2:2 (January 1936), 9.

49. P. Mattick, 'Introduction' *New Essays*, vii.

50. Ibid.

51. Formed in 1927, the Dutch Group of International Communists (GIC; *Groep van Internationale Communisten*) was the other leading councilist organisation in the post-1924 period.

52. See M. Nomad, 'The Masters of Tomorrow', *International Council Correspondence* 2:9&10 (September 1936), pp. 16–42 and D. Guérin, 'Fascist Corporatism' *International Council Correspondence* 3:2 (February 1937), pp. 14–26.

53. Perhaps the standard and authoritative historical work is H. Thomas, *The Spanish Civil War* (London: Penguin, 1990).

54. CNT-FAI, 'To All the Workers of the World', *New Essays* 2:11 (October 1936), p. 41.

55. P. Bourrinet, *The Dutch and German Communist Left*, p. 297.

56. Ethel MacDonald and Jane Patrick of the British United Socialist Movement, an organisation which included Guy Aldred and was politically close to the councilists, worked with the propaganda sections of the CNT-FAI in Barcelona during the war. See 'The Civil War in Spain' in *Class War on the Home Front* (1988): http://libcom.org/library/apcf-class-war-home-front (accessed 28 August 2009). The Dutch GIC also had one member who joined the anarchist militias fighting on the Aragon front, see P. Bourrinet, *The Dutch and German Communist Left*, pp. 295, 299.

57. P. Mattick, 'The Spanish Civil War', *New Essays* 2:11 (October 1936), 1.

58. Ibid. 9.

59. Ibid. 10.

60. Ibid. 14.

61. Ibid. 13.
62. Ibid. 14.
63. Ibid. 15.
64. Ibid. 13.
65. Of the POUM, Bolloten writes: 'A vigorous advocate of Socialist revolution and the dictatorship of the proletariat, an unrelenting critic of the Popular Front and of Stalin's trials and purges, the POUM was denounced as "trotskyist." Although some of its leaders, including Andres Nin and Juan Andrade, had once been disciples of Leon Trotsky and after the outbreak of the Civil War had favored giving him political asylum in Catalonia, the POUM was not a trotskyist party, and it frantically attempted to prove that it was not in numerous articles and speeches. Nevertheless, in accordance with the tactic used by Stalin at the Moscow trials of amalgamating all opponents under a single label, the communists denounced the dissidents of the POUM as Trotskyist agents of Franco, Hitler, and Mussolini.' Bolloten, *The Spanish Civil War*, p. 405.
66. P. Mattick, 'The Spanish Civil War', *New Essays* 2:11 (October 1936), p. 18.
67. Ibid. p. 21.
68. WRB, 'Anarchism and Marxism', Ibid. pp. 1–6.
69. D. Guérin, *Anarchism: From Theory to Practice* (New York: Monthly Review Press, 1970), p. 121.
70. I. Puente, *Libertarian Communism* (1932): http://flag.blackened.net/liberty/libcom.html (accessed 18 September 2009).
71. See V. Richards, *Lessons of the Spanish Revolution*, pp. 24–27.
72. D. Guérin, 'Preface' in G. Fontenis, *The Revolutionary Message of the 'Friends of Durruti'* (1983): http://flag.blackened.net/revolt/spain/FODtrans/preface.html (accessed 01 October 2009).
73. P. Mattick, 'The Spanish Civil War', *New Essays* 2:11 (October 1936), p. 21.
74. Ibid. pp. 21–22.
75. Berneri helped to organise the first group of Italian volunteers to fight in the Spanish Civil War, and politically, positioned himself between the CNT-FAI and the Friends of Durruti. Berneri was executed during the May Days in Barcelona in 1937.
76. N. Chomsky, 'Objectivity and Liberal Scholarship' in *American Power and the New Mandarins* (Middlesex/Victoria: Penguin Books, 1969), pp. 91–92.
77. Ibid. p. 38.
78. P. Mattick, 'What Next in Spain?', Ibid. p. 16.
79. P. Mattick, 'The Spanish Civil War', *New Essays* 2:11 (October 1936).
80. Ibid. p. 17.
81. W. D. Jones, *The Lost Debate: German Socialist Intellectuals and Totalitarianism* (Urbana: University of Illinois, 1999), p. 97.
82. K. Korsch, 'Economics and Politics in Revolutionary Spain', *New Essays* 4:3 (May 1938), p. 76.
83. Ibid.
84. Ibid. p. 77.
85. Ibid. p. 80.
86. Ibid.
87. Ibid. p. 81.
88. K. Korsch, 'Collectivization in Spain', *New Essays* 4:6 (April 1939), 179.
89. Ibid. p. 178.
90. Ibid. p. 180.

91. Ibid. p. 181.
92. K. Korsch, 'Economics and Politics in Revolutionary Spain', *New Essays* 4:3 (May 1938), p. 79.
93. P. Mattick, *Review of D.A. Santillan 'After the Revolution'*, *New Essays* 3:9&10 (October 1937), p. 29.
94. For discussions of the Barcelona May Days see H. Graham, ' "Against the State": A Genealogy of the Barcelona May Days (1937)', *European History Quarterly*, 29 (1999) pp. 485–542; B. Bolloten, *The Spanish Civil War*, pp. 414–461. For a first hand account and analysis, see G. Orwell, *Homage to Catalonia*, pp. 101–131; 216–248.
95. B. Bolloten, *The Spanish Civil War: revolution and counterrevolution*, p. 429.
96. Ibid. p. 430.
97. Ibid. p. 422.
98. Ibid. pp. 425–427.
99. Ibid.
100. H. Graham, ' "Against the State" ', p. 531.
101. P. Mattick, 'Civil War in Catalonia', *New Essays* 3:5&6 (June 1937), p. 41.
102. P. Mattick, 'Moscow Fascism in Spain: The Barricades Must be Torn Down!', *New Essays* 3:7&8 (August 1937), p. 28.
103. Ibid. p. 26.
104. Ibid. p. 29.
105. See excerpts from the FoD articles 'The problem of militarisation' and 'A Confederal Army' in G. Fontenis, *The Revolutionary Message of the 'Friends of Durruti'* (1983): http://flag.blackened.net/revolt/spain/FODtrans/fod_main2.html (accessed 15 September 2010).
106. In 1937, the FoD numbered some four to five thousand members. Balius claimed that the second issue of their main organ *El Amigo del Pueblo* (Friend of the People, which appeared in 12 issues between May 1937 and February 1938) had a distribution of nearly 15,000 copies. See letter from Jaime Balius to Burnett Bolloten, 24 June 1946 (Box 5, Folder 9 – Balius, Jaime, 1946–1949, Bolloten Collection, Stanford University).
107. Jaime Balius, *Towards a Fresh Revolution* (1938): www.flag.blackened.net/revolt/fod/towardshistory.html (accessed 16 August 2010).
108. Ibid.
109. Ronald Fraser, *Blood of Spain: An Oral History of the Spanish Civil War* (New York: Pantheon Books, 1979), p. 381, n. 1.
110. P. Mattick, *Karl Korsch: His Contribution to Revolutionary Marxism* (1967): www.marxists.org/archive/mattick-paul/1962/korsch.htm (accessed 20 July 2009).

# 8

## A 'Bohemian Freelancer'? C.L.R. James, His Early Relationship to Anarchism and the Intellectual Origins of Autonomism

*Christian Høgsbjerg*

In April 1940, in a private letter written amid a fierce faction fight then engulfing US Trotskyism, Leon Trotsky would refer in passing to Cyril Lionel Robert James (1901–1989), one of his leading comrades hailing originally from Trinidad, as a 'Bohemian freelancer'.[1] No doubt such an appellation would have caused distress to James had he heard of it at the time, for his political and intellectual evolution had owed much to Trotsky's Marxism ever since his reading of the first volume of *History of the Russian Revolution* in 1932. Yet such an appellation would, for many, both within and outside orthodox Trotskyism, seem to be vindicated by James's subsequent development as a political thinker, which would see him leave the official Trotskyist movement in 1951. Indeed, many commentators have gone much further than Trotsky, and associated James's mature political thought as much with anarchist thinking as with revolutionary Marxism. In 1981, Paul Berman declared he thought James had ultimately come up with 'a version of socialism that wittingly or unwittingly incorporates elements of anarchism within a larger Marxist framework'.[2] In 1987, James D. Young, subsequently author of *The World of C.L.R. James*, asserted 'James was always a dissident with a touch of anarchist disaffection'.[3] In 1989, after James's passing, Robin Blackburn in an obituary declared him an 'Anarcho-Bolshevik', while E.P. Thompson apparently went as far as to speak of James's writing not just being 'infused with a libertarian tendency' but of James's 'instinctive, unarticulated anarchism'.[4]

Yet there is a problem here, since James's anarchism was not simply 'unarticulated'. Rather, his writings explicitly display a casual and traditional Marxist dismissiveness of anarchism as irredeemably 'petty-bourgeois' in both theory and practice. In 1948, in *Notes on Dialectics*, James noted that 'the Proudhonists and Bakuninists represented the petty-bourgeois capitalistic influences in the proletariat' at the time of the First International which lost out to Marxism after 'the mass upheaval of the [Paris] Commune defeated the Proudhonists' because of 'the decline of the petty-bourgeois individualism in capitalism as a whole'. During the 'proletarian uprising' of the Spanish civil war, James in *Notes on Dialectics* noted that the 'the petty-bourgeois anarchist and socialist bureaucracies' allied themselves with Stalinism, which 'delivered the proletariat to Franco', commenting that 'the whole Popular Front Manoeuvre was part of the organic movement of the new petty bourgeoisie toward Stalinism'.[5] Moreover, as Berman admitted, in one of the only sustained and detailed discussions of James and anarchism in the existing scholarship, James:

> ...has always called himself, in spite of everything, a Leninist...as to anarchism, in all of his writings he condemns it forcefully. But I must say, James's forcefulness on this point reminds me of nothing so much as Rosa Luxemburg's similar forcefulness in the opening pages of *The Mass Strike* – an instance of protesting too much.[6]

The debate over James's relative intellectual affinity with or distance from anarchism is unlikely to be resolved in the near future. Given the complexity of his political and intellectual evolution, which ranged widely over both time and space, it is certainly beyond the boundaries of what is possible in one chapter to even attempt such a feat. Rather this chapter will attempt to clarify an important aspect of this question through a concrete historical exploration first of James's early relationship to anarchism and his growing openness to the idea that the Soviet Union under Stalin was 'state-capitalist' rather than socialist, and second, a briefer discussion of how his more mature political thought came to inspire and influence strands of 'autonomist' thinking during the 1950s and beyond. In making such an examination, however, it is perhaps worth stating that we will begin from the premise that James is best recognised and understood from the outset not as an anarchist thinker, but as a Marxist. Indeed, as I have suggested elsewhere, James was one of the twentieth century's most original and outstanding contributors to what Hal Draper has termed the revolutionary democratic tradition of 'socialism from below'.[7] For Paul Buhle, James's original and authorised biographer, James was 'one of the few truly creative Marxists from the 1930s to the 1950s, perhaps alone in his masterful synthesis of world history, philosophy, government, mass life and popular culture'. Buhle thought any reference to James's politics as 'anarchist' in 'its treatment of party and state' was ultimately a 'sincere but mistaken' position.[8]

The aim of this chapter however is to illuminate the evolution and intellectual influence of James's creativity as a 'dissident Marxist', to use the phrase of another biographer of James's, David Renton, not to attempt to demonstrate in detail his intellectual distance from anarchism.[9] Indeed, anarchists helped shape the political thought and historical imagination of the young James, and his life and work in 1930s Britain in particular offers a fascinating glimpse into an almost forgotten subterranean world of far-Left politics, a story of heretics and renegades, from surrealist poets to Jewish printers and anarchist booksellers. The empirical focus of the article will therefore firstly examine how the seeds of James's 'dissident Marxism' were arguably first sown in this early period, before making a brief outline of how it flowered during his US sojourn and then came to fertilise thinking on the European far-Left during the 1950s and subsequently. In the process it is hoped that some of the creative overlaps which do exist between the two traditions of Marxism and anarchism will be illuminated.

## C.L.R. James's early bohemianism

Rather than being an 'instinctive anarchist', the early politics of James, such as they were while a young teacher, journalist and writer in the British Crown Colony of Trinidad were distinctly of the gradual, practical, statist, reformist variety. He was a democrat in a country without any meaningful democracy, a parliamentary socialist in a country without a meaningful parliament. James's hero at the time, and the subject of his first book in 1932, was Captain Arthur Andrew Cipriani, the former Commanding Officer of the British West Indies Regiment in the First World War and then leader of the mass social democratic nationalist Trinidad Workingmen's Association (TWA). Inspired in part also by Gandhi and Marcus Garvey, James became a campaigner for 'West Indian self-government', but at this stage he was very far from the revolutionary Marxist and 'class struggle Pan-Africanist' he would become. If '[c]onservatism unprodded hardens into tyranny, radicalism unchecked degenerates into chaos,' he wrote in one 1931 article.[10] If anything, James was a liberal humanist who aspired to live by the tenets of the Victorian thinker and cultural critic Matthew Arnold, but his attempt to sincerely follow Arnoldian ideals led him to first implicitly, and then explicitly, criticise British colonial rule. He joined up with other writers around two literary journals, *Trinidad* and then *The Beacon*, the latter of which the editor Albert Gomes recalled 'became the focus of a movement of enlightenment spearheaded by Trinidad's angry young men of the Thirties. It was the torpor, the smugness and the hypocrisy of the Trinidad of the period that provoked the response which produced both the magazine and the defiant bohemianism of the movement that was built around it.'[11]

In this early period, then, James seems to have been something of an 'instinctive Bohemian freelancer'.[12] Arriving in Britain in 1932, witnessing the Lancashire cotton textile workers strike while up in Nelson, and then reading Trotsky's *History of the Russian Revolution* amid the conditions of the Great Depression and the triumph of Hitler's Nazis in 1933 led James to politically radicalise while working as the *Manchester Guardian*'s cricket correspondent. In 1934, James left the British Labour Party which he had joined in solidarity with Cipriani's TWA and joined the tiny British Trotskyist movement, in particular the section of it inside the Independent Labour Party (ILP), the Marxist Group.

James orientated to Trotskyism largely through his own critical independent reading, but it was while searching out Marxist classics in London in 1933 that he happened to visit a bookshop on 68 Red Lion Street, *Lahr,* owned by an anarchist from Germany, Charlie Lahr. Lahr was, according to David Goodway, 'very probably the last' in the line, 'stretching back to the late eighteenth-century', of 'great London radical booksellerscum-publishers'.[13] During the 1930s, Jonathan Rose argues, his bookshop was 'a mecca for down and out Nietzscheans and scruffy poets'.[14] James remembers Lahr soon 'got interested in what I was doing and would put aside a book or pamphlet for me he knew or thought would interest me'.[15] The two soon formed what James describes as 'a curious partnership', with Lahr helping James become acquainted with knowledge of the reactionary nature of individual Labour leaders and British trade union bureaucrats. In particular, James learned much about contemporary Germany and Hitler's rise to power.[16]

## C.L.R. James's reading of Peter Kropotkin

One might surmise that it was Lahr who also recommended James read the great anarchist Peter Kropotkin's masterful *The Great French Revolution* (1909), a pioneering volume of 'history-from-below' that was admired by Lenin and Trotsky, as part of his ongoing research on the Haitian Revolution.[17] In 1938, in his majestic classic *The Black Jacobins*, James praised Kropotkin for having a 'more instinctive understanding of revolution than any well-known book' on the subject of the French Revolution.[18] For Kropotkin, the 'true fount and origin of the Revolution' was 'the people's readiness to take up arms', noting that it was this that previous 'historians of the Revolution had not done justice – the justice owed to it by the history of civilisation'.[19] In particular, Kropotkin's stress on the revolutionary violence of the peasantry in *The Great French Revolution* seems to have influenced James when he came to understanding and analysing the liberation struggle of the enslaved black masses of French colonial Saint Domingue. For Kropotkin, 'the insurrection of the peasants for the abolition of the feudal rights and the recovery of the communal lands' in the summer of 1789 was, 'the very essence, the foundation of the great Revolution' and 'the great rising of the rural districts', the *jacquerie*, which 'lasted five years, was what enabled the Revolution to accomplish the immense work of demolition which we owe to it'.[20]

When James described the open revolt and indeed insurrection on the North Plain in Saint Domingue in August 1791, when the enslaved blacks 'neglected and ignored by all the politicians of every brand and persuasion' had 'organised on their own and struck for freedom at last' he effectively brought out the way in which their uprising resembled the contemporaneous struggles of the French peasantry:

> The slaves worked on the land, and, like revolutionary peasants every-where, they aimed at the extermination of their oppressors . . . the slaves destroyed tirelessly. Like the peasants in the Jacquerie . . . they were seeking their salvation in the most obvious way, the destruction of what they knew was the cause of their sufferings; and if they destroyed much it was because they had suffered much.[21]

By 1803, after 12 years of fighting for national independence and social libera-tion, James noted that the black rebel slave army had been forced to burn Saint Domingue 'flat so that at the end of the war it was a charred desert':

> Why do you burn everything? asked a French officer of a prisoner. We have a right to burn what we cultivate because a man has a right to dispose of his own labour, was the reply of this unknown anarchist.[22]

If other writers, above all Trotsky in his *History of the Russian Revolution*, had helped James understand the way in which the enslaved blacks acted like a 'proto-proletariat' during the Haitian Revolution, then Kropotkin's *The Great French Revolution* must have been critical to helping James understand the way in which the rebellious slave army acted like a 'proto-peasantry'.[23]

Another way in which James seems to have been influenced by Kropotkin was through his discussion of events in revolutionary France itself, particu-larly the 'Communism' in Paris between March 1793 and July 1794.[24] 'In the streets of Paris, Jacques Varlet and Roux were preaching Communism, not in production but in distribution, a natural reaction to the profiteering of the new bourgeoisie', a comment that essentially summarises Kropotkin's more detailed discussion of 'the Communist movement' in *The Great French Revolu-tion*.[25] It is possible that James's admiration and respect for Kropotkin's great work may have encouraged later assessments of his 'instinctive' anarchism. In 1963, in the revised edition of *The Black Jacobins*, James would certainly continue to praise 'Kropotkin's brief history of over fifty years ago' as 'the best general book in English [on the French Revolution] . . . Kropotkin thought the Revolution was a wonderful event and was neither afraid nor embarrassed to say so'.[26]

## C.L.R. James, anarchists in Britain and the Spanish civil war

While James's sense of fair play and critical thinking abilities led him to read widely and absorb a lot of different ideas, his political thought was also profoundly affected by the whole environment of far-Left politics in 1930s

Britain, and the eclectic milieu around the ILP, with its various traditions including Council Communism and diverse other forms of non-Leninist socialisms.[27] Moreover, fast emerging as the intellectual driving force of British Trotskyism during the 1930s, James was on reasonably good terms with one of the leading anarchists in Britain during this period, as well as anti-Stalinist communist activists like the veteran Guy Aldred who he met in Glasgow.[28] Almost by accident, James had crossed paths with Vernon Richards, a young anarchist from Italy who was editor of *Spain and the World*, the main British anarchist paper of the day (previously and subsequently called *Freedom*) which Richards had launched in London in late 1936 in solidarity with the eruption of the Spanish revolution while only 21 years old.[29] As the editor of the Trotskyist journal *Fight* (launched in October 1936), James met Richards on one of his regular visits to the printers at Narod Press in 129/131 Bedford Street, Whitechapel, which was run by a team of Jewish apprentices under 'Papa Naroditsky' and his three sons. As Richards remembered, 'apart from the boys themselves...one had the opportunity to meet other editors supervising their journals', including 'the gentle-speaking West Indian marxist C.L.R James who was producing his *Fight!* No punch-ups, political or otherwise.'[30]

James would on occasion rally to the side of the British anarchist movement against the ILP and Communist Party of Great Britain (CPGB) in *Fight*. For example, in November 1937, James took issue with leading ILP figure Fenner Brockway in *Fight* for forbidding ILP speakers to stand on the anarchist platform during the May Day celebrations in Britain that year in order to appease the CPGB In the context of the Spanish civil war then raging, James noted that in Spain 'the ILP, the Trotskyists and the Anarchists, are in their different ways, on one side of the barricade and the Stalinists on the other'; reflecting on the British context he asked rhetorically of Brockway, 'will he propose [a] united front, actively in defence of the Spanish Revolution, between the ILP, the Trotskyists and the Anarchists?'[31]

Richards's publication *Spain and the World* suggests something about the wider connection between anarchists and the tiny Pan-Africanist movement in Britain in the 1930s. In May 1937, James with his compatriot and boyhood friend, George Padmore, launched the International African Service Bureau (IASB) in London, and the title at least of the IASB's 1937 newsletter, *Africa and the World*, seems a little inspired by *Spain and the World*. The presence among the patrons of the IASB of the ILP affiliated socialist free-thinker F.A. Ridley, who called for an 'anarcho-marxist alliance' in 1938, is perhaps significant.[32] There are tantalising glimpses in Ethel Mannin's satirical 1945 novel *Comrade O' Comrade* of one key Pan-Africanist in Britain during this period, the Barbadian veteran anti-colonialist and organiser of the Colonial Seamen's Association – Chris Braithwaite – better known under his pseudonym 'Chris Jones' – speaking alongside Emma Goldman on meetings on the Spanish revolution in London during this period.[33] Such contacts and meetings meant George Padmore would later recall the period 'immediately before the outbreak of the Second World War' as 'one of the most stimulating and constructive in the history of Pan-Africanism', noting that black intellectuals made what he called a 'detailed and systematic study of European political theories and systems' including anarchism.[34]

Together with the Spanish Civil War the Moscow Trials were of importance in explaining James's later break with orthodox Trotskyism. In exposing the counter-revolutionary nature of Stalinism, both events led James to question Trotsky's characterisation of the Soviet Union. The same events were also to be critical for the political evolution of James's key intellectual collaborator during the 1940s, Raya Dunayevskaya. As Peter Hudis has suggested, the Spanish civil war in particular:

> ... presented revolutionaries with what Dunayevskaya was later to call the 'absolute contradiction' of our age – the emergence of counter-revolution from *within* revolution. It was not only the Stalinists, however, whose role was compromised by these events. For the various anti-Stalinist tendencies, be they Trotskyist, anarchist or independent, failed to successfully combat the new phenomenon of counter-revolution emerging from within revolution.[35]

In response to the apparent intellectual and political failure to have fully prepared for the new reality of Stalinist counter-revolutionary terror in Spain, Dunayevskaya, Trotsky's Russian language secretary from 1937–1938, later recalled how she first became critical of the limitations of Trotsky's analysis of the Soviet Union as a 'degenerated workers' state' during this tumultuous period. 'Out of the Spanish Civil War there emerged a new kind of revolutionary who posed questions, not only against Stalinism, but against Trotskyism, indeed against all *established* Marxisms.'[36]

James similarly began to ask questions of Trotsky's analysis of the Soviet Union in *The Revolution Betrayed*, a work which Trotsky had completed in June 1936 and so before the Moscow Trials and the Stalinist suppression of the Workers' Party of Marxist Unification (POUM)and anarchists in Barcelona. Indeed, by the time James wrote his pioneering anti-Stalinist Marxist history of 'the rise and fall of the Communist International', *World Revolution*, published in April 1937, while still formally accepting Trotsky's analysis he was already showing an openness to those arguing that the Soviet Union had become a state capitalist society. According to Special Branch operatives, when James spoke in London in defence of Trotsky after the first Moscow Trial on 9 September 1936, 'he compared the conditions of the British and Russian workers, adding that a form of capitalism was creeping into the Soviet State'.[37] In the course of researching *World Revolution*, James read the works of a number of people who felt the Soviet Union was now state-capitalist including two former leading German Communists, Arthur Rosenberg and Karl Korsch – the latter James apparently met in 1936.[38]

Another influence was the former leading French Communist Boris Souvarine. Born Boris Liefschitz in 1885 in Kiev, Souvarine, who clearly had some sort of anarchist sympathies early on as he took his name from the Russian anarchist bomb-planter in Emile Zola's *Germinal* – had been a founding member of the French Communist Party. Having known Trotsky since meeting him in Paris during the Great War, Souvarine had spoken bravely against Stalin in Moscow. Though Trotsky had high hopes of Souvarine forming a viable French Trotskyist movement, since 1929, Souvarine had broken off good relations with Trotsky, attacking Leninism and describing the Soviet Union as 'state capitalist'. Souvarine's 1935 biography of Stalin maintained that 'the Federation of Socialist Soviet Republics, the very name a fourfold contradiction of the reality, has long ago ceased to exist', and 'Soviet state capitalism', 'so-called Soviet society' rests 'on its own method of exploitation of man by man'.[39] James seems to have met up with Souvarine in Paris in 1938 and would translate his *Staline* into English in 1939, generously describing it as 'a book with an anarchist bias against the dictatorship of the proletariat but irreproachably documented, very fair, and full of insight'.[40]

Indeed, while James himself in *World Revolution* remained loyal to Trotsky's characterisation of the Soviet Union in *The Revolution Betrayed*, he also presented much evidence which suggested that Stalinist Russia could not in any way be described as a 'workers' state', even a 'degenerated' one. As James noted, 'the fiction of workers' control, after 20 years of the revolution, is dead. But the bureaucracy fears the proletariat. It knows, none better, the temper of the people it so mercilessly cheats and exploits.'[41] For Trotsky, the bureaucracy was a brutal oppressor, but was not actually exploiting the working class.[42] Yet for James, the first Five Year Plan meant that 'the remnants of workers control were wiped away'.[43] 'The Russian proletariat, after its Herculean efforts, seems to have exchanged one set of masters for another, while the very basis of the proletarian state is being undermined beneath its feet.' James declared that the methods of Stalin's industrialisation drive seemed to be just 'discovering what the capitalists knew hundreds of years ago . . . where will all this end?'[44]

Such ideas were in the air on the far-Left during the 1930s, and so James's criticisms, of the idea that state ownership of the means of production necessarily meant socialism, were not unique.[45] After writing *World Revolution*, for example, James would in 1937 write an introduction for *Red Spanish Notebook*, an eyewitness account of revolutionary Spain through the eyes of two surrealist poets who had gone to fight for the POUM, Mary Low and the Cuban Trotskyist Juan Breá. Breá had concluded by pondering the motives of the Soviet Union with respect to revolutionary Spain, noting 'let us suppose that Russia is no longer a proletarian state but is making her first steps towards capitalism'.[46] One other witness to Stalinist counter-revolution in

Spain was George Orwell, who seems to have met up with James in the summer of 1937 after returning to Britain and who once described *World Revolution* as a 'very able book'. In his 1938 classic work of revolutionary journalism, *Homage to Catalonia*, Orwell described the 'socialism in one country' being built in Russia by Stalin as little more than 'a planned state-capitalism with the grab-motive left intact'.[47]

On 3 September 1938, at the founding conference of the Fourth International, James intervened forcefully in the debate challenging the orthodox position that Trotskyists should call for the defence of the USSR in case of war.[48] A month later, James would travel to North America, meet Trotsky himself for discussions on the strategy and tactics of the black liberation struggle in the USA, and steadily establish himself as an original and creative thinker inside the US Trotskyist movement during the 1940s.[49] Trotsky's 1940 comment on James as a 'bohemian freelancer' therefore has to be seen in the context of the split in US Trotskyism, and the position James took in this split which saw him side against Trotsky and with the minority around Max Shachtman – rather than as a comment by Trotsky on James's developing ideas on the class nature of the Soviet Union. Indeed, James's subsequent embrace and development of the theory of state capitalism after Trotsky's death would steadily enable him and others to help clarify Marx's meaning of socialism itself as the self-emancipation of the working class anew, where state ownership of the means of production was not recognised as any kind of end in itself, to be equated with 'socialism', but merely a means for achieving the end goal of the emancipation of the working class through the creation of what Lenin in *The State and Revolution* had called the 'Commune-State'.[50]

James's reading of Kropotkin's *The Great French Revolution* and fraternal relationship with such anarchists as Charlie Lahr and Vernon Richards in Britain should not then detract from the fundamental importance of the towering revolutionary figure of Leon Trotsky and Trotskyism for James during the 1930s in shaping and informing his entire world view. Any criticisms of Trotskyism that James had that may have been informed in part by anarchism were not going to lead him to fundamentally break with Marxist ways of thinking. After exploring some of the ways in which James politically evolved from parliamentary socialism to a politics based on the revolutionary democratic tradition of 'socialism from below' during the 1930s, we shall now examine how his later intellectual development in the USA from 1938 to 1953 would come to influence one currently influential strand of autonomist political theory.

## The evolution of C.L.R. James's mature Marxism

In *Beyond a Boundary*, James's 1963 semi-autobiographical classic cultural history of cricket in its colonial context, he had this to say when he looked back at his political evolution after arriving from Trinidad to encounter a Europe devastated by the First World War and the economic slump and now witnessing the alarming rise of fascism:

> Fiction-writing drained out of me and was replaced by politics. I became a Marxist, a Trotskyist. I published large books and small articles on these and other kindred subjects. I wrote and spoke. Like many others, I expected war, and during or after the war social revolution. In 1938 a lecture tour took me to the United States and I stayed there 15 years. The war came. It did not bring soviets and proletarian power. Instead the bureaucratic-to-talitarian monster grew stronger and spread. As early as 1941 I had begun to question the premises of Trotskyism. It took nearly a decade of incessant labour and collaboration to break with it and reorganise my marxist ideas to cope with the post-war world. That was a matter of doctrine, of history, of economics and politics.[51]

To attempt to do justice to this 'reorganisation' of Marxism by James is impossible here, but a few words on its most crucial aspects is essential. Using his Trotskyist pseudonym, 'J.R. Johnson', James, together with Raya Dunayevskaya, or 'Freddie Forest' as she was known, and Grace Lee Boggs and others, became known collectively as the 'Johnson-Forest Tendency' inside 1940s US Trotskyism. It is noteworthy that during the Second World War and its aftermath they drew inspiration from Lenin's attempts to come to terms with the disaster that had engulfed the working-class movement during the First World War. So for example, just as the exiled Lenin in 1914 turned in despair to the library and a serious study of Hegelian dialectics to produce his 'Philosophical Notebooks', so James, Dunayevskaya and Lee in their search to find a philosophy of revolution now also spent hours engaged in serious study of the German philosopher. One product of this was James's 1948 work *Notes on Dialectics* (subtitled *Hegel, Marx, Lenin*).

Though a systematic exposition is impossible, it is vital to have some sense of how the Johnson-Forest Tendency attempted to, in James's own words 'work through Leninism' in order to try to come to terms with the crisis that had overcome not just Marxism but the wider working-class movement in a period dominated by Stalinism and Fascism.[52] This 'working through' Leninism necessitated a break with the theory and practice of 'orthodox Trotskyism', a movement James had been committed to since becoming an organised revolutionary in 1934. However, this break was conceived as a conscious attempt to not only return to classical Marxism as understood by Marx and Lenin – but also to develop that tradition so it fitted with the new realities of the post-war world. It was to make, as James put it grandly, 'our own leap from the heights of Leninism'.[53]

For Trotsky the founding of the Fourth International in 1938 represented the solution to what he called the historic 'crisis of revolutionary leadership' gripping the official political organisations of the working-class movement. Against this perspective, the Johnson-Forest Tendency during the 1940s felt the critical crisis of the age was instead what they called the 'crisis of the self-mobilisation of the proletariat', and so argued for a greater stress and focus on what James called 'free creative activity' and 'disciplined spontaneity', the self-activity of the working class itself autonomous of official political parties and trade union bureaucracies.[54]

Yet James, writing while still a member of the official Trotskyist movement, still felt in an important sense that the struggle to build a Fourth International amid a period of world-historic defeats for the international working-class movement had at least preserved the honour and the tradition of revolutionary communism associated with Marx and Lenin. The new-found stress on the self-activity of the working class in the work of the Johnson-Forest Tendency, James insisted, had not come from anarchism. As James put it in *Notes on Dialectics*,

> ... we have arrived, are arriving at Marxist ideas for our time out of Trotsky-ism. We would not come out of Stalinism, or social democracy, or anar-chism. Despite every blunder, and we have not spared them, Trotskyism was and remains in the truly dialectical sense, the only theoretical revolu-tionary current since Leninism ... we came from there and could have only come from there.[55]

However, James and the Johnson-Forest Tendency's 'Marxist ideas for our time', developed inside 1940s US Trotskyism, would ultimately come to influence the origins of a new and different current of political thought to either anarchism or Marxism in its classical forms – autonomism. As Steve Wright suggests, 'the core premises of autonomist Marxism were first de-veloped in Italy during the 1960s and 1970s' when militants first sought to confront Marx's *Capital* with 'the real study of a real factory' in 1960s Italy, beginning with Romano Alquati's pioneering 1961 'Report of the new forc-es' at F.I.A.T. However, as Wright and others including Harry Cleaver have noted, the intellectual origins of such a research project and 'autonomist Marxism' in general lie outside Italy and date back to before the 1960s.[56] During the momentous year of 1956 and for two years subsequently, for example, Daniel Mothé, a member of the French revolutionary group So-cialisme ou Barbarie around Cornelius Castoriadis and a milling machine operator at the Renault Billancourt vehicle factory, kept a diary. This was subsequently published as *Journal d'un Ouvrier, 1956–58*, and translated into Italian in 1960. Even earlier, in 1954, Danilo Montaldi, a 'dissident Marxist' sociologist had published in *Battaglia Communista* a translation of a 1947 work titled *The American Worker* by a member of the Johnson-Forest Ten-dency Phil Singer (who used the pseudonym Paul Romano). This work had first been translated into French by the comrades of Socialisme ou Barbarie who published it in their journal in parts from 1949 onwards, before being translated from the French by Montaldi.[57] It therefore seems important to explore in detail the circumstances in which Phil Singer's highly influential work came to be written.

## C.L.R. James and the making of *The American Worker*

Phil Singer was an American car worker at a General Motors plant who in his late twenties had kept a diary, which, with the help of Grace Lee Boggs, he had written up in order to portray 'Life in the Factory', 'what the workers are thinking and doing while actually at work on the bench or on the line'.[58] For Singer, most significant was his recording of not simply the degrading experience of factory work but also the everyday attempts by workers to resist at the point of production through struggles for dignity and a meaningful existence:

> This pamphlet is directed to the rank and file worker and its intention is to express those innermost thoughts which the worker rarely talks about even to his fellow workers. In keeping a diary, so to speak, of the day to day reactions to factory life, I hoped to uncover the reasons for the workers deep dissatisfaction which has reached a peak in recent years and has expressed itself in the latest strikes and spontaneous walkouts.[59]

The contribution made by Singer himself to the making of *The American Worker*, was then clearly profound – yet it would be mistaken to assume this was not essentially also a 'collective work' of the Johnson-Forest Tendency, with James himself playing a particularly critical role. As Grace Lee Boggs, who under her pseudonym Ria Stone wrote a lengthy piece of commentary titled 'The Reconstruction of Society' as an afterword to Singer's commentary in *The American Worker*, recalled:

> ...because CLR could not be publicly active, we acted as his transmission belt to the larger American community...one of CLR's great gifts was that he could detect the special abilities and interests of individuals and encourage them to use these to enrich the movement and at the same time enlarge themselves.... Phil Singer, a young GM worker, was always talking about the frustrations of the rank-and-file worker in the plant. CLR proposed that he keep a journal of his experiences. These were subsequently published in *The American Worker*.[60]

In a sense this does not sound that original, as attempting to understand society from the standpoint of working-class experience at the point of production had, ever since Marx's own *Workers' Inquiry* of 1880 if not before, at least been nominally at the heart of classical Marxism. A few months after launching *Pravda* in 1912, for example, Lenin noted that 'the chronicle of workers' life is only just *beginning* to develop into a permanent feature of *Pravda*... the workers' newspaper is a workers' forum. Before the whole of Russia the workers should raise here, one after another, the various questions of workers' life in general and of working-class democracy in particular.' Though the repressive conditions of Tsarist Russia meant Lenin's *Pravda* only lasted for a couple of years at a time of rising class struggle (1912–1914), one study of the paper by Tony Cliff noted that over 11,000 letters and items of correspondence from workers were published in a single year, or about 35 items per day.[61] As James had noted in his discussion of 'Lenin and Socialism' back in 1937 in *World Revolution*:

> The creative capacity of the masses – he [Lenin] believed in it as no other leader of the workers ever did.... The Soviet system based on the masses in the factories was to organise this creativeness not only for purpose of government but also for production, linking the two closer and closer together until ultimately the all-embracing nature of production by the whole of society rendered the State superfluous.[62]

Indeed, the British Trotskyist journal *Fight*, which James had edited in the 1930s, had carried a regular series titled 'On the Job' in 1937, featuring, for example, 'The Building Worker' by a young member of the Marxist Group who was a carpenter, Arthur Alexander Ballard, and then 'From the Engineer's Bench' by a member of the Amalgamated Engineering Union.[63] Trotsky himself in 1939 famously criticised the US Trotskyist paper, *Socialist Appeal*, on the grounds that '[it] is a paper for the workers' and not a workers' paper... . You do not hear at all how the workers live, fight, clash with the police or drink whisky... the task is not to make a paper through the joint forces of a skilled editorial board but to encourage the workers to speak for themselves.'[64]

Yet if James's encouraging of a fellow member of the Johnson-Forest Tendency to keep a diary detailing his experience at work was then not so original – the group's distinctive perspectives, particularly that of a shift towards 'state capitalism' from the 1930s on not simply in Russia but internationally, profoundly shaped what became *The American Worker*. As the leaders of the Johnson-Forest Tendency put it themselves in 1947:

> ... the Russian question is only a part of the world crisis. The decisive stage of economic development is statification of production. Statification of production is not a phrase or a description. It marks the capitulation of anarchic capitalist society to the planning of the invading socialist society. The planning, however, torn by class contradictions, repeats the fundamental features of capitalist antagonisms in their most barbarous form. Statification carries in itself the most profound social awareness of

the proletariat, and its social structure repeatedly propels the proletariat on the road to the complete transformation of society. . . . The barbarism of capitalism was concretely demonstrated in Russia. But it was the American proletariat which concretised for us the necessarily abstract conception of the creative power of the proletariat in industry as a force for the social regeneration of society. The work of American industrial psychologists and the observations of proletarian comrades whom we had developed opened this door to us. The Johnson-Forest Tendency will soon publish a pamphlet by Phil Romano and Ria Stone which will deal fully with this question from both a practical and a theoretical point of view.[65]

*The American Worker* then was about reaffirming and re-emphasising the Johnson-Forest Tendency's 'conception of the creative power of the proletariat in industry as a force for the social regeneration of society' at a time when 'socialism' had come to be seen merely as state ownership without any accompanying revolutionary democracy or workers' control.[66] In particular, James's individual contribution to developing this conception should be noted. As the American Trotskyist Stanley Weir recalled:

> . . . James was the first and only leader in the entire Trotskyist movement, from which I heard discussion of the special form of workers' control which develops in every workplace naturally and informally. He knew of the existence of informal cultures and that they were the basis from which to broach the entire question of workers' control . . . For me, he introduced the ideas which demonstrated the value of what is done socially from below on the job to get out production and to survive.[67]

## C.L.R. James, *The American Worker* and Italian workerism

We can now tentatively assess the impact of the Johnson-Forest Tendency as expressed through *The American Worker* on Italian workerism, something which as we have seen was possible thanks in no small part to the translations of Danilo Montaldi.[68] As Montaldi noted, *The American Worker* expressed:

> . . . with great force and profundity, the idea – practically forgotten by the marxist movement after the publication of *Capital* Volume 1 – that before being the adherent of a party, a militant of the revolution or the subject of a future socialist power, the worker is a being who lives above all in capitalist production and the factory; and that it is in production that the revolt against exploitation, the capacity to construct a superior type of society, along with class solidarity of other workers and hatred for exploitation and exploiters – both the classic bosses of yesterday and the impersonal bureaucrats of today and tomorrow – are formed.[69]

Moreover, for those on the anti-Stalinist far-Left in France and especially Italy during the 1950s, *The American Worker* was even more remarkable given the anti-Americanism of the Communist-dominated official Left in the context of the Cold War. As Ferrucio Gambino, a sociologist from the University of Padua and co-founder of two 1960s Italian workerist journals *Quaderni Rossi* (Red Notebooks), and *Potere Operaio* (Workers Power) recalls, after the brutal suppression of the Hungarian Revolution by Russian tanks:

> . . . tiny groups and individuals in Southern Europe discovered and read 'the American comrades' – two words that at long last it was possible to put together again – 'the American comrades' who contributed to *Socialisme ou Barbarie* . . . The conditions of the working class looked strikingly similar throughout the so-called First World – and, we argued at that time, it could not be dissimilar in the Second World. State capitalism was a living category whereby we could relate in solidarity to the people who were bearing the brunt of the opposition to 'actuated socialism'.[70]

In the 1960s, Gambino and another historian of US labour, Bruno Cartosio from Milan – would eventually establish relations with James and his loyal disciple Martin Glaberman, and the publishing of James himself into Italian began with *The Black Jacobins* in 1968 – and continued subsequently.[71] Links were established with the Jamesians in Detroit at the heart of the League of Revolutionary Black Workers while the translation of other US Jamesians followed in the 1970s.[72] As Cleaver noted in 1979, 'works by C.L.R. James, James Boggs, George Rawick, and Martin Glaberman, among others, have been translated into Italian and probably received wider circulation and discussion in Italy than in the United States'.[73]

Overall, though it has not been possible here to examine James's influence on Italian autonomism more fully, it might still be possible to draw a few conclusions. In one sense it is a pity that after helping to provide a critical focus on the self-activity of the working class at the point of production, a stress on the possibilities which flowed from wildcat strikes and other unofficial industrial action, that more of James's writings were not translated into Italian during the 1960s. It is possible that they might have ensured less of a subsequent retreat from revolutionary Marxism towards an ultimately elitist substitution of the actions of a minority for the mass action of the working class among many in the Italian autonomists. From joining the Trotskyist movement in 1934 up until his death in 1989, James – unlike say some of the current 'thought leaders' of autonomism such as Michael Hardt and Antonio Negri – never lost sight of either the central importance of working-class struggle or the need for some sort of revolutionary Marxist organisation.[74] Moreover, as Chamsy El-Ojeili has noted, compared to the majority of early Italian workerist theorists who failed adequately to consider the lives of workers outside of the purely economic battles at the point of production, James was more 'attentive to the wider cultural aspects of such an investigation of proletarian working life'.[75]

However, that said, James's own reification of spontaneity, and own gradual abandonment of the rich classical Bolshevik legacy of strategy and tactics, after his 1951 break with official Trotskyism, were not without consequences of their own. They meant that his subsequent groups of supporters, like even the best elements of the Italian autonomists, were unable to ever really satisfactorily develop a new form of revolutionary organisation able to adequately relate to the key insight of 'working class autonomy'.[76] It is possible that this was because that insight in itself, without an adequate material understanding of the wider economic and political context outside the factory, and the wider, uneven consciousness among the working class where forms of reformist politics are inevitably almost always dominant – even inside the most militant factory itself – can only reveal so much. Yet though James, the 'bohemian freelancer', ultimately failed to make his great leap forward 'from the heights of Leninism', his creative, revolutionary and democratic 'dissident Marxism' nonetheless deserves critical appreciation and study by anti-capitalist scholars and activists today.

## Conclusion

When one looks back over the last 20 years to those men who are most far sighted, who first began to tease out the muddle of ideology in our times, who were at the same time Marxist with a hard theoretical basis, and close students of society, humanists with a tremendous response to and understanding of human culture, Comrade James is one of the first one thinks of.

So spoke E.P. Thompson in 1967 at a 'National Conference on Workers Control and Industrial Democracy', after 'Comrade James' had introduced himself to the gathered assembly at Coventry in a contribution from the floor.[77] Of course, Thompson could arguably have gone further and dated James's contribution to 'teasing out the muddle of ideology in our times' back not just 20 years to 1947 but 30 years, from the publication in 1937 of James's history of the 'rise and fall of the Communist International', *World Revolution,* a pioneering critique of Stalin's ideology of 'Socialism in One Country' and its consequences for the international working-class movement.

Nevertheless, Thompson's eloquent 1967 tribute and acknowledgement of the 'hard theoretical basis' of James's Marxism arguably serves as a more accurate remembrance than his later apparent suggestion of James's 'instinctive, unarticulated anarchism'. This chapter has tried to demonstrate not simply why this is the case but also some of the complexities involved in any discussion of James's relationship to anarchism. While acknowledging that James's reading of Kropotkin and meeting individual anarchists made an impact on his early political thought, the 'Marxism for our time' developed by James and his co-thinkers in the Johnson-Forest Tendency during the 1940s was fundamentally shaped within the theoretical parameters of Marxism in order to overcome the limitations of orthodox Trotskyism in facing up to the new realities of the post-war world. The Johnson-Forest Tendency's stress on the changing nature of the worker's experience of exploitation and revolt at the point of capitalist production both anticipated and, through 'the observations of proletarian comrades' such as Phil Singer in *The American Worker*, also helped shape the ideas driving Italian workerism in the 1960s and 1970s.

James's distinctive stress on the 'free creative activity' and 'disciplined spontaneity' of the working class has often led commentators to detect an anarchist bent to his political thought. Paul Berman felt that 'anyone who has read Dolgoff's or Lehning's editions of Bakunin's writings will recognise a Bakuninist resonance to James's anti-state proletarianism', which was in full flow in for example the 1958 co-written work *Facing Reality*.[78] A Bakuninist resonance to James's mature political thought cannot be discounted, and here it is worth recalling that James himself in 1948 regarded Bakunin as 'the anarchist who believes in the spontaneous uprising of all the people to establish socialism forthwith'.[79] However, despite the assertions of E. San Juan Jr., who has suggested that 'James's belief in permanent world revolution ultimately committed him to a radical-popular democracy almost anarchic and utopian in temper and motivation', James's vision of revolutionary socialism was always shaped more by Marxism than any strand of anarchic or utopian thinking.[80] Whatever the contribution of the early anarchist thinkers to the struggle for socialism, for James, as he put it in *Notes on Dialectics*, what was of critical importance was that Marx 'sees further' than the likes of Bakunin, 'an aristocrat', and Proudhon, 'the petty-bourgeois economist of a capitalism controlled by the state'. 'He [Marx] settles down to a patient systematic preparation for the fusion of the economic and political struggles of the workers, the integration of day-to-day and revolutionary struggles. He will give the formless labour movement form.'[81]

Finally, E.P. Thompson's thoughts on the great revolutionary socialist William Morris may make for one fitting conclusion, for they are words that seem also applicable to C.L.R. James, perhaps the 'William Morris of the Twentieth Century'. As Thompson noted, 'we have to make up our minds about William Morris':

Either he was an eccentric, isolated figure, personally admirable, but whose major thought was wrong or irrelevant and long left behind by events. This could be so … on the other hand, it may be that Morris was a major intellectual figure [who] may be assimilated to Marxism only in the course of a process of self-criticism and re-ordering within Marxism itself.[82]

## Acknowledgements

I am indebted to David Goodway for some of the material quoted in this chapter, while I would also like to thank Ian Birchall, David Howell and the three anonymous reviewers of this piece in draft for their constructive, critical comments.

## Notes

1. Leon Trotsky, *In Defense of Marxism* (New York: Pathfinder Press, 1976), p. 164.
2. P. Berman, 'Facing Reality', in Paul Buhle (ed.), *C.L.R. James: His Life and Work* (London: Allison & Busby, 1986), p. 211. Berman's piece focuses on James's 1958 work *Facing Reality*, co-written with Cornelius Castoriadis and Grace Lee Boggs, a work which politically shares much common ground with Council Communism.
3. J.D. Young, 'C.L.R. James', *Journal of the Scottish Labour History Society*, 22 (1987), pp. 38–39. See also J.D. Young, *The World of C.L.R. James: His Unfragmented Vision* (Glasgow: Clydeside Press, 1999).
4. On Robin Blackburn's obituary in the *Independent* of 8 June 1989, see Ian Birchall's letter in *Revolutionary History*, 2:3 (1989), online at 'http://www.marxists.org/history/etol/revhist/backiss/vol2/no3/birchall.html'. For Thompson's obituary, see F. Rosengarten, *Urbane Revolutionary: C.L.R. James and the Struggle for a New Society* (Jackson: University Press of Mississippi, 2008), p. 26.
5. C.L.R. James, *Notes on Dialectics: Hegel, Marx, Lenin* (London: Allison & Busby, 1980), pp. 60–61, 197–199, 215. This was a document written strictly for his supporters and not a work that was published in his name while a member of the official Trotskyist movement – indeed it was not first published in a widely available format until 1980. In the co-written 1950 work *State Capitalism and World Revolution*, a work which was published while James and his comrades were still in the official Trotskyist movement, anarchism was casually included alongside liberalism, social democracy and Stalinism as an ideology of 'counter-revolution within the revolution'. See C.L.R. James, R. Dunayevskaya and G. Lee, *State Capitalism and World Revolution* (Chicago: Charles H. Kerr, 1986), p. 132.
6. Berman, 'Facing Reality', p. 208.
7. See Christian Høgsbjerg, 'C.L.R. James: The Revolutionary as Artist', *International Socialism*, 112 (2006); and Hal Draper, *The Two Souls of Socialism* (London: Bookmarks, 1996). For my brief critical discussion of two pieces of recent James-scholarship, see Christian Høgsbjerg, 'Remembering C.L.R. James, Forgetting C.L.R. James', *Historical Materialism*, 17:3 (2009), pp. 221–234
8. Paul Buhle, 'Marxism in the USA', in S. McLemee and P. Le Blanc (eds), *C.L.R. James and Revolutionary Marxism; Selected Writings of C.L.R. James, 1939–49* (New Jersey: Humanity Books, 1994), pp. 55–56.
9. David Renton, *Dissident Marxism: Past Voices for Present Times* (London: Zed Books, 2004); David Renton, *C.L.R. James; Cricket's Philosopher King* (London: Haus Books, 2007).

10. C.L.R. James, 'Michel Maxwell Philip: 1829–1888 [1931]', in S.R. Cudjoe (ed.), *Michael Maxwell Philip; A Trinidad Patriot of the 19th Century* (Wellesley: Calaloux, 1999), pp. 102–103.

11. Quoted in R.W. Sander, 'Introduction: *The Beacon* and the Emergence of West Indian Literature', in B. Samaroo (ed.), *The Beacon, Volumes I–IV, 1931–1939* (New York: Kraus, 1977), p. xvii.

12. The American labour historian George Rawick, who knew James from the 1960s, thought him a 'Victorian hippy'. Personal information from Marcus Rediker, 6 November 2007.

13. David Goodway, 'Charles Lahr', *London Magazine* (June/July 1977).

14. Jonathan Rose, *The Intellectual Life of the British Working Classes* (London: Yale University Press, 2001), p. 303.

15. C.L.R. James, 'Charlie Lahr' [1975], unpublished manuscript in the possession of David Goodway, pp. 2–3.

16. James, 'Charlie Lahr', pp. 3–4, 7. James's chapter on the rise of the Nazis in Germany in his 1937 pioneering anti-Stalinist Marxist history of 'the rise and fall of the Communist International', *World Revolution*, would owe much to Lahr's influence and would depart somewhat from Trotsky's analysis. See C.L.R. James, 'Discussions with Trotsky', in C.L.R. James, *At the Rendezvous of Victory; Selected Writings*, Vol. 3 (London: Allison & Busby, 1984); and also James, *Notes on Dialectics*, pp. 38, 149.

17. As Alfred Rosmer recalled in his 1953 work *Moscou sous Lenine*, Lenin praised *The Great French Revolution* as Kropotkin 'well understood and demonstrated the role of the people in that bourgeois revolution'. See A. Rosmer, *Lenin's Moscow* (London: Bookmarks, 1987), p. 117. Trotsky is also said to have preferred Kropotkin's history to Jaurès'. See Daniel Guérin, *Le feu du sang: autobiographie politique et charnelle* (Paris: B. Grasset, 1977), p. 133. Thanks to Ian Birchall for these references.

18. See C.L.R. James, *The Black Jacobins; Toussaint Louverture and the San Domingo Revolution* (London: Secker & Warburg, 1938), p. 320.

19. It might be noted in passing that Kropotkin's book was translated into Italian by one Benito Mussolini, then a young revolutionary socialist – and, incidentally, Kropotkin thought Mussolini's translation 'brilliant.' Peter Kropotkin, *The Great French Revolution* (Quebec: Black Rose Books, 1989), pp. xv, 15.

20. Kropotkin, *The Great French Revolution*, p. 95.

21. C.L.R. James, *The Black Jacobins; Toussaint L'Ouverture and the San Domingo Revolution* (London: Penguin, 2001), pp. 68–69, 71.

22. Ibid., p. 291.

23. For further discussion of Trotsky's critical influence on James here, see C. Høgsbjerg, 'C.L.R. James and the Black Jacobins', *International Socialism*, 126 (2010), pp. 95–120

24. James, *The Black Jacobins*, p. 112.

25. Ibid., p. 144; Kropotkin, *The Great French Revolution*, pp. 484–492.

26. See James, *The Black Jacobins*, p. 332. One should also note James's respect for and subsequent friendship with Daniel Guérin, and his unfinished attempt to translate into English what in 1963 he described as Guérin's 'brilliant, original and well documented iconoclastic study' of the French Revolution, *La Lutte de classes sous la première république, bourgeois et 'bras nus', 1793–1797* (1946). For more on James and Guérin, see Rosengarten, *Urbane Revolutionary*, p. 149.

27. G. Cohen, *The Failure of a Dream; The Independent Labour Party from Disaffiliation to World War II* (London: Taurus Academic Studies, 2007), p. 111.
28. Young, *The World of C.L.R. James*, pp. 82–83.
29. David Goodway, *Anarchist Seeds Beneath the Snow: Left-Libertarian Thought and British Writers from William Morris to Colin Ward* (Liverpool: Liverpool University Press, 2006), p. 126.
30. Vernon Richards, 'Printers We Have Known: 1936–1986', in *Freedom; Anarchist Magazine, Centenary Edition*, 47:9 (October, 1986). *Freedom*, the main British anarchist publication, then called *Spain and the World* used the Narod Press from October 1936–December 1936 and then from June 1937–September 1938. On Richards, see Goodway, *Anarchist Seeds Beneath the Snow*, p. 126.
31. 'The Struggle for the Fourth International', *Fight*, 1:11 (November, 1937).
32. F.A. Ridley, 'Anarchism and Marxism', *Controversy*, 2:23 (August 1938). On Ridley, see R. Morrell, *The Gentle Revolutionary; The Life and Work of Frank Ridley, Socialist and Secularist* (London: Freethought History Research Group, 2003).
33. E. Mannin, *Comrade O Comrade; or, Low-Down on the Left* (London: Jarrolds, 1947), p. 118. On Braithwaite, see B. Bush, *Imperialism, Race and Resistance; Africa and Britain, 1919–1945* (London: Routledge, 1999), p. 222. On Mannin, see A. Croft, 'Ethel Mannin: The Red Rose of Love and the Red Flower of Liberty', in A. Ingram and D. Patai (eds), *Rediscovering Forgotten Radicals; British Women Writers, 1889–1939* (Chapel Hill: University of North Carolina Press, 1993), pp. 205–225.
34. George Padmore, *Pan-Africanism or Communism? The Coming Struggle for Africa* (London: Dennis Dobson, 1956), p. 151. On 26 February 1943, Braithwaite was billed to speak on 'Colonial Blacks on the move' at the anarchist-run Freedom Press Rooms on 27 Belsize Road in London. See *New Leader*, 6 February 1943.
35. Raya Dunayevskaya, *The Marxist-Humanist Theory of State-Capitalism* (Chicago: News and Letters, 1992), pp. x–xi.
36. Ibid.
37. From the Special Branch file on C.L.R. James. The National Archives, London, KV/2/1824/1z. 'Stalin, he said, was striving for National Socialism, while Trotsky was upholding International Socialism.'
38. C.L.R. James, *World Revolution 1917–1936; The Rise and Fall of the Communist International* (New Jersey: Humanity Books, 1994), pp. 168, 175, 178, 185. A. Rosenberg, *A History of Bolshevism; From Marx to the First Five Years' Plan* (London: Oxford University Press, 1934), pp. viii, 236–237. James's meeting with Korsch is recorded by Kent Worcester, from an interview in 1981 with American historian George Rawick. K. Worcester, *C.L.R. James; A Political Biography* (New York: State University of New York Press, 1996), p. 30. On Korsch's analysis of state capitalism, see the discussion in M. van der Linden, *Western Marxism and the Soviet Union; A Survey of Critical Theories and Debates Since 1917* (Chicago: Haymarket Books, 2009), pp. 41–44.
39. Boris Souvarine, *Stalin: A Critical Survey of Bolshevism* (London: Secker &Warburg, 1940), pp. 564, 570. See also C. Phelps, 'C.L.R. James and the Theory of State Capitalism', in N. Lichtenstein (ed.), *American Capitalism; Social Thought and Political Economy in the Twentieth Century* (Philadelphia: University of Pennsylvania Press, 2006), p. 165.
40. James, *World Revolution*, p. 140, and Worcester, *C.L.R. James*, p. 45.
41. James, *World Revolution*, p. 371.
42. Trotsky felt the Stalinist bureaucracy was a 'temporary' phenomenon, and in 1939 argued 'Might we not place ourselves in a ludicrous position if we fixed to the

Bonapartist oligarchy the nomenclature of a new ruling class just a few years or even a few months prior to its inglorious downfall?' See Alex Callinicos, *Trotskyism* (Minneapolis: University of Minnesota Press, 1990), p. 21.

43. James, *World Revolution*, p. 296.
44. Ibid., pp. 17, 415.
45. The best general survey and discussion of state capitalist theories is Marcel van der Linden's *Western Marxism and the Soviet Union*. One former comrade of James's from the Marxist Group, Dr Ryan L. Worrall in 1939 would put forward a substantial and sophisticated state capitalist analysis in the ILP journal *Left*. Phelps, 'C.L.R. James and the Theory of State Capitalism', pp. 165–166, 331–332.
46. M. Low and J. Breá, *Red Spanish Notebook; The First Six Months of the Revolution and the Civil War* (London: Secker & Warburg, 1937), pp. 254–255.
47. P. Davison (ed.), *The Complete Works of George Orwell*, Vol. 11 (London: Secker & Warburg, 1998), p. 87. L. Cripps, *C.L.R. James; Memories and Commentaries* (London: Cornwall Books, 1997), p. 21. George Orwell, *Homage to Catalonia* (London: Penguin, 1989), p. 83. As Orwell noted of the Soviet Union in 1939, 'Is it Socialism, or is it a peculiarly vicious form of state capitalism? All the political controversies . . . for two years past really circle round this question.' Quoted in J. Newsinger, 'Destroying the Myth: George Orwell and Soviet Communism', in P. Flewers (ed.), *George Orwell: Enigmatic Socialist* (London: Socialist Platform, 2005), p. 138.
48. Socialist Platform, *C.L.R. James and British Trotskyism; An Interview* (London: Socialist Platform, 1987), p. 10. See also I. Deutscher, *The Prophet Outcast; Trotsky: 1929–1940* (Oxford: Oxford University Press, 1979), pp. 419–421.
49. For my take on these discussions, see Christian Høgsbjerg, 'The Prophet and Black Power: Trotsky on race in the US', *International Socialism*, 121 (2008), pp. 99–119
50. In 1956, James would borrow 'Every cook can govern', a phrase of Lenin's, as a title for a *Correspondence* pamphlet on 'democracy in Ancient Greece'. Ian Birchall has reminded me that it is worth remembering that Lenin's own relations with anarchism were rather more complex than is often acknowledged. *The State and Revolution* was widely accused of 'anarchism' when it was first published, and Lenin made considerable efforts to engage with visiting anarchists in Moscow, particularly at the Second Congress of the Communist International in the summer of 1920. See, for example, Rosmer, *Lenin's Moscow*, pp. 51–65.
51. C.L.R. James, *Beyond a Boundary* (London: Hutchinson & Co., 1969), p. 149.
52. James, *Notes on Dialectics*, p. 135.
53. Ibid., 150.
54. James et al., *State Capitalism and World Revolution*, pp. 58–59. James, *Notes on Dialectics*, p. 118.
55. James, *Notes on Dialectics*, p. 151.
56. Steve Wright, *Storming Heaven; Class Composition and Struggle in Italian Autonomist Marxism* (London: Pluto Press, 2002), pp. 1, 3.
57. Ibid.; H. Cleaver, *Reading Capital Politically* (Brighton: Harvester Press, 1979), pp. 50, 53, 183. On Mothé, see I. Birchall, 'Nineteen Fifty-Six and the French Left', *Revolutionary History*, 9:3 (2006), pp. 160–181.
58. P. Singer, *The American Worker (Part 1: Life in the Factory)*, online at http://www.prole.info/texts/americanworker1.html, p. 1. (accessed 25 April 2011)
59. Singer, *The American Worker*, p. 1.
60. Grace Lee Boggs, *Living for Change: An Autobiography* (Minneapolis: University of Minnesota Press, 1998), p. 62.

61. T. Cliff, *Lenin: Building the Party, 1893–1914* (London: Bookmarks, 1994), p. 342.

62. James, *World Revolution*, p. 123.

63. *Fight*, 1:3 (January, 1937) and *Fight*, 1:4 (February, 1937).

64. Trotsky, *In Defense of Marxism*, p. 112.

65. J.R. Johnson, F. Forest and M. Harvey, *Trotskyism in the United States, 1940–47: Balance Sheet; The Workers Party and the Johnson-Forest Tendency* (Detroit: Johnson-Forest Tendency, 1947), pp. 8–9. See also Worcester, *C.L.R. James*, pp. 88–89, Rosengarten, *Urbane Revolutionary*, p. 71; P. Buhle, *C.L.R. James: The Artist as Revolutionary* (London: Verso, 1993), p. 70.

66. The work was heralded as being highly original at the time. As Castoriadis later recalled, 'for the first time there was something that was absent totally from the entire Marxist tradition and from Karl Marx himself except in the *Economic and Philosophical manuscripts* of 1844: that is the acknowledgement that being a worker does not mean that one is just working or that one is just being exploited. Being a worker means living with workers, being in solidarity with other workers, living in working class quarters of the city, having women who are either workers themselves or, if they are not, their predicament is the same or even worse than that of the men.' C. Castoriadis, 'C.L.R. James and the fate of Marxism', in S.R. Cudjoe and W.E. Cain (eds), *C.L.R. James; His Intellectual Legacies* (Amherst: University of Massachusetts Press, 1995), p. 283.

67. S. Weir, 'Revolutionary Artist', in P. Buhle (ed.), *C.L.R. James: His Life and Work* (London: Allison & Busby, 1986), pp. 183–184. It is a pity Weir never seems to have had the chance to hear the Palestinian Trotskyist Tony Cliff, based in Britain, as James was not quite so unique in this. See, for example, Cliff's discussion in *The Employers' Offensive* (1970) of how the 'demand for workers' control' is 'the most important fact about modern industrial capitalism – for the "bloody-mindedness" of workers, and the thousand and one ways in which they express their demand, implicitly and explicitly, for control over their own lives, is the embryo of workers' power, of socialism.' See T. Cliff, *In the Thick of Workers' Struggle: Selected Writings*, Vol. 2 (London: Bookmarks, 2002), p. 290.

68. 'A young participant in the Resistance in Cremona, Montaldi became the bridgeman between *Socialisme ou Barbarie* and its intercontinental ramifications on the one hand and the Italian non-Stalinist groups on the left of the Italian CP and SP on the other.' See F. Gambino, 'Only Connect', in P. Buhle (ed.), *C.L.R. James: His Life and Work* (London: Allison & Busby, 1986), p. 199.

69. Quoted in Wright, *Storming Heaven*, pp. 23–24.

70. Gambino, 'Only Connect', pp. 197–198.

71. M. Glaberman (ed.), *Marxism for Our Times: C.L.R. James on Revolutionary Organisation* (Jackson: University Press of Mississippi, 1999), p. xxii. Paul Buhle, 'Political Styles of C.L.R. James: An Introduction', in Paul Buhle (ed.), *C.L.R. James: His Life and Work* (London: Allison & Busby, 1986), p. 26. Gambino was especially inspired by the League of Revolutionary Black Workers in Detroit – a Jamesian group whose first interview abroad was with Potere Operaio around the same time as *The Black Jacobins* – which had inspired the League of Revolutionary Black Workers – appeared in Italian. As Gambino recalled, 'the interview of the League [of Revolutionary Black Workers] in Potere Operaio led to more than the well-known slogan of Potere Operaio: "Turin, Detroit, Togliattigrad, class struggle will win". It signalled the death knell of the isolated within the narrow confines of the official left's "Italian road to socialism".' Gambino, 'Only Connect', p. 198.

72. George Rawick published with others including Antonio Negri – *Operai e stato* [Workers and the state] (Milan: Feltrinelli, 1972); *Lo schiavo americanodal tramonto all'alba* (Milan: Feltrinelli, 1973), with Harold Baron and Herbert Gutman, *Da schiavo a proletario (From slave to proletarian)* (Turin: Musolini, 1973). In 1976 Martin Glaberman published *Classe operaia, imperialismo, rivoluzione negli USA* [Working class, imperialism, and revolution in the USA] (Turin: Musolini), with an introduction by Bruno Cartosio. See F. Fasce, 'American Labor History, 1973–1983: Italian Perspectives', *Reviews in American History*, 14:4 (1986), pp. 602, 610–611. See also C. Taylor, 'James and those Italians', http://clrjames.blogspot.com/2008/09/james-and-those-italians.html (accessed25 April 2011); P. Buhle, 'From a Biographer's Notebook: The Field of C.L.R. James Scholarship', in S.R. Cudjoe and W.E. Cain (eds), *C.L.R. James; His Intellectual Legacies* (Amherst: University of Massachusetts Press, 1995), p. 449.

73. Cleaver, *Reading Capital Politically*, p. 184. A. Lichtenstein, 'George Rawick's "From Sundown to Sunup" and the Dialectic of Marxian Slave Studies, *Reviews in American History*, 24:4 (1996), pp. 712–725. See also the excellent comparative discussion by Nicola Pizzolato, 'Transnational radicals: labor dissent and political activism in Detroit and Turin (1950–1970)', *International Review of Social History* 56 (2011), pp. 1–30.

74. J. Fuller, 'The New Workerism; The Politics of the Italian Autonomists [1980]', *International Socialism*, 92 (2001), pp. 63–76. For some brief discussion of the possible influence of James on Hardt and Negri, see P. Hudis, 'Workers as Reason: The Development of a New Relation of Worker and Intellectual in American Marxist Humanism', *Historical Materialism*, 11:4 (2003), p. 290.

75. C. El-Ojeili, 'Book Review: "Many Flowers, Little Fruit"? the Dilemmas of Workerism', *Thesis Eleven*, 79 (2004), pp. 114–115. After they left the official Trotskyist movement, the Johnson-Forest Tendency in their newspaper *Correspondence* noted that 'From the stories we get everyday from the shops, we can see a new form of struggle emerging. It never seems to be carried to its complete end, yet its existence is continuous. The real essence of this struggle and its ultimate goal is: a better life, a new society, the emergence of the individual as a human being. . . . This is the struggle to establish here and now a new culture, a workers' culture. . . . It is this that we must be extremely sensitive to. We must watch with an eagle eye every change or indication of the things that these changes reflect'.

76. For my discussion of James's failed attempt to build a 'Marxist Group' in Britain during the tumult of 1956 after he was forced to leave McCarthyist North America in 1953, see C. Høgsbjerg, 'Beyond the Boundary of Leninism? C.L.R. James and 1956,' *Revolutionary History*, 9:3 (2006), pp. 144–159. This article explores the republication of the Johnson-Forest Tendency's 1950 work *State Capitalism and World Revolution* in the aftermath of the Hungarian Revolution in 1956, with a new preface by James, through an anarchist publisher in London, Philip Sansom. The republication of *State Capitalism and World Revolution* after the Hungarian Revolution was a collaboration by James's 'Marxist Group' with Castoriadis and Theo Massen from Socialisme ou Barbarie in France and Cajo Brendel, a Dutch 'Council Communist', then researching autonomous class struggles in Britain for a book.

77. T. Topham (ed.), *Report of the 5th National Conference on Workers' Control and Industrial Democracy held at Transport House, Coventry on June 10th and 11th, 1967* (Hull: Centre for Socialist Education, 1967), p. 55.

78. Berman, 'Facing Reality', p. 209. James at times in this work certainly seems to have an almost mystical fear of the state in itself, as opposed to a rational analysis of how the state is tied up with modern capitalist society. Raya Dunayevskaya criticised the 'stateism' of *Facing Reality*. See Worcester, *C.L.R. James*, p. 141.

79. James, *Notes on Dialectics*, p. 197.

80. E. San Juan Jr., *Beyond Postcolonial Theory* (New York: St Martin's Press, 1998), p. 249.

81. James, *Notes on Dialectics*, p. 197.

82. E.P. Thompson, *William Morris: Romantic to Revolutionary* (London: Merlin Press, 1976), pp. 801–802.

# 9

# 'White Skin, Black Masks': Marxist and Anti-racist Roots of Contemporary US Anarchism

*Andrew Cornell*

As in other parts of the world, anarchists, socialists and Marxists based in the USA have frequently influenced and borrowed from one another over the past century and a half of struggles. More research into these lines of influence is certainly called for. However, any thorough investigation of the cross-pollination of radical traditions in the USA must also consider the many ways in which the autonomous freedom struggles of people of colour have co-mingled with European-origin traditions such as Marxism and anarchism. In fact, I would suggest that it has frequently been on the terrain of campaigns opposed to white supremacy and colonialism that anarchists, socialists and Marxists have found common ground to collaborate and to develop synthetic theoretical and tactical paradigms.

In this essay, I consider the historical lineage of two tactical approaches to mass action frequently deployed by anarchist activists in the USA since the infamous anti-World Trade Organization demonstrations of 1999: 1) consensus-driven non-violent direct action, and 2) black bloc property destruction. Searching for the origins of these tactics leads us back to moments in the mid-twentieth century when support for African American freedom struggles by US anarchists brought them into conversation with three distinct forms of socialist politics. First, mass non-violent blockading at economic summit protests – and the idea that the methods of planning and carrying out such actions exemplify the movement's ideology and vision – can be traced to the use of civil disobedience tactics by opponents of racial segregation in the 1940s and 1950s. In the years following the Second World War, anarchists and democratic socialists collaborated to forge a politics of 'revolutionary non-violence' that significantly influenced the tactical and organisational orientation of this early phase of the civil rights movement in the southern USA.

Second, the practice of challenging police authority and trashing commercial centres, often in anonymous 'black blocs', owes inspiration to the example of black urban insurrections which broke out across the USA between 1964 and 1967. In the mid-1960s, a cohort of young US anarchists looked to the heterodox Marxism of the Facing Reality group, led by figures such as C.L.R. James, to help make sense of and defend the political significance of these 'race riots'. Shortly thereafter, the embrace of 'Third World Marxism' by many national liberation movements, inside and outside the USA, inspired influential counter-cultural anarchists to again embrace insurrectionary tactics in the late 1960s. Though they have been reworked by a variety of radical formations in the intervening decades, the tactical logics of non-violent direct action and trashing popularised by mid-century anti-racist insurgencies continue to deeply inform the strategic perspectives of many contemporary North American anarchists.

## Anarchism, civil rights and non-violent direct action

Between the First and Second World Wars, US anarchism had largely cleaved into a syndicalist wing influenced by the journals *Vanguard* and *Il Martello* (*The Hammer*), and an insurrectionist wing represented by the newspapers *Man!* and *L'Adunata dei Refretarri* (*The Summoning of the Unruly*). Both factions shared the traditional anarchist view of the political state and capitalist class relations as the primary sources of oppression in the modern world, but they disagreed over tactics and issues of organisation, especially whether labor unions had the potential to serve as emancipatory forces in the modern world.[1] Despite these differences, US anarchists remained fiercely anti-Communist and viewed members of the Socialist Party as reformists who had accommodated themselves to New Deal liberalism. The outbreak of the Second World War delivered a sharp blow to both tendencies, but out of this final dénouement of the 'classical' anarchism a new form arose that adopted pacifism, cultural revolution and prefigurative community-building as its strategic touchstones. A small, but intellectually vital, radical milieu developed during the war, based in large measure on formative encounters between anarchist and Gandhian war resisters. Anarchists and socialists of this milieu later collaborated to contribute important ideas and resources to the struggle for African American civil rights, and their theories of political power and strategies for social change were transformed in the process.

## The flowering of anarchist pacifism

In 1942 a half-dozen young anarchists from New York City who had been mentored by the syndicalist Vanguard Group, launched a new newspaper, *Why?*. Whereas the eminent German émigré anarchist Rudolf Rocker had persuaded most of the Vanguard Group to endorse the Allies, *Why?* soon adopted an anti-war stance and later began questioning the possibility of bringing about an anarchist society through a violent seizure of the means of production. The editors were first influenced by the positions taken by *L'Adunata die Refratari* and the British anarchist newspaper *War Commentary*, both of which denounced the sincerity of the Allies anti-Fascist intentions and called for workers in England, Italy and elsewhere to turn the crisis conditions of the war to revolutionary ends, as the Russians had done in 1917.[2] However, the *Why?* Group progressed towards a radical pacifism under the influence of Bart de Ligt, a Dutch anarchist who chaired the War Resisters International and collaborated with Mahatma Gandhi. De Ligt's 1937 treatise, *The Conquest of Violence*, argued that 'the underlying cause of modern war is the character itself of modern society [...] Our society is violent just as fog is wet.' Therefore, a far-reaching social revolution was required, but means were of the essence. 'The more violence,' he claimed, 'the less revolution.'[3]

*Why?*'s position on the war was more than a question of editorial line for the young men of the group; it directly affected their decisions about how to respond to the draft. In 1943, David Thoreau Wieck, who contributed to *Why?* while studying philosophy at Columbia University, was sentenced to three years at Danbury Prison after he refused to enlist.[4] *Why?* editors David Koven and Cliff Bennett also served time for their anti-war beliefs and draft resistance. The incarceration of anarchist draft resisters during the Second World War proved fortuitous for the future direction of the movement in the USA.

Anarchists were among the nearly 6,000 conscientious objectors (COs) and war resisters imprisoned during the Second World War. Historian James Tracy explains that, 'Of these, 4,300 were Jehovah's Witnesses with little or no political agenda. [...] The remaining seventeen hundred, however, constituted the most militant distinct group of pacifists in the country.'[5] Many COs were affiliated with the country's leading pacifist organisations, the Fellowship of Reconciliation (FOR) and the War Resisters League (WRL). During the depression years of the 1930s, the FOR had broadened its agenda to combat racial and economic inequality under the guidance of its socialist chairman, A.J. Muste, who, like other members, was inspired by Gandhi's campaigns of non-violent direct action in India.[6] Shortly after Wieck arrived, 18 Danbury COs, all of them white, launched a successful strike against racial segregation in the prison. Wieck took part in the four-month strike – refusing to work, to take his allotted time in the prison yard, or to eat meals in the segregated cafeteria. Through the strike he befriended other radical inmates, such as Jim Peck and Ralph DiGia. The Danbury strike set off a wave of similar actions in prisons and CO camps across the country, including strikes led by African American pacifists Bill Sutherland and Bayard Rustin in Lewisburg, Pennsylvania and Ashland, Kentucky, respectively. The COs experimented with Gandhian techniques such as hunger strikes and passive resistance, winning considerable media attention and support from pacifists and black political organisations outside the prisons. Besides successfully desegregating and liberalising the polices of federal penitentiaries, the wave of non-violent direct action united participants and prompted them to discuss the potential for a broad movement of 'revolutionary non-violence' against war, racism and economic inequality in the USA.[7]

Imprisonment also led the dissenters to modify their beliefs. Wieck later wrote, 'I did not go to prison as a pacifist but rather as an objector to war and conscription. It was in prison that I learned the methods of non-violence.' Afterwards, he considered himself an 'anarchist-pacifist'.[8] In turn, the influence of anarchist prisoners such as Wieck and Lowell Naeve helped move other pacifist war resisters, including DiGia, Sutherland, David Dellinger, Roy Finch and Igal Roodenko in the direction of anarchism. David Dellinger, who would later become a leading light of the New Left, kept up a lively correspondence with Holley Cantine, editor of the anarchist-pacifist journal *Retort*.[9] In letters from prison, he voiced his growing scepticism about the methods of the Socialist Party, to which he belonged. Dellinger was impressed with Cantine's assertion that revolutionaries should seek to model in the institutions they create, and in their daily lives, the type of social relations they are fighting to promote in the world at large. The imprisoned pacifist suggested that a revolutionary organisation's 'full-time workers should be men who have left their other work for 6 months, a year, or so, and will return to it again'. Not only would this avoid 'some of the problems of a centralized "leadership" [...] but others would be developed who are now kept undeveloped or are alienated'.[10] After receiving his release date, Dellinger wrote to Cantine that he was eager to meet in person so that they might discuss in more detail 'the kind of left-wing libertarian socialist movement in which we are both interested'. As his biographer Andrew Hunt asserts, 'once a Christian socialist, Dellinger had evolved into a secular anarchist in Lewisburg'.[11]

## Anarchists and socialists become non-violent revolutionaries

Most of the militant war resisters were released in the months surrounding the atomic bombing of Hiroshima and Nagasaki by the USA. Horrified by the scale of callous violence unleashed by the bomb, they expected a mass movement to arise in opposition to its use. In the August 1945 issue of *Politics*, which maintained close ties to *Why?* and *Retort*, editor Dwight MacDonald argued that the USA's willingness to use atomic weapons meant, simply, 'We must "get" the modern national state, before it "gets" us.'[12] MacDonald began his political career in the Trotskyist movement and was later considered a major figure among the 'New York Intellectuals'. The war and the bomb, however, had pushed him into the anarchist-pacifist camp.[13] Many former-COs concurred with MacDonald's anti-statism, as well as his assertion that to prevent another war, the entire society, structured in violence as it was, had to be transformed.

One key to such a transformation, they agreed, was continuing the fight against segregation and other manifestations of white supremacy. As early as 1942, the socialist radical pacifists Bayard Rustin, George Houser and James Farmer had launched the Congress of Racial Equality (CORE) to put Gandhian techniques into play to combat the segregation of restaurants, swimming pools and other public facilities. In 1947, CORE organised a Journey of Reconciliation, in which an interracial team of volunteers – including Rustin, the anarchist Igal Roodenko and Wieck's cellmate Jim Peck – travelled by bus through southern states to test compliance with a 1946 Supreme Court decision outlawing segregation in interstate transportation facilities. Some of the riders faced beatings and were sentenced to work on the chain-gang for their breach of racial protocol, but their treatment was much less severe than that encountered by participants in CORE's iconic 1961 Freedom Rides, modelled on the 1947 trip.[14]

After their release, former-COs such as Dellinger, DiGia and Sutherland also launched the Committee for Non-violent Revolution (CNVR). Two years later, in 1948, they regrouped with additional radical pacifists such as Muste and MacDonald, changing their name to Peacemakers.[15] In the late 1940s, many radical pacifists continued to maintain membership in the Socialist Party. Differences between anarchists and socialists involved with CNVR and Peacemakers were subsumed under the mantle of an emerging politics of *revolutionary non-violence*. The abstract question of whether a stateless society was possible, and what it would look like, took a back seat. However, members of both groups determined that 'decentralized democratic socialism,' a version of worker self-management, was their economic ideal and agreed that direct action, rather than electoral campaigns, should be the primary means used to force a fundamental transformation of the modern war-making nation-state. Peacemakers also sought to synthesise socialist and anarchist models of organisation: the group structured itself as a network of small cells that elected a steering committee, but operated autonomously from one another in pursuit of the organisation's defined goals. Sympathisers were encouraged to join and participate as small groups, rather than as individuals. As historian Scott Bennett writes, Peacemakers believed this form of organisation 'could challenge and eventually replace centralized, hierarchical institutions'.[16] Peacemakers, then, appears to be the first organisation in the USA in which anarchists adopted the consensus method of decision making – a process promoted by Quakers, such as Bayard Rustin, involved in the organisation.

In 1947 the militant pacifists gained control of the executive board of the War Resisters League, seating Dellinger, MacDonald, Roy Finch, Roy Kepler and other anarchists, with hopes of transforming its 10,000 person membership into non-violent revolutionaries. Although they found only modest support for their far-reaching program during the repressive McCarthy era, their presence made possible a fortuitous development in the civil rights struggle. In 1951, Rustin was fired from the staff of the Fellowship of Reconciliation and nearly drummed out of the movement, when he was arrested for having sex with two other men in the back of a parked car. Instead of accepting his resignation from the War Resisters League, the anarchists sitting on the executive board voted to hire Rustin as the organisation's full-time program director. In that capacity he would serve as a leading advisor on non-violent strategy to Martin Luther King, Jr. and other southern civil rights leaders as the struggle expanded at the end of 1955.[17]

## Revolutionary non-violence and the black freedom struggle

Despite the importance of decades of previous struggles, the 1955–1956 Montgomery Bus Boycott is often seen as marking the beginning of a new and heroic phase of the black freedom movement in the USA. Provoked by the arrest of the activist Rosa Parks, the successful year-long boycott grew to include thousands of participants and launched into national prominence the campaign's young spokesperson, Martin Luther King, Jr. Since the 1920s, many African Americans had drawn inspiration from the Indian decolonisation struggle lead by Mahatma Gandhi, who was himself influenced by the anarchists Peter Kropotkin, Leo Tolstoy and Bart de Ligt. King first learned of Gandhi's methods from talks delivered by Howard University president Mordecai Johnson and Peacemakers member A.J. Muste at Crozier Seminary in 1949 and 1950. During the Montgomery Bus Boycott, experienced non-violent revolutionaries – most notably Rustin – helped King translate Gandhian principles into a strategic plan of civil disobedience geared to the conditions of the US south.[18]

Concurrent with the launch of the bus boycott, Dellinger, Muste, Finch and Rustin collaborated to found *Liberation* magazine, which promoted their brand of libertarian socialist and pacifist politics. In its first editorial, the editors noted that:

We do not conceive the problem of revolution or the building of a better society as one of accumulating power, whether by legislative or other methods, to 'capture the state,' and then, presumably, to transform society and human beings as well. The national, sovereign, militarised and bureaucratic State and bureaucratic collectivist economy are themselves evils to be avoided or abolished.[19]

*Liberation* quickly became an important platform for participants in the civil rights movement to debate strategy. King contributed articles regularly, as did officials of the National Association for the Advancement of Colored People (NAACP) and advocates of armed self-defence, such as Robert F. Williams.

Anarchists such as Wieck, Dellinger and Paul Goodman wrote frequently for the publication, encouraging the movement to adopt strategies that relied on popular resistance rather than legal manoeuvring or the military might of the federal government.

In 1962, the governor of Mississippi attempted to block the black activist James Meredith from enrolling at the all-white state university. Pressured to respond, President John F. Kennedy deployed federal marshals to ensure Meredith's entrance. Dellinger and Rustin criticised Kennedy's true motives and claimed the incident as a missed opportunity for the movement. They co-authored an essay which concluded, 'The temptation for shortsighted men and women of good will is to rely on the Federal government to take up the slack created by their own failure to act responsibly and in social solidarity. But in the long run the Federal government must act in accord with its own nature, which is that of a highly centralised political, military, industrial and financial bureaucracy.'[20] Dellinger had earlier written in *Liberation*, 'The power of the government is not the integrating power of love but the disintegrating power of guns and prisons.'[21]

Much preferable to the deployment of troops, according to the editors of *Liberation*, was the strategy of direct resistance to racism by ordinary people emblematised by the student sit-in movement that had erupted in February 1960. The movement began as a local action when four black college students asked for service and refused to move from the segregated lunch counter of a Greensboro, North Carolina, Woolworth's department store. The protests spread and by June an estimated 50,000 students had joined the fray in more than 100 towns throughout the southern states.[22] As a contributor to the anarchist journal *Views and Comments* wrote at the time, the student sit-ins demonstrated 'how a genuine people's movement arose spontaneously, produced its own organisation, devised its own tactics and inspired everyone to participate creatively and valiantly in a common cause'. Instead of counselling reliance on a great leader, 'it arouses people from apathy and restores their belief in their own power'.[23]

## Direct action, participatory democracy and New-Left anarchism

In 1960 the experienced anti-racist organiser Ella Baker helped the student sit-in leaders develop a political organisation, the Student Non-violent Coordinating Committee (SNCC), which modelled anarchist principles in its means of operation, though members never self-identified as anarchists. In its early years, SNCC distinguished itself from existing civil rights organisations such as the NAACP and King's Southern Christian Leadership Convention by its dedication to the use of non-violent direct action and through its efforts to invent egalitarian forms of organisation, participatory decision-making processes, and what Baker termed 'group-centred leadership'. Baker concurred with Dellinger's remarks to Cantine that the mark of a good leader was his or her ability to share responsibility and develop leadership capacities in others. 'Strong people,' Baker claimed, 'don't need strong leaders.'[24]

The historian Clayborne Carson explains that early SNCC activists 'strongly opposed any hierarchy of authority such as existed in other civil rights organisations'.[25] Instead of carrying out a program designed by a few leaders, SNCC members collectively engaged in long discussions in which those not used to speaking up were supported and gently urged to participate alongside the more loquacious. The organisation attempted to reach consensus on major programme and strategy decisions – a technique introduced by participants such as James Lawson, who were affiliated with CORE and influenced by Peacemakers.[26]

As SNCC shifted its energies from direct action against segregation to organising poor black men and women to register to vote, staff members such as Bob Moses sought ways to extend the process of perpetual leadership development beyond the organisation itself to all the people SNCC staff members worked with in voter registration efforts. In this way, SNCC developed in its day-to-day organising work an ideal of *participatory democracy* that demanded ordinary people be able to make the decisions that affect their lives. SNCC organisers mobilised the poorest and least educated African Americans to demand rights from an exclusionary racial state. However, their method of building the capacities of local people to direct their own organisations in pursuit of political and economic self-determination belied an increasingly radical vision that, at least implicitly, had much in common with the various forms of direct democracy and libertarian socialism discussed throughout this book. The anarchist precepts of direct action, decentralised organisation and belief in the leadership capabilities of ordinary people, formed one significant and overlooked, but not overriding, current within the larger wellspring of religious and political traditions that shaped the black freedom movement.

The influence cut in both directions. The black freedom movement, and especially SNCC, came to serve as a new historic example of a successful *mass* movement that functioned in accordance with anarchist principles. Civil rights struggles also helped to break down traditional anarchist ideas about the primacy of class oppression and the revolutionary primacy of the working class. Recognising the power of African Americans to create fundamental social changes by organising around both racial *and* class identity, was an important step in anarchists grasping the centrality of 'race' as a social phenomenon that fundamentally structures social inequalities and everyday life. This recognition helped them to theoretically expand the object of their critique and opposition from capitalism and 'the state' to all forms of social domination.

The anti-racist campaigns of the 1940, 1950s and 1960s form a clear point of embarkation for the political sensibility that combines non-violent direct action, non-hierarchical forms of organising, and consensus-based decision-making, which contemporary anarchists continue to celebrate as central to their particular political vision. These methods, as well as the ideal of participatory democracy, were championed throughout the 1960s and early 1970s by Students for a Democratic Society and the early women's liberation movement.[27] In the 1970s and 1980s groups heavily influenced by anarchism, such as Movement for a New Society and the Clamshell Alliance, carried the tradition forward in movements against nuclear power plants, US intervention in Central America, and environmental destruction.[28] Experienced organisers from these campaigns, such as Starhawk and David Solnit, played central roles in planning and training participants in the mass demonstrations and blockades that shut down central Seattle during the World Trade Organization meetings in 1999 and re-energised the anarchist movement in the USA.[29] In turn, veterans of the global justice movement carried the tradition forward to the Occupy Wall Street encampments of 2011–2012.

## Beats, counter-culture and urban insurrection

Black blocs, like non-violent direct action and consensus, claim a relatively long lineage within the anarchist tradition. Their use can be traced to the autonomous movements of Italy, Germany and other European countries, spanning the late-1970s to the 1990s, many of which maintained deep ties to the international anarchist-punk community and other radical youth counter-cultures.[30] These movements were themselves significantly influenced by the North American counter-culture of the 1960s, however, and that counter-culture was, at its core, structured around the appreciation and appropriation of African American hip culture and, later, the celebration by white youth of forms of Marxist-inspired African, Latin American and Asian political militancy.[31] To unpack this complex lineage, it is useful to first examine the reciprocal influence of mid-century anarchist-pacifism and the writers of the Beat Generation, and to then consider the ways a variety of additional radical intellectual and political currents – especially expressions of black radicalism – contributed to the explosive growth of a heavily anarchistic youth counter-culture by 1967.

## Anarchism, jazz and the Beat generation

The anarchist-pacifists of *Liberation* magazine and the campaigns of SNCC comprise one current through which libertarian socialist ideas were transmitted to members of Students for a Democratic Society and other New Leftists. However, anarchist ideas, themes and strategies were also promoted in the 1960s by small circles of writers, activists and cultural producers that include Chicago's Rebel Worker Group, New York's Black Mask, the

Diggers of San Francisco, and the Detroit radical milieu surrounding the *Fifth Estate* newspaper, the White Panther Party, and the political rock group The MC5. Although collectively these formations were instrumental in developing the style of politics that historian Toby Boraman has termed 'carnival anarchism', none claimed purely anarchist origins or desired to promote themselves as such.[32] Instead, they integrated elements of anarcho-syndicalism, anti-vanguardist Marxism, the European avant-garde tradition, African American resistance cultures, and emergent forms of Third World Marxism into a novel form of cultural radicalism first nourished by the Beat subculture.

Beat writers such as Jack Kerouac and Allen Ginsberg provided an entry point to radical politics for many young adults across the USA in the late 1950s and early 1960s. The San Francisco Poetry Renaissance, credited with launching the Beats onto an international stage, was built in large measure by anarchist-pacifists, including many Second World War draft resisters, who formed a Libertarian Circle and a poetry forum there as early as 1946.[33] Drawing on Zen Buddhism, the Jewish mysticism of Martin Buber, and an emerging ecological consciousness, San Francisco anarchists such as Kenneth Rexroth and Robert Duncan focused on creating art and a community of like-minded dissenters, while counselling disengagement from the world of the A-Bomb and mass consumer culture.[34] Ironically, the obscenity trial against Ginsberg's 'Howl' and the commercial success of Kerouac's *On the Road* spread these ideas beyond the coastal cities to nearly every high school in North America.

In the working-class Chicago suburb of Maywood, Illinois, high school sophomore Franklin Rosemont learned of Jack Kerouac from a magazine article at the dentist's office in 1958. After devouring *On the Road* and *The Dharma Bums* (Kerouac's ode to Gary Snyder and the other Bay Area anarchist poets), Rosemont and his friends launched a high-school literary magazine, *The Lantern*, which earned them reputations as communists and beatniks. Rosemont preferred to think of his multiracial circle as 'high school hipsters'. He recalled that although *The Lantern* community was supportive of the civil rights movement, 'only with my discovery of the Beat poets, did I begin to appreciate the vitality and richness of African-American culture, and particularly jazz'.[35] Appreciation of jazz was concomitant to the Beat lifestyle, as bebop musicians provided a towering example of disdain for white bourgeois culture, and their music seemed to incarnate the anti-rationalist impulse behind Beat dissent. As literary scholar Scott Saul notes, 'The hipster was in some sense the civil rights movement's less charitable double, the face of a defiance that did not unconditionally turn the other cheek. He plugged into long-running debates in the black community about whether social protest should take direct or more evasive forms, whether it should be easily legible in its aims or should adopt the slyness of the trickster.'[36]

The Beats also lead Rosemont to explore the French surrealists – cultural revolutionaries who, beginning in the 1920s, had declared their support for decolonisation struggles and argued that revolutionaries must seek to create a world in which life is lived intensely and ecstatically, in pursuit of the sublime and the marvellous. With the discovery of surrealism, Rosemont felt that he had found a set of ideas that tied together his love of poetry, jazz and his growing interest in radical politics. 'As early as the 1950s,' he later claimed, 'some of us recognized the new jazz as the auditory equivalent of surrealism in painting [ . . . ] Our most extravagant revolutionary dreams were summed up, renewed and expanded in the untrammeled loveliness' of the music of John Coltrane, Thelonious Monk and Archie Shepp.[37] These connections helped cement a conception of musical counter-culture as an expression and method of revolutionary politics, which was expanded upon later in the decade by The MC5, and extends through the anarcho-punk scene to the present.[38]

## Workerism, rock 'n' roll and urban insurrection

Poetry and revolution also absorbed students at Chicago's Roosevelt College such as Tor Faegre, Robert and Judy Green and Penelope Bartik (soon to be Penelope Rosemont). These young poets and students, most from workingclass backgrounds, met aging members of the Industrial Workers of the World (IWW) at the union's General Headquarters, became members, and proceeded to organise migrant farm workers in southwest Michigan. In 1964 they used the IWW mimeograph machine to launch a journal, *The Rebel Worker*, which broke new ground by pairing traditional workerist politics with considerations of the revolutionary potential of art and popular culture. The young Rebel Workers learned about revolutionary unionism from long-time IWW members like Fred Thompson, but their growing analysis of capitalism and unionism also benefitted from friendly interactions with the Detroit-based heterodox Marxist organisation Facing Reality, and the British libertarian socialist organisation Solidarity. As described by Christian Høgsbjerg in this volume, Facing Reality was an organisational offshoot of the Johnson-Forest Tendency, a dissident caucus within the US Trotskyist movement during the 1930s and 1940s, grouped around the Trinidadian Marxist C.L.R. James, the Russian-American theorist Raya Dunayevskaya, and the Chinese-American philosopher Grace Lee.[39] The Johnson-Forest Tendency exchanged ideas with the French group Socialisme ou Barbarie, which had likewise broken with Trotskyism in the 1940s.[40] In the aftermath of the Hungarian uprising of 1956, James, Lee and one of Socialisme ou Barbarie's leading intellects, Cornelius Castoriadis, co-authored a treatise on anti-Stalinist and non-vanguardist Marxism, *Facing Reality*, from which the US group drew its name.[41] In the 1960s Castoriadis was the strongest influence on the political positions of the British group Solidarity, which translated, reprinted and commented on many of his articles.[42] Each of these organisations developed a criticism of 'democratic centralist' vanguard revolutionary parties, argued that labor unions had become incorporated into the postwar capitalist production system, and promoted forms of worker self-management and council democracy.[43] This constellation of mid-century libertarian socialists would deeply inform the ideas of the Situationist International (SI) and the Italian traditions of *operaismo* and autonomist Marxism.

The influence of Facing Reality and Solidarity was apparent in *Rebel Worker* articles critical of the role mainstream union officials played in policing workers' shop floor resistance. However, the group also celebrated diverse forms of resistance that they saw cropping up outside the factory gates. The journal featured articles such as Franklin Rosemont's 'Mods, Rockers, and the Revolution', which defended rock and roll music as an expression of working-class youth's 'refusal to submit to routinized, bureaucratic pressures'.[44] The Chicago radicals also kept expressions of African American resistance to white supremacy sharply in view. July 1964 saw the first of a series of massive riots in the black ghettos of northern and western cities, usually touched off by incidents of police brutality, but expressive of the generalised hostility of communities suffering from segregation, discrimination and unemployment. The *Rebel Worker* published a first-hand account of the 'Harlem insurrection' of 1964, and hailed the similar rebellion that broke out in Chicago two years later. Drawing again on the analysis provided by James, Castoriadis and their collaborators, Rosemont noted, 'Just as our labor perspective focused not on "leaders" but on "actions by the workers themselves, in or out of the unions" so too we identified ourselves strongly with the masses of black proletarian youth who outgrew the increasingly conservative older civil-rights groups and took up direct action in the streets.'[45]

## Art, anti-imperialist armed struggle and anarchism

The editors of the *Rebel Worker* recognised as political compatriots the small group of New York artists who produced the magazine *Black Mask*. *Black Mask* was founded by Ben Morea, a working-class Italian-American painter and agitator who developed his anarchist politics in a trajectory similar to that of Franklin Rosemont. Morea grew up in the Hell's Kitchen neighbourhood of Manhattan, home to Thelonious Monk and other leading bebop jazz musicians. He immersed himself in the jazz community until he picked up a heroin habit and was arrested for possession. In a prison art therapy class, he determined to take his life in a different direction. Still, he appreciated the instinct for rebellion that the jazz scene had imbued in him. 'Culturally, it was subversive,' Morea asserted:

The dominant culture, which I've never been comfortable with, could not understand jazz. It was a subculture. And so I gravitated towards subcultures. The beatniks picked up on all of that. After I quit heroin, I was about 18, I already had this subcultural context, so I struck a friendship with a lot of beatniks. Especially, first, The Living Theatre. Judith Malina and Julian Beck – they're the ones that put the name to the way I felt, [and gave me] the term *anarchist*.[46]

Malina and Beck had become anarchists in the late 1940s after attending discussions held by the Why? Group and protesting cold war air-raid drills with anarchist-pacifists from the War Resisters League and other organisations.[47] Their Brechtian theatre troupe served as an important connective tissue linking young beatniks to older New York City anarchists. Over the next few years, Morea attended meetings of a small group of old-line anarchosyndicalists known as the Libertarian League, as well as the 'Anarchos' study group formed by ecology-oriented anarchist Murray Bookchin in the early 1960s. Meanwhile he exhaustively studied the European avant-garde art tradition, including the Dada, Surrealist and Futurist movements. While the black jazz scene of the late 1950s served as a point of entry to New York's bohemian anarchist community, the explicitly political and increasingly militant black freedom movement became a key reference point and source of inspiration for Morea and his friends by the mid-1960s.

In the spring of 1965, SNCC did away with its decentralised structure and practice of consensus decision-making. Declaring the need for 'black power' the next year, the organisation also shed its commitment to non-violence and an interracial staff.[48] These shifts marked a response to the violent intransigence of southern racists and the federal government's unwillingness to defend and support civil rights organisers. Seeking an adequate response to such conditions, SNCC leaders such as James Foreman, Stokely Carmichael and H. Rap Brown increasingly looked for guidance to national liberation struggles in Africa, Asia and Latin America.[49] From writers such as Franz Fanon, Amilcar Cabral, Che Guevara and Ho Chi Minh, they ingested a 'Third World Marxist' politics that counselled tighter forms of organisation, strong leadership and, eventually, the pursuit of a strategy of armed struggle. Third World Marxist theorists shared the commitment to abolish capitalism with orthodox Marxist–Leninists, but they focused greater attention on the means by which the system of imperialism politically subjugated and derived massive profits from 'oppressed nations', overwhelmingly peoples of colour, around the world. Strategically, Third World Marxists focused less on the spread of radical unionism among industrial workers, and promoted modes of armed struggle that could simultaneously achieve the national liberation of formerly colonised territories and institute forms of state socialism.[50]

While some older anarchists, such as Wieck and Finch, were highly critical of these developments, many in the new generation welcomed the victories of insurgents such as Fidel Castro and Che Guevara as harbingers of an international revolutionary upsurge. They saw the growing militancy among African

American activists, who looked to these models, as entirely justified. In 1966, Morea and his friend Ron Hahne launched a four-page broadsheet devoted to avant-garde art and radical politics titled *Black Mask*. For Morea, the name had a number of resonances: 'There was a book written by Franz Fanon, *Black Faces, White Masks*. Well, I always thought, "white faces, black masks." I was also friends with the black nationalists, and some of them used an African mask as a symbol. The colour black was an anarchist symbol, but the mask fit the art side more, say, than Black Flag. So it was all of these things, but Franz Fanon was a big part of it.'[51] For Morea, the promotion of novel and authentic expressions of rebellion that had traction in the contemporary world took precedence over notions of theoretical purity and analytical consistency.

From the beginning *Black Mask* declared its support for the emergent forms of black radicalism. 'A new spirit is rising. Like the streets of Watts we burn with revolution [ . . . ] The guerrilla, the blacks, the men of the future, we are all at your heels,' read an early statement. The magazine's first issue also reprinted a flier from the Lowndes County Freedom Organization, the SNCC-organised project that was the first to adopt the Black Panther as its symbol.[52]

In February 1967, *Black Mask* contributors and their friends literalised the publication's name when they marched through New York City's financial district donned completely in black, wearing black ski masks, and carrying skulls on poles and a sign that read 'Wall Street is War Street'. This stark and provocative demonstration against the war in Vietnam appears to have been the first recorded deployment of the black bloc aesthetic. Like the Rebel Worker group, the *Black Mask* editors communicated, visited and traded publications with creative and militant radicals from around the world, including French situationists, Dutch Provos and the Zengakuren of Japan.[53]

In 1967, Morea and Hahne collaborated with other artists on New York City's Lower East Side to organise an 'Angry Arts' week. Police arrested participants at St. Patrick's Cathedral on Easter Sunday as they unveiled posters denouncing the cardinal's endorsement of the Vietnam War. In the aftermath of Angry Arts week, the Black Mask 'family' grew to include 10 to 15 core members, primarily white and male, including Osha Neumann, the stepson of the celebrated critical theorist Herbert Marcuse. Early in 1968, the group organised a theatrical demonstration in front of the Lincoln Center for Performing Arts, signing an explanatory leaflet, 'Up Against the Wall, Motherfucker'. The line was drawn from a poem penned by black nationalist LeRoi Jones during 'race riots' that had convulsed Newark, NJ the previous year.[54] The name stuck and the group remade itself accordingly.

Jones had contemptuously declared:

[ . . . ] you can't steal nothin from a whiteman, he's already stole it he owes you anything you want, even his life. All the stores will open if you will say the magic words. The magic words are: Up against the wall mother fucker this is a stick up.[55]

The uncompromising position of Jones and other black militants appealed to Up Against the Wall/Motherfuckers (UAWMF). Calling themselves an 'anarchist street gang' or, alternatively, 'a street gang with an analysis', UAWMF organised hippies, drop-outs, bums and Puerto Rican youth on the Lower East Side, created a free store, squatted empty buildings and regularly instigated small scale riots and brawls with the police. The group's basic strategy was to push members of the white counter-culture to increase the level of their confrontation with institutions of authority, as a means of forging another 'front' in the struggles being waged by oppressed racial groups in the USA and anti-colonial forces in southeast Asia, Africa and Latin America. Morea proudly recalled, 'We stormed the entrance to the Pentagon – the only people in history to actually penetrate into the building. *And* we cut the fences at Woodstock. So here you've got this hippie cultural [thing], and this [other thing]. And that was *us*.'[56] As Neumann put it, 'We advocated a politics of rage and tribal bonding, "flower power with thorns." '[57]

Both the Rebel Worker group and Black Mask/UAWMF were relatively short-lived formations. By 1967 members of the Rebel Worker group shifted their focus elsewhere. Penelope Rosemont joined the national staff of Students for a Democratic Society, while working with Franklin and others to develop a greater surrealist presence in the USA. The core members of UAWMF left New York City in 1971 to escape the escalating cycle of incarceration and violent protest they found themselves increasingly trapped in, dissolving soon afterwards. However, groups of radicals with similar influences, but slightly different patterns of development, such as the White Panther Party in Michigan and a variety of pro-situationist groups in California, bridged the gap between the counter-culture of the 1960s and the US anarchist movement in 1970s and 1980s.[58]

In summary, the Beat subculture of the late 1950s inured many young white North Americans to 'hip' jazz culture, which helped convince them of the desirability and possibility of cultural revolution, prompting some to embrace anarchism. They grew up watching and reading about the early, predominantly non-violent, phase of the black freedom movement. But as black anger in response to white reactionary violence lead to urban 'race riots,' and the influence of national liberation movements gave rise to the black power movement, some anarchists grew to identify people of colour willing to engage in property destruction and political violence as a radical vanguard worthy of emulation. This lead to an ideologically messy, heterodox politics that sought to combine anti-authoritarian cultural revolution with Third World Marxist-inspired armed struggle. Although pacifism predominated among anarchists in the USA between 1940 and 1965, that commitment was challenged and abandoned over the next five years. While the non-violence of Gandhi and black southerners inspired the anarchist-pacifism of the early period, the rioting and turn to armed self-defence by African Americans (and, later, groups such as the Puerto Rican Young Lords and the American Indian

Movement) in the northern and western USA revived the insurrectionist current in US anarchism by the end of the 1960s.

Through the circulation of people, publications and struggles between North America and Europe, this new sensibility mutated and multiplied over the following decades, even after the struggles against white supremacy and colonialism that had provided a key impetus had subsided. The avant-garde critique of the banality of everyday life, urban street fighting and the demand for self-management and worker's councils fused indelibly in Paris during the events of May '68, giving the situationists an international cache still far from being exhausted.[59] *Heatwave* – a British counterpart to *The Rebel Worker* – and the UK section of the SI were succeeded by King Mob, which, indebted to Black Mask/UAWMF, sought to practice an 'active nihilism' in early 1970s England.[60] They proved influential to the first wave of British punk. In 1977, what has become known as the 'autonomist Marxist' tradition emerged in Italy through a convergence of counter-cultural groups, such as the Metropolitan Indians (the influence of decolonial politics evident even in their name) and workerist organisations influenced by the Johnson-Forest/Socialisme ou Barbarie/Solidarity tradition.[61] Each of these strands of political radicalism fed into the international anarchist-punk movement of the 1980s and 1990s, which solidified sartorial youth cultures of resistance, pranks, squatting and militant street demonstrations using the black bloc tactic as defining elements of contemporary anarchism around the globe. Despite the circuitous way in which black bloc tactics developed, some contemporary anarchists and autonomists continue to defend the practice of political trashing in small, loosely organised groups by pointing to the semi-spontaneous uprisings of racialised urban communities as models of radical activity worthy of emulation. The widely circulated pamphlet *The Coming Insurrection*, for example, suggests radical intellectuals should take tactical and organisational inspiration from the French *banlieue* riots of the mid-2000s.[62]

## Conclusion

The anarchist-pacifists of the 1940s and 1950s and the cultural revolutionists of 1960s both marked fundamental departures from the traditional, class struggle based anarchism that existed in the USA prior to the Second World War. They contributed overlapping, often contradictory, anti-authoritarian sensibilities to radical social struggles in the final decades of the twentieth century and the first decade of the twenty-first. Clearly, it is impossible to fully trace and evaluate the complex pathways upon which anarchism has developed in the past half-century in a brief essay such as this. I have tried, instead, to hold a magnifying glass up to two particular moments in this history, and to then locate those moments within the broader pattern of development. What that level of magnification reveals, I hope, is the pervasive influence of a complex variety of socialisms and Marxisms, as well as many forms of people of colour-initiated struggles against white supremacy, on the political analyses, visions and strategies of contemporary anarchist movements. It likewise indicates ways that anarchist ideas and efforts have informed and bolstered black freedom struggles and other anti-racist movements. Such an analysis helps elucidate historical precedents – and therefore provides a tool for evaluating the transformative potential and possible pitfalls – of a variety of efforts aimed at reinventing the struggle for a free and equal, or libertarian socialist, world today.

## Notes

1. For more on differences between syndicalist (or mass) and insurrectionary anarchism, see, M. Schmidt and L. van der Walt, *Black Flame: The Revolutionary Class Politics of Anarchism and Syndicalism* (Oakland: AK Press, 2009).

2. See, for example, the Why? Group's translation of a pamphlet prepared by *L'Adunata*, no author, 'War or Revolution: An Anarchist Statement' (New York: Why? Publications Committee, 1944).

3. B. de Ligt, *The Conquest of Violence: An Essay on War and Revolution* (London: Pluto Press, [1937]), pp. 58, 64, 162.

4. D. T. Wieck, *Woman from Spillertown: A Memoir of Agnes Burns Wieck* (Carbondale and Edwardsville, IL: Southern Illinois University Press, 1992), p. 203.

5. J. Tracy, *Direct Action: Radical Pacifism from the Union Eight to the Chicago Seven* (Chicago: University of Chicago Press, 1996), p. 16.

6. J. K. Kosek, *Acts of Conscience: Christian Non-violence and Modern American Democracy* (New York: Columbia University Press, 2009).

7. Tracy, *Direct Action*; S. Bennett, *Radical Pacifism: The War Resisters League and Gandhian Non-violence in America, 1915–1963* (Syracuse, NY: Syracuse University Press, 2003).

8. Swarthmore College Peace Collection, Swarthmore, Pennsylvania, David Thoreau Wieck Papers, 1942–1969, memo by D. T. Wieck, 'Peace-related activities, post World War II,' no date.

9. D. Dellinger, *From Yale to Jail: The Life Story of a Moral Dissenter* (New York: Pantheon, 1993); A. Hunt, *David Dellinger: The Life and Times of a Non-violent Revolutionary* (New York: New York University Press, 2006).

10. Dachine Rainer Papers, Uncat MSS 139, Box 8, 'D-E,' letter, D. Dellinger to H. Cantine, 4 February 1945.

11. A. Hunt, *David Dellinger*, p. 86.

12. Dwight MacDonald, no title, *Politics*, 2:8 (August 1945).

13. M. Wreszin, *A Rebel in Defense of Tradition: The Life and Politics of Dwight MacDonald* (New York: Basic Books, 1994). 184 *'White Skin, Black Masks'*

14. R. Arsenault, *Freedom Riders: 1961 and the Struggle for Racial Justice* (Oxford: Oxford University Press, 2006); D. Catsam, *Freedom's Main Line: The Journey of Reconciliation and the Freedom Rides* (Lexington: University of Kentucky Press, 2009).

15. Tracy, *Direct Action*, pp. 47–75; Bennett, *Radical Pacifism*, pp. 145–55.

16. Bennett, *Radical Pacifism*, pp. 148–149.

17. J. D'Emilio, *Lost Prophet: The Life and Times of Bayard Rustin* (Chicago: University of Chicago, 2003), pp. 191–210.

18. J. Farrell, *The Spirit of the Sixties: The Making of Postwar Radicalism* (New York: Routledge, 1997), pp. 88–92.

19. Editors, 'Tract for the Times,' *Liberation*, 1:1 (1956), pp. 2–6.
20. Editors, 'Mississippi Muddle,' *Liberation*, 7:9 (1962), pp. 9–12. Reprinted with credit given to David Dellinger and Bayard Rustin in Paul Goodman (ed.), *Seeds of Liberation* (New York: George Braziller, 1964), pp. 306–316.
21. D. Dellinger, 'Are Pacifists Willing to be Negroes?' *Liberation*, 4:6 (1959), 3.
22. C. Carson, *In Struggle: SNCC and the Black Awakening of the 1960s* (Cambridge, MA: Harvard University Press, 1981), p. 11; Farrell, *Spirit of the Sixties*, p. 97.
23. E.W., 'The "Civil Rights" Struggle,' *Views and Comments*, 38 (May 1960).
24. B. Ransby, *Ella Baker and the Black Freedom Movement: A Radical Democratic Vision* (Chapel Hill: University of North Carolina Press, 2005), pp. 188–190.
25. Carson, *In Struggle*, p. 30.
26. F. Polletta, *Freedom Is an Endless Meeting: Democracy in American Social Movements* (Chicago: University of Chicago Press, 2002), p. 82.
27. Ibid, pp. 120–175; W. Breines, *Community and Organization in the New Left: The Great Refusal, 1962–1968* (New Brunswick, NJ Rutgers University Press, 1989).
28. A. Cornell, *Oppose and Propose! Lessons from Movement for a New Society* (Oakland: AK Press and Institute for Anarchist Studies, 2011); B. Epstein, *Political Protest and Cultural Revolution: Non-violent Direct Action in the 1970s and 1980s* (Berkeley: University of California Press, 1991).
29. Starhawk, *Webs of Power: Notes from the Global Uprising* (Gabriola Island: New Society Publishers, 2002); D. Solnit and R. Solnit (eds), *The Battle of the Story of 'the Battle of Seattle'* (Oakland: AK Press, 2009).
30. F. Dupuis-Déri, 'The Black Blocks Ten Years after Seattle: Anarchism, Direct Action, and Deliberative Practices,' *Journal for the Study of Radicalism*, 4:2 (2010), pp. 45–82; G. Katsiaficas, *The Subversion of Politics: European Autonomous Social Movements and the Decolonization of Everyday Life* (Oakland: AK Press, 2006); S. Lotringer and C. Marazzi, *Autonomia: Post-Political Politics* (Los Angeles: Semiotext(e), 2007).
31. On the transnational circulation of counter-cultures, see J. MacPhee and D. Greenwald, *Signs of Change: Social Movement Cultures, 1960s to Now* (Oakland: AK Press, 2010); G. McKay, *Senseless Acts of Beauty: Cultures of Resistance since the Sixties* (London and New York: Verso, 1996); R. Lumley, *States of Emergency: Cultures of Revolt in Italy from 1968 to 1978* (London and New York: Verso, 1990).
32. T. Boraman, *Rabble Rousers and Merry Pranksters: A History of Anarchism in Aotearoa/New Zealand from the Mid 1950s to the Early 1980s* (Christchurch: Kapito Books and Irrecuperable Press, 2007).
33. L. Hamalian, *A Life of Kenneth Rexroth* (New York: Norton, 1991), pp. 149–156; P. Frank, 'San Francisco 1952: Painters, Poets, Anarchism,' *Drunken Boat*, 2 (1994), pp. 136–153. *Andrew Cornell 185*
34. J. Brown, 'The Zen of Anarchy: Japanese Exceptionalism and the Anarchist Roots of the San Francisco Poetry Renaissance,' *Religion and American Culture: A Journal of Interpretation*, 19:2 (2009), 207–242; K. Knabb, 'The Relevance of Rexroth,' in K. Knabb (ed.), *Public Secrets: Collected Skirmishes of Ken Knabb: 1970–1997* (Berkeley: Bureau of Public Secrets, 1997), pp. 310–356.
35. F. Rosemont, 'To Be Revolutionary in Everything: The *Rebel Worker* Story, 1964–1968' in F. Rosemont and C. Radcliffe (eds.) *Dancin' in the Streets! Anarchists, IWWs, Surrealists, Situationists & Provos in the 1960s as Recorded in the Pages of* The Rebel Worker *and* Heatwave (Chicago: Charles H. Kerr, 2005), pp. 5–6. Also see, P. Rosemont, *Dreams and Everyday Life: André Breton, Surrealism, Rebel Worker, SDS & the Seven Cities of Cibola* (Chicago: Charles H. Kerr, 2008).

36. S. Saul, *Freedom Is, Freedom Ain't: Jazz and the Making of the Sixties* (Cambridge: Harvard University Press, 2003), p. 33. On the concept of 'hipness' and the relation between bebop jazz and the Beats, see J. Leland, *Hip: The History* (New York: Harper Collins, 2004).

37. Rosemont, 'To be Revolutionary,' p. 45.

38. John Sinclair, manager of the MC5 and a founder of the White Panther Party, tellingly named his book about the Detroit milieu *Guitar Army*. J. Sinclair, *Guitar Army: Rock and Revolution with the MC5 and the White Panther Party* (Los Angeles: Process, 2007 [1972]). See also G. McKay, *Senseless Acts of Beauty*; G. McKay, *DiY Culture: Party and Protest in Nineties Britain* (London and New York: Verso, 1998).

39. F. Rosengarten, *Urbane Revolutionary: C.L.R. James and the Struggle for a New Society* (Jackson: University of Mississippi Press, 2008); G.L. Boggs, *Living for Change: An Autobiography* (Minneapolis: University of Minnesota Press, 1998).

40. A. Hirsch, *The French Left: A History and Overview* (Montreal: Black Rose Books, 1982), pp. 108–135; H. Cleaver, *Reading Capital Politically* (Leeds and San Francisco: Anti/Theses and AK Press, 2000), pp. 59–64.

41. C.L.R. James, G. Lee and C. Castoriadis, *Facing Reality: The New Society, Where to Look for It and How to Bring it Closer* (Chicago: Charles H. Kerr, 2006 [1958]).

42. D. Goodway (ed.), *For Workers' Power: The Selected Writings of Maurice Brinton* (Oakland: AK Press, 2004).

43. M. Glaberman, *Punching Out and Other Writings*, ed. S. Lynd (Chicago: Charles H. Kerr, 2002); George Rawick, *Listening to Revolt: Selected Writings*, ed. D. Roediger and M. Smith (Chicago: Charles H. Kerr, 2010).

44. F. Rosemont, 'Mods, Rockers and the Revolution,' in F. Rosemont and C. Radcliffe (eds.) *Dancing in the Streets*, pp. 127–131.

45. Rosemont, 'To be Revolutionary,' p. 45.

46. Ben Morea, Interview with author, New York, NY, 29 March 2009.

47. J. Malina, *The Diaries of Judith Malina, 1947–1957* (New York: Grove Press, 1984).

48. Polletta, *Freedom*, 88–119; Carson, *In Struggle*, pp. 133–211; P. Joseph, *Waiting 'til the Midnight Hour: A Narrative History of Black Power in America* (New York: Henry Holt, 2006).

49. J. Foreman, *The Making of Black Revolutionaries* (Seattle: University of Washington Press, 1997 [1972]); S. Carmichael with M. Thelwell, *Ready for Revolution: The Life and Struggles of Stokely Carmichael* (Kwame Ture) (New York: Scribner, 2003); J. Al-Amin (H. Rap Brown), *Die, Nigger, Die! A Political Autobiography* (New York: Dial Press, 1969]).

50. See R. Young, *Postcolonialism: An Historical Introduction* (Oxford: Blackwell, 2001); L. Pulido, *Black, Brown, Yellow, and Left: Radical Activism in Los Angeles* (Berkeley: 186 'White Skin, Black Masks' University of California Press, 2006); M. Elbaum, *Revolution in the Air: Sixties Radicals turn to Lenin, Mao, and Che* (New York: Verso, 2002).

51. B. Morea, interview.

52. R. Hahne, *Black Mask and Up Against the Wall Motherfucker: The Incomplete Works of Ron Hahne, Ben Morea and the Black Mask Group* (Oakland: PM Press, 2011), pp. 7–12. On the Lowndes County Freedom Organization, see H. Jeffries, *Bloody Lowndes: Civil Rights and Black Power in Alabama's Black Belt* (New York: New York University Press, 2010).

53. Morea, interview.

54. O. Neumann, *Up Against the Wall Motherf\*\*ker: A Memoir of the '60s, with Notes for Next Time* (New York: Seven Stories, 2008), pp. 53–67. LeRoi Jones later changed

his name to Amiri Baraka. On Baraka and the Newark uprising, see K. Woodard, *A Nation Within a Nation: Amiri Baraka (Leroi Jones) and Black Power Politics* (Chapel Hill: University of North Carolina Press, 1999).

55. L. Jones/A. Baraka, 'Black People!' in W. J. Harris (ed.) *The Leroi Jones/Amiri Baraka Reader* (New York: Thunder's Mouth Press, 1991), p. 224.

56. Morea, interview.

57. Neumann, *Up Against the Wall*, p. 66.

58. The Diggers, *Fifth Estate* and the pro-situationist groups are among the most important of these. On the Diggers, see J. Stephens, *Anti-Disciplinary Protest: Sixties Radicalism and Postmodernism* (Cambridge, UK: Cambridge University Press, 1998); T. Hodgdon, *Manhood in the Age of Aquarius: Masculinity in Two Counter-Cultural Communities, 1965–1983* (New York: Columbia University Press, 2008). On *Fifth Estate*, see P. Werbe, 'The History of the Fifth Estate', *Fifth Estate*, 368–369 (2005), 8–19; S. Millett, 'Technology Is Capital: Fifth Estate's Critique of the Megamachine' in J. Purkis and J. Bowen (eds.) *Changing Anarchism: Anarchist Theory and Practice in a Global Age* (Manchester: Manchester University Press, 2004). On the pro-situationist groups, see K. Knabb, *Public Secrets: Collected Skirmishes of Ken Knabb, 1970–1997* (Berkeley: Bureau of Public Secrets, 1997).

59. S. Plant, *The Most Radical Gesture: The Situationist International in a Postmodern Age* (London: Routledge, 1992); K. Ross, *May '68 and Its Afterlives* (Chicago: Chicago University Press, 2002).

60. D. Wise and S. Wise, 'The End of Music' in S. Home (ed.) *What Is Situationism? A Reader* (Edinburgh: AK Press, 1996), pp. 63–102.

61. R. Lumley, *States of Emergency*; G. Katsiaficas, *The Subversion of Politics*; S. Wright, *Storming Heaven: Class Composition and Struggle in Italian Autonomist Marxism* (London: Pluto Press, 2002).

62. The Invisible Committee, *The Coming Insurrection* (Los Angeles: Semiotext(e), 2009).

# 10

# The Search for a Libertarian Communism: Daniel Guérin and the 'Synthesis' of Marxism and Anarchism

*David Berry*

> *I have a horror of sects, of compartmentalisation, of people who are separated by virtually nothing and who nevertheless face each other as if across an abyss.*
>
> Daniel Guérin[1]

Concerned that his reinterpretation of the French Revolution, *La Lutte de classes sous la Première République* (1946), had been misunderstood, Daniel Guérin wrote to the socialist Marceau Pivert in 1947 that the book was to be seen as 'an introduction to a synthesis of anarchism and Marxism-Leninism I would like to write one day'.[2] This paper aims to analyse exactly what Guérin meant by this 'synthesis', and how and why he came to be convinced of its necessity.

It must however be noted from the outset that Guérin had no pretensions to being a theorist: he saw himself first and foremost as an activist and second as a historian.[3] Indeed, from the day in 1930 when he abandoned the poetry and novels of his youth, all his research and writings were concerned more or less directly with his political commitments. His developing critique of Marxism and his later interest in the relationship between Marxism and anarchism were motivated by his own direct experience of and active participation in revolutionary struggles on a number of fronts.

Although, in some of his autobiographical writings, Guérin had a tendency to divide his life into more or less distinct 'phases', and despite the fact that his political or ideological trajectory may seem to some to be rather protean, I would argue that there was in fact an underlying ideological consistency – even if changing circumstances meant that his 'organisational options' (as he put it) changed in different periods of his life. A historical materialist all his life, he remained attached to a revolutionary socialism with a strong ethical or moral core. Although it was many years before he found an organisation which lived up to his expectations, he was always at heart a libertarian communist, developing an increasingly strong belief in the need for a 'total revolution' which would attach as much importance to issues of race, gender and sexuality as to workplace-based conflict. Whether specifically in his commitment to a libertarian communism, to anti-colonialism or to sexual liberation, or more generally in his emphasis on what today would be called intersectionality, Guérin was undoubtedly ahead of his time.

## Early influences

Despite coming from the 'grande bourgeoisie' – a background which he would come to reject – Guérin owed much to the influence of his branch of the family: humanist, liberal and cultured, both his parents had been passionately pro-Dreyfus, both were influenced by Tolstoy's ethical and social ideas, and his father's library contained the *Communist Manifesto* as well as works by Benoît Malon, Proudhon and Kropotkin.[4] The young Daniel seems to have been particularly influenced by his father's pacifism, and was also deeply affected by his own reading of Tolstoy's *Diaries* and *Resurrection*. In the context of the increasingly polarised debates of the interwar period between the far-Right and far-Left ('Maurras *versus* Marx'), he identified with the 'Marxist extreme Left' from a relatively early age.[5] His later 'discovery' of the Parisian working class and of the concrete realities of their everyday existence (to a large extent through his homosexual relationships with young workers) reinforced a profound 'workerism' which would stay with him for the rest of his life.[6]

## The bankruptcy of Stalinism and of social democracy

This workerism would lead him in 1930–31 to join the syndicalists grouped around the veteran revolutionary Pierre Monatte: typically, Guérin's first real active involvement was in the campaign for the reunification of the two major syndicalist confederations, the Confédération Générale du Travail (General Labour Confederation) and the Confédération Générale du Travail Unitaire (United General Labour Confederation). His workerism was also responsible for a strong attraction towards the French Communist Party (PCF), far more 'proletarian' than the Socialist Party (the *Section Française de l'Internationale Ouvrière*, SFIO), despite his 'visceral anti-Stalinism' and what he saw as the Party's 'crass ideological excesses, its inability to win over the majority of workers, and its mechanical submission to the Kremlin's orders'.[7] Yet Guérin was no more impressed with the SFIO, which he found petty-bourgeois, narrow-minded, dogmatically anti-communist, and obsessed with electioneering:

The tragedy for many militants of our generation was our repugnance at having to opt for one or the other of the two main organisations which claimed, wrongly, to represent the working class. Stalinism and social democracy both repelled us, each in its own way. Yet those workers who were active politically were in one of these two parties. The smaller, inter-mediate groups and the extremist sects seemed to us to be doomed to impotence and marginalisation. The SFIO, despite the social conformism of its leadership, at least had the advantage over the Communist Party of enjoying a certain degree of internal democracy, and to some extent allowed revolutionaries to express themselves; whereas the monolithic automatism of stalinism forbade any critics from opening their mouths and made it very difficult for them even to stay in the party.[8]

Hence his decision to rejoin the SFIO in 1935, shortly before the creation by Marceau Pivert of the *Gauche révolutionnaire* (Revolutionary Left) tendency within the party, of which he would become a leading member. Guérin was attracted by Pivert's 'Luxemburgist', libertarian and syndicalist tendencies.[9] He was consistently on the revolutionary wing of the *Gauche révolutionnaire* and of its successor the *Parti socialiste ouvrier et paysan* (PSOP, Workers' and Peasants' Socialist Party, created when the *Gauche révolutionnaire* was expelled from the SFIO in 1938), and, in the Popular Front period, he drew a clear distinction between what he called the 'Popular Front no. 1' – an electoral alliance between social democracy, Stalinism, and bourgeois liber-alism – and the 'Popular Front no. 2' – the powerful, extra-parliamentary, working-class movement, which came into conflict with the more moderate (and more bourgeois) Popular Front government.[10] He viewed the 'entryism' of the French Trotskyists in these years as a welcome counterbalance to the reformism of the majority of the Socialist Party.[11]

Indeed, in the 1930s, Guérin agreed with Trotsky's position on many issues: on the nature of fascism and how to stop it; on war and revolution-ary proletarian internationalism; on opposition to the collusion between 'social-patriotism' (that is, mainstream social democracy) and 'national-communism' (that is, the PCF) as well as any pact with the bourgeois Radicals; and on the need to fight actively for the liberation of Europe's colonies. As Guérin comments after recounting in glowing terms his sole meeting with Trotsky in Barbizon in 1933: 'On a theoretical level as well as on the level of political practice, Trotsky would remain, for many of us, both a stimulus to action and a teacher.'[12]

Ultimately, Guérin's experience of the labour movement and of the Left in the 1930s – as well as his research on the nature and origins of fascism and Nazism[13] – led him to reject both social democracy and Stalinism as effec-tive strategies for defeating fascism and preventing war. Indeed, the left – 'divided, ossified, negative, and narrow-minded' in Guérin's words – bore its share of responsibility and had made tragic errors.[14] The SFIO was criticised by Guérin for its electoralism and for allowing its hands to be tied by the *Parti radical-socialiste*, 'a bourgeois party whose corruption and bankruptcy were in large part responsible for the fascist explosion'; for its incomprehension of the nature of the capitalist state, which led to the impotence of Léon Blum's 1936 Popular Front government; for its failure to take fascism seriously (and to aid the Spanish Republicans), despite the warnings, until it was too late; and for its obsessive rivalry with the PCF. The PCF was equally harshly criticised by Guérin – for what seemed to him to be its blind obedience to the Comintern, the criminal stupidity of the Comintern's 'third period' and for its counter-revolutionary strategy both in Spain and in France.[15]

As for Trotsky, Guérin disagreed with him over the creation of the Fourth International in 1938, which seemed to him premature and divisive. More generally, Guérin was critical of what he saw as Trotsky's tendency continually to transpose the experiences of the Russian Bolsheviks onto contemporary events in the West, and of his 'authoritarian rigidness'. Trotskyism, Guérin argued, represented 'the ideology of the infallible leader who, in an authoritarian fashion, directs the policy of a fraction or of a party'.[16] What Guérin wanted to see was 'the full development of the spontaneity of the working class'.[17] Writing in 1963, Guérin would conclude with regard to such disputes over revolutionary tactics:

> The revolutionary organisation which was lacking in June 1936 was not, in my opinion, an authoritarian leadership emanating from a small group or sect, but an organ for the coordination of the workers' councils, growing directly out of the occupied workplaces. The mistake of the *Gauche Révolutionnaire* was not so much that it was unable, because of its lack of preparation, to transform itself into a revolutionary party on the Leninist or Trotskyist model, but that it was unable [ . . . ] to help the working class to find for itself its own form of power structure to confront the fraud that was the Popular Front no.1.[18]

So as Guérin summarised the state of the Left in the 1930s: 'Everything made the renewal of the concepts and methods of struggle employed by the French left both indispensable and urgent.'[19]

## The break from Trotskyism

Despite Guérin's reservations about Trotskyism, his analysis of the nature of the Vichy regime was very similar to that put forward by the Fourth International, and he was also impressed with Trotsky's manifesto of May 1940, 'La guerre impérialiste et la révolution prolétarienne mondiale', including it in a collection of Trotsky's writings on the Second World War he would edit in 1970.[20] He worked with the Trotskyists in the resistance, not least because they remained true to their internationalism and to their class politics, rejecting, for instance, what Guerin saw as the PCF's demagogic nationalism.[21]

However, an extended study tour of the USA in 1946–1949, which included visits to branches or prominent militants of the Socialist Workers' Party and the breakaway Workers' Party, represented a turning point in Guérin's 'Trotskyism'. In a 1948 letter to Marceau Pivert, he commented on his unhappiness with the Trotskyists' tendency to 'repeat mechanically old formulae without rethinking them, relying lazily and uncritically on the (undeniably admirable) writings of Trotsky'.[22] Looking back 30 years later, he would conclude: 'It was thanks to the American Trotskyists, despite their undeniable commitment, that I ceased forever believing in the virtues of revolutionary parties built on authoritarian, Leninist lines.'[23]

## The 'Mother of us all'

Unlike many on the Left associated with postwar ideological renewal, most of whom would focus on a revision or reinterpretation of Marxism, often at a philosophical level, Guérin the historian began with a return to what he saw as the source of revolutionary theory and praxis: in 1946, he published his study of class struggle in the First French Republic (1793–1797).[24] The aim of the book was to 'draw lessons from the greatest, longest and deepest revolutionary experience France has ever known, lessons which would help regenerate the revolutionary, libertarian socialism of today', and to 'extract some ideas which would be applicable to our time and of direct use to the contemporary reader who has yet to fully digest the lessons of another revolution: the Russian Revolution'.[25] Applying the concepts of permanent revolution and combined and uneven development, inspired by Trotsky's *History of the Russian Revolution*, Guérin argued that the beginnings of a conflict of class interest could already be detected within the revolutionary camp between an 'embryonic' proletariat – the *bras nus* (manual workers), represented by the *Enragés* – and the bourgeoisie – represented by Robespierre and the Jacobin leadership. For Guérin, the French Revolution thus represented not only the birth of bourgeois parliamentary democracy, but also the emergence of 'a new type of democracy', a form of working-class direct democracy as seen, however imperfectly, in the '*sections*' (local popular assemblies), precursors of the Commune of 1871 and the Soviets of 1905 and 1917. In the second edition of the work, he would add 'the Commune of May 1968' to that genealogy.

Guérin emphasised the political ambivalence of the bourgeois Jacobin leadership which 'hesitated continually between the solidarity uniting it with the popular classes against the aristocracy and that uniting all the wealthy, property-owning classes against those who owned little or nothing'.[26] The essential lesson to be drawn from the French Revolution was thus the conflict of class interest between the bourgeoisie and the working classes. Bourgeois, social democratic and Stalinist interpretations of the Revolution – like those of Jean Jaurès, Albert Mathiez and so many others – which tended to maintain the 'cult of Robespierre' and to reinforce the labour movement's dependence on bourgeois democracy, were thus to be rejected.[27]

*La Lutte de classes sous la Pemière République* has been described by Eric Hobsbawm as 'a curious combination of libertarian and Trotskyist ideas – not without a dash of Rosa Luxemburg'.[28] It not only shocked many academic historians of the Revolution – especially those with more or less close links to the PCF (Georges Lefebvre, and especially Albert Soboul and Georges Rudé) – but also those politicians who, in Guérin's words, 'have been responsible for perverting and undermining true proletarian socialism'.[29] The ensuing debate lasted for many years.[30] The political significance was that the Revolutionary Terror had been used as a parallel to justify Bolshevik repression of democratic freedoms and repression of more Leftist movements. Stalin had been compared to Robespierre. The Jacobin tradition of patriotism and national unity in defence of the bourgeois democratic Republic has been one of the characteristics of the dominant tendencies within the French Left, and therefore central to the political mythologies of the Popular Front and the Resistance. Guérin, as Ian Birchall has put it, 'was polemicizing against the notion of a Resistance uniting all classes against the foreign invader'.[31]

What is more, the PCF had been campaigning since 1945 for unity at the top with the SFIO, and in the 1956 elections called for the re-establishment of a Popular Front government. At a time when fascism in the form of Poujadism looked as if it might once more be a real threat, Guérin argued that what was needed was a 'genuine' Popular Front, that is, a grass roots social movement rather than a governmental alliance, a truly popular movement centred on the working classes that would bring together the labour movement and all socialists who rejected both the pro-American SFIO and the pro-Soviet PCF: 'Only a combative Popular Front, which dares to attack big business, will be able to halt our middle classes on the slope which leads to fascism and to their destruction.'[32]

## The developing critique of Leninism

Guérin's friend and translator, C.L.R. James wrote in 1958 of Guérin's reinterpretation of the French Revolution:

It is impregnated with the experience and study of the greatest event of our time: the development and then degeneration of the Russian Revolution, and is animated implicitly by one central concern: how can the revolutionary masses avoid the dreadful pitfalls of bureaucratisation and the resurgence of a new oppressive state power, and instead establish a system of direct democracy?[33]

In an important essay of 1959, 'La Révolution déjacobinisée', Guérin argued that the 'Jacobin' traits in Marxism and particularly in Leninism were the result of an incomplete understanding on Marx and Engels' part of the class nature of the Jacobin dictatorship, to be distinguished according to Guérin from the democratically controlled *'contrainte révolutionnaire'* ('revolutionary coercion') exercised by the popular *sections*.[34] Thus by applying a historical materialist analysis to the experiences of the French revolutionary movement, Guérin came to argue, essentially, that 'authentic' socialism arose spontaneously out of working-class struggle, that it was fundamentally libertarian, and that authoritarian conceptions of party organisation and revolutionary strategy had their origins in bourgeois or even aristocratic modes of thought.

Guérin insisted that Marx and Engels envisaged the 'dictatorship of the proletariat' as being exercised by the working class as a whole, rather than by an avant-garde, but that they did not adequately differentiate their interpretation from that of the Blanquists. This made possible Lenin's later authoritarian conceptions: 'Lenin, who saw himself as both a "Jacobin" and a "Marxist," invented the idea of the dictatorship of a party substituting itself for the working class and acting by proxy in its name.'[35] This, for Guérin, was where it all started to go badly wrong:

The double experience of the French and Russian Revolutions has taught us that this is where we touch upon the central mechanism whereby direct democracy, the self-government of the people, is transformed, gradually, by the introduction of the revolutionary 'dictatorship', into the reconstitution of an apparatus for the oppression of the people.[36]

Guérin's critique clearly had its sources both in his reinterpretation of the Revolution and in the conditions of his time. *La Révolution française et nous* was informed by Guérin's critique of social-democratic and Stalinist strategies before, during, and after the war. 'La révolution déjacobinisée' was written at a significant historic moment for socialists in France: after the artificial national unity of the immediate postwar years had given way to profound social and political conflict; as Guy Mollet's SFIO became increasingly identified with the defence of the bourgeois status quo and the Western camp in the cold war; as the immensely powerful postwar PCF reeled under the effects of Hungary and the Khrushchev revelations; and as the unpopular and politically unstable Fourth Republic collapsed in the face of a threatened military coup. It was this situation which made renewal of the Left so necessary. In 1959, Guérin also picked up on the results of a survey of the attitudes of French youth towards politics, which indicated to him two things: first, that what alienated the younger generation from 'socialism' was 'bureaucrats and purges', and second, that, as one respondent put it, 'French youth are becoming more and more anarchist.'37 Ever the optimist, Guérin declared:

> [T]he time has come for the French left to begin again from zero, to rethink its problems from their very foundations. [ . . . ] The necessary synthesis of the ideas of equality and liberty [ . . . ] can and must only be sought within the framework of socialist thought [ . . . ]. The failure of both reformism and stalinism imposes on us the urgent duty to find a way of reconciling (proletarian) democracy with socialism, freedom with Revolution.[38]

## From Trotskyism to New Left to anarchism

What Guérin would thus do which was quite remarkable in post-Liberation France was endeavour to separate Marxism from Bolshevism – his continued friendly and supportive relations with Trotskyists notwithstanding – and it is noteworthy that he had contact in this period with a number of prominent non-orthodox Marxists. After 1945, especially, he was involved (centrally or more peripherally) in a number of circles or networks, and according to the sociologist Michel Crozier (who regarded Guérin as a mentor) Guérin self-identified in the late 1940s and early 1950s – 'the golden age of the left intelligentsia' – as an 'independent Marxist'.[39]

C.L.R. James has already been mentioned. He and Guérin appear to have met in the 1930s; they became good friends, Guérin visited him while in the USA in 1949, and they corresponded over many years. James even translated *La Lutte de classes* into English, and described the book as 'one of the most important modern textbooks in [ . . . ] the study of Marxism' and 'one of the great theoretical landmarks of our movement'.[40]

Similarly, Guérin had first met Karl Korsch in Berlin in 1932, and visited him in his exile in Cambridge (Massachusetts) in 1947, where according to Guérin they spent many hours together.[41] The two would collaborate a decade later in their bibliographical researches on the relationship between Marx and Bakunin.[42] Also during his time in the USA, Guérin became friendly with a group of refugee Germans in Washington, D.C., dissident Marxists, 'as hospitable as they were brilliant', connected with the socalled Frankfurt School: Franz Neumann, Otto Kirchheimer and Herbert Marcuse.[43]

In France, Guérin already knew the leading figures in the Socialisme ou Barbarie group from their days in the *Parti Communiste Internationaliste* together: Guérin's papers contain a number of texts produced by the socalled Chaulieu–Montal Tendency in the late 1940s.[44] It is interesting to note that the Socialisme ou Barbarie group's theses on the Russian Revolution feature in the list of theories and authors discovered by the Algerian nationalist and revolutionary, Mohammed Harbi, thanks to his first meeting with Guérin (at a meeting of the PCI discussion group, the 'Cercle Lénine') in 1953.[45] In 1965 Guérin took part, with Castoriadis, Lefort and Edgar Morin, in a forum on 'Marxism Today' organised by Socialisme ou Barbarie (whose work Morin would describe a few years later as itself representing 'an original synthesis of Marxism and anarchism'[46]). Guérin also contributed to Morin's *Arguments* (1956–1962), an important journal launched in response to the events of 1956 with a view to a 'reconsideration not only of Stalinist Marxism, but of the Marxist way of thinking',[47] and he had been centrally involved with the French 'Titoists' around Clara Malraux and the review *Contemporains* (1950–1951).[48]

In short, Guérin was at the heart of the Left-intellectual ferment which characterised these years. He had an address book, as his daughter Anne recently put it,[49] as fat as a dictionary and he shared many of the theoretical preoccupations of many leading Marxists in the 20 years or so following the Second World War, be it the party-form, bureaucracy, alienation or sexual repression.

In the mid- to late 1950s, like other former or 'critical' Trotskyists, as well as ex-members of the FCL (the Libertarian Communist Federation, banned in 1956),[50] Guérin belonged – though 'without much conviction' – to a series of Left-socialist organisations: the *Nouvelle Gauche*, the *Union de la Gauche Socialiste*, and, briefly, the *Parti Socialiste Unifié*.[51] But it was also around 1956 that Guérin 'discovered' anarchism. Looking back on a 1930 boat trip to Vietnam and the small library he had taken with him, Guérin commented that of all the authors he had studied – Marx, Proudhon, Georges Sorel, Hubert Lagardelle, Fernand Pelloutier, Lenin, Trotsky, Gandhi, and others – 'Marx had, without a doubt, been preponderant.'[52] But having become increasingly critical of Leninism, Guérin discovered the collected works of Bakunin, a 'revelation' which rendered him forever 'allergic to all versions of authoritarian socialism, whether Jacobin, Marxist, Leninist, or Trotskyist'.[53] The discovery of Bakunin coincided with the appearance of the Hungarian workers' committees in 1956. Guérin was thus provoked into studying the councilist tradition.[54] It was also during the 1950s that Guérin, moving on from his study of the French Revolution, had begun to research the conflicts within the First International and more generally the relationship between Marxism and anarchism.

Guérin would describe the following ten years or so (that is, the mid 1950s to the mid 1960s) – which saw the publication notably of the popular anthology *Ni Dieu ni Maître* and of *L'Anarchisme*, which sold like hot cakes at the Sorbonne in May 1968 – as his 'classical anarchist phase'.[55] He became especially interested in Proudhon, whom he admired as the first theorist of *autogestion*, or worker self-management[56]; Bakunin, representative of revolutionary, working-class anarchism, close to Marxism, Guérin insisted, yet remarkably prescient about the dangers of statist communism; and Max Stirner, appreciated as a precursor of 1968 because of his determination to attack bourgeois prejudice and puritanism.

## Guérin and anarchism

Guérin had had no contact with the anarchist movement before the Second World War, other than to read E. Armand's individualist anarchist organ *L'en dehors*.[57] According to Georges Fontenis, a leading figure in the postwar anarchist movement, Guérin began to have direct contact with the Anarchist Federation (FA) in 1945, when the second edition of *Fascism and Big Business* was published. *Le Libertaire* reviewed Guérin's books favourably, and he was invited to galas of the FA and (from 1953) of the FCL to do book signings. He got to know leading anarchist militants and would drop in at the FCL's offices in Paris. Fontenis described him as being 'an active sympathiser' at that point.[58] His new-found sympathies were sufficiently well known for the US embassy in Paris to refuse him a visa to visit his wife and daughter in 1950 on the grounds that he was both a Trotskyist *and* an anarchist.[59] The ideological stance of the FCL ('libertarian Marxism') and its position on the Algerian war ('critical support' for the nationalist movement in the context of the struggle against French bourgeois imperialism) proved doubly attractive to the anti-colonialist Guérin.[60] In part for these reasons, 1954 (the beginning of the Algerian war of independence) represented the beginning of a relationship, notably with Fontenis (leading light of the FCL), which as we shall see would ultimately take Guérin into the ranks of the 'libertarian communist' movement.

In 1959, Guérin published a collection of articles titled *Jeunesse du socialisme libertaire*. This represented both a continuation of the critique of Leninism begun during the war, and Guérin's first analysis of the nineteenth-century anarchist tradition. Significantly, a copy of this collection has been found with a handwritten dedication to Maximilien Rubel, 'to whom this little book owes so much'.[61] A few years later, in 1965, he would publish both *Anarchism. From Theory to Practice* and the two volume anthology *No Gods No Masters*. The purpose was to 'rehabilitate' anarchism which 'suffered from an undeserved disrepute', and the anthology represented the 'dossier of evidence' against some common misconceptions or misrepresentations: first, the claim that 'it has no place in the modern world, a world characterised by centralisation, by large political and economic entities'; second, that it is 'essentially individualistic, particularistic, hostile to any form of organisation. It leads to fragmentation, to the egocentric withdrawal of small local units of administration and production. It is incapable of centralizing or of planning. It is nostalgic for the "golden age". [...] It suffers from a childish optimism; its "idealism" takes no account of the solid realities of the material infrastructure'; and third, that anarchism is synonymous with terrorism and assassination.[62]

Although, as we have seen, he referred to his 'classical anarchist' phase, and despite his assertion that the basics of anarchist doctrine were relatively homogeneous, elsewhere he was very clear that both books focused on a particular *kind* of anarchism. To begin with, '[t]he fundamental aspect of these doctrines' was, for Guérin, that '[a]*narchy*, is indeed, above all, synonymous with *socialism*. The anarchist is, first and foremost, a socialist whose aim is to put an end to the exploitation of man by man. Anarchism is no more than one of the branches of socialist thought [ . . . ]. For Adolph Fischer, one of the Chicago martyrs, 'every anarchist is a socialist, but every socialist is not necessarily an anarchist'.[63]

In *Pour un marxisme libertaire* (1969), Guérin described himself as coming from the school of 'anti-Stalinist Marxism', but as having for some time been in the habit of 'delving into the treasury of libertarian thought'. Anarchism, he insisted, was still relevant and still very much alive, 'provided that it is first divested of a great deal of childishness, utopianism and romanticism'.[64] He went on to comment that because of this openness towards the contribution of anarchism, his book, *Anarchism*, had been misunderstood by some, and that it did not mean that he had become an 'ecumenical' anarchist, to use Georges Fontenis' term.[65] In *Anarchisme et marxisme* (written in 1973), Guérin emphasised that his book on anarchism had focused on 'social, constructive, collectivist or communist anarchism' because this was the kind of anarchism which had most in common with Marxism.[66]

The reason Guérin gave for focusing on this kind of anarchism, as opposed to individualist anarchism, was that it was entirely relevant to the problems faced by contemporary revolutionaries: '[l]ibertarian visions of the future [ . . . ] invite serious consideration. It is clear that they fulfil to a very large extent the needs of our times, and that they can contribute to the building of our future.'[67]

But is this really 'classical anarchism', as Guérin put it, given the insistence on 'constructive anarchism, which depends on organisation, on self-discipline, on integration, on federalist and noncoercive centralisation'; the emphasis on experiments in workers' control in Algeria, Yugoslavia and Cuba; the openness to the idea that such states could be seen as socialist and capable of reform in a libertarian direction?[68] This was not the conclusion of English anarchist Nicolas Walter, whose review of *Ni dieu ni maître* and *L'Anarchisme*, though sceptical about the attention paid to Gramsci, Yugoslavia or Algeria, concluded that these two books were 'the expression of an original and exciting view of anarchism'.[69]

So Guérin's take on anarchism represented an original departure, and it is worth picking up on two taboos mentioned by Patrice Spadoni – who worked alongside Guérin in different libertarian communist groups in the 1970s and 1980s – when commenting on Guérin's 'non-dogmatism':

> The young libertarian communists that we were [ . . . ] turned pale with shock when he sang the praises of a Proudhon, of whom he was saying 'yes and no' while we said 'no and no'; then we would go white with horror, when he started quoting a Stirner whom we loathed – without having really read him . . . [70]

## Proudhon and the fundamental importance of self-management

Proudhon had already ceased to be an ideological reference for any section of the French anarchist movement by at least the time of the Great War, except for a small minority of individualists opposed to any kind of collective ownership of the means of production. Most anarchists referred to either Kropotkin or Bakunin. This was partly because of the perceived ambiguities in Proudhon's own writings regarding property, and partly because of the increasingly reactionary positions adopted by some of his 'mutualist' followers after his death in 1865.

The fact that Proudhon is so central to Guérin's 'rehabilitation' of anarchism is thus surprising and tells us something about what he was trying to do and how it is he came to study anarchism in such depth: whereas Proudhon had already for many years been commonly referred to as the 'father of anarchy', Guérin refers to him as the 'father of self-management'. This is the crux of the matter: Guérin was looking for a way to guarantee that in any future revolution, control of the workplace, of the economy and of society as a whole would remain at the base, that spontaneous forms of democracy – like the soviets, in the beginning – would not be hijacked by any centralised power.[71] Marx, Guérin insisted, hardly mentioned workers' control or self-management at all, whereas Proudhon paid it a great deal of attention.[72] Workers' control was, for Guérin, 'without any doubt the most original creation of anarchism, and goes right to the heart of contemporary realities'.[73] Proudhon had been one of the first to try to answer the question raised by other social reformers of the early nineteenth century. As Guérin put it: 'Who should manage the economy? Private capitalism? The State? Workers' organisations? In other words, there were – and still are – three options: free enterprise, nationalisation or socialisation (that is, Self-management).'[74] From 1848 onwards, Proudhon had argued passionately for the third option, something which set him apart from most other socialists of the time, who, like Louis Blanc, argued for one form or another of State control (if only on a transitional basis). Unlike Marx, Engels and others, Guérin argued, Proudhon saw workers' control as a concrete problem to be raised now, rather than relegated to some distant future. As a consequence, he thought and wrote in detail about how it might function: 'Almost all the issues which have caused such problems for present-day experiments in self-management were already foreseen and described in Proudhon's writings.'[75]

## Stirner the 'father of anarchism'?

As for Stirner – generally anathema to the non-individualist wing of the anarchist movement – the answer lies in what Guérin perceived to be Stirner's latent homosexuality, his concern with sexual liberation and his determination to attack bourgeois prejudice and puritanism: Stirner was 'a precursor of May '68' and 'the voice of all those who throw down a challenge to normality'. [76] It was Guérin's personal experience of the endemic homophobia in the labour movement and many Marxists' exclusive concern with class that accounts in large part for his sympathy with Stirner.[77]

So to the extent that Guérin insists that every anarchist is an individualist – at the same time as being a 'social' anarchist (*anarchiste sociétaire*) – to the extent that he approves of Stirner's emphasis on the uniqueness of each individual, it is because he admires the determination to resist social conformism and moral prejudice. Guérin certainly had no truck with the precious 'freedom of the individual' which was the stock mantra of those anarchists who rejected any attempt to produce a more ideologically and organisationally coherent revolutionary movement or who wished to ground their action in a realistic (or in Guérin's words 'scientific') analysis of social conditions.

## For a 'synthesis' of Marxism and anarchism

So having called himself a 'libertarian socialist' in the late 1950s before going through an 'anarchist phase' in the 1960s, by 1968 Guérin was advocating 'libertarian Marxism', a term he would later change to 'libertarian communism' in order not to alienate some of his new anarchist friends (though the content remained the same). In 1969, with Fontenis and others Guérin launched the *Mouvement communiste libertaire* (MCL), which attempted to bring together various groups such as supporters of Denis Berger's *Voie communiste*, former members of the FCL and individuals such as Gabriel Cohn-Bendit who had been associated with Socialisme ou Barbarie.[78] Guérin was responsible for the organisation's paper, *Guerre de classes* (*Class War*). In 1971, the MCL merged with another group to become the *Organisation communiste libertaire* (OCL). In 1980, after complex debates, notably over the question of trade union activity, Guérin – who rejected ultra-Left forms of '*spontanéisme*' which condemned trade unionism as counter-revolutionary – would ultimately join the *Union des travailleurs communistes libertaires* (UTCL), created in 1978. He would remain a member until his death in 1988.[79]

Looking back on those years, Fontenis would write: 'For us [the FCL], as for Guérin, "libertarian Marxism" was never to be seen as a fusion or a marriage, but as a living synthesis very different from the sum of its parts.'[80] How should we interpret this?

Guérin was always keen to emphasise the commonalities in Marxism and anarchism, and underscored the fact that, in his view at least, they shared the same roots and the same objectives. Having said that, and despite the fact that Rubel seems to have influenced Guérin, Guérin's study of Marx led him to suggest that those such as Rubel who saw Marx as a libertarian were exaggerating and/or being too selective.[81] Reviewing the ambivalent but predominantly hostile relations between Marx and Engels, on the one hand, and Stirner, Proudhon and Bakunin, on the other hand, Guérin concluded that the disagreements between them were based to a great extent on misunderstanding and exaggeration on both sides: 'Each of the two movements needs the theoretical and practical contribution of the other', Guérin argued, and this is why he saw the expulsion of the Bakuninists from the International Working Men's Association congress at The Hague in 1872 as 'a disastrous event for the working class'.[82]

'Libertarian communism' was for Guérin an attempt to 'revivify everything that was constructive in anarchism's contribution in the past'. We have noted that his *Anarchism* focused on 'social, constructive, collectivist, or communist anarchism'.[83] Guérin was more critical of 'traditional' anarchism, with what he saw as its knee-jerk rejection of organisation and simplistic, Manichean approach to the question of the 'state' in modern, industrial and increasingly internationalised societies. He became interested particularly in militants such as the Spanish anarchist Diego Abad de Santillán, whose ideas on 'integrated' economic self-management contrasted with what Guérin insisted was the naïve and backward-looking 'libertarian communism' of the Spanish CNT advocated at its 1936 Saragossa conference.[84] Such a policy seemed to Guérin to take no account of the nature of modern consumer societies and the need for economic planning and co-ordination at national and transnational level. In this connection, Guérin also became interested in the ideas of the Belgian collectivist socialist César de Paepe – who had argued against the anarchists of the Jura Federation in favour of what he called an 'an-archic state' – on the national and transnational organisation of public services within a libertarian framework.[85]

On the other hand, Guérin's libertarian Marxism or communism did not reject those aspects of Marxism which still seemed to Guérin valid and useful: (i) the notion of alienation, which Guérin saw as being in accordance with the anarchist emphasis on the freedom of the individual; (ii) the insistence that the workers shall be emancipated by the workers themselves; (iii) the analysis of capitalist society; and (iv) the historical materialist dialectic, which for Guérin remained:

... one of the guiding threads enabling us to understand the past and the present, on condition that the method not be applied rigidly, mechanically, or as an excuse not to fight on the false pretext that the material conditions for a revolution are absent, as the Stalinists claimed was the case in France in 1936, 1945 and 1968. Historical materialism must never be reduced to a determinism; the door must always be open to individual will and to the revolutionary spontaneity of the masses.[86]

Indeed, following his focus on anarchism in the 1960s, Guérin returned in the 1970s to his earlier researches on Marxism, and in his new quest for a synthesis of the two ideologies he found a fruitful source in Rosa Luxemburg. She was for Guérin the only German social democrat who had stayed true to what he called 'original' Marxism, and in 1971 he published an anthology of her critical writings on the pre-1914 SFIO, as well as a study of the notion of spontaneity in her work.[87] The following year he took part in a debate with Gilbert Badia, Michael Löwy, Madeleine Rebérioux, Denis Vidal-Naquet and others on the contemporary relevance of Luxemburg's ideas.[88] Guérin saw no significant difference between her conception of revolutionary working-class spontaneity and the anarchist one, nor between her conception of the 'mass strike' and the syndicalist idea of the 'general strike'. Her criticisms of Lenin in 1904 and of the Bolshevik Party in the spring of 1918 (regarding the democratic freedoms of the working class) seemed to him very anarchistic, as did her conception of a socialism propelled from below by workers' councils. She was, he argued, 'one of the links between anarchism and authentic Marxism', and for this reason she played an important role in the development of Guérin's thinking about convergences between certain forms of Marxism and certain forms of anarchism.[89]

Guérin was convinced that a libertarian communism which represented such a synthesis of the best of Marxism and the best of anarchism would be much more attractive to progressive workers than 'degenerate, authoritarian Marxism or old, outdated, and fossilised anarchism'.[90] But he was adamant that he was not a theorist, that libertarian communism was, as yet, only an 'approximation', not a fixed dogma:

It cannot, it seems to me, be defined on paper, in absolute terms. It cannot be an endless raking over of the past, but must rather be a rallying point for the future. The only thing of which I am convinced is that the future social revolution will have nothing to do with either Muscovite despotism or anæmic social-democracy; that it will not be authoritarian, but libertarian and rooted in self-management, or, if you like, councilist.[91]

## Conclusion

To what extent, then, can we say that Guérin succeeded in producing a 'synthesis'? Assessments by fellow revolutionaries have varied. Guérin himself used to complain that many militants were so attached to ideological pigeonholing and that quasi-tribal loyalties were so strong that his purpose was frequently misunderstood, with many who identified as anarchists criticising him for having 'become a Marxist', and *vice versa*.[92] Yet Guérin was clear that there have been many Marxisms and many anarchisms, and he also insisted that his understanding of 'libertarian communism' 'transcended' both anarchism and Marxism.[93]

Walter, apparently struggling to characterise his politics, described Guérin as 'a veteran socialist who became an anarchist' and as 'a Marxist writer of a more or less Trotskyist variety' who had gone on to attempt a synthesis between Marxism and anarchism before finally turning to 'a syndicalist form of anarchism'.[94]

George Woodcock, in a review of Noam Chomsky's introduction to the English edition of Guérin's *Anarchism*, insisted that 'neither is an anarchist by any known criterion; they are both left-wing Marxists' – their failing having been to focus too narrowly on the economic, on workers' control, on an 'obsolete', 'anarcho-syndicalist' perspective.[95] Such a judgement is clearly based on a particular and not uncontentious conception of anarchism.

The opposite conclusion was drawn by another anarchist, Miguel Chueca, who has argued that if we look at all the major issues dividing anarchists from Marxists, then 'the 'synthesis' results, in all cases, in a choice in favour of the anarchist position'.[96] Chueca seems to have based his conclusion on an essentialist view of anarchism and of Marxism, and on an identification of Marxism with Leninism. He also disregards some significant issues, such as Guérin's insistence on the historical materialist dialectic and the need for centralised (albeit 'non-coercive') economic planning.

Writing from a sympathetic but not uncritical, Trotskyist perspective, Ian Birchall suggests that ultimately Guérin's greatest achievement was his practice as a militant:

> Guérin's greatness lay in his role as a mediator rather than as a synthesist. Over six decades he had a record of willingness to cooperate with any section of the French Left that shared his fundamental goals of proletarian self-emancipation, colonial liberation and sexual freedom. He was a vigorous polemicist, but saw no fragment of the left, however obscure, as beneath his attention. [...] He was also typically generous, never seeking to malign his opponents, however profoundly he disagreed with them. [...] He was always willing to challenge orthodoxy, whether Marxist or anarchist. [...] Yet behind the varying formulations one consistent principle remained: 'The Revolution of our age will be made from below – or not at all.'[97]

Others have embraced Guérin's theoretical contribution and it is clear that his ideas on a 'libertarian Marxism' or 'libertarian communism' were enormously influential from the 1960s onwards, and many today (notably, but not only, those in France close to the organisation *Alternative libertaire*[98]) see in him a precursor and are admiring of his theoretical and practical contribution to the search for a libertarian communism – albeit as a contribution which needed further development in the context of the social struggles of the 1980s and beyond. Indeed Guérin was the first to accept that he had not yet seen the 'definitive crystalisation of such an unconventional and difficult synthesis', which would 'emerge from social struggles' with 'innovative forms which nobody today can claim to predict'[99]:

> It would be pointless today to try to paper over the cracks in the more or less crumbling and rotting edifice of socialist doctrines, to plug away at patching together some of those fragments of traditional Marxism and anarchism which are still useful, to launch oneself into demonstrations of Marxian or Bakuninian erudition, to attempt to trace, merely on paper, ingenious syntheses or tortuous reconciliations. [ ... ] To call oneself a libertarian communist today, does not mean looking backwards, but towards the future. The libertarian communist is not an exegete, but a militant.[100]

## Acknowledgements

I am grateful to the British Academy, whose Small Research Grant scheme enabled me to study Guérin's papers in the Bibliothèque de Documentation Internationale Contemporaine (BDIC, Nanterre) and the Internationaal Instituut voor Sociale Geschiedenis (IISG, Amsterdam).

## Notes

1. Daniel Guérin, *Front populaire, Révolution manquée. Témoignage militant* (Arles: Editions Actes Sud,1997), p. 29. All translations are mine unless otherwise indicated. I would like to thank Anne Guérin and Editions Agone (who will be publishing a new edition of *Front populaire, Révolution manquée* in 2013) for permission to use this quotation as an epigraph.
2. Letter to Marceau Pivert, 18 November 1947, BDIC, Fonds Guérin, F°Δ Rés 688/10/2. *La Lutte de classes sous la Première République, 1793–1797* (Paris: Gallimard, 1946; 2nd edition 1968).
3. Daniel Guérin, *A la recherche d'un communisme libertaire* (Paris: Spartacus, 1984), pp. 10–11.
4. On Malon, see K. Steven Vincent, *Between Marxism and Anarchism: Benoît Malon and French Reformist Socialism* (Berkeley: University of California Press, 1992).
5. Daniel Guérin, *Autobiographie de jeunesse, d'une dissidence sexuelle au socialisme* (Paris: Belfond, 1972), pp. 126–127. Charles Maurras was the leader of the right-wing movement, *Action Française*.

6. See my "Workers of the World, Embrace!' Daniel Guérin, the Labour Movement and Homosexuality' in *Left History*, vol.9, no.2 (Spring/Summer 2004),
pp. 11–43; and Peter Sedgwick, 'Out of Hiding: The Comradeships of Daniel
Guérin', *Salmagundi* 58:9 (June 1982), pp. 197–220.
7. Guérin, *À la recherche*, p. 9; *Front populaire*, p. 23.
8. Guérin, *Front populaire*, p. 147.
9. See Thierry Hohl, 'Daniel Guérin, 'pivertiste'. Un parcours dans la Gauche
révolutionnaire de la SFIO (1935–1938)' in *Dissidences* 2 (2007), pp. 133–149.
'*Luxembourgisme*' was an identifiable current on the French Left opposed to both
Bolshevism and social-democracy from around 1928–1931 – see Alain Guillerm's
preface to Rosa Luxembourg, *Marxisme et Dictature: La démocratie selon Lénine et
Luxembourg* (Paris: Spartacus, 1974).
10. Guérin's *Front populaire* is a classic 'revolutionist' interpretation of the Popular
Front experience.
11. 'Entryism', originally 'the French turn', was a new tactic proposed by Trotsky in
response to the growing Fascist threat, and first implemented in June 1934 in
France in order to contribute to the development of a more radical current
within the party. Daniel Bensaïd, *Les trotskysmes* (Paris: Presses Universitaires de
France, 2002), pp. 31–32; Alex Callinicos, *Trotskyism* (Minneapolis: University of
Minnesota Press, 1990), pp. 18–19.
12. Guérin, *Front populaire*, p. 104. Guérin's *Fascisme et grand capital* (Paris:
Gallimard, 1936) was inspired by Trotsky.
13. Guérin, *La Peste brune a passé par là* (Paris: Librairie du Travail, 1933), translated
as *The Brown Plague: Travels in Late Weimar and Early Nazi Germany* (Durham &
London: Duke University Press, 1994); *Fascisme et grand capital* (Paris: Gallimard,
1936), trans. *Fascism and Big Business* (New York: Monad Press, 1973). *Fascism*
has been criticised by some for tending towards reductionism: see Claude Lefort,
'L'analyse marxiste et le fascisme', *Les Temps modernes* 2 (November 1945),
pp. 357–362. Others regard Guérin's methodology as fundamentally correct: see
Alain Bihr's introduction to the 1999 edition of *Fascisme et grand capital* (Paris:
Editions Syllepse and Phénix Editions), pp. 7–14.
14. Guérin, 'Quand le fascisme nous devançait' in *La Peste brune* (Paris: Spartacus,
1996), pp. 21–22. This was originally commissioned for an issue of *Les Temps
Modernes* on the state of the Left, but was rejected by Sartre for being too critical
of the PCF. Letter from Guérin to C.L.R. James, 10 August 1955, BDIC, Fonds
Guérin, Fᵒ∆ 721/60/5.
15. Guérin, 'Quand le fascisme', p. 25.
16. Guérin, *Front populaire*, pp. 150; 156–157; 365.
17. Ibid., p. 157.
18. Ibid., p. 213.
19. Ibid., p. 23.
20. L. Trotsky, 'La guerre impérialiste et la révolution prolétarienne mondiale' in
D. Guérin (ed.), *Sur la deuxième guerre mondiale* (Brussels: Editions la Taupe,
1970), pp. 187–245; Jean van Heijenoort, 'Manifeste: La France sous Hitler
et Pétain', in Rodolphe Prager (ed.), *Les congrès de la quatrième internationale
(manifestes, thèses, résolutions)* (Paris: La Brèche, 1981) Vol.II, pp. 35–44.
21. Interview with Pierre André Boutang in *Guérin*, television documentary by
Jean-José Marchand (1985; broadcast on FR3, 4 & 11 September 1989). See
my ' "Like a Wisp of Straw Amidst the Raging Elements": Daniel Guérin in
the Second World War' in Hanna Diamond and Simon Kitson (eds), *Vichy,*

*Resistance, Liberation: New Perspectives on Wartime France (Festschrift in Honour of H. R. Kedward)* (Oxford & New York: Berg, 2005), pp. 143–154.

22. Letter to Marceau Pivert, 2 January 1948, BDIC, Fonds Guérin, F°Δ Rés 688/9/1.

23. Guérin, *Le Feu du Sang. Autobiographie politique et charnelle* (Paris: Editions Grasset & Fasquelle, 1977), p. 149. Guérin's researches led to the publication of the two-volume *Où va le peuple américain?* (Paris: Julliard, 1950–1951), published in sections as *Décolonisation du Noir américain* (Paris: Minuit, 1963), *Le Mouvement ouvrier aux Etats-Unis* (Paris: Maspero, 1968), *La concentration économique aux Etats-Unis* (Paris: Anthropos, 1971) – with a preface by the Trotskyist economist Ernest Mandel – and *De l'Oncle Tom aux Panthères: Le drame des Noirs américains* (Paris: UGE, 1973). Translations: *Negroes on the March: A Frenchman's Report on the American Negro Struggle*, trans. Duncan Ferguson (New York: George L. Weissman, 1956), and *100 Years of Labour in the USA*, trans. Alan Adler (London: Ink Links, 1979). See Larry Portis, 'Daniel Guérin et les Etats-Unis: l'optimisme et l'intelligence' in *Agone* 29–30 (2003), pp. 277–289.

24. Guérin, *Lutte de classes*. See Denis Berger, 'La révolution plurielle (pour Daniel Guérin)' in E. Balibar, J.-S. Beek, D. Bensaïd *et al.*, *Permanences de la Révolution. Pour un autre bicentenaire* (Paris: La Brèche, 1989), pp. 195–208; David Berry, 'Daniel Guérin à la Libération. De l'historien de la Révolution au militant révolutionnaire: un tournant idéologique', *Agone* 29–30 (2003), pp. 257–273; Michel Lequenne, 'Daniel Guérin, l'homme de 93 et le problème de Robespierre', *Critique communiste* 130–131 (May 1993), pp. 31–34; Julia Guseva, 'La Terreur pendant la Révolution et l'interprétation de D. Guérin', *Dissidences* 2 (2007), pp. 77–88; Jean-Numa Ducange, 'Comment Daniel Guérin utilise-t-il l'œuvre de Karl Kautsky sur la Révolution française dans *La Lutte de classes sous la première République*, et pourquoi?', *ibid.*, pp. 89–111. Norah Carlin, 'Daniel Guérin and the working class in the French Revolution', *International Socialism* 47 (1990), pp. 197–223, discusses changes made by Guérin to *La Lutte de classes* for the 1968 edition.

25. Guérin, *La Révolution française et nous* (Paris: Maspero, 1976), pp. 7–8.

26. Guérin, *La Lutte de classes* (1968), vol.I, p. 31.

27. Ibid., p. 58.

28. E.J. Hobsbawm, *Echoes of the Marseillaise: Two Centuries Look Back on the French Revolution* (London: Verso, 1990), p. 53.

29. Guérin, *La Révolution française et nous*, p. 7.

30. See Olivier Bétourné and Aglaia I. Hartig, *Penser l'histoire de la Révolution. Deux siècles de passion française* (Paris: La Découverte, 1989), esp. pp. 110–114; Antonio de Francesco, 'Daniel Guérin et Georges Lefebvre, une rencontre improbable', *La Révolution française*, http://lrf.revues.org/index162.html, date accessed 28 March 2011.

31. Ian Birchall, 'Sartre's Encounter with Daniel Guérin', *Sartre Studies International*, 2:1 (1996), p. 46.

32. Guérin, 'Faisons le point', *Le Libérateur politique et social pour la nouvelle gauche* (12 February 1956). A populist, reactionary and xenophobic anti-taxation movement of small shopkeepers founded by Pierre Poujade in 1953, 'Poujadisme' had 'more than a hint of fascism' – Rod Kedward, *La Vie en Bleu. France and the French since 1900* (London: Penguin, 2006), p. 376.

33. C.L.R. James, 'L'actualité de la Révolution française', *Perspectives socialistes: Revue bimensuelle de l'Union de la Gauche Socialiste* 4 (15 February 1958), pp. 20–21.

34. Guérin, 'La Révolution déjacobinisée', in *Jeunesse du socialisme libertaire* (Paris: Rivière, 1959), pp. 27–63.
35. Guérin, 'La Révolution déjacobinisée', p. 43.
36. Ibid., pp. 43–44.
37. Guérin, 'Preface', in *Jeunesse du socialisme libertaire*, pp. 7–8.
38. Guérin, 'La Révolution déjacobinisée', pp. 30–31.
39. Michel Crozier, *Ma Belle Epoque. Mémoires. 1947–1969* (Paris: Fayard, 2002), pp. 79;86.
40. Guérin, *Le Feu du sang*, p. 218; Kent Worcester, *C.L.R. James. A Political Biography* (Albany: SUNY, 1996), p. 201; James, letter to Guérin, 24 May 1956, BDIC, Fonds Guérin, F°∆ 721/57/2.
41. Guérin, *Le Feu du sang*, p. 189. In his account, Guérin refers positively to the collection *La Contre-révolution bureaucratique* (Paris: UGE, 1973), which contained texts by Korsch, Pannekoek, Rühle and others taken from *International Council Correspondence*, *Living Marxism* and *International Socialism*. The councilists had previously republished in translation an article of Guérin's from the French syndicalist journal *Révolution prolétarienne*: 'Fascist Corporatism', in *International Council Correspondence*, 3:2 (February 1937), pp. 14–26. (I am grateful to Saku Pinta for bringing this to my attention.) See Douglas Kellner (ed.), *Karl Korsch: Revolutionary Theory* (Austin & London: University of Texas Press, 1977).
42. Guérin/Korsch correspondence, April–June 1954, Karl Korsch Papers, IISG, Boxes 1–24.
43. Guérin, *Le Feu du sang*, p. 156.
44. Guérin Papers, IISG, Box 1, Folder 14.
45. The list included James Guillaume's history of the IWMA, Victor Serge's *Mémoires d'un révolutionnaire*, Voline's *La Révolution inconnue*, Makhno, and the many publications of the Spartacus group created by René Lefeuvre. Mohammed Harbi, *Une Vie debout. Mémoires politiques, Tome I: 1945–1962* (Paris: La Découverte, 2001), pp. 109–112. Harbi incorrectly describes the Cercle Lénine as being connected to the PCF; see *La Vérité*, 1 January 1954. On the different analyses of the nature of the USSR, see Marcel van der Linden, *Western Marxism and the Soviet Union. A Survey of Critical Theories and Debates Since 1917* (Chicago: Haymarket Books, 2007); on Castoriadis and Lefort, see pp. 116–118.
46. Edgar Morin, 'L'Anarchisme en 1968', *Magazine littéraire* 19 (1968), available at www.magazine-litteraire.com/archives/ar_anar.htm, accessed 6 October 2002.
47. See Edgar Morin, 'La réfome de pensée', in *Arguments, 1956–1962* (Toulouse: Privat, 1983), vol.I, p. ix.
48. For an explanation of why Yugoslavia's break with the soviet bloc in 1948 was so important to the extreme Left in the West, see *Le Trotskisme. Une histoire sans fard* (Paris: Editions Syllepse, 2005) by Guérin's friend and comrade Michel Lequenne.
49. Anne Guérin, 'Les ruptures de Daniel Guérin. Notice biographique', in Daniel Guérin, *De l'Oncle Tom aux Panthères noires* (Pantin: Les bons caractères, 2010), p. 9.
50. See Georges Fontenis, *Changer le monde: Histoire du mouvement communiste libertaire, 1945–1997* (Paris: Alternative libertaire, 2000); Philippe Dubacq, *Anarchisme et marxisme au travers de la Fédération communiste libertaire (1945–1956)*, *Noir et Rouge* 23 (1991).
51. Guérin, *Le Feu du sang*, p. 233.
52. Guérin, *À la recherche*, p. 9.

53. Ibid.
54. See Guérin's 1969 article, 'Conseils ouvriers et syndicalisme révolutionnaire. L'exemple hongrois, 1956' in *A la recherche*, pp. 111–115; republished as 'Syndicalisme révolutionnaire et conseillisme' in *Pour le communisme libertaire*, pp. 155–162.
55. *A la recherche*, p. 10. *L'Anarchisme, de la doctrine à la pratique* (Paris: Gallimard, 1965); *Ni Dieu ni Maître, anthologie de l'anarchisme* (Lausanne: La Cité-Lausanne, 1965). Both have been republished several times since, and *L'Anarchisme* has been translated into more than 20 languages. They have been published in English as *Anarchism: From Theory to Practice* (New York: Monthly Review Press, 1970), introduced by Noam Chomsky; *No Gods No Masters: An Anthology of Anarchism* (Edinburgh: AK Press, 1998).
56. This is not uncontentious – indeed Ernest Mandel takes issue with Guérin over this question in his anthology *Contrôle ouvrier, conseils ouvriers, autogestion* (Paris: Maspero, 1970), p. 7.
57. Letters to the author, 12 and 26 February 1986.
58. Georges Fontenis, 'Le long parcours de Daniel Guérin vers le communisme libertaire', special number of *Alternative Libertaire* on Guérin (2000), p. 37.
59. Guérin, *Le Feu du sang*, p. 228.
60. It is also noteworthy that Guérin would include a section on decolonisation in his *Anarchism* and found material from Proudhon and Bakunin which supported the FCL's position. See Sylvain Pattieu, *Les camarades des frères: Trotskistes et libertaires dans la guerre d'Algérie* (Paris: Syllepse, 2002); Sidi Mohammed Barkat (ed.), *Des Français contre la terreur d'Etat (Algérie 1954–1962)* (Paris: Editions Reflex, 2002); Sylvain Boulouque, *Les anarchistes français face aux guerres coloniales (1945–1962)* (Lyon: Atelier de création libertaire, 2003); David Porter, *Eyes to the South. French Anarchists and Algeria* (Oakland, Edinburgh, Baltimore: AK Press, 2011).
61. Editors' note in Guérin, *Pour le communisme libertaire* (Paris: Spartacus, 2003), p. 5. Rubel (1905–1996) had links with the councilist movement and published 'Marx théoricien de l'anarchisme' in his *Marx, critique du Marxisme* (Paris: Editions Payot, 1974; new edition 2000); since republished as *Marx théoricien de l'anarchisme* (Saint-Denis: Vent du ch'min, 1983; Geneva: Editions Entremonde, 2011). Rubel: 'Under the name communism, Marx developed a theory of anarchism; and further, that in fact it was he who was the first to provide a rational basis for the anarchist utopia and to put forward a project for achieving it.' 'Marx, Theoretician of Anarchism', Marxists Internet Archive, www.marxists. org/archive/rubel/1973/marx-anarchism.htm, date accessed 29 March 2011.
62. Preface of 1970 to Guérin (ed.), *Ni Dieu ni Maître. Anthologie de l'anarchisme* (Paris: La Découverte, 1999), vol. I, pp. 6–7.
63. *L'Anarchisme*, p. 21.
64. Daniel Guerin, *Pour un marxisme libertaire* (Paris: Robert Laffont, 1969), p. 7.
65. Fontenis, 'Le long parcours', p. 38.
66. 'Anarchisme et marxisme', p. 237, in *L'Anarchisme* (1981), pp. 229–252. Published in English as *Anarchism & Marxism* (Sanday, Orkney: Cienfuegos Press, 1981), and 'Marxism and Anarchism', in David Goodway (ed.), *For Anarchism. History, Theory and Practice* (London: Routledge, 1989), pp. 109–126.
67. *L'Anarchisme*, pp. 13–14.
68. *Anarchism*, p. 153.

69. Nicolas Walter, 'Daniel Guerin's anarchism', *Anarchy* 8:94, 381.
70. Patrice Spadoni, 'La synthèse entre l'anarchisme et le marxisme: «Un point de ralliement vers l'avenir»', *Alternative Libertaire* (2000), p. 43. Guérin, *Proudhon oui et non* (Paris: Gallimard, 1978).
71. See his '1917–1921, de l'autogestion à la bureaucratie soviétique', in *De la Révolution d'octobre à l'empire éclaté: 70 ans de réflexions sur la nature de l'URSS* (Paris: Alternative libertaire/UTCL, n.d.); 'Proudhon et l'autogestion ouvrière' in *L'Actualité de Proudhon* (Bruxelles: Université libre de Bruxelles, 1967), pp. 67–87; 'L'Espagne libertaire', editorial introduction to *Autogestion et socialisme*, special issue on 'Les anarchistes et l'autogestion' 18/19 (janvier–avril 1972), 81–82; 'L'autogestion contemporaine', *Noir et rouge* 31/32 (octobre1965 – février 1966), pp. 16–24.
72. See similarly critical remarks by Castoriadis: 'Marx aujourd'hui. Entretien avec Cornelius Castoriadis' *Lutter!* 5 (May 1983), pp. 15–18.
73. *L'Anarchisme*, p. 16.
74. 'Proudhon père de l'autogestion' (1965) in *Proudhon oui et non*, p. 165.
75. 'Proudhon père de l'autogestion', p. 191.
76. Guérin, *Ni Dieu ni Maître*, vol.I, p. 12 and 'Stirner, «Père de l'anarchisme»?', p. 83. Guérin began his anthology with the 'precursor' Stirner and added an appendix on him to the 1981 edition of *L'Anarchisme*. See also Guérin, *Homosexualité et Révolution* (Saint-Denis: Le Vent du ch'min, 1983), p. 12, and 'Stirner, «Père de l'anarchisme»?', *La Rue* 26 (1er et 2ème trimestre 1979), pp. 76–89.
77. See my "Workers of the World, Embrace!".
78. See Fontenis, *Changer le monde*, pp. 161–162 and 255–256.
79. The UTCL's manifesto, adopted at its Fourth Congress in 1986, was republished (with a dedication to Guérin) by the UTCL's successor organisation, Alternative Libertaire: *Un projet de société communiste libertaire* (Paris: Alternative libertaire, 2002).
80. Fontenis, *Changer le monde*, p. 80, note 1. See also my 'Change the world without taking power? The libertarian communist tradition in France today', *Journal of Contemporary European Studies* 16:1 (Spring 2008), pp. 111–130.
81. Guérin, 'Anarchisme et Marxisme' in *L'Anarchisme* (1981), p. 250.
82. Ibid., p. 248.
83. Ibid., p. 237.
84. On Abad de Santillan, see the section on 'L'Espagne libertaire' in *Les anarchistes et l'autogestion*.
85. See Guérin, *Ni Dieu ni Maître*, vol.I, 268–291.
86. Guérin, 'Anarchisme et Marxisme' in *L'Anarchisme* (1981), p. 252.
87. Rosa Luxemburg, *Le socialisme en France, 1898–1912* (Paris: Belfond, 1971), with an introduction by Guérin, pp. 7–48; *Rosa Luxemburg et la spontanéïté révolutionnaire* (Paris: Flammarion, 1971).
88. Gilbert Badia *et al.*, 'Rosa Luxemburg et nous: Débat', *Politique aujourd'hui: Recherches et pratiques socialistes dans le monde* (1972), 77–106.
89. Guérin, 'Anarchisme et Marxisme', p. 233. As the co-editor (with Jean-Jacques Lebel) of a collection titled 'Changer la Vie' for the publisher Pierre Belfond, Guérin took the opportunity to republish Trotsky's *Our Political Tasks* (1904), in which the young Trotsky was very critical of Lenin's 'Jacobinism' and of what he called the 'dictatorship over the proletariat': Léon Trotsky, *Nos tâches politiques* (Paris: Belfond, 1970). Luxemburg's 'Organizational Questions of Russian Social Democracy' is included in this as an appendix.

90. Guérin, 'Anarchisme et Marxisme', p. 252.
91. Guérin, *À la recherche*, pp. 10–11.
92. Guérin, 'Pourquoi communiste libertaire?', in *A la recherche*, p. 17.
93. Guérin, 'Un communisme libertaire, pour quoi?', *A la recherche*, pp. 123–125.
94. Walter, 'Daniel Guerin's anarchism', pp. 376–382.
95. George Woodcock, 'Chomsky's Anarchism' in *Freedom*, 16 November 1974, pp. 4–5.
96. Miguel Chueca, 'Anarchisme et Marxisme. La tentative de Daniel Guérin d'unir les deux philosophies et 'l'anarchisme' de Marx vu par Maximilien Rubel' in *Réfractions* 7, available at http://www.plusloin.org/refractions/refractions7/chueca1.htm (accessed 29 August 2006).
97. Ian Birchall, 'Daniel Guérin's Dialogue with Leninism' in *Revolutionary History* vol.9, no.2, pp. 194–222 (194–195).
98. See Irène Pereira, *Un nouvel esprit contestataire. La grammaire pragmatiste du syndicalisme d'action directe libertaire* (Unpublished PhD, Ecole des Hautes Etudes en Sciences Sociales, Paris, 2009); Patrice Spadoni, 'Daniel Guérin ou le projet d'une synthèse entre l'anarchisme et le marxisme' in *Contretemps* 6 (February 2003), 118–126. Guérin's daughter Anne has claimed recently that Guérin was the 'Maître à penser' of both Daniel Cohn-Bendit and the Trotskyist Alain Krivine – preface to Guérin, *De l'Oncle Tom aux Panthères noires*, p. 8. Christophe Bourseiller also comments that 'the politics of the *Mouvement communiste libertaire* derived largely from the theoretical reflexion of Daniel Guérin.' *Histoire générale de 'l'ultra-gauche'* (Paris: Editions Denoël, 2003), p. 484. In 1986 Guérin also contributed to the UTCL's 'Projet communiste libertaire', which was republished by Alternative Libertaire in 1993 and again in 2002. The 'Appel pour une alternative libertaire' of 1989 (which ultimately led to the creation of AL) was also co-written by Guérin: see Guérin, *Pour le communisme libertaire* (Paris: Spartacus, 2003), pp. 181–186.
99. Guérin, *A la recherche*, p. 10.
100. Guérin, 'Un communisme libertaire, pour quoi?', in *A la recherche*, p. 123.

# 11

## *Socialisme ou Barbarie* or the Partial Encounters between Critical Marxism and Libertarianism

*Benoît Challand*

For many, the French group Socialisme ou Barbarie remains associated with the name of the political theorist and psychoanalyst Cornelius Castoriadis (1922–1997). While Castoriadis played a pivotal role in the group, it also included a number of other prominent intellectuals over the course of its publishing lifetime, such as Claude Lefort (1924–2010), Jean-François Lyotard (1924–1998) and Guy Debord (1931–1994). The group's eponymous journal, published between 1949 and 1965, was dedicated to an increasingly unorthodox Trotskyist critique and it provided an important platform for debating Marxism with other strands of the ultra-Left, some of them closely associated with Left-libertarian thinking. One line of division inside the group discussed here (though to be sure, there are many others to analyse) was based on divergent views about the model of organisation and the place to be given to ideas of spontaneous self-organisation within the working class, which was influenced by precisely this Left-libertarian thinking. These issues were particularly contentious for the group and this essay will unpack the reasons why, and why they caused so many splits within SouB.[1] The primary aim of the chapter is to show that despite Castoriadis's evident legacy of Left-libertarian thinking and his radical break with orthodox Marxist-Leninism, these splits owe most to Castoriadis's original attachment to Trotskyist vanguardism. In the long run, as this chapter will illustrate, these ideological and organisational splits impeded any convergence between critical Marxism and Council Communism – Council Communism here understood as the closest SouB came to radical Left-libertarian thinking during its lifetime.

Though little space is formally dedicated to anarchism in this chapter, the analysis touches on the themes explored in this book by examining the tensions (organisational and ideological) that arise between a Leninist-inspired form of political militancy (critical Trotskyism) and a libertarian communist view of workers' organisations (Council Communism). The Council Communist position was elaborated by intellectuals such as Anton Pannekoek (1873–1960) and discussed and published by SouB. Over the course of its existence, SouB engaged in dialogue with very different political groups of the ultra-Left, but the articulations and fault-lines that emerged in the debate between Castoriadis and Pannekoek, the so-called Chaulieu–Pannekoek correspondence of 1953–1954 (Chaulieu being an alias for Castoriadis), forcefully illustrates the problems of synthesis which this collection examines. Castoriadis's own philosophy also moved from a critical Marxist–Leninist framework to a libertarian Marxist one in the 1960s and eventually became anti-Marxist in position from the 1970s onwards. At each stage Castoriadis refused a closer collaboration with Left-libertarian thinking and it is the purpose of this paper to explain why.

To this end, there are two main reasons for reinterpreting key episodes in SouB's activity in the light of the tension between Marxist and Left-libertarian schools of thought. First, Council Communism represented an important historical attempt to straddle the Marxism – anarchism divide.[2] Though Council Communism does not have the same centrality to anarchism as, say, federalism, there are historical overlaps between the two movements: both adopted an oppositional position to the orthodox Marxism of the Second International and there were important mutual contacts in German syndicalism. Council Communists tried to develop new means to accommodate centralism within a syndicalist framework and the fact that they are sometimes referred to as libertarian communists illustrates this bridging role they occupy in the history of socialism. The debate turned on the key question of workers' self-management and the role of the vanguard in revolutionary organisations. Ultimately, within SouB at least, it was the latter that won out.

In the context of SouB's editorial development, this tension can be seen in the difficult relationship of Castoriadis and Lefort, two of the group's towering figures. It is well known that the strain between these two individuals, which grew over the years and led to Lefort's departure from SouB in 1958 (after a first brief resignation in 1952), contributed to the consolidation of the positions adopted by SouB, which were originally influenced by critical Trotskyism.[3] Other militants within the group, such as Henri Simon, who were equally sympathetic to the idea of workers' self-management, played an important role in disclosing more detailed information about the failed merger of critical Marxism and libertarian communism.[4] But the theoretical roots of this tension are perfectly illustrated in the disagreement between Castoriadis and Pannekoek and their debates about the form that revolutionary movements should take – an exchange that assumes a central place in this analysis.

However, this intellectual and ideological tension within the group is best explained by the severe political exigencies of the cold war, anti-communist movements and the need for organisational and intellectual fortitude in the face of huge opposition. The intransigence of Castoriadis's position and the conflict within the group can be seen as a direct response to these conditions. However, alongside this public orthodoxy, Castoriadis was also developing a radical version of critical Marxism, one which was to be hugely significant in terms of the development of socialist thought in the second half of the twentieth century. Influencing situationist writers such as Guy Debord and the autonomist tradition more widely, the contrast between these two faces of SouB is a historical puzzle worth investigating because it shows us that ideology and organisation matter as much as, if not more than, theory.

Castoriadis is now known, in large part, as the philosopher of autonomy and the question of 'auto-institution'. The intellectual puzzle here is to understand how he married these ideas with a Leninist view of the revolutionary vanguard (based on democratic centralism) and why he kept Left-libertarian ideas at arm's length when active in SouB. Ultimately it was Castoriadis's inability to reform SouB or to abandon notions of the vanguard which ultimately consigned him to the Marxist–Leninist side of the debate. Ironically, it was only after SouB eventually dissolved that Castoriadis's ideas developed along increasingly Left-libertarian lines, in particular in his criticism of the Marxists' economism and their failure to grasp the significance of political change and the constitutive role of the social imaginary in the political process.[5]

The first substantive part of the paper will reflect on the historical conditions that made the contribution of SouB so important in the French intellectual scene and how these conditions structured the range of possible positions SouB could take. Like many groups born in the shadow of the Fourth International and the cold war, SouB experienced many splits and the paper will explore why this was the case by underlining the inherently critical nature of Trotskyism and the usefulness that this line of thinking might have had in the battle against Stalinism. The second section of the paper turns to developments and debates inside SouB and looks at Castoriadis and the internal form of the group to try explain other reasons for the failed synergies with more Left-libertarian trains of thought. The third section explores the Chaulieu–Pannekoek correspondence, using it to illustrate the interplay between ideological tensions and historical–organisational issues. Central to this discussion is the immediate post-1945 context and the period following the Hungarian crisis of 1956, as the notion of workers' self-management became very important in the evolution of critical Marxism. The fourth part of the paper returns to wider debates, Castoriadis's intellectual evolution in his final years and the demise of SouB. The conclusion will reflect on the significance of SouB for our understanding of the historiography of the Left in general. It is, without question, a singular but highly significant marker in this regard.

## The shadows of Trotskyism

The political context of the origins of SouB illustrates how two different generations of activists were recruited to this small Paris-based militant group.[6]
While the Fourth International gave qualified support to the USSR in the
second half of the 1940s, a small dissident group emerged inside the Parti
Communiste Internationaliste (PCI), the French section of the Fourth International, refusing to support the USSR and adopting a new reading of the
nature of the Soviet Union. This minority group was called the 'Chaulieu–
Montal tendency' after two of its leaders, Chaulieu being the militant name
of Cornelius Castoriadis and Montal that of Claude Lefort. It crystallised
in 1946 and 1947 and, after the support given by the PCI to Yugoslavia in
August 1948, it turned from a tendency into a new movement named after
its mouthpiece *Socialisme ou Barbarie* (a phrase taken from Rosa Luxemburg's
writings) whose first issue was published in March 1949.[7]

The main contribution of SouB at its inception was its slightly modified
Trotskyist critique of the USSR which it defined as a form of state bureaucratic capitalism, premised not on the exploitation of the propertyless by
owners of the means of production, but on the control of a subordinate
labour class of executants by a class of directors. As the manifesto printed in
the first issue of *Socialisme ou Barbarie* put it:

... [the] management of production by the workers themselves assumes
an additional importance in modern society. The entire evolution of the
modern economy tends to replace the old opposition between owners
and the propertyless with a new opposition between directors and executants in the productive process. If the proletariat does not immediately
abolish, together with the private ownership of the means of production,
the management of production as a specific function permanently carried
out by a particular social stratum, it will only have cleared the ground
for the emergence of a new exploiting stratum, which will arise out of
the 'managers' of production and out of the bureaucracies dominating
economic and political life.[8]

This analysis was a radical break with the traditional economistic focus of
Marxism–Leninism. In the course of its 16-year history, from 1949 to 1965,
SouB attracted many adherents and experienced a good deal of dissatisfaction within its ranks too. Members had a variety of different motives for
leaving the organisation. For the sake of our argument, at least two different
generations of militants involved in SouB need to be distinguished.[9] The first
generation, that of Chaulieu and Montal, can be identified on the basis of
what French historian Jean-François Sirinelli termed the *élément fondateur*.[10]
In the case of this first generation of SouB, this founding event was the Second World War and the role Stalin played in defeating Hitler. Other key

militants included Henri Simon, Daniel Mothé (the pseudonym of Jacques Gautrat, who worked in close connection with the workers of the Renault factories), Claude Lefort and Maurice Rajfus. For many of this generation the expectation of an imminent Third World War justified a radical break with the Fourth International and gave a sense of urgency to the action they thought needed to be undertaken. With the onset of the cold war and as the outbreak of a Third World War appeared to be increasingly unlikely, a second generation of militants joined SouB. For them, the *élément fondateur* took multiple forms: the 1953 East German rebellion, the Algerian war, the series of strikes in France in the summer of 1955 and the Budapest uprising of 1956. All these events gave further credence to SouB's call for more workers' self-management.[11] Among this second generation, J.-F. Lyotard (1924–1998), Pierre Souyri (1925–1979) and Guy Debord (1931–1994) were its most famous members.

This second series of founding events (in particular the 1953 and 1956 revolts) ushered in a more libertarian approach to Left-wing organisation that was increasingly critical of Leninism and argued for a stronger role for workers' councils. Contrary to the Leninist idea of a 'consciousness inculcated from without', SouB maintained in its columns that revolutionary ideals and self-organisation should stem instead from within the workers' community. As SouB gradually began to be described by some as anti-Marxist,[12] and as some of its members (Claude Lefort in particular) contributed to the discussion of anti-totalitarianism in the 1970s, it is worth remembering that a certain radical Left critique of Stalinism became an asset in the cold war battle against communism in general.

In this difficult political and social context of the post-1945 period, the Trotskyist critique of the Soviet Union regained prominence. In general, radical Marxists either supported 'progressive' forces in the name of 'socialism in one country', or criticised Stalin's autocratic style of governing. But this was a difficult issue for many Left-wing activists and intellectuals.[13] In a context defined by international tension and the nascent cold war, the image that 'Trotskyism cuts both ways' encapsulates the critical potential of this ideology in breaching the hegemonic influence of Stalinist parties while dividing further radical groups. On the one hand, Trotskyism emerged as a powerful critique of Stalinism and of the bureaucratic degeneration of the Soviet Union, appealing to radical leftists unhappy with the path that the leader of 'socialism in one country' had imposed. On the other hand, Trotskyism remained committed to Leninist ideas of the vanguard and structured party-organisation premised on democratic centralism and the limitation on pluralist ideological debates.[14]

As it turned out, the new contradictions within the different Trotskyist traditions (bureaucratic degeneration, permanent arms revolution, managerial society, entrism and so on) proved too much and paved the way to historical splits. These splits illustrate both the centrifugal and centripetal forces inside Trotskyism, since creating splits has always been a way to gain new militants (entrism), while on the other hand, the defence of some of these concepts was a means to preserve ideological purity and exclude other militants.[15] We have here a first indication of the way in which the organisational priorities and logics of SouB might have frustrated the interchange between less orthodox Marxist and libertarian ideas. In essence, doctrinal adherence to Trotskyism constrained as much as it enabled this new generation of Left-wing thinkers, but the ideological influence of Leninism hamstrung organisational development by demanding democratic centralism, or vanguardism.

The context for the continued adherence to doctrinal purity and democratic centralism can also be explained by reference to the post-1945 anti-communist struggle across the world. Even within the Trotskyist movement the split became pronounced with what Hannah Arendt called 'ex-communists' and 'former communists' and their differentiated role in organising splits in the ultra-Left. 'Former communists' were those who did not have a leading position in a Communist Party and who were mostly fellow travellers, like Picasso or Sartre. When they left the orbit of the Communist Party, their life moved on and was not centrally determined by this previous affiliation. 'Ex-communists', on the other hand, included those who had been much more engaged in the formal hierarchies of a Communist Party, for whom 'communism ... remained the chief issue of their life' once they left it.[16] Communism remained central because this group decided to fight communist ideology using their insider's knowledge. James Burnham (1905–1987), author of the *Managerial Revolution* and an influential conservative intellectual during the cold war,[17] and Arthur Koestler (1905–1983), the ex-leader of the German Communist Party (KPD) and later author of bestselling novels against the totalitarian Gulag, are two prime examples of the trajectories of 'ex-communists' Arendt describes.

It is notable that among the ex-communists, Trotskyists featured prominently. They did so for two reasons. First, many Trotskyists became Trotskyists because of their disillusionment with either the Moscow trials of the 1930s or with Stalin's inaction in the face of Fascism, or because of the post-1945 silence of communist parties in the face of Soviet repression during the popular uprisings in Central and Eastern Europe between 1953 and 1968. Second, their intellectual equipment as Trotskyists was built precisely around the criticism of the Soviet Union and was informed by a deep knowledge of the nature of its bureaucratic degeneration. It is therefore no surprise that so many ex-Trotskyists were recruited to the anti-Soviet battle of the post-1945 period. Trotskyism was both the chief method of radical critique of the trajectory of the Soviet Union and a tool in the armoury of the capitalist West against all that was worth preserving in the Soviet experiment.

Thus, many ex- and former Trotskyists *voluntarily* embraced anti-communism. In the USA in particular the list of Trotskyist 'defectors' is impressive and significant: Irving Kristol, Sidney Hook, Sol Levitas, Melvin Lasky and James Burnham (who became active in the powerful secretly funded CIA-front, the Congress for Cultural Freedom [CCF]).[18] In Europe, it was rather ex-communists that featured on the list of important anti-communist ideologues: people like Arthur Koestler, Ignazio Silone and Boris Souvarine all had a formal role in their communist parties (Germany, Italy and France respectively) but none of them were Trotskyists, while people like Raymond Aron (Claude Lefort's PhD mentor), Francois Furet (to quote two influential French intellectuals in the battle against communists) were only 'former communists' in Arendt's classification.[19]

The point to be made here is that while US ex-Trotskyists joined the anti-communist battle,[20] dozens of other small splinter groups inspired by Trotskyism arguably made an *indirect* contribution to anti-communism in Europe by constantly splitting the ultra-Left political spectrum. This climate also made any intersections between Trotskyism and anarchism even more remote – despite sharing key ideological positions as described in other chapters of this volume. Small Trotskyist factions contributed to hindering the emergence of broad Left alliances, since their declared enemies were less the bourgeois camp than orthodox communist factions and reformist socialist parties. This intellectual and historical context is vital for understanding the debates that took place within SouB.

## Ideological coherence or innovation?

Cornelius Castoriadis, the leading force of SouB, perfectly illustrates the ambiguous relation between Trotskyism and anti-communism. Castoriadis, who grew up in Athens, was active in the Greek Trotskyist party and fled his homeland for Paris at the end of 1945 where he joined the PCI, created a year earlier. Despite his very active militancy in the PCI and then as founder of SouB, he managed to work from 1949 until 1970 at the Organisation for European Economic Co-operation (OEEC, soon to become the OECD), an institution working initially for the distribution of the Marshall Plan aid, and which played an essential role in the anti-communist battle through the so-called 'counterpart' funds.[21] One wonders how he managed to remain unnoticed inside an institution working to promote capitalism and becoming, in parallel, the leader of a revolutionary group. The fact is he did, and although he frequently used the benefits of being an international civil servant by secretly using much of his salary for the publication of *Socialisme ou Barbarie*,[22] Castoriadis took significant measures to hide his true identity. For example, until his naturalisation as a French citizen in 1970, he only signed his political texts with one of his pseudonyms (the most frequent ones being Chaulieu, Cardan or Coudray).[23] Moreover, he never took part in the public events organised by SouB. And finally, he applied for French citizenship only in 1968 when all his formal political activities were over, because this type of administrative practice generally required a police inquiry into the private life of the applicant and would have jeopardised his cover.[24]

This digression on anti-communism and on the prominent role of Trotskyism in the postwar context served to highlight how external sponsors could have generated splits (for example, by providing financial means to create new organisations). In the case of SouB there is no evidence of such instrumentalisation. One therefore needs to turn to their internal discussions and their organisational debates to understand why splits happened. Alternative explanations could be found in organisational issues (group dynamics) or in a quest for theoretical improvement, and the innate tension in such a radical group looking to develop the ultimate theoretical innovation that would give it the edge over competing groups. The historian Gottraux provides a useful starting point for such analysis. He notes that:

> SouB remained trapped between the need to overtly showcase its origi-
> nality and its 'purity' on the one hand, and on the other hand, its desire
> to be open towards other groupings, albeit not in a very successful man-
> ner and by provoking disarray at times. In its attempts to open up, SouB
> finally adopted a line which aimed at maximizing profits and minimizing
> the costs: the group never departed a single second from its ideological
> coherence even as it declared itself ready to discuss with others.[25]

This duality illustrates perfectly the political exigencies of the period, but it overlooks the internal discord over the outward image SouB presented. Two examples are worth discussing. The first relates to the modality of the group's organisation. For most of its life the subtitle of *Socialisme ou Barbarie* was *Organe de critique et d'orientation révolutionnaire*. So beyond the critical dimension of SouB's writings, the publication was also meant to orientate its readers on how to become a revolutionary organisation. Its first issue and its first programmatic article are rather clear on this objective:

> Presenting ourselves today, by means of this review, before the avant-
> garde of the manual and intellectual workers, we know we are alone
> in responding in a systematic way to the fundamental problems con-
> fronting the contemporary revolutionary movement: we believe we are
> alone in taking up and pursuing the Marxist analysis of the modern
> economy; in placing the problem of the historic development of the
> workers' movement and its meaning on a scientific footing; in provid-
> ing a definition of Stalinism and of the 'workers'' bureaucracy in general;
> in characterising the Third World War; and, lastly, in proposing a revolu-
> tionary perspective, taking into account the original elements created by
> our epoch.[26]

It is this way, SouB remained dedicated to the Leninist idea of a vanguard party whose role was to help the working class in their autonomous organisation ('autonomous' here in the sense of independent from any bureaucratic Bolshevik party), geared towards the abolition of private ownership and the realisation of a socialist society, even if it criticised some of Lenin's ideas, such as inculcating revolutionary 'consciousness' from without.[27] For example, Lefort, wrote an early vitriolic piece against Trotsky, criticising him for being one of the main instigators of the bureaucratic degeneration of the Bolshevik party by virtue of his authoritarian leanings.[28] He was also the first to oppose the idea of an organised vanguard and 'placed the systematic support for workers' control at the centre of his considerations.[29] He argued that the greatest risk for this vanguard in a post-revolutionary order is to fall into the same authoritarian and bureaucratic trap as that which it seeks to replace – a reading akin to anarchism. Van der Linden suggests that:

> Castoriadis saw a dual task for the revolutionary socialists: On the one hand they should help build independent workers' organizations and papers, similar to those starting to come to the fore at Renault and at other firms; at the same time there would have to be a co-ordination of the various resistance committees and a national workers' paper. On the other hand the revolutionaries, now spread out all over the country and in numerous groups (the 'diffused vanguard'), would have to be brought together in one organization – a new type of party, based on experiences since 1917.[30]

For the first ten years of SouB this organisational debate between what Michels would have termed the 'iron law of oligarchy' and the need for a revolutionary party vanguard created tensions between the majority vanguardists spearheaded by Castoriadis and a minority critical grouping under Lefort. Lefort eventually decided to leave SouB for a few months in 1952, when it became clear that the vanguardists were the majority.[31] This issue, coupled with a growing unhappiness with the Marxist vision of history,[32] led Lefort to leave the movement definitively in 1958, along with Henri Simon, who, in addition, supported the need for truly autonomous working classes. Lefort, who never described himself as an anarchist,[33] Simon and a few others went on to create the new publication called *Informations et Liaisons Ouvrières* (ILO, soon becoming *Informations et Correspondance Ouvrières*), providing a 'forum for workers themselves to chronicle their struggles and express their pre-occupations'.[34] This autonomist line of argument was never taken up within SouB, forcing the split.

## The Chaulieu–Pannekoek correspondence

Two Dutch Council Communist militants, who had attended many of SouB's meetings in the 1950s, mapped these splits in their published observations.

Their accounts help clarify the range of positions within SouB and establish the extent to which members tried to straddle a Leninist–libertarian divide. This report, published in a Dutch militant journal, speaks of three currents within SouB: a 'Right wing' inspired by Leninism, the 'Centre' around Castoriadis, and the 'Left' around Lefort.[35] This is significant as it highlights that the majority (Centre–Right) were committed to the necessity of *organising* the vanguard party along increasingly centralist lines while the 'Left' members' arguments were gradually marginalised and eventually excluded. Their report is worth quoting at length:

> It is not the left wing which completed the break, but the right and centre, which deliberately steered for it. So deliberately, that the break came before the congress where left, centre and right were to discuss their differences of opinion. This congress was to take place in Paris on Saturday, 27 and Sunday, 28 September 1958. [...] Both right and left had prepared a text which would serve as a point of departure for the discussion. Both of these texts [...] naturally had an entirely different character; one could clearly discern the fundamental differences which had existed between the two currents for a long time: but there was nothing which indicated that the existing situation, in which the left and right worked in a single group, would shortly come to an end. [... The] differences were in no way brought to a head in the bulletin, which had been compiled by a member of the left wing. [...] The debate on both texts, which started on Thursday, 18 September, consequently had a vehement but at the same time friendly character. On Wednesday, 24 September something unexpected happened. The centre published a sequel to its text, which especially concerned the position and presentation of the left. The accent of this second paper was extremely sharp. The left were accused of propounding their theory 'while knowing better', and of 'knowingly misleading the workers'. Its behaviour was even described as 'dishonest', while the criticism of the right and the centre by the left, was turned into a downright caricature. Under these circumstances the preparatory meeting of Thursday, 25 September lost every semblance of geniality. The left expected that, at the very least, certain statements, like those concerning 'deceit' and 'deception' would be dropped immediately because upholding them would naturally make any discussion impossible. The most important spokesman of the centre refused. He declared that it was not his habit to be swayed by his emotions and that he had calmly considered every word and did not wish to take back a single word or sentence. At that the comrades of the left stood up and left the room. On Friday, 26 September they met separately and took the decision that they would not be present at the congress, which started on the 27th. Thus came the break-up.[36]

So by accusing the Left of deceit, the 'Centre–Right' managed to evict the group around Simon and Lefort, thereby destroying the potential for SouB to engage in a dialogue with the Dutch councilists. But throughout its history SouB had tried to open communication with different critical communist organisations. Anton Pannekoek, another councilist, was one of these interlocutors. Not only was he an influential theoretician of workers' councils, he also had historical experience as an activist in Germany and with the Second International before 1914. His best-known book is *De Arbeidersraden* (*Workers' Councils*), published in 1941 under the pseudonym P. Aartsz.[37] Like other Council Communists (such as Otto Ruehle, Karl Korsch or Paul Mattick), Pannekoek opposed the *diktats* of the Third International and evaluated anarchism sympathetically. In the interwar period, the Council Communists broke with social democracy and Bolshevism, while maintaining the necessity of organising the revolution by the direct control of the working class over the means of production.[38] In that sense the councilists remained Marxists and distanced themselves from the anarchist preference for federalism as a means of organisation. One sentence by Pannekoek illustrates this new orientation: 'socialism is self-direction of production, self-direction of the class-struggle, by means of workers' council'.[39]

From 1953 onwards the theme of workers' councils featured in some of *Socialisme ou Barbarie*'s articles and the group's internal debates. The debate surrounding whether these workers' councils or the vanguard party were the correct revolutionary form also featured in the exchange of letters between Anton Pannekoek and Pierre Chaulieu (one of Castoriadis's aliases), which has since generated many conflicting interpretations about the nature of the Russian Revolution and about theorising the organization of the revolutionary movement.[40]

The substance of the debate revolves around the issue of how to organize the revolutionary movement. Castoriadis argued for an organised vanguard, while Pannekoek refused this 'Bolshevik conception of the party'. The divergence also dealt with the nature of the 1917 Revolution. Castoriadis defended the idea that it was a true proletarian revolution, while Pannekoek saw in the Soviet revolution only a bourgeois revolution. In other words the disagreements could not be greater between the two authors. Castoriadis, who felt that the ideological priority for SouB should be focused elsewhere, managed to put an end to this debate, albeit only temporarily as the polemics resumed in the early 1970s.

The exchanges and debate range from the first months of 1953 to 1974.[41] The starting point came when Cajo Brendel, a militant of the Dutch Spartacus group brought issues 1–11 of *Socialisme ou Barbarie* from Paris to show to Pannekoek. The first exchange of letters at the end of October 1953 was between the two Dutch militants. This was followed a few weeks later by a letter from Pannekoek to Castoriadis, who replied personally in early 1954. The letter from Pannekoek, with Chaulieu's reply, was published in *Socialisme ou Barbarie* in the April–June 1954 issue (issue 14). The Dutch leader sent a second and third letter in August and September 1954, but these were not published. Castoriadis replied only to the second letter (August), but in the early months of 1955 Cajo Brendel states that SouB promised to publish the end of the correspondence between Pannekoek and Castoriadis.[42] This was never done.

The exchange between Pannekoek and Castoriadis is significant not only because of the content of their debate but also because of the way in which SouB handled the publication of the correspondence. Some accused Castoriadis of deliberately hiding the second letter from his companions, while in issue 15–16 (October–December 1954) SouB stated that Chaulieu had clearly shown the limits of Pannekoek's arguments and that there was therefore no need to continue the dialogue. Pannekoek wrote in the second letter that it was not meant to be published, and Castoriadis used this as a justification for not doing so. Yet Pannekoek's caution was probably more a caveat, because the text needed some editing and he was actually quite willing to continue the debate.[43] In private exchanges between Pannekoek and Brendel, both disagreed with SouB's claim that Chaulieu had won the argument,[44] and both would have liked the dialogue to go on. Pannekoek even went on to say, in the October 1953 letter, that '[t]here remain some divergences [between me and SouB]. They have not set themselves free of the Bolshevik virus with which they have been infected by Trotsky. The virus of the revolutionary party's vanguardism which must lead the revolution. On this subject, we are much ahead here in Holland.'[45]

While Pannekoek makes Castoriadis look like an old Leninist, and compared to Debord he looks like an old-fashioned second internationalist (an economist), the truth of the matter is that by this time Castoriadis had already begun to move decidedly beyond an orthodox Marxism and neither is the case. Unfortunately, it was his position within SouB and the principles that that movement originally sought to defend, with him as its figurehead, which made the interchange with both Lefts impossible. Furthermore, Castoriadis did not want to get involved in a long and protracted debate about revolutionary forms and the priority of self-organisation as he had by this time become engrossed in the analysis of the fundamental transformations underway within modern capitalism.

Indeed, Castoriadis began to express a deep dissatisfaction with *all* revolutionary organisations. Two influential articles published in 1960 and 1961 dealt with 'Le mouvement révolutionnaire sous le capitalisme moderne'.[46] Castoriadis here analysed the classical Marxist theme of political alienation but considered the depoliticisation of Western societies as a 'co-substantial part of modernization' and due to the increasing bureaucratization of social life.[47] He concluded that mainstream Marxism fails to fully grasp social change when it concentrates its attention on economic factors, thus tending to overlook the political transformation of advanced capitalist societies, the irrationality of bureaucratic management,[48] and the increasing role of so-called 'technocrats' and 'experts' leading to the gradual apathy of Western societies now living in abundance.[49] These transformations and the false trail taken by mainstream Marxism makes it, so Castoriadis argues, even more difficult for a revolutionary movement to exist and perform its task since political processes are not only economic but also social, cultural and psychological. Buried in this theoretical debate, the last thing he wanted was to be distracted by an argument about organisation.

All Castoriadis's themes influenced the subsequent generation of militants and in particular the groups that emerged in 1968 and in the 1970s: a generation keen to chant libertarian slogans, to dispute the political apathy and alienation of capitalist society, and to suggest more libertarian strategies to disrupt the dominant bourgeois order and break the Stalinist hegemony on the Left. Their view was that the proletariat no longer existed as it had done in the nineteenth century and that they were part of a transformed 'society of the spectacle'. It is no coincidence that in 1960–1961, precisely when Castoriadis made his diagnosis of working-class and revolutionary movements at a time of full employment and rapid economic growth, Guy Debord was active in the ranks of SouB. Debord took these themes to another level, that of spontaneist theory, but the intellectual filiations of Debord's ideas as part of this ultra-Left milieu that also gradually became anti-Marxist, is undisputed. Debord's new critique of the *société du spectacle*, discussed elsewhere in this volume, remains a frame of analysis in part based on intersections of red and black ideas. As in Castoriadis's 1960 and 1961 reflexions, his brand of Marxist thinking should not simply be reduced to economic and political features alone, but also explores the imaginary dimension of capitalist domination, interlinked with the continuing centrality of workers' councils in the *Internationale Situationniste*. It was the organisational imperatives of a movement originally influenced by Trotskyism that alienated Debord as much as it had done Pannekoek. Thus, in the last ten years of its existence, SouB was less a melting pot of new ideas than a springboard for their development *outside* of its organisation.

## Castoriadis' ultimate control and later evolution

Castoriadis's attempts to recapture the organisational purity of the original Leninist organisations exhibits the confluence of ideology and context, but the central role played by Castoriadis himself goes a long way to explaining the successes and failures of the group. For example, recruitment took place only by personal co-optation, limiting the capacity of the movement to expand and transform. Gottraux, on the basis of interviews and analysis of internal documents, has demonstrated that Castoriadis was what we might now call a 'control freak', constantly steering the course of the debates and imposing his personal will on the rest of the group. Castoriadis admitted that his status as international civil servant gave him a privileged amount of free time to write his militant texts. Gottraux also notes that in all the available minutes it turns out that Castoriadis never missed any of SouB's meetings.[50]

The most prominent example of Castoriadis's central (and centralising) role comes from the internal scission in 1958. In the tormented context of the dying days of the Fourth Republic, strong disagreements emerged inside SouB regarding the nature of De Gaulle's election and which interpretation to give to the PCF's ambiguous stance vis-à-vis what has been dubbed 'De Gaulle's permanent *coup d'état'*. Castoriadis, and with him the Centre and the Right wing (as discussed above), invoked 'collective discipline', and managed thus to silence the Left minority, as we have seen from the Dutch militants' reports. Lefort saw in this attitude of Castoriadis an 'avatar of democratic centralism'[51] and decided to leave the organisation in September 1958. In this context, Gottraux also observed that the minority Left had made contact with Pannekoek and the Dutch council movement, illustrating that they felt at odds and uneasy with the ways in which Castoriadis wanted to reform the organisation.[52]

In fact, some SouB positions were also premised on councilist ideas. For example, the possibility of revoking some of the rotating representation in leading committees (like the *Comité Responsable*) or the importance of the workers controlling and organising the means of production and of self-organisation.[53] The problem was that the substance and influence of Pannekoek's ideas and the idea of workers' councils did not trickle down into the organisational life of SouB *itself*. In theory, Castoriadis promoted autonomy and criticised the bureaucratic degeneration of many Marxist organisations, but in reality, the rhythm of life and the range of ideas discussed inside SouB were animated almost solely by Castoriadis. For example Castoriadis remarked during the strikes in the Renault factory in 1955 and 1956: 'We have to be alert, decide who must attend the TO [Tribune Ouvrière] meetings. These comrades must decide in advance the critiques to be made and hand in texts to TO.'[54]

It is not a coincidence that most of those who were militants and have since become influential intellectuals (such as Lefort, Debord and Lyotard) all decided to leave the organisation because of disagreements with Castoriadis. There could only be one leader and one organisational form for SouB.[55] But intellectually, again, Gottraux notes that Lefort's criticisms in the late 1950s seems to have been taken on board by Castoriadis in his reading of the events surrounding May 1968,[56] as much as Lefort also seems to acknowledge that Henri Simon was right on certain issues ten years after discussions inside ILO.[57] In certain texts from the post-SouB period, Castoriadis seems to have continued some of the dialogues that took place under the banner of SouB.[58] Despite a form of historical revisionism, it can even be argued that Castoriadis took inspiration from Pannekoek, as his 1976 reappraisal of the Hungarian revolt in *Telos* suggests. The 'Hungarian Source'[59] can be read at different levels. In part it is a vitriolic text against Ernest Mandel, the leader of the Fourth International (United Secretariat), and classical Marxism.[60] But above all, it is a cornerstone of Castoriadis's new philosophy and political theory in which autonomy becomes paramount in his elaboration of social consciousness, developed in later philosophical works, and in particular around the theme of the social imaginary.[61]

In this text, Castoriadis defines the autonomy of a society as its capacity for 'auto-institution' (a distinct phrase of Castoriadis's that does not derive directly from the anarchist idea of self-organisation).[62] The process of auto-institution implies the capacity of societies to openly 'call into question their own institution, their representation of the world, their social imaginary significations'.[63] Closure and openness are the key for Castoriadis's understanding of autonomy, envisaged as a radical project. Here, closure means the fact that it is not possible for a given society to choose the ways and means in which it reflects on itself, implying a form of heteronomy – that is, the law of others imposed on this particular society. Openness, on the other hand, is important not only in terms of a given society choosing its institutional setting but also on an 'informational and cognitive' level, in choosing the vocabulary or symbolic repertoires to express an autonomous political project.[64]

While people who remained faithful to historical materialism failed to see what was still Marxist in this new theory,[65] Castoriadis maintained that, beyond his commitment to a revolutionary praxis, at the heart of his new theoretical elaboration was the classical Marxist theme of alienation, but one also attuned to a more socially constructed and language-mediated vision of the political, one far from the strictures of historical determinism.[66] It could even be claimed that some of Pannekoek's arguments, developed in the non-published correspondence, seem to have been integrated into Castoriadis's theory of the spontaneous capacity of *society* (with the difference that back in the 1950s the central actor was the *working class*) for self-organisation. With a historical sleight of hand, Castoriadis here argues that the Hungarian revolution is fundamentally different from the previous forms of communes or council revolutions. Being of a new kind, it puts the previous communist revolts in a situation of *damnatio memoriae* – or removal from remembrance – thus realising a form of historical revisionism. This is very different from the views he expressed in the 1950s, when he argued the need for intellectuals and a revolutionary vanguard. Echoing Pannekoek, Castoriadis now states that:

> If the opposite of spontaneity (that is, of self-activity and self-organization) is *hetero*-organization (that is, organization by politicians, theoreticians, professional revolutionaries, etc.) then, clearly, the opposite of spontaneity is *counter*-revolution, or the conservation of the existing order. The revolution is exactly that: self-organization of the people.[67]

It is as if, 22 years later, Castoriadis has turned on his head. When going back to Pannekoek's second and third letters, one cannot but be struck by the parallel between the Dutch councilist's ideas and the 'new' Castoriadis:

What I am claiming is that the result of the often violent struggle is not determined by accidental circumstances, but by what is vital in the *workers' thought*, as the basis of a solid *consciousness* acquired through experience. [...] We cannot beat them [the communist parties] by following their methods. It is possible only if we follow our own methods. The true form of action for a struggling class lies in the strength of arguments, based on the fundamental principle of *autonomy of decision*. [...] The main condition for the conquest of freedom for the working class is that the concepts of *self-government* and the *self-management* of the means of production both need to be rooted in the *consciousness of the masses*.[68]

There are certainly areas of convergence between the two authors, even if more than 20 years had passed since the writing of these lines by Pannekoek. Castoriadis had also distanced himself from a stage-based vision of class struggle, because he went through its anti-Marxist period, the liquidation of historical materialism and of a rigid theory of economy as the basis of historical transformation. He remains, though, a Castoriadis dedicated to the same refined commitment to understanding how new hierarchical structures 'replaced the traditional twofold division of capitalist society into two main classes'.[69] Whether this is enough to be still considered a Marxist remains a matter for debate.

## Conclusion: Legacy beyond the organisation

SouB eventually evolved into an ultra-Left anti-Marxist movement.[70] Its influence, overall, is certainly more important for the intellectual and academic scene than the practical, political level, where its impact has remained minimal (although this is true of almost all ultra-Left organisations). That SouB achieved the notoriety and influence that it did is significant given it had such a very low number of militants, ranging from between 20 members in 1951 and 87 a decade later.[71] However, its publications influenced the work of many other French intellectual journals, and numerous French, British and US intellectuals cut their teeth in revolutionary politics while members of the group, before moving on.[72]

There are both typical and idiosyncratic elements to the story of the evolution of SouB, but neither is visible enough without the context we have given here. Ideology is not enough. As we have shown, Trotskyism in general had serious problems despite its compelling ideological critique of Stalinism, its demand for the internationalisation of political struggle, and its reading of the Soviet Union as a bureaucratic degeneration, or state capitalism. The ideological commitment to democratic centralism and a revolutionary vanguard nevertheless prohibited a fuller integration with wider Left-libertarian strands of thinking. While SouB often provided a platform for opening new avenues for political participation on the far-Left, at other times it split the political spectrum further.

We have argued that despite the substantial distancing of SouB from Trotskyism, it kept the indirect mark of its intellectual origins, in particular Castoriadis's strict (if critical) following of party discipline in the context of the ideological battles of the cold war. The need to keep a sense of intellectual purity and originality, in order to ward off detractors and to sustain the movement into the future, generated a series of splits detrimental to mutual borrowings. Intellectual cross-fertilisation took place only when members were not bound by the group's inner working logic or the power struggles between dominant and more passive figures. We have noted how Lefort and Castoriadis parted company over the group's inner organization and over their mutual philosophy of history. Yet, as individuals, they continued their dialogue on politics and theory. There was disagreement on certain topics, but on many subtle elements it is as if Lefort and Castoriadis kept developing mutual borrowings into their own independent lines of thinking.

Castoriadis's later reflections on society are caught in a battle against heteronomy on the part of an externally instituted political, social and cognitive order – a view that echoes Lefort's simultaneous work and writings against totalitarianism.[73] Both authors converge in their form of mild historical revisionism about what revolution is or should be.[74] So while SouB as a formal institution prevented creative borrowings, SouB as an informal community of intellectuals has allowed for profound and long-lasting borrowings and generated deep processes of cross-fertilisation of political ideas. This denotes the presence of strong personal ties and intellectual affinities despite the stark ideological differences which ought to be considered as the engine of subsequent theoretical innovation. *Socialisme ou Barbarie* is a case study of mid- to late twentieth-century socialism in its own right. Its lasting legacy, however, is intellectual, not organisational.

## Acknowledgements

The author would like to thank the editors and anonymous reviewers for their comments and David Berry for his assistance with the translations. Thanks to Sara Farris, Jérémie Barthas, Paul Mattick Jr. and Chiara Bottici for sharing some ideas during the writing of this chapter. All have helped to push me into rethinking in more depth what 'Red and Black' means. I obviously bear sole responsibility for remaining errors.

## Notes

1. To differentiate between the group and the publication, I use SouB for the group and *Socialisme ou Barbarie* for the journal.
2. For an overview of such elaborations inside Council Communism, see Anton Pannekoek, *Workers' Councils* (Edinburgh: AK Press, 2002).

3. Liebich is one of the first to thematise this tension. See A. Liebich, 'Socialisme ou Barbarie: A Radical Critique of Bureaucracy', *Our Generation* 12:2 (1977), pp. 55–62; M. van der Linden, 'Socialisme ou Barbarie: A French Revolutionary Group (1949–65)', *Left History* 5:1 (1997) at www.left-dis.nl/uk/lindsob.htm (accessed June 2010); and for the most detailed analysis, see P. Gottraux, *'Socialisme ou Barbarie'. Un engagement politique et intellectuel dans la France de l'après-guerre* (Lausanne: Payot, 1997).

4. See H. Simon, *Correspondance de Pierre Chaulieu (Castoriadis) et Anton Pannekoek 1953–1954* (Paris: Échanges et Mouvement, 2002). The text, with an introduction and comments, from Henri Simon is available at www.mondialisme.org/spip. php?rubrique86 (accessed July 2010).

5. See, for example, Castoriadis, *L'institution imaginaire de la société* (Paris: Seuil, 1975) and *Domaines de l'homme. Le carrefour du labyrinthe* (Paris: Seuil, 1986).

6. For a detailed description, see Gottraux, *'Socialisme ou Barbarie'*, pp. 31–40 or P. Mattick Jr., *'Socialisme ou Barbarie'*, in R.A. Gorman (ed.), *Biographical Dictionary of Neo-Marxism* (Westport, CT: Greenwood Press, 1985), pp. 387–389, for a brief overview.

7. Gottraux, *'Socialisme ou Barbarie'*, pp. 21–23.

8. Translation from Castoriadis, *Political and Social Writings*, Vol. 1: *1946–1955*, ed. and trans. David Ames Curtis (Minneapolis: University of Minnesota Press, 1988), p. 97. See also in Gottraux, *'Socialisme ou Barbarie'*, pp. 23–30, and 'An interview with Cornelius Castoriadis', *Telos* 23 (1975), pp. 131–155.

9. Gottraux (see *'Socialisme ou Barbarie'*, pp. 377–383), who provides the most detailed account of SouB life, distinguishes three generations: the war generation, the intermediary, and the Algerian war generations.

10. See J.-F. Sirinelli, *Histoire culturelle de la France* (Paris: Seuil, 2005).

11. Gottraux, *'Socialisme ou Barbarie'*, pp. 58ff.

12. See Mattick, *'Socialisme ou Barbarie'*, p. 389.

13. See P. Grémion, *Intelligence de l'Anticommunisme. Le Congrès pour la liberté de la culture à Paris 1950–1975* (Paris: Fayard, 1995); and V.R. Berghahn, *America and the Intellectual Cold Wars in Europe: Shepard Stone Between Philanthropy, Academy and Diplomacy* (Princeton, NJ: Princeton University Press, 2001).

14. This is obviously a matter of debate, and there have been Marxist intellectuals considering themselves Leninists who have nonetheless developed antiauthoritarian ideas, *in primis* Gramsci and his revised dichotomy of civil v. political society to distinguish the sphere of spontaneous association v. oppression of the bourgeois state's institutions. Moreover, Lih has recently argued that Lenin's élitist and manipulating attitude towards the workers has been overstated in the course of the last century. See L. Lih, *Lenin Rediscovered. What Is to Be Done? in Context* (Amsterdam: Brill University Press, 2006). Yet, the tragic upheaval of Kronstadt is a reminder of the little space for debate that Trotsky himself would allow inside the party.

15. There are of course counter-examples of constructive openings to other communist trends, as certain sections of the Fourth International have been in alliance with

larger communist factions, as was the case of *Bandiera Rossa* in Italy until recently. Yet it is difficult to argue that the story of the Fourth International is not replete with internal divisions.

16. H. Arendt, 'The Ex-Communists', *Commonweal* 57:24 (20 March 1953), pp. 595–599.

17. D. Kelly, *James Burnham and the Struggle for the World: A Life* (Washington, DC: ISI Books, 2008).

18. See G. Scott Smith, 'A Radical Democratic Political Offensive. Melvin J. Lasky, *Der Monat* and the CCF', *Journal of Contemporary History* 35:2 (2000), pp. 265–268; Scott Smith, *The Politics of Apolitical Culture. The Congress for Cultural Freedom, the CIA and Post-war American Hegemony* (London and New York: Routledge, 2002); F.S. Saunders, *The Cultural Cold War: The CIA and the World of Arts and Letters* (New York: New Press, 2001), pp. 47–56.

19. Our point is not to suggest that all ex-communists or ex-Trotskyists have been complacent and aware of the CIA activities in the name of anti-communism, but that there were some ties. For example, Aron was critical of these external manipulations by the CIA, as Grémion has documented in his *Intelligence de l'Anticommunisme*, pp. 429–474.

20. See Scott Smith, *The Politics of Apolitical Culture*.

21. On how a certain amount of these counterpart funds of the Marshall Plan could be used for secret operations of the US government and in particular by the CIA, see A. Carew, 'American Labor Movement in Fizzland: The Free Trade Union Committee and the CIA', *Labor History* 39:1 (1998), pp. 25–42.

22. See Gottraux, *'Socialisme ou Barbarie'*, note 38, p. 334: For a detailed trajectory of his function inside the OECD, see note 47, p. 337.

23. The full list is given on http://www.agorainternational.org/englishworksb.html. In the famous 1968 book Castoriadis, next to E. Morin and C. Lefort, signs as Jean-Marc Coudray. See Edgar Morin, Claude Lefort and Jean-Marc Coudray, Mai 68: la brèche. Premières réflexions sur les événements (Paris: Librairie Arthème Fayard, 1968). It was in 1968 that Castoriadis signed a text under his real name for the first time; however it was not a political text, but an article dealing with psychoanalysis. See Gottraux, 'Socialisme ou Barbarie', p. 336.

24. See Castoriadis, 'An Interview'. See Gottraux, *'Socialisme ou Barbarie'*, note 49, p. 337.

25. See Gottraux, *'Socialisme ou Barbarie'*, p. 253, my translation. Notes 219 and 226 also illustrate this vision of SouB thinking of itself as *super partes*. See note 219: 'Michel, approved by Chaulieu, underlines the originality of SouB's position. We do not represent a tendency polemicising from within "worker" organisations, we are outside, against them.' (trans. Dave Berry)

26. Gottraux, *'Socialisme ou Barbarie'*, p. 23.

27. See, for example, Castoriadis, *Political and Social Writings*, pp. 96–97.

28. C., Lefort, 'La contradiction de Trotsky et le problème révolutionnaire', *Les Temps Modernes* 4:39 (1948–1949), pp. 46–69.

29. Van der Linden, *'Socialisme ou Barbarie'*.

30. Ibid.
31. See Castoriadis, 'An interview', p. 134.
32. For a clear description of how their approach gradually became anti-Marxist, see both Castoriadis, 'An Interview' (esp. pp. 144–150), and 'An interview with Claude Lefort', *Telos* 30 (1976), pp. 173–192, esp. pp. 181–183. Lefort expressed strong disagreement with Castoriadis over the fact that the latter shared the views of Raya Dunayevskaya, a militant in the Johnson-Forest tendency in the USA, whose selection of texts were published in SouB in the first half of the 1950s. Lefort criticised these views as 'vaguely Hegelian' and noted that 'the close rapport between Castoriadis and Rya Stone [Raya Dunayevskaya] made me aware for the first time of profound conceptual differences between us that underlay our political differences' (177). Note that in his interview, Lefort confused Rya Stone (that is, Grace Lee Boggs) with Raya Dunayevskaya.
33. See C. Lefort, 'Alain Sergent et Claude Harmel. Recension du livre *Histoire de l'Anarchie*, vol. I', *Les Temps Modernes* 5:56 (1950), pp. 269–274.
34. Liebich, '*Socialisme ou Barbarie*', p. 58. Lefort describes the bulletin of ILO/ICO as 'as unprogrammatic as possible' (Lefort, 'An Interview', 179). Simon developed views closer to libertarian communism and was therefore very open to the suggestions made by Pannekoek, as some of his later publications demonstrated, in particular his side commentary in Simon, *Correspondance de Pierre Chaulieu*.
35. Translated and reproduced by Marcel van der Linden, '*Socialisme ou Barbarie*', note 49. The report was originally published as 'Splitsing in de Franse groep "Socialisme ou Barbarie": Brieven uit Frankrijk', *Spartacus* 18 (October–December 1958), pp. 21–25.
36. Ibid.
37. For an English imprint, see Pannekoek, *Workers' Councils*.
38. See P. Mattick Jr., 'Ruehle, Otto', in R.A. Gorman (ed.), *Biographical Dictionary of Neo-Marxism* (Westport, CT: Greenwood Press), p. 365.
39. See Pannekoek, *Workers' Councils*, p. 206. Pannekoek also had a non-deterministic reading of modern capitalism. So rather than seeing capitalism as containing the seeds of its own demise, he saw in capitalism an innate capacity of continuous adaptation allowing it to survive difficult times and transform itself into an ever stronger ideology.
40. See Gottraux, '*Socialisme ou Barbarie*', pp. 241–242; Van der Linden, '*Socialisme ou Barbarie*'; and Simon, *Correspondance de Pierre Chaulieu*. Henri Simon, who was an actor of this period, also points the finger at Castoriadis's slightly manipulating capacities. The most virulent accusation against Castoriadis can be found in *Cahier du Communisme de Conseils*, 8 (1971). Castoriadis gave his own version of the polemic in *L'expérience du movement ouvrier* (Paris: 10–18 ed. Bourgeois, 1974), pp. 261ff.
41. This chronology is adapted in large parts from Simon, *Correspondance de Pierre Chaulieu*.
42. Ibid. (see doc. 'Les voiles commencent à se lever').
43. Pannekoek's original formulation in the third letter is as follows: 'It was not my intention to see it published, or rather I had not thought when writing it that it

was for publication; if I remember rightly, I did not put much care into writing it. If, however, you believe that certain passages could provide some clarification, then I think you should select passages such that my remarks do not take up too much space in the review. I have the impression that what is said in the book *Les Conseils Ouvriers* could provide a much broader and more general base.' (trans. Dave Berry). Quoted in Simon, *Correspondance de Pierre Chaulieu* (see doc. 'Encore sur la question du parti').

44. In a note 'Socialisme ou Barbarie à l'étranger' published in *Socialisme ou Barbarie* 15–16 (October–December 1954), it states that 'The discussion between Anton Pannekoek [ ... ] and Pierre Chaulieu is of great importance from the viewpoint of the elaboration of revolutionary theory. One cannot but agree with the firm and brilliant critique which the latter provides of Pannekoek, whose positions *vis-à-vis* the Comintern are, or rather were, historically justified, but which today are as outdated as the theses against which they were a healthy reaction' (trans. Dave Berry).

45. Simon, *Correspondance de Pierre Chaulieu* (doc. 'Premiers contacts').

46. Part 1 of the article is published in SouB 31 (1960–1961), pp. 51–81, and part 2 in SouB 32 (1961), pp. 84–111.

47. Gottraux, *'Socialisme ou Barbarie'*, pp. 135–136.

48. Ibid., pp. 137–138.

49. SouB 31 (1960–1961), p. 63.

50. Gottraux, *'Socialisme ou Barbarie'*, p. 333, or n. 37, p. 334.

51. Ibid., p. 91.

52. Ibid., pp. 89–92.

53. Ibid., p. 34

54. Ibid., p. 67.

55. Mattick, *'Socialisme ou Barbarie'*, p. 388.

56. Gottraux, *'Socialisme ou Barbarie'*, p. 348.

57. See Lefort, 'An Interview', p. 185.

58. For example, Castoriadis writes: 'Things are even clearer when one considers the revolution as self-organized activity aiming at the institution of a new order, rather than an explosion and destruction of the old order. (The distinction is, of course, a separating abstraction.)' The parenthesis seems a personal aside directed against the undeterministic Lefort to tell him that the does not really believe in a before and an after of the revolutionary moment. See Castoriadis, 'The Hungarian Source', *Telos* 26 (1976), pp. 4–22 (13).

59. The text was written and published first in English and a French version was published a year later: 'La Source Hongroise' *Libre* 1 (1977), pp. 51–85.

60. Mandel is openly quoted in many places (for example, 'The Hungarian Source', 6), but some indirect criticism against Mandel's thinking can also be found throughout the text (for example, 11).

61. In particular see Castoriadis, *L'institution imaginaire,* and *Domaines de l'homme*.

62. See, for example, Castoriadis, *Domaines de l'homme*, p. 518.

63. Castoriadis, C., *World in Fragments. Writings on Politics, Society, Psychoanalysis, and the Imagination*, ed. and trans. David Ames Curtis (Stanford, CA: Stanford University Press, 1997), p. 17.

64. Castoriadis, *Domaines de l'homme*, p. 513.

65. See for example the sarcastic remarks of Henri Simon about Castoriadis's new idea of the social imaginary in Simon, *Correspondance de Pierre Chaulieu*. See also

A. Callinicos, *Trotskyism* (Minneapolis, MN: University of Minnesota Press, 1990), Section 4.3 'Castoriadis and the triumph of the will'.

66. For a succinct presentation of Castoriadis's commitment to a revolutionary praxis and the 'conscious transformation of society by the autonomous activity of men' (that is, a non-alienated society), see Castoriadis, *L'institution imaginaire*, pp. 90–92. Translation from *The Imaginary Institution of Society* (London: Polity Press, 1987, trans. K. Blamey), p. 62.

67. See Castoriadis, 'The Hungarian Source', p. 11. His emphases.

68. Pannekoek's 15 June 1954 letter to Chaulieu, reproduced in Simon, *Correspondance de Pierre Chaulieu* (doc. 'Deuxième lettre de Pannekoek'). Our emphases.

69. See Castoriadis, 'La Source Hongroise', p. 73.

70. Gottraux, *'Socialisme ou Barbarie'*, pp. 360–361, where Gottraux also notes how the Gulag effect (that is, publication of Soljenitsin's main piece) and anti-totalitarian writings in the 1970s contributed in making Castoriadis's theories appealing.

71. Gottraux, *'Socialisme ou Barbarie'*, pp. 40; 104.

72. Ibid., pp. 255–314.

73. See note 70. The journal *Constellations* held a conference shortly after the death of Lefort in 2010. Original texts presented then can be found at http://constellationsjournal.blogspot.com/search/label/Claude%20Lefort%20Memorial%20-%20TEXTS. A. Kalyvas' comparison of Castoriadis and Lefort is for our discussion illuminating but has not been included in the final publication (*Constellations* 2012, Volume 19, Issue 1).

74. For a discussion of Lefort's historical revisionism, see J. Barthas, 'Machiavelli in political thought from the age of revolutions to the present', in J. Najemy (ed.), *The Cambridge Companion to Machiavelli* (Cambridge: Cambridge University Press, 2010), pp. 269–270.

# 12
## Beyond Black and Red: The Situationists and the Legacy of the Workers' Movement

*Jean-Christophe Angaut*

## Introduction

Over the last 20 years, the situationists have often been reduced to a mere group of artists criticising everyday life, detached from any social struggle. The common description of their contribution to the events of 1968 in France was symptomatic of this reduction: either the so-called cultural orientation of these events was attributed to them, or it was said that, because the role of the situationists had been over-emphasised, these events were reduced in the collective memory to their cultural aspect.[1] Nevertheless, this understanding tends to weaken with a close reading of the situationists' texts (consisting of articles, letters, pamphlets and theoretical books).[2] From this literature, it appears that the situationists were linked with and/or opposed to most of the revolutionary groups of the 1960s.[3] For example, Debord was briefly a member of 'Pouvoir ouvrier', a group belonging to 'Socialisme ou Barbarie' in the early 1960s, and in 1966 he had connections with members of the French Anarchist Federation, which subsequently excluded the members of what was regarded as a situationist conspiracy inside the organisation. It also appears that since the beginning of the 1960s, in the two main texts of situationist theory (*The Society of the Spectacle* by Debord and *The Revolution of Everyday Life* by Vaneigem[4]) as well as in their journal *Internationale Situationniste* and during the events of 1968, the situationists pointed up slogans of the workers' councils,[5] celebrating this spontaneous revolutionary structure and its recurrence in Budapest in 1956.[6] Last but not least, they considered the events of May and June 1968 in France to be a revolutionary event, being the first general wildcat strike of workers in history, rather than a student event.[7] It is therefore interesting to investigate their relations with the history of the workers' movement, a history which led to a split between two main trends, Marxism and anarchism, or statist communism and libertarian socialism.[8]

This chapter studies the way the situationists are linked to this legacy, how they might have provided a way of going beyond this division between Marxism and anarchism and what the limits of their perspective might be. This attempt is considered in two directions. First, the situationists presented a critique of the separation between anti-capitalist and antihierarchical struggles as an ideological split rather than an objective distinction. In their relations with other revolutionary groups, this led to harsh criticisms directed at Marxist and libertarian organisations that prospered from this division. This part of the history of the situationists is beginning to be better known, but the relation of the practice to their theories is not always systematically explained. By revisiting the concepts and themes of the Young Hegelian movement – a movement to which both Marx and Bakunin belonged – the chapter then continues by showing that this attempt to go beyond the separation between black and red brings us back to a point before that separation. In other terms, the situationist claim to go beyond the Marxist and anarchist traditions is not a negation of the history of the workers' movement, but an attempt to renew this movement on the basis of its original theoretical sources.

## The critique of the separation between black and red

It is important to keep in mind that the theoretical attempts of the situationists during the 1960s cannot be isolated from their political and social context: this seems to me the best way to maintain the critical distance missing in the work of the so-called 'pro-situs' ('pro-situationists') who were attacked by Debord in 1972.[9] First of all, Debord's participation in 'Socialisme ou Barbarie', mentioned above, meant that he and other members of the group had common reference points in left communism in general, with authors such as Karl Korsch, Anton Pannekoek and Rosa Luxemburg. Furthermore, some groups close to the Situationist International (SI), especially the 'Enragés' at Nanterre University,[10] maintained links with libertarian groups, such as 'Noir et Rouge',[11] and with Council Communist groups, such as 'Informations et Correspondances Ouvrières'.[12] Moreover, in the early 1960s, the situationists were close to the philosopher, sociologist and heterodox Marxist, Henri Lefebvre, until their relationship broke down acrimoniously amid reciprocal accusations of plagiarism.[13] Situationist theories are a meeting point of at least three trends. First, a Left communist tradition which was critical of the Leninist trends in the workers' movement (in short, those who believed that the Russian Revolution was betrayed by the Bolsheviks and not just by Stalin) and which promoted the workers' councils as direct democratic organisations. Second, a tradition of anti-authoritarian critique of capitalism and so-called socialist societies. And finally, a trend of sociological reflexion aboutmodern urban life as alienated. Keeping this relation in mind does not minimise the originality of the situationist theories, but helps to understand them better, and particularly to understand the dual critique of Marxism and anarchism.

It may seem difficult to accept that the situationists were criticising the bureaucratic tendencies in the history of Marxism as well as what they saw as the historic inefficacy of anarchism, because the main references they used seemed to be more Marxist than libertarian. For example, during the summer of 1968, the group protested: 'Despite the obvious fact that the Situationist International developed a historical view deriving from Hegel and Marx, the press kept on mixing up situationists and anarchism.'[14] They also claimed filiations with what they called 'revolutionary Marxism', an expression that excluded such statist interpretations of Marxism as Leninism and social democracy. Furthermore, like Council Communists, they may also appear to be Marxists with libertarian tendencies rather than anarchists integrating Marxist scientific contributions. Moreover, even when they are dealing with social and historical experiments they agree with, where anarchists have played the main role, they refuse to reduce these experiments to the expression of anarchism as a particular trend within the workers' movement. This is made quite clear with their discussion of the 1936 Spanish revolution. In *The Society of the Spectacle*, Debord recognised that on the one hand, 'in 1936 anarchism did indeed initiate a social revolution, a revolution that was the most advanced expression of proletarian power ever realised'; but he argued that on the other hand, the uprising was not an anarchist initiative, it was a defensive reaction against a military coup, and they were unable effectively to defend the revolution against the bourgeois, the Stalinists and Fascism. Some of them even became government ministers, he noted.[15]

In *The Revolution of Everyday Life*, Raoul Vaneigem seems to be closer than Debord to libertarian ideals, for example when he explains that 'from now on, no revolution will be worthy of the name if it does not involve, at the very least, the radical elimination of all hierarchy'.[16] However, the words 'anarchism' or 'anarchy' cannot be found anywhere in the book. Vaneigem clearly speaks about *anarchists* (quoting, for example, Makhno and Durruti) but never about *anarchism*; as if individuals were worth more than their particular ideology and more than the political trend they belonged to.

Nevertheless, despite this seeming proximity to Marxism and Marxist tropes, there is very real and open critique of Marxism in these same situationist texts, a critique which not only attacks the progressive degeneration of Marxism, but also points out the germs of that degeneration in Marx's personality and work. In *The Revolution of Everyday Life*, where Marx is quoted less and in a more critical way than in Debord's texts, Vaneigem speaks, for example, about 'Marx's authoritarian attitudes in the First International'.[17] However, this criticism is also developed further in *The Society of the Spectacle*, the book which is nevertheless known as the closest to revolutionary Marxism. In Chapter IV of the book, Debord at first gives the impression, like other French left-wing Marxists of the time,[18] that his criticisms are of the incorrect use of Marx by those who claimed filiation with him. But Debord goes on to explain that in Marx's thought, there is a 'scientific-determinist aspect' which 'made it vulnerable to ideologisation'.[19] That drift towards economism (for, as Marx put it, economics is 'the historical science *par excellence*') always postpones the moment of revolutionary practice and the advent of the historical subject by claiming that the correct objective conditions are not present. For Debord, Marxism as it evolved emphasised a tendency which was already there in embryo in Marx, consisting principally in separating the theory (especially the economics) from the revolutionary practice, just as Marx isolated himself 'by cloistered scholarly work in the British Museum'.[20] According to Debord, that lack in Marxist theory also has its roots in the fact that this theory was the faithful expression of the revolutionary movement at that time, and also of the insufficiencies of this movement. This movement missed something that could not come from the theory, but had to emerge from the concrete form of organisation that arose spontaneously from the proletarian struggles: the workers' councils, the *soviets*.

When Marx elaborated his theory, the working-class organisation he promoted could be nothing other than that which was in accord with his separate theoretical work, and that form has two failures. First, it mimics the bourgeois revolutions, in the sense that the main task of the proletariat would be to take power as it exists in bourgeois society: Debord explains that 'the theoretical shortcomings of the *scientific* defence of proletarian revolution (both in its content and in its form of exposition) all ultimately result from identifying the proletariat with the bourgeoisie *with respect to the revolutionary seizure of power*'.[21] The self-criticism contained in Marx's work on the Paris Commune, which corrects some formulations of the *Manifesto of the Communist Party* (1848), seems here to be clearly recognisable. According to the *Communist Manifesto*, the proletariat was supposed to seize the State machine as it was in order to make it work for the benefit of the proletariat. In Chapter II, we read: 'The proletariat will use its political supremacy to wrest, by degree, all capital from the bourgeoisie, to centralise all instruments of production in the hands of the State, i.e., of the proletariat organised as the ruling class; and to increase the total productive forces as rapidly as possible'.[22] Later, in *The Civil War in France*, which was written just after the end of the Paris Commune (1871), Marx argues that 'the working class cannot simply lay hold of the ready-made state machinery, and wield it for its own purposes', but has to destroy it immediately, replacing it with the Commune, which is 'the political form at last discovered under which to work out the economical emancipation of labour'.[23] However, Debord does not repeat the praise of the Commune as 'the political form at last discovered', and even when he praises the workers' councils, he does not speak about them as 'political forms'. To understand this point, it is therefore important to consider his critique of political parties, which takes us to the second failure in Marxism.

This second failure is the lack of a conception of the organisation which would have been truly revolutionary, that is, without any echo of statist or bourgeois forms. In summary, Marxism (and all Marxist groups) had failed in their thinking about what the revolutionary organisation should be. The following passage deserves quoting at length:

> The proletarian class is formed into a subject in its process of organ-ising revolutionary struggles and in its reorganisation of society at the *moment of revolution* [...]. But this crucial question of organisation was virtually ignored by revolutionary theory during the period when the workers' movement was first taking shape – the very period when that theory still possessed the *unitary* character it had inherited from historical thought (and which it had rightly vowed to develop into a unitary his-torical *practice*). Instead, the organisational question became the weakest aspect of radical theory, a confused terrain lending itself to the revival of hierarchical and statist tactics borrowed from the bourgeois revolution. The forms of organisation of the workers' movement that were devel-oped on the basis of this theoretical negligence tended in turn to inhibit the maintenance of a unitary theory by breaking it up into various spe-cialised and fragmented disciplines. This ideologically alienated theory was then no longer able to recognise the practical verifications of the uni-tary historical thought it had betrayed when such verifications emerged in spontaneous working-class struggles; instead, it contributed to repressing every manifestation and memory of them.[24]

With this quotation, which describes the process of degeneration of Marxism, we understand the *relative* legitimacy of the anarchist critique for the situationists. At its foundation (deeply rooted in an original relation with the Hegelian current in both Marx and in Bakunin, as we shall see), revolu-tionary theory was ahead of the time of the revolutionary practice it infers – and that is part of the original theory of the avant-garde the situationists developed at that time. Initially, that theory was unitary, but because of the lateness of the revolutionary practice, a revolutionary conception of the organisation as the junction of practice and theory was lacking. Revolu-tionary theory thus adopted bourgeois and statist patterns of organisation. Obviously, Debord has the party system in mind, in which the different pow-ers are separated as if the parties were small states and where parties compete for power like states, and his critique has to be seen in relation to that devel-oped by socialist and trade union thinkers at the beginning of the twentieth century, especially in Germany.[25] But Debord also suggests something more difficult to understand about the link between the internal organisation of the political parties and the separations that occurred inside what he called revolutionary theory. Indeed, following Debord, it seems that the separation of different powers (the classical division into a legislature, an executive and a judiciary), that was available inside political parties, in turn influenced the theory, separating the theory from the practice, and the theory itself in different fields, so that the unitary character of the theory could not be maintained, giving way to specialisation and bureaucratism. And finally, when in historical practice there arises a form of organisation which is in accord with the originally unitary theory, the latter, which is alienated in the division of labour involved in activism, crystallised in bureaucratic organisations and sometimes submitted to a state, is unable to recognise this right form and prevents its manifestation.

The emergence of the workers' councils during the Hungarian uprising of 1956 is a key contextual fact to explain Debord's praise of the workers' councils and the reasons why he does not repeat Marx's praise of the Commune. As a merely political form, the Commune would imply a separation of politics as a particular activity. As a goal to attain, it would imply a separation between the form of organisation that is desired and the form of organisation by which the goal is supposed to be attained. In short, the Commune could maintain a separation between the revolutionary subject and their representation.[26] On the other hand, the workers' councils compensate for the two failures of the organisation promoted by Marxism. Workers' councils are indeed organisations of struggle *and* prefigurations of the coming social organisation. In a workers' council based on direct democracy, there is neither hierarchy nor separate function, and that is why it is a form of organisation radically different from the State. This explains why, in an article written for the last issue of the journal *Internationale Situationniste*, René Riesel wrote that 'the victory of the councils has its place not at the end, but at the very beginning of the revolution'.[27] The councils are not an aim which could be contemplated as the dreamt for political form for the day following the revolution: they are a way of organising which is effective in the very process of the revolution and which prevents the harmful action of bureaucratic organisations (parties and trade unions). The Commune was thus *not* an adequate revolutionary instrument.

In May and June 1968 the situationists formed a Council for the Maintenance of the Occupations (Conseil pour le maintien des occupations, or CMDO) with the *Enragés*, and in several situationist texts, one can detect the ambition of making the SI into an organisation that would prefigure such a coming organisation. It is particularly clear in a text which is both the testament and the obituary of the SI, namely the *Theses on the Situationist International and Its Time* written by Debord in 1972 and published the same year in *The Veritable Scission in the International*.[28] The *Theses* are particularly remarkable in their definition of revolutionary organisations:

> The revolutionary organisation of the proletarian age is defined by different moments of the struggle, where it must succeed each time, and in each of these moments, it must succeed in never becoming a separate

power. [...] Whenever it is able to act, the revolutionary organisation unites practice and theory, which constantly proceed together, but it never believes that it can accomplish this through a mere voluntarist proclamation of the necessity of their total fusion. When the revolution is still distant, the major task of the revolutionary organisation is above all *the practice of theory*. When the revolution begins, its major task increasingly becomes *the theory of practice*, but then the revolutionary organisation has taken on an entirely different character. In the former circumstances, very few individuals are *avant-garde*, and they must prove it by the coherence of their general project, and by the practice that enables them to know and communicate this project; in the latter situation, the mass of workers are *of their time*, and must remain so as its only possessors by mastering the totality of their theoretical and practical weapons, notably by refusing all delegation of power to a separate avant-garde. In the former circumstances, a dozen effective people can be enough to begin the self-explanation of an age that contains in itself a revolution that it still does not yet know about, and that seems to it everywhere to be absent and impossible; in the latter, the vast majority of the proletarian class must hold and exercise all power by organising itself into permanent deliberative and executive assemblies, which allow nothing to remain in the form of the old world and the forms that defend it.[29]

First, it appears from the above that the main theme of the revolutionary organisation is negative: something has to be avoided, namely the separation of the organisation as an autonomous power. That signals the opposition of the situationists to any Leninist or social democratic conception of the organisation. Nevertheless, revolutionary organisation cannot be defined once and for all and admits of two main stages, which form a chiasmus, constituted by the 'practice of theory' and the 'theory of practice'. 'Practice of theory' defines the 'avant-garde' stage of revolutionary organisation, and means not only that the practice of the avant-garde consists only in the theoretical explanation of the revolution, which is contained as a virtuality in a certain society at a certain time, but also that its practice is determined by the theory it builds. Therefore, the main task of the avant-garde is to experiment with a new kind of life, in harmony and coherence with the revolutionary project. The avant-garde is no ruling elite, but a prefiguration of future organisation. 'Theory of practice', which defines the second stage of revolutionary organisation, signifies that theory is no longer in advance of practice and from then on only has to be in harmony with revolutionary practice – in other terms, theory becomes somehow minor, and the main task is to practically prevent the emergence of a separate power. The most remarkable characteristic of this definition of revolutionary organisations is the conception of the avant-garde it promotes. Against the Leninist conception of organisation, developed for instance in *What Is*

*To Be done?* (1902) and criticised by Rosa Luxemburg, the situationists built an original theory of the avant-garde which results from the importing of an artistic conception of avant-garde into the field of politics. Therefore, in so far as it is not a general staff, the avant-garde does not lead, but conducts experiments, expresses what is still unsaid and prefigures the coming social organisation.

One can therefore understand the critical description of the split between anarchism and Marxism around this very question of the organisation's form that can be found in *The Society of the Spectacle*. Debord explicitly turns back to the conflict between Marx and Bakunin inside the International Workingmen's Association and describes it as the opposition between two ideologies, 'each containing a partially true critique, but each losing the unity of historical thought and setting itself up as an ideological *authority*'.[30] Those two criticisms are partially true because they apply on two different fields: the power inside a revolutionary society and the organisation of the revolutionary movement. Bakunin and his friends are right when they see the threat of a bureaucratic dictatorship behind the idea of a temporary proletarian state, but Marx and his friends are also right when they denounce Bakunin's conspiracy plans. If we stand at this point, this double criticism could be qualified as libertarian as it denounces the authoritarian tendencies in both theories. But this libertarian criticism is paired with a historical criticism which owes a lot to Marx but targets the two organisations which followed these two main orientations, the Black and the Red: the Spanish FAI (*Federación Anarquista Ibérica*, Iberian Anarchist Federación) and the German SPD (*Sozialdemokratische Partei Deutschlands*, Social Democratic Party of Germany).

Paragraph 92–94 of *The Society of the Spectacle* are devoted to anarchism but must be read in the context of the tense relations between the SI and libertarian organisations, since young members of the French Anarchist Federation had declared their great interest in the situationist theses around 1966 and 1967.[31] The French Anarchist Federation was obsessed at that time with the possible infiltration of Marxist elements into its ranks, since it had already split a few years earlier with the departure of the libertarian communists. The young libertarians were forced to quit the Federation and *The Society of the Spectacle* perhaps echoes this episode, especially in §92 when Debord explains why the anarchist critique remains only partial. In particular, he claimed, the criticism of the political struggle by the anarchists remained abstract as they promoted a purely economic struggle based on the pattern of the instantaneous general strike – which means that Debord is thinking here of anarcho-syndicalism. According to Debord, anarchists only see struggle as the realisation of an ideal, opposed to reality, without questioning the practical means of realisation of this ideal, and in each struggle, they constantly repeat the same things, which leads to their presenting themselves as guardians of the temple and self-proclaimed specialists of freedom (§93).

The meaning of this criticism is clear: the theoretical basis of the libertarian organisations, theoretical anarchism, is an outdated stage in the history of revolutionary theory, the stage of the ideological conflict with authoritarian socialism, which is also the stage of the separation between black and red and between the proletariat and its representation. Therefore libertarian organisations such as the French and (later) the Italian Anarchist Federations and the rebuilt Spanish CNT (*Confederación Nacional del Trabajo*, National Confederation of Labour) are, for Debord,[32] remnants of the past, small churches having no relation with the contemporary revolutionary movement, seeking to perpetuate themselves by constantly repeating the same ideological antitheses (which is why those who proclaimed their affinity with situationist theses were expelled). On the contrary, according to the situationists, workers' councils, as they arose spontaneously (that is to say: independently of any preconceived theory) in revolutionary Russia and spread in Germany and Spain, as a unitary practice, are supposed to be in accord with the unity of revolutionary theory. And this theoretical unity is to be found before the separation between black and red, before the split which gave birth to Marxism and anarchism as two partial truths, which means in revolutionary theory as expressed in the 1840s.

## Before black and red: The situationists and the Young Hegelians

In this section, I provide a critical reconstruction of the situationist attempt to theorise the antecedent theory to the separation between Marxism and anarchism and from that examine the parallels between their theoretical practices and those of the Young Hegelian movement of the 1840s. This means showing the proximity between the two movements in their relation to Hegel, questioning the knowledge the situationists had about the Young Hegelians and seeing which Young Hegelian themes are reactivated by situationist theories.

According to §78 of *The Society of the Spectacle*, the unity of the revolutionary theory is to be found in an original critical relation with Hegelian thought among the Young Hegelians in the 1840s: 'All the theoretical currents of the *revolutionary* working-class movement – Stirner and Bakunin as well as Marx – grew out of a critical confrontation with Hegelian thought.'[33] The situationists reactivate this critical confrontation which characterises Young or Left Hegelianism, and they do it, first, by using some Hegelian texts which also found favour with the Young Hegelians. Each of the two main situationist books written by Debord contains a quotation from the *Phenomenology of the Spirit*, which was, among Hegel's works, the one the Young Hegelian movement, from its very beginnings, admired the most.[34]

The final chapter of *The Society of the Spectacle*, which describes what a society beyond the society of the spectacle could be, is introduced with this sentence: 'Self-consciousness exists in and for itself when, and by the fact that, it so exists for another; that is, it exists only in being acknowledged'.[35] In accordance with the situationist concept of '*détournement*' (misappropriation or twisting), the Hegelian theory of acknowledgment, once moved onto the appropriate field (from an idealistic description of the development of self-consciousness to a prospective description of a desired society), gains its real meaning: such expressions as 'self-consciousness' and 'acknowledgment' cannot find their meaning inside the society of the spectacle, which is rather characterised by alienation and the lack of any self-consciousness.

*La véritable scission dans l'Internationale*[36] (*The Veritable Scission in the International*) begins with another Hegelian quotation:

> One party proves itself to be victorious by the fact that it breaks up into two parties; for in that fact it shows it possesses within it the principle it combats, and consequently shows it has abolished the one-sidedness with which it formerly made its appearance. The interest which was divided between it and the other, now falls entirely within it, and forgets the other, because that interest finds lying in it alone the opposition on which its attention is directed. At the same time, however, the opposition has been lifted into the higher victorious element, where it manifests itself in a clarified form. So that the schism that arises in one party, and seems a misfortune, demonstrates rather its good fortune.[37]

Initially, Hegel was describing the victory of the Enlightenment in its struggle against superstition, and the best proof of this victory was that superstition had disappeared and that, instead of a struggle between Enlightenment and superstition, there was from then on a struggle inside the Enlightenment between two opposite principles, pure thought and pure matter. In 1972, Debord uses this quotation in order to describe the split inside the SI. The SI has accomplished its historical task as avant-garde, and the best proof of this accomplishment is the split, not between Marxists and Bakuninists, but between two trends concerning the very question of the spectacle: the SI begins to be contemplated by spectators who describe themselves as 'pro-situs' ('pro-situationist'), and that is why it has to disappear.[38] This manner of using Hegel is one of the ways in which situationists can be compared with Young Hegelians.[39]

It is difficult to determine precisely what knowledge the situationists had of the Young Hegelian movement, beyond the young Marx's writings. Nevertheless, we know that in 1973 Debord published a translation (by Michel Jacob) of one of the first texts of that movement, August Cieskowski's *Prolegomena to a Historiosophy*[40] (1838), and ten years later even wrote a preface for a possible republication of the book.[41] In this text, he considers the Polish philosopher as 'the dark point around which all historical thought has turned for the last century and a half'. Moreover, in Debord and in Vaneigem, we can find hidden quotations of Young Hegelian texts – in particular of *Die Reaktion in Deutschland* (*The Reaction in Germany*, 1842), Michael Bakunin's seminal article, which has not yet been entirely translated into French.[42]

What the situationists take from Young Hegelianism is the fact that Marxist communism and individualistic and collectivist variants of anarchism both have their roots in an original confrontation with Hegelian thought. I will briefly study three Young Hegelian themes, reactivated, updated and sometimes 'twisted' by the situationists: the connections between theory and practice, the primacy of the negative moment in the dialectical process, and finally the theme of alienation. I do not claim, in doing so, to exhaust the philosophical content of situationist writings, or the meaning of their relation with Marx or Hegelian thought. I would just like to show how the situationist conception of the unity of revolutionary theory relates to the history of philosophy and therefore support the hypothesis of a specific situationist attempt to renew revolutionary thought beyond the separation between black and red from the common source of both currents.

Now, their conception of theory (and the postulation of its unity with a historical practice) is already the reactivation of a Young Hegelian theme. For example, when Debord characterises Hegel as 'the *philosophical* culmination of philosophy',[43] he reactivates a theme that can be found in three main figures of Young Hegelianism. First in Cieskowski for whom a thought of history, a philosophy of practice (the 'historiosophy'), has to go beyond the split between being and thought which characterises the old philosophy: Hegel's philosophy of history is a philosophy of the past, while historiosophy is a philosophy of the future which depends on a practice.[44] A similar conception can be found in *The Reaction in Germany*, Bakunin's first revolutionary writing: Hegel is claimed to have 'already gone above theory, but inside the theory itself' and to have 'postulated a new, practical world'[45] so that in Hegel, the theory itself, separated from the practice under the name of philosophy, finds its own limit. And last but not least, Marx's *Introduction* to the *Critique of Hegel's Philosophy of Right* (1843) explains that it is time to 'realise philosophy': the first task of philosophy was to criticise religion, 'the prerequisite of all criticism',[46] thus a critique of social alienation, leading to the ultimate 'transcendence of the proletariat', the 'dissolution of society as a particular estate'.[47] In the situationist theories, the aim of this postulated unity between theory and practice is to object to theoretical specialisation, which they saw as the germ of degeneration in Marxism, leading ultimately to authoritarian forms. This degeneration ends up in a relation of subordination between theory and practice, where, as I discussed above, the theory becomes unable to recognise the revolutionary form of organisation and ignores the rationality inherent in practice.[48]

Second, in Debord and in Vaneigem, the critical confrontation with Hegelian thought is re-performed by asserting the predominance of the negative in the dialectical process. Once again, the situationists take this theme from the Young Hegelians. Bakunin's article explains that the category of opposition, which is for him the centre of Hegelian philosophy, is 'a preponderance of the Negative' over the Positive[49]: the negative, identified as the party of the revolution, is what the positive, identified as the reaction, tries to reject from itself, so that the positive is only the negation of the negative, the negation of the destructive movement. The assertion of the preponderance of the negative is a central theme in Young Hegelianism, also found in Bruno Bauer.[50] For Bakunin however, it is important to recognise the positivity of the negative, that is to say the new world which is supposed to arise in the very process by which the old world perishes. In §114 of *The Society of the Spectacle*, Debord similarly identifies the revolutionary proletariat as the negative party[51] and at the same time, he asserts the primacy of the negative in the Hegelian dialectical process – and, as it is written in §206, the style of the dialectical theory has to express this primacy.[52] Similarly, in *The Revolution of Everyday Life*, Vaneigem explains that the negative has to become positive.[53] This theme was brilliantly illustrated in Bakunin's article with the famous sentence: 'The passion for destruction is a creative passion, too'.[54] This sentence is quoted (without any source reference) in the chapter which relates the situationists' contribution to the events of May and June 1968 in France,[55] as it was in Vaneigem's book.[56] This reading of the Hegelian dialectical process has a precise meaning in situationism: revolutionary theory, unitary theory, expresses the global rejection of the actual world, and a new world can be born only from the global negation of this world.

Like other Marxists of the 1960s (notably Herbert Marcuse), the situationists came to use the concept of alienation extensively. They owe this use to a particular reading of Marx's *Economic and Philosophical Manuscripts of 1844* as a seminal work which contains Marx's philosophy, which later developed throughout the rest of his writings. This reading is a reconstruction of Marxism based on a philosophy of alienation, in which the theme of commodity fetishism is central (in Debord particularly[57]). The theme of alienation is especially used in Vaneigem's book, without any mention of its Marxian or Hegelian origin. Actually, the concept of alienation is transformed by the situationists in two ways. In Marx, the concept of alienation, which translates two German words: *Entäußerung* – giving something up by alienating it – and *Entfremdung* – when the alienated object has become stranger, is the result of a transfer from the field of the critique of religion to the field of social and political critique.[58] Marx had read this transfer in Moses Hess's *On the Essence of Money*. In the same way that in Christianity (according to Feuerbach) human essence is alienated, so that humanity is unable to recognise what it is oppressed by, the human being in capitalist societies alienates its vital activity in money, which is another form of oppression.[59] In the situationist appropriation of this theme, the first transformation is a historicisation: in *The Revolution of Everyday Life*, Vaneigem explains that 'history is the continuous transformation of natural alienation into social alienation',[60] which would suggest that religious alienation is natural. The second transformation is a widening. In Marx's *Manuscripts*, alienation applies to the process of production: the worker becomes the machine's slave and is dispossessed of the fruit of his labours. Situationists expand this theme to the alienation of the consumer. Alienation is commodity alienation: it happens in commodity production (workers lose control of their labour and of the fruits of their labours) and also in commodity consumption, particularly in the spectacle as the ultimate commodity, according to Debord.[61] Spectacle is alienation in so far as 'the passive contemplation of images, which have moreover been chosen by someone else, substitutes for what is experienced and for the determination of the events by the individual itself'[62] and, eventually dominates the individual.

## Conclusion: The present relevance of a critique

Situationist critique is often reduced to its negative dimension and its attempt to go beyond outdated oppositions, such as black and red. This reduction gave the impression that situationist theories were radically new and radically separated from the history of the workers' movement. Yet, such a position bears little relation with situationist theories. While the pro-situs tended to consider that situationist theses as a spontaneous historical form, without antecedent, the aim of this chapter has been to link situationism back to its Hegelian roots, roots shared by both anarchists and Marxists. In other words, in denouncing the 'pro-situs'[63] in 1972 Debord objected to creating a new object of contemplation, and the last object of spectacular domination out of the SI. Preventing the dominated from remembering the history of their revolts is one of the most powerful effects of the society of the spectacle. For that very reason, it is important to recall that the situationists attempted to go beyond the opposition between black and red for the sake of a revolutionary theory whose unity had to be restored, integrating the social and historical experiment of the workers' councils and beyond the alienation of theory in bureaucratic economism. So this would be the situationist answer to Bismarck's anxiety about a possible reunification of black and red after the split of 1872: black is dead, red is dead, but the unification of both trends is still the manifestation of workers' democracy and, if we follow Bakunin's first words as a revolutionary, has to be kept 'at the top of the agenda of history'.[64]

What did the situationist attempt to repeat and extend the seminal moves of revolutionary thought from the 1840s bring to revolutionary movements of the 1960s? Basically, the reactivation of Young Hegelian themes provided a renewed theory of alienation which made possible the critique of both capitalist society and false oppositions to it. Capitalist society was from then on criticised not only as a society in which workers are exploited, but also as a society in which consumers are passive. The category of alienation enables us to criticise both aspects: workers are alienated in so far as they have no control over production, and consumers are alienated in so far as they are in a passive relation to the commodity. But the theme of alienation is also a weapon against representative conceptions of democracy or 'vanguardist' conceptions of revolution,[65] in which people are separated from their representation and are unable to act effectively. By showing that opposition to the capitalist system can also take alienated forms, the situationists pointed out that the realisation of a society without alienation begins in the very process of opposition to it.

Yet we cannot bury our head in the sand about certain limits of the situationist attempt to go beyond black and red. The first one concerns the question of the revolutionary organisation. Their theoretical criticism of Marxism and anarchism on this very question is as acute as one could wish. Nevertheless, their practical attempt to prefigure another kind of organization deserves in turn to be criticised in many respects. As Challand's chapter shows in this volume, like the group *SouB*, the *SI* had its own authoritarianisms. Debord explained the many expulsions that occurred in the history of the SI by reference to the need to keep the group small and thereby also forcing those excluded to be free on their own.[66] Nevertheless, there is also evidence that some of the exclusions can be explained by personal resentments.[67] And what kind of prefiguration can be implied by the almost exclusively male composition of the group, or the objective domination of the French section?

Moreover situationist concepts of unity and totality have to be questioned. There are very solid reasons to think that capitalist society has to be entirely rejected, and in that respect a unitary theory can be very useful, but a question remains: is there only one alternative to this society? Black and red today mean the multiplicity of real social alternatives, avoiding hierarchy and the rule of the commodity. In addition, we have to recognise which elements of our societies remain outside that rule, such as public services, which could be self-managed by the workers and users. These aspects of our society are a kind of collective inheritance which escaped partially from the rule of the commodity but always risks being caught up in it.

## Notes

1. For a critique of this view and another interpretation, see Jean-Christophe Angaut 'La fin des avant-gardes: les situationnistes et Mai 68', *Actuel Marx*, 41 (2009), pp. 149–161.
2. In the 1990s, several high quality books about the Situationist International were published and have corrected the picture of a merely artistic avant-garde. The first ones were Pascal Dumontier *Les Situationnistes et Mai 68 – Théorie et pratique*

*de la révolution* (Paris: Éditions Gérard Lebovici, 1990), Anselm Jappe *Guy Debord* (Paris: Denoël, 2001 – originally published in Italian, Pescara: Edisioni Tracce, 1992), Gianfranco Marinelli *L'amère victoire du situationnisme* (Arles: Gulliver, 1998) and Shigenobu Gonzalvez, *Guy Debord ou la beauté du négatif* (Paris: Nautilus, 2002). Among the numerous books published since then, Laurent Chollet *L'insurrection situationniste* (Paris: Dagorno, 2000), Fabien Danesi *Le Mythe brisé de l'Internationale Situationniste: l'aventure d'une avant-garde au coeur de la culture de masse (1945–2008)* (Dijon: Les Presses du Réel, 2008) and Patrick Marcolini, *Le mouvement situationniste: une histoire intellectuelle* (Montreuil: L'Échappée, 2012) must especially be mentioned.

3.  That does not mean, however, that the situationists should be considered as an artistic avant-garde that became purely political. It would be more correct to say that they refused the separation between art and politics. For a discussion of this point, see Chollet, *L'insurrection situationniste*, p. 84 and Danesi, *Le Mythe brisé*, pp. 21–29, 229–233, and for the implications of this double label over the concept of avant-garde used by the situationists, see below.

4.  Raoul Vaneigem *Traité de savoir-vivre à l'usage des jeunes générations* (Paris: Gallimard, 1992). The book (translated into English as *The Revolution of Everyday Life*) was actually written between 1963 and 1965 but was published only in 1967, the same year as Debord's book. English translations of both texts can be found on the Internet: www.marxists.org/reference/archive/debord/society.htm; http://library.nothingness.org/articles/SI/en/pub_contents/5.

5.  See René Riesel 'Préliminaires sur les conseils et l'organisation conseilliste', *Internationale Situationniste*, 12 (1969), in *Internationale Situationniste* (Paris: Fayard, 1997), pp. 632–641.

6.  In May 1968, several situationists, including Debord, had control of the occupation committee at the Sorbonne and in its name sent telegrams to such correspondents as the International Institute of Social History in Amsterdam or the politburo of the Communist Party of the Soviet Union. To the latter, they wrote this funny and insulting telegram: 'TREMBLE BUREAUCRATS STOP THE INTERNATIONAL POWER OF THE WORKERS COUNCILS WILL SOON SWEEP YOU AWAY STOP HUMANITY WILL BE HAPPY ONLY WHEN THE LAST BUREAUCRAT HAS BEEN HANGED WITH THE GUTS OF THE LAST CAPITALIST STOP LONG LIVE THE STRUGGLE OF THE KRONSTADT SAILORS AND OF THE MAKHNOVTCHINA AGAINST TROTSKY AND LENIN STOP LONG LIVE THE COUNCILIST INSURRECTION OF BUDAPEST IN 1956 STOP DOWN WITH THE STATE STOP LONG LIVE REVOLUTIONARY MARXISM STOP', in René Viénet, *Enragés et Situationnistes dans le mouvement des occupations* (Paris: Gallimard, 1968), p. 275. A similar telegram was sent to the Chinese Communist Party. Unless otherwise indicated, all translations are my own.

7.  See Guy Debord 'Le commencement d'une époque', *Internationale Situationniste*, 12 (1969), in Guy Debord *OEuvres* (Paris: Gallimard, 2004), pp. 917–963.

8.  In this paper, socialism is not intended as a particular trend beside syndicalism or communism but as a generic notion including both syndicalism and communism as particular socialist trends.

9.  Debord *OEuvres*, pp. 1104–1125. Debord's critique of the 'pro-situs' is the response to what he perceived as the transformation of the SI, after 1968, into a kind of collective star, a new object of contemplation, and therefore a new source of alienation.

10. Regarding Nanterre University in the pre-'68 period, see Jean-Pierre Duteuil *Nanterre 1965–66–67–68: Vers le Mouvement du 22 Mars* (Mauléon: Acratie, 1988).

11. The members of the *Noir et rouge* group (including future MEP Daniel Cohn-Bendit) had been expelled from the French Anarchist Federation in 1967 after accusations of Marxist conspiracy. The connections between the SI and the (mainly French) anarchist movement are thoroughly exposed in Miguel Amoros, *Les situationnistes et l'anarchie* (Villasavary: Éditions de la Roue, 2012).

12. ICO (*Informations et correspondances ouvrières*) was founded in 1958 by former members of 'Socialisme ou Barbarie' Claude Lefort and Henri Simon.

13. According to the situationists, Lefebvre had plagiarised one of their texts on the Paris Commune. See the 1963 tract 'Aux poubelles de l'histoire' in Debord *OEuvres*, pp. 624–634. But according to Lefebvre, the text was jointly written by him and several situationists who visited him at his home in the Pyrenees. See Henri Lefebvre 'On the Situationist International', Interview by Kristin Ross (1983), *October*, 79 (1997), pp. 77–78.

14. Viénet, *Enragés et situationnistes*, p. 18. Actually, that book was written by René Viénet, Guy Debord, Mustapha Kayati, Raoul Vaneigem and René Riesel.

15. Debord *OEuvres*, p. 803. And again in 1980, the text 'Aux libertaires' evokes 'the 1936 proletarian revolution, the greatest which ever began in history until today, and so the one which also best prefigures the future. The only organised force which had the will and the ability to prepare and to make the revolution, and to defend it – although with less lucidity and consistency – was the anarchist movement [ . . . ].' Ibid., p. 1515. Similarly, when they speak about black flags in the giant demonstration of May 13, 1968, the situationists refuse to see it as a sign of significant anarchist presence inside the demonstration: 'More than a hundred black flags were mixed with the many red flags, realising for the first time this junction of the two flags which was about to become the sign of the most radical trend inside the occupation movement, not as an affirmation of an autonomous anarchist presence, but as a sign of workers' democracy.' Viénet *Enragés et Situationnistes*, p. 73.

16. Vaneigem *Traité*, p. 100.

17. Ibid., p. 216. I rectify the current English translation which speaks about 'authoritarian positions' where the French original text says 'les attitudes autoritaires de Marx'.

18. One of the most famous is the editor of Marx's works in the prestigious collection 'Bibliothèque de la Pléiade', Maximilien Rubel. See Maximilien Rubel *Marx critique du marxisme* (Paris: Payot, 2000) in which one of the chapters is titled 'Marx, théoricien de l'anarchisme' ('Marx as anarchist theoretician').

19. Debord *OEuvres*, p. 797.

20. Ibid., p. 798.

21. Ibid., Italics in the original.

22. Karl Marx, *Manifeste du parti communiste* (Paris: Éditions Sociales, 1966), p. 67 (English translation from the Marxists Internet Archive website www.marxists. org/archive/marx/works/1848/communist-manifesto/ch02.htm).

23. Karl Marx, *La Guerre civile en France* (Paris: Éditions Sociales, 1968), p. 59 (English translation from the MIA website www.marxists.org/archive/marx/works/1871/civil-war-france/ch05.htm).

24. Debord *OEuvres*, p. 800. Italics in the original.

25. At the end of his life, in a letter to Jean-Pierre Baudet, published in Jean-François Martos, *Correspondance avec Guy Debord* (Paris: Le Fin Mot de l'Histoire, 1998), Debord recommended the reading of Robert Michels' famous critique of political parties. This letter of 18 December 1987 is part of the letters that are unavailable

248 Beyond Black and Red

because of the dispute between Debord's widow and Jean-François Martos. The latter had published his own correspondence with Debord in 1998, but the book was withdrawn from sale after Alice Debord was recognised as the sole claimant of Debord's work. In retaliation, Jean-Pierre Baudet opposed the publication of Debord's letters that were sent to him in the 'official' edition of his correspondence. That added another shortcoming to an edition which also omits all the letters sent *to* Debord.

26. Actually, Debord, Kotanyi and Vaneigem did praise the Paris Commune in a 1962 text ('Sur la Commune', republished in *Internationale Situationniste*), but as an historical experiment, and not as a political form.

27. Debord *Internationale Situationniste*, p. 641.

28. Actually, the book was signed by Debord and Gianfranco Sanguinetti, member of the Italian section of the Situationist International, in order to protest against the deportation of the latter from France by decision of the Minister of the Interior. An English translation of the *Theses* can be found on the Internet: www.notbored.org/theses-on-the-SI.html.

29. Debord *Œuvres*, pp. 1127–1128. Italics in the original.

30. Ibid., p. 801. Italics in the original.

31. See Guy Bodson *La F.A. et les Situationnistes – 1966–1967, ou mémoire pour discussion dans les familles après boire* (Paris: 1968) and Miguel Amoros, *Les situationnistes et l'anarchie*.

32. On the Italian Anarchist Federation, see Debord, *Œuvres*, pp. 1147–1456; about the Spanish CNT, see ibid., pp. 1514–1515.

33. Ibid., p. 794.

34. In the first affirmation of Left Hegelianism, *Phenomenology of the Spirit* is mentioned as the only Hegelian book that can be used for a Left interpretation of Hegelian thought. See David Friedrich Strauss, *Streitschriften zur Verteidigung meiner Schirft über das Leben Jesu und zur Charakteristik der gegenwärtigen Theologie* (Tübingen: 1838), p. 65. See also for English translation David Friedrich Strauss, *In Defense of My Life of Jesus Against the Hegelians*, Archon Books, 1983.

35. Debord *Œuvres*, p. 856. See also Georg Wilhelm Friedrich Hegel, *Phénoménologie de l'Esprit*, trans. Bernard Bourgeois (Paris: Vrin, 2006), p. 201, and Georg Wilhelm Friedrich Hegel, *Phenomenology of the Spirit*, trans. A.V. Miller (Oxford: Oxford University Press, 1979), p. 111.

36. The title of this book is a *détournement* from the title of the pamphlet written by Marx and Engels in the name of the General Council of the International after the Congress of The Hague in 1872 and the exclusion of Bakunin's friends: Karl Marx and Friedrich Engels *Les Prétendues Scissions dans l'Internationale* (Genève: Imprimerie Coopérative, 1872). English translation on the MIA website: www.Marxists.org/archive/Marx/works/1872/03/fictitious-splits.htm.

37. Debord *Œuvres*, p. 1087. See also Hegel, *Phénoménologie*, p. 490 and Hegel, *Phenomenology*, p. 350.

38. It is interesting to note that Bakunin, possibly remembering Hegel, used the same conception in 1870, during the war between France and Germany, when he thought that a civil war in France could propagate in Germany. See Michel Bakounine *Œuvres complètes*, vol. VII, 'La guerre franco-allemande et la révolution sociale en France (1870–1871)' (Paris: Champ Libre, 1979), pp. 59–60, and Jean-Christophe Angaut 'Marx, Bakounine et la guerre franco-allemande', *Sens public. Cosmopolitique* (2005), www.sens-public.org/article.php3?id_article=131.

39. Other ways of comparison are possible, especially from a sociological point of view. See the description of Young Hegelians as a literary bohemia and as an avant-garde in Wolfgang Essbach *Die Junghegelianer: Soziologie einer Intellektuellengruppe* (München: W. Fink, 1988).

40. See August von Cieszkowski *Prolégomènes à l'historiosophie* (Paris: Champ Libre, 1973). Partially translated in Lawrence S. Stepelevitch (ed.), *The Young Hegelians* (Cambridge: Cambridge University Press, 1983), pp. 57–90.

41. 'Présentation inédite des *Prolégomènes à l'historiosophie* d'August von Cieszkowski' [1983], in Debord, *Œuvres*, pp. 536–537.

42. Viénet *Enragés et Situationnistes*, p. 57 about the barricades night of 10–11 May 1968: 'the passion of destruction had never shown itself to be more creative' (a hidden quotation of the conclusion of Bakunin's article: 'the passion of destruction is also a creative passion'). See also Vaneigem *Traité de savoir-vivre*, p. 152 (Chapter XIII) about 'the pleasure of creating and the pleasure of destroying'.

43. Debord *Œuvres*, p. 793. Italics in the original.

44. August von Cieszkowski, *Prolégomènes*, p. 116 and Stepelevitch (ed.), *The Young Hegelians*, p. 77: 'Philosophy must descend from the height of theory to the plane of praxis. [...] To be [...] the development of *truth* in *concrete activity* – this is the future fate of philosophy in general.' (Italics in the original).

45. A French translation of Bakunin's article can be found in Jean-Christophe Angaut, *Bakounine jeune hégélien: la philosophie et son dehors* (Lyon, ENS Éditions, 2007), p. 123 for the quotation and pp. 91–95 for a commentary. See also Paul McLaughlin *Mikhail Bakunin; The Philosophical Basis of His Anarchism* (New York: Algora, 2002), pp. 21–61.

46. Karl Marx *Critique du droit politique hégélien*, trans. Albert Baraquin (Paris: Éditions Sociales, 1975), p. 197 (English translation from the MIA website www.marxists. org/archive/marx/works/1843/critique-hpr/intro.htm).

47. Marx *Critique du droit politique hégélien*, pp. 211–212.

48. Vaneigem *Traité*, p. 353.

49. Angaut *Bakounine jeune hégélien*, p. 125.

50. For a comparison of Bakunin's and Bauer's views on this point, see McLaughlin, *Mikhail Bakunin*, pp. 68–71.

51. Debord *Œuvres*, p. 816.

52. Ibid., p. 853.

53. Vaneigem *Traité*, pp. 266, 352.

54. Angaut *Bakounine jeune hégélien*, p. 136.

55. Viénet *Enragés et Situationnistes*, p. 57, about the 'night of the barricades' (May 10, 1968): 'Never had the passion of destruction been so creative.'

56. Vaneigem *Traité*, p. 152: '*People may be forced to swing back and forth across the narrow gap between the pleasure of creating and the pleasure of destroying, but this very oscillation suffices to bring Power to its knees.*' (Italics in the original).

57. See Jappe *Guy Debord*, pp. 29–31. It is more difficult to agree with Anselm Jappe when he asserts that situationists take a lot here from Lukács, who had indeed emphasised the concept of commodity fetishism in Marx's *Capital* but could not have been familiar with the 1844 *Manuscripts*, which were published later (first in Russian in 1927, then in German in 1932), after the publishing of *Geschichte und Klassenbewusstsein* (*History and Class Consciousness*, 1923). In Lukács, reification is more important than alienation.

58. About this transfer, see David Wittmann 'Les sources du concept d'aliénation', in Emmanuel Renault (ed.), *Lire les Manuscrits de 1844* (Paris: Presses Universitaires

de France, 2008), pp. 91–110 and Jean-Christophe Angaut 'Un Marx feuer-bachien?', in Renault (ed.), *Lire les Manuscrits de 1844*, pp. 51–70.

59. Significantly, Feuerbach is the first author quoted in *The Society of the Spectacle*.
60. Vaneigem *Traité*, p. 96.
61. About 'the alienation of the spectator to the profit of the contemplated object', see Debord *Œuvres*, p. 774
62. Jappe, *Guy Debord*, p. 21.
63. Debord *Œuvres*, pp. 1107–1125.
64. Angaut *Bakounine jeune hégélien*, p. 111
65. In a paper read at the Université du Québec à Montréal in June 2010 ('Les situationnistes et le concept d'avant-garde: art, politique et stratégie'), I tried to show what the differences were between Leninist and situationist conceptions of the avant-garde: basically, Lenin understands the avant-garde as a general staff and not as an advanced detachment. See http://halshs.archives-ouvertes.fr/docs/00/65/07/60/PDF/Les_situationnistes_entre_avant-garde_artistique_et_avant-garde_politique.pdf (last consultation: 06/27/2012).
66. See Debord's letter to Asger Jorn, August 23, 1962, in Guy Debord *Correspondance*, vol. II, 'Septembre 1960–Décembre 1964' (Paris: Fayard, 2001), pp. 93–94.
67. On the question of the exclusions, the best reference is Marinelli *L'amère victoire*. One can also find interesting self-criticism in Raoul Vaneigem, *Entre le deuil du vieux monde et la joie de vivre* (Paris: Verticales, 2008).

# 13

# Carnival and Class: Anarchism and Councilism in Australasia during the 1970s

*Toby Boraman*

Anarchism and 'councilism', a form of libertarian socialism that was influenced heavily by council communism, converged in Australasia during the 1970s. Many anarchists drew upon councilism in order to update anarchism. Councilists sought to rejuvenate socialism from below and to re-evaluate Marx. In so doing, they took an anarchistic turn. Overall, two loose anarchist/councilist tendencies emerged. The first was that of 'class-struggle anarchists' and councilists. The second was a bohemian, anti-work current represented by 'carnival anarchists' and situationist groupings influenced by the Situationist International (SI).

This chapter examines the perspectives these currents held on class. Both tendencies, following the councilist analysis of 'bureaucratic capitalism', asserted that the fundamental problem with society was the lack of control people had over their everyday lives. Consequently, they believed that the major division in society was between 'order-givers' and 'order-takers' rather than between the capitalist class and the working class. This analysis represented a shift away from seeing class exploitation as central to the everyday maintenance and reproduction of capital. As Greg George of the Brisbane Self-Management Group (SMG) suggested, it might be called a 'hierarchical analysis' based on power relationships of 'dominance/submission' rather than a 'class analysis' based on exploitative social relations derived from property.[1] Notwithstanding this convergent analysis, a lasting synthesis between anarchism and councilism did not develop in practice.

The tendencies' broader relationship with the multifarious forms of class struggle of the 1970s is also explored. This relationship shaped their tensions, attempts at co-operation and their praxis. Placing the small revolutionary groups studied in this piece in their wider context is important because it shows how they were influenced (or not) by this context and offers a yardstick by which their relevance and effectiveness can roughly be judged. The councilist/class-struggle anarchist tendency attempted to relate to working-class revolts in the workplace and community against capitalist, state, union and leftist bureaucracies. In contrast, carnivalists and followers of the SI (or 'situs') generally attempted to relate imaginatively to working-class resistance by disaffected sub-cultural youth, 'delinquents' and the unwaged.

This chapter presents a case study of the relationship between anarchism and councilism in Australasia during the 1970s, outlining their attempts at co-operation and their clashes. It is based on extensive research, including many interviews, into this milieu in New Zealand,[2] and on a preliminary and incomplete investigation into the corresponding milieu in Australia. Furthermore, this piece aims to shed some light on little-known anarchist and libertarian socialist movements, as Anglophone studies of anarchism and unorthodox Marxism tend to neglect movements outside the UK, France and the USA. While much has been written about Solidarity in the UK and particularly Socialisme ou Barbarie (SouB) in France, nothing has been published about their Australian counterpart, the Brisbane SMG, even though the SMG had a comparable or probably larger membership than both.[3]

## International context and definitions

While endeavouring to develop their own praxis, Australasian anarchists and councilists often took their main inspiration from movements in other 'advanced' capitalist countries, especially from the UK, France, the USA and the Netherlands. Given this level of influence, what occurred in Australasia cannot be dismissed as peculiarly Antipodean. To some extent this research offers a picture in microcosm of developments elsewhere. It is therefore important to outline the international context in which these currents arose. This shall be done briefly while defining councilism, class-struggle anarchism and carnival anarchism.

The coalescence between councilism and anarchism was shaped by two major developments in the class struggle. First, workers' councils appeared during the Hungarian revolution of 1956, which created a surge of interest in council communism and anarchism among New Leftists searching for an anti-bureaucratic alternative to Stalinism and social democracy.

Second, the explosive global events of 1968, and particularly the massive revolt in France, sparked an astonishingly broad upturn in class struggle until about the mid-1970s. Broadly speaking, workers took direct action, sometimes outside official organisational forms (union or party), to press their demands. This revolt was mutually interlinked with a wider community-based struggle against other forms of social control in society – such as patriarchy, racism and sex roles, for instance – and in particular, mass opposition to the Vietnam War. As direct action in the community and workplace became commonplace, many non-Leninist revolutionary groupings emerged which were influenced loosely by a melange of left communism, situationism, council communism and anarchism.[4]

Defining councilism requires an outline of its Marxist antecedent, council communism. Marcel van der Linden defines council communism, which arose during the German revolution following the First World War, as aiming for the abolition of capitalism through workers establishing 'a democracy of workers' councils'. To create these councils, the capitalist class was not the only group that had to be 'consistently resisted'. Parliamentary 'democracy', unions, social democratic parties and Bolshevik parties needed to be treated similarly, as they were viewed as organs that manipulated the working class and promoted capitalism.[5] Philippe Bourrinet adds that council communists opposed nationalism and cross-class popular fronts, and rejected 'substitutionism, which sees the communist party as the general staff and the proletariat as a passive mass blindly submitting to the orders of this general staff'.[6]

In the 1940s and 1950s, several Western European groups emerged which drew upon the legacy of council communism. Those with most influence in Australasia were Solidarity, SouB and the SI. Bourrinet maintains that Solidarity, SouB and other similar groups represented a new 'councilist' tendency that was largely distinct from the historic council communist movement.[7]

Councilists diverged from council communism predominantly due to their innovative attempt to transcend Marxism for the changed material conditions of the postwar era. As explored below, they believed that class struggle had taken a new form: the struggle of 'order-takers' against bureaucratic 'order-givers'. In this vein, the term 'councilism' is used in this chapter to distinguish it from council communism. Bourrinet also believes, when compared with council communism, the broader councilist milieu of the post-1968 era lacked coherent theoretical positions, was organisationally loose and ephemeral, and was theoretically eclectic, as they often borrowed from anarchism.[8] Yet unlike Bourrinet, the term councilism is not employed to imply an anarchist degeneration of council communism, nor theoretical or organisational looseness. Nor is it meant to suggest councilists deviated from council communism completely. Indeed, they accepted most of its core assumptions noted above.[9]

The SI can perhaps be considered part of this broad councilist current. While the SI began as an artistic movement, by the early 1960s it had adopted the fundamentals of councilist praxis.[10] For instance, as Challand shows in this volume, the SI redefined the proletariat as those who had no power over their lives, and understood revolution as a process through which it regained this control. However, the SI was influenced by an eclectic mixture of traditions, such as Western Marxism and radical artistic currents. With its analysis of commodity fetishism, it was more Marxist than SouB and Solidarity.

When anarchism revived in the 1960s and 1970s, it took many different forms. This chapter focuses upon the two main types that drew upon councilism. The first was 'class-struggle anarchism', a term that was beginning to be used in the 1970s to denote anarchists who rejected liberal and individualist anarchism. The term encompasses forms of anarchism – especially anarchist communism and anarcho-syndicalism – that place emphasis on the centrality of class struggle for the revolutionary overthrow of capitalism, hierarchy and the state.[11] This renewal of class-struggle anarchism has been mostly overlooked, yet as Nicolas Walter has noted 'most of the new anarchist organisations formed during and after the revival of the 1960s have been of a traditional kind.'[12] By traditional, he meant anarchist communist or anarcho-syndicalist.

Nonetheless, this revival was far from traditional. Many of the new class-struggle anarchists drew eclectically from Marxism and especially from councilism to the dismay of traditional anarchists, many of whom simplistically equated all forms of Marxism with Stalinism. In France, councilism was highly influential. Daniel Cohn-Bendit, for instance, declared that he was an 'anarchist...along the lines of "council socialism"'.[13] Noir et Rouge, which included Cohn-Bendit, stated in 1968 that:

> The real cleavage is not between 'Marxism' or what is described as such, and anarchism, but rather between the libertarian spirit and idea, and the Leninist, Bolshevik, bureaucratic conception of organization... We feel closer to 'Marxists' in the Council Communist movement of the past...than we do to official 'anarchists' who have a semi-Leninist conception of party organization.[14]

The other type of anarchism that drew upon councilism was carnival anarchism. During the 1960s, the Dutch groups the Provos and Kabouters helped to popularise carnival anarchism globally.[15] Carnival anarchism was both a distinctive style and type of anarchism. It aimed to combine the cultural revolution with a socio-economic one, and synthesise personal transformation with collective transformation. Theoretically and organisationally, it valued eclecticism, creativity, informality and spontaneity. Carnivalists were provocative tactically, mixing absurdist humour with direct action. In brief, they wanted revolution and fun too. The term 'carnival anarchist' was first used in Australia. There 'serious anarchists' employed it largely as a derogatory term during the 1970s, but in this chapter it is not used to suggest that carnivalists were frivolous, disruptive 'chaoticists'.[16] Today, the current is represented – albeit in a modified form – by groups such as the French insurrectionists Tiqqun and the Invisible Committee, and CrimethInc in the USA.[17]

# The Australasian context

In the 1950s and 1960s, most working-class Australians and New Zealanders experienced rising living standards, full employment and widespread 'affluence' (although most indigenous people were still trapped in deprivation). In both countries, from about 1968, this Keynesian class compromise began to break down largely due to an upsurge in proletarian dissent. The percentage of the workforce participating in strike activity rose dramatically in the late 1960s, peaking in about the mid-1970s in Australia and during the late 1970s in New Zealand.[18]

However, this militancy was confined to a minority. During the 1970s, an average of 16.5 per cent of the New Zealand workforce went on strike.[19] The Australian working-class was much more combative than its New Zealand counterpart.[20] Yet in neither country did this upsurge reach the radical proportions of France 1968, Italy 1969, nor Britain 1974 when miners helped to bring down a government.

This workplace rebellion was interlinked with the 'protest movement', which peaked in the late 1960s and early 1970s. The Vietnam War was a significant issue in Australasia, as both New Zealand and Australian troops fought in Vietnam, and conscription was introduced in Australia. The unwaged, such as students, played an important part in the protest movement. Furthermore, that movement contributed to the emergence of a broader youth rebellion, which concurrently helped to create the counterculture. Protest began to dissipate because of the election of mildly reforming social democratic governments during the early 1970s in both countries.

These workplace and community revolts seemingly challenged almost every form of authority in society. This upheaval also had an anti-bureaucratic aspect: many people pushed for greater control over their workplaces, educational institutions and communities, thus challenging the unprecedented growth of corporate and state – and sometimes union – bureaucracies that had occurred under the postwar Keynesian class compromise.

From the early to mid-1970s, economic decline set in. Living standards fell, mass unemployment arrived, and while workplace rebellion continued, it became more defensive in nature.[21] Yet women's liberation, anti-apartheid, anti-racist, indigenous and ecology movements blossomed in both countries. During the late 1970s in Aotearoa/New Zealand, many Maori occupied land to protest against the ongoing alienation from the little of it that remained in their possession.

Belligerent governments attempted to counteract this generalised revolt, such as Joh Bjelke-Petersen's state government in Queensland, Australia, and Robert Muldoon's government in New Zealand. Both governments curtailed many civil liberties, were confrontational towards dissenters and increased police power. Bjelke-Petersen even banned street marches in 1977.

The Australasian left throughout this time was dominated by mass social democratic parties and unions. While militant workers, the New Left and various social movements challenged this orthodoxy, their contestation was gradually recuperated. In both countries, revolutionaries were few if not minuscule in number relative to overseas. Of these, Leninist parties were dominant. Anarchists and councilists had less impact, apart from in a few cities where Leninists had not gained ascendency, such as Brisbane. They were often starting from scratch, particularly in New Zealand, which lacked both a continuous and notable anarchist tradition, and a council communist current whatsoever. The much smaller New Zealand anarchist and councilist milieu developed close links with its Australian counterpart, hence developments in New Zealand often closely mirrored those in Australia.

## Class-struggle anarchist and councilist groups

This section examines the relevant views of three Australasian groups – the Christchurch Anarchy Group (CAG), the Brisbane Self-Management Group (SMG) and the Auckland-based Revolutionary Committee – to illustrate the relationship between class-struggle anarchists and councilists, and to appraise these organisations' relationship with, and perspectives on, class.

Solidarity – and thus SouB, from whom Solidarity took much of its inspiration – exerted a significant influence upon the 1970s New Zealand anarchist milieu. While no specifically anarcho-syndicalist or anarchist communist groups were established, numerous anarchist groupings drew heavily from Solidarity. These included CAG, the People's Revolutionary Movement (Wellington), Solidarity (Auckland), the anarchist wing of the anarcho-situationist magazine *KAT* (Wellington) and *Anarchy* magazine (Christchurch). All of these groups were tiny in size, with most numbering half a dozen members.

In Australia, an anarcho-syndicalist current was established that concentrated on restarting the Industrial Workers of the World from 1975, as well as building small anarcho-syndicalist propaganda groups. Even then, many anarchist organisations were also influenced by Solidarity, as can clearly be seen in the Melbourne publication *Solidarity*.

CAG's relationship with councilism demonstrates well the crossover between anarchism and councilism that transpired in the 1970s. CAG, which existed from 1975 to c.1978, identified with Solidarity to such an extent that they believed Solidarity was, for all intents and purposes, anarchist. CAG defined anarchism as centrally involving workers' councils:

Anarchists propose a society based upon local and industrial peoples assemblies, federating with elected and revocable delegates in workers councils. History shows that such workers councils are developed by everyday people whenever they seek to take control of their life in revolution...It is because our daily lives are increasingly unliveable that we must collectively take control of them.[22]

Anarchism meant a dual 'struggle against the state and for self-management'.[23] They claimed that Solidarity referred to themselves as 'libertarian socialists' rather than 'anarchists' only because:

> They do not wish to become identified with the more 'individualistic' faction of the anarchist movement. Solidarity do work closely with anar-chist groups in Britain with whom they share a common theory and basis for action. Solidarity have had a considerable influence on the anarchist movement in Britain.[24]

This overlooked Solidarity's critical attitude towards anarchism, including class-struggle anarchists such as Kropotkin and Bakunin.[25] As with many anarchists, CAG assumed councilism was anarchist rather than engaging critically with it. For example, Richard Bolstad of CAG, in a pamphlet which summarised Cornelius Castoriadis' *Workers' Councils and the Economics of a Self-Managed Society*, presumed that Castoriadis' 'central assembly of delegates' which would run a future socialist society was anarchist in nature. He did not question whether such a proposal centralised too much power in a relatively small body.[26]

Solidarity made such an impression on CAG for numerous reasons. Solidarity publications, like those of the SI, seemed fresh and innovative. Solidarity published an impressive series of up-to-date and easy-to-read pamphlets, including histories which uncovered little-known episodes of workers' self-management. Their focus upon workers' self-organisation, rather than the activities of party or union bureaucrats, seemed validated by the uprisings of the time, such as Hungary (1956), France (1968), Czechoslovakia (1968) and Portugal (1974–1975). In contrast, class-struggle anarchism seemed stuck in the past, constantly reliving the defeat of the Spanish revolution of 1936–1937. Class-struggle anarchist literature at the time consisted predominantly of either tired reprints of classics, or restatements of basic principles.

Solidarity and SouB's anti-bureaucratic analysis of postwar 'advanced' capitalist society appealed to CAG because of its anarchistic nature. Castoriadis, perhaps the main theoretician of SouB, contended that society had become dominated by a complex pyramid-like hierarchical structure, one that affected all aspects of social life. People had become manipulated by bureaucrats at work, in consumption and in everyday life. The working class had become thoroughly alienated from any control over their lives. Yet they did not passively accept this. Class struggle had taken a new tendency: proletarians were attempting to assert some form of control over their daily lives, inside and outside the workplace.[27] Hence, to SouB and Solidarity, socialism meant the full realisation of *autogestion* throughout society via workers' councils. Both groups argued that working-class self-organisation constantly transformed capital, and that this autonomy was the basis for social revolution.

Bolstad was also drawn to Solidarity because of its well-thought-out proposals for a future society based on a network of workers' councils. He compared his involvement in the carnivalesque New Left group the Christchurch Progressive Youth Movement (PYM) during the early 1970s with his later involvement in CAG. In the PYM, it felt like 'revolution is around the corner', while CAG was 'more thought-out, more planned and focused upon how to build up support and links' based on what he perceived to be Solidarity's model of a revolutionary organisation that shared people's experiences and established mutual trust.[28]

Another reason why CAG was attracted to Solidarity was because of Solidarity's trenchant critique of the traditional left, especially Leninism. Solidarity lambasted Leninist parties for being rigidly hierarchical and bureaucratic, and acting on behalf of the working class, instead of encouraging working-class self-emancipation.[29] This critique resonated with CAG because much of the Christchurch PYM shifted from anarchism to non-party Maoism in the early 1970s.[30] Those PYMers were attracted to 'direct action Maoism' because they believed that China was a near paradise where no class divisions or state bureaucracy existed. CAG expended much energy criticising this viewpoint, criticism which drew from a Solidarity pamphlet by Council Communist Cajo Brendel.[31]

In the early 1970s, two councilist groups strongly influenced by Solidarity and SouB emerged in Australasia. One was the Brisbane Self-Management Group (1971–1977). The other was the awkwardly named 'Revolutionary Committee of the CPNZ (Expelled)' (1968–c.1974), which was based in Auckland. Examining the two groups, who were in correspondence with each other, makes for an interesting contrast.

Both organisations emerged from conflict with Leninists, and hence placed paramount importance on rejecting vanguardism. Indeed, the Revolutionary Committee was formed after it was expelled from the Maoist Communist Party of New Zealand (CPNZ), for opposing the CPNZ's lack of internal freedom and its participation in elections.[32] The SMG originated from the campus-based Brisbane New Left. Specifically, it emanated from the short-lived Revolutionary Socialist Party (RSP), a party which also contained a Trotskyist tendency. After the Trotskyists departed from the RSP, it was renamed the SMG.[33]

The SMG, which called itself 'libertarian socialist' and sometimes 'libertarian communist' in orientation,[34] was the largest and most influential councilist or anarchist organisation in Australasia during the 1970s. It grew during a period of sharp decline in Brisbane street protest. Estimates of its size vary from less than 100 to 300 people involved in its cells, with a smaller core membership that attended general assemblies of somewhere between

30 and 70.[35] It had a mixed base of workers and students. It formed struggle-based cells where members lived, worked or studied, such as in high schools, universities and workplaces. These cells were formal sub-groups which then reported back to the SMG's monthly general assembly. The SMG was activist in orientation: it has been claimed that the SMG 'led Brisbane's marches' against the Vietnam War, apartheid and the repressive measures imposed by the Bjelke-Petersen government.[36] The SMG involved many prominent and capable activists, such as Drew Hutton and especially Brian Laver. It agitated, with limited success, for struggles to be controlled by open assemblies.

In contrast, the Revolutionary Committee was a tiny non-student-based discussion group. They claimed 'our expulsion from the C.P.N.Z. and our "splendid isolation" has its obverse side in that we have had unrestricted freedom to think and draw conclusions'.[37] Subsequently, they mostly focused upon discussing theory and producing their magazine *Compass*.

However, the SMG was not anti-intellectual, and the Revolutionary Committee were not armchair revolutionaries. The former prolifically produced material (mainly leaflets, but also a few pamphlets) and operated their own printshop and bookshop (the Red and Black Bookshop); and members of the latter went on a hunger strike against the Vietnam War in a central city park.

The Revolutionary Committee distanced itself from the anarchist milieu. Indeed, Steve Taylor of the Committee wrote that he had 'no affiliation express or implicit' with anarchism.[38] In contrast, after initially being hostile to anarchism on much the same grounds as Solidarity, the SMG developed contacts with local anarchists, and attempted to co-operate with them. SMG delegates attended a few Australian anarchist conferences in an effort to seek revolutionary allies, but soon they stopped participating in these gatherings after they found them fraught with internal contradictions, and after they clashed with carnival anarchists (see below). Greg George of the SMG said that they generally found anarchism more attractive in theory than in practice because the Australian anarchists seemed disorganised.[39]

The SMG was drawn to certain aspects of anarchism because they thought they complemented councilism. In a pamphlet, George dismissed orthodox Marxist objections to anarchism. Instead, he praised anarchism for being practical and relevant to society:

> It offers complexity and variety rather than bureaucratic narrowness... it offers self-activity, initiative and autonomy balanced by co-operation and responsibility, it offers real democracy and an end to alienation, it offers... equality between specialists and experts and others, and it offers equal sharing of our riches.[40]

As the SMG looked towards working-class rebellions involving self-management as their historical legacy, they were especially attracted to anarchism because they viewed the Spanish revolution and the Makhnovist uprising as significant examples of self-management in action.[41]

Yet they were not uncritical of anarchism. For example, George criticised individualist anarchism because he argued it was terrorist and elitist; anarchist communism because it fetishised the spontaneous, insurrectionary creativity of the working class; and anarcho-syndicalism because it was bureaucratic, vanguardist and overlooked the council form. Overall, he viewed anarchism as inadequate and in need of being superseded by council communism.[42]

Anarchist influence on the SMG became more pronounced by the mid-1970s, and some members began to identify with anarchism. This development can be seen in several of its offshoots. In 1977, the SMG split into the Libertarian Socialist Organisation (LSO), the Self-Management Organisation (SMO) and the 'Marxist tendency' (many of whom joined the Trotskyist International Socialists). The first two groups, which were by far the largest, viewed anarchism positively. The SMO was explicitly anarchist, while the LSO was sympathetic to anarchism. The latter published *You Can't Blow up a Social Relationship: The Anarchist Case Against Terrorism* with several other Australian libertarian socialist or anarchist groups.[43] The pamphlet was a revised version of an earlier article written by George for the SMG's publication *Libertarian*.[44] It became an internationally recognised, perhaps classic, publication after it was republished by many anarchist groups outside Australia. When Joe Toscano of the SMG moved to Melbourne in about 1976, he helped found the councilist group the Libertarian Workers for a Self-Managed Society. Yet by 1978 that group had become anarchist in orientation under the influence of local anarchists. Toscano was drawn to anarchism because he considered it a more diverse, vibrant current with a richer history than councilism, which he contended had been formed only since 1968.[45]

## Relationship with and perspectives on class

In the UK, Solidarity formed a network of militant workers, developed many contacts in the shop stewards' movement and had some influence in important disputes. In contrast, the New Zealand councilist-influenced milieu did not seemingly participate in, or support, workplace struggles. For instance, instead of building a workers' network, CAG attempted to build a nationwide *anarchist* network, and as such their newsletter did not contain any items about domestic workplace disputes. Instead, it contained mainly news stories about anarchist groups abroad.

Of all the Solidarity-influenced groupings in New Zealand, only Solidarity (Auckland) became involved in workplace-based struggles, and even then its involvement was minimal. For example, its contribution to the Auckland ferry dispute of 1974, a significant workplace conflict which threatened briefly to mushroom into a nationwide wildcat general strike, was to distribute a leaflet at a union meeting.

In comparison, the SMG gained considerable influence in several workplaces. It tapped into the loose rank-and-file network that already existed within many Brisbane unions, and many militants joined the SMG. Part of the SMG's appeal was their robust criticism of union bureaucrats, which they nicknamed 'TUBs' (Trade Union Bureaucrats). The SMG had many active industry-based cells, such as its health-care, teachers, white-collar and industrial cells. The industrial cell contained workers at Cairncross Dock and the Evans Deakin shipyards, among other worksites. At the shipyards, the SMG had a substantial presence that took part in numerous go-slows and strikes. The university cell participated heavily in a large-scale strike at the University of Queensland in 1971. The health-care cell contained workers at several worksites in both the public and private sectors. It did not act within unions or professional associations because it believed, like the rest of the SMG, that these organisations were undemocratic, bureaucratic and capitalist.[46]

The SMG's workplace strategy had its limitations, however. It was often based around propagandising the abstract idea of workers' self-management, idealistically presenting that idea as a panacea for all situations.[47] They seemingly spent more energy on mass leafleting this ideal than attempting to build solidarity and self-organisation within and across workplaces.

Importantly, the SMG – like other councilists – developed a broader view of class than orthodox Marxists. Workers without any real power in 'industrial, agricultural, white-collar, service (including housewives) and intellectual labour' were considered part of the proletariat.[48] Furthermore, George argued that most people worked in non-industrial workplaces.[49] As such, the SMG placed emphasis on agitating within white-collar workplaces, and distributed well-received propaganda criticising the boredom and alienation of office work. They saw libertarian socialism as a many-sided struggle to change not only work, but also everyday life. The SMG adopted Solidarity's manifesto 'As We See It' wherein it was stated that socialism meant 'a radical transformation in all human relations'.[50] Hence they pushed for increasing the 'quality of life' by overcoming sexism and racism, experimenting with communal living, creating a 'broader cultural life', advocating the decentralisation of cities, preventing ecological destruction and espousing equal wages for all (including wages for those performing domestic work, and the unwaged in general).[51] The Revolutionary Committee likewise advocated wages for housework.[52]

However, councilists questionably asserted that the chief problem with capitalism was the way it was managed. Controversially, they believed that the fundamental contradiction in society was between order-givers and order-takers. Subsequently, class was anarchistically seen as being produced by social relations of authority or hierarchy, rather than the more classical socialist view that class derives from social relations of exploita-tion.[53] Councilists viewed capitalists as bosses whose main task was to order workers around – they maintained the chief problem with capitalists was their control of the workplace. This is problematic because it overlooks how the ownership of property and resultant extraction of surplus value from labour creates exploitative social relations. Workplace authority and management are necessary products of class exploitation in order to mon-itor, speed-up and control workers, rather than being the cause of this exploitation.

Gilles Dauvé and François Martin argue that 'Socialism is not the man-agement, however "democratic" it may be, of capital, but its complete destruction'.[54] Workers could run their workplaces themselves, and yet be forced to compete with other worker-owned enterprises via the market, thus forcing these enterprises to lessen costs (such as by firing workers or reducing wages) and to make workers work harder in order to stay competitive, even if all workers were paid the same wage and had equal decision-making power. Consequently, fundamentally transforming the decision-making processes of society is not enough in itself; private property, the market and the wage system also need to be abolished.

Several other difficulties with the councilists' conception of class can be noted. As was argued in an Australian anarchist magazine, their class anal-ysis was unwieldy since many if not most workers were on some level both order-takers and order-givers.[55] Moreover, self-management as an aim tends to appeal to a minority of workers: that of skilled technical workers who desire control over the production process, an aim that is generally not shared by Taylorised assembly-line workers nor casualised workers.[56]

The danger of self-managed exploitation was not recognised by Australasian councilists or anarchists.[57] Nor did everyone accept this refor-mulation of class. For instance, Steve Taylor of the Revolutionary Committee retained a Marxist definition of the proletariat as those 'dependent for its support on the sale of its labour', while at the same time redefining it as 'resting squarely' on unpaid domestic labour performed mainly by women.[58]

## Bohemian councilism and carnival anarchism

This section presents a brief overview of the stormy relationship between situationist-influenced individuals and anarchists, especially the carnival anarchists. It then examines the 'situ' and carnivalist relationship with (or lack of relationship with) the broader class struggle, and their perspectives on class.

As the works of the SI became readily available in English during the early-mid 1970s, many revolutionaries were attracted to their ideas. A few formed 'situ' groups. In Australia, one such situationist grouping was founded in Perth and then migrated to Sydney. It produced many leaflets under different names. One such leaflet was their 'vandal's license', which was published under the name of the 'Free Association of Australasian Shoplifters and the Disturbed Citizens for the Redistribution of Punishment'. It read:

IS THIS REALLY LIVING? ...

Are you tired of work, consume, be silent, die?

WE ARE!

The DISTURBED CITIZENS for the REDISTRIBUTION of PUNISHMENT is combating the futility of everyday life; by mounting a campaign to promote VANDALISM ...

*Break up* the barriers that separate your desires from reality

To learn how to build; first we must learn how to *destroy*

Ever noticed how your good intentions seemed to be *smashed* on the reef of workaday routine?

Why not start the day off by *hurling* your clock through your TV set

Then begin a festival of *looting, burning* and *busting up* the boredom!

Imagine your local shopping centre, workplace, home ... in *ruins*!

Can you think of a better way to spend the day?[59]

This leaflet encapsulated the wishful insurrectionary immediatism of 'situ' groups and the carnival anarchists they influenced. In New Zealand, no situationist group was formed, despite the attempts of Grant McDonagh. Instead, McDonagh operated as an individual on the periphery of the anarchist milieu, co-operating with anarchists to publish several magazines, such as *Anarchy* and *KAT*. The latter called itself 'an anti-authoritarian spasmodical' of the 'libertarian ultra-left (situationists, anarchists and libertarian socialists)'.[60] McDonagh argued that the situationist current was 'only a minority current in the broader Anarchist milieu between 1975 and 1979, but potent in that context and beyond'.[61] Undoubtedly this tendency had much impact on the anarchist milieu, but it was not 'potent', as many anarchists found situationist writing impenetrable.[62]

McDonagh was originally an anarchist, yet soon became a situationist. However, he viewed the SI as part of the broad anti-authoritarian left.[63] He believed that the 'Situationists attempted more successfully than anyone else to supersede the split first occurring in the 1st International between the Marxists and the Bakuninists, by reinventing revolution itself, with results well known in the [French] occupation movement of May and June '68'.[64] Indeed, he thought that the SI was more anti-authoritarian than the vast majority of anarchists, and maintained that the SI had criticised authoritarian forms of Marxism far more effectively and coherently than anarchists had.[65]

In practice, instead of overcoming the rigid division between anarchism and Marxism, bitter clashes occurred between anarchists and McDonagh. McDonagh critiqued the anarchist milieu for lacking radical and intellectual content, for an 'anaemic' opportunistic involvement in various protest movements, and for being authoritarian. Anarchist ideology, he argued, causes anarchists 'to deal with power by choosing to believe that he/she is somehow immune to it. Perhaps by the magical talismanic qualities of the mere word anarchy'.[66] He dismissed attendees to the 1978 anarchist 'unconvention' as 'corpses, hacks, closet authoritarians, masochists, intellectual midgets & retarded reformists'.[67]

Anarchists reciprocated with their own criticisms. For example, Andrew Dodsworth, who was involved in *KAT*, thought that McDonagh's politics were incomprehensible to working-class people. Likewise, anarchists overseas commonly viewed the SI and its followers as hopelessly sectarian, dogmatic and hierarchical. For example, Franklin Rosemont of the Chicago-based anarchist publication *The Rebel Worker* castigated US 'situ' groups not only along these lines, but also for having 'full time non-involvement in real struggle'.[68]

Hence the tension between 'situs' and anarchists resulted from anarchists dismissing 'situs' for being too intellectual and isolated, and 'situs' scolding anarchists for indulging in an easily co-optable mindless activism. Despite these clashes, of all the tendencies within anarchism, the SI and their followers exerted most influence over the carnival anarchists (who, interestingly enough, were very much activists).

Numerous carnival anarchist groupings were formed in Australasia. In New Zealand, they included the Auckland Anarchist Activists (AAA), the *Lumpen* grouping in Auckland and the Dunedin Anarchist Army. In Melbourne, according to Toscano, they included the Working People's Association (which produced the paper *Dingo*) and the Collingwood Freestore (members of whom had earlier produced the magazine *Solidarity*).[69] In Sydney, they included the Sydney Anarchist Group (members of whom produced *Rising Free* and *The Plague*), Fruity Together, Bondi Vandals and the Panic Merchants. Frequently, the name of their group would change with each new action they took. Most of these groups had a loose membership of half a dozen to a dozen people, with a much larger social group occasionally participating in their activities.

The carnival anarchists drew eclectically from many different tendencies, including councilism. For example, Peter McGregor, a central figure in the Sydney carnival anarchist scene, noted that he was influenced by SouB, Solidarity and the SMG.[70] McGregor helped found the Sydney Anarchist Group (SAG) in about 1974 largely based on the SMG's platform. As a result, SAG reprinted articles by Carl Boggs and Situationist René Riesel on workers' councils.[71] Likewise, the AAA, the major carnival anarchist grouping in New Zealand, defined anarchism as a 'real socialist society built from below. Built by working people who are directly involved, through workers councils, in making the decisions which affect their lives'.[72]

Carnivalists were drawn to situationist praxis, including rejecting work and everyday boredom, and emphasising the festival-like nature of riots and revolutions. This was because they generally saw the SI's ideas as complementing and bolstering their attempts to fuse art with politics, and to fuse the counterculture with the revolutionary project.

Accordingly, they were more attracted to the SI's 'radical subjectivist' wing represented poetically by Raoul Vaneigem, rather than the SI's 'objectivist' wing represented by Guy Debord, whose writing was more analytical and Marxist. For example, Terry Leahy, an Australian carnivalist, stressed Vaneigem's idea that revolution begins from everyday life by people fulfilling their own desires, rejecting rigid roles and playing games. Leahy wrote 'spontaneous creativity and the sense of festivity are the keys to revolutionary practice'.[73]

In this Vaneigemist vein, carnivalists such as McGregor attempted to live a creative lifestyle free from self-sacrifice by refusing to reproduce capital in everyday life:

> In the purist spirit of Charles Fourier's *Some Advice Concerning the Next Social Metamorphosis*: 'Never sacrifice a present good to a future good. Enjoy the moment; don't get into anything which doesn't satisfy your passions right away.' ... So, since property was theft, why not squat; and since work was wage-slavery, then don't.[74]

McGregor saw interpersonal relations as the primary site of politics, rather than self-sacrificing activism for an *external* cause.

Jean Barrot (Dauvé) perceptively argues that these Vaneigemist lifestyles *'cannot be lived'*. He continues: 'either one huddles in the crevices of bourgeois society, or one ceaselessly opposes to it a different life which is impotent because only the revolution can make it a reality'.[75] The carnivalists did not overcome this dilemma. Overall, the carnivalists' borrowing from the SI was haphazard. Often they were more attracted to the aggressive style of the SI rather than its substance. They frequently reduced situationist ideas to slogans such as 'everyday life has been reduced to a commodity'.[76] What ultimately mattered to carnivalists was not careful analysis, or theoretical exposition, but what you were *doing* in the here and now.

### Relationship with and perspectives on class

'Situs' like McDonagh unambiguously promoted working-class resistance. Yet McDonagh took signs of proletarian dissent to signify the possibility of the *immediate* revolutionary establishment of the 'total democracy' of workers' councils.[77] For example, in a leaflet criticising a 'cover-up' by Prime Minister Muldoon, McDonagh wildly asserted that the proletariat would, in response, unleash a 'fury' only hinted at in previous struggles and storm the palace.[78] Further, 'None…can stomach Bosses or cops anymore. The fragmentary radicalism and the moments of poetry it stumbled hesitantly towards in 1978 must in '79 fuse into an insatiable lust for the totality if we are to gain everything.'[79] Unsurprisingly, this 'lust for the totality' never materialised – although in 1979 a one-day general strike involving about one-third of the workforce occurred. This was the first genuinely nationwide general strike in New Zealand history. However, it did not produce radical class-wide confrontations with capital. In Australia, the working class was likewise non-insurrectionary, with a few notable exceptions, such as in 1973 when auto-workers rioted in Melbourne.[80]

It was hardly a practical suggestion to call for the *immediate* formation of workers' councils during a non-revolutionary period, and indeed, in a country without a revolutionary tradition where workers' councils have never appeared, nor looked likely to appear. Dodsworth elaborates further:

> Our contact with, and understanding of, the workers who we were urging to seize power (Grant [McDonagh] was particularly fond of spraypainting the slogan 'All power to the workers' councils', overlooking the trivial objection that there were no workers' councils to seize power, even if any other of the preconditions for this had been met) was practically non-existent. [...] We didn't actually *do* anything except produce *Kat* [...] put up a few posters and spraypaint a few walls [with] utterly incomprehensible [slogans].[81]

Hence their idealistic immediatism was a product of their isolation from workers.

Carnival anarchists were much more ambiguous about class than the 'situs'. On the one hand, some declared that class was a dogmatic and outdated leftist belief. Workers were seen as passive, while protesters, students, youth, hippies and the 'lumpenproletariat' were considered the new rebellious 'classes'. For example, The Lunatic Fringe, a carnival anarchist group from Melbourne, wrote:

> The basis of a revolution must be cultural as well as being political and social. Therefore, we urge all dropouts, alcoholics, lunatics, junkies, bludgers, neurotics, prisoners, inmates, schizophrenics, the unemployed, the insane, the psychologically unsound, the freaks, the lazy, and other assorted maniacs to…make the revolution.[82]

Consequently, much of the exuberant energy of carnivalists went into somewhat random attempts to push the protest movement in a more radical direction (they participated in a wide variety of movements – in New Zealand, these included anti-Vietnam War marches, pro-abortion rallies, anti-apartheid demonstrations, land occupations by Maori and protests against the deportation of Pacific Island migrant labour), as well as building inner-city communities of largely 'lumpenproletarian' counter-cultural youth. While most of these movements can be considered expressions of class struggle to a large extent, carnivalists did not see them as such; indeed, they often saw them as something beyond and against class.

On the other hand, many carnival anarchists were supportive of class struggle. While their views appear to be individualistic, they sought to synthesise individual and collective interests.[83] Most were from working-class backgrounds. Their activism included strike support, and a few were involved in rank-and-file workplace groups, although these attempts at workplace organising were carried out on an individual, isolated and intermittent basis.[84] *Dingo* and *Rising Free* covered workplace disputes. Most carnivalists espoused workers' self-management as a core aim.

The stunts of the carnival anarchists were reminiscent of the group Class War in the UK. For example, in New Zealand, a carnivalist was caught while attempting to steal a ballot box during the 1981 cliff-hanger election. His aim was to demand, in return for the votes, a 100 per cent increase in wages for all workers during the then wage-freeze. In Australia, carnivalists formed the 'Dairy Liberation Front' which stole milk from rich suburbs and redistributed it to community organisations in working-class suburbs. Sydney carnivalists penned a letter that purported to be the Leichardt Town Council Mayor's resignation letter. The letter advocated an anarchist revolution and encouraged the formation of workers' and residents' councils. At the time, corruption allegations had been made against Council Officers regarding the rezoning of areas for high rise development.[85]

Furthermore, New Zealand carnivalists were heavily involved in helping to organise part of the unwaged wing of the working class, namely the unemployed. They formed several unemployed groups, such as the Auckland City Unemployed Group (ACUG), an energetic group that involved about 30 people, including many Polynesians. It distributed material in several different languages in industrial working-class South Auckland, and picketed racist capitalists.[86]

For carnival anarchists, becoming involved in the unemployed movement was a class-based response to the economic downturn of the mid-1970s. It was also a product of their rejection of work and the work ethic. Oliver Robb, of the AAA and ACUG, wrote, 'Why should a person work? Why should a person be forced to work at a dull, humiliating job?'[87]

Yet paradoxically this 'dole autonomy' also represented a retreat from class. It led to self-marginalisation from the waged working class, who could be looked down upon for having a job and not adopting a creative lifestyle on the dole.[88] Urging workers to 'drop-out' was hardly a relevant suggestion for those who had to work in order to survive. Indeed, many carnivalists worked for a few months at a time at various menial jobs in order to save money, then quit to live off the proceeds. Like dole autonomy, such a practice did not challenge class exploitation; it was more a method of survival under capitalism.

In Australia, carnival anarchists clashed with anarcho-syndicalists and councilists, such as the SMG, over the worth of workplace-based strategies, resulting in somewhat riotous scenes and bitter splits at anarchist conferences. The Libertarian Socialist Federation summed up the quarrel:

> Those people who were arguing for the Anarchist movement to become involved in trade union and industrial work were accused of neglecting other forms of struggle. Wherever this position was advanced the people doing so were denounced for idolizing the working class, ignoring its conservatism, 'laying heavy moral views', and pressurizing others to become factory workers.[89]

While some anarcho-syndicalists and councilists unfairly demanded that people who refused to work become workplace militants, and some anarcho-syndicalists belittled 'the revolutionary significance' of students and the unemployed,[90] the carnivalist assertion that the working class was conservative is dubious. In 1976, 38 per cent of the Australian workforce participated in strikes, including a general strike against the removal of universal health insurance.[91] Many carnival anarchists, who could be quite inward-looking, seemed out of touch with dissent in broader Australian society. Additionally, the councilists and anarcho-syndicalists thought that the carnivalists were 'chaoticist', individualist, anti-organisational and aimless. In response to the carnivalists, the SMG defended the need for formal organisation, planning, internal democracy and a coherent political programme.[92] While similar tensions existed in New Zealand, they did not produce splits.

## Conclusions

Councilism and anarchism loosely merged into 'libertarian socialism', offering a non-dogmatic path by which both council communism and anarchism could be updated for the changed conditions of the time, and for the new forms of proletarian resistance to these new conditions.

It has been argued that 1970s anarchism was influenced predominantly by the New Left, 'new social movements', the counter-culture and sometimes classical anarchism.[93] Yet councilism arguably had just as much impact on anarchism as these movements did. There is much truth in George's assessment that 'since the Spanish revolution no major theoretical advances have been made by anarchism. Council Communists have provided most of the new energy and new analysis of modern society in the general libertarian movement.'[94] Because anarchists generally lacked in-depth and up-to-date

theoretical analysis, they were content to merely republish councilist literature. Councilism was considered just one more anti-authoritarian ingredient
to be added uncritically into the anarchist melting pot.

In turn, councilists were much influenced by anarchism, to the extent
that some claimed to be more anti-authoritarian than anarchists, and others
became either anarchists or highly sympathetic to anarchism. Councilists
were attracted by anarchism's rich history of self-management, and because
they were a new tendency that lacked support, and so needed revolutionary
allies and sympathisers. Indeed, they often operated on the fringes of a larger
anarchist milieu.

However, this synthesis between anarchism and councilism was undeveloped. Indeed, anarchists and councilists clashed over many issues. Instead
of these tensions resulting in a healthy redevelopment of anarchist and
councilist praxis, they caused acrimonious and personalised disputes.

The anarchist and councilist milieu was too small, youthful and ephemeral
to develop a sophisticated synthesis or critical engagement. Differences
between anarchists and councilists – for example, on the worth of anarcho-
syndicalist unions versus workers' councils and extra-union networks, and
the worth of decentralisation or centralisation – were set aside because these
currents were largely *oppositional* in nature. They were brought together
more for what they were against (such as order-givers of any ideological hue,
especially Leninist bureaucrats), rather than what they were for.

In terms of their relationship to class, councilism *and* class-struggle anarchism were helpfully redeveloped into a praxis that questioned not only
the ownership of the means of production, but also capital's colonisation of
everyday life. With their focus upon the alienation and boredom produced
by 'bureaucratic capitalism' or by the 'spectacle-commodity economy',
they transcended vulgar economism. Additionally, in response to changes in
class composition, they importantly considered non-managerial white-collar
workers and the unwaged to be part of the working class.

Yet both tendencies anarchistically argued that the central problem with
capital was its *hierarchy*. This is highly debateable, as the central contradiction within capital is still *class exploitation*, not bureaucratic or managerial
control, or boredom. Councilism was developed during a time of expanding bureaucracy in both the capitalist West and 'communist' East, which
produced an increased demand for skilled, technical labour. Since the imposition of neo-liberalism, class exploitation has intensified, labour has become
more precarious and casualised, and bureaucracy has been arguably reduced.
Consequently, councilist theories seem outdated.

The responses of the councilists and carnival anarchists to the upsurge in
workplace struggle of the 1970s stand in contrast. Councilists such as the
Revolutionary Committee urged the formation of extra-union shop committees. While their strategy was not influential, and they remained in
'splendid isolation', the industrious SMG was more effective. Their grassroots

strategy based on their network of cells had much potential to link community and workplace struggle together. Nevertheless, their contributions were transitory and often idealistic. The councilist milieu soon faded away by the late 1970s in New Zealand, and by the mid-1980s in Australia. Many Australian councilists became anarchists (some later became involved in the Institute for Social Ecology in Brisbane), community activists or Green Party members.

In contrast, the 'situs' and carnival anarchists believed impatiently that total revolution (social, economic, cultural and psychological) needed to occur immediately. Situationists dismissed the dissent of the time as being fragmentary and lacking radical content, hence making it easily recuperable. Certainly, this was largely true, but they tended to differentiate 'a pure, autonomous class from the "external" institutions of the workers' movement (unions, leftist parties), and in so doing, end[ed] up concluding that the class has been duped by the ideology of these external forces',[95] or by the spectacle. 'Situs' – as with other councilists – froze the high points of class struggle, in particular the emergence of workers' councils, and used it as a principle to judge the present. Their critique did not relate to the daily *contradictory* relationship that exists between capital and workers, where 'both the acceptance and refusal of capitalist labour coexist, where workers' passive objectification and subjective (collective) resistance coexist within the subsumption of labour-power to the productive process'.[96] It was thus unsurprising that the groups and projects of the 'situs' were highly ephemeral and ineffectual.

The carnival anarchists were ambiguous towards class. They were not simply individualist bohemians, nor lifestyle anarchists. They refused to work, formed unemployed groups, went on picket lines and supported workers' self-management. Yet in their despair over the decline of the protest movement and the alleged conservatism of the working class, they turned inward. Their attempt to live the most radical lifestyle possible in their everyday lives was often elitist and self-marginalising. Their experiments became self-destructive. Subsequently, their squats and affinity groups collapsed, often without trace.

Nonetheless, the carnivalists went beyond the SI in one respect. In their challenge to the solemn seriousness of leftists, they attempted to put certain Situationist ideas into *everyday practice*. This was well articulated by Franklin Rosemont: 'At the time it always seemed to me that the Situationists *wrote* and *talked* and *theorized* about playing and having fun, while *we* – still just kids, in a sense – were actually *playing* and *having the fun*.'[97]

Class-struggle anarchists and anti-Leninist revolutionary Marxists today continue to converge and clash. Yet there is still much untapped scope for a two-way synthesis, or at least for sustained critical engagement between the two currents. For example, councilists analysed the importance of bureaucracy and managerial authority in class struggle, a factor that Marxists have tended to downplay. In this regard, a genuine synthesis could offer considerable insight into the heavily disputed subject of the 'middle class': that is, those 'contradictory class locations' where workers such as managers are exploited *and* yet also wield considerable power over other workers.

## Acknowledgements

Many thanks to Viola Wilkins, Tim Briedis, Gavin Murray, Joe Toscano and Greg George for enlightening me about Australian councilism and anarchism. Thanks also to everyone who participated in my earlier New Zealand research, and to Steve Wright and the editors for their rigorous comments on earlier drafts.

## Notes

1.  Greg George, *Essay Aimed at Discovering Anarchism's Relevance to Modern Society* (Brisbane: Self-Management Group (SMG), c.1974), p. 8.
2.  Toby Boraman, 'The New Left and Anarchism in New Zealand from 1956 to the Early 1980s' (PhD dissertation, University of Otago, 2006), and Toby Boraman, *Rabble Rousers and Merry Pranksters: A History of Anarchism in Aotearoa/New Zealand from the Mid-1950s to the Early 1980s* (Christchurch: Katipo Books, 2007).
3.  Although precise membership figures for these organisations are lacking, estimates claim that the SMG had more than 200 members and Solidarity had between 80 and 100 members in the 1970s. SouB's discussion meetings in the late 1950s were attended by more than 100 people. Tim Briedis personal correspondence, May 2010; Louis Robertson, 'Reflections of My Time in Solidarity', http://libcom.org/library/recollections-solidarity-louisrobertson [accessed 01/03/12]; and Marcel van der Linden, 'Socialisme ou Barbarie: A French Revolutionary Group (1949–65)', *Left History* 5(1) (1997), p. 36 n. 50.
4.  Philippe Bourrinet, *The Dutch and German Communist Left (1900–68)* (N.p.: Philippe Bourrinet, 2008), pp. 319–322.
5.  Marcel van der Linden, 'On Council Communism', *Historical Materialism*, 12(4) (2004), pp. 30–31.
6.  Bourrinet, *The Dutch and German Communist Left*, p. 324.
7.  Ibid.
8.  Ibid., pp. 209, 322.
9.  Richard Gombin, *The Origins of Modern Leftism* (Harmondsworth: Penguin, 1975) goes further and argues that councilism was part of the council communist tradition.
10. While rejecting the term councilism as a frozen and dogmatic *ideology* 'which restrains and reifies their [workers' councils] total theory and practice'. René Riesel, 'Preliminaries on the Councils and Councilist Organization', in Ken Knabb (ed.) *Situationist International Anthology* (Berkeley: Bureau of Public Secrets, 1981), p. 274.
11. See also Benjamin Franks, *Rebel Alliances* (Edinburgh and San Francisco: AK Press, 2006), pp. 12–13.
12. NicolasWalter, 'Has Anarchism Changed? Part Two', *Freedom* (26 June 1976), p. 9. For this revival, see Alexandre Skirda, *Facing the Enemy: A History of Anarchist Organization from Proudhon to May 1968* (Edinburgh, San Francisco, and London: AK Press and Kate Sharpley Library, 2002).

13. Daniel Cohn-Bendit, 'Interview', *Anarchy*, 99 (May 1969), p. 153.
14. Quoted in George Woodcock, *Anarchism* (London: Penguin, 1986), p. 271.
15. See Peter Stansill and David Mairowitz (eds), *BAMN: Outlaw Manifestos and Ephemera 1965–70* (Harmondsworth: Penguin, 1971).
16. The term is borrowed from John Englart, 'Anarchism in Sydney 1975–1981: Part I', *Freedom* (12 June 1982), yet used differently from Englart www.takver. com/history/sydney/syd7581.htm [accessed 01/03/12].
17. See CrimethInc Workers' Collective, *Days of War, Nights of Love* (Atlanta: CrimethInc, 2001) and the Invisible Committee, *The Coming Insurrection* (Los Angeles: Semiotext(e), 2009).
18. See for instance Tom Bramble, *Trade Unionism in Australia* (Cambridge: Cambridge University Press, 2008), and Brian Roper, *Prosperity for All? Economic, Social and Political Change in New Zealand Since 1935* (Melbourne: Thomson/Dunmore Press, 2005).
19. Calculated from *Industrial Stoppages Report* (Wellington: New Zealand Department of Labour, 1970–1980). This figure includes political stoppages, which have been excluded from other statistical series.
20. See Chris Briggs, 'Strikes and Lockouts in the Antipodes', *New Zealand Journal of Employment Relations* 30(3) (2005).
21. For the decline in living standards and rise in unemployment, see Tom O'Lincoln, *Years of Rage: Social Conflicts in the Fraser Era* (Melbourne: Bookmarks, 1993) and Roper, *Prosperity for All?*
22. Christchurch Anarchy Group (CAG), 'Peoples Rights – Self-Management Is the Only Answer' (leaflet, Christchurch, c.1977).
23. Ibid.
24. CAG, *Anarchy Information Sheet*, 2 (c.1976).
25. See Maurice Brinton, *For Workers' Power*, ed. David Goodway (Edinburgh and Oakland: AK Press, 2004), pp. 81, 85–89, 215.
26. Richard Bolstad, *The Industrial Front* (Christchurch: CAG, c.1978), p. 41 and Cornelius Castoriadis, *Workers' Councils and the Economics of a Self-Managed Society* (Philadelphia: Wooden Shoe, 1984).
27. See for instance, Paul Cardan [Castoriadis], *Redefining Revolution* (London: Solidarity, n.d.).
28. Richard Bolstad interview with author, May 1996.
29. Solidarity 'As We See It', in Brinton *For Workers' Power*, p. 153.
30. For an analysis of this shift towards Maoism see Boraman, *Rabble Rousers*, pp. 56–58.
31. Richard Bolstad, *An Anarchist Analysis of the Chinese Revolution* (Christchurch: CAG, 1976) and Cajo Brendel, *Theses on the Chinese Revolution* (London: Solidarity, 1974).
32. The CPNZ was one of the few 'communist' parties in the 'advanced' capitalist world to side with China after the Sino-Soviet split.
33. Tim Briedis, '"A Map of the World That Includes Utopia": The Self-Management Group and the Brisbane Libertarians' (BA Hons. thesis, University of Sydney, 2010), p. 43.
34. For example, George of the SMG claimed that libertarian socialism, libertarian communism and council communism meant the same thing. George, *Essay Aimed at Discovering Anarchism's Relevance*, p. 2.
35. Briedis, 'A Map of the World that Includes Utopia', p. 10; Joe Toscano personal correspondence, May 2010; and Greg George interview with author, June 2010.

36. Hamish Alcorn, 'No Organised Anarchists in Brisbane?' www.ainfos.ca/99/apr/ainfos00118.html [accessed 01/03/12].

37. *Compass* 6 (September 1971).

38. CAG, *Anarchy Newsletter* (August 1977).

39. George interview.

40. George, *Essay Aimed at Discovering Anarchism's Relevance*, p. 13.

41. See SMG, *Workers' Councils Democracy, Not Parliamentary* (Brisbane: SMG, n.d.), pp. 2,4.

42. George, *Essay Aimed at Discovering Anarchism's Relevance*.

43. *You Can't Blow Up a Social Relationship: The Anarchist Case Against Terrorism* (Brisbane, Melbourne and Adelaide: Libertarian Socialist Organisation, Libertarian Workers for a Self-Managed Society, Monash Anarchist Society and Adelaide Libertarian Socialists, c.1978).

44. Greg George, 'You Can't Blow Up a Social Relationship', *Libertarian*, 2 (May/June 1976). George's article was subtitled 'The Case against Terrorism' rather than 'The Anarchist Case against Terrorism'.

45. Toscano personal correspondence.

46. Briedis, 'A Map of the World That Includes Utopia', p. 62; Briedis personal correspondence; George interview; Toscano personal correspondence; and SMG, *Workers' Councils Democracy*.

47. Briedis, 'A Map of the World That Includes Utopia', pp. 66–67.

48. SMG, 'Equal Wages – Equal Power' (leaflet, Brisbane, 1976).

49. George, *Essay Aimed at Discovering Anarchism's Relevance*, p. 9.

50. 'As We See It' quoted in SMG, *Workers' Councils*, p. 3.

51. SMG, *Workers' Councils*, p. 3.

52. Steve Taylor, *The Anatomy of Decision* (Auckland: Compass, c.1974), pp. 24, 41.

53. George, *Essay Aimed at Discovering Anarchism's Relevance*, p. 8.

54. Gilles Dauvé and François Martin, *The Eclipse and Re-emergence of the Communist Movement* (London: Antagonism Press, 1997), p. 73.

55. 'Some Provisional Points of Disagreement with the Comrades of the Brisbane S.M.G.', *Federation of Australian Anarchists Bulletin* (1975), in *Melbourne Anarchist Archives Volume II* (Melbourne: Melbourne Anarchist Archives, 1979), p. 37.

56. 'Decadence: The Theory of Decline or the Decline of Theory? Part Two', *Aufheben*, 3 (Summer 1994), http://libcom.org/library/decadence-aufheben-3 [accessed 01/03/12].

57. With the exception of 'Workers' Councils, Self-Management and Syndicalism', *Federation of Australian Anarchists Bulletin* (1974) in *Melbourne Anarchist Archives*, p. 28.

58. Taylor, *The Anatomy of Decision*, p. 41.

59. Leaflet Sydney, c. late 1970s, original emphasis.

60. *KAT* 1 (1978), p. 13, 2 (1978), p. 1.

61. Grant McDonagh, 'My Involvement in an Ultra-Leftist Tendency' (MSS, Nelson: 1981).

62. Boraman, *Rabble Rousers*, p. 122.

63. McDonagh, interview with author, July 1996.

64. McDonagh, 'My Involvement'.

65. McDonagh, personal correspondence, December 1997.

66. McDonagh, 'Tableau in a Morgue', *KAT*, 5 (1978), pp. 5–6.

67. Ibid., p. 5.

68. Rosemont in Franklin Rosemont and Charles Radcliffe, *Dancin' in the Streets!* (Chicago: Charles H. Kerr, 2005), pp. 61–62, 68.
69. Joe Toscano, 'Carnival Anarchism in Melbourne 1970–75', www.takver.com/history/melb/carnival1970_75.htm [accessed 01/03/12].
70. Peter McGregor, *Cultural Battles: The Meaning of the Viet Nam – USA War* (Melbourne: Scam Publications, 1988), p. 16.
71. *Workers' Councils* (Sydney: Rising Free Reprint, n.d.)
72. Auckland Anarchist Activists, *Anarchy and the State* (Auckland: AAA, c.1976).
73. Terry Leahy, 'Pre-War Anarchists and the Post-War Ultra-Left' (MSS, Sydney, c.1981), p. 32.
74. Anonymous, http://en.wikipedia.org/wiki/Peter_McGregor [accessed 01/03/12].
75. Jean Barrot [Gilles Dauvé], *What Is Situationism?* (Fort Bragg: Flatland, 1991), p. 25, original emphasis.
76. *Black Mail* 2 (1982), p. 15.
77. For instance, see McDonagh, 'Tableau in a Morgue' and 'The Year of the Goat', *KAT*, 7 (1978), p. 3.
78. McDonagh, 'Irresponsibility vs Poverty: The Valkay Affair' (leaflet, Christchurch, 1979).
79. McDonagh, 'The Year of the Goat', p. 3.
80. Iain McIntyre, *Disturbing the Peace* (Melbourne: Homebrew Books, 2005), pp. 35–41.
81. Andrew Dodsworth, personal correspondence, February 1997, original emphasis.
82. Lunatic Fringe, 'Pre-Moratorium Leaflet (1970)', www.takver.com/history/melb/maa40.htm [accessed 01/03/12].
83. Graeme Minchin interview with author, February 1997.
84. Gavin Murray interview with author, June 2010.
85. Englart, 'Anarchism in Sydney'.
86. Frank Prebble interview with author, May 1996.
87. Oliver Robb, *Anarchy in Albert Park: An Attack on the 'Work Ethic'* (Christchurch: Christchurch Anarchy Group, 1976).
88. Aufheben, 'Unemployed Recalcitrance and Welfare Restructuring in the UK Today', in *Stop the Clock! Critiques of the New Social Workhouse* (Brighton: Aufheben, 2000).
89. Quoted in Englart, 'Anarchism in Sydney'. The LSF was formed as a 'libertarian/syndicalist' split from the Federation of Australian Anarchists. It did not involve the SMG.
90. 'The Split – A Monash Anarchist Perspective', *Federation of Australian Anarchists Bulletin* (1976) in *Melbourne Anarchist Archives*, p. 30.
91. Briggs, 'Strikes and Lockouts', p. 9.
92. SMG, 'Editorial', *Federation of Australian Anarchists Bulletin* (1975), in *Melbourne Anarchist Archives*, pp. 31–34.
93. See for instance Peter Marshall, *Demanding the Impossible: A History of Anarchism* (London: Fontana Press, 1993), pp. 539–558.
94. George, *Essay Aimed at Discovering Anarchism's Relevance*, pp. 1–2. However, it is doubtful that councilists provided most of the energy.
95. ' "We Have Ways of Making You Talk!" Review Article', *Aufheben*, 12 (2004), p. 59.
96. Sandro Studer quoted in 'We Have Ways,' p. 60.
97. Rosemont, *Dancin' in the Streets!*, p. 378, original emphasis.

# 14
# Situating Hardt and Negri

*David Bates*

## Introduction

To what extent is it possible to situate Hardt and Negri's thought? Are they best regarded as 'anarchists', 'socialists', 'communists', 'Marxists', 'Leninists', 'post-Marxists' or 'post-anarchists'? Answering this question is no mere intellectual exercise. As Wittgenstein once remarked, 'words are deeds'.[1] On the radical Left, much blood has been spilled through those deeds, careers ended and reputations shattered. Of course, today a great deal is made of the claim that we live in 'post-ideological' times, 'new times' where 'class struggle' does not have the importance it once had; postmodern times, where meanings and identities are constantly subject to the contestation of 'discourse'. Now, while the costs of labelling are not what they once were, there are still costs. Labelling instigates a kind of 'symbolic violence' over discursive space. Rival ideologies are constructed as 'straw men', as 'crude', 'naïve', as 'elitist' or 'authoritarian' and so on. This process neglects any philosophical sophistication, common ground, or indeed the interpenetration of 'rival ideologies'. One danger of labelling is that we move beyond healthy criticism to a desire to relegate our theoretical interlocutors to the status of the 'other'. Accordingly, they become an opponent we seek to dismiss, in order to give positive identity to ourselves, rather than a potential ally in the struggle against the exploitative mechanisms of global capitalism. Where labelling is also connected with the construction of orthodoxies, it can lead to what Skinner has termed a 'mythology of coherence' (and of incoherence) produced often by those wishing to defend the integrity of their specific ideological projects.[2]

While seeking to avoid the excesses of such 'symbolic violence', this chapter aims to locate Hardt and Negri's work within the cross-cutting currents of modern socialism, and crucially to understand the labelling strategies which they themselves deploy in the field of revolutionary politics. Why specifically, do they find it necessary to reject the label of 'anarchism'? Why do they make often rather cryptic reference to 'Leninism'? What game are they playing, and why do they feel a need to play it? What are their intentions? How can we read Hardt and Negri? Antonio Negri has paid a higher price than most in the struggle against global capitalism and we can learn a great deal both from his work and activism.[3] That said, in what follows I will subject his work – along with Michael Hardt's – to a robust critique, drawing on Marxist, anarchist, post-Marxist, and post-anarchist thinking, so as to assess the cogency of their arguments in the context of radical politics today.

## Labels and the Left

Hardt and Negri are difficult authors to situate. The immediate context in which Negri's work emerged was the Italian autonomist movement of the 1960s and 1970s, a movement in which he was one of the leading intel-lectuals. Autonomism has been viewed by such diverse figures as Bologna and Callincos as embodying an attempt to 'refuse' or 'reject' the rule of the Leninist party model in the context of contemporary revolutionary politics.[4] This challenge to Leninism – perhaps in part as a result of the weakness of Italian Trotskyism – resulted in a strong libertarian anti-statist aspect in autonomist thought in general, and Negri's thought in particular.[5] More-over, we see in Negri's more recent work with Hardt, the combination of this with an emphasis on that old Marxian foe the 'lumpenproletariat'. Accordingly, the well-respected scholar of Marxism David McLellan, and the post-anarchist S. Newman, have each regarded Hardt and Negri as at least unacknowledged anarchists, albeit for Newman of a post-anarchist flavour.[6]

Yet Hardt and Negri have refused the label of 'anarchist'. They have writ-ten: 'No, we are not anarchists but communists.'[7] This refusal also leads Hardt and Negri to adopt a complex response to the discourse of Leninism, one which – in contrast to Bologna – goes beyond simple 'refusal'. Rather, Lenin is treated as 'the most complete representation of... the "actuality of the revolution"'.[8] Indeed, in *Empire*, Hardt and Negri have written of an 'alternative implicit in Lenin's work: *either world communist revolution or Empire*'.[9] The question to be addressed here is 'what is the practice of these statements?' Elsewhere, Negri has written – this time very clearly:

> To me, Leninism is the price we paid for the political composition of the Italian proletariat. There was no way to talk politics other than via Leninism.... It was the class lingua franca: it could cause trouble, but you could make headway with the class (and with no one else) only by using it.[10]

And of course, this 'lingua franca' is anti-anarchist to the very core. To under-stand this in more detail, we need to look first at the nature and prac-tice of the 'divide' between anarchism and Marxism, and then how this came to feed in to the discourse of Marxism–Leninism. This divide is not illusory. There are some very real differences between anarchist and Marxist approaches. But such differences are heightened as problematic when used as textual 'orthodoxy' to establish the 'party line'. To achieve this, a 'return' to Marx was often viewed as the only 'scientific' way forward. This 'return' inevitably focuses on Marx's hostile polemics with Proudhon and Bakunin, and hence a clear critical line comes do be drawn between Marxism and anarchism. Yet it must be pointed out – albeit briefly – that these polemics were complex in nature. Thus, while it is the case that Marx came to criticise the 'petty-bourgeois' and 'non-dialectical' character of Proudhon's work,[11] he had earlier regarded Proudhon's 1840 text *What Is Property?* as a great scientific advance.[12] And, while Marx wrote of Bakunin that: 'He does not understand a thing about social revolution, only the political phrases about it; its economic conditions do not exist for him'[13], he had also considered there to be many advances in Bakunin's early economic materialism. And Bakunin for his part had written of Marx that he 'advanced and proved the incontrovertible truth, confirmed by the entire past and present history of human society, nations and states, that economic fact has always preceded legal and political right'.[14]

Indeed, we might comment that both Marx and Bakunin opposed the institution of private property; both were committed to the revolutionary overthrow of the capitalist mode of production; both considered economic conflict – specifically class struggle – to be a fundamental driving force of historical development; both thought capitalist states to be rooted in sys-tems of class domination, and should therefore be abolished; and both explicitly stressed proletarian self-emancipation as a necessary feature of the forthcoming social revolution.[15]

Yet, a clear textual basis for the construction of the official state ideology of Marxism–Leninism came to be viewed as self-evident. Consider how in his 1901 *Thesis on Anarchism and Socialism,* Lenin wrote that: 'Anarchism, in the course of the 35 to 40 years (Bakunin and the *International*, 1860) of its existence (and with Stirner included, in the course of many more years) has produced nothing but general platitudes against exploitation.'[16] For Lenin, anarchism failed to understand the 'causes' of this exploitation. In 1905, he wrote that: 'The philosophy of the anarchists is bourgeois philosophy turned inside out. Their individualistic theories and their individualistic ideal are the very opposite of socialism.'[17] Similarly, in 1912, at the Italian Socialist Congress, he claimed that the working-class movement was 'rapidly ridding itself of the sickness... of anarchism'.[18]

The words of Lenin can be situated here in the context of the central-ist theory of organisation that he had articulated in texts such as *What Is to Be Done?* (1902), and *One Step Forwards, Two Steps Backwards* (1904).[19] Here Lenin, as is well known, put forward the controversial thesis – building on the arguments of Kautsky – that the working classes, left to their own devices, would never reach beyond 'trade union consciousness'. Political consciousness came to the class from outside the economic struggle, the vehicle of revolutionary theory being party intellectuals.

Although anarchists have often seized on this to explain the deviations of the Soviet system, a few words of caution must be made. First, it would be a mistake to argue that there is a simple continuity between Leninism and Stalinism. After all in 1922 Lenin stated in his 'Last Testament' that 'Comrade Stalin [...] has unlimited authority concentrated in his hands, and I am not sure whether he will always be capable of using that authority with sufficient caution.'[20] Second – a fact ignored by the Stalinists – Lenin's view was amenable to change. Bloody Sunday in 1905 had helped to mobilise the masses against the Tsarist state. And in *The State and Revolution* (written between August and September of 1917), Lenin had stated the case for a more open form of organisational structure, and indeed for the rapid abolition of the state.[21]

Of course post-revolutionary history led to different outcomes. The 'new dawn' after October 1917 was rapidly to pass, as the political and ideological differences between the communists and the anarchists came to be accentuated. The Leninist attempt to establish hegemony over the revolutionary movement led to suppression of alternative voices.

This brings us back to Negri's point about the 'price' of Leninism – for one price was undoubtedly his (and Hardt's) refusal of the label anarchism. Intellectually, too, the price was the dishonesty – however 'necessary' – of dogma. Indeed, it would be a distortion to think of Lenin's view of revolutionary organisation as being hegemonic, even among communists. Trotsky and others had very different views. Revolutionary Marxists such as Rosa Luxemburg voiced significant concerns about the type of centralism advocated by Lenin, questioning specifically its suitability even for 'Russian conditions'.[22] This is not to say that Luxemburg was a 'naïve' spontaneist; certainly, she had faith in the revolutionary potential of the proletariat, but this was a spontaneity in a definite material context, and with a clear and democratic organisational structure, serving to militate against the possible excesses of centralised party structures.

Negri's 'orthodoxy' is far from the usual kind; there is no 'application' of Lenin's theory. Rather, Negri claims to rethink the 'contemporaneity' of Lenin, a Leninism for the epoch of global capitalism, a Lenin whose analysis shifts in accordance with the specificity of the context in which he is embedded, but who nevertheless enables us to 'think' revolutionary subjectivity. Indeed, Negri's account of Lenin involves periodisation. Thus we have the Lenin of 1890–1900, of 1900–1910 and of 1910–1917.[23] In the first period, Lenin focuses on providing an analysis of the 'determinate social formation'; here his aim is to understand the specificity of working-class composition – that is the 'actual standpoint' of the working class. The goal of political economy here is to be judged through its practical-political efficacy, or its contribution to the constituent power of the proletariat. In the second period, characterised by *What Is to Be Done?*, Lenin was concerned with 'organisational' questions. In the third period Lenin wrote of the need to eradicate the bourgeois state. We see this most clearly in Lenin's *The State and Revolution*.

So, this problematic periodisation of Lenin, which we have just outlined, needs to be thought in terms of the contemporaneity of Lenin – a Lenin for the realities of global capitalism, a Lenin against Empire. As early as 1973, Negri wrote against the crude application of the Leninist party form to the contemporary context, insisting that the political composition of the working class had now been substantially modified.[24] And in a recent article, Negri claims that we must understand Lenin's 'biopolitics'; we need, he claims, to grasp 'new revolutionary corporealities, the powerful base of the production of subjectivity...', 'of the communist 'general intellect'. We need to 'move into the realm of Lenin beyond Lenin'.[25]

Thus we arrive at an important question: to what extent is Hardt and Negri's somewhat unconventional (post-)Leninist communism actually anti-anarchist in a way that is comparable with the anti-anarchism of orthodox 'Marxism-Leninism'? Here we need to explore in greater detail what Hardt and Negri have to say about anarchism and communism.

## Anarchism and communism

Negri writes in *Reflections on Empire*: '[I]t is a pity that the anarchist conception has never been attentive to the issue of homology with the state [...] so that it produces in its concept of insurrection and in that of the abolition of the state a revolutionary imprint that is fiercely empty of alternative proposals and full of resentment.'[26] Earlier in the same text, he criticises the anarchists for refusing 'to define a time or space as privileged moments of uprising; they live in the chaos of the world of exploitation, illustrating destructively its institutions, but failing to put forward a positive strategy of transformation'.[27]

There is no explicit engagement with the 'texts' of anarchism here; no discussion of the wide range of subtle and not so subtle differences in the anarchist 'canon'. And there is most definitely no attempt to explore the common ground between Marx and his 'classical' anarchist contemporaries such as Bakunin. Instead we have an opposition to a Leninist (indeed Stalinist) construction of anarchism, which enables Hardt and Negri to maintain their communist credentials, and thus – perhaps strategically – to distract their more orthodox comrades from what is in many ways an approach which resonates theoretically with themes present both in 'classical' as well as 'post'-anarchism.

So, as we have seen, Hardt and Negri view themselves not as anarchists but as communists, communists who have seen 'how much repression and destruction of humanity has been wrought by liberal and socialist big government'.[28] New co-operative 'circuits' have however generated radical possibilities. Hardt and Negri insist how:

> Today productivity, wealth and the creation of social surpluses take the form of cooperative interactivity through linguistic, communicational, and affective networks. In the expression of its own creative energies, immaterial labor thus seems to provide the potential for a kind of spontaneous elementary communism.[29]

This is a communism based in love and communality, and *'irrepressible lightness and joy'*, a communism rendered possible by the information age and the communication networks instigated therein.[30]

Some of both Hardt and Negri's recent writings are of interest to us here. In a collection of essays responding to the work of Alain Badiou, the authors argue for what we might term an anti-statist understanding of communism. Of course, a usual argument put forward by liberal capitalist and anarchist opponents of communism is that it is statist, and as such serves to undermine the freedom of the individual. Both Hardt and Negri develop a challenging rereading of this line of thought. For them, communism is opposed to 'state socialism' (which might be equated with 'actually existing socialism'). In a way which shows something of the rhetorical flourish of Giddens's 'Third Way',[31] Hardt writes that: 'We need to explore another possibility: neither the private property of capitalism nor the public property of socialism but the common in communism.'[32] And Negri writes:

> Being communist means being against the State. The State is the force that organizes, always normally yet always exceptionally, the relations that constitute capital and discipline the conflicts between capitalists and the proletarian labour force.[33]

State socialism according to this argument is akin to a type of state capitalism. Public ownership is state ownership – alienated ownership – which operates against 'the common'. As such the constitutive power of proletarian labour is alienated, indeed neutralised.[34]

Thus we have a move from a type of strategic (post-)Leninism, to a strong opposition to actually existing state socialism, and embrace of the 'common' in communism. In making the case for this anti-state vision of communism, the rejection of anarchism continues. For, Negri writes: '...there is no revolution without organization [...] there still is no rational design that invests and involves the moments of rupture with the power of organization'.[35]

Some critical points need to be both emphasised and re-emphasised here. Hardt and Negri's self-identification as anti-anarchists is based on a misrepresentation of anarchism and hence a sectarianism which undercuts their critique of capitalism; this problem is exacerbated when we turn to their critique of socialism. Hardt and Negri's characterisation of socialism is in some ways more fitting for an author such as Phillip Blond, than for authors so deeply embedded in progressive radical political struggle.[36] But what possible purpose can such anti-socialism have in the struggle against capitalism? For one thing, does socialism really undercut the constitutive power of the proletariat? Maybe so with certain forms of what used to be termed 'actually existing socialism', and aspects of European social democracy. But it must also be acknowledged that socialism was – and still is – a product of mass struggle, a struggle often against a laissez faire form of capitalism that has been quite happy to see workers starve in the name of liberal 'freedoms'. It was a system which pushed for the reduction of the working day, the abolition of child labour, the creation of free public education and health care – all developments resisted by the bourgeoisie, cutting as it did into capitalist valorisation and the production of surplus value.

Accordingly, an effective anti-capitalist counter-hegemony must oppose such sectarian lines of reasoning. It must engage honestly and widely with the revolutionary Left, drawing on the rich history of emancipatory struggle therein. The political 'purpose' which such labelling once served no longer resonates.

## A 'postmodern' politics?

But what of the understanding of politics which Hardt and Negri propose? This is a politics which results from the shift from modernity to postmodernity, a new politics grounded in the realities of globalisation. But how cogent is their account?

In *Empire*, Hardt and Negri write: 'The passage to Empire emerges from the twilight of modern sovereignty [...] It is a decentred and deterritorializing apparatus of rule that progressively incorporates the entire global realm within its open, expanding frontiers.'[37] The modernist understanding of 'sovereignty', the 'nation state' and the 'people', come to be challenged. Thus Negri insists: 'Today, on the contrary, it is the crisis of the nation state as induced by globalisation that the general crisis of political categories of modernity manifests, opening thought to the relation between Empire and multitudes.'[38]

For Hardt and Negri, 'classical' anarchists, socialists and Marxists alike are trapped inside a 'modernist' problematic, where power is understood only in relation to its univocal, or at best dualistic, exercise. For 'classical' anarchists this is the exercise of repressive state power over essentially free individuals. For Marxists, this is a causally determinant economic power, which produces a particular state form and which serves both to justify and maintain the exploitative status quo. And for 'socialists' this is a state which can be seized for revolutionaries and for reformists, transformed in order to defend and promote a progressive conception of the public – put in the kind of language which Hardt might use – a 'state of love'. As we have already noted, for Hardt and Negri, the erosion of the very logic of the nation state is making (technologically) real the communist utopia, as a new conception of the postmodern 'commons' emerges in the context of globalisation. It is to this theme that I now turn.

Hardt and Negri radicalise the Foucauldian language of biopower, and harness it to the cause of radical politics in a context of 'postmodernity'. Foucault wrote of biopower's 'influence on life' that it 'endeavours to administer, optimize, and multiply it, subjecting it to precise controls and comprehensive regulations'.[39] Hardt and Negri write of biopower as 'a form of power that regulates social life from its interior, following it, interpreting it, absorbing it, and rearticulating it'.[40] To this extent, the authors are on the same theoretical terrain as post-anarchism and post-Marxism. Take Saul Newman's claim that:

> We can no longer imagine a clear conceptual distinction between society and the state, between humanity and power, as power is reproduced through everyday relationships and practices – such as educating, healing, governing – and through a variety of social institutions...'[41]

This is in many ways the irony of postmodern analyses of power – that power is decentred, multivocal, but also more totalising than it has ever been. So, for Laclau, as social closure is an 'impossibility', power's grasp is never complete, but nor are we ever outside the discourse of power relations. Following an Althusserian theme, the very subject of power is constituted in the context of power relations; as such the abstract liberal individual subject comes to be problematised. For the post-anarchist Saul Newman, power is endemic in everyday social practices, such that the liberal distinction between state and society can no-longer be sustained, while for Hardt and Negri, *Empire* and biopower subjugates more than a state-centred imperialism ever could.

What then of the possibility of resistance – and in particular, how does an understanding of Hardt and Negri's view on this issue enable us to situate their thought? A key feature that unites Foucault, post-Marxism and post-anarchism is an opposition to a 'grand narrative' of resistance, and of emancipation. The totalising effect of power means that all attempts to resist its subjugation will be temporary and partial. Here, much attention is given to what we might term 'micro-practices', embodied perhaps most clearly in Foucault's claim that we have to 'create ourselves as a work of art'.[42] Accordingly, the large projects of social transformation held up alike by Bakunin, Marx and Lenin, are looked on as at best outmoded.

Yet there are clear differences in post-Marxist and post-anarchist approaches. Where for post-anarchists such as Newman, the concern is with a non-hegemonic prefigurative politics of the 'here and now', post-Marxists stress the importance of a post-Gramscian hegemonic politics which seeks to weld various complex struggles into a concrete – and always precarious – historic bloc.[43]

But how 'radical' is Newman's alternative? In some ways it is strangely conservative. Newman writes: 'Radical transformation – and here we recall Bakunin's "urge to destroy", which for him was also a creative urge – should be accompanied by a sensitivity to what exists, and a desire to conserve what needs to be conserved.'[44] Hardt and Negri are more clearly radical in the language they use. But there is no account of hegemonic politics, either in 'statist' or non-statist forms.[45] Instead there is a stress on the autonomist notion of 'refusal'.[46] In his earlier writings, Negri provided a theorisation of refusal which he at least considered to have a firm Marxian grounding – located that is in a specific and novel reading of Marx's *Grundrisse*.[47] In this reading, the autonomous and unified power of labour against capital is clearly asserted.[48]

In what they regard as distinguishing their work from anarchism, Hardt and Negri have made the argument, in *Empire* and elsewhere, for a constructive ontology of resistance, a 'refusal' which contains the seeds of a possible 'communist' future. So they write: '[S]uch destruction only grasps the passive, negative limit of sovereign power. The positive, active limit is revealed most clearly with respect to labor and social production.'[49] To this extent, Hardt and Negri write of the creation of 'constellations of powerful singularities'.[50]

Here the notion of biopolitics is important. Biopolitics rallies against the exploitive totalisation of the contemporary capital form. It seeks to reincorporate a form of production which resists the imposition of the rule of 'measure' – a form of communal production against Empire. Hardt and Negri draw a distinction between 'constituent' and 'constitutional' power. The former is 'an institutional form that develops a common content; it is a development of force that defends the historical progression of emancipation and liberation; it is, in short, an act of love'.[51] The latter, on the other hand, seeks to constrain, to subjugate, to legalise. Just as there is no one site of Empire, there is no one site of (constructive) resistance to Empire. In the same way that Empire can be considered a totalising mode of exploitation, so too resistance is everywhere. The 'Party' can no longer represent a unitary site of struggle. The working class are just one exploited group among many. We are all the 'multitude'.

Stressing the complexity of these new modes of struggle, Hardt and Negri write that 'as production becomes increasingly biopolitical [...] an isolation of economic issues makes less and less sense'.[52] A revolutionary approach must be levelled against the social bios as a whole, not at 'the economy' (in the limited sense) or 'the state', and exploitation must be attacked in all its differential manifestations. But this for Hardt and Negri is a positive attack. So, they write: 'We need to create weapons that are not merely destructive but are themselves forms of constituent power, weapons capable of constructing democracy and defeating the armies of Empire.'[53]

## The multitude and revolution

In this section, I interrogate further Hardt and Negri's concept of the multitude, in order to assess their understanding of the form of revolutionary agency and subjectivity made possible in the context of Empire. Hardt and Negri have challenged the restrictive identification of the contemporary proletariat with wage labourers, which they associate with Marxism. Hardt and Negri write:

> The exclusions of other forms of labor from the working class are based on the notion that there are differences of kind between, for example, male industrial labor and female reproductive labor, between industrial labor and peasant labor, between the employed and the unemployed, between workers and the poor.[54]

Marx it is true provides a somewhat restricted relational understanding of the proletariat. Moreover, Ernesto Laclau has pointed out that Marx's proletariat involves a substantial revision – indeed redefinition – of that concept. Whereas the proletariat was a 'poor outside any stable social ascription',[55] it comes now to be associated with a radical and transformative conception of agency.[56]

The proletariat, according to the definition in the *Communist Manifesto*, are wage labourers, and the bourgeoisie owners of the means of production, and purchasers of labour. Moreover, they were labourers capable of their own emancipation from the constraints of the capitalist economy, despite the forms of fetishism therein.[57] Of course the paradigmatic and most advanced mode of wage labour in Marx's time was industrial, and a discussion of industrial wage labour comprises much of the content of his later analyses of political economy. More recent Marxists,[58] motivated by a political desire to conform to certain party orthodoxies, have maintained that a necessary condition for wage labour to be proletarian is that it produces so-called 'material' commodities. For Poulantzas, 'Non-material' white-collar labour was largely 'petty bourgeois' in character.[59] But Marx explicitly opposed such an approach; it did not matter for him whether you worked in a 'sausage factory' or a 'teaching factory'. Proletarian labour was defined simply as 'wage labour', labour which politically may be more or less 'advanced'.[60]

To return to the theme of exclusion, let us take the 'unpaid' labourers to which Hardt and Negri refer. Marx uses the term 'lumpenproletariat' to refer to aspects of this category, for in constructing a theory of the revolutionary proletariat, it was necessary for Marx to exclude as 'other', all that which he considered to be 'reactionary'/'counter-revolutionary'. The lumpenproletariat exist outside of the binary opposition between exploiter and exploited, conceived as the bourgeoisie and the proletariat. They were the class that was not a class, to the extent that, as Hayes has noted: 'They were a class only in so far as they were lumped together by their last contact with the dialectic, their common exclusion from the relations of production.'[61] So too, Ernesto Laclau writes that: 'In order to maintain its credentials as an "insider" of the main line of historical development, however, the proletariat had to be strictly differentiated from the absolute "outsider": the lumpenproletariat.'[62]

We can look in more detail at Marx and Engels' work to see how they go about constructing this understanding of the outsider. Engels wrote: 'The *lumpenproletariat*, this scum of depraved element from all classes, with headquarters in the big cities, is the worst of all possible allies. This rabble is absolutely venal and absolutely brazen.'[63] In *The Communist Manifesto*, Marx and Engels referred to the lumpenproletariat as 'the social scum, that passively rotting mass thrown off by the layers of old society'.[64] For Marx, key aspects of the lumpenproletariat sat outside the (directly) exploitative mechanisms of the capitalist system. They were the parasitic groupings. They were the reactionary forces likely set back the historical cause of the proletariat. But they were more than (permanently) unemployed workers. They were the 'organ grinders', the 'criminals', the 'prostitutes'. Marx even discusses the finance aristocracy in this context, writing that 'where money, filth and blood commingle. The finance aristocracy, in its mode of acquisition as well as in its pleasures, is nothing but the *rebirth of the lumpenproletariat on the heights of bourgeois society*.'[65]

Bakunin's work represented a contemporary and immediate challenge to Marx and Engels' views on the lumpenproletariat. But his challenge was based on an understanding of a further 'exclusion'. The forces of reaction were for Bakunin to be found not in the 'lumpenproletariat', but within Marx's hallowed 'advanced' sections of the proletariat. Accordingly, Bakunin turned his back on the industrially 'advanced' proletariat, and embraced the 'lumpenproletariat', the 'flower' of the proletariat. 'By the flower of the proletariat I mean precisely that eternal "meat" for governments, that great rabble of people ordinarily designated by Messrs. Marx and Engels by the phrase at once picturesque and contemptuous of "lumpenproletariat"'[66]

Both accounts attract the criticism of post-Marxists and post-anarchists. Laclau considers that Marx's concept of the lumpenproletariat represents the boundary of his theory of class struggle and historical materialism, a tension between an 'economic essentialism' and a recognition of the discursive character of political identity. Marx considered class identity as constructed through the internal antagonisms of the mode of production. Yet the discourse of proletarian identity is the result of an a 'antagonism' external to the social 'totality', what Laclau would term a 'constitutive outside', this 'other', itself being the product of a contradictory discursive operation of

Marxism. To this extent, all political identities result from antagonistic discursive processes, rather than the unfolding of the historical or economic dialectic.[67] But if this is so, Bakunin's view is hardly an 'advance' on the one put forward by Marx. Bakunin explicitly stated – despite a tendency in his work to reify the significance of state forms – that he shared with Marx a belief in the economic determinants of the historical process. If, as Bakunin argued, the lumpenproletariat was the 'flower of the proletariat', this flower would seem spontaneously to bloom outside of the operation of politics.

Newman has levelled the charge of determinism against Marx and Bakunin. He writes that: 'Bakunin's political thought can be seen as a scientific-materialist philosophy combined with a dialectical view of historical development'.[68] Yet Bakunin receives a far better treatment from Newman than does Marx. This is in part because Bakunin's 'essentialism' is mitigated by the negative character of his dialectics – a dialectics where there is a thesis, anti-thesis, but no synthesis. This is a dialectics of opposition to politics, a dialectics of destruction, a dialectics of refusal.[69]

As we have seen, the theme of refusal runs through Hardt and Negri's understanding of the 'multitude'. Let us explore this multitude in more detail. Hardt and Negri propose a conception of revolutionary agency which is more fitting to the 'realities' of contemporary global capitalism in the information age, or the period of 'Empire'. In place of 'traditional' manual labour Hardt and Negri point to the increasing significance of what they term 'immaterial labour'. Thus they write of 'the communicative labour of industrial production that has newly become linked in informational networks, the interactive labour of symbolic analysis and problem solving, and the labour of the production and manipulation of affects.'[70] These are broad categories, uniting the labour of high tech and service industry, for example, the flight attendant's 'service with a smile'. For Hardt and Negri – and to this extent they follow the theorists of the 'information age' such as Bell and Castells[71] – these modes of labour are generated through an unfolding logic of the global capitalist economic system.

Their view, then, is not that there are no determinant processes which generate an ontological resistance to capitalism but, rather, that the ontological understanding produced by Marxism has been displaced; the need is for a new understanding of revolutionary agency in a contemporary 'postmodern' context. It is again worth making a comparison here with Laclau and Mouffe's post-Marxism. Laclau and Mouffe write: 'Only if we renounce any epistemological prerogative based on the ontologically privileged position of a universal class will it be possible seriously to discuss the present degree of validity of the Marxist categories. At this point we should state quite plainly that we are now situated on post-marxist terrain.'[72] Having made this assertion, Laclau and Mouffe find no agent with which to replace the working class. In contrast, as we have seen, when Hardt and Negri bid farewell to the 'old working class' they say hello to the new proletariat – the 'multitude'. However, this notion of the multitude is difficult to grasp. At once, it becomes 'the class of those who refuse the rule of capital'.[73] They maintain that:

> The concept rests [...] on the claim that there is no political priority among the forms of labor: all forms of labor are today socially productive, they produce in common, and share too a common potential to resist the domination of capital [...] The multitude gives the concept of the proletariat its fullest definition as all those who labour and produce under the rule of capital.[74]

The 'immanence' of the multitude brings with it a certain political potentiality, a potentiality of common collaboration.

So, the multitude are the exploited who nevertheless have the potential power to *refuse* the rule of capital. Let us look a little more at some of those Hardt and Negri place under this banner. The traditional working class are part of the multitude. Those who perform domestic labour – women in the household – are part of the multitude. The health care worker is part of the multitude. The agricultural worker in the developing country is part of the multitude. The sex worker is part of the multitude. The 'poor' are part of the multitude. The unemployed are part of the multitude. For, as Hardt and Negri write: '[j]ust as social production takes place today equally inside and outside the factory walls, so too it takes place equally inside and outside the wage relationship'.[75] At one point, Hardt and Negri insist that: 'All of the multitude is productive and all of it is poor.'[76] And elsewhere Hardt and Negri write: 'The poor [...] refers not to those who have nothing but to the wide multiplicity of all those who are inserted into the mechanisms of social production regardless of social order or property.'[77]

Whereas for Hardt and Negri the use of the term lumpenproletariat by Marxists served to 'demonise' the poor, '*only the poor has the ability to renew being*'.[78] As the authors put it: 'these classes are in fact included in social production [...] the poor are not merely victims but powerful agents [...] they are part of the circuits of social and biopolitical production'.[79] The 'lumpenproletariat' are not a reactionary 'other' to the proletariat, but rather a constituent element of it.

Leaving aside the issue of whether the 'poor' really can be regarded as having such transformative potential,[80] it remains difficult to see how the multitude can be regarded as a site of possible transformation of the social bios as a whole. That is, without a hegemonic project bringing together the unemployed, sex workers, service workers, material and manual labourers, as well as the lumpenproletariat, immigrants, and indigenous residents, it is difficult to see how a meaningful challenge to the power of the capitalist state can be mounted. Indeed, the fact that Hardt and Negri reject engagement with the state form means that their prefigurative politics of resistance – as with post-anarchism – will always be constrained.

Problems are exacerbated further by some of the approaches to refusal which Hardt and Negri have suggested. These seem to owe more to a postmodern understanding of identity politics, than to an effective politics of anti-capitalism. Accordingly, they write of the subversion of 'conventional norms of corporeal and sexual relations between and within genders'.[81] They enthuse about the subversion implied by 'dressing in drag'. Indeed, 'Bodies themselves transform and mutate to create new posthuman bodies.'[82] Speaking about these types of approaches in general, the resoundingly modernist Marxist Terry Eagleton writes of how: 'Socialism has lost out to sado-masochism. Among the students of culture, the body is an immensely fashionable topic, but it is usually the erotic body, not the famished one. There is a keen interest in coupling bodies, but not in labouring ones.'[83]

That said, there is at least for Hardt and Negri a stress on exploitation as a key determinant of revolutionary capacity, setting their work apart from the more extreme excesses of postmodern understandings of politics. However, the lack of analytical precision at the heart of the category of the multitude does throw into doubt the idea that Hardt and Negri's work really does represent an advance on traditional Marxian categories. Indeed, the rich tradition of Marxist class analysis has attempted to interrogate in detail – and through a rich theoretical and empirical analysis – the revolutionary potential created in the context of particular modes of exploitation, and social relations.[84] For Hardt and Negri, if we are all part of the multitude, there is no scope at all for class analysis.

## Conclusion

The task of locating Hardt and Negri's thought is far from straightforward. Nevertheless, a number of provisional conclusions can be drawn. First, Negri's rereading of Lenin is both strategic and far from orthodox. In going 'beyond' Lenin, we see a Leninist basis to Hardt and Negri's anti-anarchist communism, and therefore how Hardt and Negri's polemical approach might be situated. Yet, second, the account which Hardt and Negri give of communism, particularly as this relates to the opposition to 'socialism' in their recent work, is to say the least curious. How can two authors so embedded in the radical tradition hold such disappointing views of socialism, its history, and its advances? What game are they playing? Third, despite their preoccupation with the theme of exploitation, it seems that when it comes to 'politics', the authors are closer to their anarchist straw man than they would like. They claim that anarchism lacks strategic awareness, yet they too fail to articulate a conception of revolutionary strategy. Rather, they see in the multitude the immanent possibility of spontaneous revolutionary activity, an activity without centre and therefore without 'authority', without 'identity'. Unfortunately, this is activity without direction. Of course, we might finally regard Hardt and Negri's displacement of the problematic and ontological centrality of the working class as situating them close to the post-Marxist end of the spectrum. This is an interpretation further reinforced by their radicalisation of the Foucauldian conception of biopower. Yet, at least for the post-Marxists, Hardt and Negri's multitude fails to take account of how political identity is a 'discursive' product, a product of hegemony. Perhaps then they are post-anarchists? However we choose to label their thought, Hardt and Negri's go a long way towards subverting many of the labels which have done so much to carve up the space of radical politics. The realities of contemporary global capitalism do necessitate revisiting some of these labels, if radical resistance to exploitation in all its forms is to be possible.

## Acknowledgements

This idea for this chapter initially emerged from a discussion of Hardt and Negri's thought with Professor David McLellan, a discussion for which I am grateful. An early version of the chapter was presented at the Manchester Workshops in Political Thought, Manchester Metropolitan University, September 2010. I would like to thank all those who attended for their comments – and particularly Benjamin Franks for making me think of the historical relationship between Marxism and anarchism in a different way. I would also like to thank the editors of this volume for their exceptionally challenging but also generously constructive comments. Any errors and omissions remain my own.

## Notes

1. Wittgenstein in J. Tully (ed.) *Meaning and Context: Quentin Skinner and his Critics* (Cambridge: Polity, 1988), p. v.
2. Q. Skinner, 'Meaning and Understanding in the History of Ideas', in J. Tully (ed.), p. 39.
3. See A. Callinicos, 'Toni Negri in Perspective', in G. Balakrishnan (ed.) *Debating Empire* (London: Verso, 2003), pp. 121–143.
4. See Callinicos (2003) and Steve Wright, 'A Party of Autonomy?', in T.S. Murphy and A.-K. Mustapha (eds) *The Philosophy of Antonio Negri: Volume 1, Resistance in Practice* (London: Pluto, 2005), pp. 73–106.
5. On Italian Trotskyism, see R.J. Alexander, *International Trotskyism, 1929–1988: A Documented Analysis of the Movement* (Durham, NC: Duke University Press, 1991).
6. The post-Marxist Ernesto Laclau considers that Hardt and Negri do not sufficiently break with the essentialism of Marxist class politics. For Laclau, revolutionary identity is the product of strategic thinking, that is a form of politics which goes beyond the immediacy of what May terms 'tactics'. See David McLellan, *Marxism After Marx* (Fourth Edition) (London: Palgrave, 2007);

S. Newman, *The Politics of Postanarchism* (Edinburgh: Edinburgh University Press, 2010). Ernesto Laclau 'Can Immanence Explain Social Struggles?', in P.A. Passavant and J. Dean (eds.) *Empire's New Clothes: Reading Hardt and Negri* (London: Routledge, 2004), pp. 21–30; and T. May, *The Political Philosophy of Poststructuralist Anarchism* (Pennsylvania: The Pennsylvania State University Press, 1994).

7.  Hardt and Negri, *Empire*, p. 350.
8.  A. Negri 'Lesson One: From the Factory of Strategy', available online at http://antonionegriinenglish.wordpress.com/2010/09/06/lesson-1-from-33-lessons-on-lenin-for-a-marxist-reading-of-lenins-marxism/ (Accessed 20 June 2011).
9.  Hardt and Negri, *Empire*, p. 234.
10. Negri, cited in Michael Hardt (2005) 'Into the Factory: Negri's Lenin and the Subjective Caesura (1968–1973)', in Timothy Murphy and Abdul-Karim Mustapha, *The Philosophy of Antonio Negri: Volume I – Resistance in Practice* (London: Pluto Press, 2005), p. 13.
11. K. Marx, *The Poverty of Philosophy* (Moscow: Progress Publishers, 1975).
12. K. Marx, 'The Holy Family', in D. McLellan (ed.), *K. Marx: Selected Writings* (Second Edition) (Oxford: Oxford University Press: 2000), pp. 145–169.
13. K. Marx, 'On Bakunin's Statism and Anarchy', in David McLellan (ed.), *Karl Marx: Selected Writings* (Oxford: Oxford University Press, 2000), p. 607. See also Engels' letter to Cuno of 1872, where Engels writes: 'Bakunin maintains that it is the state which has created capital, that the capitalist has his capital only by the grace of the state. As, therefore, the state is the chief evil, it is above all the state which must be done away with and then capitalism will go to blazes of itself.' F. Engels, 'Letter to Theodore Cuno in Milan in 1872', in *Marx-Engels: Selected Correspondence* (Moscow: Progress Publishers, 1975), p.257.
14. M. Bakunin, *Statism and Anarchy*, M. Shatz (ed.) (Cambridge: Cambridge University Press, 1990) p. 142.
15. See E. H. Carr, *Michael Bakunin* (London: London, 1937). See also A.W. Gouldner, 'Marx's Last Battle: Bakunin and the International', *Theory and Society* (Vol. 11, No. 6, 1982) pp. 853–884.
16. V.I. Lenin, (1901) 'Theses on Anarchism and Socialism', available online at http://www.marxists.org/archive/lenin/works/1901/dec/31.htm (Accessed 18 April 2011).
17. V.I. Lenin, (1905) 'Socialism and Anarchism', available online at http://www.marxists.org/archive/lenin/works/1905/nov/24.htm (Accessed 18 April 2011). Stalin, writing in 1906–1907, took seriously Lenin's line of critique. Thus he wrote that: 'Some people believe that Marxism and anarchism are based on the same principles and that disagreements between them concern only tactics, so that, in the opinion of these people, it is quite impossible to draw a contrast between these two trends [. . .] This is a great mistake [. . .]We believe that anarchists are the real enemies of Marxism.' J. Stalin 'Anarchism or Socialism', available online at http://www.marxists.org/reference/archive/stalin/works/1906/12/x01.htm (Accessed 23 May 2011).
18. V.I. Lenin, (1912) 'The Italian Socialist Congress', available online at http://www.marxists.org/archive/lenin/works/1912/jul/15b.htm (Accessed 18 April 2011).
19. V.I. Lenin, *What Is to Be Done?* (Moscow: Progress Publishers, 1947); *One Step Forwards, Two Steps Backwards* (Moscow: Progress Publishers, 1947).
20. V.I. Lenin (1922) 'Letter to Congress', available online at http://www.marxists.org/archive/lenin/works/1922/dec/testamnt/congress.htm (Accessed 22 May 2011).
21. V.I. Lenin (1917) *The State and Revolution*, available online at http://www.marxists.org/archive/lenin/works/1917/staterev/ (Accessed 22 May 2011).

22. R. Luxemburg 'Organisational Questions of the Social Democracy'; and 'The Mass Strike, the Political Party and the Trade Unions', in M.A. Waters (ed.), *Rosa Luxemburg Speaks* (New York: Pathfinder Press, 1970), pp. 112–130 and 153–218 respectively.

23. See Hardt, 'Into the Factory'; David Bates (2009) 'Reading Negri', *Critique*, 49 (31/3) pp. 465–482.

24. A. Negri, 'Workers' Party Against Work', in T. S. Murphy (ed.), *Books for Burning: Between Civil War and Democracy in 1970s Italy* (London: Verso, 2005) pp. 51–117.

25. A. Negri 'What to Do Today withWhat Is to Be Done?, or Rather: The Body of the General Intellect', in S. Budgen, S. Kouvelakis and S. Žižek (eds.) *Lenin Reloaded: Towards a Politics of the Truth* (Durham and London: Duke University Press, 2007), p. 301.

26. A. Negri, (2008) *Reflections on Empire* (Cambridge: Polity, 2008), pp. 145.

27. Negri, *Reflections on Empire*, pp. 144–145.

28. Hardt and Negri, *Empire*, p. 350.

29. Ibid., p. 294.

30. Ibid., p. 413.

31. A. Giddens, *The Third Way* (Cambridge: Polity, 1998).

32. M. Hardt 'The Common in Communism', in C. Douzinas and S. Žižek (eds.) *The Idea of Communism* (London: Verso, 2010), p. 131.

33. A. Negri 'Communism: Some Thoughts on the Concept and Practice', in Douzinas and Žižek, *The Idea of Communism*, p. 159.

34. Ibid., pp. 158–159.

35. Ibid., p. 161.

36. To the extent at least that Blond maintains that 'state socialism' undermined a working-class capacity for 'self-help' and self-organisation – a capacity which had been particularly strong in the nineteenth century. For Blond, of course, the working class ought still to know its place. For Negri, statism stifles revolutionary capacity. See P. Blond, *Red Toryism* (London: Faber and Faber, 2010), especially Chapter 5.

37. Hardt and Negri, *Empire*, pp. xii–xii.

38. A. Negri, *The Porcelain Workshop* (Los Angeles, CA: Semiotext(e), 2008), p. 22.

39. M. Foucault, *The History of Sexuality*, Volume One (London: Allen Lane, 1979), p. 137.

40. Hardt and Negri, *Empire*, pp. 23–24.

41. Newman, *The Politics of Postanarchism*, p. 62.

42. Michel Foucault, cited in J. Bernauer and M. Mahon, 'The Ethics of Michel Foucault', in G. Gutting (ed.) *The Cambridge Companion to Foucault* (Cambridge: Cambridge University Press, 1994), p. 153.

43. Newman, *The Politics of Postanarchism*, p. 93. E. Laclau and C. Mouffe, *Hegemony and Socialist Strategy* (London: Verso, 1985). A brief word of caution against Newman's reading of Laclau and Mouffe, for Laclau and Mouffe do not, I think, fall prey to the type of state reductionism which Newman suggests. Gramsci – on whom Laclau and Mouffe draw heavily, if critically – formulated his concept of the 'integral state' to move beyond a liberal understanding of sovereignty. And Laclau and Mouffe take this line of thought further, arguing for a discursive 'anti-essentialist' understanding of power, where power is an effect of discursive practices which permeate every aspect of the 'impossible object' called 'society'. This involves a rejection of the base-superstructure 'metaphor', and any *a priori* understanding of power, whether this emphasises 'the state' or 'the economy'.

This said, I would argue that the political project of 'radical democracy' emerging from Laclau and Mouffe's thought, in the end, is radical in name only, for the authors reject all types of large-scale social transformation, or meta-narrative of human emancipation.

44. Newman, The *Politics of Postanarchism*, p. 178.
45. Hardt and Negri, *Multitude*, p. 54.
46. See K. Weeks 'The Refusal of Work as Demand and Perspective', in Murphy and Mustapha, *The Philosophy of Antonio Negri*, pp. 109–135.
47. K. Marx, *Grundrisse* (Harmondsworth: Penguin, 1973).
48. Negri, 'Workers' Party Against Work (1973)', p. 75.
49. Hardt and Negri, *Multitude*, p. 54.
50. Hardt and Negri, *Empire*, p. 61.
51. Hardt and Negri, *Multitude*, p. 351.
52. Ibid., p. 136.
53. Ibid., p. 347.
54. Ibid., p. 106.
55. E. Laclau, *On Populist Reason* (London: Verso, 2005), p. 143.
56. Stallybrass writes: 'Before Marx, *proletarian* [*prolétaire*] was one of the central signifiers of the passive spectacle of poverty. In England, Dr Johnson had defined *proletarian* in his *Dictionary* (1755) as 'mean; wretched; vile; vulgar', and the word seems to have had a similar meaning in France in the early nineteenth century, where it was used virtually interchangeably with *nomade*'. Staylbrass, cited in Laclau, *On Populist Reason*, p. 143.
57. See H. Draper, 'The Principle of Self-Emancipation in Marx and Engels', R. Miliband and J. Saville (eds.) *The Socialist Register* (London: Merlin, 1971), pp. 81–109; C. Johnson 'The Problem of Reformism in Marx's Theory of Fetishism', *New Left Review*, 119 (January–February 1980), pp. 71–96.
58. See E. Mandel, *Late Capitalism* (London: New Left Books); N. Poulantzas, *Classes in Contemporary Capitalism* (London: New Left Books, 1975).
59. Poulantzas, *Classes in Contemporary Capitalism, especially* chapters 3, 4 and 5.
60. K. Marx, *Capital*: Volume One (Harmondsworth: Penguin, 1976).
61. P. Hayes, 'Utopia and the Lumpenproletariat: Marx's Reasoning in "The Eighteenth Brumaire of Louis Bonaparte" ', *The Review of Politics*, 50/3 (1988), p. 447.
62. Laclau, *On Populist Reason*, pp. 143–144.
63. F. Engels, 'Preface to The Peasant War in Germany', in *Marx and Engels: Selected Works* (London: Lawrence and Wishart, 1968), p. 229.
64. K. Marx and F. Engels, *The Communist Manifesto*, in D. McLellan (ed.) *Karl Marx: Selected Writings* (London: Penguin, 2000), p. 254.
65. Marx in Hayes, 'Utopia and the Lumpenproletariat', p. 449.
66. M. Bakunin, *Marxism, Freedom and the State*, K. J. Kenafick (ed. and trans.) (London: Freedom Press, 1990), p. 48.
67. See, for example, Laclau, *On Populist Reason*, p. 146.
68. Newman, *The Politics of Postanarchism*, p. 38.
69. See S. Newman, *From Bakunin to Lacan* (Plymouth: Lexington Books, 2007), p. 28.
70. Hardt and Negri, *Empire*, p. 30.
71. D. Bell, *The Coming of the Post-Industrial Society* (New York: Basic Books, 1999); M. Castells, *The Rise of the Network Society*, Volume 1 (Second Edition) (London: Blackwell, 2000).
72. Laclau and Mouffe, *Hegemony and Socialist Strategy*, p. 4.
73. Hardt and Negri, *Multitude*, p. 106.

74. Ibid., p. 107.
75. Ibid., p. 135.
76. Ibid., p. 134.
77. M. Hardt and A. Negri, *Commonwealth* (Cambridge, MA: Harvard University Press), p. 40.
78. Hardt and Negri, *Empire*, p. 157.
79. Ibid., p. 129.
80. See D. Byrne, *Social Exclusion* (Buckingham: Open University Press, 1999); W. J. Wilson, *The Truly Disadvantaged* (Chicago: Chicago University Press, 1987).
81. Hardt and Negri, *Empire*, p. 215.
82. Ibid., p. 215.
83. T. Eagleton, *After Theory* (London: Penguin, 2003), p. 2.
84. See, for example, E. O. Wright, *Class Counts* (Cambridge: Cambridge University Press, 1997).

# 15

# Conclusion: Towards a Libertarian Socialism for the Twenty-First Century?

*Saku Pinta and David Berry*

> There is something that has amazed and even shocked me for a long time. There is a tragicomical paradox in the spectacle of people who claim to be revolutionary, who wish to overthrow the world and at the same time try to cling at all costs to a reference system, who would feel lost if the author or the system which guarantees the truth of what they believe, were to be taken away from them. How is it possible not to see that these people place themselves by their own volition in a position of mental subjection to a work which is already there, which has mastered a truth which henceforth can only be interpreted, refined, patched up?
>
> Cornelius Castoriadis[1]

It is difficult to imagine the 'Black and Red' conference (in which this volume originated) having been conceived of, were it not for the epochal events of the 1980s and 1990s and the subsequent depolarisation of global politics, the generalised ideological crisis of the Left and the increased 'illegibility' of many social struggles since then, the emergence of movements of resistance to globalised capital such as *zapatismo* (seen by some as 'post-ideological'[2]) and the blossoming of the worldwide 'movement of movements' and the associated Social Forums.[3] The corollary of this seems to have been not only a renewed interest in the history and theory of anarchisms (in Europe and North America, at least), but also a new willingness to revisit the essentialist tribalism that has arguably always (but especially since the Comintern's 'Bolshevisation' of the mid-1920s) characterised the Left. Many would concur with John Holloway's remark that 'One thing that is new and exciting about the re-articulation of ideas is that the old divisions between anarchism and Marxism are being eroded.'[4] These re-examinations of how anarchist and communist theories and practices interact – and how some of the old divisions within the radical Left milieu might be overcome – have acquired a renewed sense of urgency following the 2008 economic and financial crisis and the search for a new emancipatory politics. David Harvey, in a recent discussion of the changing nature of present-day anticapitalist movements, stated:

> Contemporary attempts to revive the communist hypothesis typically abjure state control and look to other forms of collective social organisation [...]. Horizontally networked, as opposed to hierarchically commanded, systems of coordination between autonomously organised and self-governing collectives of producers and consumers are envisaged as lying at the core of a new form of communism. [...] All manner of small-scale experiments around the world can be found in which such economic and political forms are being constructed. In this there is a convergence of some sort between the Marxist and anarchist traditions that harks back to the broadly collaborative situation between them in the 1860s in Europe before their break-up into warring camps after the Paris Commune in 1871 and the blow-up between Karl Marx and one of the leading radicals of the time, the anarchist Michael Bakunin, in 1872.[5]

The reference to the hoary old story of Marx *versus* Bakunin might seem tiresome, but interestingly echoes the theme of a conference held in Paris a few years ago – organised largely by militants associated with the Trotskyist *Ligue Communiste Révolutionnaire*, the libertarian communist *Alternative Libertaire* and syndicalists from the SUD (Solidaires Unitaires Démocratiques) unions – which took as its starting point a return to the history of the First International. The point, however, was not to rehearse the divergences and conflicts, or to attempt to apportion blame – all of which has been done quite enough already by both 'sides'. It was to hold up the story of the International Working Men's Association as 'an interesting example for the future', 'a democratic, multiple, diverse, internationalist movement' in which both Marxists and anarchists (among others) participated, and where 'it was possible for distinct, if not opposed, political options to converge in reflection and in action over several years, playing a major role in the first great modern proletarian revolution. An International where libertarians and Marxists were able – despite conflicts – to work together and engage in common actions.'[6]

The purpose of this collection of papers has been similarly to provide a back-story, as it were, to these developments: to rediscover the lost histories of a libertarian socialist tradition – an ideological current effectively blurring the boundaries between anarchist and Marxist variants of revolutionary socialist thought – and to open up debate about the development of socialist ideologies by re-examining the relationship between Marxism and anarchism – or rather between Marxisms and anarchisms – emphasising the complexities and the convergences, but also engaging with the very real divergences not only between Marxism and anarchism, but also between different Marxisms and between different anarchisms.

Indeed, as was noted in the introduction to this volume and has been made abundantly clear by more than one contribution, one of the standard features of established socialist and labour historiography has been to reduce the complexity of multiple anarchisms and multiple Marxisms. The result has been an ahistorical portrayal of 'anarchism' that routinely lumps individualists together with advocates of collective social action, and an equally ahistorical and reductionist 'Marxism' that fails to differentiate between separate trends in this tradition, often assumed to be Leninist, similarly to the way in which 'communism' is often equated with Stalinism by antisocialists or anticommunists. Articles and books which draw a bold, unbroken and unproblematic line between 'authoritarian' and 'anti-authoritarian' socialisms are legion.[7]

One of the conclusions that may be drawn from the examinations of revolutionary socialist theory and history offered in this volume, is that any such schematic division of the Left along anarchist and Marxist lines is highly problematic, and furthermore, that if we are to accept a dividing line in the socialist tradition between 'libertarian' and 'authoritarian' currents, then this does not neatly correspond to anarchist and Marxist ideological designations. In addition to the fact that multiple anarchisms and Marxisms throughout the late nineteenth and twentieth centuries have been, and continue to be, internally divided on a variety of strategic and theoretical matters, it is equally clear that those currents on both 'sides' of the anarchist-Marxist 'divide' most concerned with working-class self-organisation have displayed a remarkable degree of commonality, as have, ironically perhaps, variants of both traditions that have routinely been viewed as diametrically opposed. One could argue, for example, that there is a similarity between the 'substitutionism' of anarchist 'illegalists' or proponents of 'propaganda by the deed' – substituting the exemplary actions of activists as the spark which will ignite spontaneous mass revolt – with the leadership role assigned by some Leninists to an avant-garde party composed of enlightened professional revolutionaries substituted for a similarly conceived mass of followers. Victor Serge, more than any other historical revolutionary figure, perhaps best exemplifies this unusual convergence of perspectives, shifting from a vocal and active advocate of individualist anarchism to, at a later stage, a member of the Russian Communist Party (employed as a journalist, editor, and translator with the Communist International) – ending his political trajectory as a Trotskyist and an anti-Stalinist socialist critic of the Soviet Union. Historically, it has proved quite possible to make the rather short conceptual leap from a Stirnerite or Nietzschean idea of a ruthless egoist or overman – and associated negative or paternalistic attitudes towards the 'mass' or 'herd' – to the embrace of a powerful political elite.[8] Conversely, the evolutionary approach typically identified with the reformist tendencies in social democracy – focused on gradual and piecemeal changes to the existing system – have certain parallels with 'liberal' anarchisms which similarly advocate the construction of various counter institutions and lifestyles as a moral rebellion against the state and capital.

Tensions and debates, common to both anarchists and Marxists, surrounding appropriate forms of organisation have frequently arisen, although often employing different political vocabulary. The 'party' as interpreted by anti-parliamentary Marxists – as an organisation uniting the most politically advanced and conscious elements of the working class – has parallels with, for example, the General Union of Anarchists as elaborated by the platformist-Makhnovists; similarly, there are parallels between the outright rejection of these political formations – in favour of looser groupings or strictly autonomous labour combinations – both by Marxists such as Otto Rühle as well as by anarchists such as Voline.[9] (Indeed it is perhaps worth mentioning here that before the term 'party' acquired its modern meaning, and in particular prior to its association with Bolshevik conceptions, anarchist-communists such as Errico Malatesta and Peter Kropotkin spoke of forming anarchist 'parties', and the term 'vanguard' – adopted as the name of one US anarchist-communist journal[10] – was embraced by anarchists.)

Debates surrounding the 'transitional period' – describing, or speculating, how a society might undergo the transformation from capitalism to communism and what (if any) intermediate steps are to be deemed necessary in this process – have proved to be another traditional dividing point between some anarchists and Marxists, raising further matters of contention – crucially, the role of the state in social change (and the nature of that state). Again, this matter is not always so clear cut. One variation of the 'transition period', the 'two stage' theory most closely associated with the Social Democratic parties of the Second International as well as with Stalinist orthodoxy, suggests that societies (above all economically 'underdeveloped' societies) would first have to pass through a capitalist stage of economic development in order to build the industrial and technological foundations necessary to support a socialist economy – 'socialist' meaning yet another transitional stage of state ownership of productive assets prior to the emergence of full-blown communism.[11] Although couched in Marxist terminology the stagist strategy, the emphasis which it placed on the state as a key instrument for social change, and its political consequences were not accepted by all Marxists. Moreover, while it is true that Marx himself remained rather vague or ambiguous about how he envisaged the process of a revolutionary transformation (at least up to the Paris Commune in 1871), the familiar accusation of a thoroughly 'determinist' and 'teleological' Marx has also been contested.[12] Another variation on the 'transitional period' theme, the 'dictatorship of the proletariat', is often understood to mean an authoritarian and centralised state controlled by a political elite. Anarchists have criticised this political form as totalitarian and as tending towards a permanent (rather than transitional) existence, and claimed that the results of this transitional period were foreseen by Bakunin in his warnings of Marx's 'red bureaucracy'. Instead, anarchists have posed the alternative of an immediate dissolution of the state following a revolutionary upheaval. However, the interpretation of the 'dictatorship of the proletariat' as the armed suppression of bourgeois counter-revolution under the direction of democratic workers' councils, embraced by councilists and other anti-state Marxist groupings, also finds (controversial) parallels in anarchist praxis in the militias of revolutionary Ukraine and Spain.

These theoretical or practical convergences, if routinely ignored or unacknowledged, are unsurprising when considering the variety of interpretations and geographic spread of these ideas and practices since the mid-nineteenth century. However, convergences are all the more notable when considering those currents, such as the ones primarily discussed in this volume, associated with working-class movements. If one were to exclude from consideration, on the one hand, individualist, anti-organisational, market-oriented or non-socialist currents from the broad anarchist tradition, and on the other, reformist, electoralist or state-centric approaches most often associated with the two dominant expressions of Marxism in the twentieth century (social democracy and Bolshevism), the grey area between these positions – what has sometimes been referred to as 'libertarian socialism' or 'libertarian communism' (despite the lack of any universally accepted usage of these terms) – display a number of common commitments and considerations: the role assigned to the working class as the social grouping most clearly associated with carrying out the task of human liberation; an anti-parliamentary disposition, rejecting the formal political democracy (as opposed to, and distinct from, economic democracy) of bourgeois parliaments or participation in electoral activity as effective methods for advancing social change; working-class self-activity and direct action as both a method for circumventing mediating bureaucracies, argued to stifle initiative and channel grievances into acceptable areas, and as a way to forge solidarities and create a sense of collective workers' power.

Few sustained or conscious instances of such an alliance – the merger of an anarchistic insistence on non-hierarchical organisation and antiauthoritarian praxis and a Marxist critique of alienation and capitalist social relations – are evident through the late nineteenth and twentieth centuries. The 'revolutionary industrial unionism' of the Industrial Workers of the World (IWW) – distinct from, but with more than a passing family resemblance to, revolutionary syndicalism – is one prominent example.[13] Indeed for union organiser and labour historian Fred Thompson, the IWW represented a working-class 'Marxism in overalls'.[14] Small wonder, then, that the IWW has served as a major reference point for multiple anarchist and Marxist currents.[15]

Syndicalism early on, itself a fairly heterogeneous form of working-class radicalism, was viewed by many as a synthesis of anarchist and Marxist perspectives through the avowal of class struggle combined with a rejection of electoralism (see Lewis Mates' contribution to this volume). French 'anarcho-Marxist' syndicalist Georges Sorel was but one theorist who, as Renzo Llorente points out, acknowledged an intellectual debt to both Marx and the anarchists. The Hungarian revolutionary Ervin Szabó (1877–1918) would be another example. However, as syndicalism began to adopt a more consciously anarchist political orientation in the 1920s, theorists such as Rudolf Rocker began to distance themselves from Marxist contributions to syndicalist theory (and for their open acceptance of Marxist categories and terminology, the IWW was excluded by Rocker from the anarcho-syndicalist tradition).[16]

'The revolutionary syndicalism of the early twentieth century,' writes historian Vadim Damier, 'was not born in the heads of theoreticians,' but rather developed through 'the practice of the workers' movement which sought its own doctrine – above all, the practice of direct action' and only subsequently was it theorised.[17] Similarly, periods of revolutionary up-heaval and collective action, more than philosophical speculation, have contributed to the forging of common perspectives between self-identi-fied revolutionary anarchists and Marxists in the years following the First World War. Specifically, the workers' council, as a directly democratic social form prefiguring postcapitalist economic and social arrangements emerging from actual workers' struggles, became a central organisational concept through the interwar period (and beyond). The workers' councils were embraced by revolutionary Marxists (ranging from the ideas of Rosa Luxemburg and the Dutch-German council communists to the defenders of the Italian factory occupations like Antonio Gramsci); anarchists such as the Ukrainian Makhnovschina or the positions adopted by the Friends of Durruti group in the Spanish Revolution and Civil War in 1937; as well as more variegated political constellations, for example, the Kronstadt naval mutineers in 1921 and their demands for democracy in the soviets against single-party rule. In the late 1940s, council communist theorist Anton Pannekoek came to the view that the workers' council form had effectively synthesised anarchist notions of liberty and spontaneity with Marxist con-ceptions of class struggle and working-class organisation, and as a result, had transcended the limitations of both pre-war 'classical anarchism' and 'orthodox Marxism'.[18]

Also drawing inspiration from workers' councils, in the postwar era, were groups of activists such as Socialisme ou Barbarie and the situationists in France, the Facing Reality group in the USA, Solidarity in the UK, and others who saw the continued relevance of this social form in its re-emergence in the Hungarian workers' struggle in 1956.[19] Indeed, for some the Hungarian workers' councils – like the 1905 soviets and the soviets or workers' coun-cils thrown up during and immediately after the First World War – were a revelation and it is clear from a number of the contributions to this volume how important they were in the development of new thinking among revolutionaries. This was not only important with regard to the development of non-Leninist Marxism, but also for many on the radical Left who were committed to creating something new and innovative beyond standard divisions. An editorial written by the Aberdeen Solidarity group expressed this desire to overcome sectarian divisions, stating that 'It is often said by Solidarists that Marxists call us anarchists and anarchists call us Marxists. This paradox is a result of the inability of traditional revolutionaries to understand anything which falls outwith their own outdated categories.'[20]

The recovery of the workers' councils paved the way for a renewed interest in self-management or *autogestion* in the 1960s and 1970s and beyond. For many this was connected to an analysis of post-1945 technocratic modernisation, managerialism, bureaucratisation: self-management thus acquired heightened importance, implying the need to abolish not just capitalist property relations but also the bureaucratic/manager 'class' – what Michael Albert and Robin Hahnel would later call 'co-ordinatorism'.[21] The critique of the domination of economic and political life by 'bureaucratism' became a major focus of both anarchists and Marxists, and was directed by many at both modern capitalism/state capitalism and Leninist organisational conceptions. This was often connected, as we can see in the papers by Jean-Christophe Angaut, Toby Boraman and Benoît Challand, to a reflection on alienation in modern capitalist society, and a new focus on the quality of everyday life. Modern capitalism was to be analysed as a total social, cultural and even aesthetic system – a system that had extended its dominance beyond the immediate 'point of production'. As Guérin remarked (in 1969) when quizzed by a journalist about the simultaneous appearance of two of his books, one on libertarian Marxism and the other on the sexual revolution: 'The libertarian critique of the bourgeois regime is not possible without a critique of bourgeois mores. The revolution cannot be simply political. It must be, at the same time, both cultural and sexual and thus transform every aspect of life and of society . [. . .] The revolt of the spring of 68 rejected all the faces of subjugation.'[22]

If there are many examples of convergence and overlap, there are also clearly a number of tensions which go beyond reciprocated complaints of caricatural misrepresentation. An important one – perhaps the fundamental one – is the question of the limits to individual freedom, a point discussed here by Paul Blackledge, and also raised by Ruth Kinna in the context of Morris' criticism of the anarchists, who for him were all individualists. This has historically been a matter of debate and even a source of conflict between anarchists, too, with the platformists notably arguing that the insistence on the absolute freedom of the individual so beloved of many anarchists was incompatible with the effectiveness of a revolutionary movement. (Indeed Matthew Wilson has recently argued convincingly that an unacknowledged problem in contemporary anarchism is that the concept of freedom is inadequately worked out.[23]) Like Paul Thomas before him, Blackledge argues that this represents a fundamental philosophical divide between Marxism and anarchism – even social anarchism.[24] He nevertheless concedes that there was greater convergence between Marx and Bakunin than there had been between Marx and Proudhon – Donald Clark Hodges, as Renzo Llorente points out, described Bakunin as 'the first anarcho-Marxist'[25] – and it is surely clear from a number of contributions to this volume that some Marxist currents' views have been entirely compatible with the anarchist critique of hierarchy, centralisation and authoritarian organisation.

Another issue which has continued to be much debated – although as much between anarchists as between anarchists and Marxists – has been the question of the historic agent of change. C. Wright Mills and others associated with the New Left were critical of what seemed to them to be the 'labour metaphysic' of European revolutionaries, condemning it as 'a legacy from Victorian Marxism' which had become 'unrealistic' in the light of economic, social and cultural change.[26] For such activists, the modern radicals were the intelligentsia, in particular the young intelligentsia. Although some anarchists, especially individualists, have always been drawn to social marginals, the so-called 'lumpenproletariat', to *déclassé* bohemians – the 'outsider' as the title of E. Armand's individualist organ *l'en dehors* had it – anarchist communists and syndicalists have tended to be just as oriented towards the working class and organised labour as Marxists. As is made clear in contributions to this collection, redefinitions of the working class prompted both by social change and by shifts in analytical frames have represented an area of (qualified) convergence between social anarchists, syndicalists and Marxists in the twentieth and twenty-first centuries. Andrew Cornell, emphasising the importance of the conditions that produce convergence (often movements of opposition to racism, colonialism and war), points out the impact of the US civil rights movement in breaking down some anarchists' attachment to a focus on class and state. The same can of course be said of second-wave feminism.

Can the often violent history of Left sectarianism be overcome in the interests of the common objective of realising an emancipatory society in which 'the free development of each is the condition for the free development of all'? Perhaps the answer to this question lies less in the activities and mutual recriminations of groupuscules and revolutionary formulae concocted in sterile theoretical laboratories, and more in relating to, learning and drawing inspiration from social struggles. History, it might be said, is a good teacher but a poor master in that we can only draw lessons from our collective experiences but should be wary of colouring our expectations of the future too neatly with past events.

## Notes

1. Cornelius Castoriadis, 'Marx aujourd'hui. Entretien avec Cornelius Castoriadis', *Lutter!* 5 (May–August 1983), pp. 15–18; quotation 18. Original translation by Franco Schiavoni for the January 1984 issue of the Australian magazine *Thesis*

*Eleven*, amended and corrected by Castoriadis himself for *Solidarity. A Journal of Libertarian Socialism* no.17 (Summer 1988), pp. 7–15. Available online: http://www.rebeller.se/m.html (accessed 12 June 2012). I would like to thank the editors of this site, *Tankar från rebeller*, for permission to reproduce this quotation as an epigraph. (All other translations from the French are by David Berry.)

2. Simon Tormey, *Anti-capitalism* (Oxford: Oneworld, 2004).
3. Léon Crémieux, 'Mouvement social, anti-mondialisation et nouvelle Internationale', *Contretemps* 6 (February 2003), pp. 12–18.
4. ' "Walking, We ask Questions": An Interview with John Holloway', by Marina A. Sitrin in *Perspectives on Anarchist Theory* (Fall 2004), available online: http://www.leftturn.org/?q=node/363 (accessed 26 July 2010).
5. *The Enigma of Capital and the Crises of Capital* (London: Profile Books, 2010), p. 225. See also 'Andrej Grubačić: Libertarian Socialism for the Twenty-First Century' in Sasha Lilley, *Capital and its Discontents. Conversations with Radical Thinkers in a Time of Tumult* (Oakland, CA: PM Press, 2011), pp. 246–257.
6. Philippe Corcuff and Michaël Löwy, 'Pour une Première Internationale au XXIe siècle', *Contretemps* 6 (February 2003), 9.
7. For a detailed analysis, see Saku Pinta, *Towards a Libertarian Communism: A Conceptual History of the Intersections between Anarchisms and Marxisms* (Unpublished PhD thesis, Loughborough University, 2012).
8. See Part I of David Berry, *A History of the French Anarchist Movement, 1917–1945* (Oakland, CA: AK Press, 2009).
9. Otto Rühle, 'The Revolution Is Not A Party Affair' (1920), Marxists Internet Archive, http://www.Marxists.org/archive/ruhle/1920/ruhle02.htm [19 November 2011]. Voline, *The Unknown Revolution, 1917–1921* (New York: Free Life Editions, 1974 [first published in 1947, in French]).
10. *Vanguard: A Libertarian Communist Journal*, edited by Sam Dolgoff *et al.*, was published in New York, 1932–1939.
11. As Maximilien Rubel points out 'The terms "socialism" and "communism" ' may be used interchangeably 'as there is no distinction between society and the community, so social ownership and communal ownership are equally indistinguishable. Contrary to Lenin's assertions, socialism is not a partial and incomplete first stage of communism.' Maximilien Rubel and John Crump (eds), *Non-Market Socialism in the Nineteenth and Twentieth Centuries* (London: MacMillan Press, 1987), 1.
12. See Kevin B. Anderson, *Marx at the Margins: On Nationalism, Ethnicity, and Non-Western Societies* (Chicago and London: University of Chicago Press, 2010); Teodor Shanin (ed.), *Late Marx and the Russian Road: Marx and 'the Peripheries of Capitalism'* (New York: Monthly Review Press, 1983).
13. See Marcel van der Linden and Wayne Thorpe (eds), *Revolutionary Syndicalism: An International Perspective* (Aldershot: Scolar, 1990); Ralph Darlington, *Syndicalism and the Transition to Communism: An International Comparative Study* (Aldershot: Ashgate, 2008); Vadim Damier, *Anarcho-Syndicalism in the 20th Century* (Edmonton: Black Cat Press, 2009); Wayne Thorpe, 'Uneasy Family: Revolutionary Syndicalism in Europe from the *Charte d'Amiens* to World War I' in David Berry and Constance Bantman (eds), *New Perspectives on Anarchism, Labour and Syndicalism: The Individual, the National and the Transnational* (Newcastle upon Tyne: Cambridge Scholars Publishing, 2010), pp. 16–42.
14. Quoted in Franklin Rosemont, *Joe Hill: The IWW & the Making of a Revolutionary Workingclass Counterculture* (Chicago: Charles H. Kerr, 2003), pp. 19.

15. For the IWW and autonomist Marxists see Steve Wright, *Storming Heaven: Class Composition and Struggle in Italian Autonomist Marxism* (London and Sterling, Virginia: Pluto Press, 2002), pp. 176–196.

16. Rudolf Rocker, *Anarcho-Syndicalism* (London and Sterling, Virginia: Pluto Press, 1989), pp. 137.

17. Vadim Damier, *Anarcho-Syndicalism in the* 20th *Century*, p. 23.

18. John Gerber, *Anton Pannekoek and the Socialism of Workers' Self-Emancipation 1873–1960*. (Dordrecht, Boston, London: Kluwer Academic Publishers and Amsterdam: International Institute of Social History, 1989), pp. 198.

19. On Solidarity, see Maurice Brinton, *For Workers' Power. The Selected Writings of Maurice Brinton* (Edinburgh: AK Press, 2004), ed. David Goodway. Brinton's writings can be found both on the Libcom website (http://libcom.org/tags/maurice-brinton) and on the Marxists Internet Archive (http://www.Marxists.org/archive/brinton/index.htm).

20. 'Editorial' in *Solidarity Aberdeen* 3 (1969), pp. 1–2.

21. Michael Albert & Robin Hahnel, *Looking Forward: Participatory Economics For The Twenty First Century* (Cambridge, MA: South End Press, 1991); see also their *Unorthodox Marxism. An Essay on Capitalism, Socialism and Revolution* (Cambridge, MA: South End Press, 1978).

22. *Le Monde*, 15 November 1969.

23. Matthew Wilson, *Rules without Rulers: The possibilities and limits of anarchism* (Unpublished PhD thesis, Loughborough University, 2011).

24. Paul Thomas, *Karl Marx and the Anarchists* (London: RKP, 1980).

25. Donald Clark Hodges, *The Literate Communist: 150 Years of the Communist Manifesto* (New York: Peter Lang, 1999), pp. 113. Daniel Guérin often referred approvingly to the argument in favour of a synthesis of Marx and Bakunin by H.-E. Kaminski in his *Bakounine. La vie d'un révolutionnaire* (Paris: La Table Ronde, 2003 [1938]).

26. C. Wright Mills, 'Letter to the New Left', *New Left Review* 5, September-October 1960, http://www.Marxists.org/subject/humanism/mills-c-wright/letter-new-left.htm [20 November 2011].

# BIBLIOGRAPHY

## Manuscripts and Archival Material

Dachine Rainer Papers. Yale Collection of American Literature. Beinecke Rare Book and Manuscript Library, Yale University.

Daniel Guérin Papers. International Institute for Social History, Amsterdam.

David Thoreau Wieck Papers, 1942–1969. Peace Collection, Swarthmore College.

Fonds Guérin. Bibliothèque de Documentation Internationale Contemporaine, Nanterre.

James, C.L.R. 'Charlie Lahr' [1975]. Unpublished MS in the possession of David Goodway.

Karl Korsch Papers. International Institute for Social History, Amsterdam.

Leahy, Terry. *Pre-War Anarchists and the Post-War Ultra-Left*. MS, Sydney, 1981.

McDonagh, Grant. *My Involvement in an Ultra-Leftist Tendency*. MS, Nelson, 1981.

National Archives, London. KV/2/1824/1z.

Paul Mattick Papers. International Institute for Social History, Amsterdam.

Subject Vertical File. Labadie Collection, University of Michigan.

## Newspapers and Magazines

*Alternative Libertaire*

*Christchurch Anarchists Newsletter* (New Zealand)

*Daily News* (London)

*Fight* (London)

*Freedom* (London)

*The Industrial Front* (New Zealand)

*Justice* (London)

*KAT* (New Zealand)

*La Vérité* (Paris)

*Liberation* (United States)

*Libertarian* (New Zealand)

*Liberty* (London)

*Politics* (United States)

*The Rebel Worker* (United States)

*Solidarity Aberdeen* (Scotland)

*Vanguard: A Libertarian Communist Journal* (United States)

*Views and Comments* (United States)

## Interviews

Lefebvre, Henri. 'On the Situationist International', Interview by Kristin Ross (1983). *October* 79 (Winter 1997), pp. 69–83.

Morea, Ben. Interview with Andrew Cornell. New York City, March 29, 2009.

Zinn, Howard. Interview with Sasha Lilley, available online: http://www.youtube.com/watch?v=DbaizDSg1YU (accessed 19 February 2017).

# Film

Boutang, Pierre-André. *Daniel Guérin: 1904–1988: Mémoires*. Sodaperaga, La Sept, 1985; broadcast on FR3, 1989.

# Books and Journals

Albert, Michael, and Robin Hahnel. *Looking Forward: Participatory Economics for the Twenty First Century*. Cambridge, MA: South End Press, 1991.

Albert, Michael, and Robin Hahnel. *Unorthodox Marxism: An Essay on Capitalism, Socialism and Revolution*. Cambridge, MA: South End Press, 1978.

Allen, Grant. 'Individualism and Socialism'. *Contemporary Review* LV (1889), pp. 730–734.

*Alternative Libertaire, Un projet de société communiste libertaire*. Paris: Alternative libertaire, 2002.

Althusser, Louis. *For Marx*. London: Penguin, 1965.

Amorós, Miquel. *La revolución traicionada: La verdadera historia de Balius y los Amigos de Durruti*. Barcelona: Virus editorial, 2003.

Anderson, Benedict. *Under Three Flags: Anarchism and the Anti-Colonial Imagination*. London: Verso, 2005.

Anderson, Kevin J. *Marx at the Margins: On Nationalism, Ethnicity, and Non-Western Societies*. Chicago and London: University of Chicago Press, 2010.

Anderson, Perry. 'The Antinomies of Antonio Gramsci'. *New Left Review* 100 (1976–1977), pp. 5–78.

Angaut, Jean-Christophe. *Bakounine jeune hégélien. La philosophie et son dehors*. Lyon: ENS Éditions, 2007.

Angaut, Jean-Christophe. 'La fin des avant-gardes: les situationnistes et Mai 68'. *Actuel Marx* 41 (2009), pp. 149–161.

Angaut, Jean-Christophe. 'Marx, Bakounine et la guerre franco-allemande'. *Sens public. Cosmopolitique* (2005), available online: www.sens-public.org/article.php3?id_article=131 (accessed 6 February 2017).

Antliff, Allan. *Anarchist Modernism: Art, Politics and the first American Avant-Garde*. London: University of Chicago Press, 2001.

Apter, David E. 'Anarchism Today'. *Government and Opposition* 5:4 (1970), pp. 397–409.

Apter, David E., and James Joll. *Anarchism Today*. London: Macmillan, 1971.

Arendt, Hannah. 'The Ex-Communists'. *Commonweal* 57:24 (1953), pp. 595–599.

Armaline, William T., and Deric Shannon. 'Introduction: Toward a More Unified Libertarian Left'. *Theory in Action* 3:4 (2010), available online: http://www.transformativestudies.org/publications/theory-in-action-the-journal-of-tsi/past-issues/volume-3-number-4-october-2010/ (accessed 16 February 2017).

Arsenault, Raymond. *Freedom Riders: 1961 and the Struggle for Racial Justice*. Oxford: Oxford University Press, 2006.

Atkins, John. *Neither Crumbs nor Condescension: The Central Labour College, 1909–1915*. Aberdeen: Aberdeen People's Press, 1981.

Auckland Anarchist Activists. *Anarchy and the State*. Auckland: Auckland Anarchist Activists, 1976.

Audenino, Patrizia. 'Non più eterni iloti: valori e modelli della pedogogia socialista'. In *Cultura, istruzione e socialismo nell'età giolittiana*. Lino Rossi (ed.). Milan: Franco Angeli, 1991, pp. 27–54.

Avrich, Paul. *The Modern School Movement: Anarchism and Education in the United States*. Oakland: AK Press, 2006.

Avrich, Paul. *The Russian Anarchists*. Princeton: Princeton University Press, 1967.

Badaloni, N. *Il marxismo di Gramsci: dal ito alla ricomposizione politica*. Turin: Einaudi, 1975.

Badia, Gilbert, et al. 'Rosa Luxemburg et nous: Débat'. *Politique aujourd'hui: Recherches et pratiques socialistes dans le monde* (1972), pp. 77–106.

Bakounine, Michel. 'La guerre franco-allemande et la revolution sociale en France (1870–1871)'. In *Œuvres complètes*, Volume 7. Paris: Champ Libre, 1979.

Bakunin, Michael. *God and the State* (1867), available online: http://dwardmac. pitzer.edu/anarchist_archives/bakunin/godandstate/godandstate_ch1.html (accessed 16 February 2017).

Bakunin, Michael. *Power Corrupts the Best* (1867), available online: http:// dwardmac.pitzer.edu/anarchist_archives/bakunin/bakuninpower.html (accessed 16 February 2017).

Bakunin, Mikhail. 'Geneva's Double Strike'. In *From Out of the Dustbin: Bakunin's Basic Writings, 1869–1871*, Robert M. Cutler (ed. and trans.). Ann Arbor, Michigan: Ardis, 1985.

Bakunin, Mikhail. 'The International and Karl Marx'. In *Bakunin on Anarchy*, Sam Dolgoff (ed. and trans.). New York: Alfred A. Knopf, 1972, pp. 286–320.

Bakunin, Mikhail. *Marxism, Freedom and the State*, K.J. Kenafick (ed. and trans.). London: Freedom Press, 1990.

Bakunin, Mikhail. 'The Paris Commune and the Idea of the State'. In *Bakunin on Anarchy*, Sam Dolgoff (ed.). London: Allen and Unwin, 1973, pp. 259–273.

Bakunin, Mikhail. *Statism and Anarchy*, M. Shatz (ed.). Cambridge: Cambridge University Press, 1990.

Bakunin, Mikhail. *Statism and Anarchy*. Cambridge: Cambridge University Press, 2000.

Balius, Jaime. *Towards a Fresh Revolution* (1938), available online: https://libcom. org/library/towards-fresh-revolution-friends-durruti (accessed 16 February 2017).

Baratta, Giorgio. *Antonio Gramsci in contrappunto. Dialoghu al presente*. Rome: Carocci, 2007.

Barkat, Sidi Mohammed (ed.). *Des Français contre la terreur d'État (Algérie 1954–1962)*. Paris: Editions Reflex, 2002.

Barker, Colin. 'Robert Michels and the "Cruel Game"'. In *Leadership and Social Movements*, Colin Barker, Alan Johnson, and Michael Lavalette (eds.). Manchester: Manchester University Press, 2001, pp. 24–43.

Barrot, Jean [Gilles Dauvé]. *What Is Situationism?*. Fort Bragg: Flatland, 1991.

Barthas, Jérémie. 'Machiavelli in Political Thought from the Age of Revolutions to the Present'. In *The Cambridge Companion to Machiavelli*, John M. Najemy (ed.). Cambridge and New York: Cambridge University Press, 2010, pp. 256–273.

Bates, D. 'Reading Negri'. *Critique*, 7:3 (2009), pp. 465–482.

Bell, Daniel. *The Coming of the Post-Industrial Society*. New York: Basic Books, 1999.

Bellamy Joyce M., and John Saville. *Dictionary of Labour Biography*, Volume VII. London: Macmillan, 1984.

Bellamy, Richard, and Darrow Schecter. *Gramsci and the Italian State*. Manchester: Manchester University Press, 1993.

Bennett, Scott H. *Radical Pacifism: The War Resisters League and Gandhian Nonviolence in America, 1915–1963*. Syracuse, NY: Syracuse University Press, 2003.

Benvenuti, Francesco, and Silvio Poms. 'L'Unione Sovietica nei Quarderni del Carcere'. In *Gramsci e il novecento*, G. Vacca (ed.). Rome: Carcocci, 1999.

Bergami, Giancarlo. *Il giovane Gramsci e il marxismo: 1911–1918*. Milan: Feltrinelli, 1977.

Berger, Denis. 'La révolution plurielle (pour Daniel Guérin)'. In *Permanences de la Révolution. Pour un autre bicentenaire*, Étienne Balibar et al. Paris: La Brèche, 1989, pp. 195–208.

Berghahn, Volker R. *America and the Intellectual Cold Wars in Europe: Shepard Stone Between Philanthropy, Academy and Diplomacy*. Princeton: Princeton University Press, 2001.

Berkman, Alexander. *What Is Communist Anarchism?*. London: Phoenix Press, 1989.

Berman, Paul. 'Facing Reality'. In *C.L.R. James: His Life and Work*, Paul Buhle (ed.). London: Allison & Busby, 1986, pp. 206–211.

Bernauer, James, and Michael Mahon. 'The Ethics of Michel Foucault'. In *The Cambridge Companion to Foucault*, Gary Gutting (ed.). Cambridge: Cambridge University Press, 1994, pp. 141–158.

Berneri, Marie-Louise. *Neither East nor West: Selected Writings 1939–1948*. London: Freedom Press, 1988.

Berry, David. 'Change the World without Taking Power? The Libertarian Communist Tradition in France Today'. *Journal of Contemporary European Studies* 16:1 (Spring 2008), pp. 111–130.

Berry, David. 'Daniel Guérin à la Libération. De l'historien de la Révolution au militant révolutionnaire: un tournant idéologique'. *Agone* 29–30 (2003), pp. 257–273.

Berry, David. *A History of the French Anarchist Movement, 1917–1945*. Westport, CT: Greenwood Press, 2002; 2nd edition, Oakland: AK Press, 2009.

Berry, David. '"Like a Wisp of Straw Amidst the Raging Elements": Daniel Guérin in the Second World War'. In *Vichy, Resistance, Liberation: New Perspectives on Wartime France (Festschrift in Honour of H.R. Kedward)*, Hanna Diamond and Simon Kitson (eds.). Oxford and New York: Berg, 2005, pp. 143–154.

Berry, David. '"Workers of the World, Embrace!" Daniel Guérin, the Labour Movement and Homosexuality'. *Left History* 9:2 (Spring/Summer 2004), pp. 11–43.

Berta, Giuseppe. 'The Interregnum: Turin, Fiat and Industrial Conflict between War and Fascism'. In *Challenges of Labour: Central and Western Europe 1917–1920*, Chris Wrigley (ed.). London: Routledge, 1993, pp. 105–124.

Berti, Giuseppe (ed.). 'Problemi del movimento operaio. Scritti critiche e storiche inediti di Angelo Tasca'. *Annali della Biblioteca G.G. Feltrinelli* 10 (1968).

Bertolo, Amedeo. 'Democracy and Beyond'. *Democracy and Nature: An International Journal of Inclusive Democracy*, 5:2 (1999), available online: http://www.democracynature.org/vol5/vol5.htm (accessed 4 February 2017).

Bétourné, Olivier, and Aglaia I. Hartig. *Penser l'histoire de la Révolution. Deux siècles de passion française*. Paris: La Découverte, 1989.

Bihr, Alain. 'Introduction' to *Fascisme et grand capital*, by Daniel Guérin. Paris: Editions Syllepse and Phénix Editions, 1999.

Birchall, Ian. 'Letter'. *Revolutionary History* 2:3 (1989), available online: http://www.marxists.org/history/etol/revhist/backiss/vol2/no3/birchall.html (accessed 17 February 2017).

Birchall, Ian. 'Nineteen Fifty-Six and the French Left'. *Revolutionary History* 9:3, (2006), available online: http://www.revolutionary-history.co.uk/index.php/187-articles/articles-of-rh0903/8314-french-2 (accessed 6 February 2017).

Birchall, Ian. 'Sartre's Encounter with Daniel Guérin'. *Sartre Studies International* 2:1 (1996), pp. 41–56.

Blackledge, Paul. 'Anarchism, Syndicalism and Strategy: A Reply to Lucien van der Walt'. *International Socialism* 131 (2011), pp. 189–206.

Blackledge, Paul. 'Marxism and Anarchism'. *International Socialism* 125 (2010), pp. 131–159.

Blackledge, Paul. 'Marxism and Ethics'. *International Socialism* 120 (2008), pp. 125–150.

Blackledge, Paul. *Marxism and Ethics*. New York: SUNY Press, 2012.

Blackledge, Paul. 'Marxism, Nihilism and the Problem of Ethical Politics Today'. *Socialism and Democracy* 24:2 (2010), pp. 101–123.

Bloch, Ernst. *The Principle of Hope*. Oxford: Blackwell, 1986.

Blond, Phillip. *Red Tory*. London: Faber and Faber, 2010.

Bock, Hans Manfred. *Syndikalismus und Linkskommunismus von 1918 bis 1923. Zur Geschichte und Soziologie der Kommunistischen Arbeiterpartei Deutschlands (K.A.P.D.), der Allgemeinen Arbeiterunion (A.A.U.D.) und der Freien Arbeiterunion (F.A.U.D.)*. Meisenheim: Verlag Anton Hain, 1969.

Bodson, Guy, *La F.A. et les situationnistes: 1966–1967, ou Mémoire pour discussion dans les familles après boire*. Paris: self-published, 1968, available online: https://situationnisteblog.wordpress.com/tag/guy-bodson/ (accessed 6 February 2017).

Boggs, Carl. *Gramsci's Marxism*. London: Pluto Press, 1976.

Boggs, Grace Lee. *Living for Change: An Autobiography*. Minneapolis: University of Minnesota Press, 2016 [1998].

Bolloten, Burnett. *The Spanish Civil War: Revolution and Counterrevolution*. Chapel Hill: University of North Carolina Press, 1991.

Bolstad, Richard. *An Anarchist Analysis of the Chinese Revolution*. Christchurch: Christchurch Anarchy Group, 1976.

Bonacchi, Gabriella M. 'The Council Communists Between the New Deal and Fascism' (1976), available online: https://libcom.org/library/council-communism-new-deal-fascism (accessed 16 February 2017).

Bookchin, Murray. 'The Communalist Project'. *The Harbinger* 3:1 (2002), pp. 20–35.

Bookchin, Murray. *Post-Scarcity Anarchism*. 2nd edition. Montreal: Black Rose Books, 1986.

Bookchin, Murray. *Social Anarchism or Lifestyle Anarchism: An Unbridgeable Chasm*. Edinburgh: AK Press, 1995.

Bookchin, Murray. *The Third Revolution: Popular Movements in the Revolutionary Era*, Volume 3. London: Continuum International Publishing Group, 2004.

Boos, Florence. 'William Morris's Socialist Diary'. *History Workshop* 13 (1982), pp. 1–78.

Boothman, Derek. 'The Sources of Gramsci's Concept of Hegemony'. *Rethinking Marxism* 20:2 (2008), pp. 201–215.

Boraman, Toby. *The New Left and Anarchism in New Zealand from 1956 to the Early 1980s*. PhD thesis, University of Otago, 2006.

Boraman, Toby. *Rabble Rousers and Merry Pranksters: A History of Anarchism in Aotearoa/New Zealand from the Mid 1950s to the Early 1980s*. Christchurch: Kapito Books and Irrecuperable Press, 2007.

Boulouque, Sylvain. *Les anarchistes français face aux guerres coloniales (1945–1962)*. Lyon: Atelier de création libertaire, 2003.

Bourrinet, Philippe. *The Dutch and German Communist Left: A Contribution to the History of the Revolutionary Movement*. London: Porcupine Press, 2001.

Bourrinet, Philippe. *The Dutch and German Communist Left (1900–68)*. Philippe Bourrinet, 2008.

Boykoff, Jules. *Beyond Bullets: The Suppression of Dissent in the United States*. Oakland: AK Press, 2007.

Bramble, Tom. *Trade Unionism in Australia: A History from Flood to Ebb Tide*. Cambridge: Cambridge University Press, 2008.

Brendel, Cajo. *Theses on the Chinese Revolution*. London: Solidarity, 1974.

Brendel, Cajo (ed.). 'Une correspondence entre Anton Pannekoek et Pierre Chaulieu'. *Cahiers du communisme de conseils* 8 (1971), pp. 15–35.

Brenkert, George G. *Marx's Ethics of Freedom*. London: Routledge, 1983.

Brennan, Timothy. *Wars of Position: The Cultural Politics of Left and Right*. New York: Columbia University Press, 2006.

Brienes, Wini. *Community and Organization in the New Left: The Great Refusal, 1962–1968*. New Brunswick: NJ: Rutgers University Press, 1989.

Briggs, Chris. 'Strikes and Lockouts in the Antipodes'. *New Zealand Journal of Employment Relations*, 30:3 (2005), pp. 1–15.

Brinton, Maurice. *For Workers' Power: The Selected Writings of Maurice Brinton*, David Goodway (ed.). Oakland: AK Press, 2004.

Broué, Pierre. *The German Revolution, 1917–1923*. Chicago: Haymarket Books, 2006.

Brown, Geoff. *The Industrial Syndicalist*. Nottingham: Spokesman Books, 1974.

Brown, H. Rap [Jamil Abdullah Al-Amin.]. *Die, Nigger, Die! A Political Autobiography* New York: Dial Press, 1969.

Brown, James. 'The Zen of Anarchy: Japanese Exceptionalism and the Anarchist Roots of the San Francisco Poetry Renaissance'. *Religion and American Culture: A Journal of Interpretation*, 19:2 (2009), pp. 207–242.

Buci-Glucksmann, Christine. *Gramsci et l'État*. Paris: Librairie Arthème Fayard, 1975.

Buck-Morss, Susan. 'Hegel and Haiti'. *Critical Inquiry* 26 (2000), pp. 821–865.

Buhle, Paul (ed.). *C.L.R. James: The Artist as Revolutionary*. London: Verso, 1993.

Buhle, Paul. 'From a Biographer's Notebook: The Field of C.L.R. James Scholarship'. In *C.L.R. James: His Intellectual Legacies*, Selwyn Reginald Cudjoe and William E. Cain (eds.). Amherst: University of Massachusetts Press, 1995, pp. 435–451.

Buhle, Paul. 'Marxism in the USA'. In *C.L.R. James and Revolutionary Marxism: Selected Writings of C.L.R. James, 1939–49*, Scott McLemee and Paul Le Blanc (eds.). New Jersey: Humanity Books, 1994, pp. 55–76.

Buhle, Paul. 'Political Styles of C.L.R. James: An Introduction'. In *C.L.R. James: His Life and Work*, Paul Buhle (ed.). London: Allison & Busby, 1986, pp. 22–29.

Burgmann, Meredith, and Verity Burgmann. *Green Bans, Red Union: Environmental Activism and the New South Wales Builders Labourers' Federation*. Sydney: University of New South Wales Press, 1998.

Bush, Barbara. *Imperialism, Race, and Resistance: Africa and Britain, 1919–1945*. London: Routledge, 1999.

Byrne, David. *Social Exclusion*. Buckingham: Open University Press, 1999.

Caldwell, John Taylor. *Guy A. Aldred (1886–1963)*. Glasgow: The Strickland Press, 1966.

Callinicos, Alex (ed.). *Marxist Theory*. Oxford University Press, 1989

Callinicos, Alex. 'Toni Negri in Perspective'. *International Socialism* 92 (2001), pp. 33–61.

Callinicos, Alex. *Trotskyism*. Minneapolis: University of Minnesota Press, 1990.

Cardan, Paul [Cornelius Castoriadis]. *Redefining Revolution*. London: Solidarity, n.d.

Carew, Anthony. 'American Labor Movement in Fizzland: The Free Trade Union Committee and the CIA'. *Labor History* 39:1 (1998), pp. 25–42.

Carlin, Norah. 'Daniel Guérin and the Working Class in the French Revolution'. *International Socialism* 47 (1990), pp. 197–223.

Carmichael, Stokely, with Michael Ekwueme Thelwell. *Ready for Revolution: The Life and Struggles of Stokely Carmichael (Kwame Ture)*. New York: Scribner, 2003.

Carr, E.H. *Michael Bakunin*. London: Macmillan, 1937.

Carr, E.H. *Studies in Revolution*. London: Frank Cass & Co. Ltd., 1962.

Carson, Clayborne. *In Struggle: SNCC and the Black Awakening of the 1960s*. Cambridge, MA: Harvard University Press, 1981.

Carver, Terrell. 'Editor's Introduction' to *Marx: Later Political Writings*. Cambridge: Cambridge University Press, 1996.

Castells, Manuel. *The Rise of the Network Society*, Volume 1. London: Blackwell, 2000.

Castoriadis, Cornelius. 'C.L.R. James and the Fate of Marxism'. In *C.L.R. James: His Intellectual Legacies*, Selwyn Reginald Cudjoe and William E. Cain (eds.). Amherst: University of Massachusetts Press, 1995, pp. 277–297.

Castoriadis, Cornelius. *Domaines de l'homme. Le carrefour du labyrinthe*. Paris: Éditions du Seuil, 1986.

Castoriadis, Cornelius. 'The Hungarian Source'. *Telos* 26 (1976), pp. 4–22; published in French, with slight modifications and a few translation mistakes, as 'La Source Hongroise'. *Libre* 1 (1977), pp. 51–85.

Castoriadis, Cornelius. 'An Interview with Cornelius Castoriadis'. *Telos* 23 (1975), pp. 131–155.

Castoriadis, Cornelius. *L'expérience du movement ouvrier*. Paris: 10–18, 1974.

Castoriadis, Cornelius. *L'institution imaginaire de la société*. Paris: Éditions du Seuil, 1975.

Castoriadis, Cornelius. 'Le mouvement révolutionnaire sous le capitalisme moderne, Part 1'. *Socialisme ou Barbarie,* 31 (1960), pp. 51–81.

Castoriadis, Cornelius. 'Le mouvement révolutionnaire sous le capitalisme moderne, Part 2'. *Socialisme ou Barbarie,* 32 (1961), pp. 84–111.

Castoriadis, Cornelius. 'Marx aujourd'hui. Entretien avec Cornelius Castoriadis'. *Lutter!* 5 (May 1983), pp. 15–18.

Castoriadis, Cornelius. *Political and Social Writings, Volume 1, 1946–1955*, David Ames Curtis (ed. and trans.). Minneapolis: University of Minnesota Press, 1988.

Castoriadis, Cornelius. *Workers' Councils and the Economics of a Self-Managed Society*. Philadelphia: Wooden Shoe, 1984.

Castoriadis, Cornelius. *World in Fragments: Writings on Politics, Society, Psychoanalysis, and the Imagination*, David Ames Curtis (ed. and trans.). Stanford: Stanford University Press, 1997.

Catone, Andre. 'Gramsci, la tradizione socialista e il problema della mancata recezione del marxismo'. In *Gramsci e l'Italia*, R. Giacomo, D. Losurdo and M. Martelli (eds.). Naples: La Città del Sole, 1994.

Catsam, Derek. *Freedom's Main Line: The Journey of Reconciliation and the Freedom Rides*. Lexington: University of Kentucky Press, 2009.

Challinor, Ray. 'Jack Parks, Memories of a Militant'. *Bulletin of the North-East Group for the Study of Labour History* 9 (1975), pp. 34–42.

Challinor, Ray. *The Origins of British Bolshevism*. London: Croom Helm, 1977.

Charzat, Michel. 'A la source du "marxisme" de Gramsci'. In *Georges Sorel*, M. Charzat (ed.). Paris: Éditions de l'Herne, 1986, pp. 213–222.

Chattopadhyay, S., and B. Sarkar. 'The Subaltern and the Populat'. *Postcolonial Studies* 8:4 (2005), pp. 357–363.

Chollet, Laurent. *Les situationnistes: l'utopie incarnée*. (Paris: Gallimard, 2004).

Chollet, Laurent., *L'insurrection situationniste* (Paris: Dagorno, 2000).

Chomsky, Noam. *American Power and the New Mandarins*. Middlesex/Victoria: Penguin Books, 1969.

Chomsky, Noam. *Government in the Future*. New York: Seven Stories Press, 2005.

Chomsky, Noam. 'Introduction' to *Anarchism*, by Daniel Guérin. New York: Monthly Review, 1970, pp. vii–xx.

Chomsky, Noam. 'Preface' to *Anarcho-Syndicalism*, by Rudolf Rocker. London: Pluto, 1989, pp. vi–vii.

Christie, Stuart, and Albert Meltzer. *The Floodgates of Anarchy*. 2nd edition. Oakland, PM Press, 2010 [1970].

Church, Roy, and Quetin Outram. *Strikes and Solidarity: Coalfield Conflict in Britain, 1889–1966*. Cambridge: Cambridge University Press, 2002.

Cieszkowski, August von. *Prolégomènes à l'historiosophie*, Michel Jacobs (trans.). Paris: Champ Libre, 1973.

Cirese, Alberto Maria. 'Gramsci's Observations on Folklore'. In *Approaches to Gramsci,* Anne Showstack Sassoon (ed.). London: Writers and Readers Publishing Cooperative, 1982, pp. 212–247.

Clark, Martin. *Antonio Gramsci and the Revolution that Failed*. New Haven: Yale University Press, 1977.

Clarke, J.F. 'An Interview with Sir Will Lawther'. *Bulletin of the Society for the Study of Labour History* 18 (1969), pp. 14–21.

*Class War on the Home Front* (1998), available online: http://libcom.org/library/apcf-class-war-home-front (accessed 6 February 2017).

Cleaver, Harry. *Reading Capital Politically*. Brighton: Harvester Press, 1979; Oakland: AK Press, 2000.

Cliff, Tony. *In the Thick of Workers' Struggle: Selected Writings,* Volume 2. London: Bookmarks, 2002.

Cohen, G.A. *Karl Marx's Theory of History: A Defence*. Oxford: Oxford University Press, expanded edition 2000.

Cohen, Gidon. *The Failure of a Dream: The Independent Labour Party from Disaffiliation to World War II*. London: Taurus Academic Studies, 2007.

Cohn-Bendit, Daniel. 'Interview'. *Anarchy* 99 (May 1969), pp. 153–159.

Cohn-Bendit, Daniel. *Obsolete Communism: The Left-Wing Alternative*, Arnold Pomerans (trans.). London: André Deutsch, 1968.

Cole, G.D.H. *A History of Socialist Thought, 1789–1939* (7 volumes). London: Macmillan, 1953–1961.

Collini, Stefan. *Liberalism and Sociology: L.T. Hobhouse and Political Argument in England 1880–1914*. Cambridge: Cambridge University Press, 1983.

Collins, Henry, and Chimen Abramsky. *Karl Marx and the British Labour Movement*. London: Macmillan, 1964.

Corcuff, Philippe, and Michael Löwy. 'Pour une Première Internationale au XXIe siècle'. *Contretemps* 6 (February 2003), pp. 8–10.

Cornell, Andrew. *'For a World without Oppressors': U.S. Anarchism from the Palmer Raids to the Sixties*. PhD dissertation, New York University, 2011.

Cornell, Andrew. *Oppose and Propose! Lessons from Movement for a New Society*. Oakland: AK Press, 2011.

Crehan, Kate. *Gramsci, Culture and Anthropology*. London: Pluto Press, 2002.

Crémieux, Léon. 'Mouvement social, anti-mondialisation et nouvelle Internationale'. *Contretemps* 6 (February 2003), pp. 12–18.

Cripps, Louise. *C.L.R. James: Memories and Commentaries*. London: Cornwall Books, 1997.

Croft, Andy. 'Ethel Mannin: The Red Rose of Love and the Red Flower of Liberty'. In *Rediscovering Forgotten Radicals: British Women Writers, 1889–1939*, Angela Ingram and Daphne Patai (eds.). Chapel Hill: University of North Carolina Press, 1993, pp. 205–225.

Crouch, Colin, and Alessandro Pizzorno (eds.). *The Resurgence of Class Conflict in Western Europe since 1968* (2 volumes). London: Macmillan, 1978.

Crozier, Michel. *Ma belle époque. Mémoires. 1947–1969*. Paris: Fayard, 2002.

Dainotto, Roberto M. 'Gramsci Now: Philology and Philosophy of Praxis'. In *Perspectives on Gramsci: Politics, Culture and Social Theory*, Joseph Francese (ed.). London: Routledge, 2009, pp. 50–68.

Damier, V. *Anarcho-Syndicalism in the 20th Century*. Edmonton: Black Cat Press, 2009.

Danesi, Fabien. *Le mythe brisé de L'Internationale Situationniste: L'aventure d'une avant-garde au cœur de la culture de masse (1945–2008)*. Dijon: Les Presses du Réel, 2008.

Darlington, Ralph. *Syndicalism and the Transition to Communism: An International Comparative Analysis*. Aldershot: Ashgate, 2008.

Dauvé, Gilles, and François Martin. *The Eclipse and Re-emergence of the Communist Movement*. London: Antagonism Press, 1997.

Davidson, Alastair. 'The Uses and Abuses of Gramsci'. *Thesis Eleven* 95 (2008), pp. 68–94.

Davies, David Keith. *The Influence of Syndicalism, and Industrial Unionism in the South Wales Coalfield 1898–1921: A Study in Ideology, and Practice*. PhD thesis, University of Wales, 1991.

Davis, Laurence. 'Everyone an Artist: Art, Labour, Anarchy and Utopia'. In *Anarchism and Utopianism*, Laurence Davis and Ruth Kinna (eds.). Manchester: Manchester University Press, 2009, pp. 73–98.

Davison, Peter (ed.). *The Complete Works of George Orwell*, Volume 11. London: Secker & Warburg, 1998.

Day, Richard J.F. *Gramsci Is Dead: Anarchist Currents in the Newest Social Movements*. London: Pluto Press, 2005.

Dean, Jodi. *Crowds and Party: How Do Mass Protests Become an Organised Activist Collective?*. London: Verso, 2016.

Debord, Guy. *Correspondance, Volume 2, Septembre 1960–Décembre 1964*. Paris: Fayard, 2001.

Debord, Guy. *La société du spectacle*. Paris: Folio, Gallimard, 1967.

Debord, Guy. *Œuvres*. Paris: Gallimard, 2004.

Debord, Guy. *A Sick Planet*, Donald Nicholson-Smith (trans.). Oxford and New York: Seagull Books, 2008.

'Decadence: The Theory of Decline or the Decline of Theory?', Part 2. *Aufheben*, 3 (1994), available online: http://libcom.org/library/decadence-aufheben-3 (accessed 16 February 2017).

Dellinger, David. *From Yale to Jail: The Life Story of a Moral Dissenter*. New York: Pantheon, 1993.

Dellinger, David, and Bayard Rustin. 'Mississippi Muddle'. In *Seeds of Liberation*, Paul Goodman (ed.). New York: George Braziller, 1964, pp. 306–316.

D'Emilio, John. *Lost Prophet: The Life and Times of Bayard Rustin*. Chicago: University of Chicago, 2003.

de Francesco, Antonio. 'Daniel Guérin et Georges Lefebvre, une rencontre improbable'. *La Révolution française*, available online: http://lrf.revues.org/index162.html, (accessed 6 February 2017).

de Ligt, Bart. *The Conquest of Violence: An Essay on War and Revolution*. London: Pluto Press, 1989 [1937].

de Llorens, Ignacio. *The CNT and the Russian Revolution*. London and Berkeley: Kate Sharpley Library, 2007.

Deutscher, Isaac. *The Prophet Outcast: Trotsky: 1929–1940*. Oxford: Oxford University Press, 1979.

Dolgoff, Sam. *Fragments: A Memoir*. Cambridge, UK: Refract Publications, 1986.

Dongen, Luc van. '"De toute façon la gauche était contrôlée": agents provocateurs, infiltrations et subversion de droite à l'intérieur des mouvements sociaux'. In *Mourir en manifestant. Répressions en démocratie*, Charles Heimberg, Stéfanie Prezioso, and Marianne Enckell (eds.). Lausanne: Editions d'En Bas, 2008, pp. 159–183.

Donnisthorp, Wordsworth. *Socialism Analyzed: Being a Critical Examination of Mr. Joynes's 'Socialist Catechism'*. London: Liberty and Property Defence League, 1888.

D'Orsi, Angelo (ed.). *Egemonie*. Naples: Libreria Dante & Descartes, 2008.

Draper, Hal. *The Dictatorship of the Proletariat*. New York: Monthly Review, 1988.

Draper, Hal. *Karl Marx's Theory of Revolution, Volume I: State and Bureaucracy*. New York and London: Monthly Review Press, 1977.

Draper, Hal. *Karl Marx's Theory of Revolution, Volume II: The Politics of Social Classes*. New York and London: Monthly Review Press, 1978.

Draper, Hal. *Karl Marx's Theory of Revolution, Volume III: The Dictatorship of the Proletariat*. New York Monthly Review, 1978.

Draper, Hal. *Karl Marx's Theory of Revolution, Volume IV: Critique of Other Socialisms*. New York: Monthly Review Press, 1990.

Draper, Hal. 'The Principle of Self-Emancipation in Marx and Engels'. In *The Socialist Register 1971*, Ralph Miliband and John Saville (eds.). London: The Merlin Press, 1971, pp. 81–109.

Draper, Hal. *The Two Souls of Socialism*. London: Bookmarks, 1996.

Dubacq, Philippe. *Anarchisme et marxisme au travers de la Fédération communiste libertaire (1945–1956)*. Pantin, France: Noir et Blanc, 1991.

Dubofsky, Melyvyn, and Joseph A. McCartin. *We Shall Be All: A History of the Industrial Workers of the World*. Chicago: Quadrangle, 1969.

Ducange, Jean-Numa. 'Comment Daniel Guérin utilise-t-il l'œuvre de Karl Kautsky sur la Révolution française dans *La Lutte de classes sous la première République*, et pourquoi?'. *Dissidences* 2 (2007), pp. 89–111.

Dumontier, Pascal. *Les situationnistes et mai 68: Théorie et pratique de la revolution*. Paris: Éditions Gérard Lebovici, 1990.

Dunayevskaya, Raya. *The Marxist-Humanist Theory of State-Capitalism*. Chicago: News and Letters, 1992.

Dupuis-Déri, Francis. 'The Black Blocs Ten Years after Seattle: Anarchism, Direct Action, and Deliberative Practices'. *Journal for the Study of Radicalism* 4:2 (2010), pp. 45–82.

Duteuil, Jean-Pierre. *Nanterre 1965-66-67-68: Vers le mouvement du 22 mars*. Mauléon: Acratie, 1988.

Eagleton, Terry. *After Theory*. London: Penguin, 2003.

Editorial Staff of Why?. *War or Revolution: An Anarchist Statement*. New York: Why? Publications Committee, 1944.

Egan, David. 'The Miners' Next Step'. *Labour History Review*, 38 (1979), pp. 10–11.

Elbaum, Max. *Revolution in the Air: Sixties Radicals Turn to Lenin, Mao, and Che*. New York: Verso, 2002.

el-Ojeili, Chamsy. 'Book Review: "Many Flowers, Little Fruit"? The Dilemmas of Workerism'. *Thesis Eleven*, 79 (2004), pp. 114–115.

Engels, Frederick. 'A Critique of the Draft Programme of 1891'. In Karl Marx and Frederick Engels, *Collected Works,* Volume 27. London: Lawrence and Wishart, 1990, pp. 217–232.

Engels, Frederick. 'Engels, to Theodore Cuno in Milan', 1872. In *Marx-Engels: Selected Correspondence*. Moscow: Progress Publishers, 1975.

Engels, Frederick. 'Introduction to Karl Marx's *The Civil War in France*'. In Karl Marx and Frederick Engels, *Collected Works,* Volume 27. New York: International Publishers, 1990, pp. 179–191.

Engels, Frederick. 'Preface to the 1888 English Edition of the *Manifesto of the Communist Party*'. In Karl Marx and Frederick Engels, *Collected Works*, Volume 26. New York: International Publishers, 1990, pp. 512–518.

Engels, Frederick. 'Preface to The Peasant War in Germany'. In Karl Marx and Frederick Engels, *Marx and Engels: Selected Works*. London: Lawrence and Wishart, 1968, pp. 224–236.

Engels, Frederick. 'Programme of the Blanquist Commune Refugees'. In Karl Marx and Frederick Engels, *Collected Works*, Volume 24. New York: International Publishers, 1998, pp. 12–18.

Englart, John. 'Anarchism in Sydney 1975–1981, Part I'. *Freedom* (June 1982), available online: www.takver.com/history/sydney/syd7581.htm (accessed 17 February 2017).

Epstein, Barbara. 'Anarchism and the Alter-Globalization Movement'. *Monthly Review* 53:4 (2001), available online: http://www.monthlyreview.org/0901epstein.htm (accessed 6 February 2017).

Epstein, Barbara. *Political Protest and Cultural Revolution: Nonviolent Direct Action in the 1970s and 1980s*. Berkeley: University of California Press, 1991.

Essbach, Wolfgang. *Die Junghegelianer: Soziologie einer Intellektuellengruppe*. München: W. Fink, 1988.

Farrell, James J. *The Spirit of the Sixties: The Making of Postwar Radicalism*. New York: Routledge, 1997.

Fasce, Ferdinando. 'American Labor History, 1973–1983: Italian Perspectives'. *Reviews in American History* 14:4 (1986), pp. 601–608.

Fiori, Giuseppe. *Antonio Gramsci: Life of a Revolutionary*. London: NLB, 1970.

Fontenis, Georges. *Changer le monde: Histoire du mouvement communiste libertaire, 1945–1997*. Paris: Alternative libertaire, 2000.

Fontenis, Georges. 'Le long parcours de Daniel Guérin vers le communisme libertaire'. *Alternative Libertaire* (2000), pp. 36–38.

Fontenis, Georges. *The Revolutionary Message of the 'Friends of Durruti'* (1983), available online: https://libcom.org/history/revolutionary-message-friends-durruti%E2%80%99 (accessed 6 February 2017).

Foreman, James. *The Making of Black Revolutionaries*. Seattle: University of Washington Press, 1997 [1972].

Foucault, Michel. *The History of Sexuality*, Volume 1. London: Allen Lane, 1979.

Foucault, Michel. *Power/Knowledge: Selected Interviews and Other Writings, 1972–1977*, Colin Gordon (ed.). New York: Pantheon, 1980.

Frank, Patrick. 'San Francisco 1952: Painters, Poets, Anarchism'. *Drunken Boat* 2 (1994), pp. 136–153.

Franks, Benjamin. 'Between Anarchism and Marxism: The Beginnings and Ends of the Schism'. *Journal of Political Ideologies* 17:2 (2012), pp. 207–227.

Franks, Benjamin. *Rebel Alliances: The Means and Ends of Contemporary British Anarchisms*. Oakland: AK Press, 2006.

Fraser, Ronald (ed.). *Blood of Spain: An Oral History of the Spanish Civil War*. New York: Pantheon Books, 1979.

Freeden, Michael. *Ideologies and Political Theory: A Conceptual Approach*. Oxford: Clarendon 1996.

Freeden, Michael. 'Thinking Politically and Thinking Ideologically'. *Journal of Political Ideologies* 13:1 (2008), pp. 1–10.

Freeman, Jo. *The Tyranny of Structurelessness* (1970), available online: http://struggle.ws/pdfs/tyranny.pdf (accessed 17 February 2017).

Fuller, Jack. 'The New Workerism: The Politics of the Italian Autonomists [1980]'. *International Socialism*, 92 (2001), available online: http://pubs.socialistreviewindex.org.uk/isj92/fuller.htm (accessed 17 February 2017).

Furiozzi, Gian Biagio. *Sorel e l'Italia*. Florence: D'Anna,1975.

Gagnier, Regenia. *Individualism, Decadence and Globalization*. London: Palgrave Macmillan, 2010.

Gambino, Ferruccio. 'Only Connect'. In *C.L.R. James: His Life and Work*, Paul Buhle (ed.). London: Allison & Busby, 1986, pp. 195–199.

Ganser, Daniele. *NATO's Secret Armies: Operation Gladio and Terrorism in Western Europe*. London and New York: Frank Cass, 2005.

García Salvatecci, H. *Georges Sorel y Mariátegui. Ubicación ideológica del Amauta*. Lima: Delgado Valenzuela 1979.

Gemie, Sharif. 'Anarchism and Feminism: A Historical Survey'. *Women's History Review* 5:3 (1996), pp. 417–444,

George, Greg. *Essay Aimed at Discovering Anarchism's Relevance to Modern Society*. Brisbane: Self-Management Group, 1974, available online: http://libcom.org/library/essay-aimed-discovering-anarchisms-relevance-modern-society (accessed 6 February 2017).

Gerber, John. 'From Left Radicalism to Council Communism: Anton Pannekoek and German Revolutionary Marxism'. *Journal of Contemporary History* 23 (1988), pp. 169–189.

Gerber, John. *Anton Pannekoek and the Socialism of Workers' Self-Emancipation 1873–1960*. Dordrecht, Boston, London: Kluwer Academic Publishers, 1989.

Ghosh, Peter. 'Gramscian Hegemony: An Absolutely Historicist Approach'. *History of European Ideas* 27 (2001), pp. 1–43.

Giddens, Anthony. *Runaway World: How Globalisation Is Shaping Our Lives*. London: Profile Books, 2002.

Glaberman, Martin (ed.). *Marxism for Our Times: C.L.R. James on Revolutionary Organisation*. Jackson: University Press of Mississippi, 1999.

Glaberman, Martin. *Punching Out and Other Writings*, Staughton Lynd (ed.). Chicago: Charles H. Kerr, 2002.

Gluckstein, Donny. *The Paris Commune: A Revolution in Democracy*. Chicago: Haymarket, 2011.

Goldman, Emma. 'Anarchism: What It Really Stands For' and 'Syndicalism: Its Theory and Practice'. In *Red Emma Speaks: Selected Writings and Speeches by Emma Goldman*, Alix Kates Shulman (ed.). New York: Vintage Books, 1972, pp. 61–77, 87–100.

Gombin, Richard. *The Origins of Modern Leftism*. Harmondsworth: Penguin, 1975.

Gombin, Richard. *The Radical Tradition: A Study in Modern Revolutionary Thought*. London: Methuen & Co Ltd., 1978.

Gonzalvez, Shigenobu. *Guy Debord ou la beauté du négatif*. Paris: Nautilus, 2002.

Goodway, David. *Anarchist Seeds Beneath the Snow: Left-Libertarian Thought and British Writers from William Morris to Colin Ward*. 2nd edition. Oakland: PM Press, 2012 [2006].

Goodway, David. 'Charles Lahr'. *London Magazine* (June/July 1977).

Goodway, David (ed.). *For Workers' Power: The Selected Writings of Maurice Brinton*. Oakland: AK Press, 2004.

Goodway, David. 'Introduction' to *For Anarchism*, David Goodway (ed.). London: Routledge, 1989, pp. 1–22.

Gordon, Uri. *Anarchy Alive! Anti-Authoritarian Politics from Practice to Theory*. London: Pluto, 2008.

Gorman, Robert A. 'Sorel, Georges'. In *Biographical Dictionary of Neo-Marxism*, Robert A. Gorman (ed.). Westport, CT: Greenwood Press, 1985, pp. 390–392.

Gorter, Herman. *Open Letter to Comrade Lenin, A Reply to 'Left-Wing' Communism, an Infantile Disorder* (1920), available online: www.marxists.org/archive/gorter/1920/open-letter/index.htm (accessed 17 February 2017).

Gottraux, Philippe. *"Socialisme ou Barbarie". Un engagement politique et intellectuel dans la France de l'après-guerre*. Lausanne: Payot, 1997.

Gouldner, Alvin W. 'Marx's Last Battle: Bakunin and the First International'. *Theory and Society* 11:6, Special Issue in Memory of Alvin W. Gouldner (1982), pp. 853–884.

Graeber, David. *Direct Action: An Ethnography*. Oakland: AK Press, 2010.

Graeber, David. 'The New Anarchists'. *New Left Review* 13 (2002), pp. 61–73.

Graeber, David. 'Why Is the World Ignoring the Revolutionary Kurds in Syria?'. *Guardian* (8 October 2014), available online: https://www.theguardian.com/commentisfree/2014/oct/08/why-world-ignoring-revolutionary-kurds-syria-isis (accessed 30 January 2017).

Graeber, David, and Andrej Grubačić. 'Anarchism or the Revolutionary Movement for the 21st Century', available online: https://zcomm.org/znetarticle/anarchism-or-the-revolutionary-movement-of-the-twenty-first-century-by-david-graeber/ (accessed 6 February 2017).

Graham, Helen. 'Against the State: A Genealogy of the Barcelona May Days (1937)'. *European History Quarterly* 29 (1999), pp. 485–542.

Gramsci, Antonio. 'Address to the Anarchists'. In Antonio Gramsci, *Selections from Political Writings 1910–1920*. London: Lawrence and Wishart, 1970, available online: https://libcom.org/history/address-anarchists-antonio-gramsci-1920 (accessed 17 February 2017).

Gramsci, Antonio. *Cronache torinesi*, Sergio Caprioglio (ed.). Turin: Rinaudi, 1980.

Gramsci, Antonio. *Il nostro Marx: 1918–1919*, Sergio Caprioglio (ed.). Turin: Einaudi, 1984.

Gramsci, Antonio. *La città future: 1917–1918*, Sergio Caprioglio (ed.). Turin: Einaudi, 1980.

Gramsci, Antonio. *Pre-Prison Writings*, Richard Bellamy (ed.). Cambridge: Cambridge University Press, 1994.

Gramsci, Antonio. *Quaderni del carcere*, Volume 1. Turin: Einaudi, 1975.

Gramsci, Antonio. *Selections from Political Writings, 1910–1920*, Quintin Hoare (ed.). London: Lawrence and Wishart, 1977.

Gramsci, Antonio. *Selections from the Prison Notebooks*, Quintin Hoare and Geoffrey N. Smith (eds. and trans.). London: Lawrence and Wishart, 1971.

Gray, John. *Post-Liberalism: Studies in Political Thought*. New York and London: Routledge, 1993.

Green, Maurice E. 'Gramsci Cannot Speak: Deconstruction and Interpretation of Gramsci's Concept of the Subaltern'. *Rethinking Marxism* 13:1 (2001), pp. 1–24.

Green, Maurice E., and Peter Ives. 'Subalternity and Language: Overcoming the Fragmentation of Common Sense'. *Historical Materialism*, 17:3 (2009), pp. 3–30.

Grémion, Pierre. *Intelligence de l'Anticommunisme. Le Congrès pour la liberté de la culture à Paris 1950–1975*. Paris: Fayard, 1995.

Grubačić, Andrej. 'Libertarian Socialism for the Twenty-First Century'. In Sasha Lilley, *Capital and Its Discontents. Conversations with Radical Thinkers in a Time of Tumult*. Oakland: PM Press, 2011, pp. 246–257.

Guérin, Daniel. *A la recherche d'un communisme libertaire*. Paris: Spartacus, 1984.

Guérin, Daniel. *Anarchism and Marxism*. Sanday, Orkney: Cienfuegos Press, 1981.

Guérin, Daniel. *Anarchism: From Theory to Practice*, Mary Klopper (trans.). New York: Monthly Review Press, 1970.

Guérin, Daniel. *Autobiographie de jeunesse, d'une dissidence sexuelle au socialisme*. Paris: Belfond, 1972.

Guérin, Daniel. *The Brown Plague: Travels in Late Weimar and Early Nazi Germany*, Robert Schwartzwald (trans.). Durham & London: Duke University Press, 1994.

Guérin, Daniel. *De l'Oncle Tom aux Panthères: Le drame des Noirs américains*. Paris: UGE, 1973.

Guérin, Daniel. *Décolonisation du Noir américain*. Paris: Minuit, 1963.

Guérin, Daniel. 'Faisons le point'. *Le Libérateur politique et social pour la nouvelle gauche* (12 February 1956).

Guérin, Daniel. *Fascism and Big Business*. New York: Monad Press, 1973.

Guérin, Daniel. *Fascisme et grand capital*. Paris: Gallimard, 1936.

Guérin, Daniel. 'Fascist Corporatism'. *International Council Correspondence* 3:2 (February 1937), pp. 14–26.

Guérin, Daniel. *Front populaire, Révolution manquée. Témoignage militant*. Arles: Editions Actes Sud, 1977.

Guérin, Daniel. *Homosexualité et Révolution*. Saint-Denis: Le Vent du ch'min, 1983.

Guérin, Daniel. *Jeunesse du socialisme libertaire*. Paris: Rivière, 1959.

Guérin, Daniel. *L'Anarchisme, de la doctrine à la pratique*. Paris: Gallimard, 1965; 1981.

Guérin, Daniel. 'L'autogestion contemporaine'. *Noir et rouge* 31/32 (October 1965–February 1966), pp. 16–24.

Guérin, Daniel. 'L'Espagne libertaire', editorial introduction to part of special issue on 'Les anarchistes et l'autogestion'. *Autogestion et socialisme* 18/19 (January–April 1972), pp. 81–82.

Guérin, Daniel. *La concentration économique aux États-Unis*. Paris: Anthropos, 1971.

Guérin, Daniel. *La Lutte de classes sous la Première République, 1793–1797* (2 volumes). Paris: Gallimard, 1968 [1946].

Guérin, Daniel. *La Peste brune*. Paris: Spartacus, 1996.

Guérin, Daniel. *La Peste brune a passé par là*. Paris: Librairie du Travail, 1933.

Guérin, Daniel. *La Révolution française et nous*. Paris: Maspero, 1976.

Guérin, Daniel. *Le Feu du sang. Autobiographie politique et charnelle*. Paris: Editions Grasset & Fasquelle, 1977.

Guérin, Daniel. *Le Mouvement ouvrier aux Etats-Unis*. Paris: Maspero, 1968.

Guérin, Daniel (ed.). *Léon Trotski, Sur la deuxième guerre mondiale*. Brussels: Editions la Taupe, 1970.

Guérin, Daniel. 'Marxism and Anarchism'. In *For Anarchism. History, Theory and Practice*, D. Goodway (ed.). London: Routledge, 1989, pp. 109–126.

Guérin, Daniel. *Negroes on the March: A Frenchman's Report on the American Negro Struggle*, Duncan Ferguson (trans.). New York: George L. Weissman, 1956.

Guérin, Daniel. *Ni Dieu ni Maître, anthologie de l'anarchisme*. Lausanne: La Cité-Lausanne, 1965.

Guérin, Daniel. '1917–1921, de l'autogestion à la bureaucratie soviétique'. In *De la Révolution d'octobre à l'empire éclaté: 70 ans de réflexions sur la nature de l'URSS*. Paris: Alternative libertaire/UTCL, n.d.

Guérin, Daniel. *No Gods No Masters: An Anthology of Anarchism*, Paul Sharkey (trans.). Edinburgh: AK Press, 1998.

Guérin, Daniel. *100 Years of Labour in the USA*, Alan Adler (trans.). London: Ink Links, 1979.

Guérin, Daniel. *Où va le peuple américain?*. Paris: Julliard, 1950–1951.

Guérin, Daniel. *Pour le communisme libertaire*. Paris: Spartacus, 2003.

Guérin, Daniel. *Pour un marxisme libertaire*. Paris: Robert Laffont, 1969.

Guérin, Daniel. 'Proudhon et l'autogestion ouvrière'. In Centre national d'étude des problèmes de sociologie et d'économie européennes, *L'Actualité de Proudhon*. Bruxelles: Université libre de Bruxelles, 1967, pp. 67–87.

Guérin, Daniel. *Proudhon oui et non*. Paris: Gallimard, 1978.

Guérin, Daniel. *Rosa Luxemburg et la spontanéité révolutionnaire*. Paris: Flammarion, 1971.

Guérin, Daniel. 'Stirner, "Père de l'anarchisme"?'. *La Rue* 26 (1er et 2ème trimestre 1979), pp. 76–89.

Guérin, Daniel. *Towards a Libertarian Communism* (1988), available online: http://libcom.org/library/towards-libertarian-communism-daniel-guerin (accessed 6 February 2017).

Guillamón, Augustin. *The Friends of Durruti Group: 1937–1939*. Edinburgh and San Francisco: AK Press, 1996.

Guillerm, Alain, 'Preface' to Rosa Luxembourg, *Marxisme et Dictature: La démocratie selon Lénine et Luxembourg*. Paris: Spartacus, 1974.

Guseva, Julia. 'La Terreur pendant la Révolution et l'interprétation de Daniel Guérin'. *Dissidences* 2 (2007), pp. 77–88.

Hahne, Ron. *Black Mask and Up Against the Wall Motherfucker: The Incomplete Works of Ron Hahne, Ben Morea, and the Black Mask Group*. Oakland: PM Press, 2011.

Hahnel, Robin. *Economic Justice and Democracy: From Competition to Cooperation*. New York: Routledge, 2005.

Hamalian, Linda. *A Life of Kenneth Rexroth*. New York: Norton, 1991.

Hannavy, John (ed.). *Encyclopedia of Nineteenth-Century Photography*. London: Routledge, 2008.

Harbi, Mohammed. *Une Vie debout. Mémoires politiques, Tome I: 1945–1962*. Paris: La Découverte, 2001.

Harding, Neil. *Leninism*. Durham, NC: Duke University Press, 1996.

Hardt, Michael. 'The Common in Communism'. In *The Idea of Communism*, Costas Douzinas and Slavoj Žižek (eds.). London: Verso, 2001, pp. 131–144.

Hardt, Michael. 'Into the Factory: Negri's Lenin and the Subjective Caesura (1968–1973)'. In *The Philosophy of Antonio Negri: Resistance in Practice*, Timothy S. Murphy and Abdul-Karim Mustapha (eds.). London: Pluto, 2005, pp. 7–37.

Hardt, Michael, and Antonio Negri. *Commonwealth*. Cambridge, MA: Harvard University Press, 2009.

Hardt, Michael, and Antonio Negri. *Empire*. Cambridge, MA: Harvard University Press, 2000.

Hardt, Michael, and Antonio Negri. *Labour of Dionysus: A Critique of the State Form*. Minneapolis: University of Minnesota Press, 1994.

Hardt, Michael, and Antonio Negri. *Multitude*. London: Penguin, 2005, pp. 7–37.

Harvey, David. *The Enigma of Capital and the Crises of Capital*. London: Profile Books, 2010.

Harvey, David. 'Value Production and Struggle in the Classroom: Teachers Within, Against and Beyond Capital'. *Capital and Class* 88 (2006), pp. 132.

Haug, Wolfgang Fritz. 'From Marx to Gramsci, from Gramsci to Marx: Historical Materialism and the Philosophy of Praxis'. *Rethinking Marxism* 13:1 (2001), pp. 69–82.

Hayes, Peter. 'Utopia and the Lumpenproletariat: Marx's Reasoning in "The Eighteenth Brumaire of Louis Bonaparte"'. *Review of Politics* 50:3 (1988), pp. 445–465.

Hegel, G.W.F. *Phénoménologie de l'Esprit*, Bernard Bourgeois (trans.). Paris: Vrin, 2006.

Hegel, G.W.F. *Phenomenology of the Spirit*, A.V. Miller (trans.). Oxford University Press, 1979.

Herbert, Auberon. *The Voluntaryist Creed: Being the Herbert Spencer Lecture Delivered at Oxford, June 7, 1906*. London: Henry Frowde,1908.

Hill, Deb J. *Hegemony and Education: Gramsci, Post-Marxism and Radical Democracy Revisited*. Lanham, MD: Lexington Books, 2007.

Hirsch, Arthur. *The French Left: A History and Overview*. Montreal: Black Rose Books, 1982.

Hirsch, Steven J., and Lucien van der Walt. (eds.). *Anarchism and Syndicalism in the Colonial and Postcolonial World, 1870–1940: The Praxis of National Liberation, Internationalism, and Social Revolution*. Leiden: Brill, 2010.

Hobsbawm, Eric. *The Age of Extremes: The Short Twentieth Century, 1914–1991*. London: Abacus, 1999.

Hobsbawm, Eric. *Echoes of the Marseillaise: Two Centuries Look Back on the French Revolution*. London: Verso, 1990.

Hobsbawm, Eric. *Primitive Rebels: Studies in Archaic Forms of Social Movement in the 19th and 20th Centuries*. Manchester: Manchester University Press, 1959.

Hobsbawm, Eric. *Revolutionaries*. London: Quartet Books, 1977.

Hodgdon, Tim. *Manhood in the Age of Aquarius: Masculinity in Two Counter-Cultural Communities, 1965–1983*. New York: Columbia University Press, 2008.

Hodges, Donald Clark. *The Literate Communist: 150 Years of the Communist Manifesto*. New York: Peter Lang, 1999.

Høgsbjerg, Christian. 'Beyond the Boundary of Leninism? C.L.R. James and 1956'. *Revolutionary History* 9:3 (2006), pp. 144–159.

Høgsbjerg, Christian. 'C.L.R. James and the Black Jacobins'. *International Socialism* 126 (2010), pp. 95–120.

Høgsbjerg, Christian. 'C.L.R. James: The Revolutionary as Artist'. *International Socialism* 112 (2006), pp. 163–182.

Høgsbjerg, Christian. 'The prophet and Black Power: Trotsky on race in the US'. *International Socialism* 121 (2008), pp. 99–119.

Høgsbjerg, Christian. 'Remembering C.L.R. James, Forgetting C.L.R. James'. *Historical Materialism* 17:3 (2009), pp. 221–234.

Hohl, Thierry. 'Daniel Guérin, "pivertiste". Un parcours dans la Gauche révolutionnaire de la SFIO (1935–1938)'. *Dissidences* 2 (2007), pp. 133–149.

Holloway, John. *Change the World without Taking Power*. London: Pluto Press, 2002; 2nd edition 2005.

Holota, W. *Le Mouvement machnoviste ukrainien 1918–1921 et l'évolution de l'anarchisme européen à travers le débat sur la plate-forme 1926–1934*. Strasboug: Université des sciences humaines, 1975.

Holton, Bob. *British Syndicalism 1900–1914: Myths and Realities*. London: Pluto, 1976.

Horowitz, Irving L. *The Anarchists*. New York: Dell Publishing Co., Inc., 1964.

Horowitz, Irving L. *Radicalism and the Revolt Against Reason*. New York: The Humanities Press, 1961.

Howson, Richard. 'From Ethico-Political Hegemony to Postmarxism'. *Rethinking Marxism* 19:2 (2007), pp. 234–244.

Hudis, Peter. 'Workers as Reason: The Development of a New Relation of Worker and Intellectual in American Marxist Humanism'. *Historical Materialism*, 11:4 (2003), pp. 267–293.

Hunt, Andrew E. *David Dellinger: The Life and Times of a Nonviolent Revolutionary*. New York: New York University Press, 2006.

Huxley, T.H. 'Government: Anarchy or Regimentation' (1890). In *Collected Essays*, available online: http://aleph0.clarku.edu/huxley/CE1/G-AR.html (accessed 17 February 2017).

Hyman, Richard. 'Strikes'. In *A Dictionary of Marxist Thought*, Tom Bottomore (ed.). Cambridge, MA: Harvard University Press, 1983, pp. 470–471.

*Internationale situationniste*. Amsterdam: Van Gennep, 1970; republished Paris: Fayard, 1997.

Isserman, Maurice. *The Other American: The Life of Michael Harrington*. New York: Public Affairs, 2000.

Ives, Peter. *Gramsci's Politics of Language. Engaging the Bakhtin Circle and the Frankfurt School*. Toronto: University of Toronto Press, 2004.

Ives, Peter. *Language and Hegemony in Gramsci*. London: Pluto, 2004.

Ives, Peter, and Rocco Lacorte (eds.). *Gramsci, Language and Translation*. Lanham, MD: Lexington Books, 2010.

James, Bob (ed.). *Anarchism in Australia: An Anthology*. Melbourne: Bob James, 1986.

James, C.L.R. *Beyond a Boundary*. London: Hutchinson & Co., 1969.

James, C.L.R. *The Black Jacobins: Toussaint L'Ouverture and the San Domingo Revolution*. London: Penguin, 2001 [1938].

James, C.L.R. 'Discussions with Trotsky'. In *At the Rendezvous of Victory: Selected Writings*, Volume 3. London: Allison & Busby, 1984, pp. 33–64.

James, C.L.R. 'L'actualité de la Révolution française'. *Perspectives socialistes: Revue bimensuelle de l'Union de la Gauche Socialiste* 4 (15 February 1958), pp. 20–21.

James, C.L.R. 'Michel Maxwell Philip: 1829–1888 [1931]'. In *Michael Maxwell Philip: A Trinidad Patriot of the 19th Century*, Selwyn R. Cudjoe (ed.). Wellesley: Calaloux, 1999, pp. 87–103.

James, C.L.R. *Notes on Dialectics: Hegel, Marx, Lenin*. London: Allison & Busby, 1980.

James, C.L.R. *World Revolution 1917–1936: The Rise and Fall of the Communist International*. New Jersey: Humanity Books, 1994.

James, C.L.R., Grace Lee Boggs, and Cornelius Castoriadis. *Facing Reality: The New Society, Where to Look for It and How to Bring It Closer*. Chicago: Charles H. Kerr, 2006 [1958].

James, C.L.R., Raya Dunayevskaya, and Grace Lee Boggs. *State Capitalism and World Revolution*. Oakland: PM Press, 2013 [1950].

Jaspe, Anselm. *L'avant-garde inacceptable: Réflexions sur Guy Debord*. Paris: Lignes–Éditions Léo Scheer, 2004.

Jaspe, Anselm. *Guy Debord*. Pescara: Edisioni Tracce, 1992; republished Paris: Denoël, 2001.

Jay, Anthony. *Oxford Dictionary of Political Quotations*. Oxford: Oxford University Press, 1996.

Jeffries, Hasan Kwame. *Bloody Lowndes: Civil Rights and Black Power in Alabama's Black Belt*. New York: New York University Press, 2010.

Jennings, Jeremy. 'Introduction' to *Reflections on Violence*, by Georges Sorel, Jeremy Jennings (ed.). Cambridge: Cambridge University Press, 1999, pp. vii–xxi.

Jennings, Jeremy. 'Sorel, Georges'. In *A Dictionary of Marxist Thought*, Tom Bottomore (ed.). Cambridge, MA: Harvard University Press, 1983, p. 509.

Johnson, Carol. 'The Problem of Reformism in Marx's Theory of Fetishism'. *New Left Review* 119 (January–February 1980), pp. 71–96.

Johnson, J.R., Forest, F., and Harvey, M. *Trotskyism in the United States, 1940–47: Balance Sheet: The Workers Party and the Johnson-Forest Tendency*. Detroit: Johnson-Forest Tendency, 1947.

Joll, James. *The Anarchists*. 2nd edition. Cambridge, MA: Harvard University Press, 1980.

Jones, LeRoi/Amiri Baraka. 'Black People!'. In *The LeRoi Jones/Amiri Baraka Reader*, William J. Harris (ed.). New York: Thunder's Mouth Press, 1991, p. 224.

Jones, William D. *The Lost Debate: German Socialist Intellectuals and Totalitarianism*. Urbana: University of Illinois, 1999.

Joseph, Peniel E. *Waiting 'Til the Midnight Hour: A Narrative History of Black Power in America*. New York: Henry Holt, 2006.

Kain, Philip J. *Marx and Modern Political Theory*. Lanham, MD: Rowman & Littlefield, 1993.

Kamenka, Eugene. 'Marxism and Ethics – A Reconsideration'. In *Varieties of Marxism*, Shlomo Avineri (ed.). The Hague: Martinus Nijhoff, 1977, pp. 119–146.

Kaminski, Hanns-Erich. *Bakounine. La vie d'un révolutionnaire*. Paris: La Table Ronde, 2003 [1938].

Karatani, Kojin. *Transcritique*. Cambridge, MA: MIT Press, 2003.

Katsiaficas, Georgy. *The Subversion of Politics: European Autonomous Social Movements and the Decolonization of Everyday Life*. Oakland: AK Press, 2006.

Kellner, Douglas (ed.). *Karl Korsch: Revolutionary Theory*. Austin: University of Texas Press, 1977.

Kelly, Daniel. *James Burnham and the Struggle for the World: A Life*. Washington: ISI Books, 2008.

Kergoat, Jacques. *Marceau Pivert, 'socialiste de gauche'*. Paris: Les Editions de l'Atelier/Editions Ouvrières, 1994.

Kinna, Ruth. *Anarchism*. Oxford: Oneworld, 2005.

Kinna, Ruth. 'Anarchism and the Politics of Utopia'. In *Anarchism and Utopianism*, Laurence Davis and Ruth Kinna (eds.). Manchester: Manchester University Press, 2009, pp. 221–240.

Kinna, Ruth, 'Morris, Anti-statism and Anarchy'. In *William Morris: Centenary Essays*, Peter Faulkner and Peter Preston (eds.). Exeter: University of Exeter Press, 1999, pp. 215–228.

Kinna, Ruth, and Alex Prichard. 'Anarchism: Past, Present and Utopia'. In *Contemporary Anarchist Studies: An Introductory Anthology of Anarchy in the Academy*, Randall Amster et al (eds.). London: Routledge, 2009, pp. 270–279.

Kirby, David. *War, Peace and Revolution: International Socialism at the Crossroads 1914–1918*. London/Aldershot: Gower, 1986.

Klein, Naomi. *No Logo*. London: Flamingo, 2001.

Knabb, Ken (ed.). *Situationist International Anthology*. Berkeley: Bureau of Public Secrets, 1981.

Knabb, Ken. 'The Relevance of Rexroth'. In *Public Secrets: Collected Skirmishes of Ken Knabb: 1970–1997*. Berkeley: Bureau of Public Secrets, 1997, pp. 310–356.

Knapp, Michael, Anja Flach, and Ercan Ayboga. *Revolution in Rojava: Democratic Autonomy and Women's Liberation in Syrian Kurdistan*. London: Pluto, 2016.

Kołakowski, Leszek. *Main Currents of Marxism, Volume 2: The Golden Age*, P.S. Falla (trans.). Oxford: Oxford University Press, 1981.

Kolpakidi, Aleksander, and Jaroslav Leontiev. 'Il peccato originale: Antonio Gramsci e la fondazione del PCd'I'. In *P.C.I. La storia dimentica*, S. Bertelli and F. Bigazzi (eds.). Milan: Arnaldo Mondadori, 2001, pp. 25–60.

Korsch, Karl, Paul Mattick, Antonie Pannekoek, Otto Rühle, and Helmut Wagner. *La Contre-révolution bureaucratique*. Paris: UGE, 1973.

Kosek, Joseph Kip. *Acts of Conscience: Christian Nonviolence and Modern American Democracy*. New York: Columbia University Press, 2009.

Kropotkin, Peter. *Ethics: Origin and Development*, Louis S. Friedland and Joseph R. Piroshnikoff (trans.). Montreal: Black Rose Books, 1992.

Kropotkin, Peter. *The Great French Revolution*. Quebec: Black Rose Books, 1989.

Kropotkin, Peter. *Kropotkin's Revolutionary Pamphlets*, Roger N. Baldwin (ed.). New York: Dover, 1970.

Kropotkin, Peter. 'Revolutionary Government'. In *Peter Kropotkin: Anarchism*, Roger N. Baldwin (ed.). New York: Dover, 2002, pp. 236–250.

Laborde, Cécile. *Pluralist Thought and the State in Britain and France, 1900–1925*. Basingstoke: Palgrave, 2000.

Labriola, Antonio. *Socialism and Philosophy*, Paul Piccone (trans.). St. Louis: Telos Press, 1980.

Laclau, Ernesto. 'Can Immanence Explain Social Struggles'. In *Empire's New Clothes: Reading Hardt and Negri*, Paul A. Passavant and Jodi Dean (eds.). London: Routledge, 2004, pp. 21–30.

Laclau, Ernesto. *On Populist Reasoning*. London: Verso, 2005.

Laclau, Ernesto, and Chantal Mouffe. *Hegemony and Socialist Strategy*. London: Verso, 1985.

Landauer, Gustav. *Revolution and Other Writings: A Political Reader*. Gabriel Kuhn (ed. and trans.). Oakland: PM Press, 2010.

Lefort, Claude. 'Alain Sergent et Claude Harmel. Recension du livre *Histoire de l'Anarchie*, 1'. *Les Temps Modernes* 5:56 (1950), pp. 2269–2274.

Lefort, Claude. 'An interview with Claude Lefort'. *Telos* 30 (1976), pp. 173–192.

Lefort, Claude. 'L'analyse marxiste et le fascisme'. *Les Temps modernes* 2 (November 1945), pp. 357–362.

Lefort, Claude. 'La contradiction de Trotsky et le problème révolutionnaire'. *Les Temps Modernes* 4:39 (1948–1949), pp. 46–69.

Lefort, Claude. *Les formes de l'histoire. Essais d'anthropologie politique*. Paris: Folio essais, 1978.

Leland, John. *Hip: The History*. New York: Harper Collins, 2004.

Lenin, V.I. *April Theses* (1917), available online: www.marxists.org/archive/lenin/works/1917/apr/04.htm (accessed 7 February 2017).

Lenin, V.I. 'Draft Programme'. In *Collected Works,* Volume 2. Moscow: Progress Publishers, 1972, p. 97.

Lenin, V.I. *The Italian Socialist Congress* (1912), available online: http://www.marxists.org/archive/lenin/works/1912/jul/15b.htm (accessed 7 February 2017).

Lenin, V.I. *Left-Wing Communism: An Infantile Disorder* (1920), available online: www.marxists.org/archive/lenin/works/1920/lwc/ (accessed 7 February 2017).

Lenin, V.I. 'Materialism and Empirio-Criticism'. In *Collected Works*, Volume 14. Moscow: Progress Publishers 1972.

Lenin, V.I. *One Step Forward, Two Steps Back*. Moscow: Progress Publishers, 1947.

Lenin, V I. 'The Proletarian Revolution and the Renegade Kautsky'. In *Collected Works,* Volume 28. Moscow: Progress Publishers, 1974.

Lenin, V.I. *Socialism and Anarchism* (1905), available online: http://www.marxists. org/archive/lenin/works/1905/nov/24.htm (accessed 7 February 2017).

Lenin, V.I., 'The State and Revolution' (1918). In *Selected Works*. Moscow: Progress Publishers, 1968, pp. 263–348, available online: www.marxists.org/archive/ lenin/works/1917/staterev (accessed 7 February 2017).

Lenin, V.I. *Anarchism and Socialism* (1901), available online: http://www.marxists. org/archive/lenin/works/1901/dec/31.htm (accessed 7 February 2017).

Lenin, V.I., *What Is to Be Done?*. Moscow: Progress Publishers, 1947.

Lenin, V.I., *What Is to Be Done?*. In *Collected Works,* Volume 5. Moscow: Progress Publishers/London: Lawrence and Wishart, 1961.

Lequenne, Michel. 'Daniel Guérin, l'homme de 93 et le problème de Robespierre'. *Critique communiste* 130–131 (May 1993), pp. 31–34.

Lequenne, Michel. *Le Trotskisme. Une histoire sans fard*. Paris: Editions Syllepse, 2005.

Levy, Carl. *Antonio Gramsci: Machiavelli: Marxism and Modernism*. Cambridge: Polity, 2012.

Levy, Carl. 'Anarchism, Internationalism and Nationalism in Europe, 1860–1939'. *Australian Journal of Politics and History* L (2004), pp. 330–342.

Levy, Carl. 'Charisma and Social Movements: Errico Malatesta and Italian Anarchism'. *Modern Italy* 3:2 (1998), pp. 205–217.

Levy, Carl (ed.). 'Colin Ward: Special Issue', *Anarchist Studies* 19:2 (2011).

Levy, Carl. *Gramsci and the Anarchists*. Oxford and New York: Berg, 1999.

Levy, Carl. 'Gramsci's Cultural and Political Sources: Anarchism in the Prison Writings'. *Journal of Romance Studies*, 12:3 (2012), pp. 44–62.

Levy, Carl. 'A New Look at the Young Gramsci'. *Boundary 2* 24:3 (1986), pp. 31–48.

Levy, Carl. 'The People and the Professors: Socialism and the Educated Middle Classes in Italy, 1870–1914'. *Journal of Modern Italian Studies* VI:2 (2001), pp. 193–208.

Levy, Carl. '"The Rooted Cosmopolitan": Errico Malatesta, Syndicalism, Transnationalism and the International Labour Movement'. In *New Perspectives on Anarchism, Labour and Syndicalism: The Individual, the National and the Transnational*, David Berry and Constance Bantman (eds.). Newcastle: Cambridge Scholars Press, 2010, pp. 61–79.

Levy, Carl. '"*Sovversivismo*": The Radical Political Culture of Otherness in Liberal Italy'. *Journal of Political Ideologies* 12:2 (2007), pp. 147–161.

Levy, J.H. 'Appendix' to *Auberon Herbert, Taxation and Anarchism: A Discussion between the Hon. Auberon Herbert and J.H. Levy*. London: Personal Rights Association, 1912, available online: http://oll.libertyfund.org/titles/herbert-taxation-and-anarchism-a-discussion-between-the-hon-auberon-herbert-and-j-h-levy (accessed 7 February 2017).

Lichtenstein, Alex. 'George Rawick's "From Sundown to Sunup" and the Dialectic of Marxian Slave Studies'. *Reviews in American History* 24:4 (1996), pp. 712–725.

Lichtheim, George. *The Concept of Ideology and Other Essays*. New York: Random House, 1967.

Lichtheim, George. *From Marx to Hegel*. New York: The Seabury Press, 1971.

Lichtheim, George. *Marxism: An Historical and Critical Study*. 2nd edition. New York: Praeger, 1965.

Liebich, Andre. 'Socialisme ou Barbarie: A Radical Critique of Bureaucracy'. *Our Generation* 12:2 (1977), pp. 55–62.

Liguori, Guido. 'Common Sense in Gramsci'. In *Perspectives on Gramsci: Politics, Culture and Social Theory*, Joseph Francese (ed.). London: Routledge, 2009, pp. 122–133.

Lih, Lars T. *Lenin Rediscovered.* What Is to Be Done? *in Context*. Amsterdam: Brill University Press, 2006.

Lindemann, Albert S. *'The Red Years': European Socialism and Bolshevism, 1919–1921*. Berkeley: University of California Press, 1974.

Linden, Marcel van der. 'On Council Communism'. *Historical Materialism*, 12:4 (2004), available online: https://www.marxists.org/subject/left-wing/2004/council-communism.htm (accessed 8 February 2017).

Linden, Marcel van der. 'Second Thoughts on Revolutionary Syndicalism'. *Labour History Review* 63:2 (1998), pp. 182–196.

Linden, Marcel van der. 'Socialisme ou Barbarie: A French Revolutionary Group (1949–65)'. *Left History* 5:1 (1997), available online: www.left-dis.nl/uk/lindsob.htm (accessed 8 February 2017).

Linden, Marcel van der. *Western Marxism and the Soviet Union: A Survey of Critical Theories and Debates Since 1917*. Chicago: Haymarket Books, 2009.

Linden, Marcel van der, and Wayne Thorpe (eds.). *Revolutionary Syndicalism: An International Perspective*. Aldershot: Scolar Press, 1990.

Lo Piparo, Franco. *Lingua intellettuali egemonia in Gramsci*. Bari: Laterza, 1979.

Lotringer, Sylvère, and Christian Marazzi. *Autonomia: Post-Political Politics*. Los Angeles: Semiotext(e), 2007.

Low, Mary, and Juan Breá. *Red Spanish Notebook; The First Six Months of the Revolution and the Civil War*. London: Secker & Warburg, 1937.

Löwy, Michael. 'Rosa Luxemburg, un marxisme pour le XXIe siècle'. *Contretemps* 8 (2010), pp. 59–63.

Lucarini, Federico. 'Socialismo, riformismo e scienze sociali nella Torino del giovane Gramsci (1914–21)'. In *Gramsci e il suo tempo*, Francesco Giasi (ed.). Rome: Carocci, 2008, pp. 219–240.

Lukács, György. *History and Class Consciousness*. London: Merlin Press, 1976.

Lumley, Robert. *States of Emergency: Cultures of Revolt in Italy from 1968 to 1978*. London and New York: Verso, 1990.

Lussana Fiamma, and Giulia Pissarello. (eds.). *La lingua/le lingue di Gramsci e delle sue opera. Scrittura, riscritture, letture in Italia e nel mondo*. Soveria Mannelli: Rubbettino, 2008.

Luxemburg, Rosa. *Le socialisme en France, 1898–1912*. Paris: Belfond, 1971.

Luxemburg, Rosa. 'The Mass Strike, the Political Party and the Trade Unions'. In *Rosa Luxemburg Speaks*, Mary-Alice Waters (ed.). New York: Pathfinder Press, 1970, pp. 53–218.

Luxemburg, Rosa. *The Mass Strike, the Political Party, and the Trade Unions* and *The Junius Pamphlet*. London: Harper and Row, 1971.

Luxemburg, Rosa. 'Organisational Questions of the Social Democracy'. In *Rosa Luxemburg Speaks*, Mary-Alice Waters (ed.). New York: Pathfinder Press, 1970, pp. 153–218.

Luxemburg, Rosa. 'Our Program and the Political Situation'. In *The Rosa Luxemburg Reader*, Peter Hudis and Kevin B. Anderson (eds.). New York: Monthly Review Press, 2004, pp. 357–373.

Luxemburg, Rosa. *Reform or Revolution*. New York: Gordon Press, 1974.

Luxemburg, Rosa. *The Russian Revolution* (1918), available online: http://www.marxists.org/archive/luxemburg/1918/russian-revolution/ (accessed 7 February 2017).

MacIntyre, Alasdair. *A Short History of Ethics*. London: Routledge, 1967.

Mack, Eric. 'Voluntaryism: the Political Thought of Auberon Herbert'. *Journal of Libertarian Studies* 2:4 (1978), pp. 299–309.

MacPhee, Josh, and Dara Greenwald. *Signs of Change: Social Movement Cultures, 1960s to Now*. Oakland: AK Press, 2010.

Maggi, Michele. *La filosofia della rivoluzione. Gramsci, la cultura e la guerra Europea*. Rome: Edizione di storia letteratura, 2008.

Malatesta, Errico. 'Syndicalism: An Anarchist Critique'. In *The Anarchist Reader*, George Woodcock (ed.). Glasgow: Fontana Paperbacks, 1977, pp. 223–225.

Malatesta, Errico. 'Syndicalism and Anarchism'. In *The Anarchist Revolution: Polemical Articles 1924–1931*, Vernon Richards (ed.). London: Freedom Press, 1995, pp. 23–27.

Malatesta, Errico. *Democracy and Anarchy* (1924), available online: http://www.marxists.org/archive/malatesta/1924/03/democracy.htm (accessed 18 February 2017).

Malatesta, Errico. *Neither Democrats nor Dictators: Anarchists* (1926), available online: http://www.marxists.org/archive/malatesta/1926/05/neither.htm (accessed 18 February 2017).

Malina, Judith. *The Diaries of Judith Malina, 1947–1957*. New York: Grove Press, 1984.

Mandel, Ernest. *Contrôle ouvrier, conseils ouvriers, autogestion*. Paris: Maspero, 1970.

*Manifesto of English Socialists*. London: Twentieth Century Press, 1893.

Mannin, Ethel. *Comrade O Comrade; or, Low-Down on the Left*. London: Jarrolds, 1947.

Marcos, Subcomandante. 'I Shit on All the Revolutionary Vanguards of This Planet', (January 2003), available online: http://flag.blackened.net/revolt/mexico/ezln/2003/marcos/etaJAN.html (accessed 27 January 2017).

Marcuse, Herbert. *A Study on Authority*. London: Verso, 2008.

Mariátegui, José Carlos. *Mariátegui total*, Volume 1. Lima: Empresa Editora Amauta S.A., 1994.

Marinelli, Gianfranco. *L'amère victoire du situationnisme*. Arles: Gulliver, 1998.

Marshall, Craig. *Levels of Industrial Militancy and the Political Radicalisation of the Durham Miners, 1885–1914*. MA thesis, Durham University, 1976.

Marshall, Peter. *Demanding the Impossible: A History of Anarchism*. London: Harper Collins, 1992; 2nd edition 1993; 3rd edition 2008.

Martin, Charles. *Towards a Free Society*. London: Freedom Press, 1960.

Martin, James J. 'Editor's Introduction' to *The Ego and His Own*, by Max Stirner. New York: Dover, 2005, pp. vii–xvi.

Martos. Jean-François. *Correspondance avec Guy Debord*. Paris: Le Fin Mot de l'Histoire, 1998.

Marx, Karl. *Capital*, Volume 1. Harmondsworth: Penguin, 1976.

Marx, Karl, 'The Civil War in France'. In Karl Marx, *The First International and After*. London: Penguin, 1974, pp. 187–268.

Marx, Karl. *Critique du droit politique hégélien*, Albert Baraquin (trans.). Paris: Éditions sociales, 1975.

Marx, Karl, 'Critique of the Gotha Programme'. In Karl Marx, *The First International and After*. London: Penguin, 1974, pp. 339–359.

Marx, Karl. 'Critique of the Gotha Programme'. In Karl Marx and Frederick Engels, *Collected Works*, Volume 24. New York: International Publishers, 1989, pp. 75–99.

Marx, Karl. 'Drafts of the Civil War in France'. In Karl Marx and Frederick Engels, *Collected Works*, Volume 22. New York: International Publishers, 1986, pp. 437–514.

Marx, Karl. 'The Eighteenth Brumaire of Louis Bonaparte'. In *Marx and Engels: Selected Works*. London: Lawrence and Wishart, 1968, pp. 97–180.

Marx, Karl. *Grundrisse*. Harmondsworth: Penguin, 1973.

Marx, Karl. *La Guerre Civile en France*. Paris: Éditions Sociales, collection 'Classiques du marxisme', 1968.

Marx, Karl. *Manifeste du Parti Communiste*. Paris: Éditions Sociales, collection 'Classiques du marxisme', 1966.

Marx, Karl. 'On Bakunin's Statism and Anarchy'. in *Karl Marx: Selected Writings*, D. McLellan (ed.). Oxford: Oxford University Press, 2000, pp. 606–609.

Marx, Karl. 'On the Jewish Question'. In *Marx: Early Political Writings*, .Joseph O'Malley (ed.). Cambridge: Cambridge University Press, 1994, pp. 28–56.

Marx, Karl. 'On the Jewish Question'. In Karl Marx and Frederick Engels, *Collected Works*, Volume 3. New York: International Publishers, 1975, pp. 146–174.

Marx, Karl. *The Poverty of Philosophy*. Moscow: Progress Publishers, 1975.

Marx, Karl. 'Provisional Rules of the Association'. In Karl Marx and Frederick Engels, *Collected Works*, Volume 20. New York: International Publishers, 1985, pp. 14–16.

Marx, Karl. 'Speech at the Anniversary of the *People's Paper*'. In Karl Marx and Frederick Engels, *Collected Works*, Volume 14. New York: International Publishers, 1980, pp. 655–656.

Marx, Karl. 'Theses on Feuerbach'. In Karl Marx, *Early Writings*. London: Penguin, 1975, pp. 421–423.

Marx, Karl, and Friedrich Engels. 'Circular Letter'. In *Karl Marx: Selected Writings*, David McLellan (ed.). Oxford: Oxford University Press, 2000, pp. 620–622.

Marx, Karl, and Frederick Engels. 'Circular Letter to August Bebel, Wilhelm Liebknecht, Wilhelm Bracke and Others'. In Karl Marx and Frederick Engels, *Collected Works*, Volume 24. New York: International Publishers, 1989, pp. 253–269.

Marx, Karl, and Friedrich Engels. 'The Communist Manifesto'. In *Karl Marx: Selected Writings*, David McLellan (ed.). Oxford: Oxford University Press, 2000, pp. 245–272.

Marx, Karl, and Frederick Engels. *The German Ideology*. In Karl Marx and Frederick Engels, *Collected Works*, Volume 5. New York: International Publishers, 1976, pp. 19–539.

Marx, Karl, and Frederick Engels. *The Holy Family, or Critique of Critical Criticism.* In Karl Marx and Frederick Engels, *Collected Works,* Volume 4. New York: International Publishers, 1975, pp. 5–211.

Marx, Karl, and Frederick. 'Manifesto of the Communist Party'. In Karl Marx, *The Revolutions of 1848.* London: Penguin, 1973, pp. 62–98.

Marx, Karl, Frederick Engels, and V.I. Lenin. *Marx, Engels, Lenin: Anarchism and Anarcho-Syndicalism.* Moscow: Progress Publishers, 1972.

Mates, Lewis H. *From Revolutionary to Reactionary: The Life of Will Lawther.* MA thesis, Newcastle University,1996.

Mates, Lewis H. *The Spanish Civil War and the British Left: Political Activism and the Popular Front.* London: I.B. Tauris, 2007.

Mattick, Paul. 'Anti-Bolshevist Communism in Germany' (1947). *Telos 26* (Winter 1975–1976), available online: www.libcom.org/library/anti-bolshevist-communism-germany-paul-mattick (accessed 8 February 2017).

Mattick, Paul. *Die Todeskrise des kapitalistischen Systems und die Aufgaben des Proletariats* (1933), available online: www.workerseducation.org/crutch/pamphlets/todeskriese.html (accessed 18 February 2017).

Mattick, Paul. 'Introduction'. *New Essays: A Quarterly Dedicated to the Study of Modern Society.* Westport, CT: Greenwood Reprint Corporation, 1969.

Mattick, Paul. *World-wide Fascism or World Revolution? Manifesto and Program of the United Workers Party of America.* Chicago: United Workers Party of America, 1934, available online: www.marxists.org/archive/mattick-paul/1934/fascism-revolution.htm (accessed 18 February 2017).

Mattick, Paul, Jr. 'Karl Korsch: His Contribution to Revolutionary Marxism' (1962), available online: www.marxists.org/archive/mattick-paul/1962/korsch.htm (accessed 8 February 2017).

Mattick, Paul, Jr. 'Ruehle, Otto'. In *Biographical Dictionary of Neo-Marxism*, Robert A. Gorman (ed.). Westport, CT: Greenwood Press, 1985, p. 365.

Mattick, Paul, Jr. 'Socialisme ou Barbarie'. In *Biographical Dictionary of Neo-Marxism* R.A. Gorman (ed.). Westport, CT: Greenwood Press, 1985, pp. 387–389.

Maximov, Giorgi Petrovitch. *Syndicalists in the Russian Revolution* (n.d., c.1940), available online: www.libcom.org/library/syndicalists-in-russian-revolution-maximov (accessed 18 February 2017).

May, Todd. 'Anarchism from Foucault to Rancière'. In *Contemporary Anarchist Studies* Randall Amster et al. (eds.). London: Routledge, 2009, pp. 11–17.

May, Todd. 'Friendship in the Age of Economics'. *New York Times*, July 4, 2010, available online: https://opinionator.blogs.nytimes.com/2010/07/04/friendship-in-an-age-of-economics/ (accessed 18 February 2017).

May, Todd. *The Political Philosophy of Poststructuralist Anarchism.* Pennsylvania: Pennsylvania State University Press, 1994.

McElroy, Wendy. *The Debates of Liberty: An Overview of Individualist Anarchism, 1881–1908.* Lanham, MD: Lexington Books, 2003.

McGregor, Peter. *Cultural Battles: The Meaning of the Viet Nam – USA War.* Melbourne: Scam Publications, 1988.

McIntyre, Iain. *Disturbing the Peace: Tales from Australia's Rebel History.* Melbourne: Homebrew Books, 2005.

McKay, George. *DiY Culture: Party and Protest in Nineties Britain*. London and New York: Verso, 1998.

McKay, George. *Senseless Acts of Beauty: Cultures of Resistance since the Sixties*. London: Verson, 1996.

McKay, Iain (ed.). *Property Is Theft! A Pierre-Joseph Proudhon Anthology*. Oakland: AK Press, 2011.

McLaughlin, Paul. *Michael Bakunin: The Philosophical Basis of His Anarchism*. New York: Algora, 2002.

McLellan, David. *Marxism After Marx*. 3rd edition. Houndmills and London: Macmillan Press Ltd, 1998; 4th edition. London: Palgrave, 2007.

McLellan, David. *The Young Hegelians and Karl Marx*. London: Macmillan, 1969.

McNally, David. *Against the Market*. London: Verso, 1993.

Medici, Rita. 'Giacobinismo'. In *Le parole di Gramsci. Per un lessico di Quardern del Carcere*, Fabio Frosini and Guido Liguori (eds.). Rome: Carocci, 2004, pp. 112–130.

Meikle, Scott. *Essentialism in the Thought of Karl Marx*. La Saale: Open Court, 1985.

Meltzer, Albert. *The Anarchists in London 1935–1955*. Sanday: Cienfuegos Press, 1976.

Mészáros, Istvan. *Lukács' Concept of Dialectic*. London: Merlin, 1972.

Mészáros, Istvan. *Marx's Theory of Alienation*. London: Merlin, 1975.

Michelini, Luca. 'Antonio Gramsci e il liberismo italiano (1913–1919)'. In *Gramsci e il suo tempo*, Volume 1, Francesco Giasi (ed.). Rome, Carocci, 2008, pp. 175–196.

Michels, Robert. *Political Parties*. New York: Collier Press, 1962.

Miliband, Ralph. 'Reply to Nicos Poulantzas'. In *Ideology in Social Science: Readings in Critical Social Theory*, Robin Blackburn (ed.). London: Fontana, 1972, pp. 253–262.

Miliband, Ralph. *The State in Capitalist Society*. New York: Basic Books, 1969.

Miller, David. *Anarchism*. London: Dent, 1984.

Millett, Steve. 'Technology Is Capital: *Fifth Estate*'s Critique of the Megamachine'. In *Changing Anarchism: Anarchist Theory and Practice in a Global Age*, Jonathan Purkis and James Bowen (eds.). Manchester: Manchester University Press, 2004, pp. 73–98.

Mills, C.W. 'Letter to the New Left'. *New Left Review* 5 (September–October 1960), available online: http://www.marxists.org/subject/humanism/mills-c-wright/letter-new-left.htm (accessed 8 February 2017).

*Minutes of the Second Congress of the Communist International* (1920), available online: www.marxists.org/history/international/comintern/2nd-congress/ch07.htm (accessed 8 February 2017).

Morabito, G. 'Antonio Gramsci e l'idealismo guridico italiano. Due tesi a confronto'. *Storia e politica* VI:4 (1979), pp. 744–755.

Morera, Esteve. 'Gramsci's Critical Modernity'. *Rethinking Marxism* 12:1 (2000), pp. 16–46.

Morin, Edgar. 'L'Anarchisme en 1968'. *Magazine littéraire* 19 (1968).

Morin, Edgar. 'La réfome de pensée'. In *Arguments, 1956–1962*, Volume 1. Toulouse: Privat, 1983), pp. ix–xi.

Morin, Edgar, Claude Lefort, and Jean-Marc Coudray. *Mai 68: la brèche. Premières réflexions sur les événements*. Paris: Librairie Arthème Fayard, 1968.

Morland, David. 'Anarchism, Human Nature and History'. In *Twenty-First Century Anarchism*, Jonathan Purkis and James Bowen (eds.). London: Cassell, 1997, pp. 8–23.

Morland, David. *Demanding the Impossible? Human Nature and Politics in Nineteenth-Century Social Anarchism*. London: Cassell, 1997.

Morrell, Robert. *The Gentle Revolutionary: The Life and Work of Frank Ridley, Socialist and Secularist*. London: Freethought History Research Group, 2003.

Morris, William. *The Collected Letters of William Morris, Volume III: 1889–1892*, Norman Kelvin (ed.). New Jersey: Princeton University Press, 1996.

Morris, William. *The Collected Letters of William Morris, Volume IV: 1893–1896*, Norman Kelvin (ed.). Princeton, NJ: Princeton University Press, 1996.

Morris, William. 'The Dream of John Ball'. In *Three Works by William Morris*, A.L. Morton (ed.). London: Lawrence and Wishart, 1986, pp. 33–113.

Morris, William. *Journalism: Contributions to Commonweal 1885–1890*, Norman Salmon (ed.). Bristol: Thoemmes Press, 1996.

Morris, William. *News From Nowhere*, D. Leopold (ed.). Oxford: Oxford University Press, 2003.

Morris, William. *Political Writings: Contributions to Justice and Commonweal*, Nick Salmon (ed.). Bristol: Thoemmes Press, 1994.

Morris, William. *Statement of Principles of the Hammersmith Socialist Society*. London: Kelmscott Press, 1890.

Morris, William. *The Story of the Glittering Plain*, Norman Talbot (ed.). Bristol: Thoemmes Press, 1996.

Morton, Adam David. 'Waiting for Gramsci: State Formation, Passive Revolution and the International'. *Millennium* 35:3 (2007), pp. 597–621.

Mukherjee, Subrata, and Sushila Ramaswamy. *A History of Socialist Thought: From the Precursors to the Present*. Delhi: Sage 2000.

Murray, Christopher John (ed.). *Encyclopedia of Modern French Thought*. New York and London: Fitzroy Dearborn, 2004.

Natoli, Claudio. 'Grande Guerra e rinnovamento del socialismo negli scritti del giovane Gramsci (1914–1918)'. In *Gramsci e il sup tempo*, Volume 1, Francesco Giasi (ed.). Rome: Carocci, 2008, pp. 51–76.

Negri, Antonio. 'Communism: Some Thoughts on the Concept and Practice'. In *The Idea of Communism*, Costas Douzinas and Slavoj Žižek (eds.). London: Verso, 2010, pp. 155–165.

Negri, Antonio. 'Lesson One: From the Factory of Strategy', available online: http://antonionegriinenglish.wordpress.com/2010/09/06/lesson-1-from-33-lessons-on-lenin-for-a-marxist-reading-of-lenins-marxism/ (accessed 18 February 2017.

Negri, Antonio. *Marx Beyond Marx*. London: Autonomedia/Pluto, 1991.

Negri, Antonio. *The Porcelain Workshop*. Los Angeles: Semiotext(e), 2006.

Negri, Antonio. *Reflections on Empire*. Cambridge: Polity, 2008.

Negri, Antonio. *Time for Revolution*. London: Continuum, 2003.

Negri, Antonio. 'What to Do Today with What Is to Be Done?, or Rather, The Body of the General Intellect'. In *Lenin Reloaded: Towards a Politics of Truth*, Sebastian Budgen, Stathis Kouvelakis, and Slavoj Žižek (eds.). Duke University, 2007, pp. 297–307.

Negri, Antonio. 'Workers' Party Against Work' (1973). In Antonio Negri, *Books for Burning*. London: Verso, 2005, pp. 51–117.

Nelson, Joel I. *Post-Industrial Capitalism*. London: Sage, 1995.

Nettlau, Max. *A Short History of Anarchism*, Heiner M. Becker (ed.), Ida Pilat Isca (trans.). London: Freedom Press, 1996.

Neumann, Osha. *Up Against the Wall Motherf**ker: A Memoir of the '60s, with Notes for Next Time*. New York: Seven Stories, 2008.

Newman, Saul. *From Bakunin to Lacan: Anti-Authoritarianism and the Dislocation of Power*. Plymouth: Lexington Books, 2007.

Newman, Saul. *The Politics of Postanarchism*. Edinburgh: Edinburgh University Press, 2010.

Newsinger, John. 'Destroying the Myth: George Orwell and Soviet Communism'. In *George Orwell: Enigmatic Socialist*, Paul Flewers (ed.). London: Socialist Platform, 2005, pp. 55–80.

Nun, José. 'Elements for a Theory of Democracy: Gramsci and Common Sense'. *Boundary 2* 14:3 (1986), pp. 197–230.

O'Lincoln, Tom. *Years of Rage: Social Conflicts in the Fraser Era*. Melbourne: Bookmarks, 1993.

Ollman, Bertell. *Alienation: Marx's Conception of Man in Capitalist Society*. Cambridge: Cambridge University Press, 2nd edition 1976.

Olssen, Mark. 'Foucault and Marxism: Rewriting the Theory of Historical Materialism'. *Policy Futures in Education*, 2/2–3 (2004), pp. 454–482.

Orwell, George. *Homage to Catalonia*. London: Penguin, 1989.

Padmore, George. *Pan-Africanism or Communism? The Coming Struggle for Africa*. London: Dennis Dobson, 1956.

Page Arnot, R., *South Wales Miners to 1914*. London: George Allen and Unwin, 1967.

Paggi, Loenardo. *Le strategie del potere in Gramsci*. Rome: Riuniti, 1984.

Pannekoek, Anton. *Workers' Councils*. Oakland: AK Press, 2003.

Paris, Robert. 'Mariátegui: un sorelismo ambiguo'. In *Mariátegui y los orígenes del marxismo latinoamericano*, José Aricó (ed.). Mexico City: Pasado y Presente, 1978, pp. 155–161.

Pattieu, Sylvain. *Les camarades des frères: Trotskistes et libertaires dans la guerre d'Algérie*. Paris: Syllepse, 2002.

Pattison, Gary. 'Anarchist Influence in the Durham Coalfield Before 1914'. *The Raven* 11 3:3 (1990), pp. 239–243.

Paz, Abel. *Durruti in the Spanish Revolution*. Oakland: AK Press, 2007.

Pennetier, Claude (ed.). *Dictionnaire biographique: mouvement ouvrier, mouvement social de 1940 à mai 1968*. Paris: Editions de l'Atelier, 2010.

Perkins, Stephen. *Marxism and the Proletariat*. London: Pluto, 1993.

Phelps, Christopher. 'C.L.R. James and the Theory of State Capitalism'. In *American Capitalism: Social Thought and Political Economy in the Twentieth Century*, Nelson Lichtenstein (ed.). Philadelphia: University of Pennsylvania Press, 2006, pp. 157–174.

Piccone, Paul. 'From Spaventa to Gramsci'. *Telos* 31 (1977), pp. 35–66.

Pinta, Saku. *Towards a Libertarian Communism: A Conceptual History of the Intersections between Anarchisms and Marxisms*. Unpublished PhD thesis, Loughborough University, 2012.

Pizzolato, Nicola. 'Transnational radicals: labor dissent and political activism in Detroit and Turin (1950–1970)'. *International Review of Social History* 56 (2011), pp. 1–30.

Plant, Sadie. *The Most Radical Gesture: The Situationist International in a Postmodern Age*. London: Routledge, 1992.

Polletta, Francesca. *Freedom Is an Endless Meeting: Democracy in American Social Movements*. Chicago: University of Chicago Press, 2002.

Portis, Larry. 'Daniel Guérin et les Etats-Unis: l'optimisme et l'intelligence'. *Agone* 29–30 (2003), pp. 277–289.

Poulantzas, Nicos. *Classes in Contemporary Capitalism*. London: New Left Books, 1975.

Poulantzas, Nicos. 'The Problem of the Capitalist State'. In *Ideology in Social Science: Readings in Critical Social Theory*, Robin Blackburn (ed.). London: Fontana, 1972, pp. 238–253.

Prager, Rudolphe (ed.). *Les congrès de la quatrième internationale (manifestes, thèses, résolutions)* (2 volumes). Paris: La Brèche, 1981.

Price, Wayne. *The Abolition of the State: Anarchist and Marxist Perspectives*. Bloomington IN/Milton Keynes: Authorhouse, 2007.

Prichard, Alex, and Owen Worth. 'Left-wing convergence: An introduction'. *Capital & Class* 40/1 (2016), pp. 3–17.

Procacci, Giuliano. 'Antonio Labriola e la revisione del marxismo atrraverso l'epistolario con Bernstein a con Kautsky, 1895–1904'. *Annali della Bibilioteca Giangiacomo Feltrinelli* III (1960), pp. 264–331.

*Programme of the Communist Workers Party of Germany* (KAPD) (1920), available online: www.libcom.org/library/programme-communist-workers-party-germany-kapd-1920 (accessed 8 February 2017).

Progressive Geographies. 'Simon Springer and David Harvey debate Marxism, anarchism and geography', available online: https://progressivegeographies.com/2015/06/10/simon-springer-and-david-harvey-debate-marxism-anarchism-and-geography/ (accessed 27 January 2017).

Proudhon, Pierre-Joseph. *General Idea of the Revolution in the Nineteenth Century*. London: Pluto, 1989.

Proudhon, Pierre-Joseph. *What Is Property?*. Cambridge: Cambridge University Press, 1994.

Puente, Isaac. *Libertarian Communism*. Sydney: Monty Miller Press, 1985 [1932], available online: http://flag.blackened.net/liberty/libcom.html (accessed 8 February 2017).

Pulido, Laura. *Black, Brown, Yellow, and Left: Radical Activism in Los Angeles*. Berkeley: University of California Press, 2006.

Quail, John. *The Slow Burning Fuse: The Lost History of British Anarchists*. London: Paladin, 1978.

Rachleff, Peter J. *Marxism and Council Communism: The Foundation for Revolutionary Theory for Modern Society*. Brooklyn: Revisionist Press, 1976.

Radcliffe, Charles. 'Two Fiery Flying Rolls – The *Heatwave* Story, 1966–1970'. In *Dancin' in the Streets! Anarchists, IWWs, Surrealists, Situationists & Provos in the 1960s as recorded in the Pages of* The Rebel Worker *and* Heatwave, Franklin

Rosemont and Charles Radcliffe (eds.). Chicago: Charles H. Kerr, 2005, pp. 327–380.

Ramnath, Maia. *Decolonizing Anarchism: An Antiauthoritarian History of India's Liberation Struggle*. Oakland: AK Press, 2011.

Ramsay, Maureen. *What's Wrong with Liberalism?*. London: Leicester University Press, 1997.

Ransby, Barbara. *Ella Baker and the Black Freedom Movement: A Radical Democratic Vision*. Chapel Hill: University of North Carolina Press, 2005.

Rawick, George P. *Listening to Revolt: Selected Writings*, David Roediger and Martin Smith (eds.). Chicago: Charles H. Kerr, 2010.

Read, Christopher. *Revolution, Religion and the Russian Intelligentsia*. Basingstoke: Macmillan, 1979.

Renault, Emmanuel (ed.). *Lire les Manuscrits de 1844*. Paris: PUF, 2008.

Renton, Dave. *C.L.R. James: Cricket's Philosopher King*. London: Haus Books, 2007.

Renton, Dave. *Dissident Marxism: Past Voices for Present Times*. London: Zed Books, 2004.

Richards, Vernon. *Lessons of the Spanish Revolution*. London: Freedom Press, 1995.

Richards, Vernon. 'Printers We Have Known: 1936–1986'. *Freedom, Centenary Edition* 47:9 (1986), pp. 28–29.

Richter, Eugene. *Pictures of the Socialistic Future*. London: Swan Sonnenschein & Co. 1907, available online: http://www.econlib.org/library/YPDBooks/Richter/rchtPSF.html (accessed 18 February 2017).

Ridley, Frank Ambrose. 'Anarchism and Marxism'. *Controversy* 2:23 (August 1938), pp. 214–217.

Rioux, Jean-Pierre, and Jean-François Sirinelli (eds.). *Histoire culturelle de la France*, Tome 4. Paris: Editions du Seuil, 2005.

Robb, Oliver. *Anarchy in Albert Park: An Attack on the 'Work Ethic'*. Christchurch: Christchurch Anarchy Group, 1976.

Robertson, Louis. *Reflections of My Time in Solidarity*, available online: http://struggle.ws/disband/solidarity/recollections.html (accessed 8 February 2017).

Robinson, Cedric. *Black Marxism: The Making of the Black Radical Tradition*. Chapel Hill: University of North Carolina Press, 2000 [1983].

Rocker, Rudolf. *Anarcho-Syndicalism*. London: Pluto Press, 1989.

Rocker, Rudolf. 'The Ideology of Anarchism'. In *The Anarchists*, Irving Louis Horowitz (ed.). New Brunswick: Aldine Transaction, 2005, pp. 183–193.

Romano, Paul. *The American Worker (Part 1: Life in the Factory)*, available online: www.prole.info/pdfs/americanworker.pdf (accessed 19 February 2017).

Roper, Brian S. *Prosperity for All? Economic, Social and Political Change in New Zealand since 1935*. Melbourne: Thomson/Dunmore Press, 2005.

Rorty, Richard. *Contingency, Irony, and Solidarity*. Cambridge University Press, Cambridge, 1989.

Rose, Jonathan. *The Intellectual Life of the British Working Classes*. London: Yale University Press, 2001.

Rosemont, Franklin. *Joe Hill: The IWW & the Making of a Revolutionary Workingclass Counterculture*. Chicago: Charles H. Kerr, 2003.

Rosemont, Franklin, and Charles Radcliffe (eds.). *Dancin' in the Streets! Anarchists, IWWs, Surrealists, Situationists & Provos in the 1960s as recorded in the pages of* The Rebel Worker *and* Heatwave. Chicago: Charles H. Kerr, 2005.

Rosemont, Penelope. *Dreams and Everyday Life: André Breton, Surrealism, Rebel Worker, SDS & the Seven Cities of Cibola.* Chicago: Charles H. Kerr, 2008.

Rosenberg, Arthur. *A History of Bolshevism; From Marx to the First Five Years' Plan.* London: Oxford University Press, 1934.

Rosengarten, Frank. *Urbane Revolutionary: C.L.R. James and the Struggle for a New Society.* Jackson: University Press of Mississippi, 2008.

Rosmer, Alfred. *Lenin's Moscow.* London: Bookmarks, 1987.

Ross, Kristin. *May '68 and Its Afterlives.* Chicago: Chicago University Press, 2002.

Rossi, Angelo, and Giuseppe Vacca. *Gramsci tra Mussolini e Stalin.* Rome: Fazi, 2007.

Rossini, Daniela. *Woodrow Wilson and the American Myth in Italy: Culture, Diplomacy and War Propaganda.* Cambridge, MA.: Harvard University Press, 2008.

Roth, Jack Joseph. *The Cult of Violence: Sorel and the Sorelians.* Berkeley: University of California Press, 1980.

Rouse, Joseph. 'Power/Knowledge'. In *The Cambridge Companion to Foucault,* Gary Gutting (ed.). Cambridge: Cambridge University Press, 1994, pp. 95–122.

Rowbotham, Sheila. *Dreamers of a New Day: Women Who Invented the Twentieth Century.* London: Verso, 2010.

Rubel, Maximilien. *Marx, critique du Marxisme.* Paris: Editions Payot, 1974; new edition 2000.

Rubel, Maximilien. *Marx théoricien de l'anarchisme.* Saint-Denis: Vent du ch'min, 1983; Geneva: Editions Entremonde, 2011.

Rubel, Maximilien. 'Marx, Theoretician of Anarchism'. *L'Europe en formation,* no. 163–164 (1973), available online: http://www.marxists.org/archive/rubel/1973/marx-anarchism.htm, (accessed 19 February 2017).

Rubel, Maxmilien. *Rubel on Karl Marx,* Joseph J. O'Malley and Keith W. Algozin (eds. and trans.). Cambridge: Cambridge University Press, 1981.

Rubel, Maximilien, and John Crump (eds.). *Non-Market Socialism in the Nineteenth and Twentieth Centuries.* London: MacMillan Press, 1987.

Rühle, Otto. *From the Bourgeois to the Proletarian Revolution* (1924), available online: www.marxists.org/archive/ruhle/1924/revolution.htm (accessed 8 February 2017).

Rühle, Otto. *The Revolution is Not a Party Affair* (1920), available online: www.marxists.org/archive/ruhle/1920/ruhle02.htm (accessed 8 February 2017).

Rustin, Michael. 'Empire: A Postmodern Theory of Revolution'. In *Debating Empire,* Gopal Balakrishnan (ed.). London: Verso, 2003, pp. 1–18.

Ryan, Michael. 'Epilogue' to *Marx Beyond Marx,* by Antonio Negri. London: Automedia/Pluto, 1991, pp. 191–221.

Saccarelli, Emanuele. *Gramsci and Trotsky in the Shadow of Stalin: The Political Theory and Practice of Opposition.* London: Routledge, 2008.

Samuel, Raphael (ed.). *Miners, Quarrymen and Salt Workers.* London: Routledge & Kegan Paul, 1977.

San Juan, E., Jr. *Beyond Postcolonial Theory.* New York: St Martin's Press, 1998.

Sander, Reinhard W. 'Introduction: *The Beacon* and the Emergence of West Indian Literature'. In *The Beacon, Volumes I–IV, 1931–1939*, Brinsley Samaroo (ed.). New York: Kraus, 1977, pp. xv–xxv.

Sassoon, Donald. *One Hundred Years of Socialism: The West European Left in the Twentieth Century*. London: Fontana, 1996.

Saul, Scott. *Freedom Is, Freedom Ain't: Jazz and the Making of the Sixties*. Cambridge: Harvard University Press, 2003.

Saunders, Frances Stonor. *The Cultural Cold War: The CIA and the World of Arts and Letters*. New York: New Press, 2001.

Sayer, Derek. *The Violence of Abstraction*. Oxford: Blackwell, 1987.

Sayers, Sean. 'Marxism and the Dialectical Method: A Critique of G. A. Cohen'. *Radical Philosophy* 36 (1984), pp. 4–13.

Sayers, Sean. *Marxism and Human Nature*. London: Routledge, 1998.

Schecter, Darrow. *Gramsci and the Theory of Industrial Democracy*. Aldershot: Ashgate, 1991.

Schecter, Darrow. *The History of the Left from Marx to the Present: Theoretical Perspectives*. London: Continuum, 2007.

Schecter, Darrow. 'Two Views of Revolution: Gramsci and Sorel, 1916–1920'. *History of European Ideas* 22 (1990), pp. 636–653.

Schirru, Giancarlo (ed.). *Gramsci, le culture e il mondo*. Rome: Viella, 2009.

Schmidt, Michael, and Lucien van der Walt. *Black Flame: The Revolutionary Class Politics of Anarchism and Syndicalism*. Oakland: AK Press, 2009.

Scott-Smith, Giles. *The Politics of Apolitical Culture: The Congress for Cultural Freedom, the CIA and Post-War American Hegemony*. London and New York: Routledge, 2002.

Scott-Smith Giles. 'A Radical Democratic Political Offensive: Melvin J. Lasky, *Der Monat* and the CCF'. *Journal of Contemporary History* 35:2 (2000), pp. 263–280.

Sedgwick, Peter. 'Out of Hiding: The Comradeships of Daniel Guérin'. *Salmagundi* 58:9 (June 1982), pp. 197–220.

Self-Management Group. *Workers' Councils Democracy, Not Parliamentary*. Brisbane: Self-Management Group, n.d.

Semprún, Jorge. *Communism in Spain in the Franco Era: The Autobiography of Federico Sanchez*. Helen R. Lane (trans.). Sussex: Harvester, 1980.

Service, Robert. *Lenin: A Biography*. Basingstoke: Macmillan, 2000.

Settembrini, Domenico. 'Mussolini and the Legacy of Revolutionary Socialism'. *Journal of Contemporary History* 11:4 (1976), pp. 239–268.

Shanin, Teodor (ed.). *Late Marx and the Russian Road: Marx and 'the Peripheries of Capitalism'*. New York: Monthly Review Press, 1983.

Shannon, David. *The Socialist Party of America*. Chicago: Quadrangle, 1955.

Sharkey, Paul. *The Friends of Durruti – A Chronology* (1984), available online: http://flag.blackened.net/revolt/spain/fod_chron.html (accessed 19 February 2017).

Shilliam, Robbie. 'Jacobinism: The Ghost in the Gramscian Machine of Counter-Hegemony'. In *Gramsci, Political Economy and International Relations Theory: Modern Princes and Naked Emperors*, Alison J. Ayers (ed.). Basingstoke: Palgrave Macmillan, 2008, pp. 239–260.

Silver, Beverly J. *Forces of Labor: Workers' Movements and Globalization Since 1870*. New York: Cambridge University Press, 2003.

Simon, Henri. *Correspondance de Pierre Chaulieu (Castoriadis) et Anton Pannekoek 1953–1954*. Paris: Échanges et Mouvement, 2002, available online: www.mondialisme.org/spip.php?rubrique86 (accessed 19 February 2017).

Sinclair, John. *Guitar Army: Rock and Revolution with the MC5 and the White Panther Party*. Los Angeles: Process, 2007 [1972].

Singh, Nikhil Pal. *Black is a Country: Race and the Unfinished Struggle for Democracy*. Cambridge: Harvard University Press, 2004.

Sitrin, Marina A. '"Walking, We Ask Questions": An Interview with John Holloway'. *Perspectives on Anarchist Theory* (Fall 2004), available online: http://www.leftturn.org/%E2%80%9Cwalking-we-ask-questions%E2%80%9D-interview-john-holloway (accessed 17 February 2017).

Skinner, Quentin. 'Meaning and Understanding in the History of Ideas'. in *Meaning and Context: Quentin Skinner and His Critics*, James Tully (ed.). Cambridge: Polity, 1988), pp. 29–67.

Skinner, Quentin. *Visions of Politics, Volume 1: Regarding Method*. Cambridge: Cambridge University Press, 2002.

Skirda, Alexandre. *Facing the Enemy: A History of Anarchist Organization from Proudhon to May 1968*. Oakland: AK Press, 2002.

Smith, Kylie. 'Gramsci at the Margins: Subjectivity and Subalternity as a Theory of Hegemony'. *International Gramsci Journal* 1:2 (April 2010), pp. 39–50.

Smith, R. 'Obituary Article: Sir William Lawther'. *Bulletin of the North-East Group for the Study of Labour History* 10 (1976), pp. 27–33.

Soave, Sergio. 'Gramsci e Tasca'. In *Gramsci nel suo tempo*, Volume 1, Francesco Giasi (ed.). Rome: Carocci, 2008, pp. 99–125.

Socialist Platform, *C.L.R. James and British Trotskyism; An Interview*. London: Socialist Platform, 1987.

Solnit, David, and Rebecca Solnit (eds.). *The Battle of the Story of the Battle of Seattle*. Oakland: AK Press, 2009.

Sonn, Richard D. *Sex, Violence, and the Avant-Garde: Anarchism in Interwar France*. Pennsylvania State University Press, 2010.

Sorel, Georges. *Matériaux d'une théorie du proletariat*. Paris and Geneva: Slatkine Genève-Paris, 1981.

Sorel, Georges. *Reflections on Violence*, Jeremy Jennings (ed.). Cambridge: Cambridge University Press, 1999.

Sorel, Georges. 'The Socialist Future of the Syndicates'. In *From Georges Sorel*, John L. Stanley (ed.). New York: Oxford University Press, 1976, pp. 71–93.

Souvarine, Boris. *Stalin: A Critical Survey of Bolshevism*. London: Secker & Warburg, 1940.

Spadoni, Patrice. 'La synthèse entre l'anarchisme et le marxisme: "Un point de ralliement vers l'avenir"'. *Alternative Libertaire* (2000), pp. 40–44.

Srnicek, Nick, and Alex Williams. *Inventing the Future: Postcapitalism and a World Without Work*. London: Verso, 2015.

Stalin, J.V. "Anarchism or Socialism?" (1907), available online: https://www.marxists.org/reference/archive/stalin/works/1906/12/x01.htm (accessed 19 February 2017).

Stallybrass, Peter. 'Marx and Heterogeneity: Thinking the Lumpenproletariat'. *Representations* No. 31, Special Issue: 'The Margins of Identity in Nineteenth Century England' (Summer 1990), pp. 69–95.

Stanley, John L. 'Editor's Introduction' to *From Georges Sorel*. New York: Oxford University Press, 1976, pp. 1–61.

Stansill, Peter, and David Zane Mairowitz, D. (eds.). *BAMN: Outlaw Manifestos and Ephemera 1965–70*. Harmondsworth: Penguin, 1971.

Starhawk. *Webs of Power: Notes from the Global Uprising*. Gabriola Island: New Society Publishers, 2002.

Stephens, Julie. *Anti-Disciplinary Protest: Sixties Radicalism and Postmodernism*. Cambridge, UK: Cambridge University Press, 1998.

Stirner, Max. *The Ego and His Own*. New York: Dover, 2005.

Strauss, David. *Die Streitschriften zur Verteidigung meiner Schrift über das Leben Jesu und zur Charakteristik der gegenwärtigen Theologie*. Tübingen: Osiander, 1838.

Strauss, David. *In Defense of My Life of Jesus Against the Hegelians*. North Haven, CT: Archon Books, 1983.

Tame, Chris R. 'The Libertarian Tradition no. 1: Auberon Herbert'. *Free Life: The Journal of the Libertarian Alliance* 1:2 (1980), pp. 1–3.

Tasca, Angelo. 'Preface' to *Nascita e avvento del fascismo*. Florence: Le Monnier, 1950.

Taylor, Charles. 'Foucault on Freedom and Truth'. *Political Theory* 13:2 (May 1984), pp. 152–183.

Taylor, Chris. 'James and those Italians' [2009], available online: http://clrjames. blogspot.co.uk/2008/09/james-and-those-italians.html (accessed 19 February 2017).

Taylor, Steve. *The Anatomy of Decision*. Auckland: Compass, c.1974.

Thomas, Hugh. *The Spanish Civil War*. London: Penguin, 1990.

Thomas, Paul. *The Gramscian Moment: Philosophy, Hegemony and Marxism*. Leiden: Brill, 2009.

Thomas, Paul. *Karl Marx and the Anarchists*. London: Routledge & Kegan Paul, 1980; 2nd edition 1985.

Thomas, Paul. *Marxism and Scientific Socialism: From Engels to Althusser*. London: Routledge, 2008.

Thorpe, Wayne. 'Uneasy Family: Revolutionary Syndicalism in Europe from the *Charte d'Amiens* to World War I'. In *New Perspectives on Anarchism, Labour and Syndicalism: The Individual, the National and the Transnational*, David Berry, and Constance Bantman (eds.). Newcastle upon Tyne: Cambridge Scholars Publishing, 2010, pp. 16–42.

Tognarini, Ivan. 'Giacobinismo e bolschevismo: Albert Malthiez e l'Ordine Nuovo'. *Ricerche storiche* VI (1976), pp. 523–549.

Tormey, Simon. *Anti-Capitalism*. Oxford: Oneworld, 2004.

Toscano, Joe. 'Carnival Anarchism in Melbourne 1970–75', available online: http://www.takver.com/history/melb/carnival1970_75.htm (accessed 19 February 2017).

Tracy, James. *Direct Action: Radical Pacifism from the Union Eight to the Chicago Seven*. Chicago: University of Chicago Press, 1996.

Trotsky, Leon. *In Defense of Marxism*. New York: Pathfinder Press, 1976.

Trotsky, Léon. *Nos tâches politiques*. Paris: Belfond, 1970.

Turkeli, Süreyya. 'Introduction: How New Anarchism Changed the World (of Opposition) after Seattle and Gave Birth to Post-Anarchism'. In *Post-Anarchism: A Reader*, Duane Rousselle and Süreyya Turkeli (eds.). London: Pluto, 2011, pp. 1–19.

Turkington, Don J. *Industrial Conflict: A Study of Three New Zealand Industries*. Methuen: Wellington, 1976.

Turnbull, Les. *Chopwell's Story*. Gateshead: Gateshead Borough Council, 1978.

'Unemployed Recalcitrance and Welfare Restructuring in the UK Today'. In *Aufheben*, 9, Stop the Clock! Critiques of the New Social Workhouse (2000), pp. 12–21, available online: http://libcom.org/library/aufheben/pamphlets-articles/stop-the-clock-critiques-of-the-new-social-workhouse (accessed 21 February 2017).

Unofficial Reform Committee of the South Wales Miners' Federation. *The Miners Next Step* [1912], reprinted with introduction by Dave Douglass. Doncaster: Germinal and Phoenix Press, 1991.

Vaneigem, Raoul. *Entre le deuil du monde et la joie de vivre*. Paris: Verticales, 2008.

Vaneigem, Raoul. *L'ère des créateurs*. Bruxelles: Complexe, 2002.

Vaneigem, Raoul. *Traité de savoir-vivre à l'usage des jeunes generations*. Paris: Gallimard, 1967 [1992].

Viénet, René. *Enragés et situationnistes dans le mouvement des occupations*. Paris: Gallimard, 1968.

Vincent, K. Steven. *Between Marxism and Anarchism: Benoît Malon and French Reformist Socialism*. University of California Press, 1992.

Voline, *The Unknown Revolution, 1917–1921*. New York: Free Life Editions, 1974.

Walker, Geoff. 'George Harvey and Industrial Unionism'. *Bulletin of the North-East Group for the Study of Labour History* 17 (1983), pp. 21–24.

Walker, Geoff. *George Harvey: The Conflict between the Ideology of Industrial Unionism and the Practice of its Principles in the Durham Coalfield*. MA thesis, Ruskin College, 1982.

Walt, Lucien van der. 'Anarchism, Black Flame, Marxism and the IST: debating power, revolution and Bolshevism', available online: https://lucienvanderwalt.wordpress.com/2011/07/04/journal-anarchism-black-flame-marxism-and-the-ist-debating-power-revolution-and-bolshevism/ (accessed 8 February 2017).

Walt, Lucien van der. 'Counterpower, participatory democracy, revolutionary defence: debating *Black Flame*, revolutionary anarchism and historical Marxism'. *International Socialism: A Quarterly Journal of Socialist Theory* 130 (2011), available online: http://isj.org.uk/revolutionary-anarchism-and-historical-marxism/ (accessed 19 February 2017).

Walt, Lucien van der. 'Debating Black Flame, Revolutionary Anarchism and Historical Marxism'. *International Socialism* II/130 (2011), pp. 193–207.

Walter, Nicolas. 'Daniel Guerin's anarchism'. *Anarchy* 8:94 (12 December 1968), pp. 376–382.

Walter, Nicolas. 'Has Anarchism Changed?' Part 2. *Freedom* (26 June 1976), pp. 9–10.

Ward, Colin. *Anarchy in Action*. London: Allen & Unwin, 1973.

Weeks, Kathi. 'The Refusal of Work as Demand and Perspective'. In *The Philosophy of Antonio Negri, Volume 1: Resistance in Practice*, Timothy S. Murphy and Abdul-Karim Mustapha (eds.). London, Pluto, 2005, pp. 109–135.

Weir, Stanley. 'Revolutionary Artist'. In *C.L.R. James: His Life and Work*, Paul Buhle (ed.). London: Allison & Busby, 1986, pp. 180–184.

Werbe, Peter. 'The History of the *Fifth Estate*'. *Fifth Estate* 368–369 (2005), pp. 8–19.

'What was the USSR? Part I: Trotsky and state capitalism'. *Aufheben* #06 (Autumn 1997), available online: http://libcom.org/library/what-was-the-ussr-aufheben-1 (accessed 19 February 2017).

White, Stuart. 'Making Anarchism Respectable: The Social Philosophy of Colin Ward'. *Journal of Political Ideologies* 12:1 (2007), pp. 11–28.

Wieck, David Thoreau. *Woman from Spillertown: A Memoir of Agnes Burns Wieck*. Carbondale and Edwardsville, IL: Southern Illinois University Press, 1992.

Williams, R.C. *The Other Bolsheviks: Lenin and his Critics, 1904–1919*. Bloomington: University of Indian Press, 1986.

Wilson, Matthew. *Rules without Rulers: The Possibilities and Limits of Anarchism*. Winchester, UK: Zero Books, 2014.

Wilson, William Julius. *The Truly Disadvantaged*. Chicago: Chicago University Press, 1987.

Wise, David, and Stuart Wise. 'The End of Music'. In *What Is Situationism? A Reader*, Stewart Home (ed.). Edinburgh: AK Press, 1996, pp. 63–102.

Wood, Ellen Meiksins. *Empire of Capital*. London: Verso, 2003.

Wood, Ellen Meiksins. 'A Manifesto for Global Capital?'. In *Debating Empire*, Gopal Balakrishnan (ed.). London: Verso, 2003, pp. 61–82.

Wood, Ellen Meiksins. *The Retreat From Class*. London: Verso, 2nd edition 1998.

Woodard, Komozi. *A Nation Within a Nation: Amiri Baraka (Leroi Jones) and Black Power Politics*. Chapel Hill: University of North Carolina Press, 1999.

Woodcock, George. *Anarchism: A History of Libertarian Ideas and Movements*. Harmondsworth: Penguin, 1963; 2nd edition 1986).

Woodcock, George. 'Syndicalism Defined'. In *The Anarchist Reader*, G. Woodcock (ed.). Glasgow: Fontana-Collins, 1978.

Worcester, Kent. *C.L.R. James: A Political Biography*. Albany NY: SUNY Press, 1996.

Wreszin, Michael. *A Rebel in Defense of Tradition: The Life and Politics of Dwight MacDonald*. New York: Basic Books, 1994.

Wright, Erik Olin. *Class Counts*. Cambridge: Cambridge University Press, 1997.

Wright, Steve. 'A Party of Autonomy?'. In *The Philosophy of Antonio Negri, Volume 1: Resistance in Practice*, Timothy S. Murphy and Abdul-Karim Mustapha (eds.). London: Pluto, 2005, pp. 73–106.

Wright, Steve. 'Radical traditions: council communism'. *Reconstruction* 4 (1995), available online: www.libcom.org/library/radical-traditions-council-communism-steve-wright (accessed 19 February 2017).

Wright, Steve. *Storming Heaven: Class Composition and Struggle in Italian Autonomist Marxism*. London: Pluto Press, 2002.

*You Can't Blow Up a Social Relationship: The Anarchist Case Against Terrorism*. Brisbane, Melbourne and Adelaide: Libertarian Socialist Organisation,

Libertarian Workers for a Self-Managed Society, Monash Anarchist Society and Adelaide Libertarian Socialists, c.1978.

Young, James D. 'C.L.R. James'. *Journal of the Scottish Labour History Society*, 22 (1987), pp. 38–39.

Young, James D. *The World of C.L.R. James: His Unfragmented Vision*. Glasgow: Clydeside Press, 1999.

Young, Robert J.C. *Postcolonialism: An Historical Introduction*. Oxford, UK: Blackwell, 2001.

Zanardi, Learco. *Luigi Molinari. La Parola, l'azione, il pensiero*. Mantua: Sometti, 2003.

Zimmer, Kenyon. 'Premature Anti-Communists?: American Anarchism, the Russian Revolution, and Left-Wing Libertarian Anti-Communism, 1917–1939'. *Labor: Studies in Working-Class History of the Americas* 6:2 (Summer 2009), pp. 45–71.

# Index

PM Press was founded at the end of 2007 by a small collection of folks with decades of publishing, media, and organizing experience. PM Press co-conspirators have published and distributed hundreds of books, pamphlets, CDs, and DVDs. Members of PM have founded enduring book fairs, spearheaded victorious tenant organizing campaigns, and worked closely with bookstores, academic conferences, and even rock bands to deliver political and challenging ideas to all walks of life. We're old enough to know what we're doing and young enough to know what's at stake.

We seek to create radical and stimulating fiction and non-fiction books, pamphlets, T-shirts, visual and audio materials to entertain, educate, and inspire you. We aim to distribute these through every available channel with every available technology—whether that means you are seeing anarchist classics at our bookfair stalls; reading our latest vegan cookbook at the café; downloading geeky fiction e-books; or digging new music and timely videos from our website.

PM Press is always on the lookout for talented and skilled volunteers, artists, activists, and writers to work with. If you have a great idea for a project or can contribute in some way, please get in touch.

# FRIENDS OF PM

These are indisputably momentous times—the financial system is melting down globally and the Empire is stumbling. Now more than ever there is a vital need for radical ideas.

In the many years since its founding—and on a mere shoestring—PM Press has risen to the formidable challenge of publishing and distributing knowledge and entertainment for the struggles ahead. With hundreds of releases to date, we have published an impressive and stimulating array of literature, art, music, politics, and culture. Using every available medium, we've succeeded in connecting those hungry for ideas and information to those putting them into practice.

Friends of PM allows you to directly help impact, amplify, and revitalize the discourse and actions of radical writers, filmmakers, and artists. It provides us with a stable foundation from which we can build upon our early successes and provides a much-needed subsidy for the materials that can't necessarily pay their own way. You can help make that happen—and receive every new title automatically delivered to your door once a month—by joining as a Friend of PM Press. And, we'll throw in a free T-shirt when you sign up.

Here are your options (all include a 50% discount on all webstore purchases):
- $30 a month: Get all books and pamphlets
- $40 a month: Get all PM Press releases (including CDs and DVDs)
- $100 a month: Superstar—Everything plus PM merchandise and free downloads

For those who can't afford $30 or more a month, we have Sustainer Rates at $15, $10, and $5. Sustainers get a free PM Press T-shirt and a 50% discount on all purchases from our website.

Your Visa or Mastercard will be billed once a month, until you tell us to stop. Or until our efforts succeed in bringing the revolution around. Or the financial meltdown of Capital makes plastic redundant. Whichever comes first.

PM Press • PO Box 23912 • Oakland CA 94623
510-658-3906 • www.pmpress.org